# PARADISE LOST

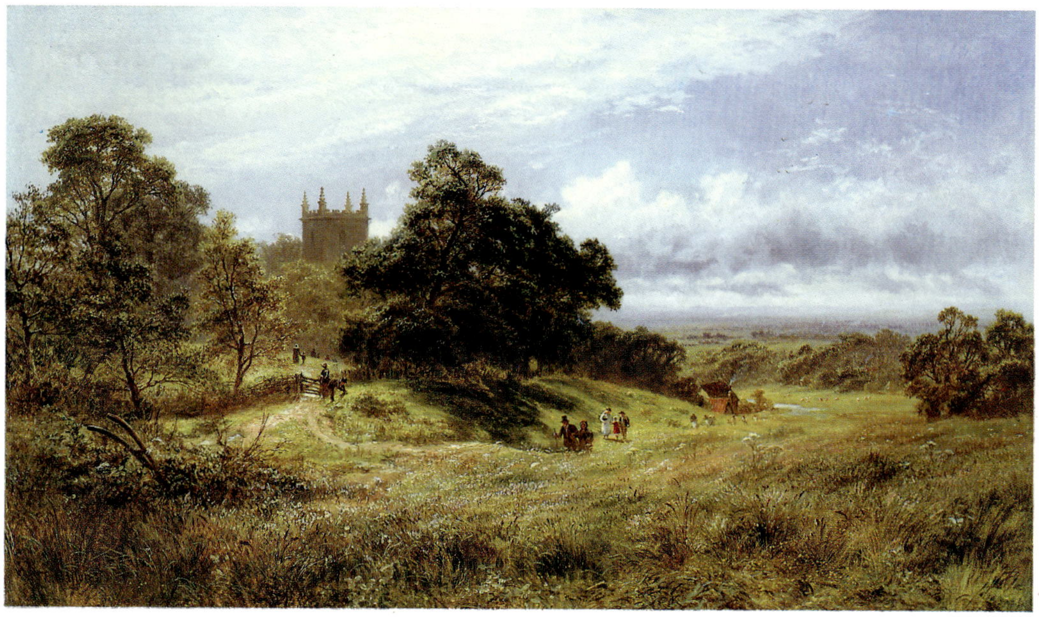

1
ROBERT GALLON
*On the Way to Church, the South Downs*

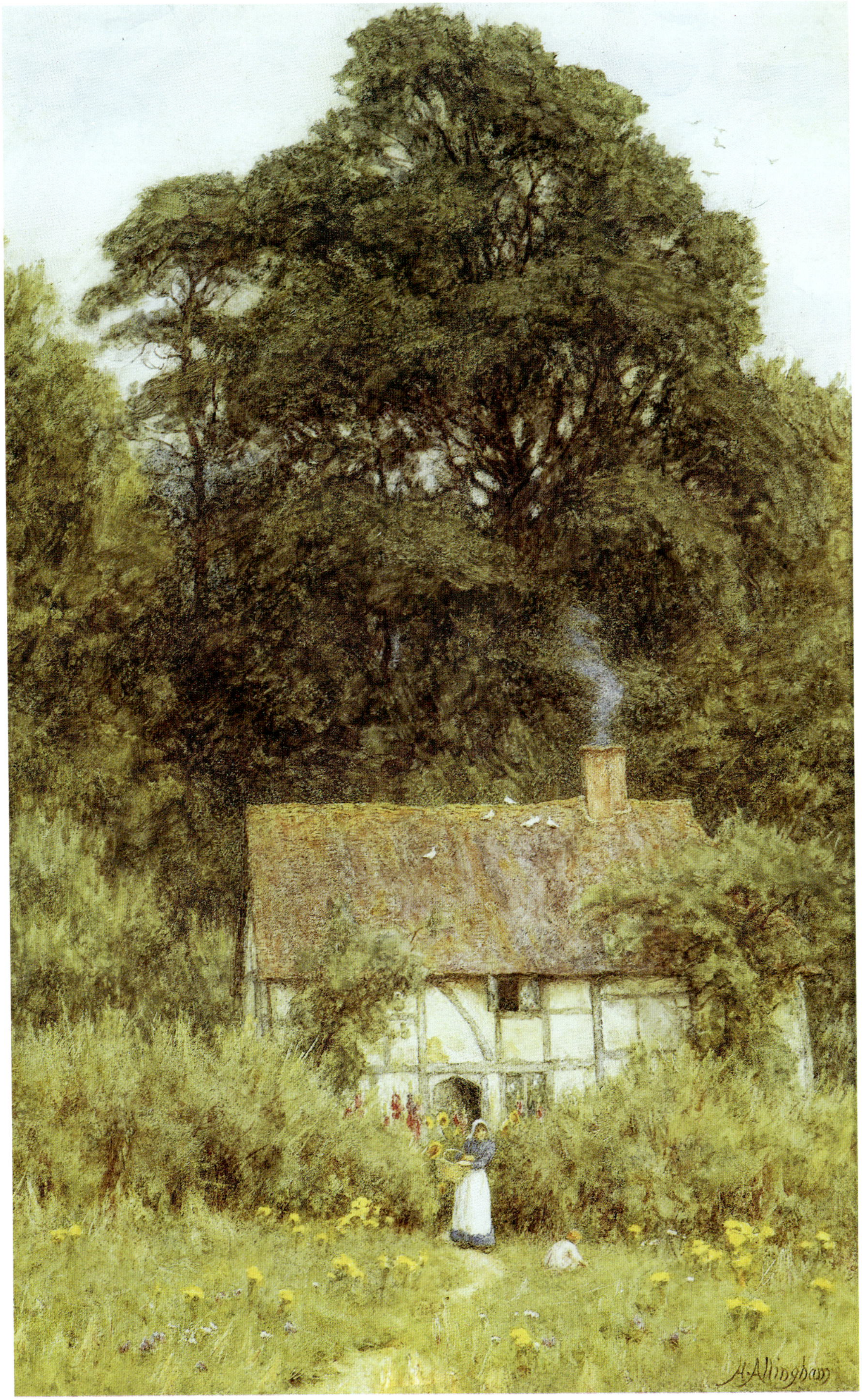
H. Allingham

# PARADISE LOST

## Paintings of English Country Life and Landscape 1850–1914

CHRISTOPHER WOOD

2
HELEN ALLINGHAM
*Cottage at Brook, near Witley*

Grange Books

This edition published 1993
by Grange Books, an imprint of
Grange Books PLC, The Grange,
Grange Yard, London SE1 3AG

First published in Great Britain in 1988 by
Barrie & Jenkins Ltd
20 Vauxhall Bridge Road, London SW1V 2SA



British Library Cataloguing in Publication Data
Wood, Christopher, *1941-*
Paradise lost : paintings of English
country life and landscape 1850-1914.
1. English landscape paintings, 1850-1914
I. Title
758.1'0924

ISBN 1-85627-480-2

Typeset by SX Composing Limited
Printed and bound in China

# Contents

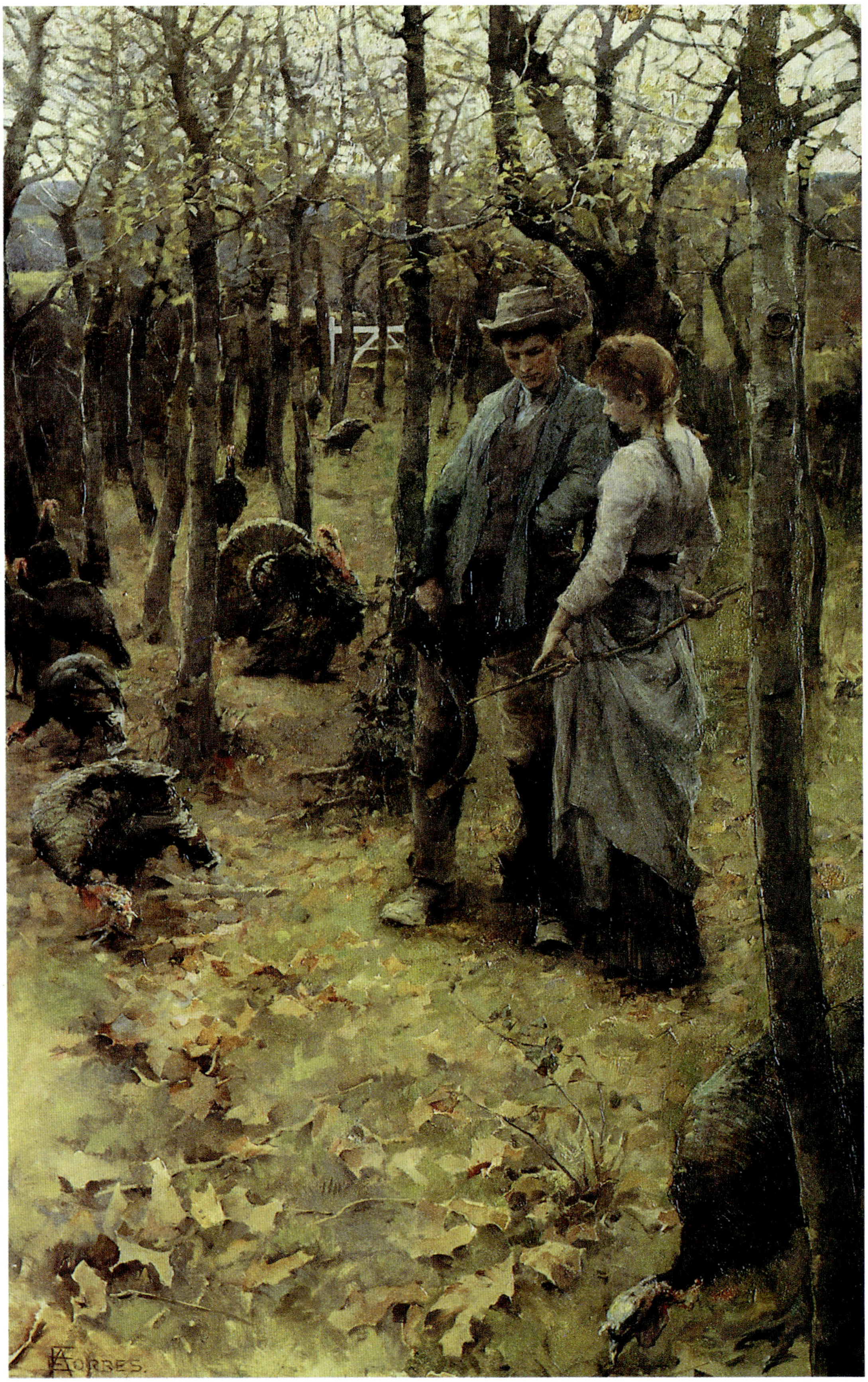


ELIZABETH STANHOPE FORBES
*The Edge of the Wood*

## Introduction

# VICTORIAN ART ~ AND THE ~ COUNTRYSIDE

THIS BOOK IS ABOUT COUNTRY LIFE IN THE LATE nineteenth and early twentieth centuries – from about 1850 to 1914 – as seen through the eyes of its painters. Artistically speaking, this is a huge tract of territory, from the Pre-Raphaelites at one end, to the Newlyn School and George Clausen at the other. The idea, however, is to focus on these pictures, not only as pictures, but also as social and historical documents, to see what they tell us about the countryside and country life. I have therefore arranged the pictures by subject, not by date, nor with any particular art-historical continuity. This book does not follow a strict chronological pattern. The chapter headings – the village, the cottage, the farm, and so on – have been suggested by the pictures themselves, and each one forms a kind of mini-survey of its own, reflecting the attitudes and preoccupations of the artists towards that specific subject. By looking at the pictures in this way, we can explore much more easily what Victorian painters actually thought about the countryside and country life. What subjects did they like to paint, and what subjects did they avoid? How concerned were they about social conditions, if at all? How do their pictures compare with the writings of Victorian social historians and novelists? Do their pictures correspond to the reality of country life? Was it really a rural paradise? These are some of the questions this book sets out to answer.

Most Victorian artists were painters of pretty pictures first, and social historians second. They do not present us with a completely truthful, realistic or comprehensive picture, either of the countryside, or of life as it was really lived by country people. That, in any case, is not the function of art. Beautiful, evocative and informative their pictures certainly are, but the overwhelming impression they create is one of a rural paradise. This is not because I have deliberately chosen the most ideal-

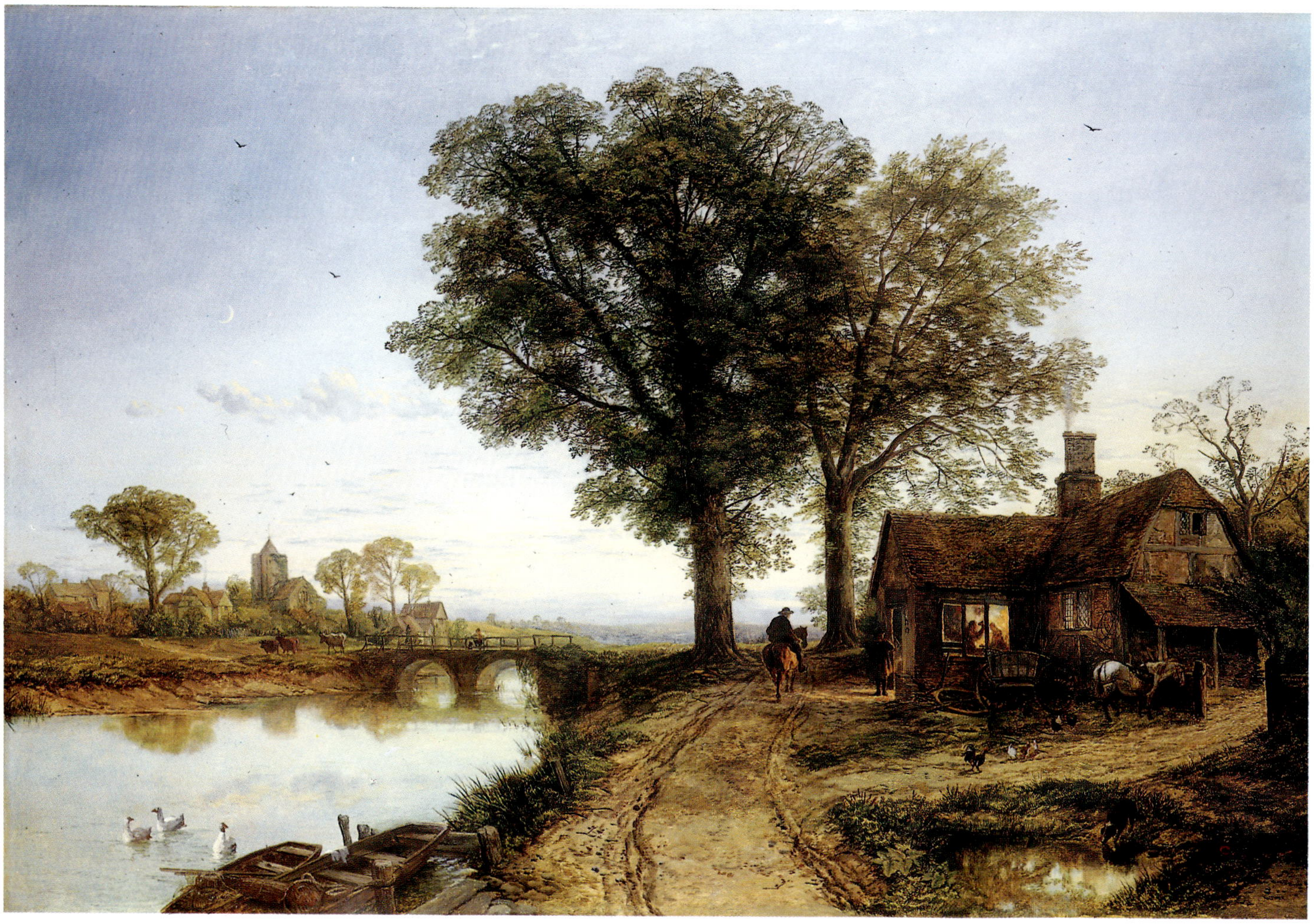

4
THOMAS CRESWICK
*The Village Smithy*

ised and rosy pictures of country life; it is because that is how most Victorian artists saw it, and how their patrons wanted to see it. Victorian landscape paintings, like so much of Victorian art, tell us just as much about the Victorians as they do about the countryside of the nineteenth century. They are a mirror in which the middle-class attitudes and values of the age are clearly reflected. The underlying paradox – and just about everything in the Victorian age is riddled with paradox – is that although the countryside may have looked like a paradise it was certainly not a paradise for most of the people who lived and worked in it. The Victorians, of course, knew this. Any intelligent reader of newspapers, magazines or novels would know that poverty, illness, ignorance and exploitation were rife in the English countryside. But like many men faced with the unpleasant or the unacceptable, they simply ignored it. They preferred their own image of the countryside – a beautiful, healthy, pure, innocent arcadia, where peasants went happily about their labours, children played on the village green and mothers sat by the fireside in neat, picturesque little cottages, all watched over by a benevolent gentry and clergy.

The Victorians preferred their rusticity idyllic for another, deeper reason. During the nineteenth century, England changed from a rural society to an urban one. For the first time in history, the population of the towns overtook that of the countryside. The effect on country life was devastating. Centuries-old patterns of life and tradition began suddenly to disappear. Old habits, customs and dialects seemed simply to melt away. 'Village tradition,' wrote Thomas Hardy, 'a vast amount of unwritten folk-lore, local chronicle, local topography, and nomenclature – is absolutely sinking, has nearly sunk, into eternal oblivion.' The countryside was steadily depopulated; the huge new cities grew uncontrollably. The Victorians watched all this with alarm and frustration, as there was nothing they could do to stop it. They clung

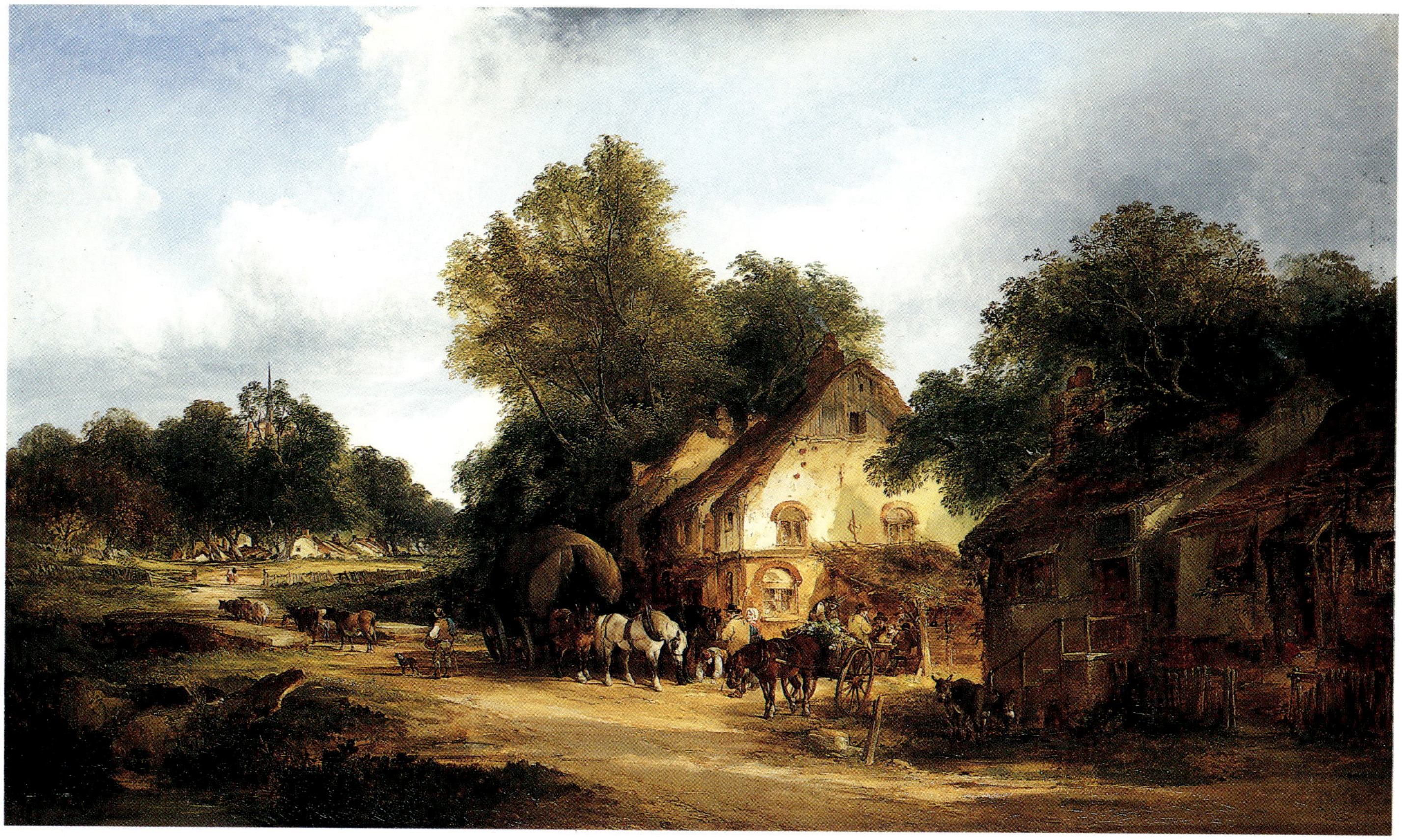

5
EDWARD CHARLES WILLIAMS AND
WILLIAM SHAYER
*An Old Roadside Inn in Kent*

ever more desperately to the vanishing ideals of country life because they knew they were in danger of losing them. The Victorians were just as concerned about the countryside, and about country life, as we are today. Many of the preservation societies were founded in the late nineteenth century, including the National Trust. They were maybe even more concerned than we are, because they were the first to feel the effects of the industrial revolution. For them the railway, the factory and the city were completely new experiences. The feeling that 'man made the town, God made the country' was therefore particularly strong and it lies behind most of the art and literature of the period. It is also the spirit that motivates most Victorian pictures of country life. Even those artists and writers, such as Frank Holl or Thomas Hardy, who depicted the harsher side of country life, still subscribed to the view that the country was a purer, simpler and healthier place than the smoky new towns. It is an idea deeply rooted in the English character, and certainly seems to be just as prevalent today as it was then.

Victorian patrons subscribed to the same view. Most townsmen were first-generation town dwellers and would have been born in the country. Successful merchants and businessmen, who formed the bulk of the Victorian picture-buying public, might well have recalled country childhoods or country forebears, and therefore liked to buy pictures that reminded them of their rural roots. They certainly did not want to be reminded about the nasty things that went on in the countryside. The ideal picture was a pleasant scene, painted in good weather, suitable for all the family, and making few mental demands on the viewer. It is no accident that the most productive of all Victorian painters was Thomas Sidney Cooper, who exhibited pictures of sheep and cows at the Royal Academy for over sixty years without a break – still a record. His pictures found their way not into farms or country houses, but into the

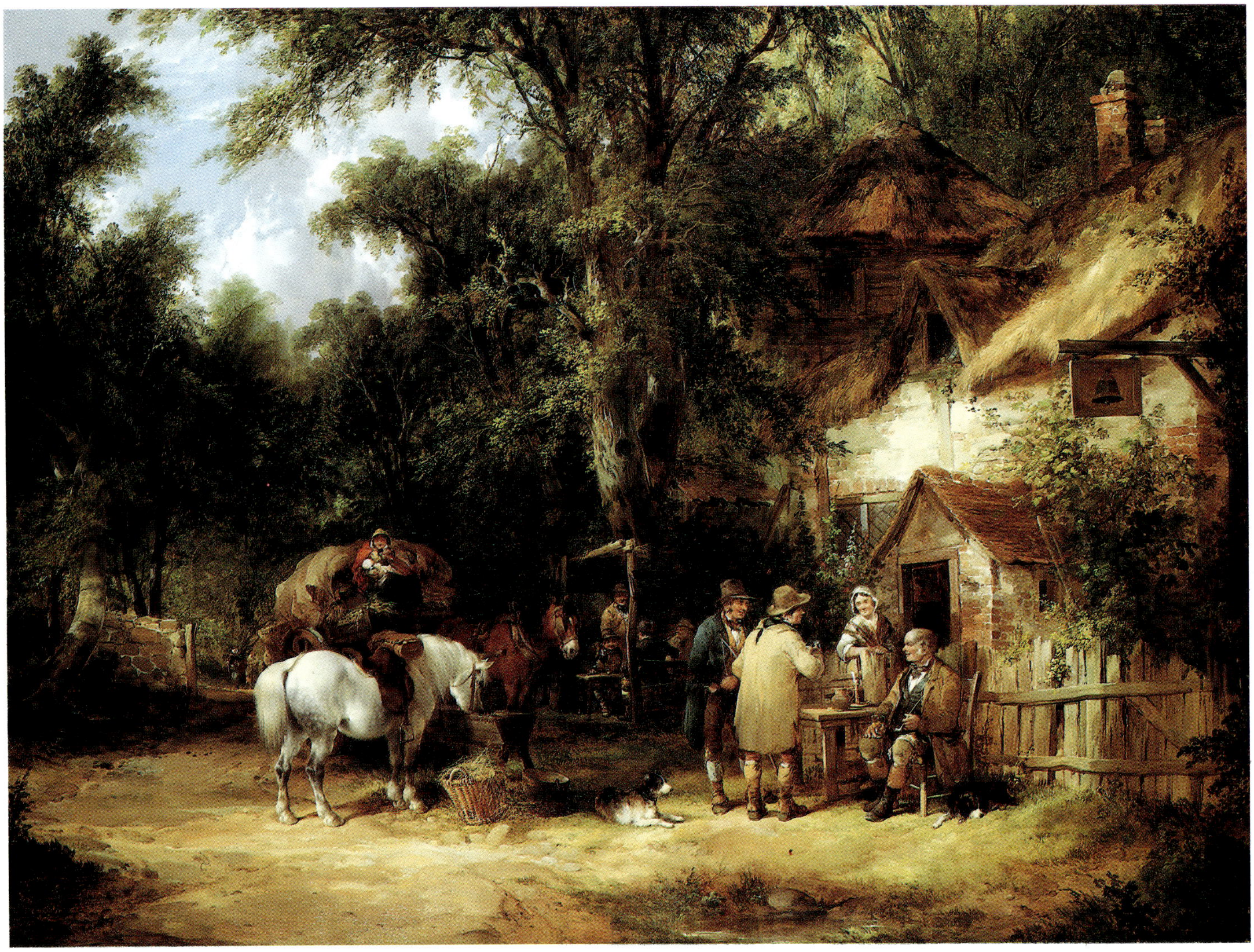

6
WILLIAM SHAYER
*At the Bell Inn, Cadnam, New Forest*

suburban villas of the newly-rich middle classes. Most Victorian painters seem to have shared the tastes and the attitudes of their patrons anyway, so their relationship was a uniquely harmonious one. Painter and patron were united in their devotion to the artistic fiction of the rural paradise. George Eliot, one of the most perceptive writers about Victorian country life, expressed the situation perfectly in an article in the *Westminster Review* in 1856: 'The notion that peasants are joyous, that the cottage matrons are usually buxom, and village children are necessarily rosy and merry, are prejudices difficult to dislodge from the artistic mind. . . . The painter is still under the influence of idyllic literature, which has always expressed the imagination of the cultivated and town-bred, rather than the truth of country life.' Victorian landscapes were mostly painted by townsmen for townsmen, and they therefore have an inevitable tendency to soothe and confirm the prejudices of the middle-class buyer, comfortably ensconced in an armchair in his cosy suburban villa.

This book is mainly about people in landscapes, not about pure landscape. English landscape painting in the nineteenth century is a vast subject in itself, and would need another book. Although the Victorian period produced no great landscape painters of the stature of Constable or Turner, it did produce a large number of very good landscape artists, whose true worth has yet to be recognised. Some, like John Linnell or Benjamin Williams Leader, may one day be regarded as great painters. The Pre-Raphaelite movement also produced some of the most remarkable landscapes in English art. Turner died in 1851, well into the Victorian period. Although his late work was regarded as the incomprehensible eccentricities of an old man, his reputation remained high throughout the nineteenth century, and his pictures always commanded greater admiration and higher prices than Constable's. John Constable died in

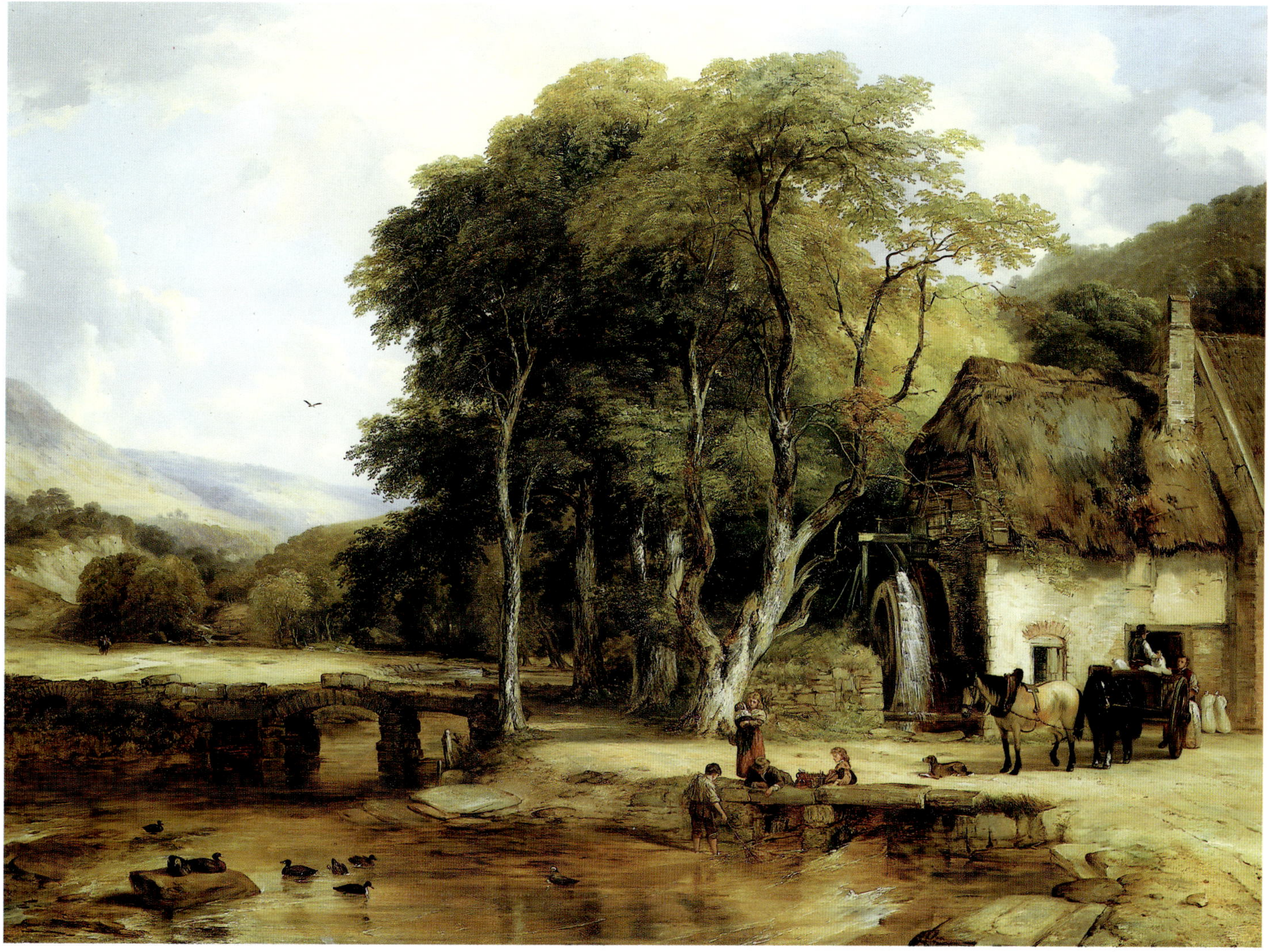

7
FREDERICK RICHARD LEE
*Devonshire Scenery*

1837, the year of Queen Victoria's accession to the throne. His work was neglected for most of the century, mainly because of Ruskin's dislike of it. A few collectors and connoisseurs were perceptive enough to admire Constable, but the Victorian taste was for a more romantic, idyllic style of landscape. Constable's work was too rugged, too impressionistic and too honest to find favour with most Victorian collectors. Other artists admired him, and he had one faithful pupil, Frederick William Watts. But the Victorians preferred the sentimental rusticity of William Collins, the highly-charged romanticism of Linnell, the gentle lyricism of B.W. Leader, or the Pre-Raphaelite intensity of John Brett and William Dyce.

At a more popular level, the love of the Victorian townsman for the countryside also produced an avalanche of pretty landscapes and rural scenes, to fill the parlours of the new bourgeoisie. Landscapes formed the majority of pictures at the Royal Academy throughout the Victorian period. So many were painted that they are still filling salerooms up and down the country every week even now. High honours and high prices were accorded then, and still are now, to painters like William Shayer, Vicat Cole, Thomas Creswick, B.W. Leader, the Williams family, and countless others who catered for the insatiable demand for pretty, idealised landscapes, peopled with contented and picturesque peasants going about their work or their rustic pleasures. In general, the Victorian public wanted a pleasing landscape in which the figures blended happily into the background. They liked a nice view of their own beautiful English countryside, like Mr Millbank, the industrialist in Disraeli's novel *Coningsby*, who preferred 'a fine free landscape by Lee, that gave him the broad plains, the green lanes, and running streams of his own land'. Doubtless Mr Millbank, like most Victorian buyers, did not want to be troubled with what the peasants were doing in his pictures, or might be thinking. For preference, they chose the well-mannered cows and sheep

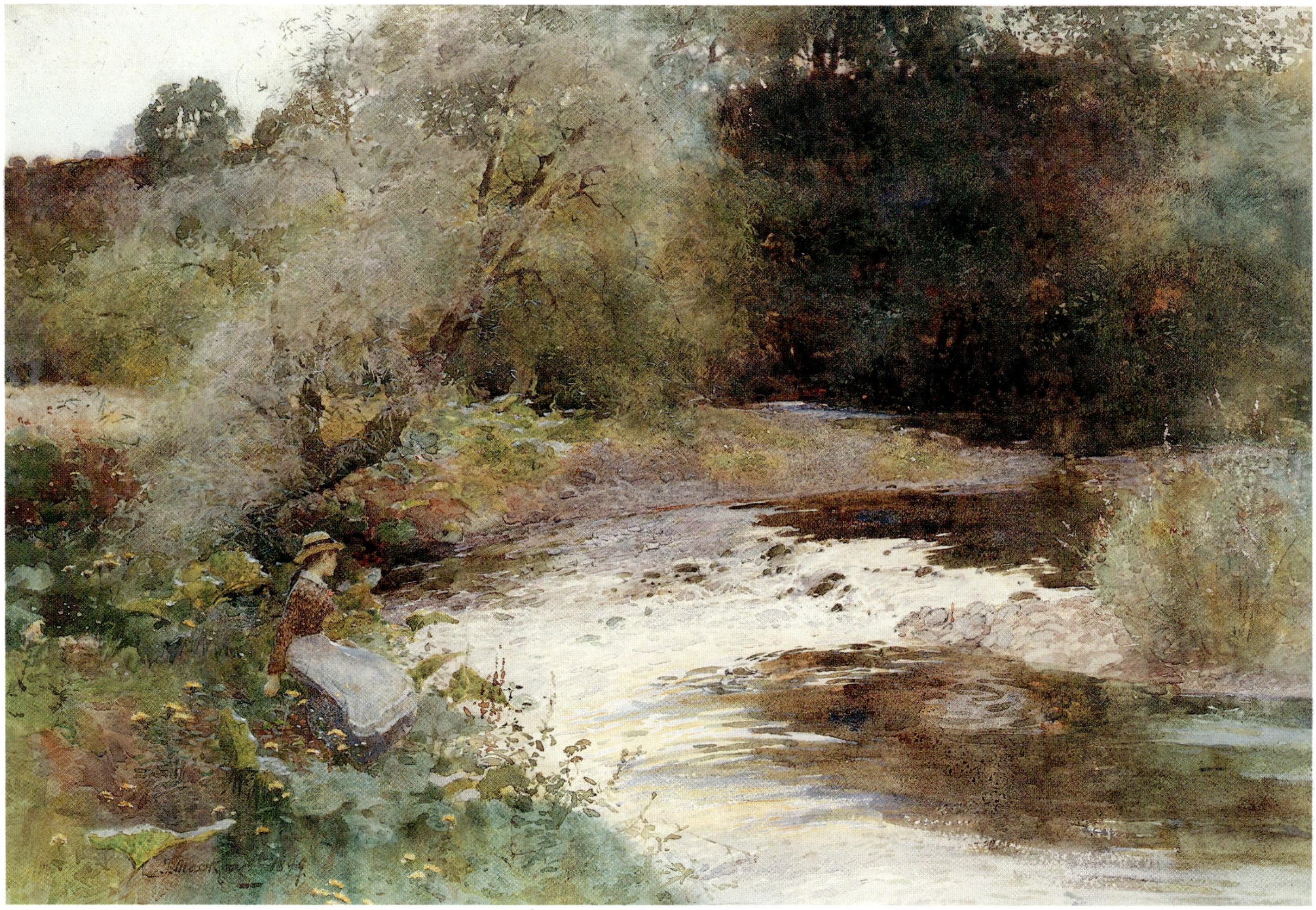

8
THOMAS MACKAY
*By the Stream*

of T.S. Cooper, or the farmyards of John Frederick Herring, neat, orderly, well-manicured, with no sign of any real mud or manure. 'Farmyard Friends' was a favourite title, applicable to almost the entire output of artists like Edgar or Walter Hunt. In pictures like these, the business of farming is converted into something quaint, picturesque and innocuous. They represent a kind of mainstream of conventional, middle-class, middle-of-the-road, taste. But the Victorian period is nothing if not surprising, and there were other artists who, as we shall see, painted the countryside and country life with real honesty and sincerity. Some were even brave enough to face up to some of the unpleasant facts about country life, and the reaction of the critics and the public could be violent. These painters were always an unpopular minority, but their work is of great importance, warning us against accepting too readily the idyllic image presented by most Victorian painters. They show us that the rural paradise had its darker, Miltonic regions too.

It is difficult to resist the charge, therefore, that the majority of Victorian landscapes are machines for evasion. They might be pleasant, competent and harmonious; they might display considerable artistry and skill; but they do not try and tell the truth. Paradoxically, Victorian painters were often great sticklers for realistic detail, especially during the Pre-Raphaelite period. No trouble was too great to get details exactly right, no labour spared to pose the right models. Detail was an article of faith, a sign that the artist had worked hard and conscientiously. Ruskin, who always carried a magnifying glass with him to exhibitions, loved detail because of 'the sense of human labour and care spent on it'. The trouble to which Victorian painters went to make their pictures authentic is legendary. William Shakespeare Burton, for example, a minor Pre-Raphaelite landscape painter, actually dug a hole in the ground so that he could sit in it and paint the daisies and the grass at eye-level.

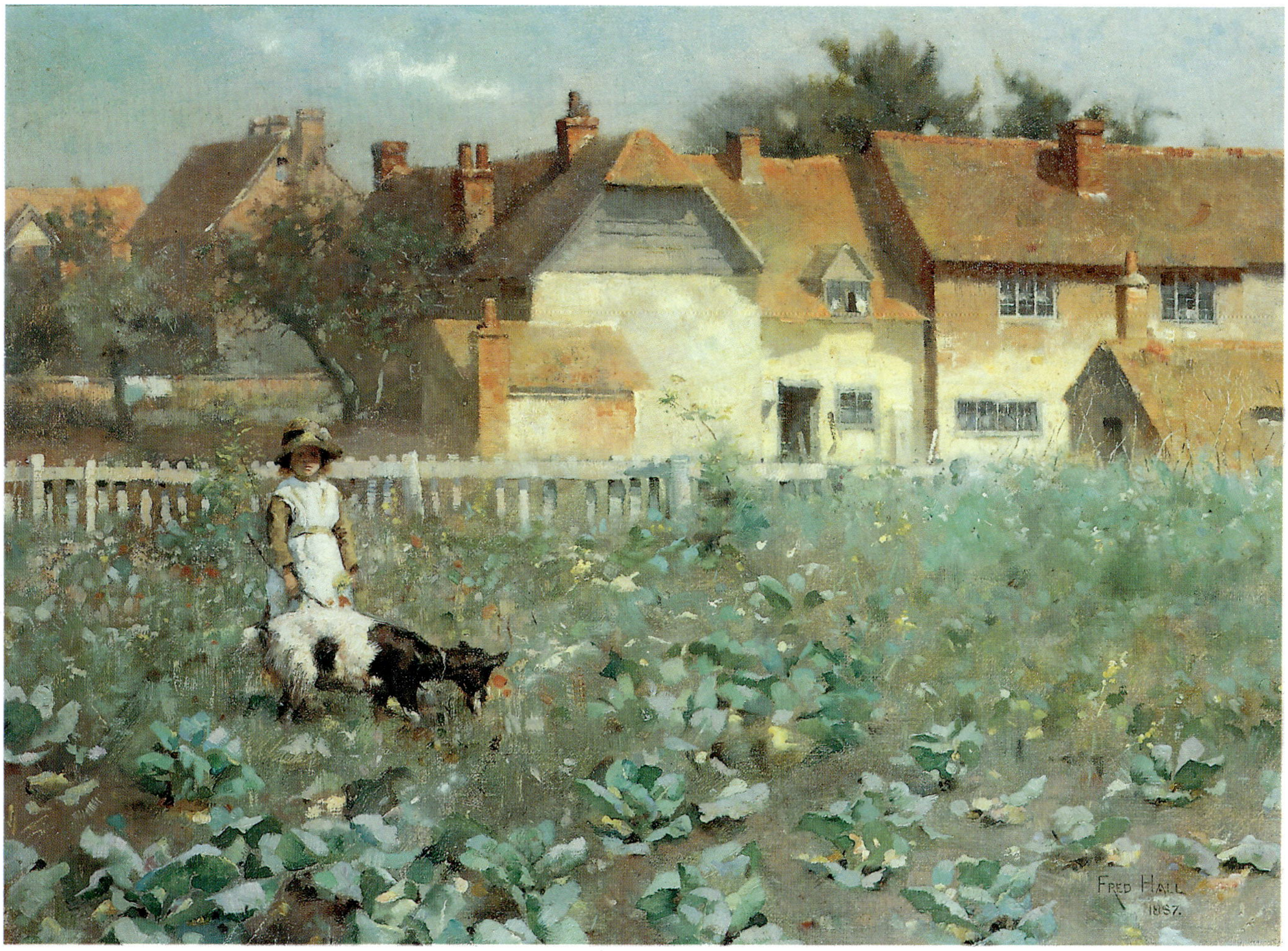


9
FREDERICK HALL
*The Cabbage Field*

But however hard a Victorian artist might try to make his pictures realistic and truthful, he was still hampered by two important limitations – his own artistic and moral attitudes and the attitudes of the Victorian public, many of whom, like Dickens's appalling governess Mrs General in *Little Dorrit*, believed that 'nothing disagreeable should ever be looked at'. The German art historian Richard Muther perceptively described Victorian art as 'art based on luxury, optimism and aristocracy . . . the ascendant view that a picture ought in the first place to be an attractive article of furniture for the sitting room . . . everything must be kept within the bounds of what is charming, temperate and prosperous, without in any degree suggesting the struggle for existence'. Facts, therefore, had to be tailored to suit this prevailing atmosphere. There is an unwillingness to face up to such unpleasant realities as poverty, death, exploitation or seduction. Painters would often study a subject in detail, such as a cottage interior, as if devotion to realism in small matters licensed evasion in larger ones. Most cottage scenes, for example, are unremittingly cheerful and happy, in spite of the fact that most cottage dwellers in the nineteenth century lived in great poverty, often without adequate food, clothing or sanitation, and with very little security of tenure. Any artist brave enough to tackle these taboo subjects would invariably meet with the wrath of the critics. The public could exercise their disapproval in an even more effective way, by not buying the picture. The artist Charles West Cope, for example, painted early in his career a large and serious picture depicting a meeting of Poor Law Guardians. To his great disappointment, it did not sell at the Academy. He therefore abandoned modern-life subjects, and turned to the safer pastures of historical and domestic scenes. He went on to become rich, an R.A., and write his memoirs, in the index of which there are 23 references to fly-fishing, and only two to Italy, an interesting indication of his artistic prior-

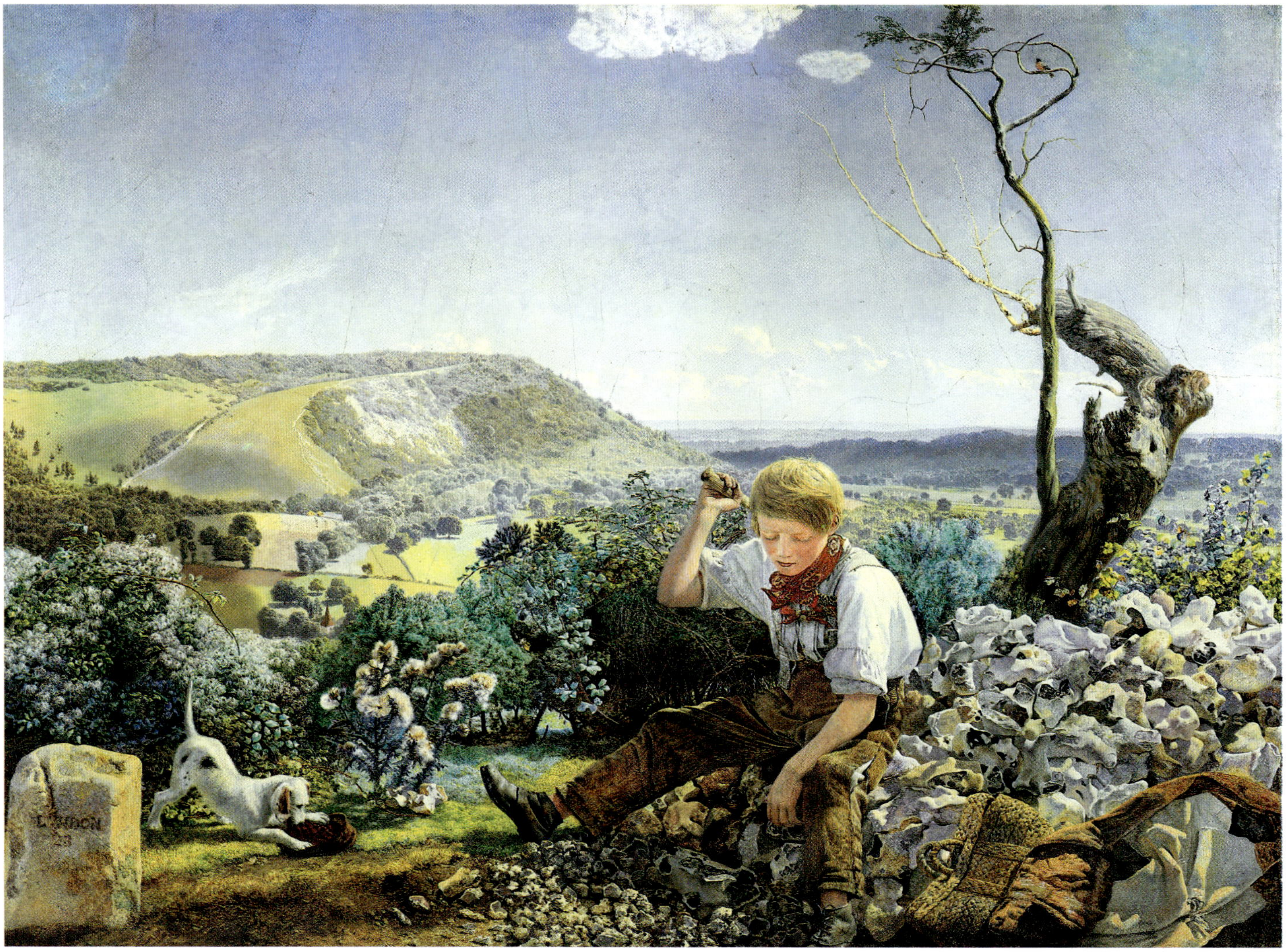

10
JOHN BRETT
*The Stonebreaker*

ities. But Cope had learned an important lesson: it was wiser to give the Victorian public what it wanted.

Not all critics and writers were happy about this. 'Who is not weary of simpering rusticity?' wrote an *Art Journal* critic in 1856. Many critics complained of the superficial nature of many Victorian pictures of country life, but it did little to change the tastes of either patrons or artists. Ragged, barefoot, but resolutely cheerful children continued to grin out from countless canvases; suspiciously pretty girls went on haymaking, filling up pitchers of water, or flirting over stiles. One might be forgiven for thinking that all Victorian farm workers were married to artists' models. Poverty was thereby converted into something picturesque and harmless, arousing a sympathetic tear rather than a desire for social revolution. The truth was rather different. 'The women grew prematurely old,' wrote George Bourne, in *Change in the Village* (1912), 'the children early lost their charm: the loveliness of the girls was gone almost before they had grown up . . . the waste of beauty was heart-rending.'

Critics may have been weary of simpering rusticity, but they did not like the reality much either. Any artist who dared to tackle the forbidden subjects of poverty and distress too realistically was invariably attacked. The works of Redgrave, Fred Walker, Luke Fildes, Herkomer and Holl, for example, were constantly criticised, and always for the same reason. Again and again, reading reviews of Victorian exhibitions, we find critics dismissing any attempt at social realism as not a suitable subject for art, and not suitable to hang in drawing rooms. It was simply felt that it was not the painter's job to draw attention to such things, or to suggest the struggle for existence. The *Art Journal* was a particularly consistent upholder of this viewpoint. 'We protest against his continually dismal selection of themes apart from the highest and holiest purpose of art,' wrote one reviewer of Henry Wallis's *Stonebreaker* of 1857. 'A subject

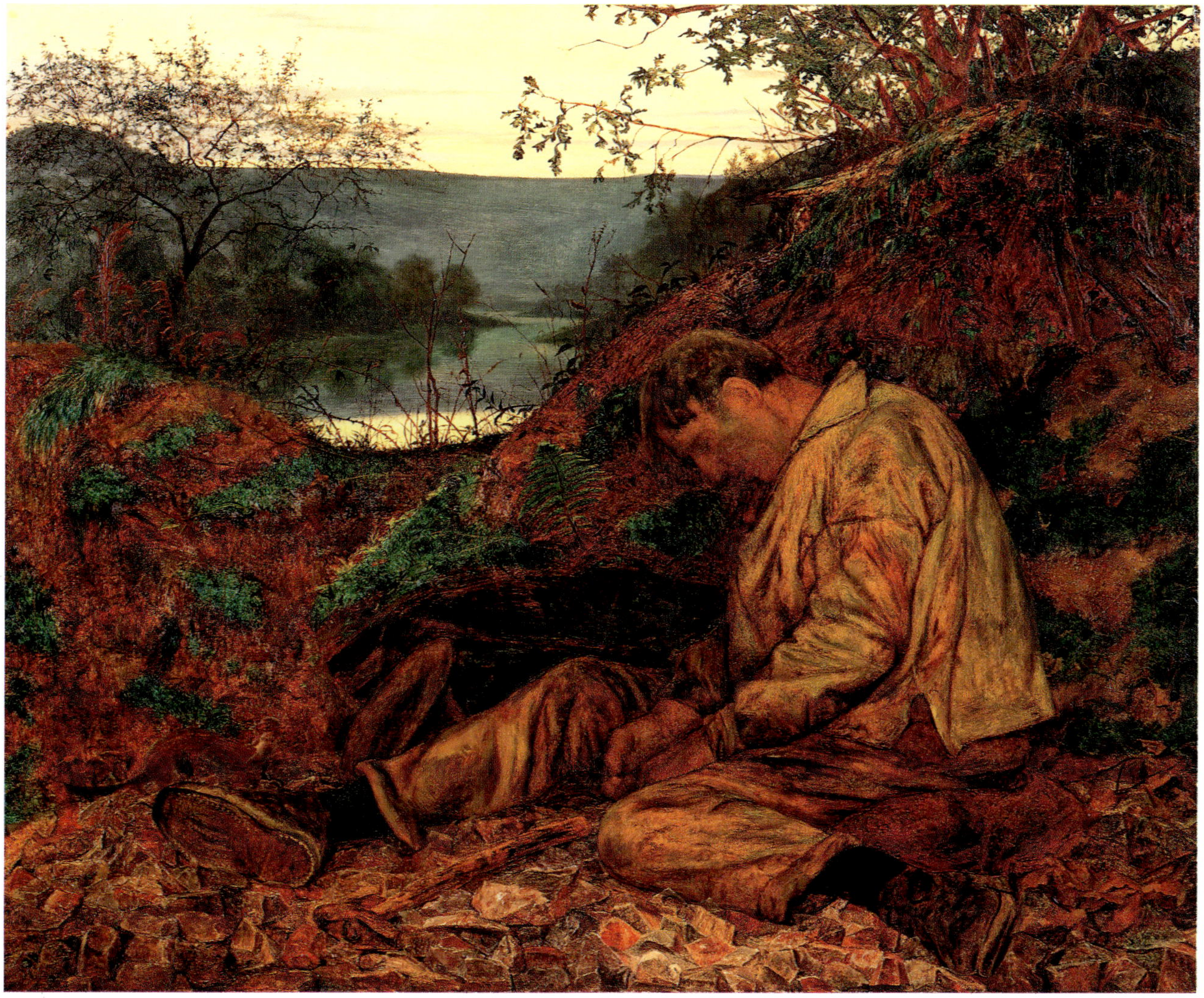

11
HENRY WALLIS
*The Stonebreaker*

almost too painful for a picture: defects in nature should not be brought within the sphere of art,' wrote another of a picture by James Collinson. 'We think it a pity Mr Crowe wasted his time on such unattractive materials' – this about Eyre Crowe's most famous picture *The Dinner House, Wigan*. But in spite of all this, artists did persevere with such subjects, and gradually social realist pictures began to be accepted, particularly during the 1870s and 1880s. In a sense, the history of Victorian narrative painting is the history of the gradual acceptance of social realist subjects, in spite of bitter opposition. This book will therefore record some of the battles fought along the way. But it has to be borne in mind that the social realist pictures, and those which faced up to the grimmer side of country life, were always in a minority. For every one of them there might be fifty of the rosy variety. Victorian pictures of country life can be said to divide themselves into the rosy school or the misery school, with very little in between. No better contrast between the two schools could be found than the two pictures of stonebreakers, one painted by John Brett (10), the other by Henry Wallis (11), and both exhibited by a curious coincidence at the Royal Academy exhibition of 1858. Brett's picture shows a boy and his dog cheerfully at work in a beautiful sunny landscape on Box Hill in Surrey. Wallis's picture, by contrast, is a grim twilight scene, showing a stonebreaker who has died while at work on a heap of stones. Ruskin praised both pictures, describing Brett's as 'a boy hard at work at his heap in the morning', and Wallis's as 'an old man dead on his heap at night'. Everything depended on your point of view. Brett was an optimist, a Pre-Raphaelite, and a disciple of Ruskin; Wallis was a pessimist, also a Pre-Raphaelite, but an admirer of the writings of Carlyle.

Victorian literature offers many parallels with Victorian paintings of country life, and I explore some of these in the text. But it also has to be remembered that Victorian novels and poems about the countryside are part of an artistic fiction just

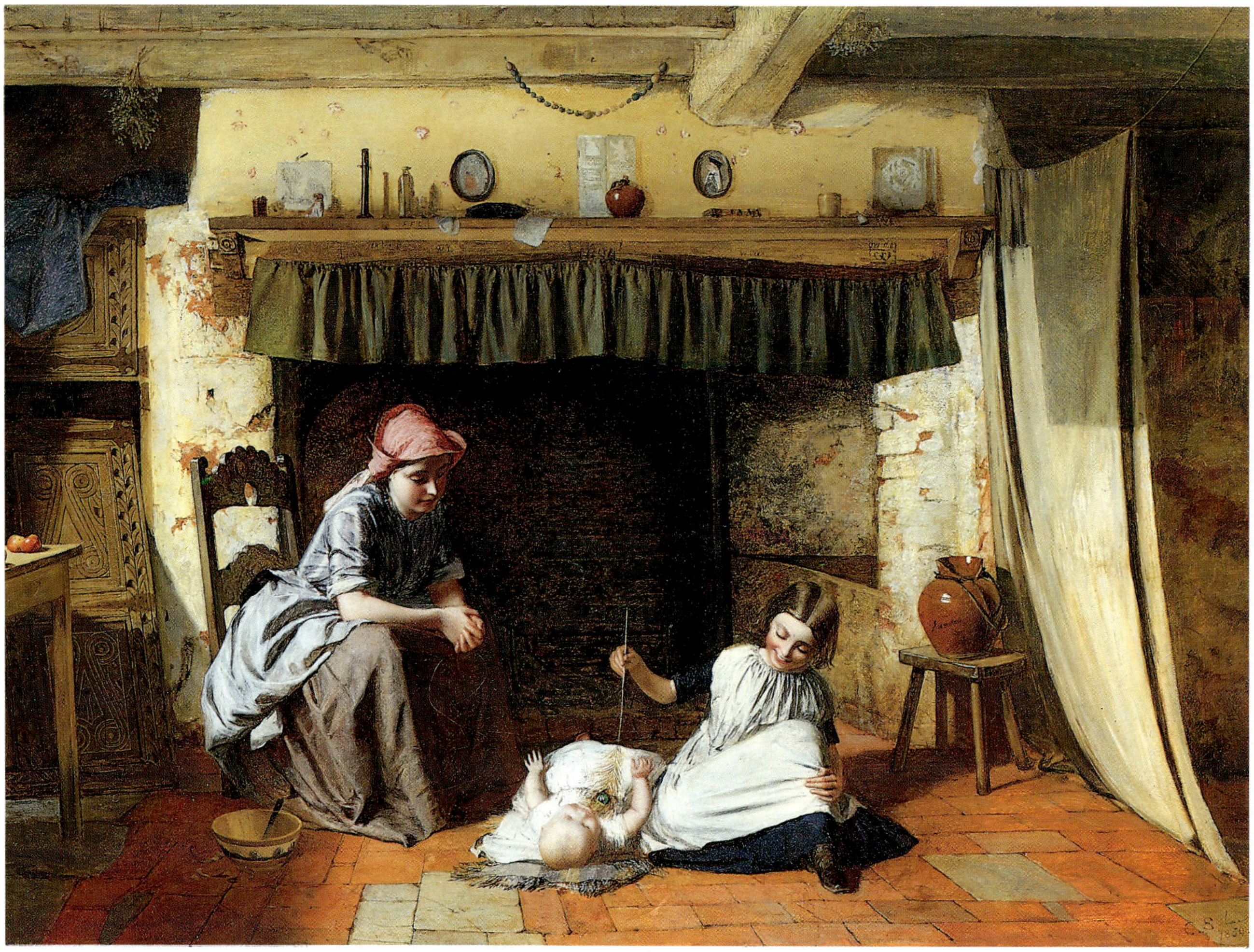

12
CHARLES SILLEM LIDDERDALE
*Happy*

as removed from reality as Victorian painting. They do not tell us the truth about Victorian England any more than Verdi's opera *Aida* tells us about life in ancient Egypt. A reviewer writing about George Eliot's *Silas Marner* in 1861 complained that the poor in Victorian novels about country life 'are always looked at from the point of view of the rich. . . . They have no existence apart from the presence of the curate and a district visitor. They live in order to take tracts and broth.' And, one might add, to form the subjects of endless pretty Victorian pictures of cheerful peasants. George Eliot's novels were thought to depict country life and country people as they really were, for the first time, but she herself was always well aware of the gulf between fiction and reality. She knew that her novels, like Victorian paintings, appealed to the imagination of the cultivated town-dweller, even though he might be outraged by *Tess of the D'Urbervilles* or the paintings of Frank Holl. There are therefore many parallels between Victorian paintings and novels by such writers as Eliot, Charles Kingsley and Thomas Hardy. Both novelists and painters tended to set their works in a period about fifty years earlier, around the early years of the nineteenth century. In many Victorian paintings, such as Luke Fildes's *Village Wedding*, we are not looking at Victorian country life, but at some idyllic, pre-industrial age, such as most mid-Victorians might remember from their childhood.

Even more relevant are the diarists, country writers and journalists – Richard Jefferies, Alexander Somerville, Francis Kilvert, Flora Thompson, Rider Haggard. In their books, we will find people and scenes described which mirror almost exactly many of the paintings in this book. Perhaps the most reliable of all these writers is Flora Thompson, whose great book *Lark Rise to Candleford* gives the most truthful and realistic picture of life in a small village in late nineteenth-century England. Many of her descriptions of village life could form captions to the pictures in this book, and I have therefore

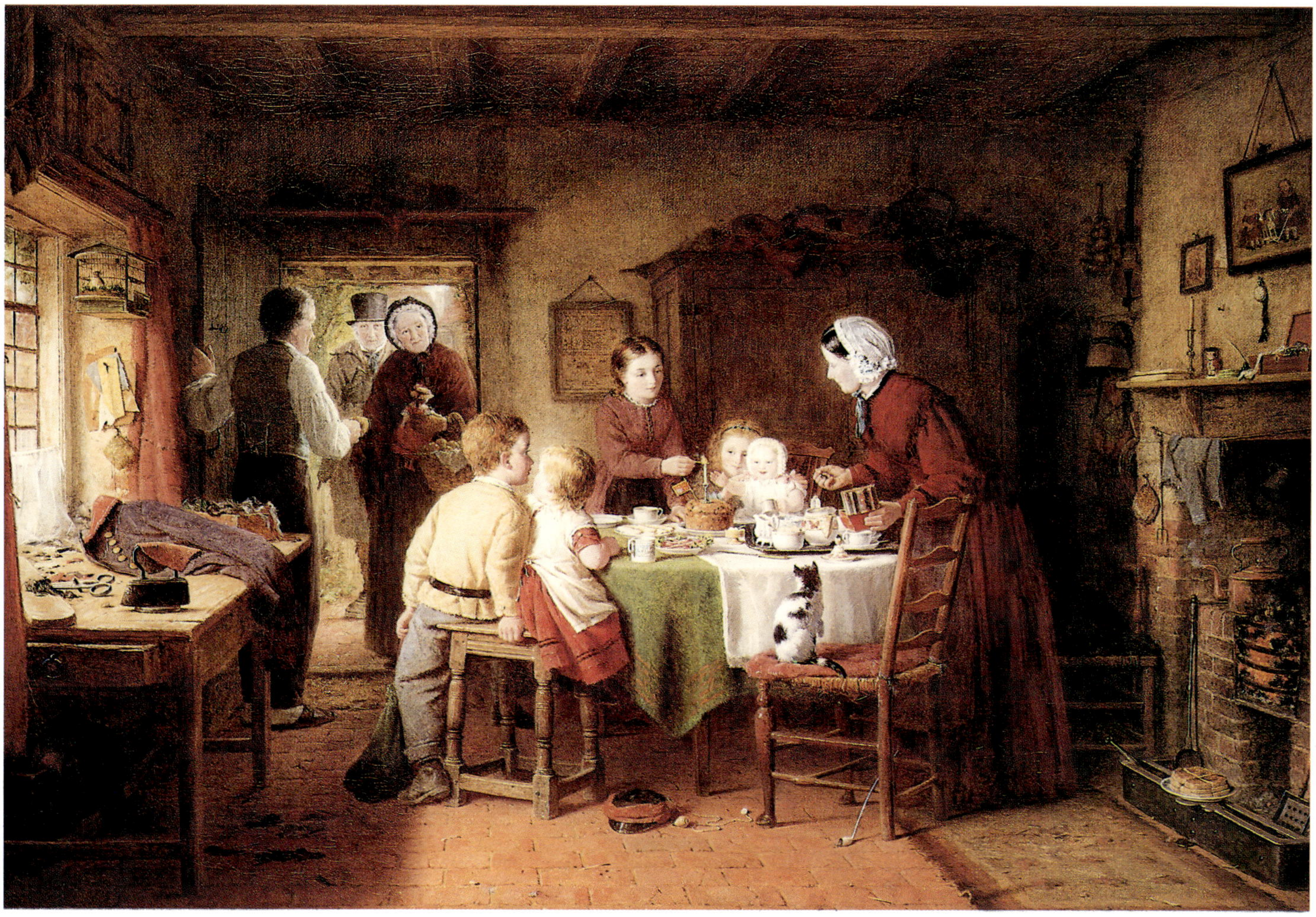

13
FREDERICK DANIEL HARDY
*The First Birthday Party*

quoted her copiously. But even she has been accused in some quarters of sentimentalising, of dwelling on pleasant and happy facts, and leaving out unpleasant ones. Perhaps no-one can be totally truthful about their childhood.

'In the life of the English agricultural labourers, there is absolutely no poetry, no colour.' Thus wrote Richard Jefferies, one of the most passionate and committed Victorian writers about the countryside. This might make a suitable caption to Wallis's *Stonebreaker*, but how is one to reconcile this statement with the watercolours of Helen Allingham and Birket Foster? Obviously, there is a vast gulf between the reality of English country life and the artistic expression of it. Almost every picture in this book is full of poetry and colour. But writers like Cobbett, Jefferies and Somerville were propagandists, seething with rage at the injustice, poverty and oppression which they found in the countryside. They were looking for misery, and would certainly have had little trouble finding it in nineteenth-century England. They would certainly have had no time for the artistic view of the countryside, which they would have regarded as absurdly idealised, inaccurate and hypocritical. Seeing a particularly depressed group of female workers on a farm, Jefferies wrote sarcastically, 'Do you suppose these women moved in rhythmic measures to Bacchanalian song and pastoral pipe?' Between art and the hard facts of social and agricultural history, there is bound to be a disparity; to explore this disparity will be one of the functions of this book. The more we know of the social, historical and literary background, the better we shall be able to appreciate and understand the pictures. Art history is, in a sense, a branch of social history, as it reflects the society which produced it. So this book is something of a hybrid – art history, social history, agricultural history and literary history combined. But art is also about myths. And the most potent of all Victorian myths was the myth of the rural paradise – the green and pleasant land.

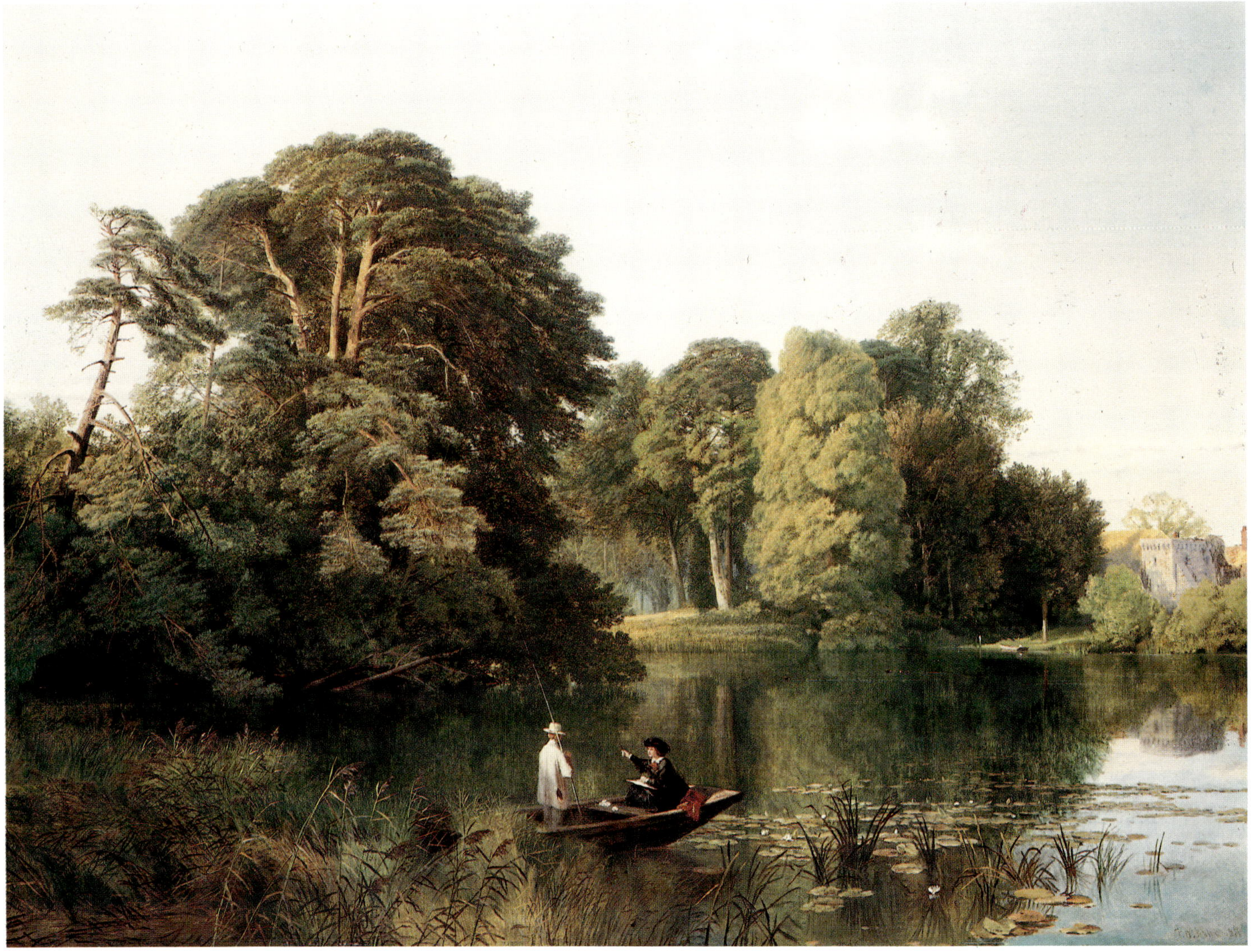

14
Frederick William Hulme
*A Quiet Retreat, Surrey*

# Chapter One

# A GREEN AND PLEASANT LAND

This blessed plot, this earth, this realm,
this England.

William Shakespeare, *Richard II*

The English countryside must have looked at its most beautiful in the mid-nineteenth century. It was the last golden age of English agriculture, the period when 'high farming' was at its peak, employing a work force of over two million people. Before the agricultural depressions of the 1880s and 90s, which were to drive so many people away into the towns, it was a time of general prosperity. The land had never been so intensely cultivated, and never employed so many people. Very little machinery was used and chemicals were unknown. All farm work was done by men and horses, using methods that had hardly changed for centuries. The countryside must have looked greener, lusher and more idyllic than it is possible to imagine now. Roads were mostly small and unsurfaced, and the only traffic was horse-drawn. Villages were bustling, industrious places, full both of farm workers and of local craftsmen, and with a strong local culture and dialect. The squires and great landowners, who still owned nearly 90% of the land, were at the height of their power and influence. To the average, town-dwelling Victorian artist, the countryside must have seemed like an unspoiled paradise, and on the surface it was.

This prosperity had been achieved at the expense of the small, independent farm worker by means of the enclosures. The enclosure of the old common lands had begun in the eighteenth century, and gathered pace in the nineteenth. Although this brought more land under cultivation, and increased the efficiency and productivity of agriculture, it had reduced the farm labouring class to a state of servile dependence on wages. Both farmers and landowners conspired to keep wages as low as possible, and this was the source of most of the evils of the Victorian countryside. As the century went by, people looked back more and more wistfully to the old pre-enclosure days. As early as 1833, the poet Ebenezer Elliot lamented:

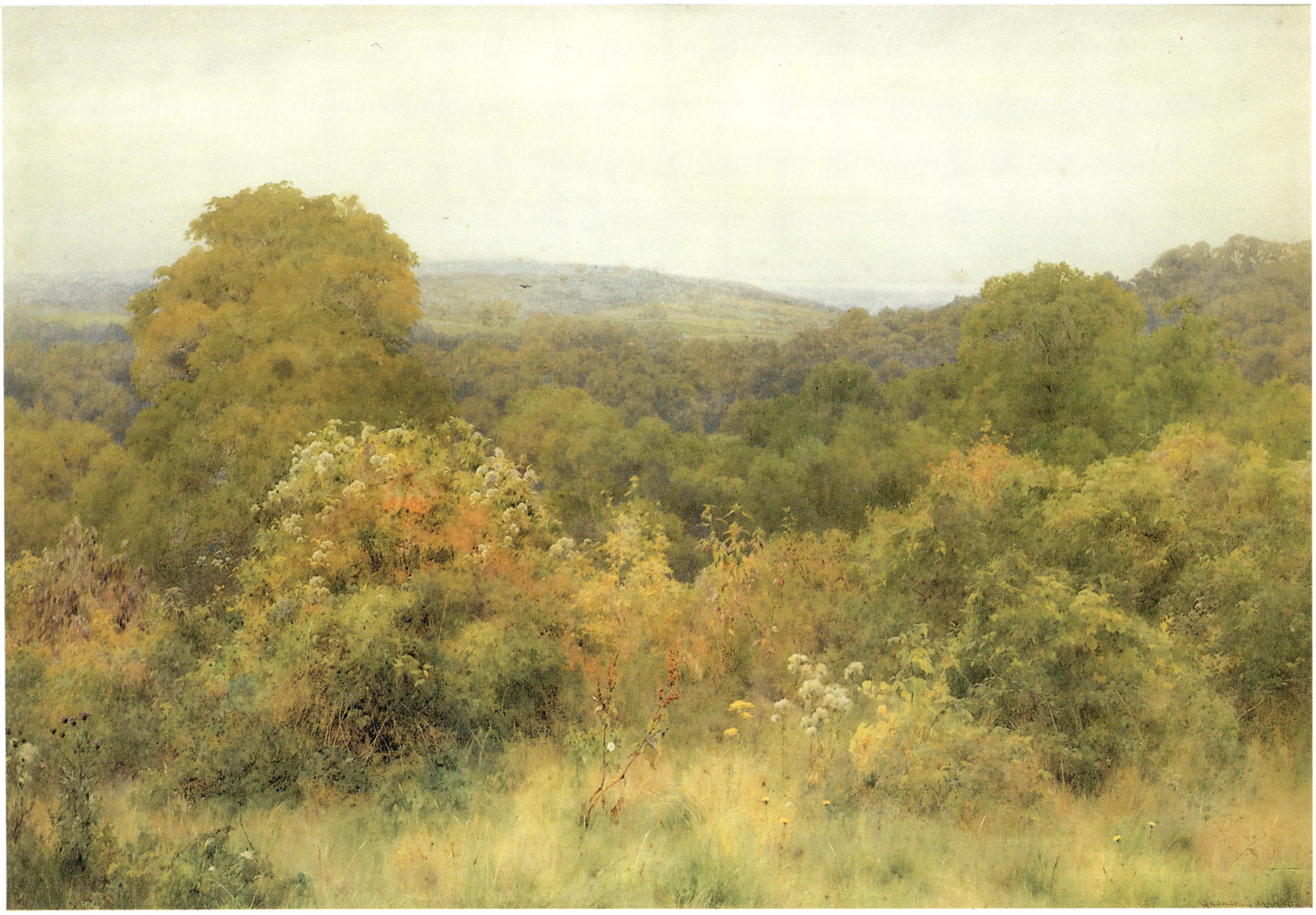

15
George Marks
*Nature's Garden*

Where is the common, once with blessings rich -
The poor man's common? Like the poor man's flitch
And well fed ham, which erst his means allowed,
'Tis gone to bloat the idle and the proud.

Old Sally, one of the old women of Flora Thompson's Lark Rise, could remember when the village was surrounded by common land, on which any inhabitant of the village could keep cows, sheep, pigs or geese. 'It was strange to picture Sally,' wrote Flora Thompson, 'a little girl, running with her switch after the great hissing birds on the common, especially as both common and geese had vanished as completely as though they had never been.' Concern over the future of the common lands, heaths, moors and swamps led to the founding of the Commons Preservation Society in 1865, and was also one of the reasons for the founding of the National Trust in 1895. Thereafter the pace of enclosure finally slowed down, but as George Bourne was to write in *Change in the Village* in 1912, 'to the enclosure of the common more than any other cause may be traced all the changes that have subsequently passed over the village.'

The response of Victorian artists to the countryside, as we shall see, bore little relation to these practical or political concerns. Most artists and writers in the nineteenth century were opposed to change and modernisation in the countryside. They simply wanted to keep it the way it was, the way it had always been. For them the countryside was a place of beauty, tranquillity and tradition, a paradise of refreshment for thirsty urban souls. Their attitudes were also heavily influenced by the romantic movement in literature; as George Eliot warned, 'the painter is still under the influence of idyllic literature'. Landscape painters at the beginning of Victoria's reign were mainly concerned to make their pictures as sentimental and pretty as possible.

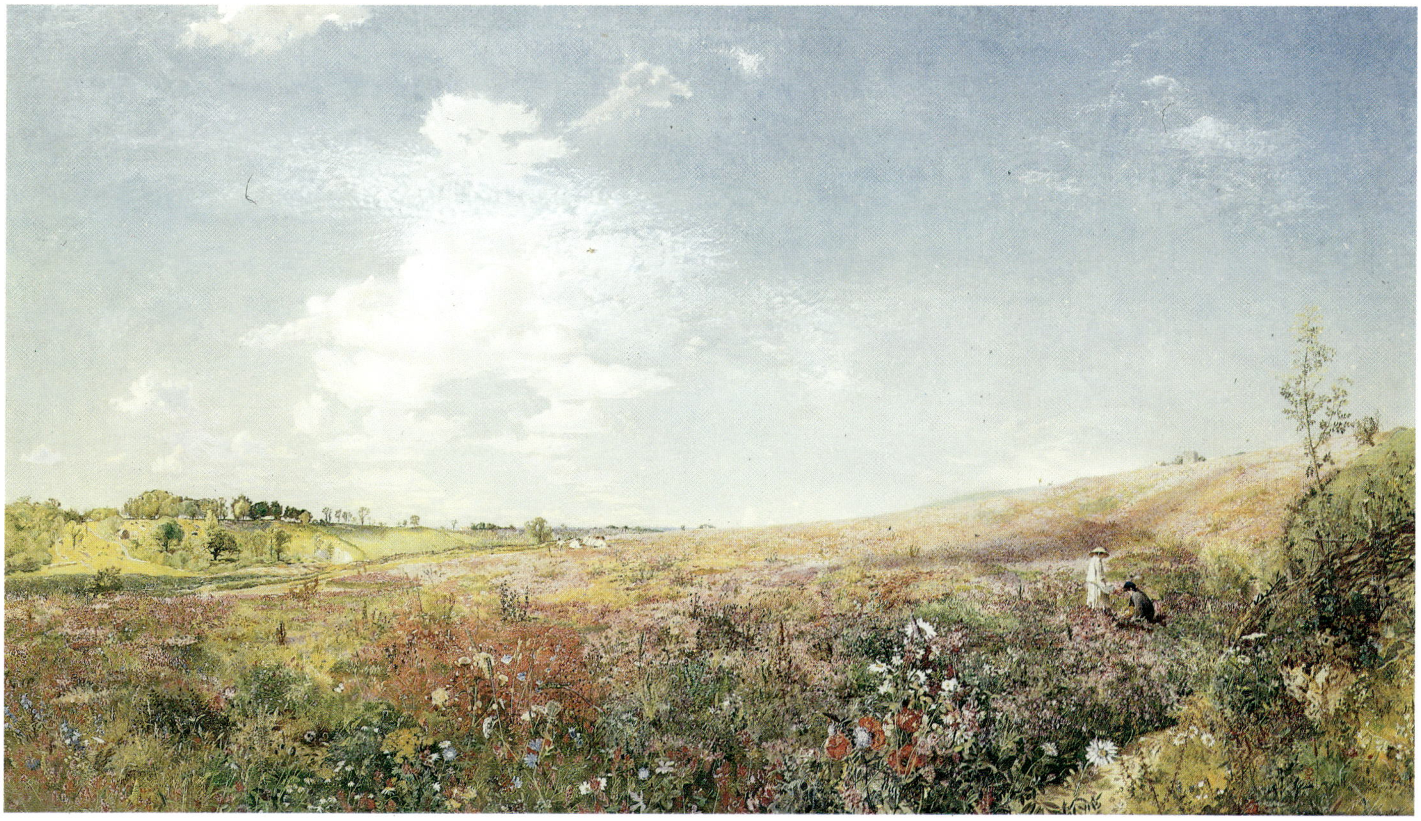

16
JOHN SAMUEL RAVEN
*Summer Landscape*

The most popular artist of the day was William Collins, a painter of idyllic country scenes populated by cheerful and pretty children. His most famous picture showed a smiling and deferential child holding open a gate, with the title *Rustic Civility*. Other leading artists of the 1840s included William F. Witherington, William Shayer, Frederick Richard Lee (the one so admired by Disraeli's Mr Millbank), Thomas Creswick, and Frederick William Hulme. All were extremely competent painters of the English scene, and Hulme's *A Quiet Retreat* (14) may stand as a typical example of the genre. It was painted rather later, in 1860, and already shows a Pre-Raphaelite influence in the intense colouring. It is above all a Victorian townsman's view of the country paradise, painted in Surrey, a county much beloved of the Victorians and still quite unspoiled up to the end of the century. The man has his fishing rod, the lady her sketchbook; the punt sits among waterlilies; all around the lake are tall trees, and beyond is a glimpse of an old castle. This type of pretty, conventional scene was to remain popular with 'mainstream' Victorian artists throughout the century. This was their answer to the naturalism of John Constable.

The two writers who had the greatest influence on nineteenth century landscape painting were Wordsworth and Ruskin. Both in their different ways worshipped nature with religious intensity. Nature was God's work, and was good for the soul of man. Landscape was *Nature's Garden*, the appropriate title of a watercolour by the Kentish artist George Marks (15). Marks, who worked in Kent and Surrey in the 1880s and 1890s, produced soft but intensely lyrical watercolours which are eloquent testimony to the Victorian nostalgia for the unspoiled beauties of nature. Ruskin, a botanist and geologist by training, carried Wordsworth's philosophy into art, exhorting the landscape painter to 'go to Nature in all singleness of heart, and walk with her laboriously and trustingly, having no other thoughts but how best to penetrate her meaning . . .

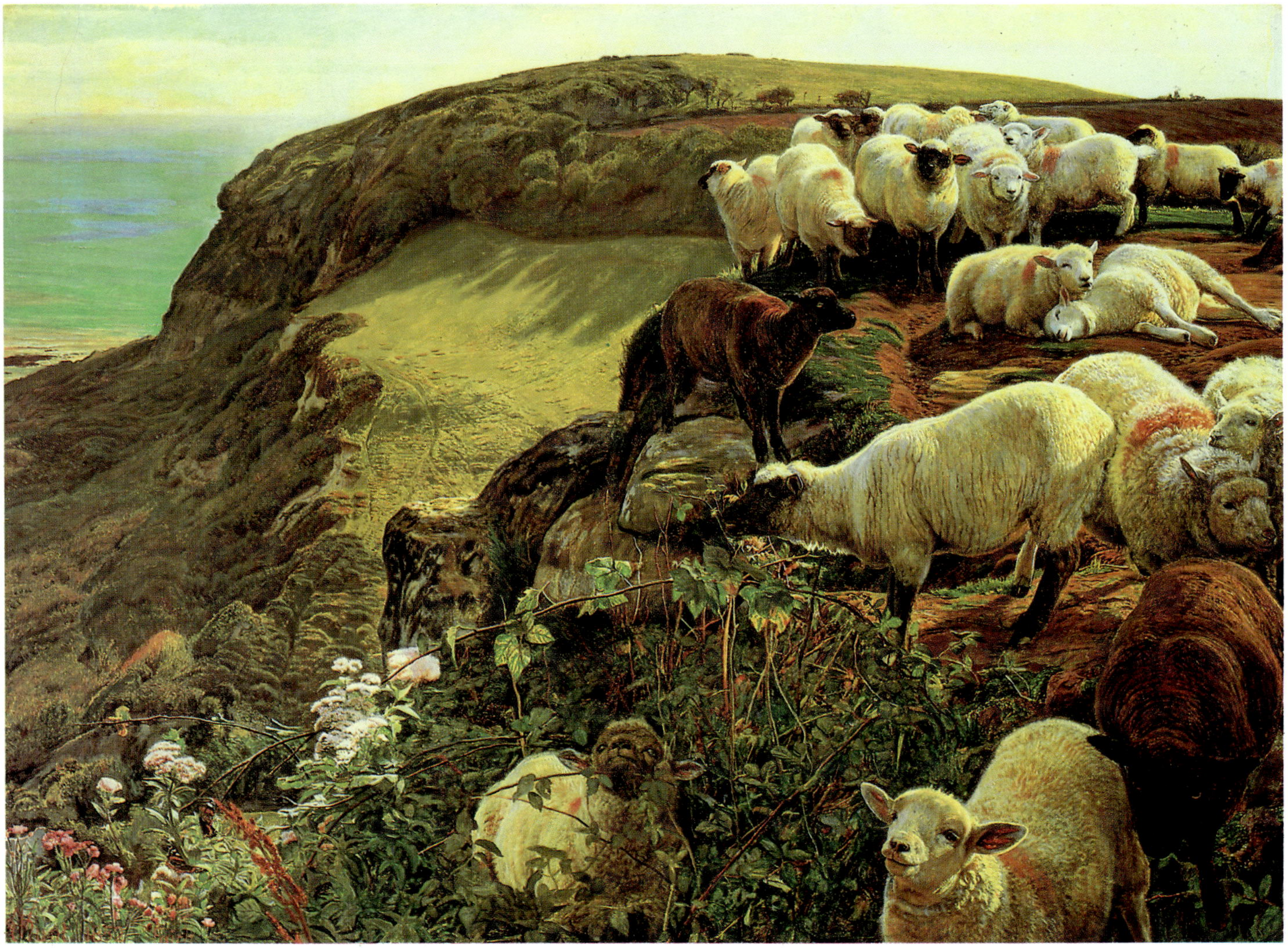

17
William Holman Hunt
*Strayed Sheep*

rejecting nothing, selecting nothing and scorning nothing; believing all things to be right and good, and rejoicing always in the truth'. The biblical tone of this famous passage from *Modern Painters* is typical of Ruskin's passionate and moralistic reverence for nature. The artist who trusted to nature would automatically produce landscape that was noble and good. Nature would take him by the hand and show him the right way. Like many Victorian intellectuals who had lost their religious faith, Ruskin substituted a vaguely pantheistic nature-worship in its place. Nature was less a manifestation of God's greatness than a kind of holy book wherein the good student might read, learn and seek guidance. This incredibly earnest, didactic approach to art is the essence of Ruskin's philosophy, and it is an attitude shared to some degree by a great many of the landscape painters of his time. A picture had not merely to be pretty, it had to do good. A Ruskinian landscape was a moral landscape.

Ruskin's writings were to have an immense influence on Victorian landscape painting for the rest of the century, but his most devoted followers were the Pre-Raphaelites. Among the Brotherhood, Millais and Holman Hunt were the first to attempt landscape based on entirely new, Ruskinian principles. Their ideas were, first, total fidelity to nature, to be achieved by painting out-of-doors in natural daylight. Secondly, painting should be in clear colours over a white ground with the minimum of shadows. This microscopic, inch-by-inch delineation of every leaf and flower was an extremely slow and laborious way of painting. Because it required them to work out-of-doors in all weathers, many a Victorian artist's diaries and letters complain of long hours out in the fields, tormented by heat, cold, rain, wind or insects. A whole day's work might result in an area of only a few square inches being completed. This relentless accumulation of compressed details was often achieved at the expense of the overall composition – a common

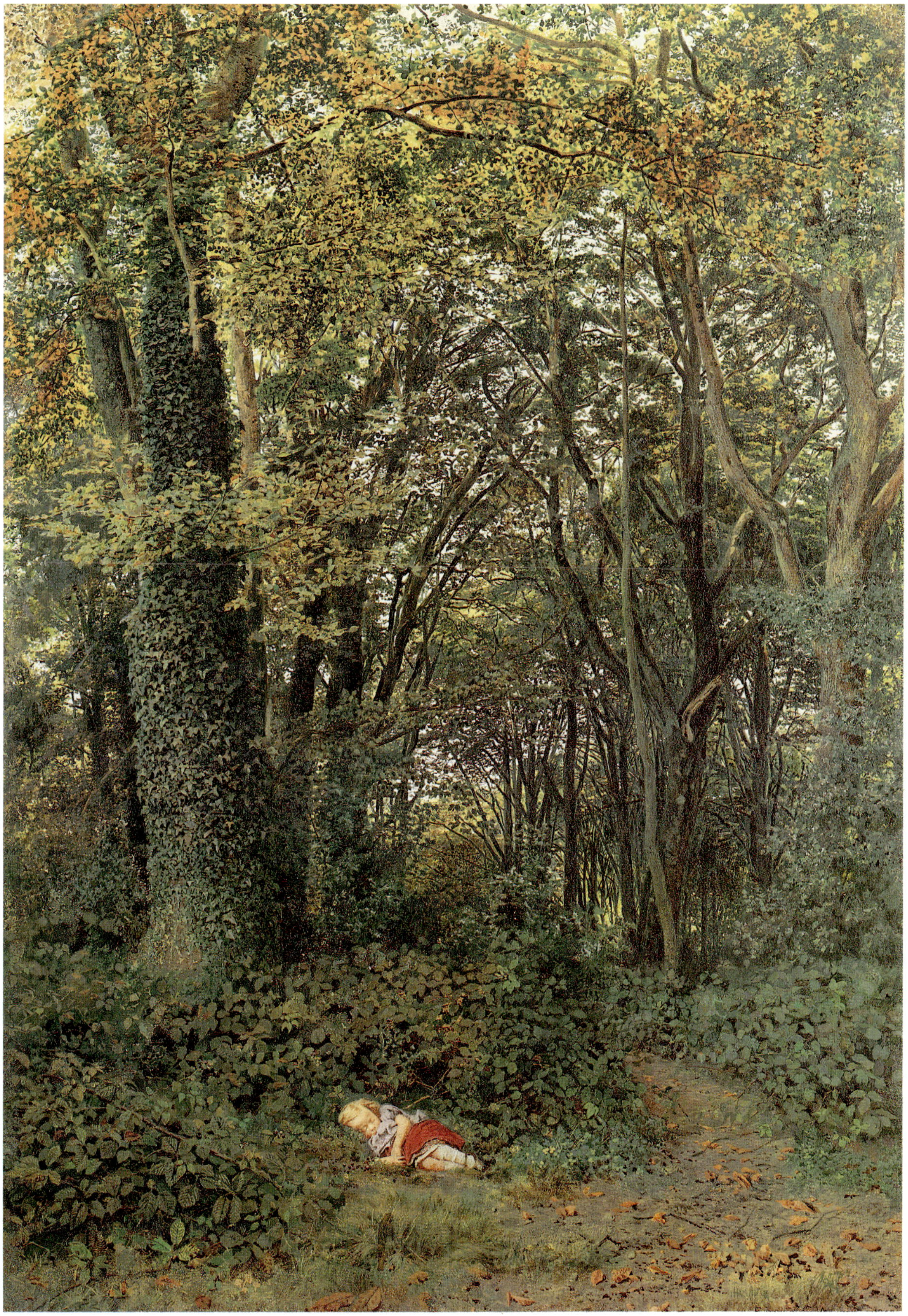

18
EDMUND GEORGE WARREN
*Lost in the Woods*

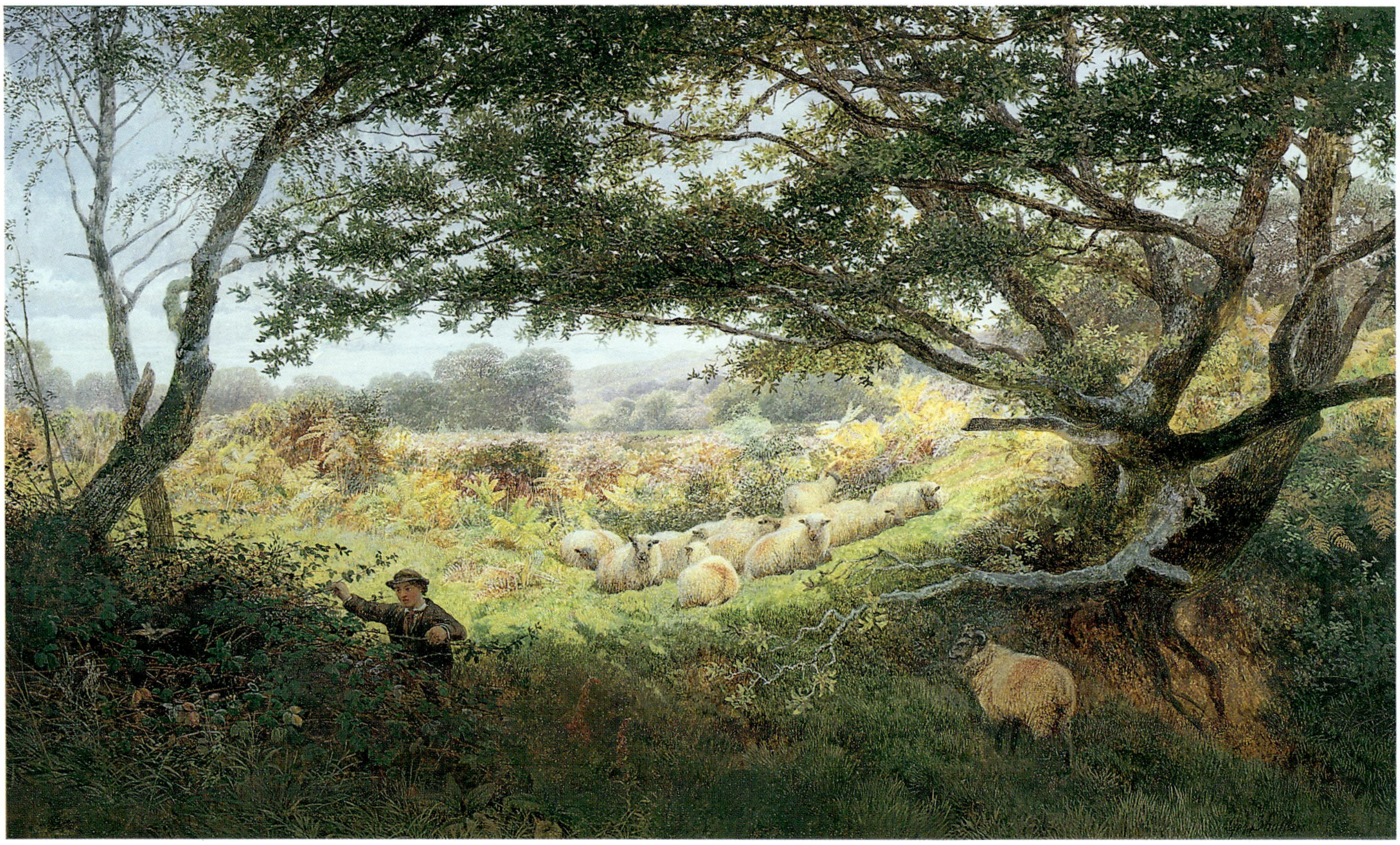

19
GEORGE SHALDERS
*The Shepherd Boy*

fault in Pre-Raphaelite landscapes, but a sacrifice they thought worth making in their search for greater truth and integrity. Many critics argue that to treat every inch of the canvas with equal importance was unnatural, as the human eye could not take in so much detail at once. The lack of shadows also tended to produce an airless, artificial atmosphere that is more surrealistic than realistic. By breaking completely with the English landscape tradition of Constable and David Cox and insisting on total realism, they were condemning themselves to a dead end. But while it lasted the Pre-Raphaelite experiment breathed a new vitality and intensity into Victorian landscape painting. Even after the Pre-Raphaelite influence declined, in the 1860s and 1870s, some landscape painters, especially watercolourists, continued to imitate their style and methods right up to the end of the century. After the Pre-Raphaelites, English landscape painting was never the same again.

Neither Holman Hunt nor Millais, however, were ever pure landscape painters. Some of their most brilliant landscapes were only settings for figures, such as Hunt's *Hireling Shepherd* or *The Light of the World*, or Millais' *Ophelia* or *Blind Girl*. The nearest Hunt ever came to a pure landscape was *Strayed Sheep* (17) of 1852. Painted on the south downs at Fairlight, near Hastings, and exhibited at the Royal Academy in 1853, it is the most remarkable example of a Pre-Raphaelite landscape painted in full sunlight on a summer's day. We know from Hunt's letters and drawings that he in fact suffered appalling weather, and frequently had to work in wind and rain. Throughout every inch of the picture he has studied the effect of sunlight and shadow as they fall on each surface, even down to the veins of the sheeps' ears. The shadows in the landscape are full of surprising blues and violets. The sheep's wool is made up of tiny strokes of many different colours. It is the most intensely scientific and Ruskinian of all Hunt's landscapes, painted, as it were, with a microscope in one hand and a bible

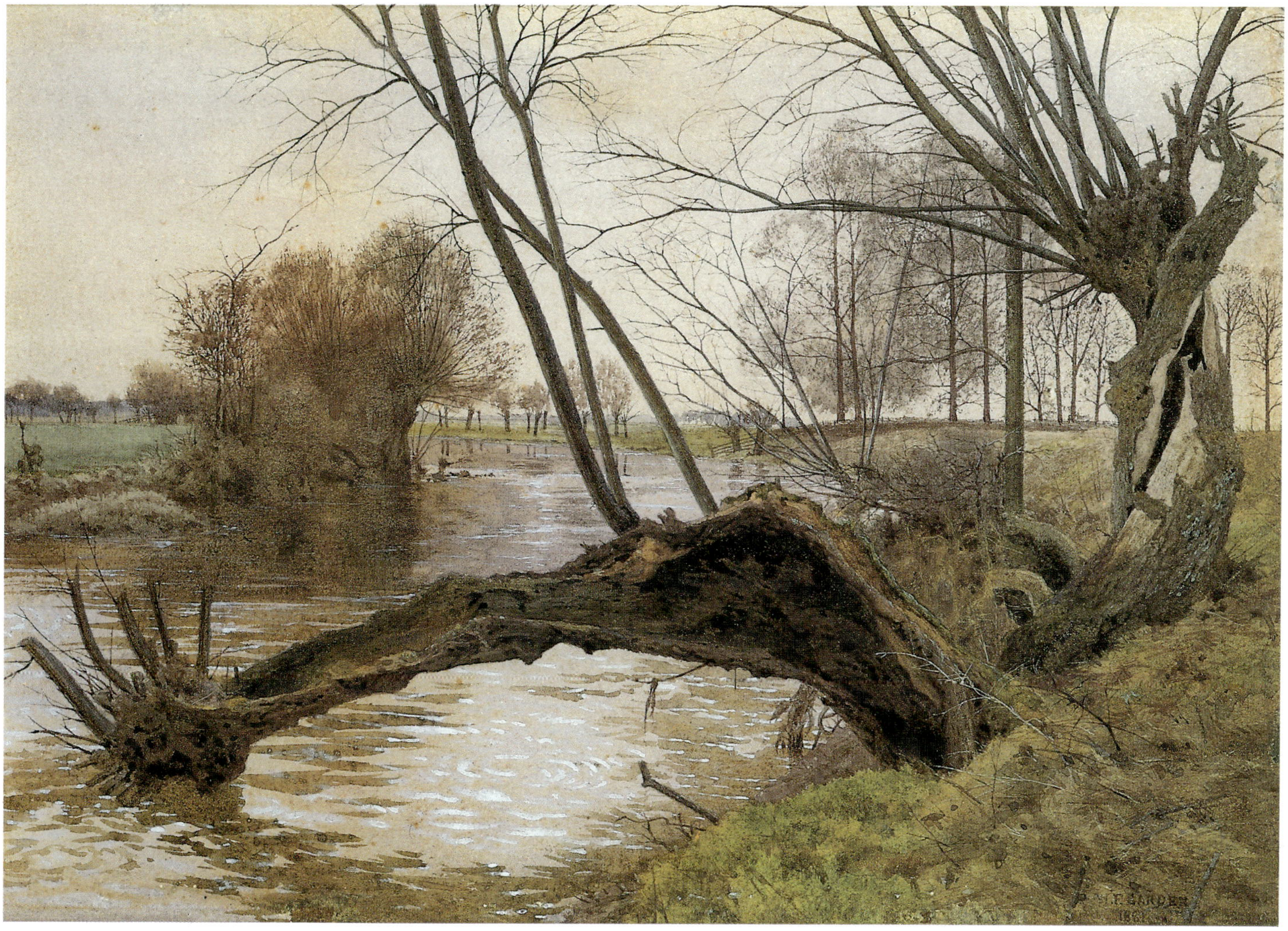

20
WILLIAM FRASER GARDEN
*Willows on the Ouse*

in the other. Its relentless exploration of light and colour anticipates many later developments in French art – not only Impressionism but also Pointillism. Even Delacroix, who saw it at the *Exposition Universelle* of 1855, wrote in his Journal 'I am really astounded by Hunt's Sheep'.

There were some Pre-Raphaelites who did devote themselves to pure landscape, notably Ford Madox Brown, John Brett, William Dyce, William Bell Scott, John William Inchbold and Atkinson Grimshaw. Most of them were encouraged, lectured and bullied by Ruskin. Many younger artists were inspired by the Pre-Raphaelite example to produce an occasional brilliant work. John Samuel Raven's *Summer Landscape* (16) is a case of this. It is also a reminder of the incredible wealth of wild flowers to be found in the Victorian countryside. Pre-Raphaelite techniques could be applied equally well to watercolour, and resulted in many works of astonishing intensity and beauty. Edmund George Warren's *Lost in the Woods* (18), for example, is as good a study of woodlands as any picture by the more famous Pre-Raphaelites.

Warren was one of an artistic tribe. His father, Henry Warren, was a watercolourist, as were his two brothers, H. Clifford and Bonomi Edward. All three of the brothers particularly liked painting the interiors of dark, mysterious woods, with the sunlight filtering through the trees on to the foliage below. England's woodlands and forests must have been infinitely wilder and more beautiful than they are now, and they provided the perfect landscape for a dedicated Pre-Raphaelite, prepared to paint it leaf by leaf. Ruskin, unpredictable as usual, was critical of E.G. Warren's work in his *Academy Notes*, describing his trees as 'pleasant fly-traps to draw public attention, but without refined work or feeling'. Ruskin frequently criticised painters for using precisely the methods he had advocated in his books. Also decidedly Ruskinian is *The Shepherd Boy* (19) by George Shalders, this time a view out of woodlands

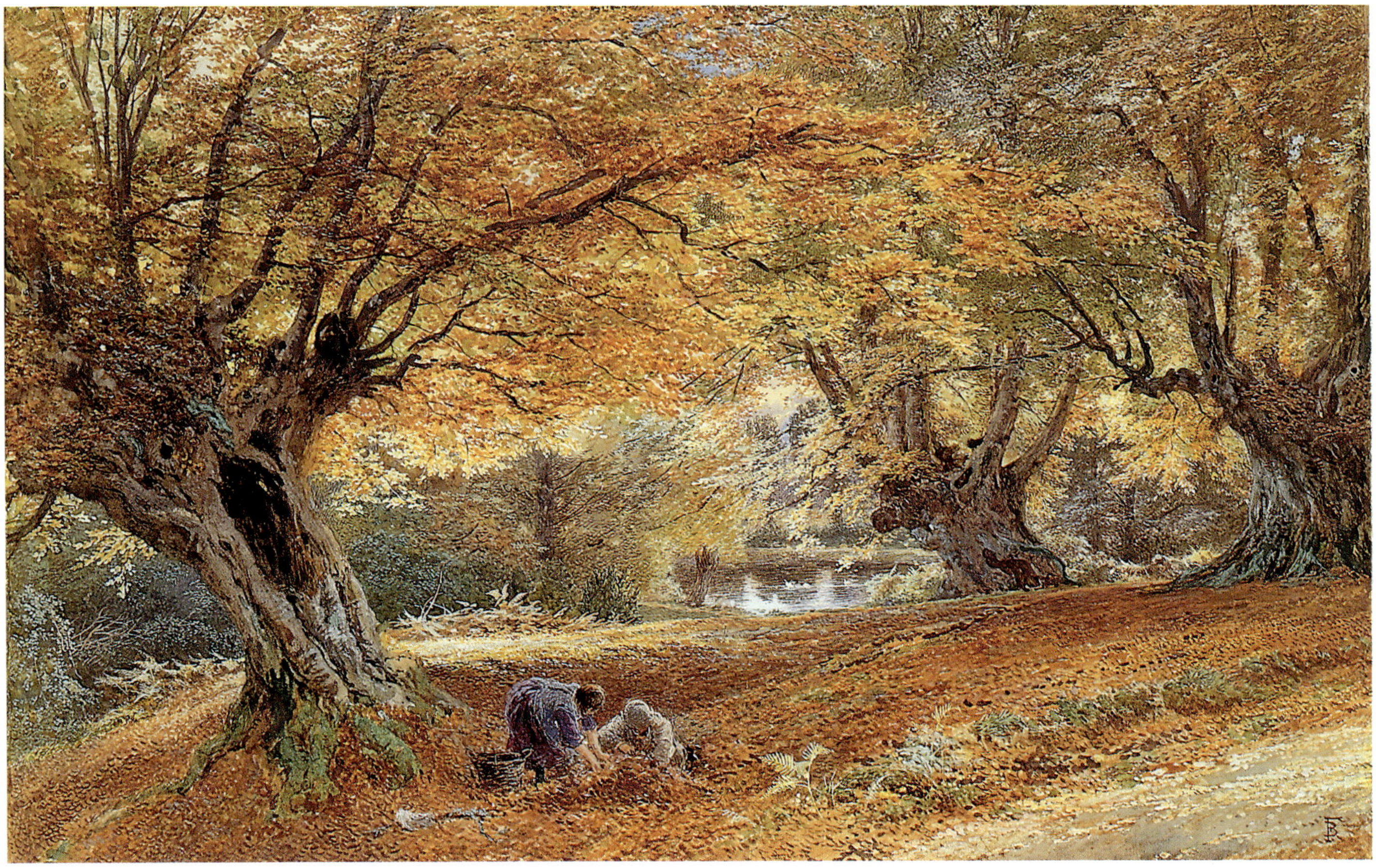

21
MYLES BIRKET FOSTER
*Burnham Beeches*

into a brilliantly sunlit landscape. Shalders was one of the many landscape painters to fall under Pre-Raphaelite influence in the 1850s and 60s, but whose other work is much more conventional. The work of the Huntingdon artist William Fraser Garden (20), working towards the end of the century, has an extraordinary, almost surrealistic stillness and intensity that still owes much to the Pre-Raphaelite vision.

After the Pre-Raphaelites, landscape painting becomes infinitely complex, but a few definitions can be attempted. Probably the most popular landscape painter from the 1860s onwards was Birket Foster. Foster was a wood engraver and book illustrator by training, and he brought the sharpness and minuteness of an engraver's eye to bear on the art of watercolour. One of the books he illustrated was the *Year Book of the Country* by William and Mary Howitt, authors of many popular mid-Victorian books about the countryside, such as *The Rural Life of England* (1838). Finding the traditional colour wash style uncongenial, Foster adopted the Pre-Raphaelite method of working over a white ground, using a stipple technique with very fine brushes. His methods were very similar to those of the still-life painter William Henry Hunt, whose works Foster both admired and collected. Foster's enchanting visions of the English countryside, with their picturesque cottages, happy villagers and cheerful children, are some of the most enduringly popular of all images of England. The Victorians loved them; a successful businessman with any pretensions to artistic taste had to own one. Their appeal has remained constant throughout the twentieth century, even through the darkest days of modernism. Foster's works will appear elsewhere in this book, but *Burnham Beeches* (21) is an example of his landscape style. Burnham Beeches is a wood famed for its ancient gnarled trees, and was much beloved of Victorian painters. On a sunny day there must have been rows of them at their easels, painting away.

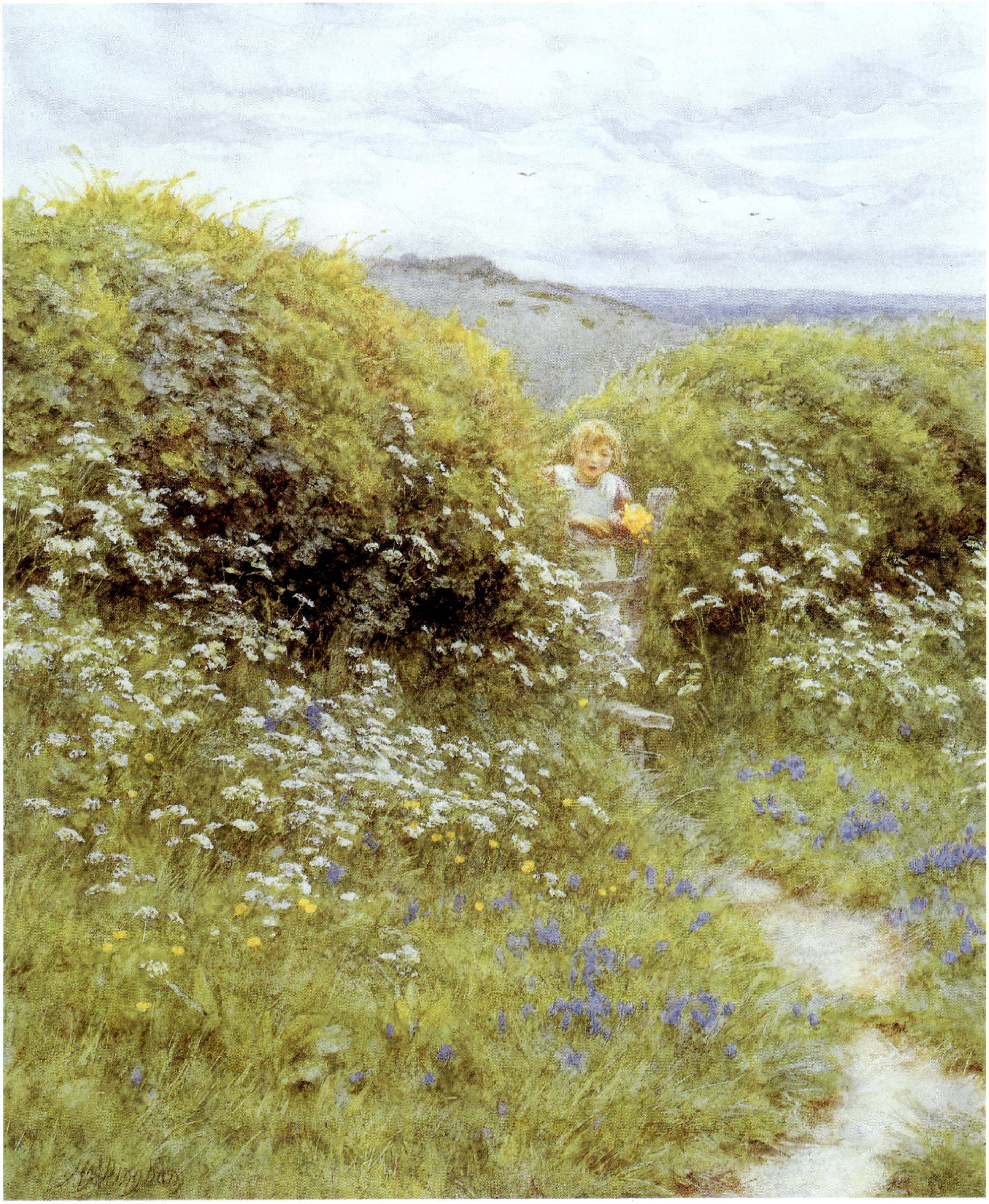

22
HELEN ALLINGHAM
*Cow Parsley and Bluebells*

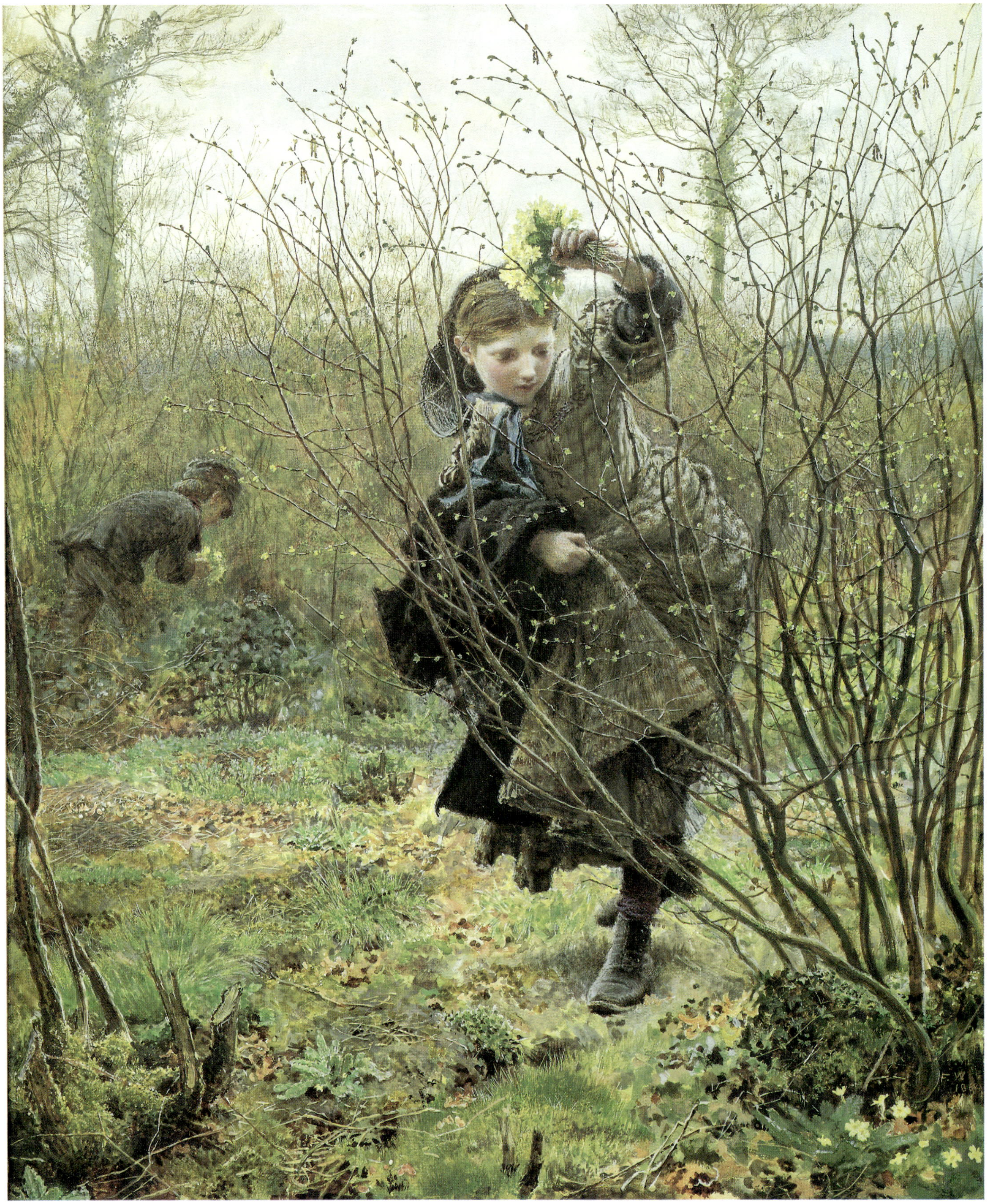

23
FREDERICK WALKER
*Spring*

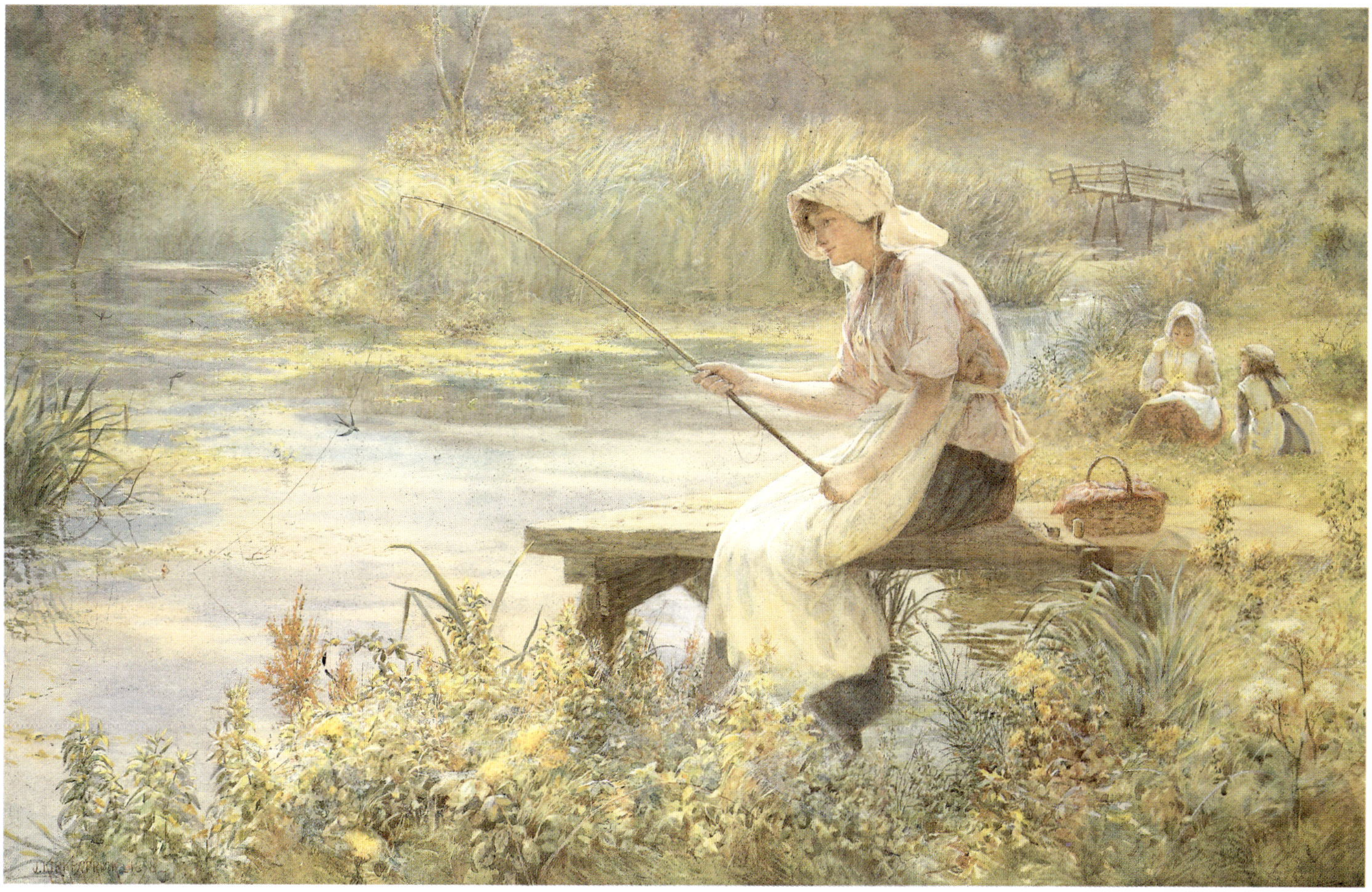

24
JOSEPH KIRKPATRICK
*The Gentle Art*

Fine old trees have always been recognised as an essential element in the beauty of the English countryside. Francis Kilvert, writing about another famous wood, Moccas Park, on the Wye, was awed by its ancient oaks:

> I fear those grey old men of Moccas, huge, strange, long-armed, deformed, hunch-backed, misshapen oak men . . . with such tales to tell, as when they whisper them to each other in the midsummer nights, make the silver birches weep and the poplars and aspens shiver and the long ears of the hares and rabbits stand on end. No human hand planted those oaks. They are 'the trees which the Lord hath planted'. They look as if they had been at the beginning and making of the world, and they will probably see its end.

Kilvert's vivid words recall the animated and menacing trees of Arthur Rackham. By the middle of the century, the building of wooden ships had largely ended, so the oak trees were simply left to grow. In many cases they remained to adorn the parks of country houses. Many Victorian landowners were keen tree-planters, and the planting of woodlands actually increased in the second half of the century. They were equally keen to continue the tradition of laying out parks around their houses. In 1892 England possessed no less than four hundred deer parks.

Foster had innumerable followers in the 1860s and 70s, who were generally referred to as the pastoral or idyllic school. The best-known is Helen Allingham (22). Perhaps no-one has painted wild flowers growing naturally in the fields with such skill and delicacy as Allingham. She particularly liked fields of ox-eye daisies, and carpets of bluebells or primroses. It was old cottages, however, that were to become her trademark, and these will feature in another chapter. Birket Foster's influence remained pervasive for the rest of the century. The vogue for

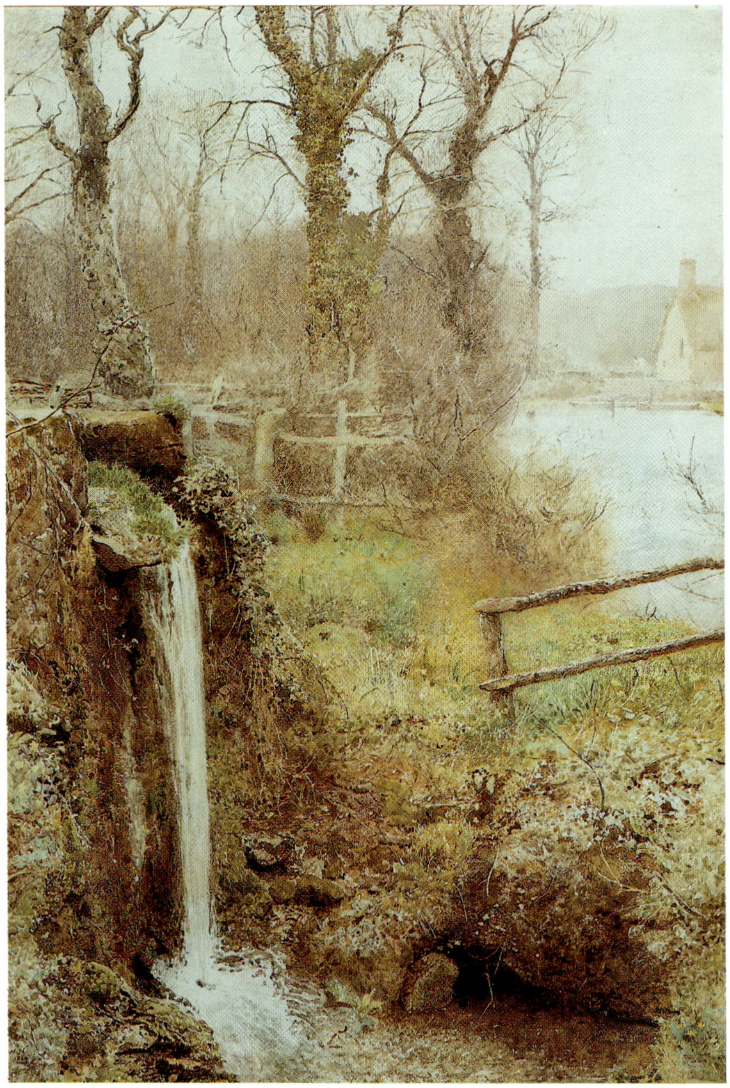

25
JOHN WILLIAM NORTH
*A Woodland Spring*

pretty, summery pictures of girls in white dresses and bonnets seemed limitless, as evinced by Joseph Kirkpatrick's enchanting *The Gentle Art* (24) of 1898. Kirkpatrick was a Liverpool artist who studied in Paris under Bouguereau, but he seems to have preferred the countryside of his native land to French academicism. The same idyllic, almost ecstatic celebration of that brief phenomenon the English summer is evident in literally thousands of late Victorian watercolours, of which the strangely-named Roberto Angelo Kittermaster Marshall's *Summer Landscape* (26) is a fine example. The work of Birket Foster and his followers is really a combination of the Pre-Raphaelite and the sentimental. It was to prove a popular recipe.

A more serious follower of Birket Foster was the influential but short-lived Frederick Walker, who died in 1875 aged only 35. In his watercolours, such as the famous *Spring* (23) in the Victoria and Albert Museum, he tried to inject more serious and symbolic figures into the pastoral settings of Foster and Allingham. His approach was simpler and less sentimental, and he attempted subjects involving distress, poverty and old age – a path down which the more prudent Birket Foster would never have followed. Through his work for the *Graphic* magazine, founded in 1869, Walker influenced a whole generation of painters and watercolourists, including the young Van Gogh, who lived in London between 1873 and 1876. One of his closest friends and followers was John William North (25), whose particularly delicate style of pastoral landscape owes much to Walker. Another follower was Robert Walker MacBeth, whose watercolour illustrated here (27), with its idyllic mood, and carefully composed figures, is typical of the Walker style. MacBeth also painted more heroic pictures of peasants toiling, in what Ruskin mockingly called 'galvanised-Elgin' attitudes, which have been compared to the novels of Thomas Hardy. The landscape style of Fred Walker, North, MacBeth, George Hemming Mason, and others like them, is the landscape of the

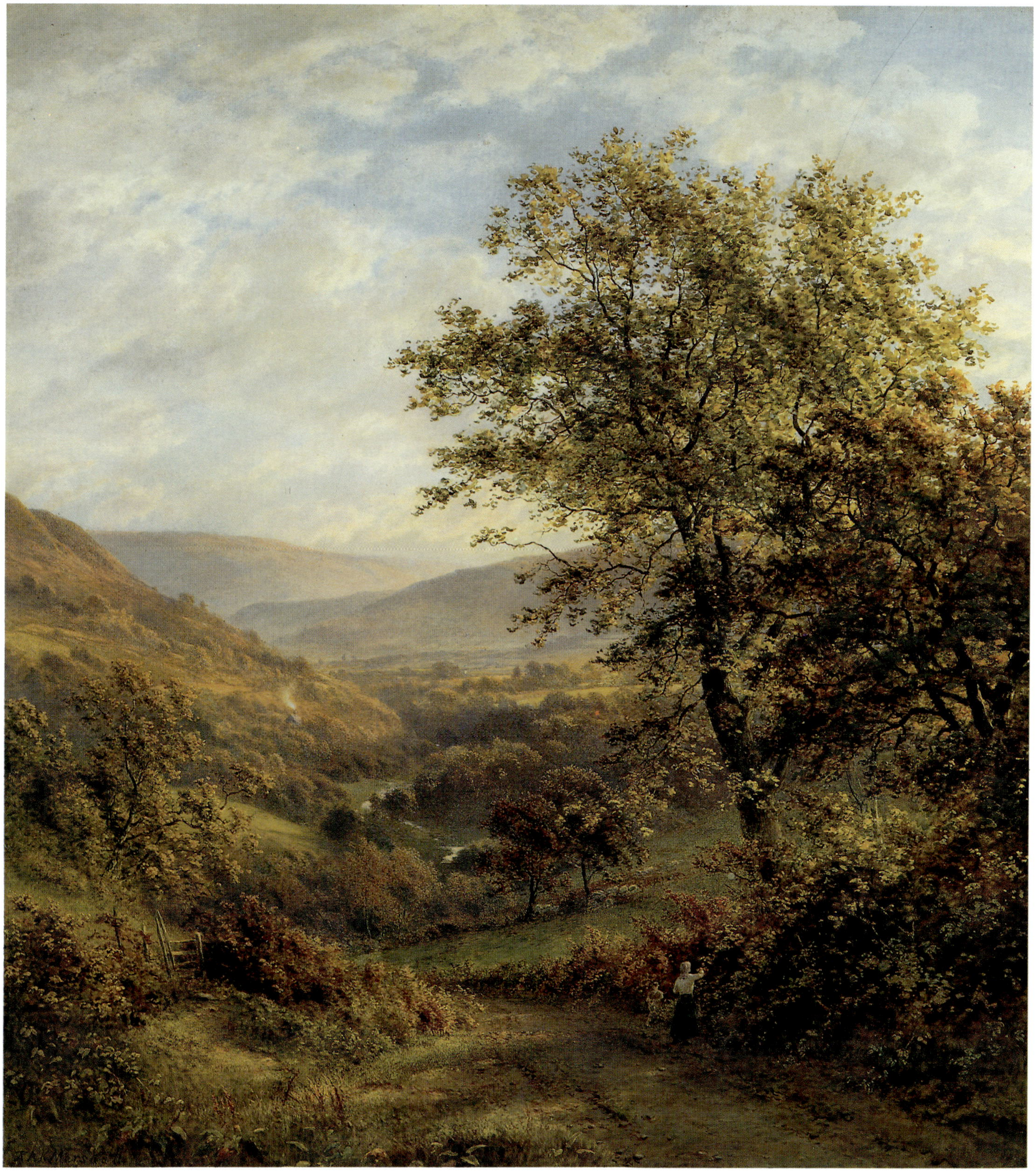

26
ROBERT A.K. MARSHALL
*Summer Landscape*

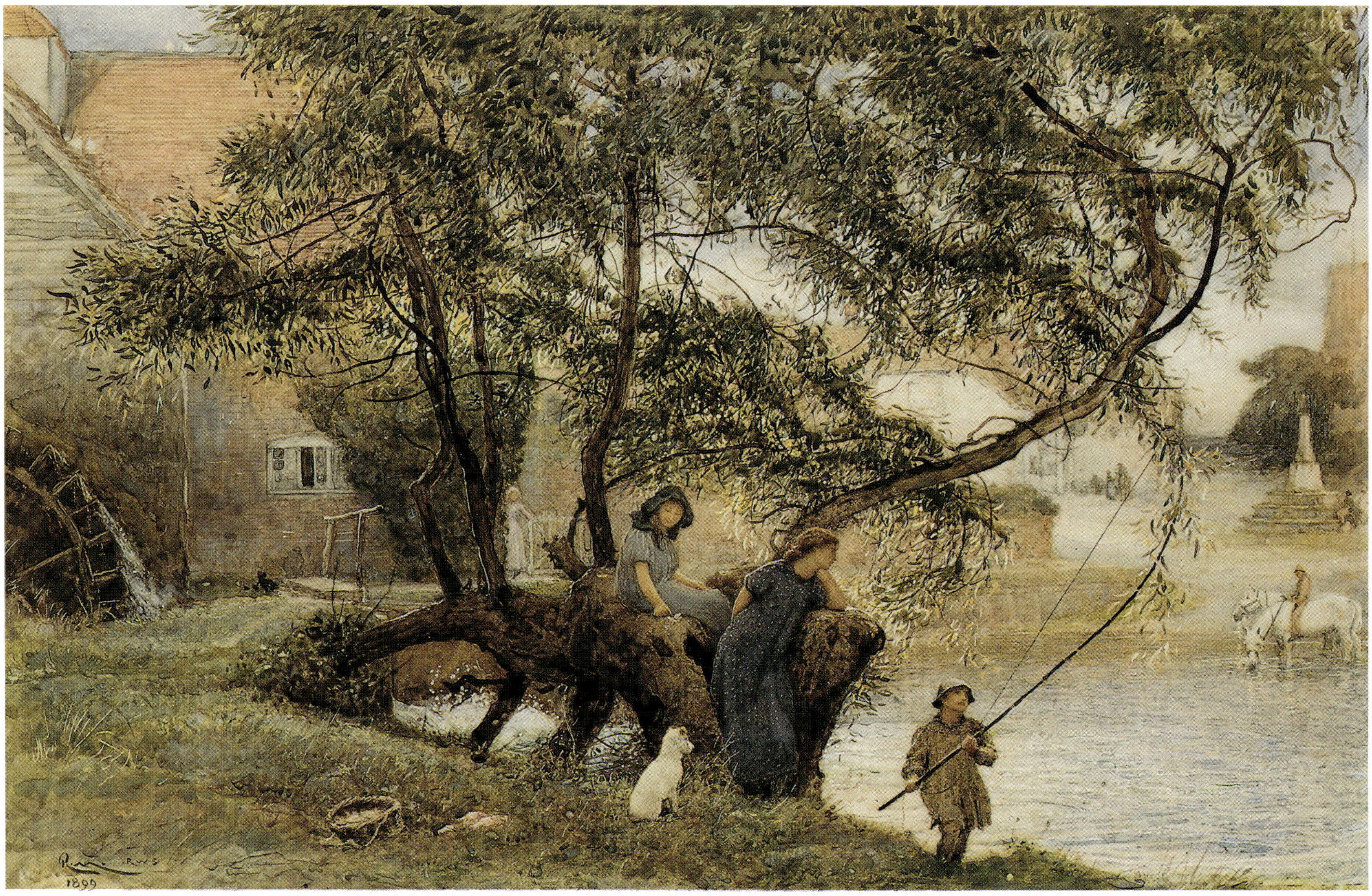

27
Robert Walker MacBeth
*By the River*

aesthetic movement – refined, poetic, intelligent, cultured, and with a tinge of underlying concern about social issues.

Some equally serious landscape painters, like John Linnell, are difficult to fit into any category. Linnell, a friend and pupil of William Blake, and father-in-law of Samuel Palmer, was a survivor of the romantic movement. From 1807 until his death in 1882, he exhibited at the Royal Academy his own distinctively romantic visions of the English countryside, and although his work was enormously admired he was a lonely figure who created a style entirely his own.

After Linnell, one of the most revered landscape painters was Benjamin Williams Leader. He was as productive and as long-lived as Linnell, dying in 1923. Like any artist whose life spans a huge period, his work goes through different phases. As a young man he was much influenced by the Pre-Raphaelites, but later he changed to a lighter, more naturalistic style. His later work becomes steadily more impressionistic, but he was always admired for his honest and literal renderings of the landscape. England's rivers are another of its glories, and Leader was a great lover of river scenes (29), especially on the Severn near his native Worcester, and in North Wales. Leader's lifelong devotion to English scenery always assured him a wide following, and he was brave enough to paint one of the wettest pictures in English art, *February Fill Dyke*, now in Birmingham City Art Gallery. Spring, summer and autumn all had their devotees, but very few artists have cared to paint the miseries of a wet winter's day in England.

Another artist who had no fear of a gloomy subject was Frank Holl. 'Give me a grey day' was one of his frequent sayings. During the 1870s Holl, Hubert von Herkomer and Luke Fildes, all illustrators for the *Graphic*, began to paint social realist subjects with a directness and honesty that most Victorians found shocking. Most of their famous pictures are of urban subjects – Fildes's *Applicants for Admission to a Casual Ward*,

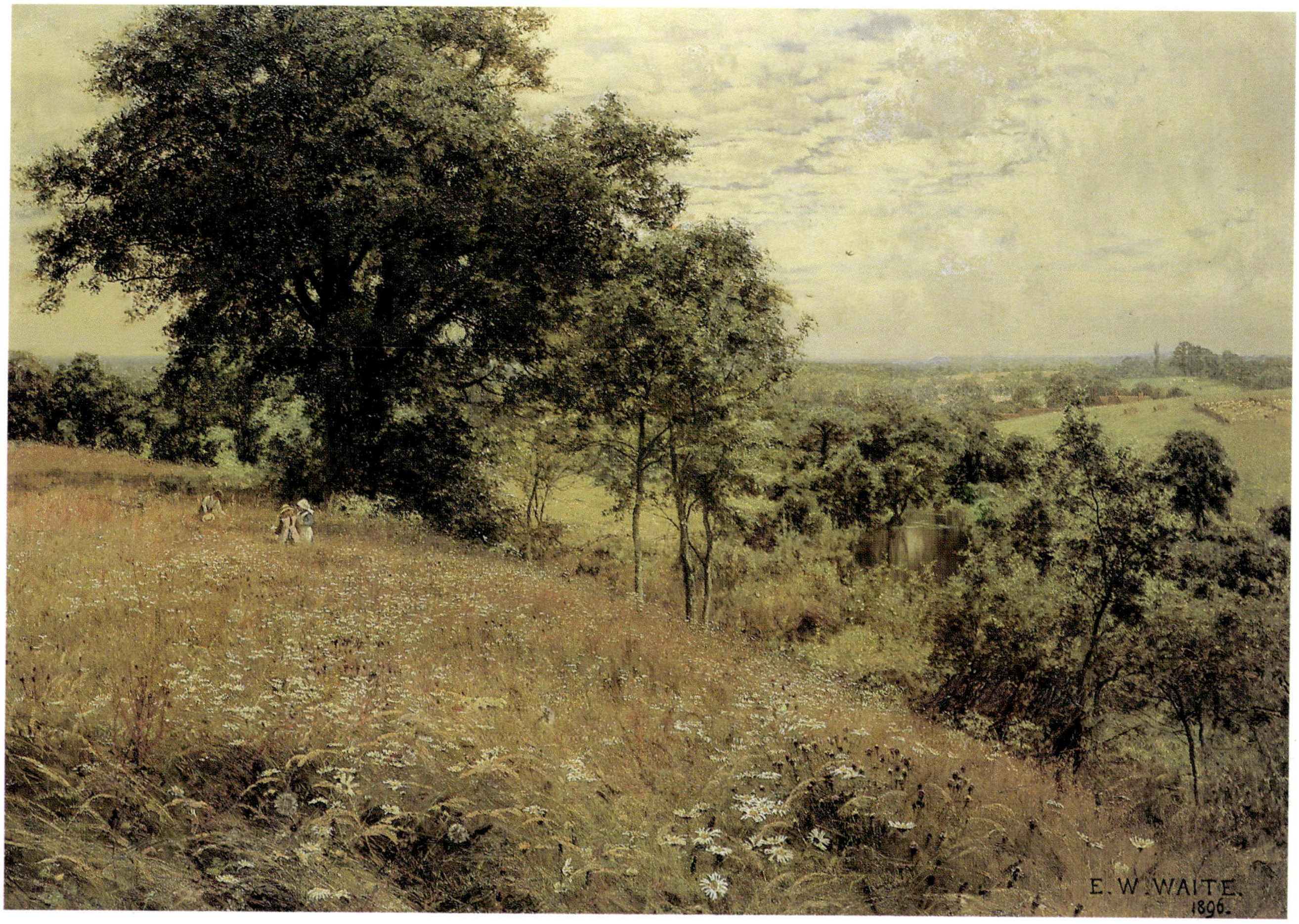


28
EDWARD WILKINS WAITE
*In the Meadow*

Holl's *Newgate, Committed for Trial* or Herkomer's *On Strike* – but all of them painted country subjects as well, the most famous being Herkomer's *Hard Times.* This, and the works of Holl and Fildes, will appear in later chapters. The social realists, although hardly a full-scale school or movement, influenced a great many artists in the later years of the century. Their work forms a vital contrast to the avalanche of idyllic rusticity which engulfs most of Victorian landscape painting, and it reminds us that there was always a Victorian social conscience.

All the artists I have mentioned so far are essentially English figures. From the 1860s onward, artists began to travel more, and study on the continent and foreign influences become more evident. The Grosvenor Gallery was founded in 1877 as a focal point for new, avant-garde ideas, including European ones. In 1886 came the New English Art Club, dedicated to promoting French impressionism. In 1899 Stanhope Forbes and his wife Elizabeth founded the Newlyn School in Cornwall, already a flourishing artistic colony devoted to painting fisherfolk in the French *plein-air* style of Millet and Bastien-Lepage. The Barbizon School had its admirers too, such as Alfred East and John Arnesby Brown. Even the gigantic animal pictures of Rosa Bonheur were imitated by H.W.B. Davis and others. The Hague School in Holland was also influential, especially in Scotland among the Glasgow School and others. By 1900 Robert Bevan was painting Exmoor in the brilliant fauvist colours of Gauguin. Victorian landscape really runs across the whole gamut of nineteenth-century artistic movements. The work of nearly all these different schools, except fauvism, will be found among the later illustrations in this book.

The influence of the Impressionists was most widespread in the last twenty years of the century, and can be seen at work in the watercolours of even a provincial artist like Thomas

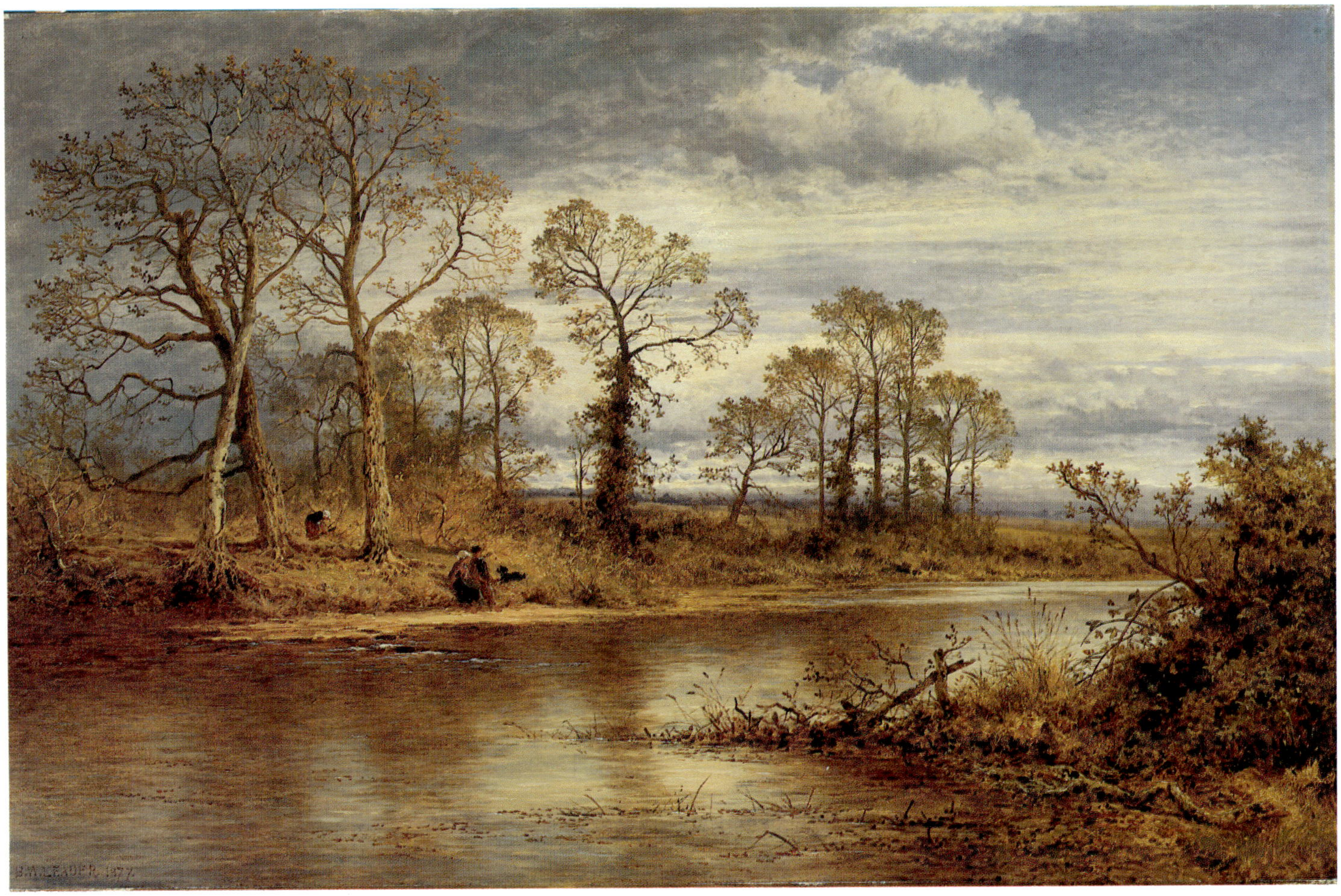

29
BENJAMIN WILLIAMS LEADER
*An English River in Autumn*

Mackay (8). Mackay was a Liverpool artist, painting in Cheshire and North Wales, who developed a charming and distinctively English style of impressionistic watercolour. With a painter like Edward W. Waite (28) we find several different strands combined – impressionist technique, a robust love of English scenery, and a touch of Helen Allingham in the white bonnets and wild flowers.

Even this brief survey suggests just how incredibly rich and varied English landscape painting was in the nineteenth century. Never can the English countryside have been studied so intensely, and with such a variety of stylistic results. The invention of photography, contrary to expectations, seems to have spurred landscape painters on to even greater efforts. The whole Pre-Raphaelite landscape movement can be seen as an attempt by painters to prove that painting could do everything that photography could do and do it better. It was widely thought that photography, with its ability to reproduce nature exactly, would actually kill off the art of painting altogether, but instead Victorian landscape painting flourished more than ever. It was a period when almost anything seemed possible. One artist, John Brandon Smith, spent his whole career painting waterfalls – and is now known as Waterfall Smith; William Henry Hunt painted birds' nests, so is known as Birdsnest Hunt. But enough of landscape. It is time to move on to the more serious business of work. We begin with the place where most rural labour was based – the farm itself.

# Chapter Two

# THE FARM

Few years are past, since, on the paddock green,
Beneath the hill, that old farm-house was seen,
Round which the barley-mows and wheat ricks rose,
And cattle sought refreshment and repose.

William Holloway, *The Peasant's Fate*

The Victorian idea of a farmer was Farmer Giles, a genial if occasionally crotchety figure, in clothes of an antique cut, muddy boots and gaiters, with a strong regional accent, and usually carrying a large stick. This is how the painter John Evan Hodgson saw him, in *The Farmer's Dream* (30). With his clay pipe and glass of ale, he dreams of the harvest being gathered in to his splendid old timbered barns, in a farmyard teeming with livestock. It is a surprising picture for Hodgson, who usually devoted himself to historical pictures and Arab subjects. He was one of the so-called St John's Wood group of artists, the 'school of slashed breeches' as Swinburne described them, and was more at home painting cavaliers and roundheads. Another member of the group was William Frederick Yeames, painter of the famous *And when did you last see your Father?*

There are many farmers in Victorian literature. Here is Alfred Williams's description of a typical Farmer Giles, in his book *In a Wiltshire Village*:

Farmer Tull was one of the very old school, who had done fairly well in his time, but had not the faculty of making the most of his earnings. . . . He lived well, paid high wages, cared for no man and was fond – perhaps over-fond – of little drops of gin. . . . The old man was tall and stout; his shoulders were round with fat, his face rather sour-looking and flabby, his eyes were grey and steely . . . square forehead, heavy brows, thick nose, mouth pursed up disagreeably, double chin, frosty pate. He always wore a suit of light, large check and hobbled about on two crab-sticks, for he was afflicted with gout. . . . But the old man was wondrously good-natured. There was a hot cooked supper at night; bread and cheese and ale in abundance. . . . His old wife – as kind a body as ever lived – was so stout she could not walk straight through doors in the farmhouse, but had to negotiate them sideways.

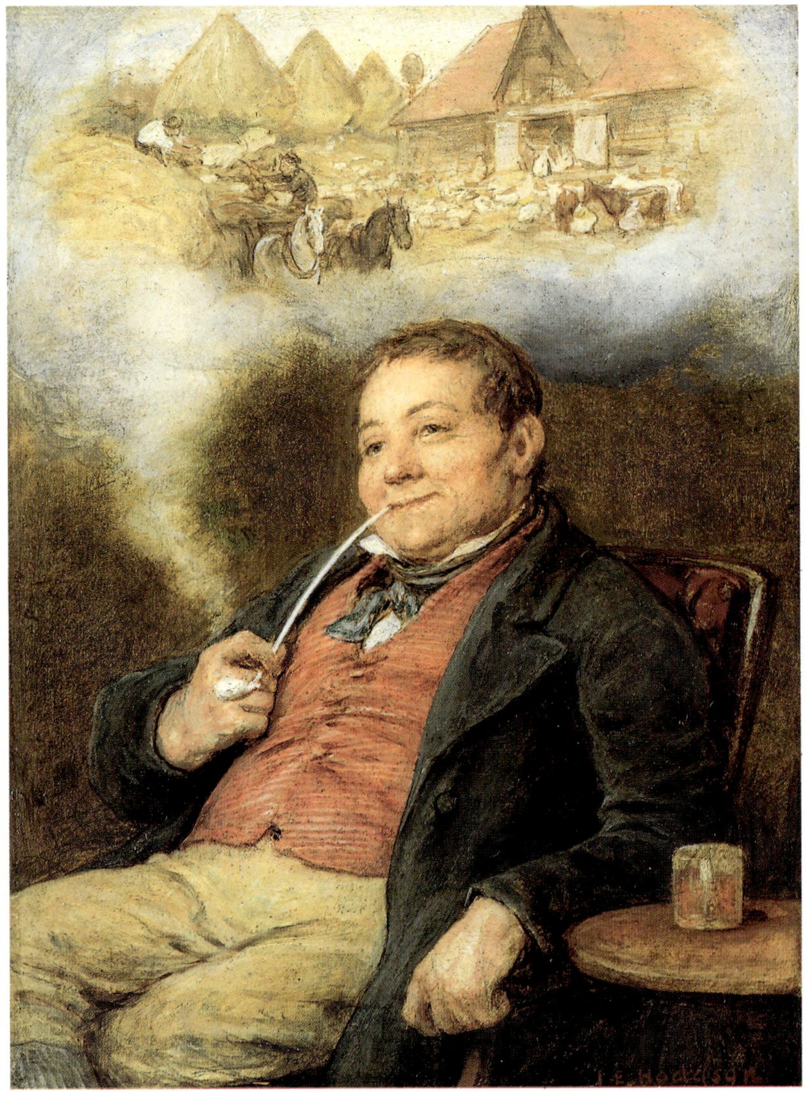

30
JOHN EVAN HODGSON
*The Farmer's Dream*

Conditions on any farm varied enormously from county to county, village to village, even from farm to farm. Much might depend on the character and generosity of the farmer himself. Williams observed that 'those farmers who are strong and hearty in health, fond of a bite and a sup, and whose cellars are well stocked with cider and ale, are always the best natured. Teetotal farmers are usually parsimonious and near, ready to extract the last ounce of labour from the individual. . . .'

Most Victorian farmers were smallholders, farming as little as five to fifty acres. The great majority were tenants, and in general deferential to their landlords, except in matters of religion and education on which they were likely to maintain a stubborn independence. Farmers tended to be methodists, or chapel goers, their landlords Church of England, or Catholic. On larger estates the landowner might insist on his tenants attending the same church as himself. Up to about 1870, farmers had in general become exceedingly prosperous, and there had been a steady rise in their social status. Some, like John Pullett in George Eliot's *Mill on the Floss*, were even rich and cultured enough to mix with the gentry. The average Victorian farmer, however, was probably a more down-to-earth character, like Tennyson's *Northern Farmer*, or Richard Jefferies's John Hodson. The pub and the market were his social centres. Market-day dinners, or 'ordinaries' – meetings held in local pubs to discuss farming matters, local events and politics – were the highlights of a farmer's year. At home, he would still keep to the ancient custom of eating together with his workers, several of whom lived in the house. Gradually this began to change: farmers and their wives preferred to eat on their own, banishing their labourers to out-buildings or cottages. William Cobbett particularly deplored this development, abhorring the gentleman farmer, with 'a painted lady for a wife, sons apeing the young squires and lords; a house crammed up with sofas, pianos, and all sorts of fooleries'. Like so many champions of

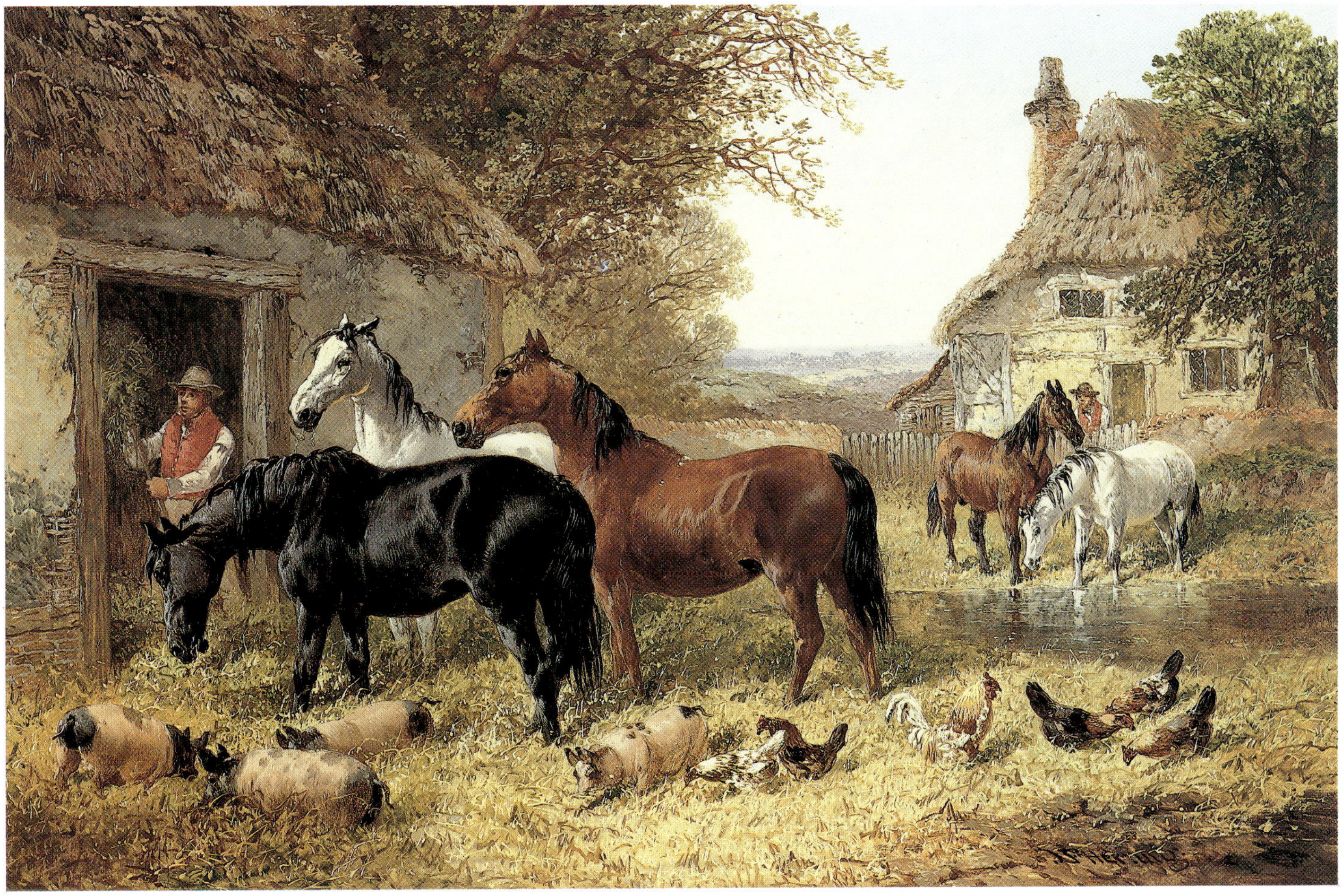

31
John Frederick Herring, Junior
*Horses in a Farmyard*

the working class, Cobbett found it intolerable that they should want to improve themselves socially. Although many farmers prospered, and built new houses and even halls for themselves, the old ways survived on small farms and in remote parts of the country. In the north especially, the old wide chimney with oak settles was still the centre of the farmhouse; the farmer and his wife and daughters sat on one side, with the men on the other side with their shoes off.

A Victorian farmyard must have been a messy, muddy and smelly place, but this was not the view presented by Victorian painters. For them it was invariably picturesque and cheerful, an essential element in the rural paradise. Thomas Baker's *Old Park Farm* (32) for example looks prosperous and orderly, with fine old buildings and trees, and neat green meadows full of contented cows and sheep. Baker was a Leamington artist, and painted country scenery in his native Warwickshire. He presents us with an accurately painted, if idealised, picture of the Midlands countryside. The most prolific of all Victorian painters of farmyards was John Frederick Herring, Junior, son of the famous sporting and racing artist of the same name. Herring Junior imitated his father's style closely, but developed his own inimitable vision of the farmyard (31). The buildings are invariably ancient, usually thatched; the farmyard is entirely free of mud or manure; and an unlikely assortment of animals rootle about among suspiciously clean straw, which the farmer seems to have laid thoughtfully in the farmyard itself – hardly good or normal farming practice. Unlikely or not, the Herring farmyard proved an immensely popular recipe, and he painted literally hundreds of them. They were also much copied: this was clearly the type of farmyard that a successful manufacturer or merchant wanted to have hanging in his villa.

Perhaps closer to reality, but still very idealised, is the Kentish farmyard painted by Thomas Sidney Cooper (33). Although many new farm buildings were erected in the nineteenth

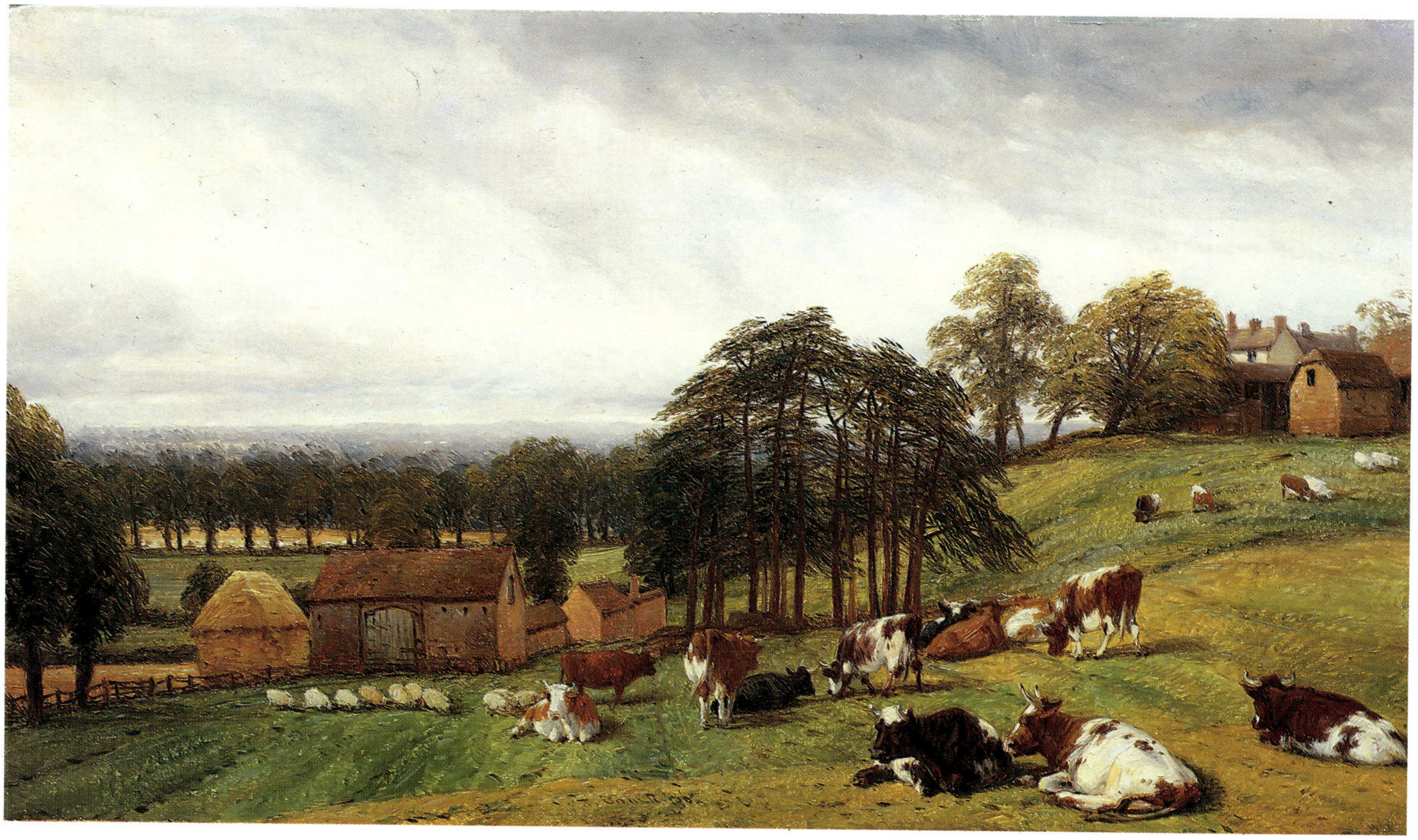

32
THOMAS BAKER
*Cattle and Sheep at Old Park Farm*

century, Herring and Cooper were not exaggerating in their pictures of old farm buildings – timbered and thatched affairs, some many hundreds of years old. In *Middlemarch*, George Eliot describes Dagley's farmhouse: 'The mossy thatch of the cow-shed, the broken, grey barn-doors, the pauper labourers in ragged breeches. . . could have made a sort of picture which we have all paused over as "a charming bit", touching other sensibilities than those which are stirred by the depression of the agricultural interest.' Old buildings, and old methods, including ploughing with oxen and threshing by hand with a flail, still survived on many farms right through the century.

T.S. Cooper was one of the longest-lived and best-known of all Victorian painters, born in 1803 and dying in 1902, just short of his century. He studied in Brussels with the famous Belgian artist Eugene Verboeckhoven, whose style much influenced his own. Both artists were followers in the great Dutch tradition of animal painting, established in the seventeenth century by Paulus Potter and Aelbert Cuyp. Cooper's Kentish farmyard is a Victorianisation of the Dutch tradition, more sentimental and picturesque than any Potter or Cuyp would have been. But Cooper's best pictures of sheep and cows (34, 36) have a monumentality and technical finish that set him apart from most of his contemporaries. Cooper did for the cow what Landseer did for the stag. He even painted a large picture entitled *Monarch of the Meadows*, showing a large Potter-like bull surrounded by docile, recumbent heifers. This picture was considered valuable enough to be stolen from its owner, and later recovered, the whole affair attracting sensational publicity.

Cooper not only outlived most of his contemporaries, he simply wore them down by sheer bovine productiveness. From 1833 to 1902, he exhibited 266 pictures at the Royal Academy, never missing a year. This is still a record for unbroken exhibition at the Academy, and one never likely to be surpassed. He

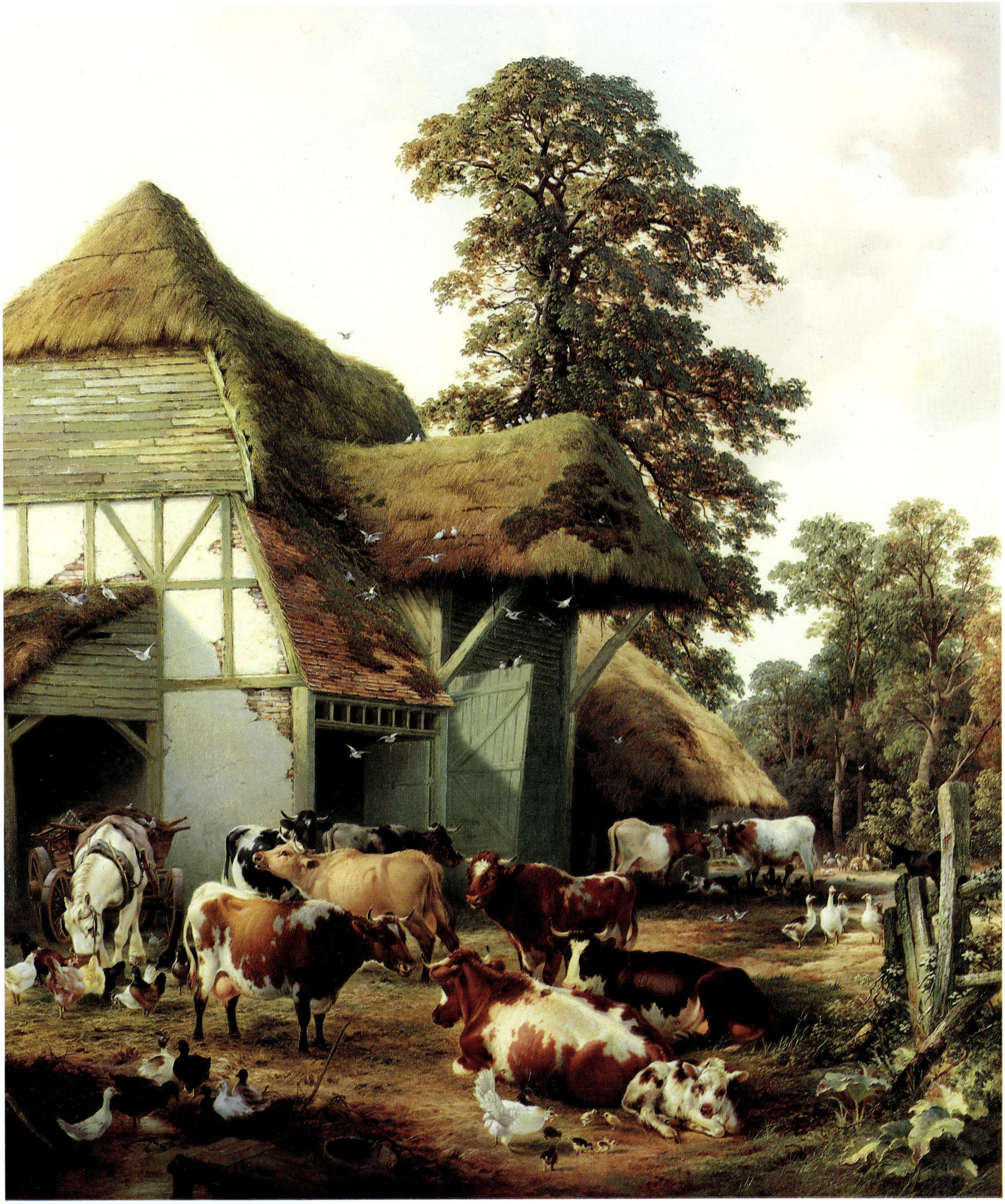

33
Thomas Sidney Cooper
*A Farm in Kent*

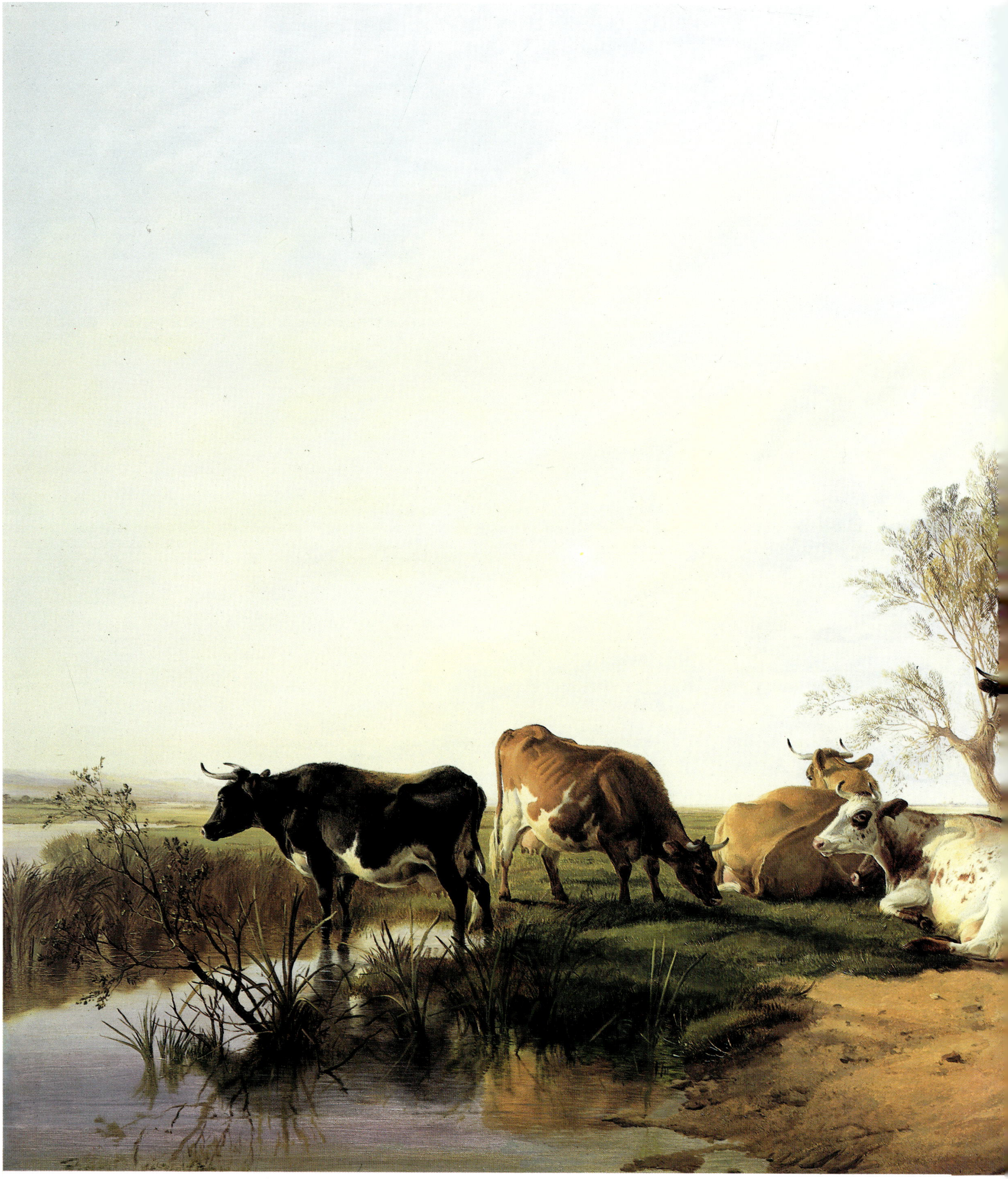

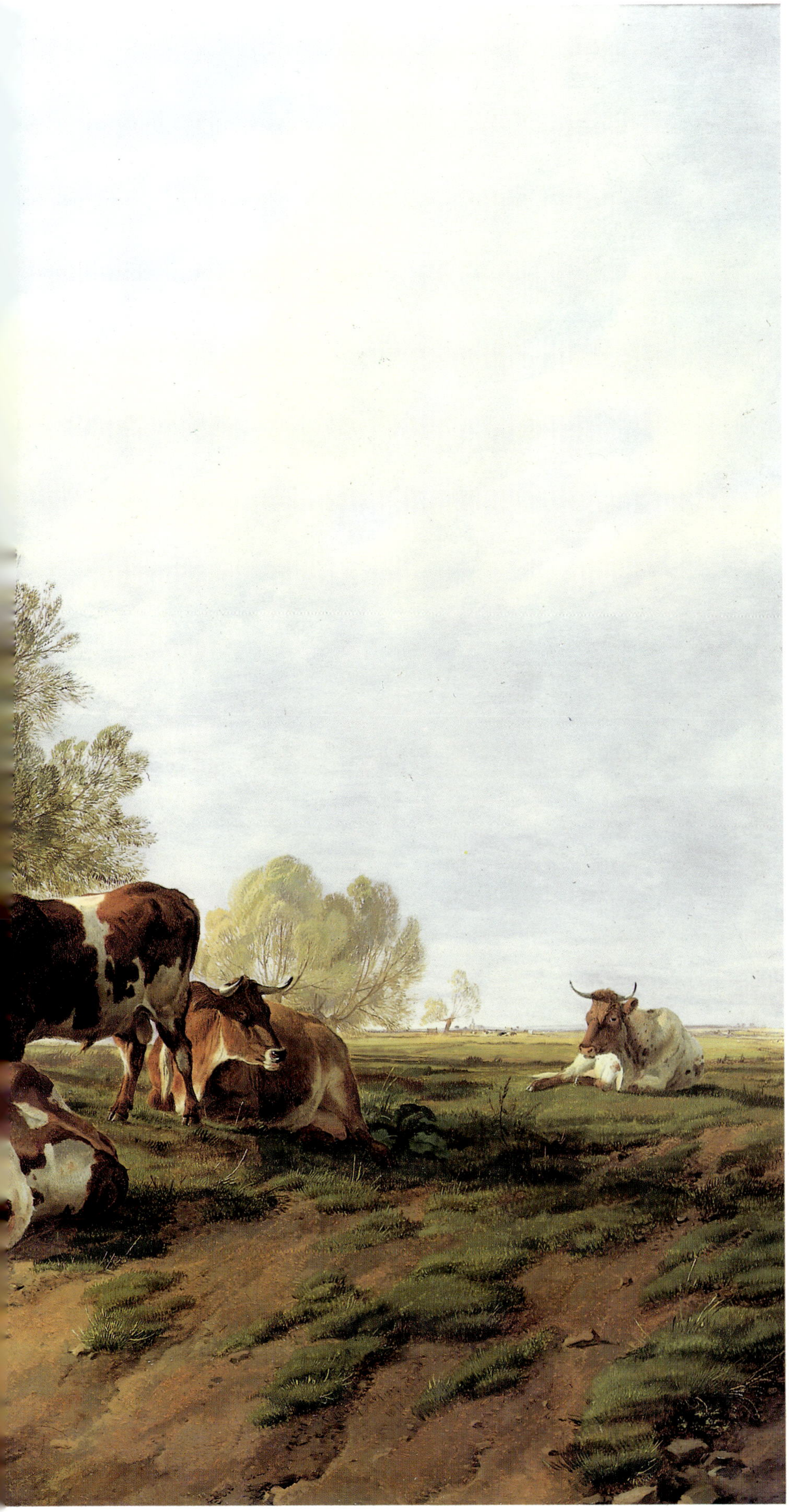

34
THOMAS SIDNEY COOPER
*By a Sedgy Brook*

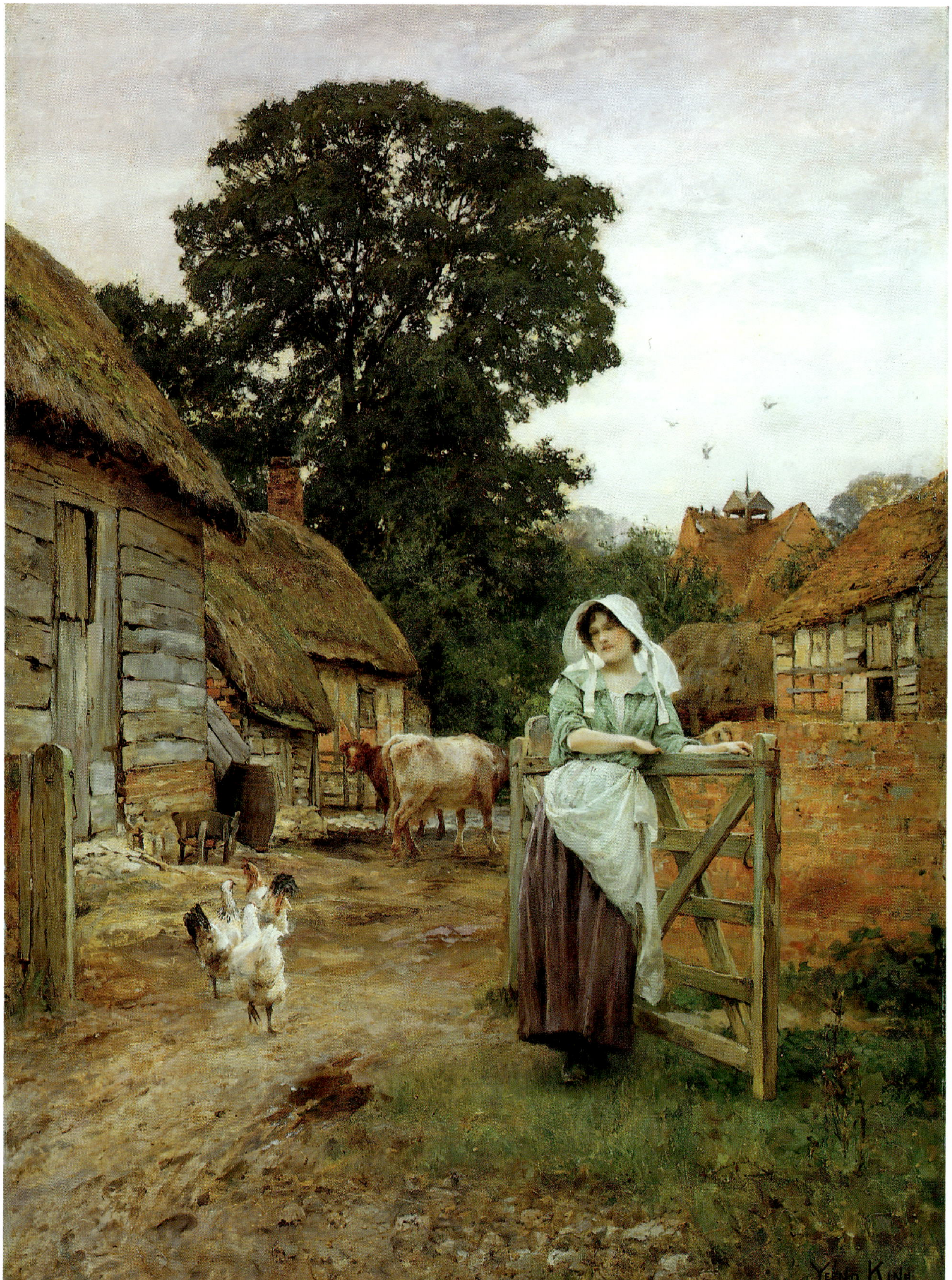

35
HENRY JOHN YEEND KING
*At the Farm Gate*

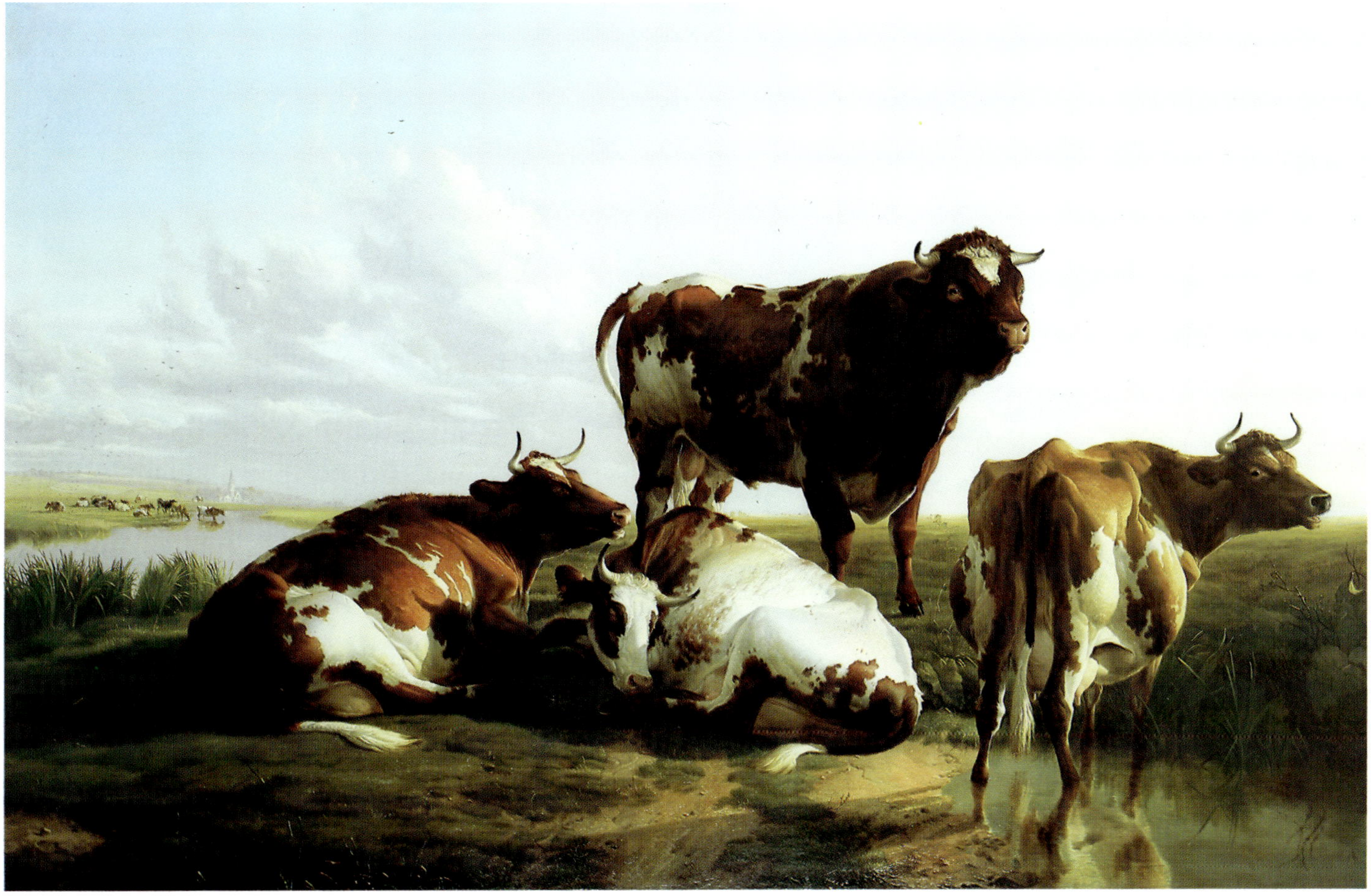

36
THOMAS SIDNEY COOPER
*On a Dairy Farm*

never seemed to tire of cows and sheep, and even lent a hand to other artists, such as Thomas Creswick and F.R. Lee, painting the cows and sheep in their landscapes. In 1890 he published the regulation two-volume autobiography, entitled simply *My Life*, with the *Monarch of the Meadows* embossed in gold on the covers. Like most Victorian artists' memoirs, it is a long-winded and sanctimonious catalogue of a lifetime of ceaseless, blameless endeavour, and quite unreadable. Born in great poverty in Canterbury, Cooper worked his way up to prosperity and respectability, like a character out of Samuel Smiles's *Self-Help*. Hard work was his recipe for success; he was always in his painting room by seven in the morning, and reckoned to have two pictures well under way before breakfast. Eventually he became a rich and respected citizen of his native Canterbury, owning several properties, 'all freehold', he wrote proudly. He also recorded in his memoirs the inevitable sale to Queen Victoria, and visit to Osborne, where he painted the Queen's favourite cow, Buffie. The Queen was delighted with it, and exclaimed 'Oh yes, that is my Buffie.'

Cooper very rarely introduced figures into his pictures. Henry John Yeend King, on the other hand, was rather a specialist in pretty farm girls (35). This pretty maid, like Tess of the D'Urbervilles at Talbothays, stands invitingly at a half-open gate, leading to a farmyard full of picturesque, half-timbered old buildings, with the farmhouse roof glimpsed beyond, surrounded by a dovecot. Yeend King was trained in Paris, which shows in his technique, but his subject-matter remained unequivocally English, and tailored to the Victorian market. His brother-in-law was Robert Gallon, the landscape painter. In 1898 his picture *Milking Time* was bought by the Tate Gallery, but has not been seen again. T.S. Cooper and Yeend King are among that multitude of Victorian painters, much admired in their day, whose pictures have languished in museum basements ever since.

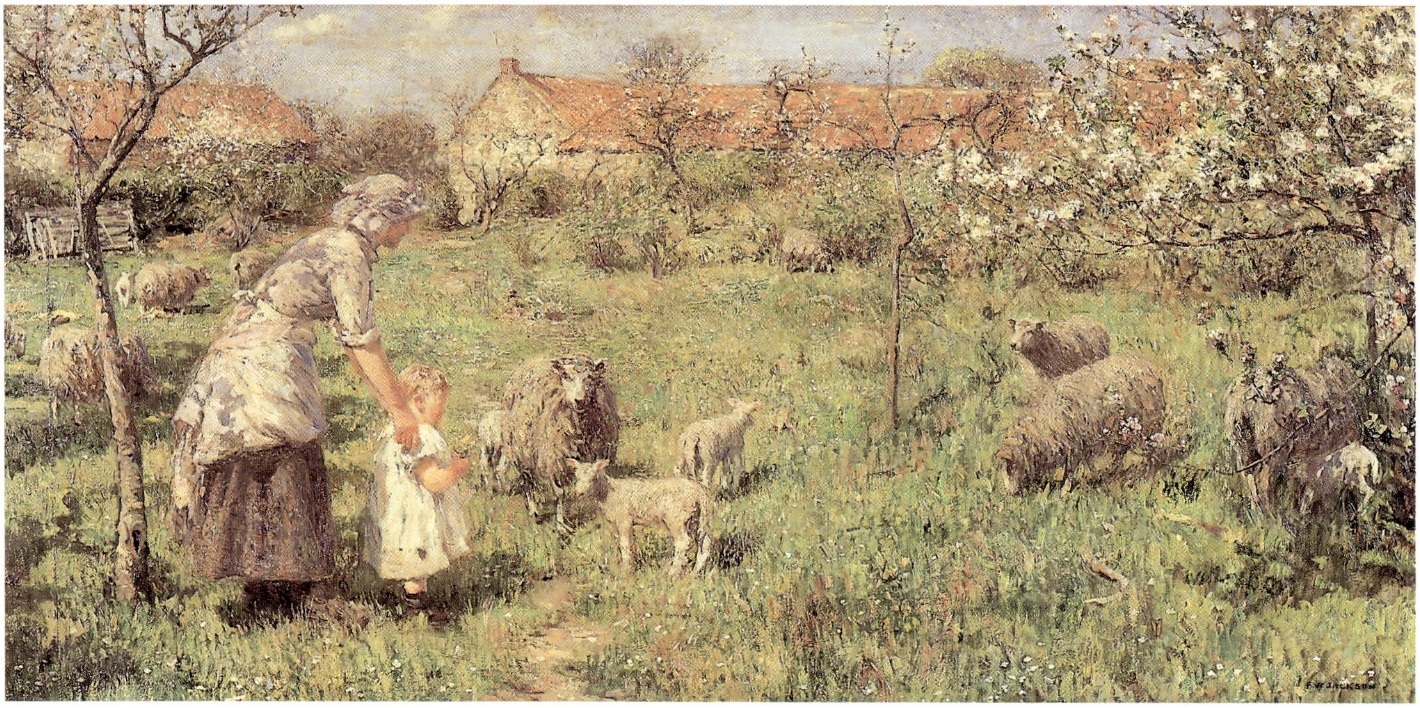

37
FREDERICK WILLIAM JACKSON
*In the Springtime*

Frederick William Jackson is the kind of late-Victorian impressionist painter whose works are now being dusted off and taken out of the basement (37). Jackson, like so many English painters after 1870, studied in Paris, and travelled extensively in Europe and North Africa. He then returned to his native Yorkshire, and painted the countryside in a charmingly French impressionist style. Painters of Jackson's type were interested in light, colour, a pretty, idyllic subject, and making Yorkshire look as much like Normandy as possible. They particularly liked orchards in spring, for that reason, with picturesque figures and farm animals in the foreground, and a glimpse of mellow red roofs beyond. This is typical of the type of impressionist picture produced in England in the last quarter of the nineteenth century; impressionism with a distinctly English accent. These farms, and the orchards and meadows around them, contain no sign of labour and toil, let alone of hardship. The reality, however, was rather different.

# Chapter Three

# WORK

A spade! A rake! A hoe!
A pickaxe or a bill!
A hook to reap, or a scythe to mow,
A flail, or what ye will -
And here's a ready hand
To ply the needful tool,
And skill'd enough, by lessons rough
In labour's rugged school.

THOMAS HOOD, *The Lay of the Labourer*

AGRICULTURAL LABOUR IN THE NINETEENTH century was certainly 'a rugged school'. The hours were long, the work backbreaking, the pay low. Absolutely all the agricultural writers, Jefferies, Alexander, Somerville, Rider Haggard, Friedrich Engels, were united in their condemnation of the oppressed state of the Victorian farm labourer. Orwin and Whetham's *History of British Agriculture 1846-1914* (1964) summarised it thus – 'He was given starvation wages, overlong hours of work, disgraceful housing, little or no education, and was generally treated as of lowly estate and as being of no account, an object of charity, perhaps, but with no prospect of improving his lot.' Conditions certainly varied in different parts of the country – the north was in general more prosperous than the south, with Wiltshire, Dorset and Somerset at the bottom of the wages and conditions scale. Conditions also varied from estate to estate, or farm to farm. But the lot of the average farm worker, at least to modern sensibilities, was still incredibly hard. Richard Jefferies in *Toilers of the Field* (1892) describes the farm worker's day:

The ordinary adult farm labourer commonly rises at from four to five o'clock; if he is a milker, and has to walk some little distance to his work, even as early as half-past three. Four was the general rule, but of late years the hour has grown later. He milks till five or half-past, carries the yokes to the dairy, and draws water for the dairymaid, or perhaps chops up some wood for her fire to scald the milk. At six he goes to breakfast, which consists of a hunch of bread and cheese as a rule, with now and then a piece of bacon, and as a milker he receives his quart of beer. At breakfast there is no hurry for half-an-hour or so; but some time before seven he is on at the ordinary work of the day. If a milker and very early riser, he is not usually put at the heavy jobs, but allowances are made for the work he has already done. The other men

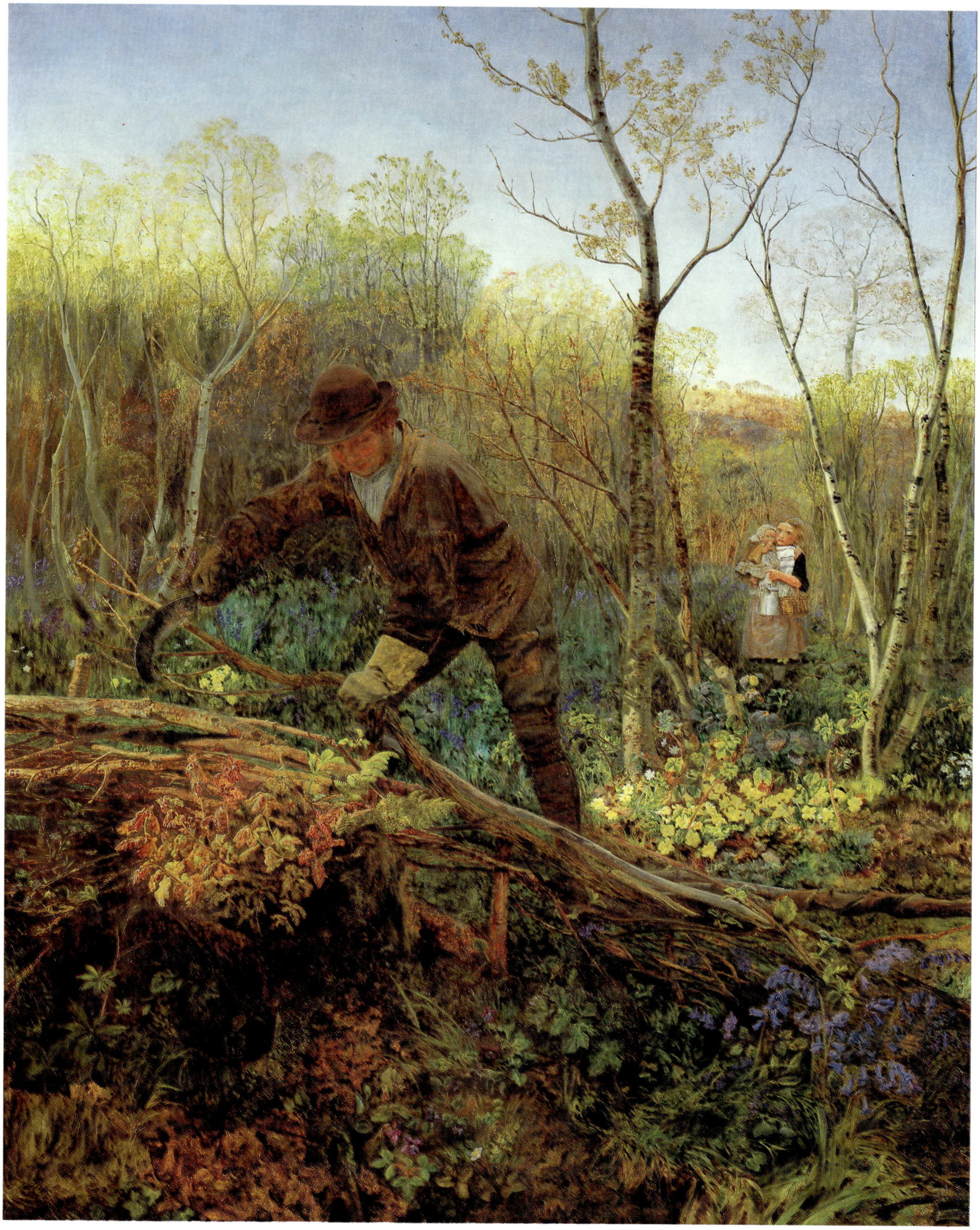

38
John Brett
*The Hedger*

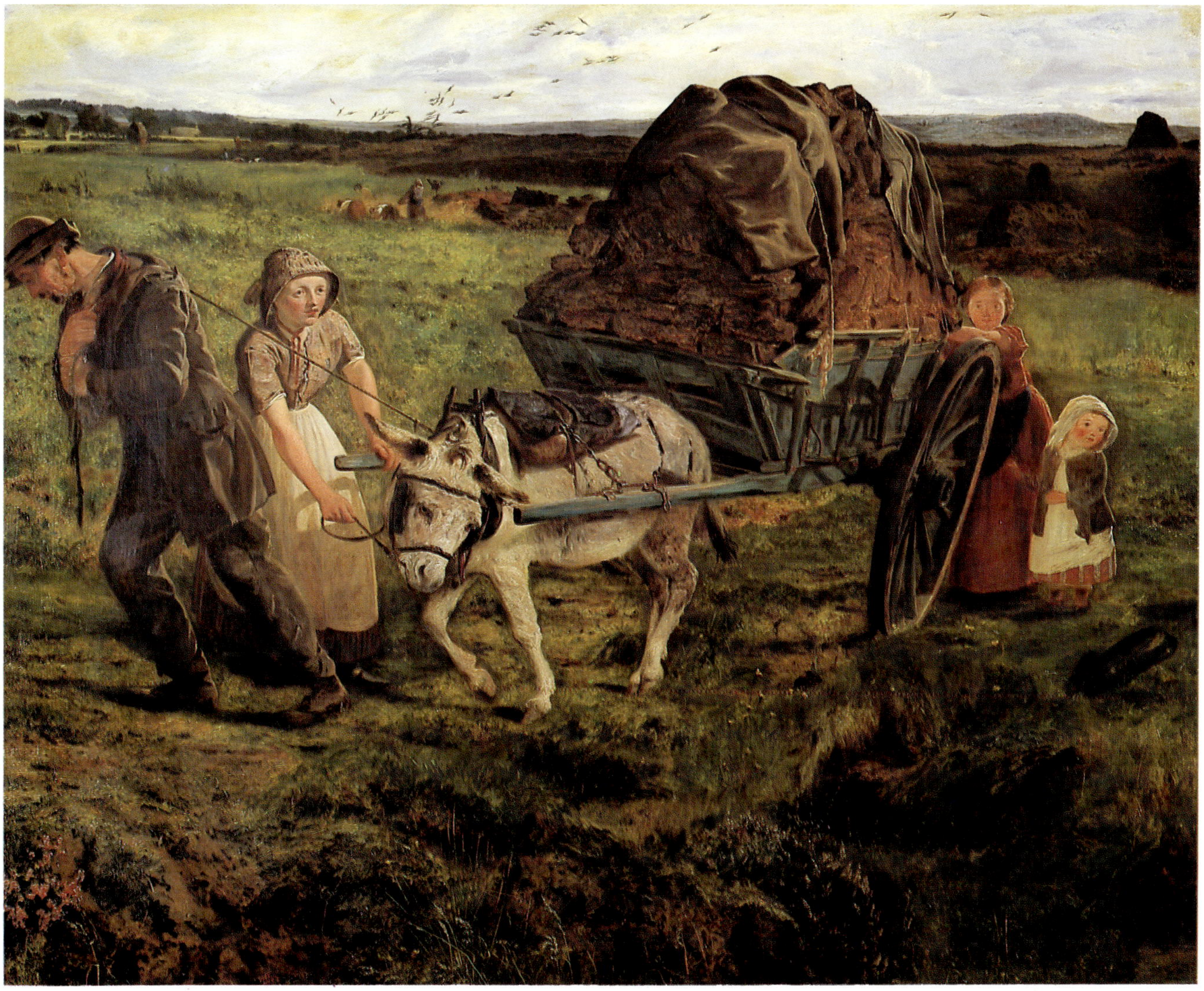

39
THOMAS WADE
*Carting Turf from the Moss*

on the farm arrive at six. At eleven, or half-past, comes luncheon, which lasts a full hour, often an hour and a quarter. About three o'clock the task of milking again commences; the buckets are got out with a good deal of rattling and noise, and yokes fitted to the shoulders, and away he goes for an hour or hour and a half of milking. That done, he has to clean up the court and help the dairymaid put the heavier articles in place; then another quart of beer, and away home. The time of leaving off work varies from half-past five to half-past six. At ordinary seasons the other men leave at six, but in hay-making or harvest time they are expected to remain till the job in hand that day is finished, often till eight or half-past.

At the end of the day, the farm labourer must have had his supper and fallen into bed exhausted.

Wages were low, and diet meagre. In times of depression, from the 1870s on, farm labourers and their families rarely had enough to eat. 'I couldn't tell you how we do live,' said one Mrs West in 1913, 'it's a mystery.' Housing conditions were often appalling, and as the cottages usually belonged to farmers and landowners there was no security of tenure. Most workers were hired for limited periods only, usually at the great hiring fairs that took place in county towns at Michaelmas, so there was little job security either. For some, life was likely to end in the dreaded workhouse.

The typical Victorian farm worker was called Hodge. He was likely to be large and heavy of build, slow of speech, and with a deliberate plodding walk from following the plough through muddy fields. Although knowledgeable about country matters, he would know absolutely nothing about the outside world, beyond his local town, which he might only visit very rarely. Jefferies, who wrote a book entitled *Hodge and his Masters* in 1880, described the average farm labourer as having 'an oriental absence of inspiration'.

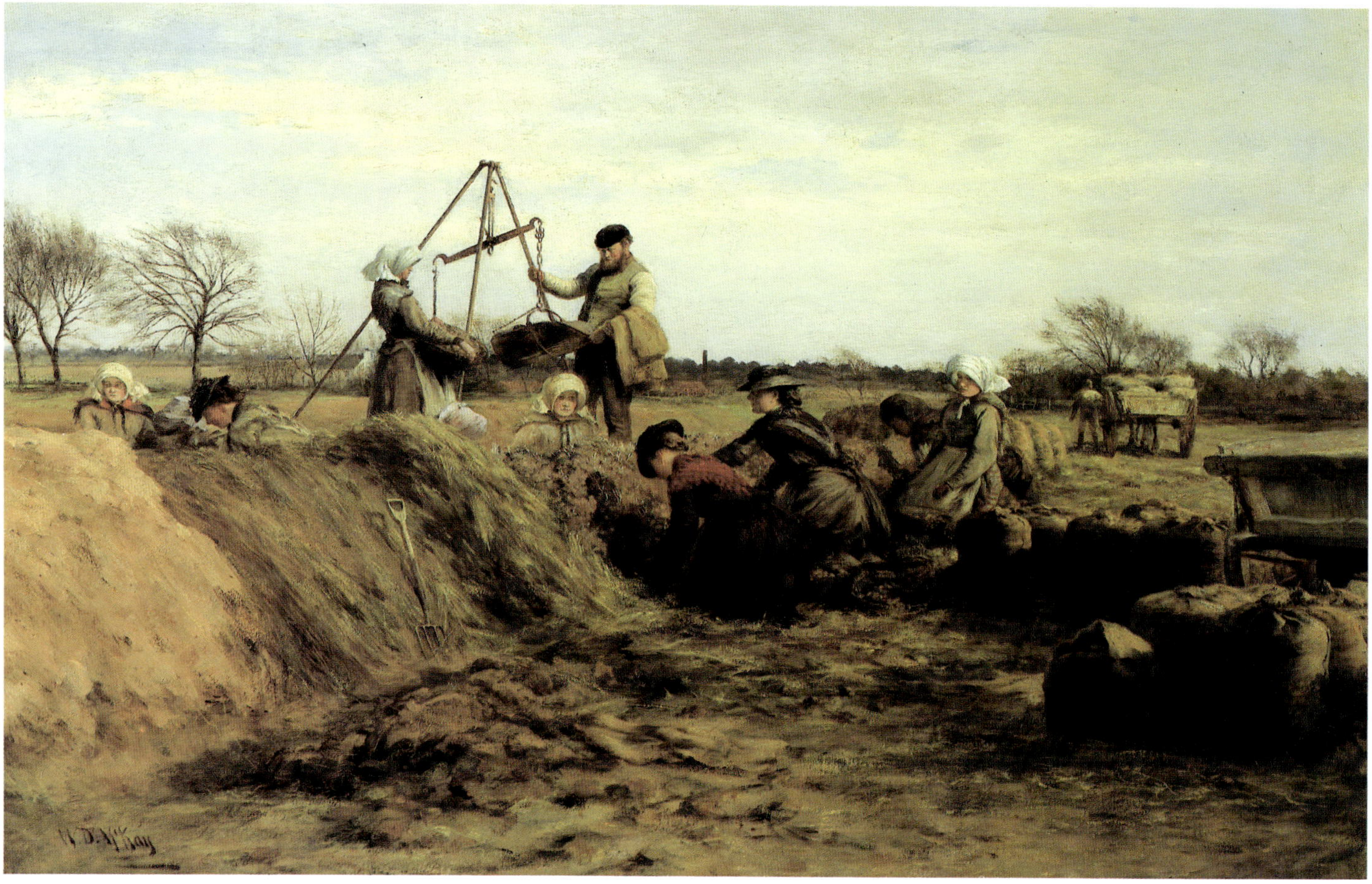

40
WILLIAM DARLING MACKAY
*Field Working in Spring – at the Potato Pits*

Although the reality of rural life was so grim, painters responded to it in many different ways. Most concentrated on the glories of the unspoiled countryside, with farm workers only seen as small and distant figures. The labourer is merely a decorative appendage, much the same as a sheep or a cow. Groups of farm workers might be seen, but usually resting rather than actually working. If they are working, they always look extremely happy and cheerful about it. Other painters, like Clausen and La Thangue, saw the worker as a heroic, monumental figure, at home in his environment, at one with nature. Victorian pictures of farm work extend to both extremes of realism and sentimentality.

In spite of the Pre-Raphaelite Brotherhood's concern for social issues, very few of their paintings are to do with farm work. Holman Hunt's *Hireling Shepherd* is about flirtation; his *Strayed Sheep* is all about sheep; so is Madox Brown's *Pretty Baa-Lambs*. In *The Woodman's Daughter* by Millais and *The Woodman's Child* by Arthur Hughes the emphasis is on the children, with the woodman seen as a distant figure at work in the background. Almost the only major Pre-Raphaelite to show an interest in farm work was John Brett. His *Stonebreaker* of 1858, as we have seen, is a happy picture of what was generally considered a degrading form of labour. Most farm workers would only take to it after all other occupations had failed. Alfred Williams described an old stonebreaker, Johnny Garret, whose real skills were those of hedge-cutter, haymaker and harvester. But when work was short, he would turn to 'snopping' stones by the roadside. 'He brought four hammers to the stonebreaking – a sledge, a middle-sized one, and two smaller. After sledging the heap, or a part of it, he knelt on an old sack and "snopped" away.' Brett also painted a picture of a *Hedger* (38). Here again the emphasis is on the beauty of the flowers, the hedge, and the woods in the background. The heroic pose of the hedger dominates the picture, but he seems quite happy

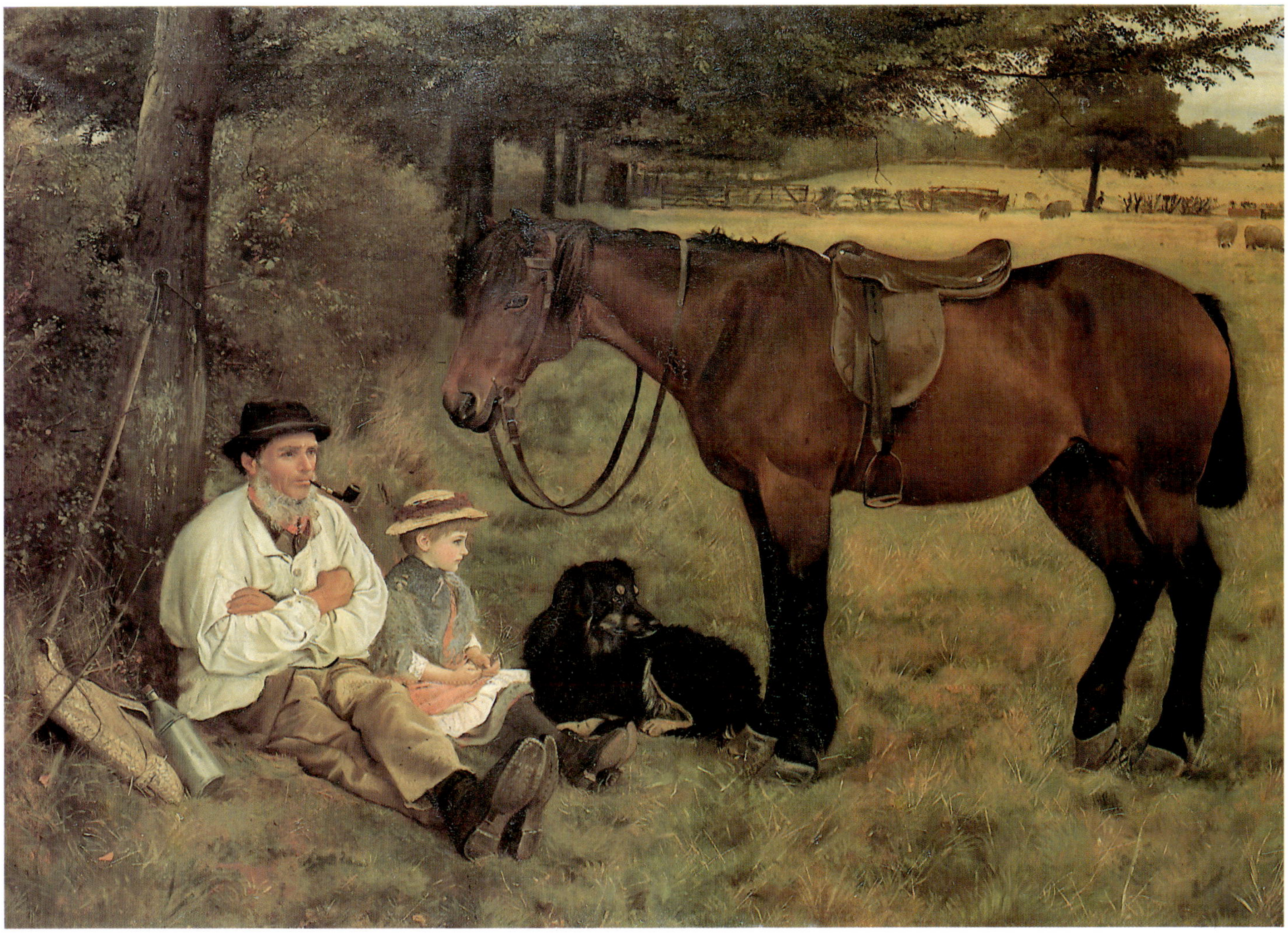

41
WILLIAM EDWARD MILLNER
*Resting*

with his work. The mood and colouring are restrained compared with the summery brilliance of the *Stonebreaker*, but the atmosphere is one of gentle harmony between man and nature. Hedge-cutting was one of the traditional skills of the farm worker. John Clare wrote of

> The hedger soaked in the dull weather, chops
> On at his toils which scarcely keeps him warm
> And every stroke he takes, large swarms of drops
> Patter about him like an April storm.

The Pre-Raphaelite movement threw up other surprising social realist pictures, such as Thomas Wade's *Carting Turf from the Moss* (39). Wade lived in Preston, Lancashire, and imbibed his Pre-Raphaelite ideas from Madox Brown who had a number of followers and admirers among the Liverpool school. *Carting Turf* combines a beautiful Pre-Raphaelite landscape with a feeling of intense sympathy for the hard life of the agricultural poor. It also reminds us that women and children did a great deal of farm labouring. A worker with an able wife and children was often preferred for a job for that reason, and many farmers made it a condition of employment that the women and children would help out at busy times of year. In William Darling Mackay's *Field Working in Spring* (40) all the workers are women, except for the overseer, or grieve, who is weighing the potatoes on a scale. Women continued to do farm work, especially in Scotland and the north of England, for most of the nineteenth century, until machinery, higher wages and the agricultural depressions drove them off the land. In Northumberland, the system of 'bondagers', or hired gangs of female labourers, survived even into the twentieth century.

The midday meal, usually carried by the farm workers

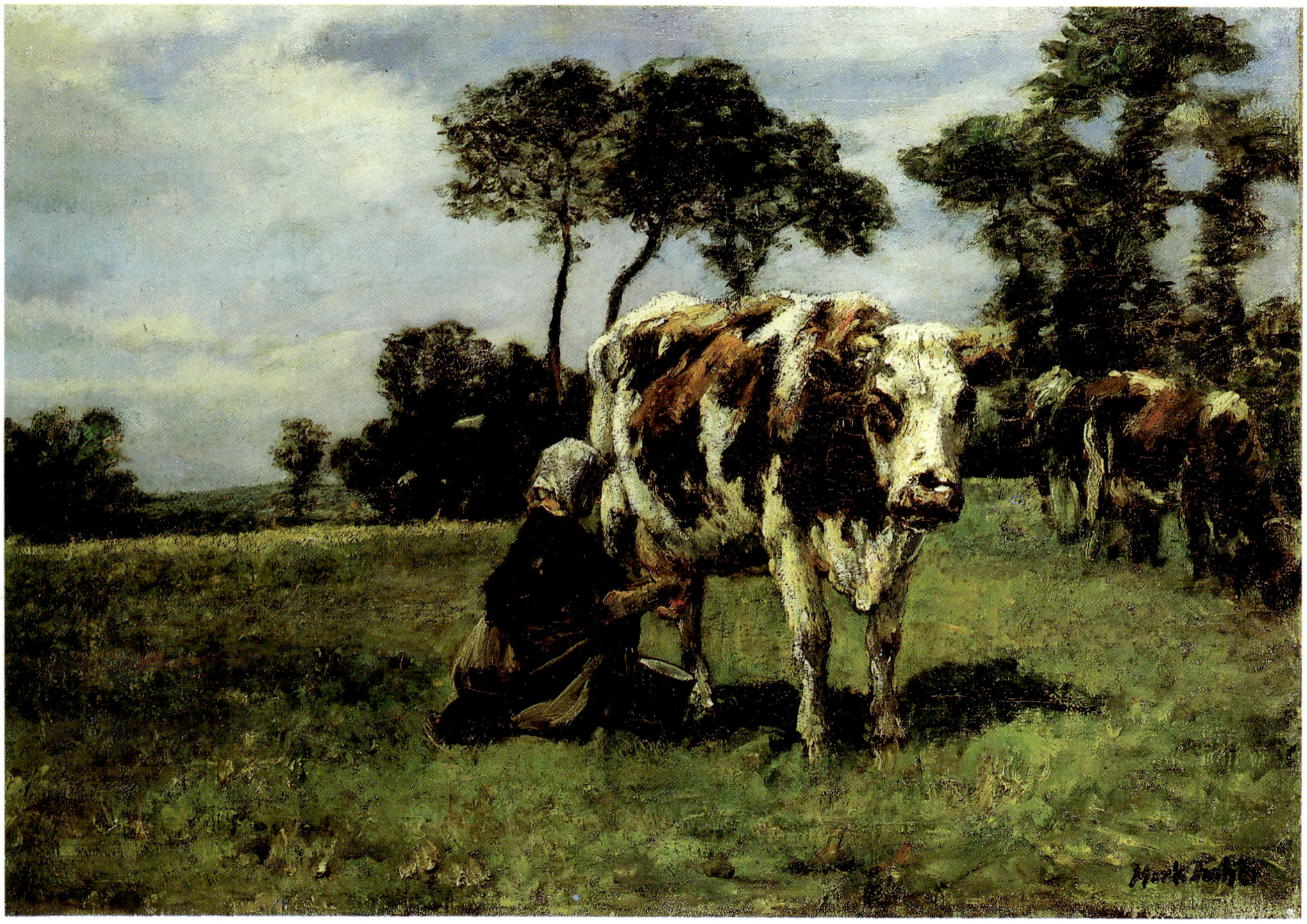

42
MARK FISHER
*The Milkmaid*

and eaten in the fields, was a favourite subject for painters. William Edward Millner's *Resting* (41) is an appealingly honest and unsentimentalised example. Millner lived and worked all his life in Gainsborough, Lincolnshire, and must therefore have known farming at first hand. Many of his pictures are country scenes involving farm work, which he depicts with an unusual honesty and sympathy. Proggings, beever, bait, baggings, snaps, drinkings, muncheon, crib, tommy, nammet – these are just a few of the extraordinary variety of names given to the packed lunch or midday snack. It was washed down with beer or cider, carried in stone jars, or cold tea in a metal can.

Milking was another popular subject, offering the combination of a picturesque scene and a pretty milkmaid. Mark Fisher's *Milkmaid* (42) avoids the temptation to emphasise the prettiness of the milkmaid, which is the real theme of most pictures of the subject. The growth of the Victorian cities led to a huge demand for milk, and dairy farming was on the increase. Much of the milk was brought in by train, and the Great Western Line became known as the 'milky way'. Fisher was a late Victorian landscape painter much influenced by Corot and the Barbizon school. His landscapes with cattle look remarkably similar to those of the French landscape painter, Daubigny. The dairy, with its milkmaids, cheese and butter, was for the Victorians a potent symbol of the supposed purity of country life. Many progressive landowners, including Queen Victoria and Prince Albert, built elaborate dairies, often architect-designed, and full of artistic tiles and friezes. George Eliot described Hetty Sorrel's dairy as 'a scene to sicken for with a sort of calenture in hot and dusty streets – such coolness, such purity, such fragrance of new-pressed cheese, of firm butter, of wooden vessels perpetually bathed in pure water. . . .' Much mystery surrounded the churning of the butter, and Hardy recorded in *Tess of the D'Urbervilles* how the dairymen resorted

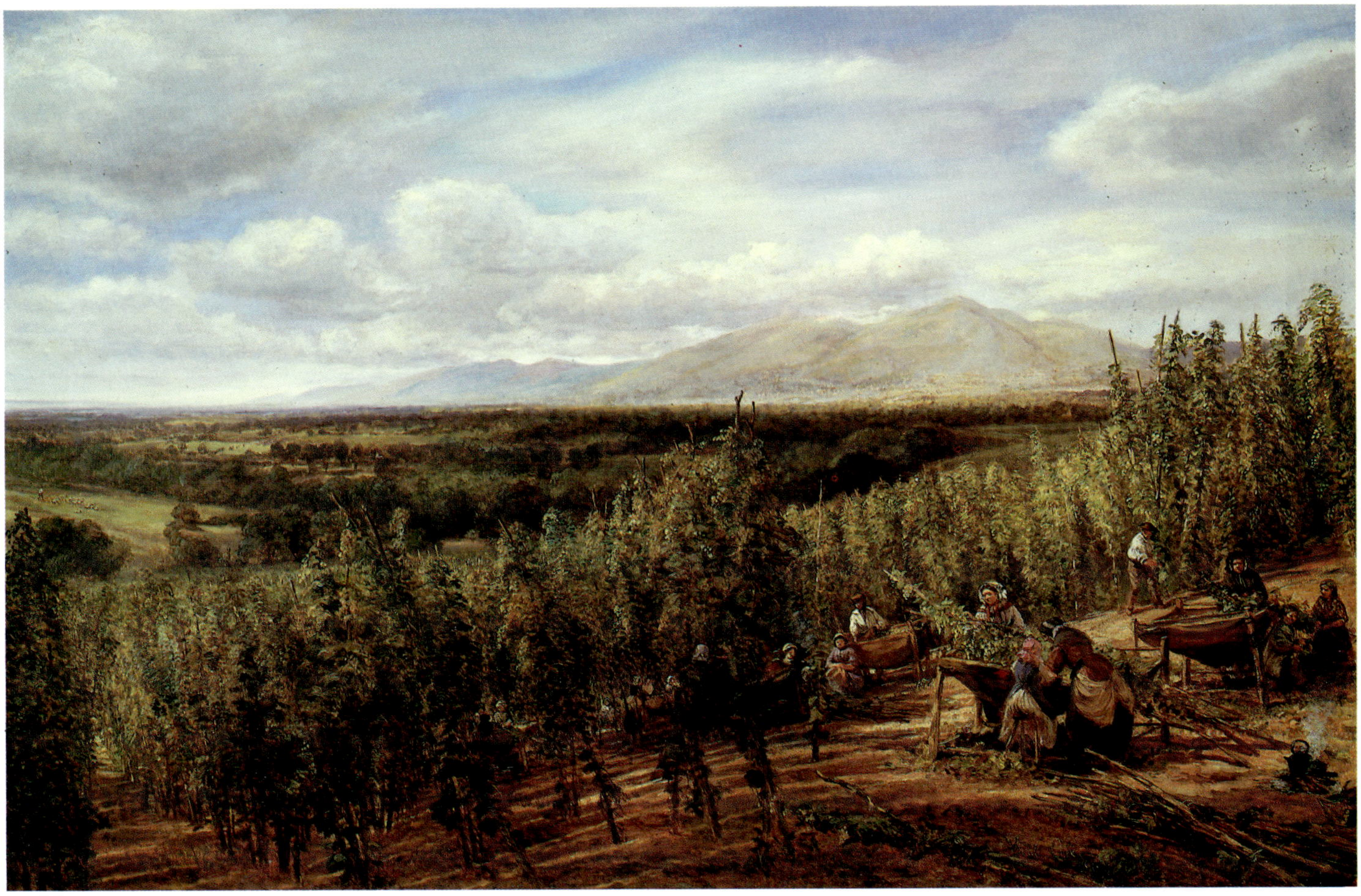

43
GEORGE VICAT COLE
*The Hop Gardens*

to magicians and sorcerers when the butter refused to 'make' or solidify.

Another activity surrounded with much tradition and ritual was the growing of hops, used for flavouring beer, and still widely grown in Kent and Sussex. The harvesting was usually done by gangs of workers, mainly women and children, from the east end of London. It provided them with a useful source of extra income and a taste of country life. Hop-picking was therefore regarded as a particularly cheerful activity, and conditions in the hop fields were not as hard as in other jobs, such as ploughing or harvesting. This is certainly reflected in Vicat Cole's *Hop Gardens* of 1862 (43). Cole was the son of another landscape painter, George Cole, and was almost as popular and successful as Leader. He was particularly known for his harvesting scenes, and hop-picking was not a common subject for him. After picking, the hops were taken to the oast houses for drying. The typical conical roofs of these buildings can clearly be seen in the background of Birket Foster's *Farm Cart* (44). Here we are at the extreme edge of the sentimental, pastoral vision of the countryside. The figures in Birket Foster's pictures seem to be enjoying their work so much that they look as if they were on a perpetual holiday. Even the gipsy cabin on the left, with a child asleep inside it, looks positively inviting and cosy. Much the same spirit animates *Returning from Market* (45), another favourite subject of the period. Painters like Foster could avoid the realities of farm work by concentrating on such peripheral activities as going to or from the market, and preferred to show country people resting or relaxing.

A great feature of the English countryside in summer was the arrival of the Irish workers. These were gangs of annual immigrants who came over every year to earn extra money by helping with the harvest. In general, they were well-behaved and popular, as Flora Thompson has recorded: 'They were a wild-looking lot, dressed in old clothes, and speaking a brogue

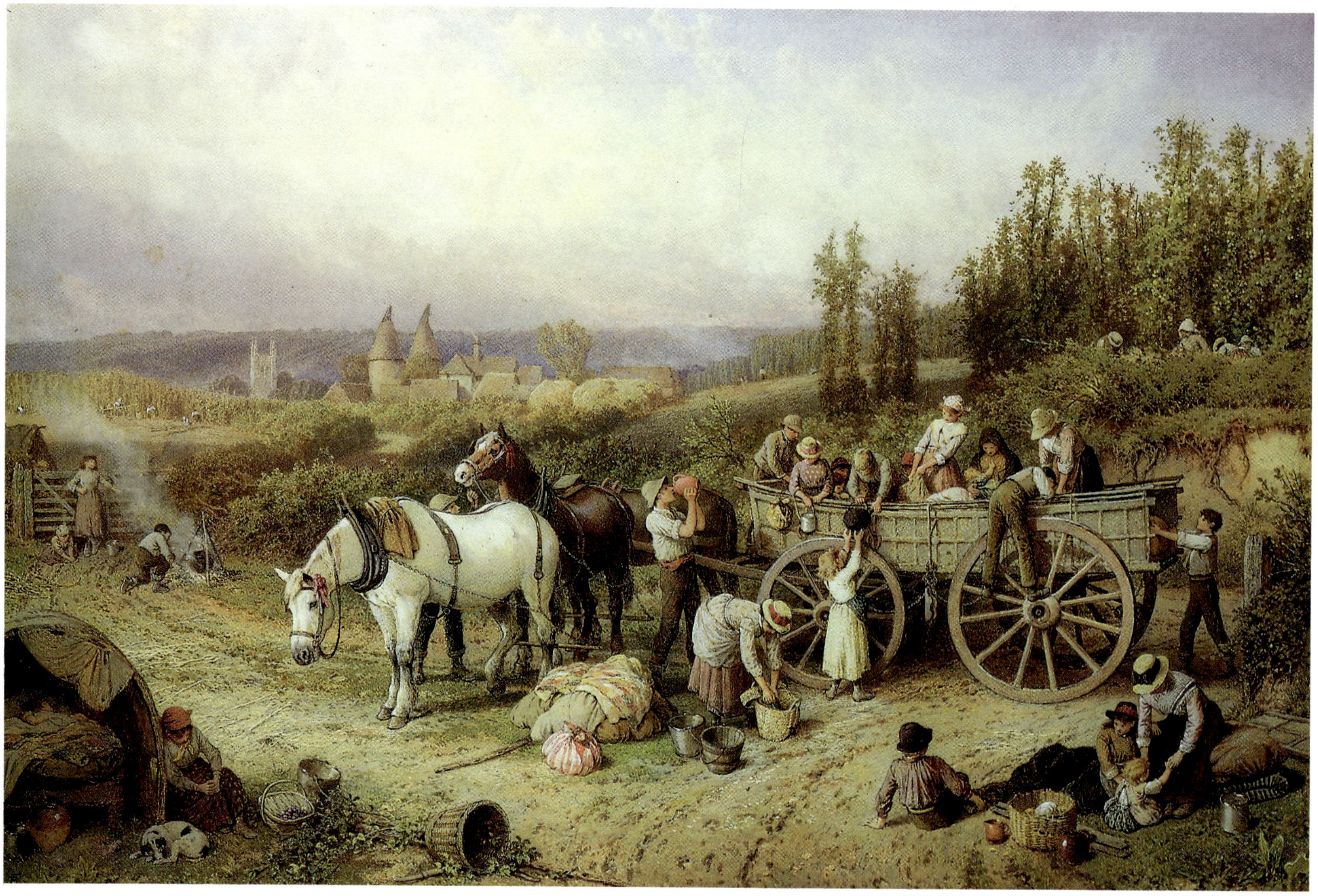

44
MYLES BIRKET FOSTER
*The Farm Cart*

so thick that the natives could only catch a word here and there. . . . All they desired was to earn as much money as possible to send home to their wives, to have enough left for themselves to get drunk on a Saturday night, and to be in time for Mass on a Sunday morning.' Later, at Candleford Post Office, she sold them postal orders out of hours, so that they could send their wages off to their wives at weekends. Erskine Nicol, a Scottish artist who lived in Ireland and painted many pictures of Irish life, has left us an amusing picture of an Irish emigrant in 1841 (46). To the urchins on the quayside he is a figure of fun, and the boot-boy mockingly suggests that he polish his boots for him. The Irish came over not only to work on the harvest, but also as navvies on the railways and other building projects. As Engels commented, 'The rapid extension of English industry could not have taken place if England had not possessed in the numerous and impoverished population of Ireland a reserve at command.'

At the opposite extreme from Birket Foster and the pastoralists is Herkomer's great picture of 1885, *Hard Times* (47), one of the most memorable of all English social realist pictures. Although agricultural workers got the vote in 1884, the agricultural depression brought great hardship the following year. Herkomer wrote in his autobiography that 'hundreds of honest workers wandered through the country in search of work . . . it was such a group, resting by the wayside of a country lane, that I depicted. The lane, with winding roadway and high-trimmed hedges of hawthorn, lay on my very door at Bushey. It was named by the students "Hard Times Lane".' Herkomer and his family had suffered great poverty themselves, after emigrating from Germany, first to America, then to England, and *Hard Times* reveals a true sympathy for the sufferings and hardships of the poor. But having known poverty Herkomer's desire for fame and riches gave him no rest, and led him away from social realist pictures down the primrose path to fashionable portrait

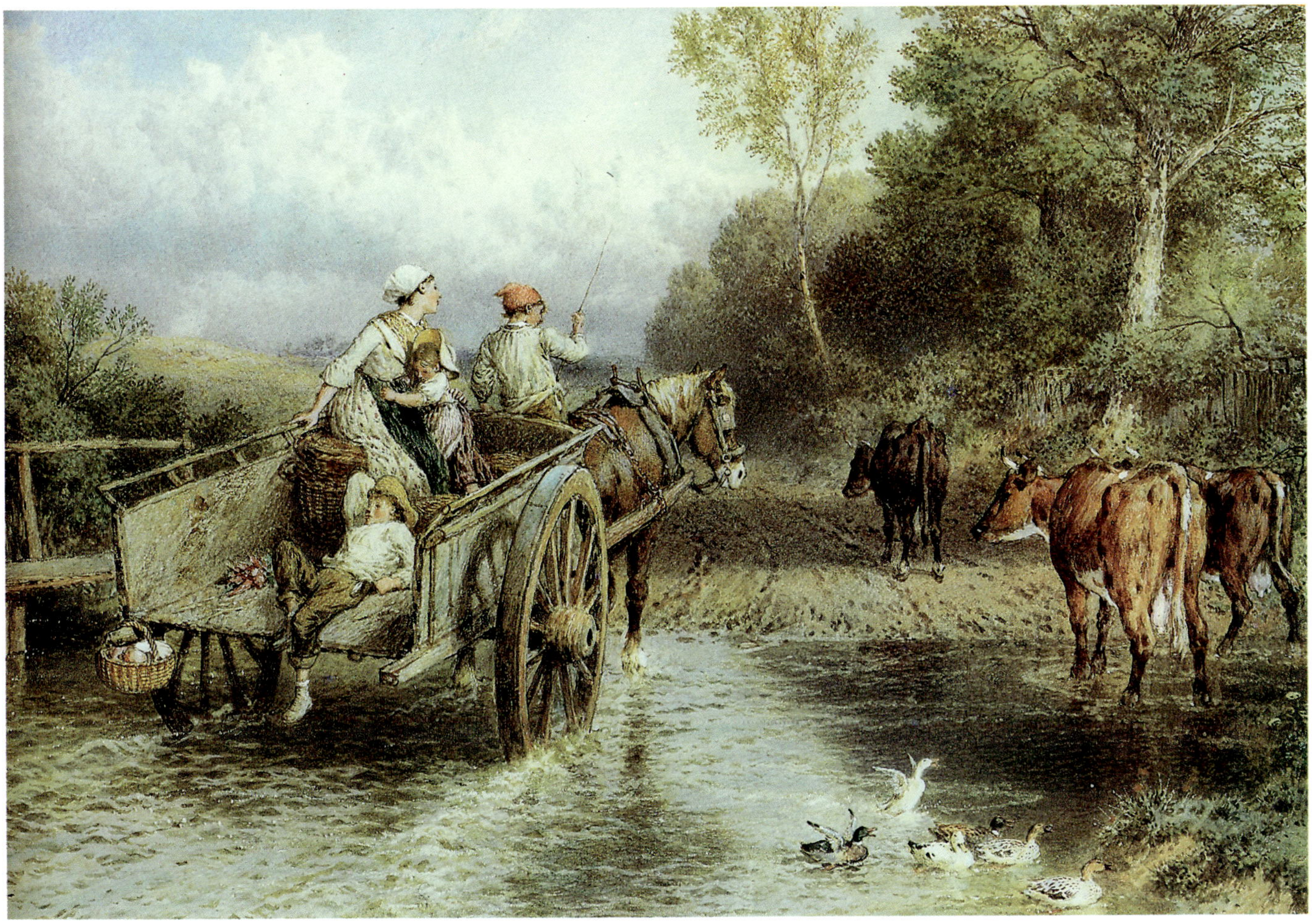

45
MYLES BIRKET FOSTER
*Returning from Market*

painting. Honours were showered upon him – the CVO, a knighthood, even a German title from the Kaiser. He founded an art school at Bushey, where he constantly lectured the students about his early hardships and the need for hard work. Nearby he built a monstrous Germanic house called Lululand, and in Germany erected a Wagnerian tower in memory of his mother. He became Slade Professor, wrote operas, and lived to design both for the stage and the cinema. He died in 1914, a veritable pillar of the art establishment. In his memoirs he wrote that in England 'truth in art should be enhanced by sentiment'. Concealed by sentiment would have been more accurate.

But as a young man, Herkomer had worked on the *Graphic*, and was much influenced by Luke Fildes and Fred Walker. Although Walker had been dead for ten years by 1885, the heroic pose of the workman leaning against the gate strongly recalls some of Walker's figures. The figures were modelled from a local workman, James Quarry, his wife Annie, and their two children. Quarry was actually an employed labourer at the time, and the bundle of tools on the ground is a reminder that workmen were expected to bring their own tools in the nineteenth century. Although the picture exudes a feeling of suffering and hardship, it is in fact a highly contrived work of art. The models were posed, and the picture finished in the studio. The composition has highly respectable artistic precedents; the pose of the workman is 'an Apollo or Hermes incarnated in the shape of an English "out of work",' as Herkomer's biographer J. Saxon Mills wrote; the group of the mother and children recalls the Madonna in *The Rest on the Flight into Egypt*. The purposeful stance of the workman, as he looks away down the winding road, suggests hope and strength, and it is strongly implied that he will triumph over adversity and eventually find work. The picture is an allegory rather than a polemic against the sufferings of the Victorian

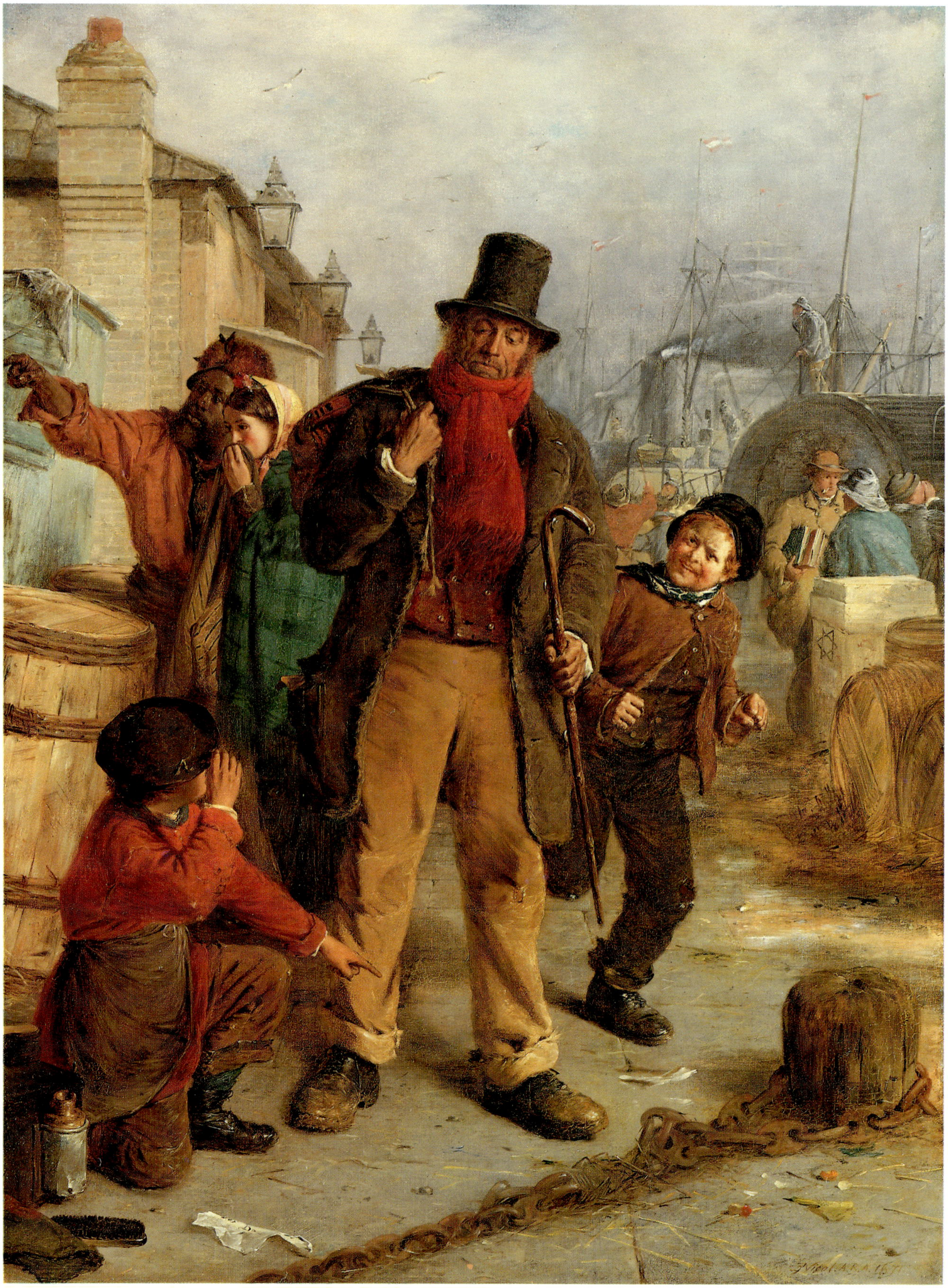

46

Erskine Nicol

*An Irish Emigrant Landing at Liverpool*

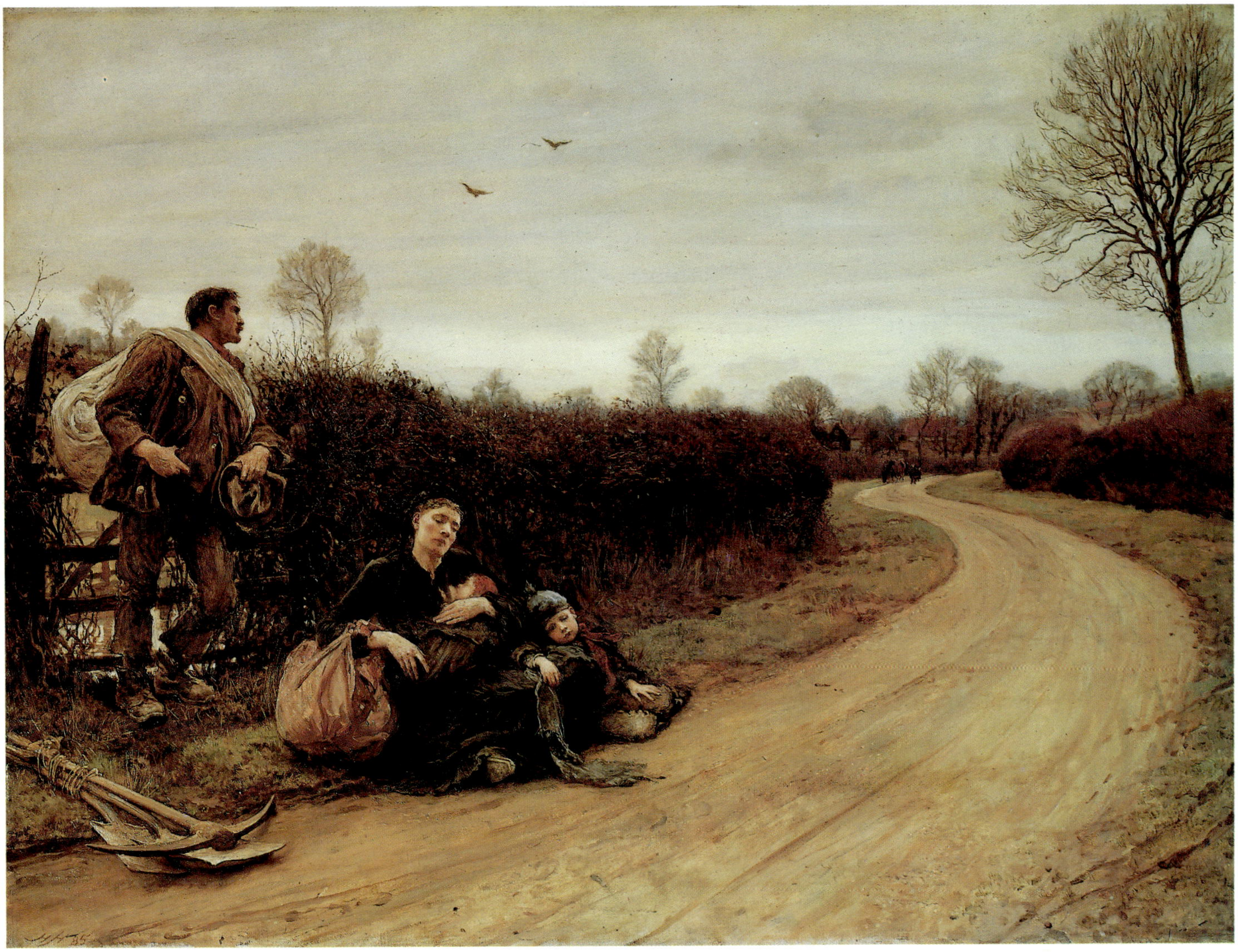

47
Sir Hubert von Herkomer
*Hard Times*

poor, and ultimately transmits a message of hope. Nonetheless, it is a powerful image, and for future generations it is likely to remain a potent symbol of the sufferings of the Victorian rural working class.

Even more allegorical are the landscapes of John Linnell. Linnell was not only a survivor of the romantic movement, pupil of Blake and father-in-law of Samuel Palmer, but he was also deeply religious. His landscapes are imbued with a mystical sense of the grandeur of nature. 'The business of art,' he wrote, 'should be to create spiritual perceptions.' In his *Timber Waggon* (48), for example, the figures blend completely into the scenery. They have no individuality, no character, no personality – they are simply absorbed into the background, part of the landscape. In the same way, the characters in Hardy's later novels are seen as helpless creatures, in the grip of natural forces which they cannot understand or control. The figures in any of Linnell's landscapes could be Jude the Obscure.

At first, Linnell worked as a portrait painter and watercolourist, but in 1820 he decided to become a landscape painter. He moved out of London and settled at Redhill, in Surrey, where he raised a large family, several of them artists. At first he painted landscapes with actual biblical subjects, such as *Noah*, or *The Halt by the Jordan*, but since he had never been abroad they always had English landscape settings. The dealers complained that these landscapes did not sell, so he turned instead to the pastoral landscapes for which he is best known and which were immensely popular in his own day. Through these pastoral scenes, he tried to convey the same religious feelings as he had in his biblical subjects, showing men and animals in a deliberately timeless environment. In Wales, he wrote, 'I could almost fancy myself living in the times of Jacob and Esau, and might expect to meet their flocks.' That is exactly what the Victorian spectator did feel, looking at Linnell's landscapes. The Holy Land, for Linnell, was mainly situated in

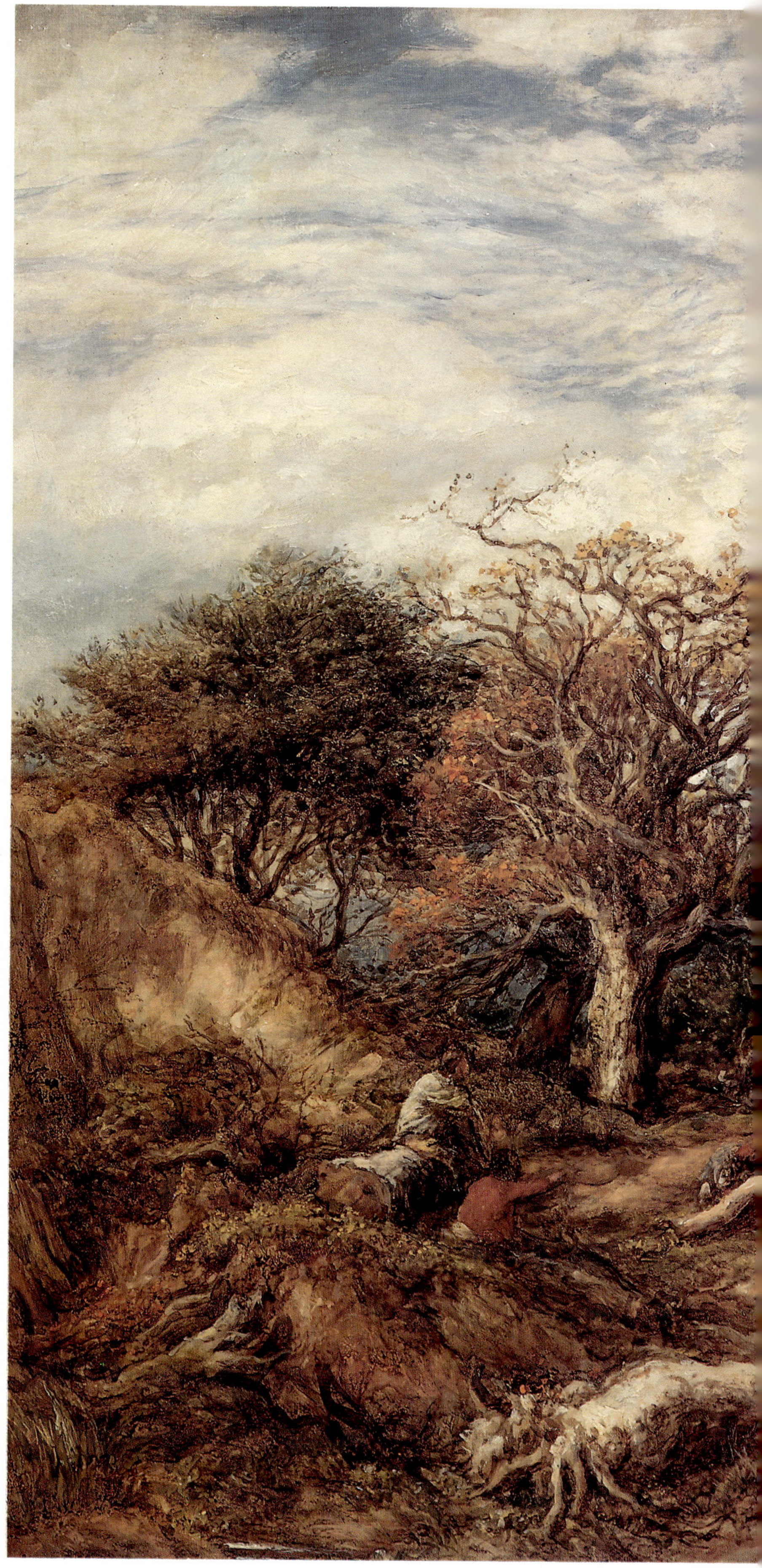

48
JOHN LINNELL
*The Timber Waggon*

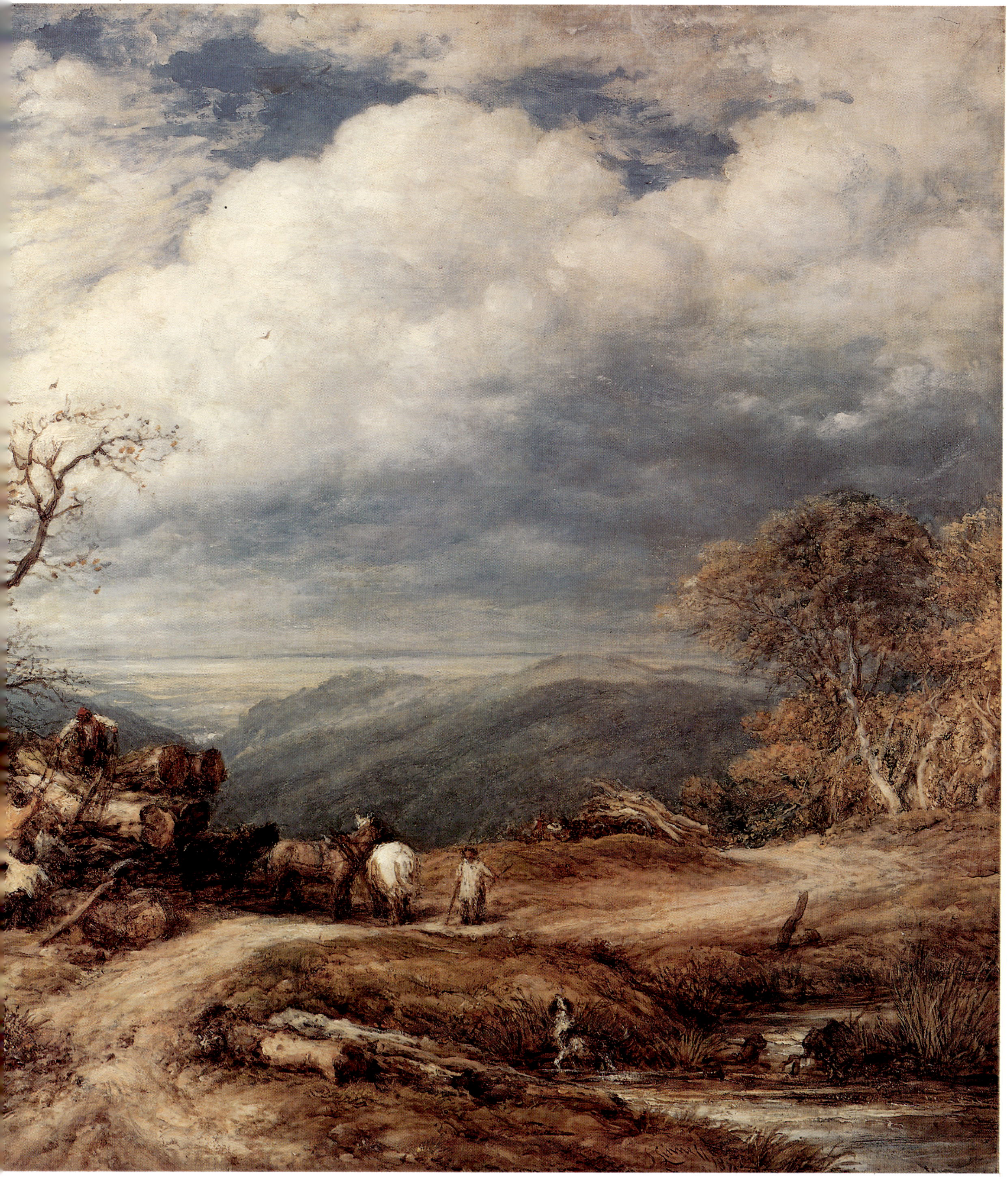

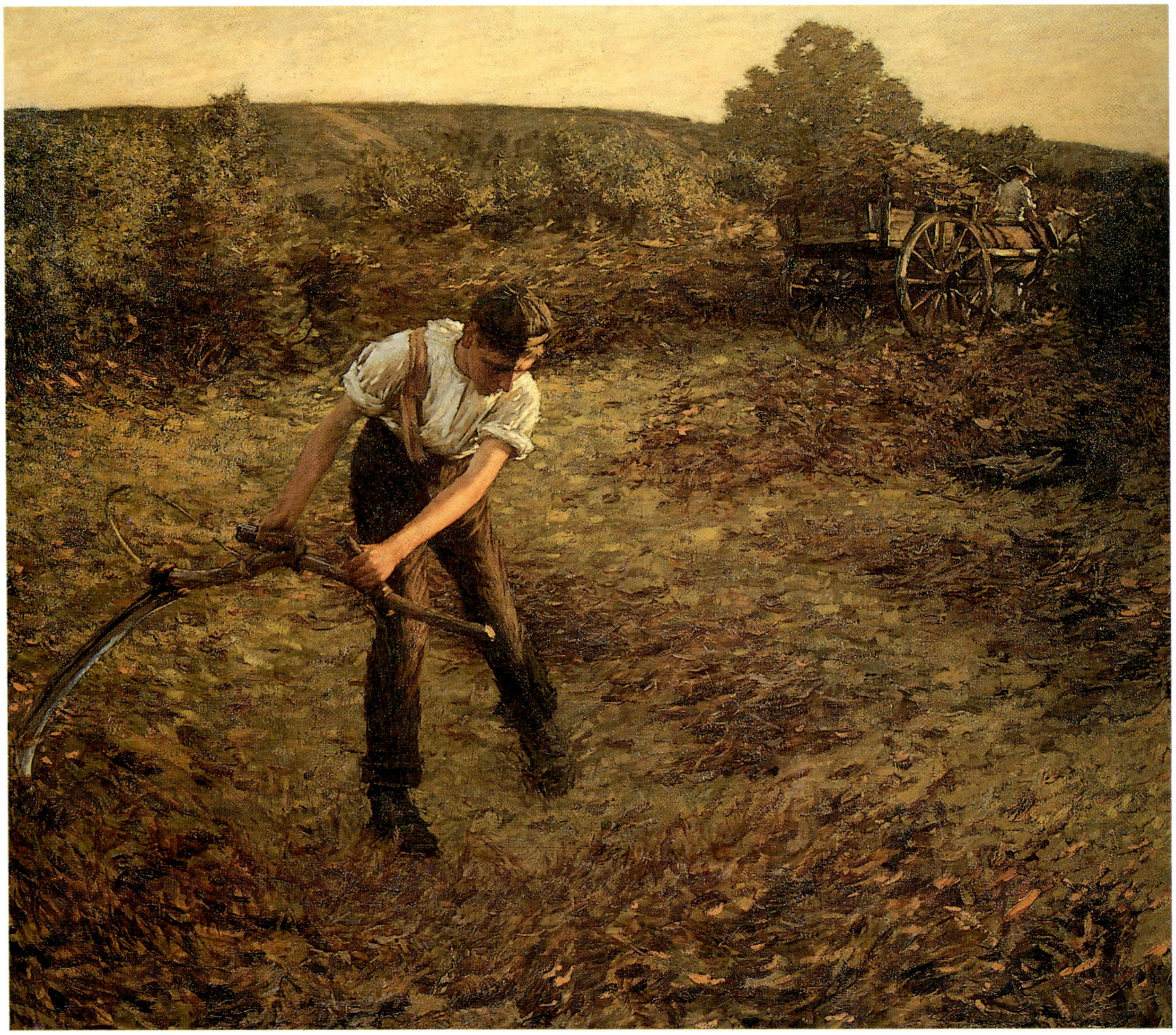

49
HENRY HERBERT LA THANGUE
*Mowing Bracken*

Surrey. His pictures are distinctive for their browny-yellow colours, impressionist technique, and fleecy masses of clouds. One of his favourite subjects was *A Coming Storm*, in which the black, threatening clouds become almost apocalyptic, dwarfing the puny humans who scurry like ants below.

Linnell himself was a stubbornly independent character, and a typical mid-Victorian. At first he became a Baptist, then joined the Plymouth Brethren, then abandoned all religious denominations, preferring to rely on his own personal interpretation of the scriptures. Born poor, he worked hard for his success, and was a fanatical believer in the virtues of hard work and self-help. His clients were probably much the same sort of men – self-made, hardworking, non-conformist businessmen, who believed in combining piety with profits. A convinced egalitarian, Linnell refused in later life to join the Royal Academy, which he regarded as a social clique. This led to some embarrassment among the Academicians, who felt that such a famous artist should be one of their number. When he died in 1882, he was widely regarded as the greatest English landscape painter since Turner (who had died in 1851). Somewhat unfairly, he has also been blamed for Palmer's lack of success after 1839. Linnell undoubtedly was an overbearing father-in-law, and may have bullied poor Palmer into changing his style to a more conventional and acceptable one, in the hope of making it more saleable.

Linnell's figures are dwarfed and absorbed by the landscape, bathed in nature's aura; whereas in the landscapes of Henry Herbert La Thangue the human figure dominates. La Thangue studied in Paris under Gerome, but was more influenced by the French painters of peasant life, such as Bastien-Lepage and Dagnan-Bouveret. On his return he settled at Bosham, in Surrey, but he was also a friend of Stanhope Forbes, the founder of the Newlyn School in Cornwall. Although not a member of the Newlyn School, La Thangue was

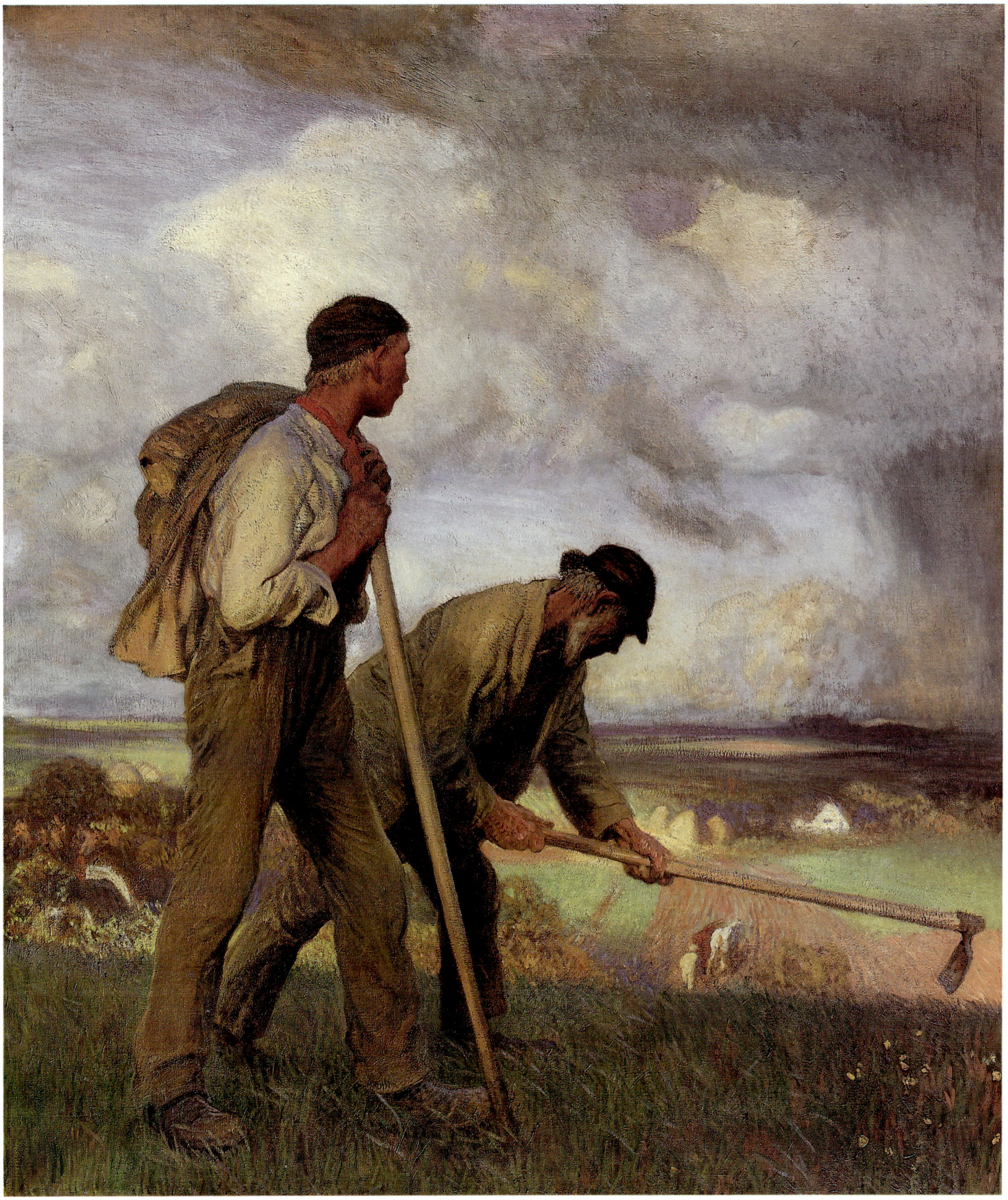

50
SIR GEORGE CLAUSEN
*The Boy and the Man*

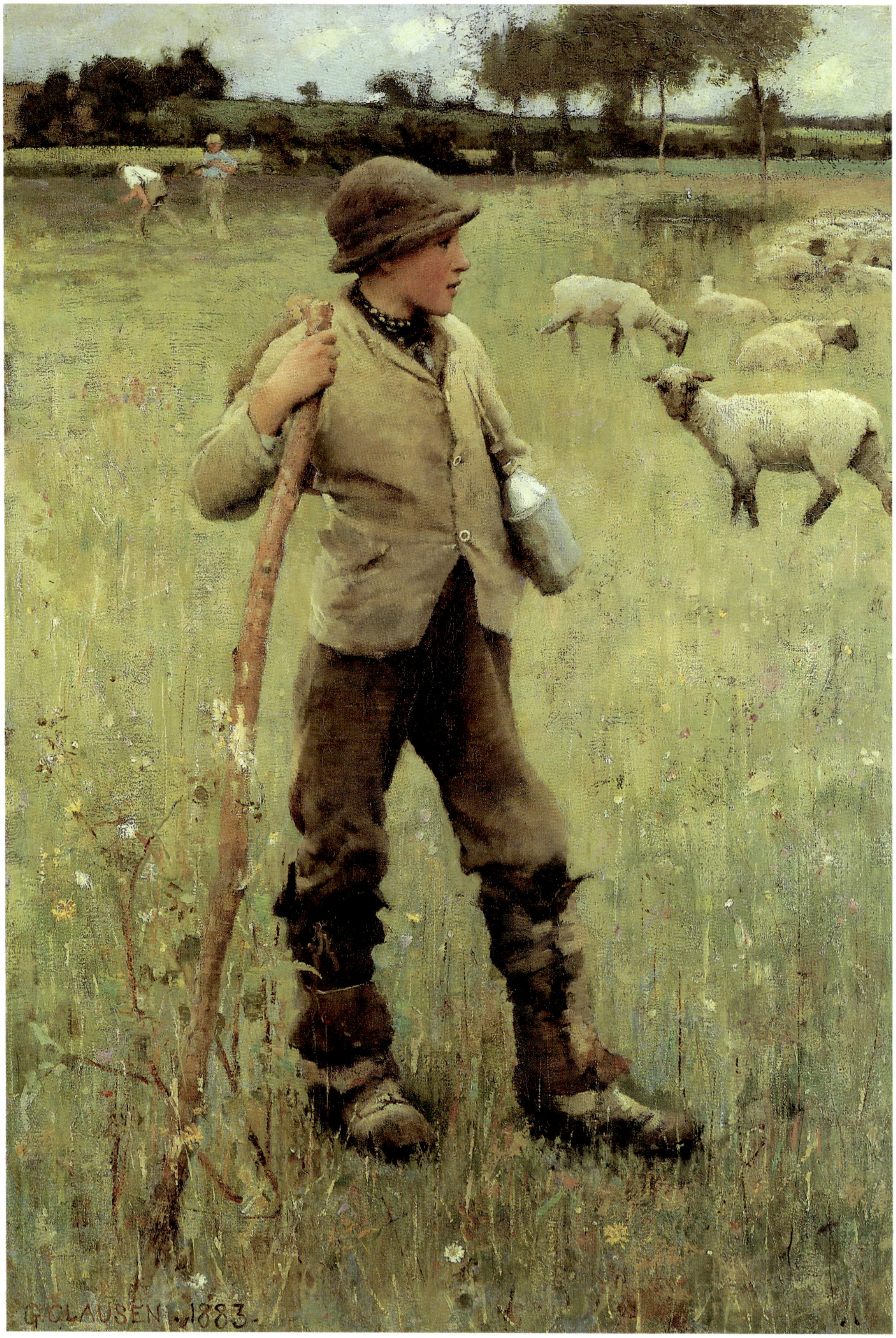


51
Sir George Clausen
*The Shepherd Boy*

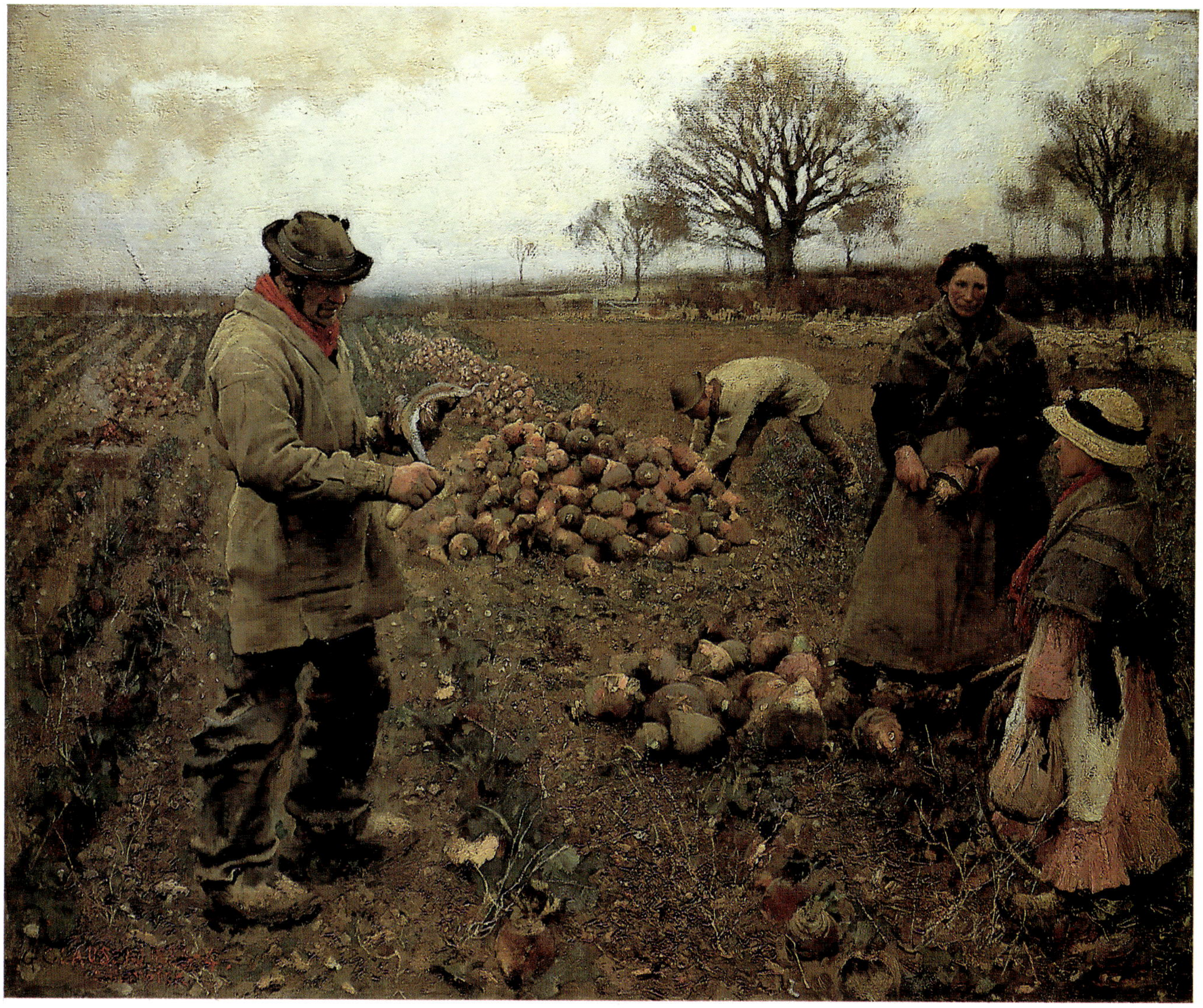

52
Sir George Clausen
*Winter Work*

much in sympathy with their aims and ideas. He shared their tendency to represent the worker as a heroic, timeless figure, part of the landscape yet dominating it. La Thangue painted many fine, sympathetic pictures of people at work in the countryside, of which *Mowing Bracken* (49) is a good example. Unlike *Hard Times*, there is no sense of deprivation or hardship here. As in most of his work there is a sense of the dignity of labour. Less strenuous is Fred Hall's delightful *Cabbage Field* (9). Hall was a member of the Newlyn School, and his pictures are typical of the gently pastoral impressionism so common in the late years of the century.

Even more monumental and heroic are the figures in the pictures of George Clausen. In his large picture, *The Boy and the Man* (50), the huge figures dominate the landscape, the low viewpoint adding to their impressive size. Clausen was almost the only Victorian painter to devote himself wholeheartedly to the theme of the farm worker. His pictures of men in the fields, harvesters, ploughmen, shepherds and bird-scarers, are among the most memorable of all images of country life in English art, and since the major exhibition of his work at the Royal Academy in 1980 they have become deservedly better known. Clausen's work is important to our theme, and several of his pictures will appear in other chapters, as well as here.

George Clausen was born in London in 1852, the son of a Danish sculptor. He visited Holland and Belgium in 1876, and his earliest pictures show strong Dutch influence. He was even referred to at this period as 'a very clever Dutch painter'. He then studied in Paris where, like his friend La Thangue, he was much impressed by the naturalist painter Bastien-Lepage. After his return to London, he and La Thangue were both involved in the founding of the New English Art Club in 1886. It was during the 1880s and 90s that Clausen painted some of his finest studies of English agricultural life, all of which show strong French influence. One of the best of these, *The Girl at the*

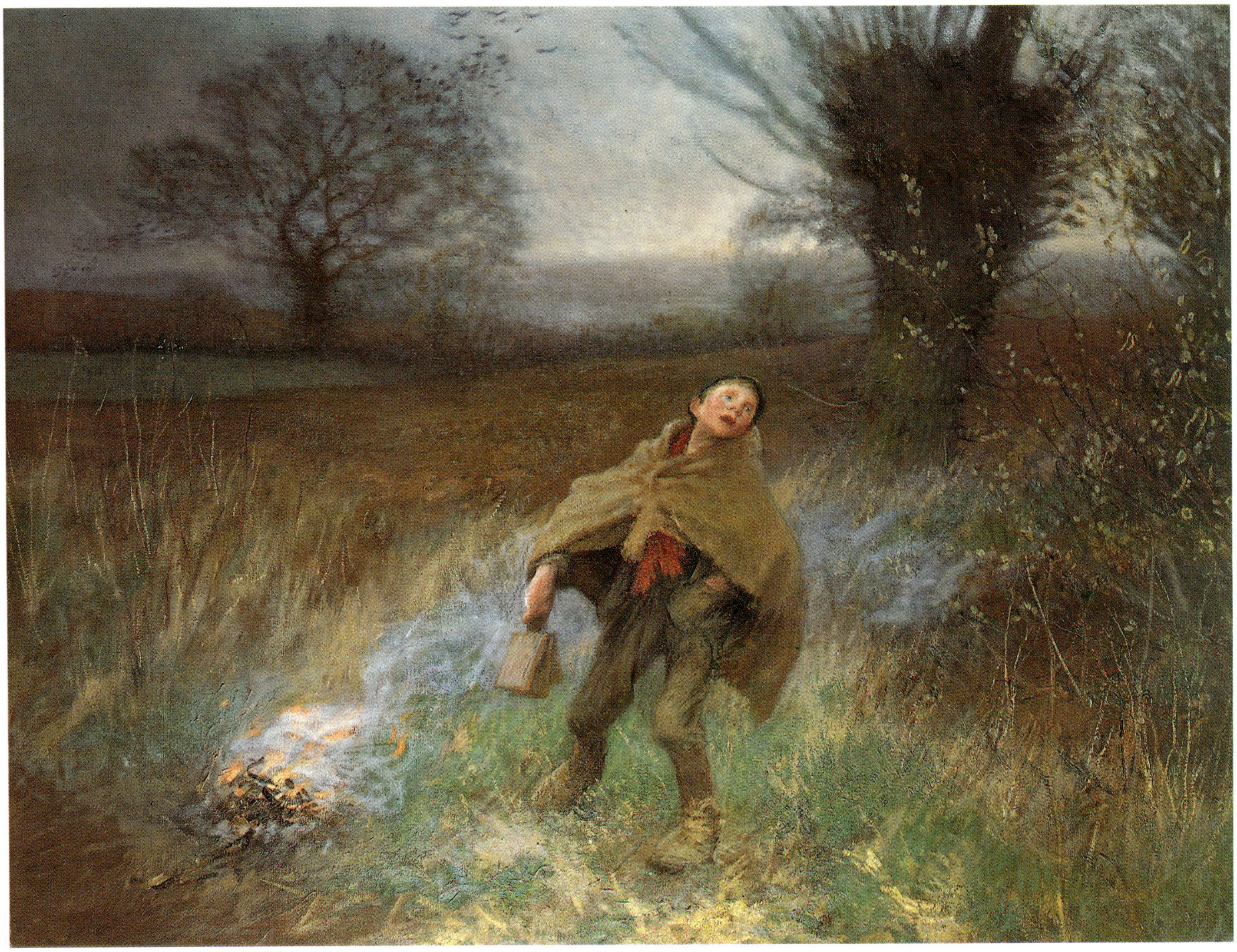

53
SIR GEORGE CLAUSEN
*Bird-Scaring*

*Gate*, was purchased in 1890 for the Tate Gallery by the trustees of the Chantrey Bequest.

Many of the finest of Clausen's early works are simply single figures, like *The Shepherd Boy* (51) of 1883. With his tattered trousers, leggings and short jacket, he is a marvellously strong and unsentimental figure, a far cry from the 'simpering rusticity' of so much earlier Victorian painting. Looking after the sheep was a job often done by boys or girls, and Clausen painted several young shepherdesses in a similar style. Another job done by children was *Bird-Scaring* (53). This is one of Clausen's most memorable images. When it was first exhibited in 1896, the *Times* and other critics thought the boy 'ugly' and 'uncouth', but the *Graphic* rightly praised it as 'a very true type of English rustic character'. Many writers have recorded the miseries of bird-scaring, which involved spending long and lonely hours in the fields, and was traditionally done by young boys. M.K. Ashby, in her biography of her father, *Joseph Ashby of Tysoe 1859-1919* (1961), wrote that 'From the time he was nine Joseph would spend long, lonely days in school vacations and on Saturdays scaring crows off the short green corn. He had a wooden clapper, but if he saw no-one for hours he took to shouting so as to hear a human voice.' Joseph Arch, founder of the National Union of Agricultural Labourers, also recalled working as a crow-scarer, for which he was paid fourpence a day. He also remembered the farmer creeping up on him, to catch him idling or wandering outside the field, and getting 'a smart taste of the farmer's stick'. Clausen's picture is the only one to give any idea of the loneliness and hardship that this job entailed.

Clausen liked painting boys and old men together, to contrast youth and age. In *The Return from the Fields* (54), a watercolour of 1882, he shows an old man and a boy carrying bundles of brushwood, probably to be used for hedging, firelighting, or making sheep hurdles. It is not only a beautiful

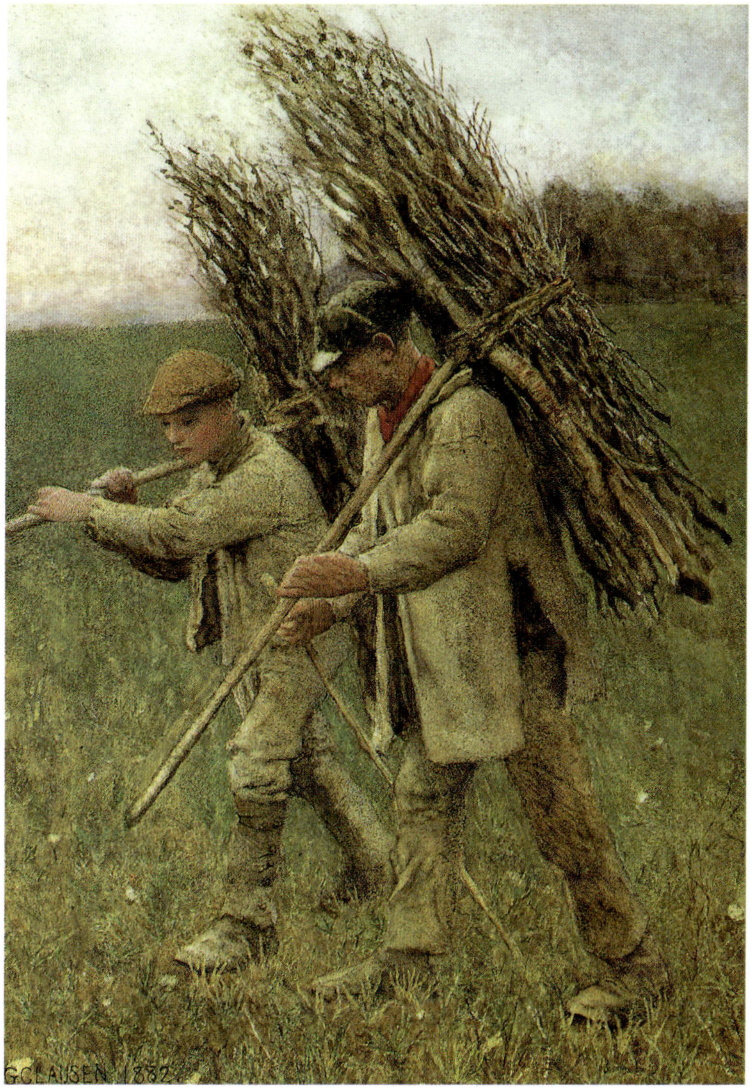

54
Sir George Clausen
*The Return from the Fields*

watercolour, but reminds us that nearly all farming skills were transmitted from father to son, or from old to young. There was no other way of learning them. The proper title of this picture is probably *Boy and Man*, as cutting brushwood was a winter task, not a summer one. When it was exhibited at the Royal Institute in 1882, the *Magazine of Art* critic praised it as 'the most artistic work on the walls . . . so tender and full of feeling that it arrests attention more powerfully than the other pictures together'. Painted in Clausen's characteristically soft tones of green and brown, it is indeed one of the most successful of all translations of the Millet style into an English idiom.

Even more monumental and impressive is his large *Winter Work* (52), showing turnip-cutters at work in a wet and muddy field. Perhaps more than any other picture of the nineteenth century, this painting conveys how it really felt to work in the fields in an English winter. Turnip-pulling and turnip-cutting were the hardest and most unpopular of all winter jobs, and are described by Hardy, both in *Tess*, and in his poem *We Field-Women*:

How it rained
When we worked at Flintcomb Ash,
And could not stand upon the hill
Trimming swedes for the slicing mill.
The wet washed through us – plash, plash, plash:
How it rained!

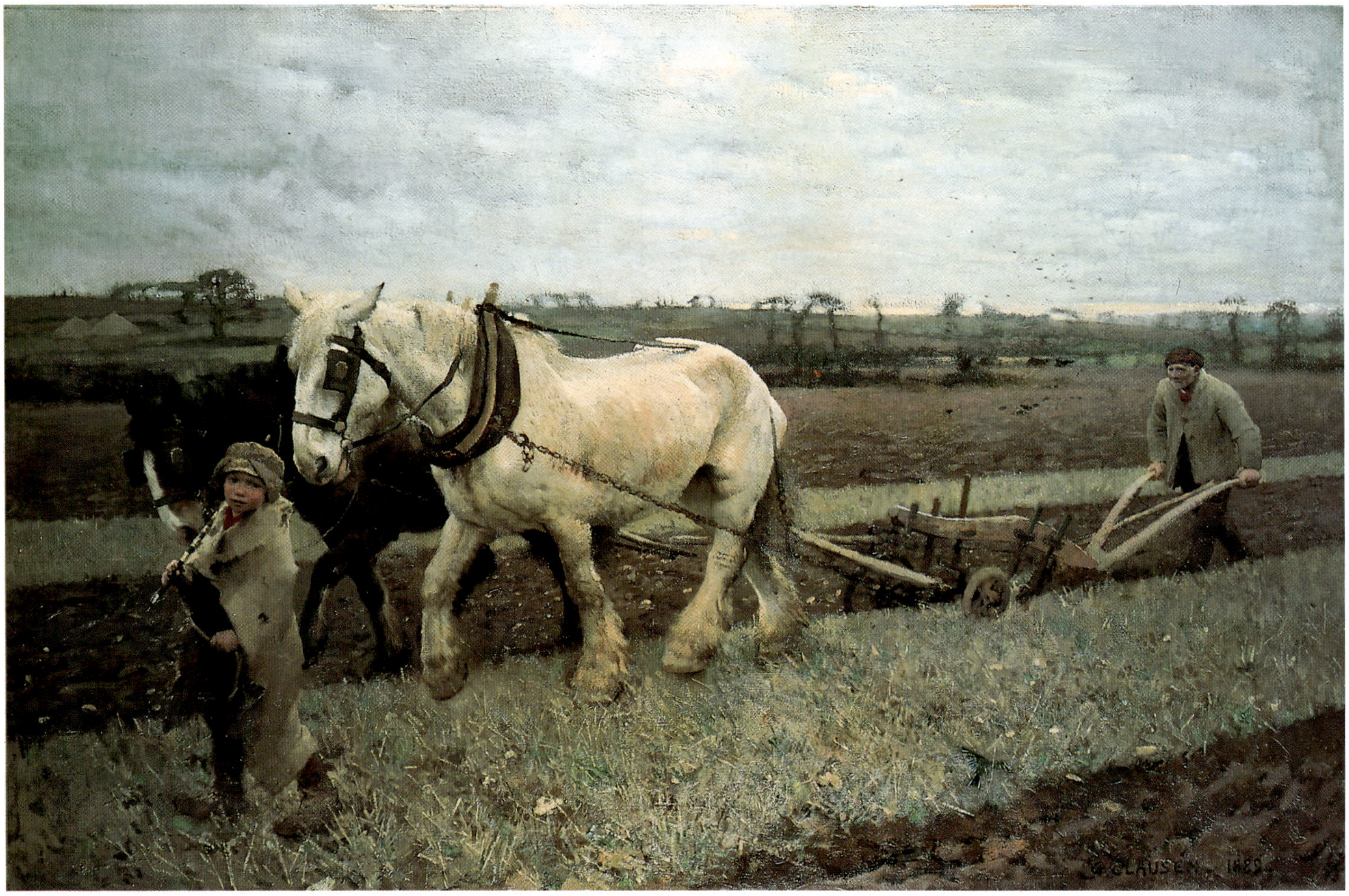

55
SIR GEORGE CLAUSEN
*Ploughing*

# Chapter Four

# ~ HORSES ~

Come all you jolly ploughboys, come
listen to my lays
And join with me in chorus, I'll sing the
ploughboy's praise.

TRADITIONAL

Although it is now difficult to imagine, the horse played as important a role in human affairs in the nineteenth century as the motor car has in the twentieth. A Victorian looked at a horse in much the same way as we now look at a car, both as a symbol, and as an object of practical use. And for most of the twentieth century the cylinder capacity of motor cars has been calculated in terms of horse-power. There is a story of an elderly and eccentric duke, who in the early twentieth century decided to replace his horses and carriages with motor cars. He asked his head groom to calculate exactly how many cars would be needed to replace the total horse-power of his horses. After much mathematical calculation, the duke purchased ten cars.

Even after the invention of the railway, the horse continued to play an important role in transport, both in the country and the town. For country people, the local carrier with his horse and cart was often the only link with the local town. On the farm, the horse was the main source of pulling power for the heavy machinery that performed such essential tasks as ploughing, harrowing, sowing, haymaking and harvesting, and for the heavy wooden farm carts. During the century, the number of horses used both in farming and in transport reached its apogee, and only began to decline after the First World War. Horses needed men to guide them and look after them, so around the horse grew up a whole mystique of skills and related trades to supply and maintain them.

On the farm, the horsemen enjoyed a higher status than ordinary labourers. 'Them horse chaps', as the other men referred to them, regarded themselves as an élite and usually enjoyed higher wages and better conditions. The head horseman was a respected and important figure on any farm, with his teams of horses, and his own men under him, among whom

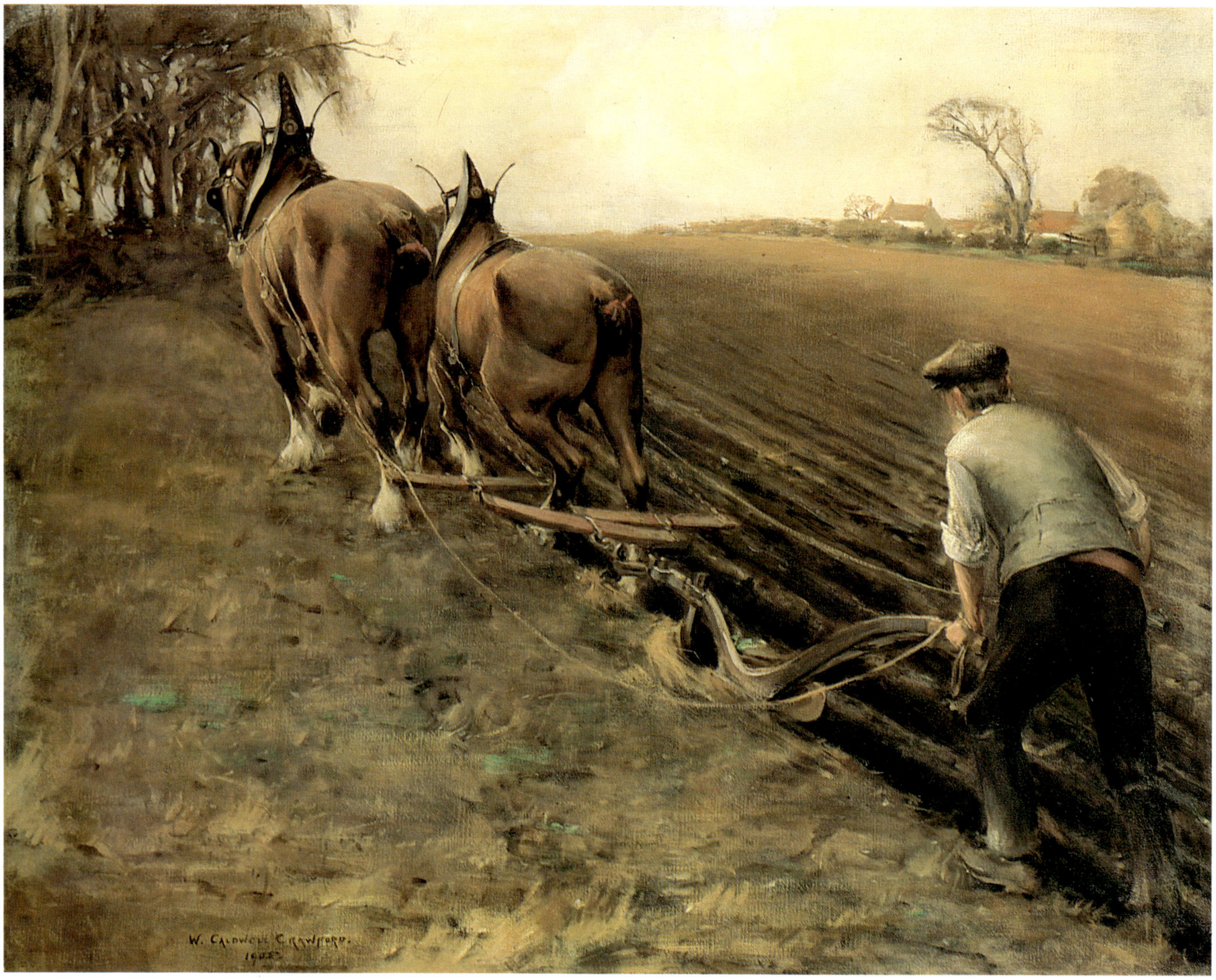

56
William Caldwell Crawford
*Ploughing*

a strict hierarchy prevailed. Every horseman had his own special vocabulary of words to control the horses, some doubtless of very ancient origin. He also had his own special ways of calming down a difficult or bad-tempered horse, and his own secret medicine chest of remedies for their ailments. Every head horseman took a pride in the glossy and smart appearance of his team, and often the harness and the horse brasses might be his own property. He also saw to it that the horses were properly fed, even if this meant stealing extra hay or corn from the store.

Horses naturally appear in many Victorian pictures of farming. The strength and beauty of the huge cart horses was admired, and a team of them made a picturesque subject. But it was ploughing that appealed most and this was the subject of innumerable oils and watercolours throughout the century. It also inspired one of Clausen's finest early pictures, his *Ploughing* (55) of 1889. This large and wonderful picture represents the summit of his achievement in the Bastien-Lepage style, before he began to move towards a lighter palette and a more impressionistic technique. The critics were impressed, and the *Art Journal* wrote that 'The light of the cold March day lies round the figures of the boy and the horses in a remarkably truthful manner.' Less poetic, but equally forceful in its suggestion of strain and movement, is William Caldwell Crawford's picture of the same title (56). Crawford was a Scottish painter who mostly exhibited his work at the Scottish Academy, and is consequently little known in England. In these pictures only one or two horses are being used. In Flora Thompson's description, 'There were usually three or four ploughs to a field, each of them drawn by a team of three horses, with a boy at the head of the leader and the ploughman behind at the shafts. All day, up and down they would go, ribbing the pale stubble with stripes of dark furrows which, as the day advanced, would get wider and nearer together, until, at length, the whole field lay a vel-

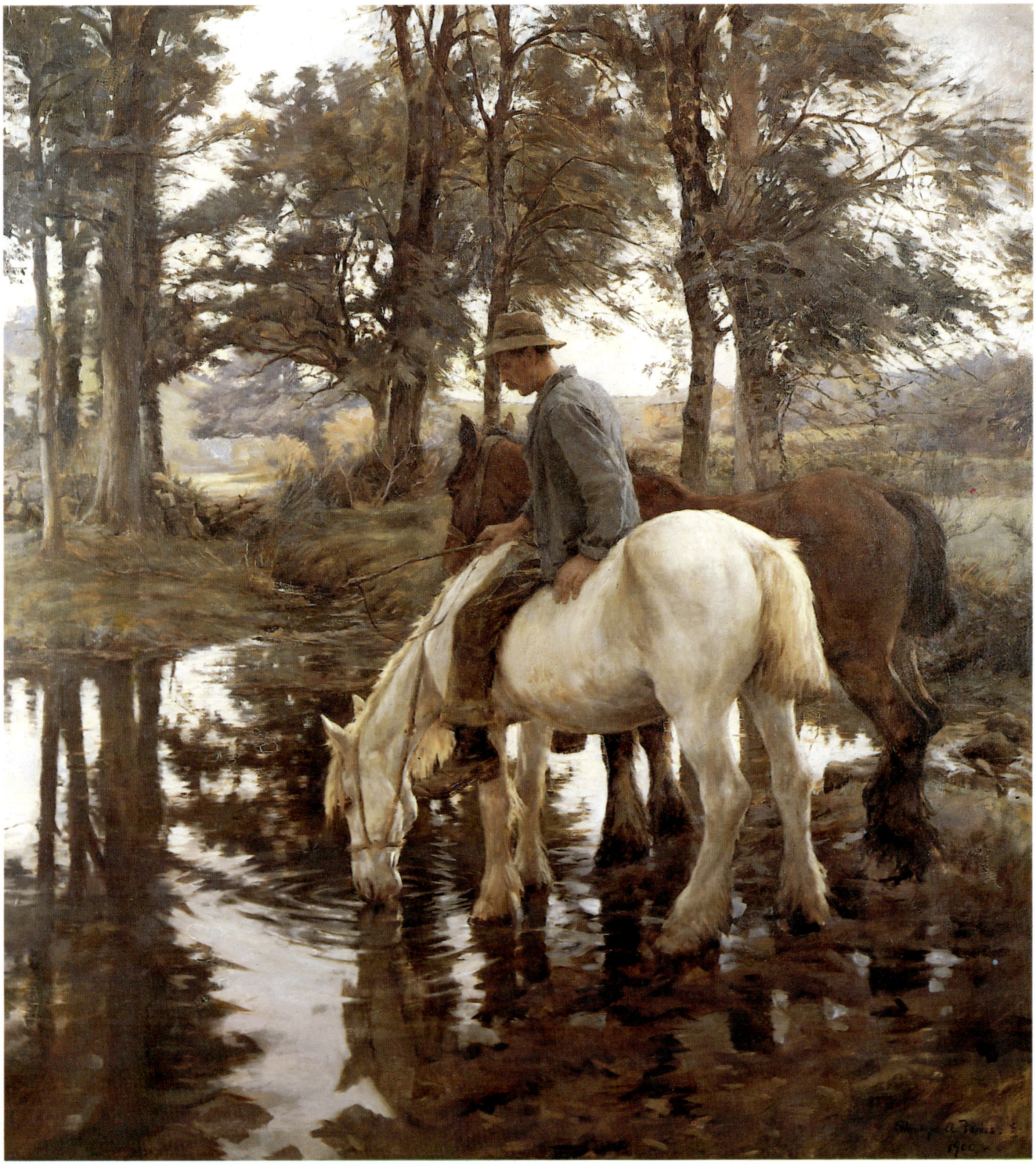

57
STANHOPE FORBES
*The Drinking Place*

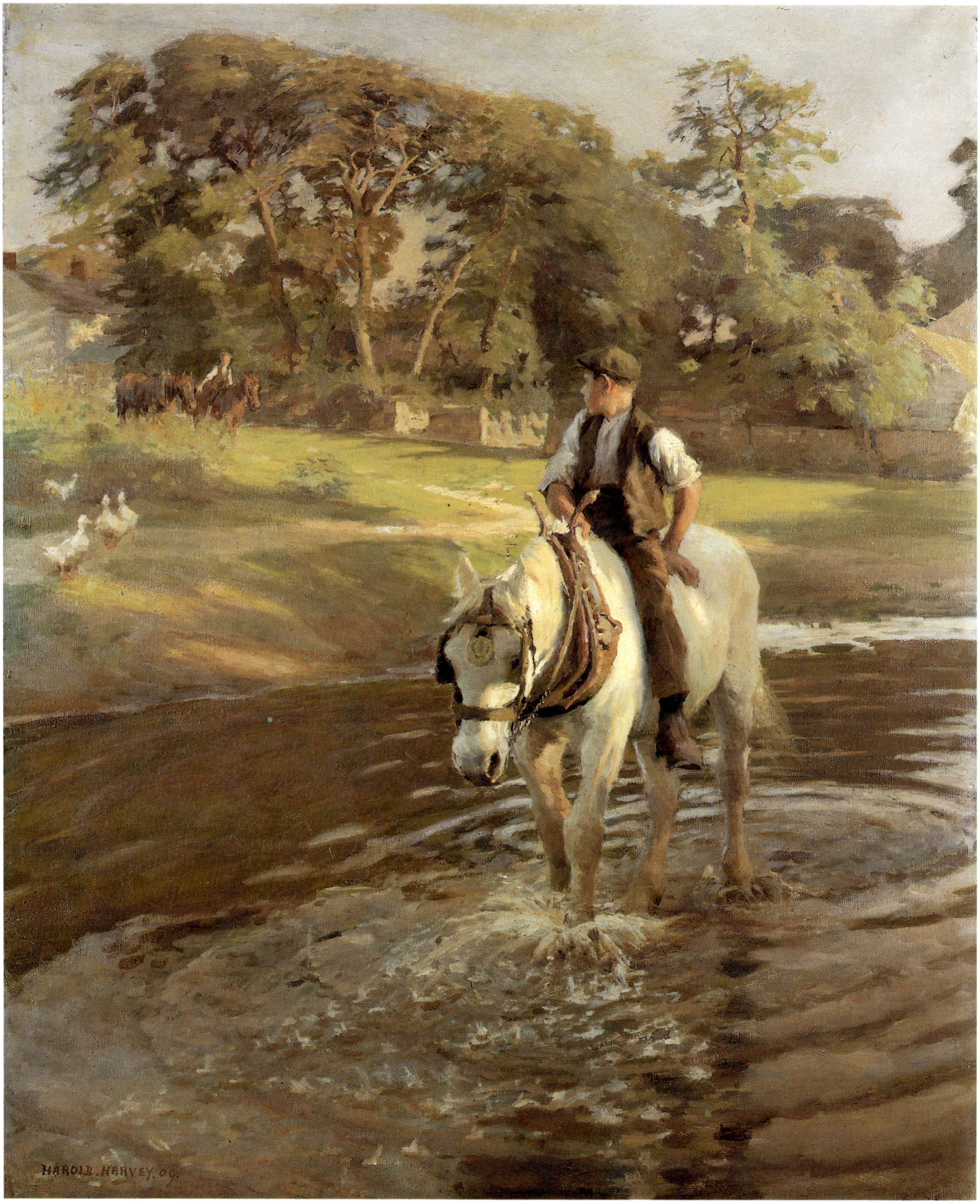


58
HAROLD HARVEY
*Watering the Horse*

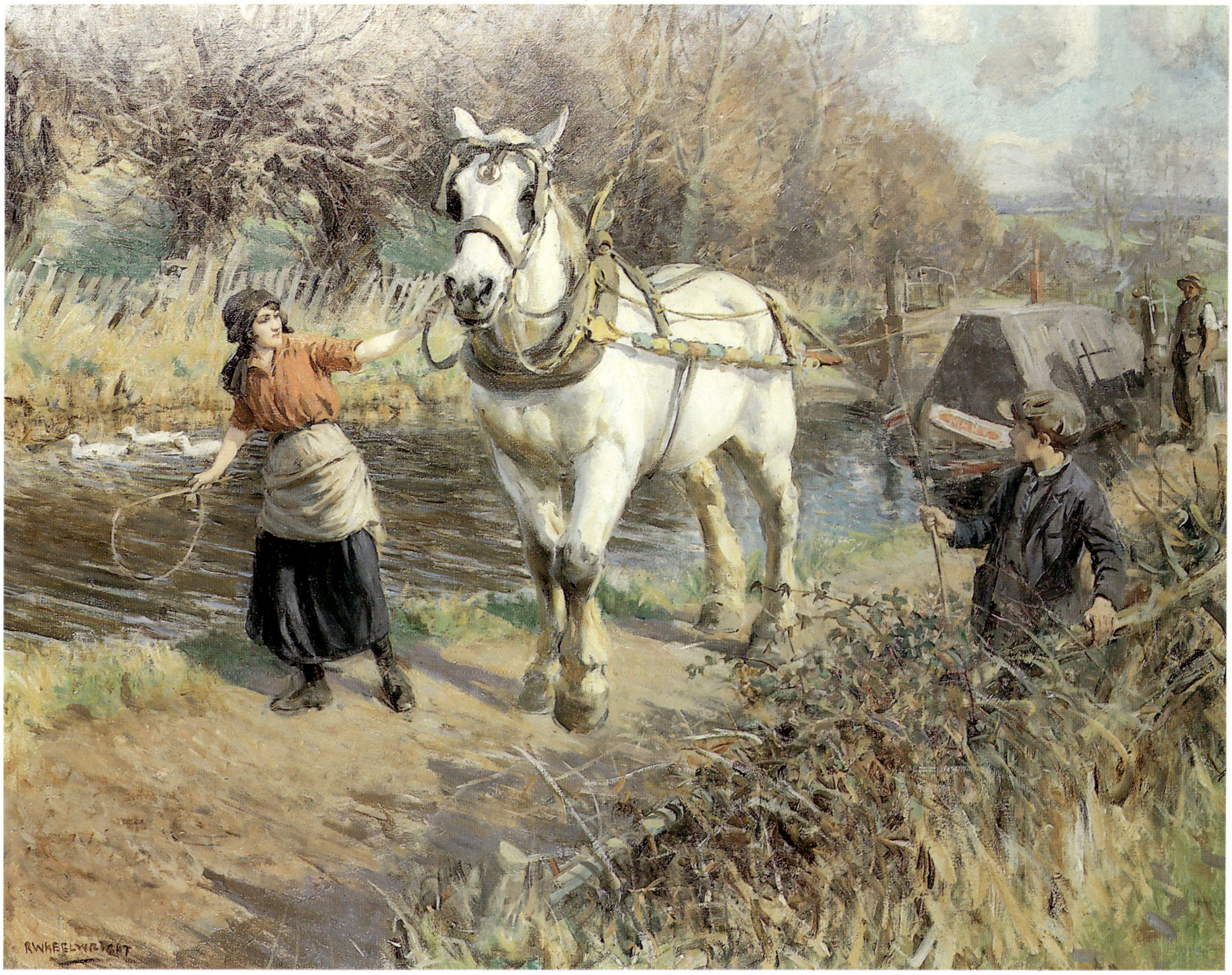

59
ROWLAND WHEELWRIGHT
*On the Towpath*

vety plum colour.' Many poems too were inspired by ploughing, such as *Harry Ploughman* by Gerard Manley Hopkins, and also part of *The Everlasting Mercy* by John Masefield:

> A ploughman's voice, a clink of chain,
> Slow hoofs, and harness under strain,
> Up the slow slope a team came bowing,
> Old Callow at his autumn ploughing. . . .

Horses drinking was another popular subject, offering the opportunity to combine horses with water and trees. One of Herring Junior's most popular pictures was the heads of three horses at a trough. Many other artists copied this subject, even calling it *A Temperance Society*, thus trying to cash in on both the horse market and the teetotaller. Stanhope Forbes made better use of it in his fine picture *The Drinking Place* (57) of 1900. Forbes was the father of the Newlyn School, and spent nearly all his life painting there, founding the Art School in 1899. He studied in Paris with his friends Arthur Hacker and H.H. La Thangue. Like them, he was deeply impressed with the French naturalist painters, and all three went to Brittany in search of suitably picturesque village subjects. He returned to France for several years running, but in 1884 decided to look for new painting grounds in England. He made his first visit to Cornwall, and was immediately captivated by the unspoiled fishing village of Newlyn. More artists followed him there, and before long a regular colony was established. In 1885, Forbes exhibited his famous *Fish Sale on a Cornish Beach* at the Royal Academy, and its success gave a great impetus to the Newlyn School. Forbes painted not only fishermen, but other aspects of village life too, such as *The Village Philharmonic* and *The Health of the Bride*, both illustrated in future chapters. Forbes believed in realism, and painting in the open air, but also in wholesome,

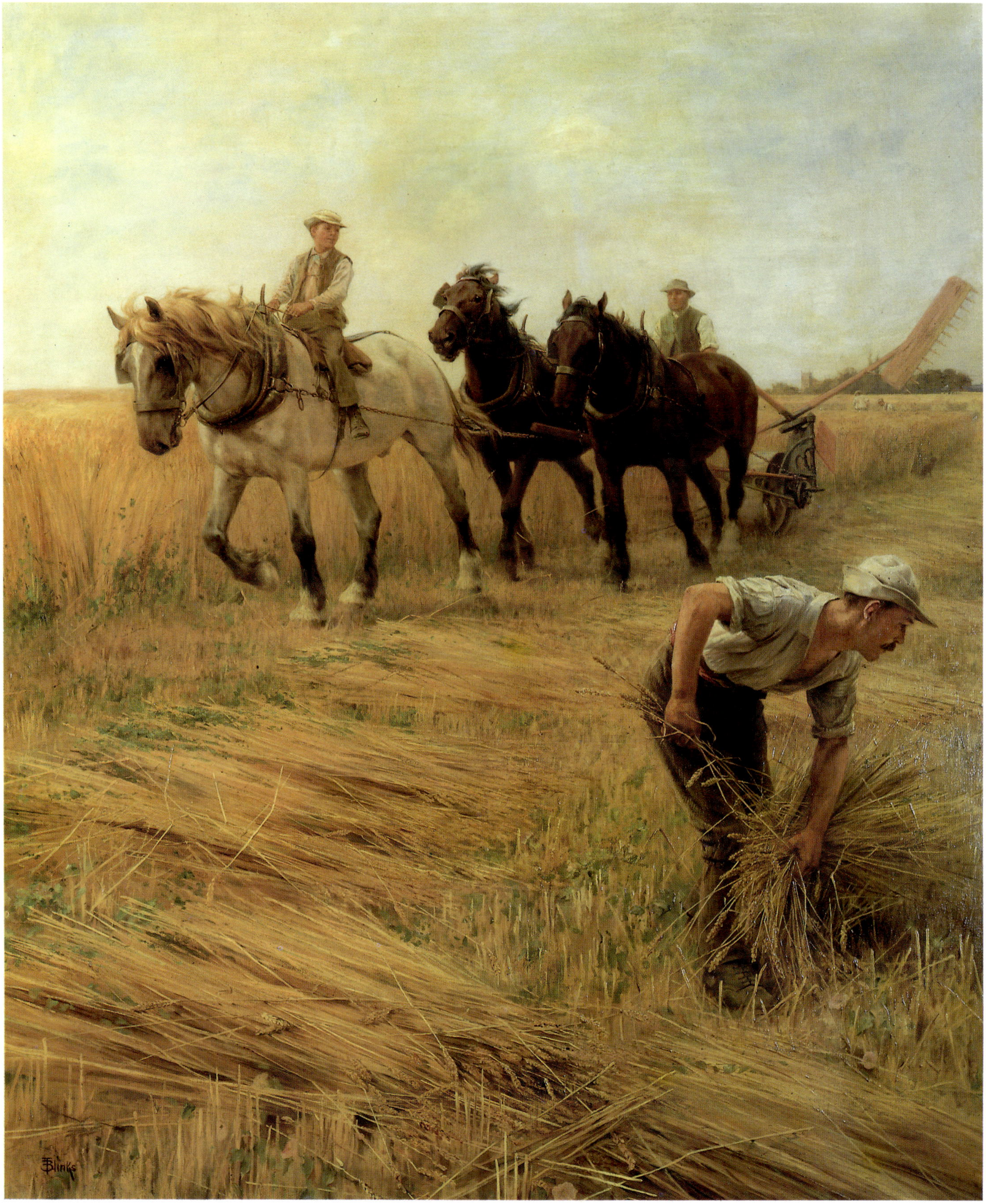

60
THOMAS BLINKS
*Bread Winners*

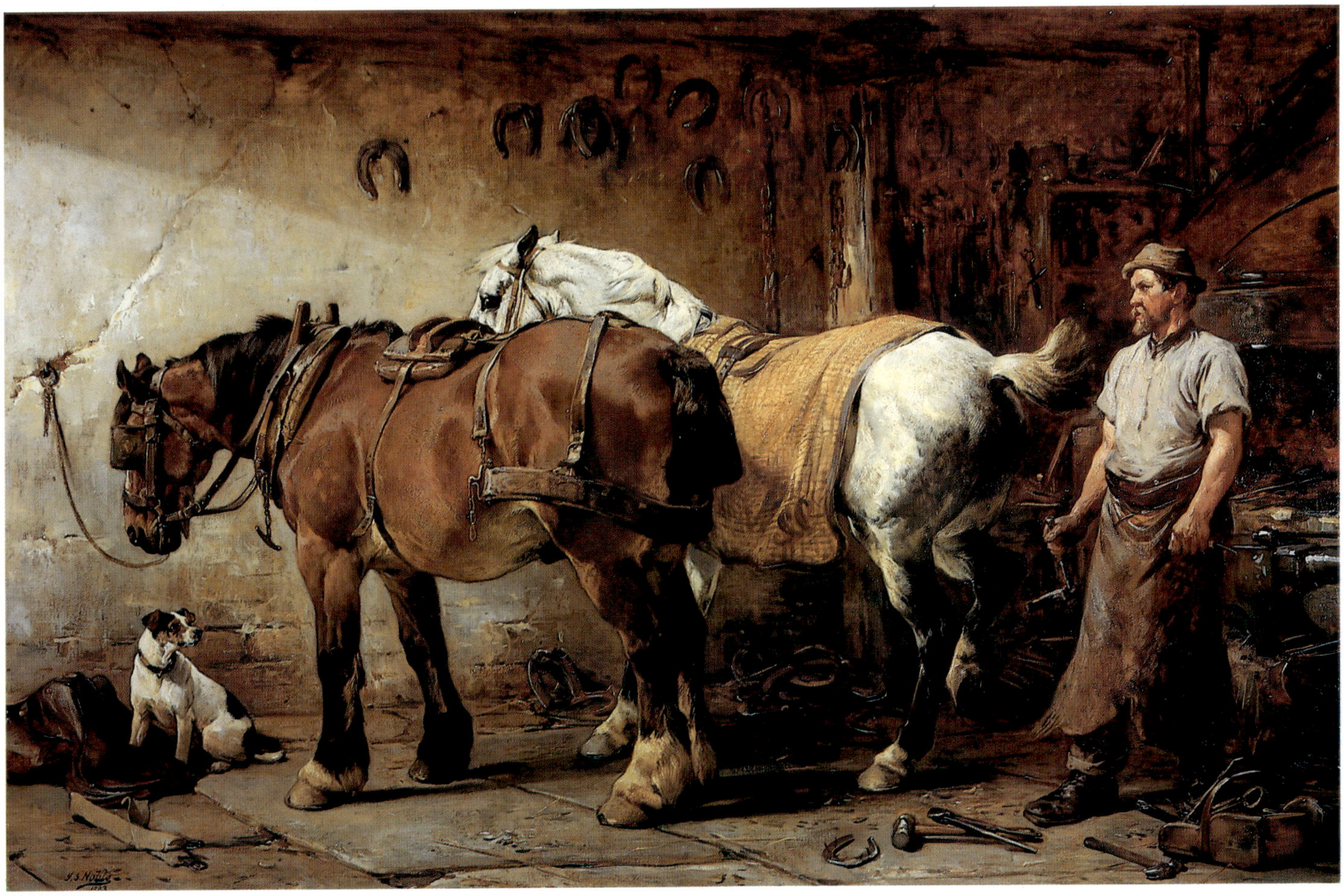

61
JOHN SARGENT NOBLE
*At the Blacksmith's*

healthy subjects. Sickert and the Camden School were anathema to him; he dismissed them as 'tawdry', and 'vulgar'. Forbes and his followers, such as Walter Langley, Fred Hall, Frank Bramley, and Thomas Cooper Gotch, influenced a whole generation of painters in the last twenty years of the century.

Another Forbes follower was Harold Harvey, who painted his *Watering the Horse* (58) in 1909. Harvey belonged to a younger generation than Forbes, but was a native of Cornwall, born in Penzance. He studied with another Newlyn painter, Norman Garstin, and then in Paris in the 1880s. He then settled in Cornwall for the rest of his life. His early work is much influenced, in style and subject, by Stanhope Forbes, but later he changed to a brighter, more decorative style.

Almost an exact contemporary of Harvey's was Rowland Wheelwright, who was born in Australia, and studied with Herkomer in Bushey. He painted a wide range of historical and mythological subjects, but also country scenes. His *On the Towpath* (59) is a fine essay in the Stanhope Forbes style, remarkably similar in colouring to the Harvey. Horses were widely used for towing barges along canals, and for towing heavy loads, such as timber and building materials. The canal system was at its height in the early Victorian period, providing a very cheap way of transporting both goods and passengers.

The title of Thomas Blinks s picture *Bread Winners* (60) of 1905 implies that it is the horses who are the heroes. Here a team of three horses pull an old-fashioned, sail-type reaper, while the man in the foreground gathers up the corn to bind it into sheaves. Blinks was a well-known sporting painter, best known for his hunting scenes and pictures of hounds. *Bread Winners* is one of his very few attempts at a country life subject; one only wishes that he had painted more of them. Also a sporting artist, and well-known for dog subjects, was John Sargent Noble. His *At the Blacksmith's* (61) reveals that he could paint horses equally well. The blacksmith in most villages was

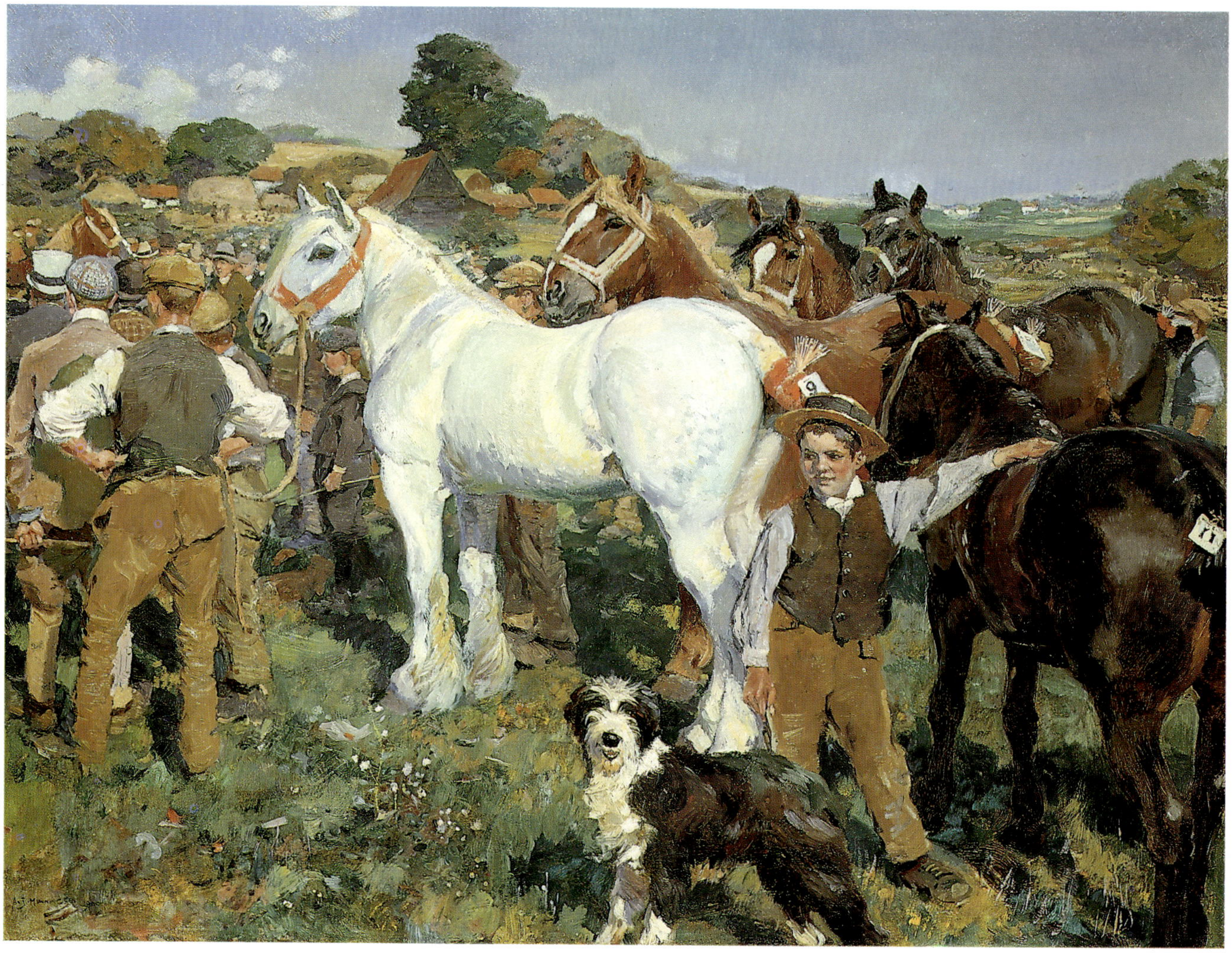

62
SIR ALFRED MUNNINGS
*A Michaelmas Sale on a Suffolk Farm*

also the farrier, and was therefore an important person in the country. Almost every village of any size had a blacksmith's shop, which was inevitably a centre of village life and local gossip. At Candleford Green, Flora Thompson's postmistress, Miss Dorcas Lane, also owned the blacksmith's next door. The foreman and his three young shoeing-smiths would all come into Miss Lane's for lunch each day, looking bashful, and 'rolling their leather aprons up around their waists as they tiptoed to their places at table'. Outside,

All kinds of horses came to the forge to be shod: heavy cart horses, standing quiet and patient; the baker's and the grocer's and butcher's van horses; poor old screws belonging to gipsies or fish-hawkers; and an occasional hunter. . . . The local horses were all known to the men and addressed by them by name. Even the half-yearly bills were made out: To So-and-So Esq., for shoeing Violet, or Poppet, or Whitefoot, or The Grey Lady, 'all round', or 'fore', or 'hind'. . .

When the smithy was empty, Laura would slip in there to 'inhale the astringent scents of iron and oil and ashes and hoof-parings. . . pull the bellows handle and see the dull embers turn red. . . .'

The importance of horses meant that horse fairs were significant business and social occasions. Many artists painted fairs and race-meetings, but the excitement and bustle of a horse sale has perhaps never been conveyed better than by the young Alfred Munnings, painting in his native Suffolk (62). In his autobiography, *An Artist's Life*, he wrote excitedly of his first visit to Lavenham Horse Fair. 'What a sight! This famous fair of heavy draught-horses eclipsed anything of its kind I had ever seen . . . packed with a breed of men long since gone: men with fat jowls, wearing wide-brimmed bowlers or half-high hats, who came from London to buy heavy horses for London work – for railway companies' vans, brewers' drays and a host of other trades.'

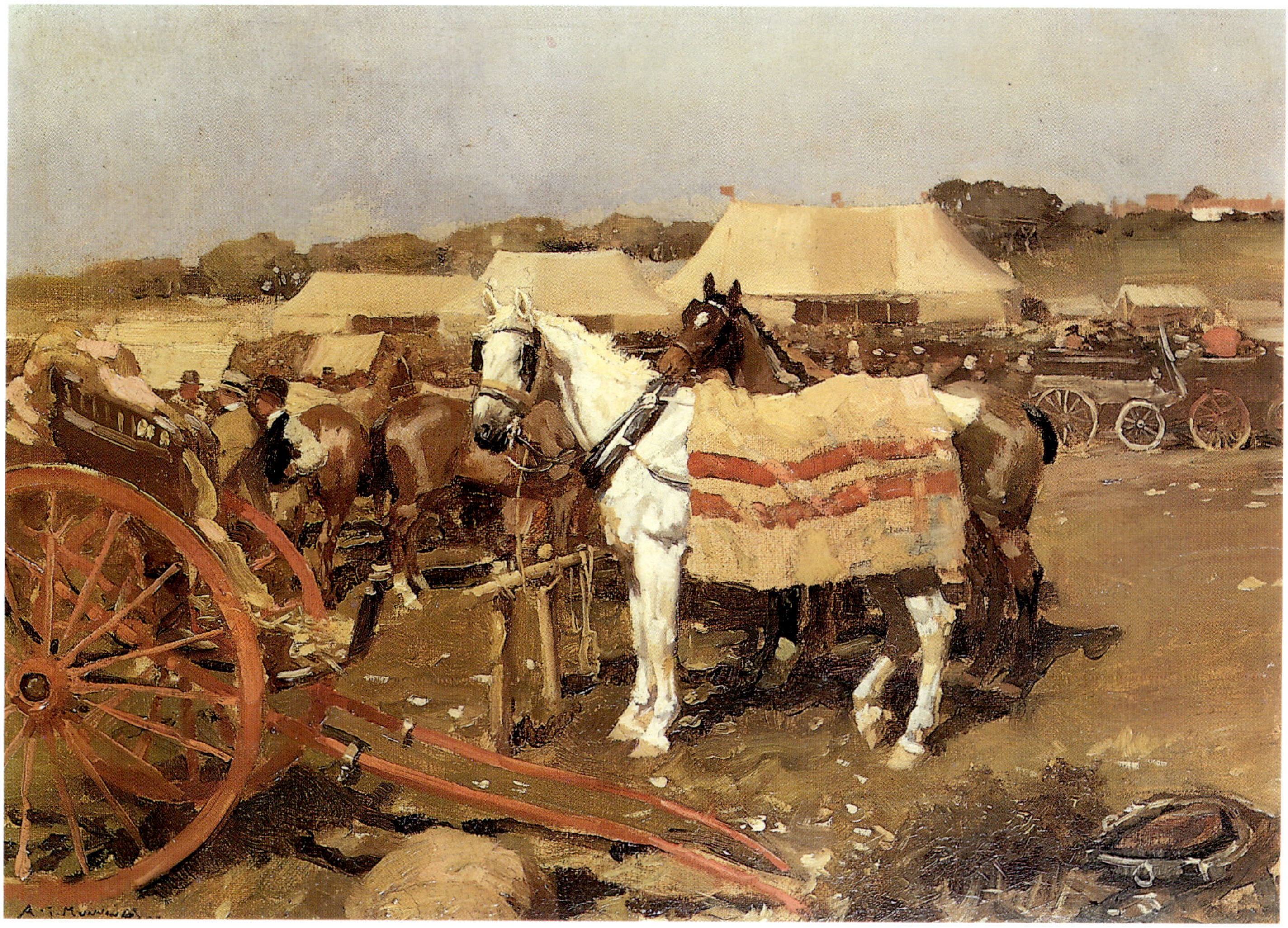

63
Sir Alfred Munnings
*Bungay Races*

Munnings was a lifelong lover of horses and racing, and recorded in his book his first visit to a race-meeting, Bungay Races, also to be the subject of several pictures (63).

I had known horse sales in Norwich, local races and regattas; but what were they compared to this vast fair and meeting combined on Bungay Common? There were roundabouts, shooting-galleries, swinging-boats and coconut shies; large eating and drinking tents, flags flying, and thousands of oranges blazing on stalls in the sun. I had never seen such droves of ponies and gipsy lads. But all this, with music and noise, died away and dwindled to nothing when I saw the thoroughbred horses and jockeys – professional and gentlemen riders – in bright silk colours, going off down the course.

Munnings went on to become England's most famous painter of racehorses in the twentieth century. But his words conjure up the glamour and excitement that must have surrounded these fairs and race meetings in Victorian times. They really were a place where all classes of society could mix. At Newmarket dukes and commoners met on equal terms, and an ex-prizefighter like John Gulley could become both an MP and the owner of three Derby winners. The numerous small meetings – described disparagingly by Surtees as run by landlords and bookies – united the town and country. The Victorians, as with so many things, tried to clean up racing. Reformers such as Lord George Bentinck and Admiral Rous began to introduce tighter rules; the disorderly and crooked steeple-chase of the early Victorian period was transformed into the more decorous and organised point-to-point. But in 1885 it was still possible for the saddle and bridle of a fallen horse to be immediately stolen by the crowd at the Heythrop point-to-point. In the Victorian age, racing spanned the widest social spectrum of any sport, from the aristocratic to the criminal.

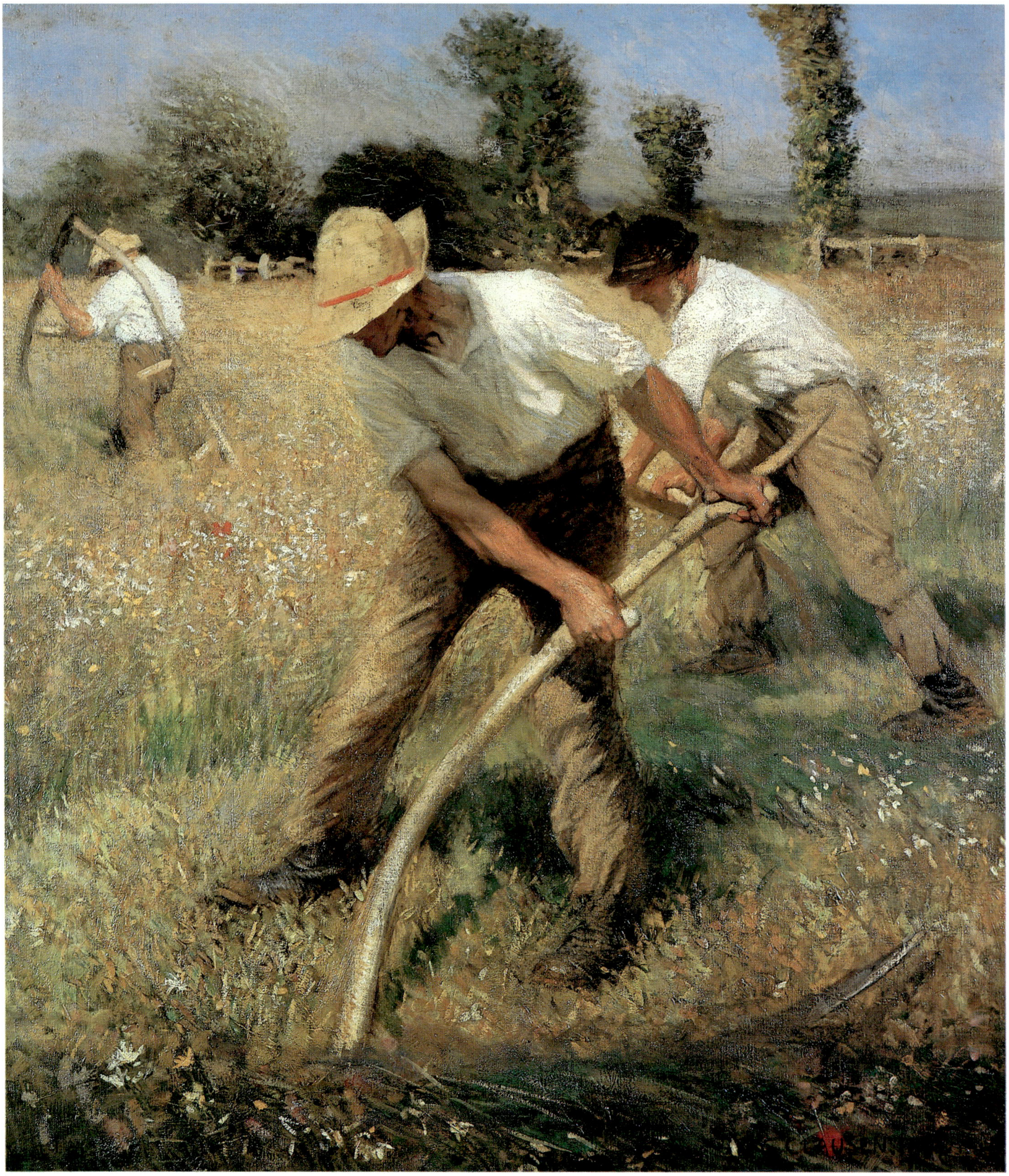

64
Sir George Clausen
*The Mowers*

Chapter Five

# HAYMAKING AND HARVESTING

The corn is all ripe and the reapings begin,
The fruits of the earth, O we gather them in . . .

TRADITIONAL

HAYMAKING IN ENGLAND HAS ALWAYS BEEN thought of as synonymous with having a good time. In Victorian times it was also extremely hard work. Until the use of mechanical reapers became general, the cutting of hay was done by hand, often during very hot weather. 'Today the heat was excessive,' wrote Francis Kilvert, 'and as I sat reading under the lime I pitied the poor haymakers toiling in the burning Common where it seemed to be raining fire.' Victorian painters seemed in general to share the common view that making hay was the jolliest and most cheerful activity possible. A typical painting by Birket Foster, *In the Hayfield*, shows a group of girls and children settling down for their picnic in the hayfield. All sense of sweat and toil has been eliminated; this is something more like a day's holiday than actual work. Arthur Hopkins's version (65) is much more realistic; this is what Victorian haymaking must really have looked like. Arthur Hopkins was the brother of the poet Gerard Manley Hopkins, and clearly both had a keen appreciation of the beauties of the English countryside.

There are many beautiful descriptions of haymaking in the nineteenth century. One of the best and most detailed is by Alfred Williams. He recalled that the farmer would send down to the school for boys and girls to help. The reaping was by this time done by a mechanical reaper. 'The first day the grass lay untouched. . . . The second day the haymakers proper appeared, little Betsy and her school, the laughing boys and girls, the fogger too, and his young men. Some came with rakes and some with prongs, and pulled the swath over; others shook the thick heaps about; it was laugh and chatter, tease and prattle all the time. . . .' It does sound remarkably like a Birket Foster scene. Then lunch would be taken in the shade of a tree, with plenty of lemonade and beer supplied by the farmer. If the

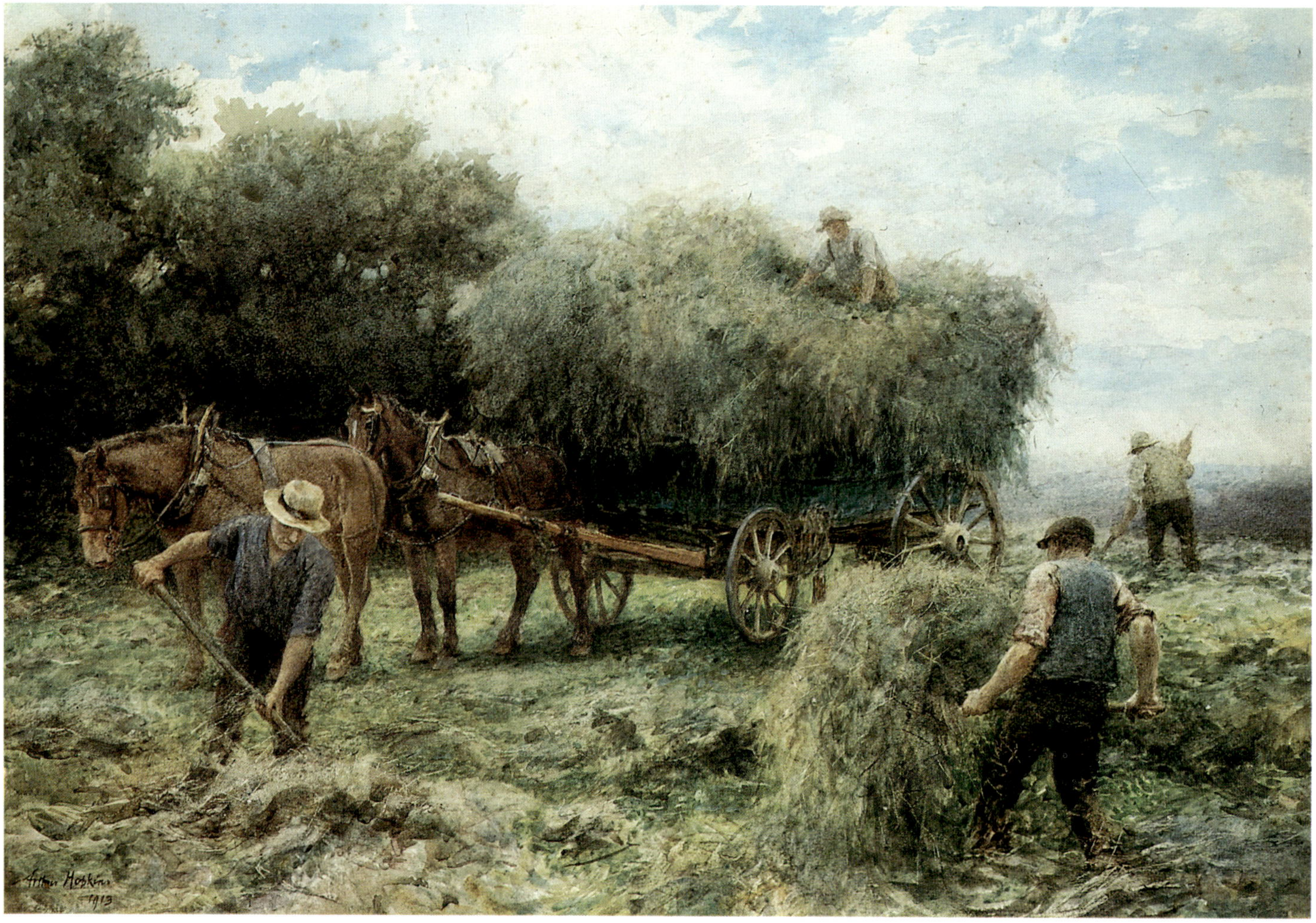

65
ARTHUR HOPKINS
*Loading Hay*

hay was dry enough after two days, 'Then the waggons came out for gathering up the hay. There was one, or perhaps two pitchers, and there might be two loaders.' Their job was to load up each waggon, throwing the sheaves, or 'wakes' as they were called in Wiltshire, up on to the waggon. Back at the farm the bed of the rick had already been prepared, and a mechanical elevator brought up if they had one. When the hayrick was complete, it would be clipped and thatched by the foggers, making it both tidy and weathertight. Vicat Cole's picture shows what the completed hayrick might look like (66), although this one has already been partly used. The keeping of hay in good condition was vital for a farmer with stock to feed through the winter.

Haymaking generally lasted about two or three weeks, and when it was finished everyone involved was invited to the 'hay-home' supper, sometimes a glorified tea, sometimes a full-scale meal. Flora Thompson has described a hay-home supper, the centrepiece of which was 'a great round joint, being the whole neck of a pig, cut and cured specially. . . . It was lavishly stuffed with sage and onions and was altogether very rich and highly flavoured. Afterwards there were invariably speeches, toasts and songs, to which everyone had to make some contribution.

The hay at Candleford Green was not cut by a reaper but by hand, by a team of men with scythes. The farmers and men already knew of the existence of the mechanical reaper, but it was still thought of 'as an auxiliary, a farmer's toy'. The tallest and most skilled man in the gang was selected as leader, who was then called 'The King of the Mowers. . . . With a wreath of poppies and green bindweed trails around his wide, rush-plaited hat, he led the band down the swathes as they mowed and decreed when and for how long they should halt for "a breather" and what drinks should be had from the yellow stone jar they kept under the hedge. . . .

The title of 'King of the Mowers' could well apply to

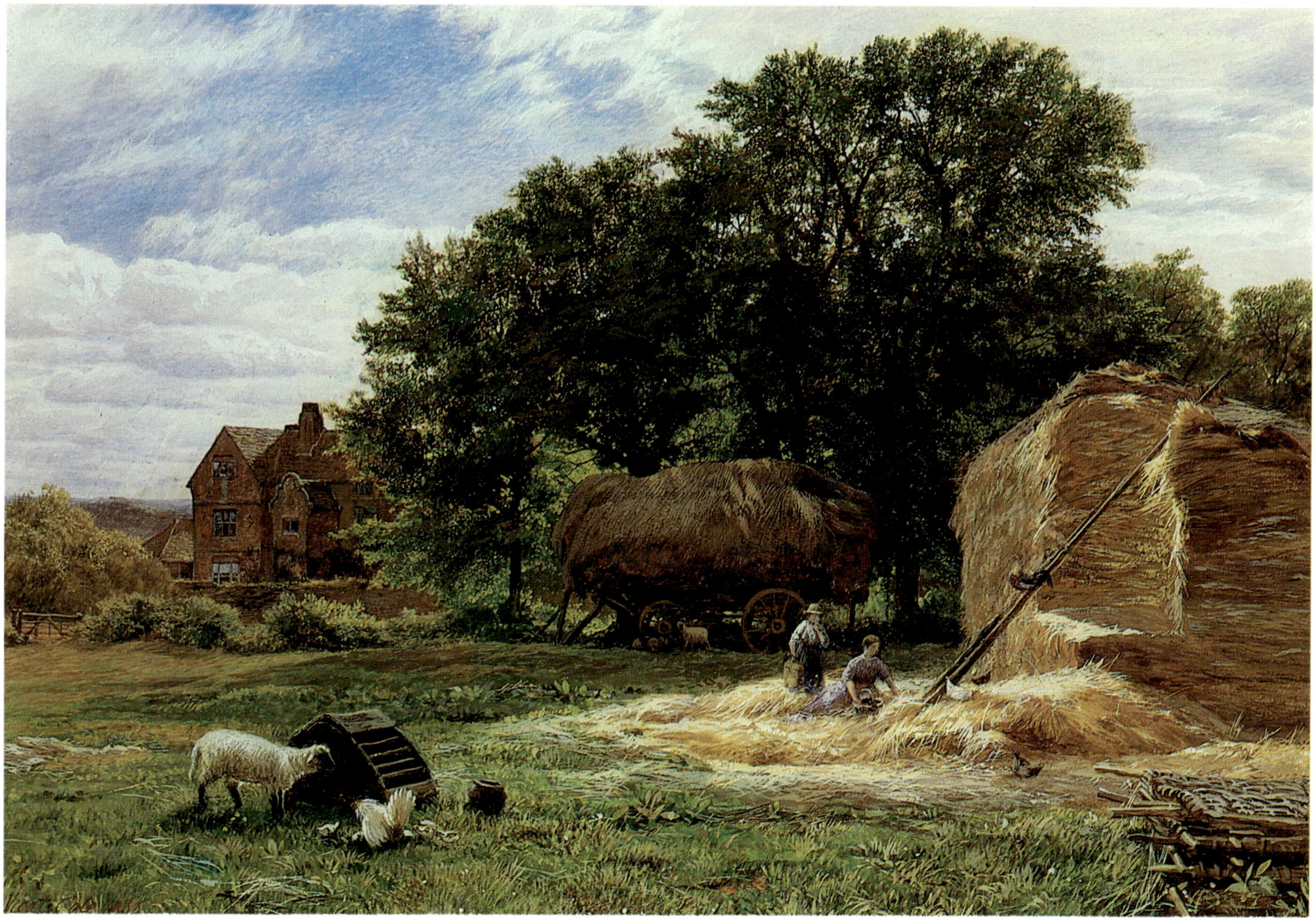

66
GEORGE VICAT COLE
*The Hayrick*

Clausen's magnificent picture of 1891 (64). Unlike Birket Foster or Arthur Hopkins, who were primarily interested in a picturesque scene, Clausen has again created a noble and resonant image of the farm worker. When it was exhibited at the Royal Academy in 1892, the critics immediately recognised that Clausen was moving away from his earlier Bastien-Lepage style, towards a lighter, more impressionistic manner. Although the figures are still monumental, the flickering brushwork gives a wonderful impression of sunlight and movement. The *Saturday Review* wrote that Clausen 'has long been a student of nature, now he has discovered beauty'. This picture is surely one of the greatest achievements of English Impressionism.

Some critics wrote that the position of the man scything in the foreground was incorrect. Clausen countered this, and wrote a reply to the *Magazine of Art* himself, enclosing a diagram proving that the stance of the mower, who is at the very end of his stroke, was correct. Although Clausen's picture is heroic, it is not entirely unsentimental, for by 1891 mechanical reapers were already widely in use. Clausen preferred to depict the old-fashioned mowers, not only for aesthetic reasons but doubtless for nostalgic reasons too. He would have appreciated M.K. Ashby's description of her father Joseph Ashby of Tysoe, out harvesting, starting as early as four in the morning: 'Their scythes went singing through the grass, and the triumph of the scythe and the rhythmic fall of the swath continued like a long, slow, sacred dance.'

The harvest was the high point of the farming year, and for painters it was therefore an irresistibly picturesque and symbolic subject. Like haymaking, it was generally seen to be a cheerful activity, but invested with rather more solemnity and significance. In haymaking, the keynote seems to be hilarity and fun; with the harvest, the emphasis is on the important rituals, such as *The Last Load* or the *Harvest Supper*. The harvest inspired some beautiful pictures, many of them by artists

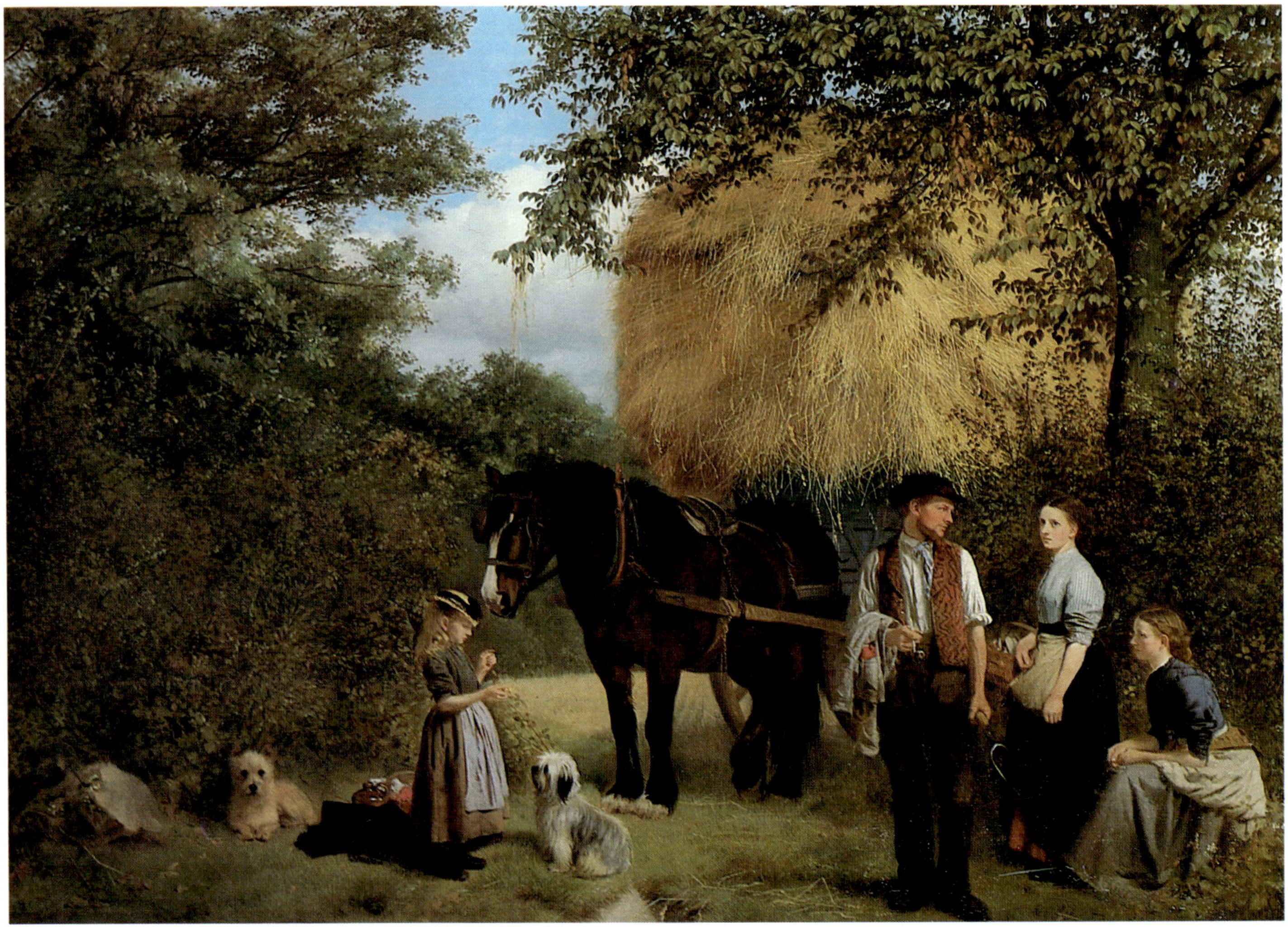

67
WILLIAM EDWARD MILLNER
*The End of the Day*

already mentioned – E.G. Warren, W.E. Millner, Vicat Cole, John Linnell, La Thangue and Clausen.

England was still a great corn-growing country in the nineteenth century, but between 1850 and 1885 'King Corn' was actually in decline. This was the period of 'down corn, up horn', with arable land gradually giving way to pasture. Cheap foreign imports of corn drove the price down to the point where farmers were forced to diversify into other areas. Mixed farming increased throughout the period – beef, dairy products, sheep, orchards, market gardening, root crops, hop grounds. Sir James Caird, in his survey of British agriculture carried out for *The Times* in 1850, observed that in general the south and east were the main corn-growing areas, whereas cattle and sheep predominated in the north and west; but mixed farming was on the increase in all areas.

The harvest has always been surrounded with custom and ritual, and one of these was observed by William Maw Egley in his picture *Hullo, Largess! A Harvest Scene in Norfolk* (68). Egley stayed in Norfolk in 1860 with his friend John Rose, who is seen on the left, with his children, horse and dog. In his diary, Egley explained this old East Anglian custom. If, during harvest-time, the farmer has a visitor, 'the head man among the labourers usually asks for a largess. They then collect in a circle, and "Hullo Largess!" is given as loud and long as their lungs will allow, at the same time elevating their hands as high as they can, and still keeping hold. This is done three times, and immediately followed by three successive whoops.' The two groups form an interesting contrast: the well-to-do farmer on the left, with his very smartly turned-out daughters; on the right the rustics, in their corduroy trousers and leggings; and in the middle, one of the workers' children holding out her hand for the largess.

Egley's fascinating picture is a reminder of just how much women and children were employed in farm work in Victorian

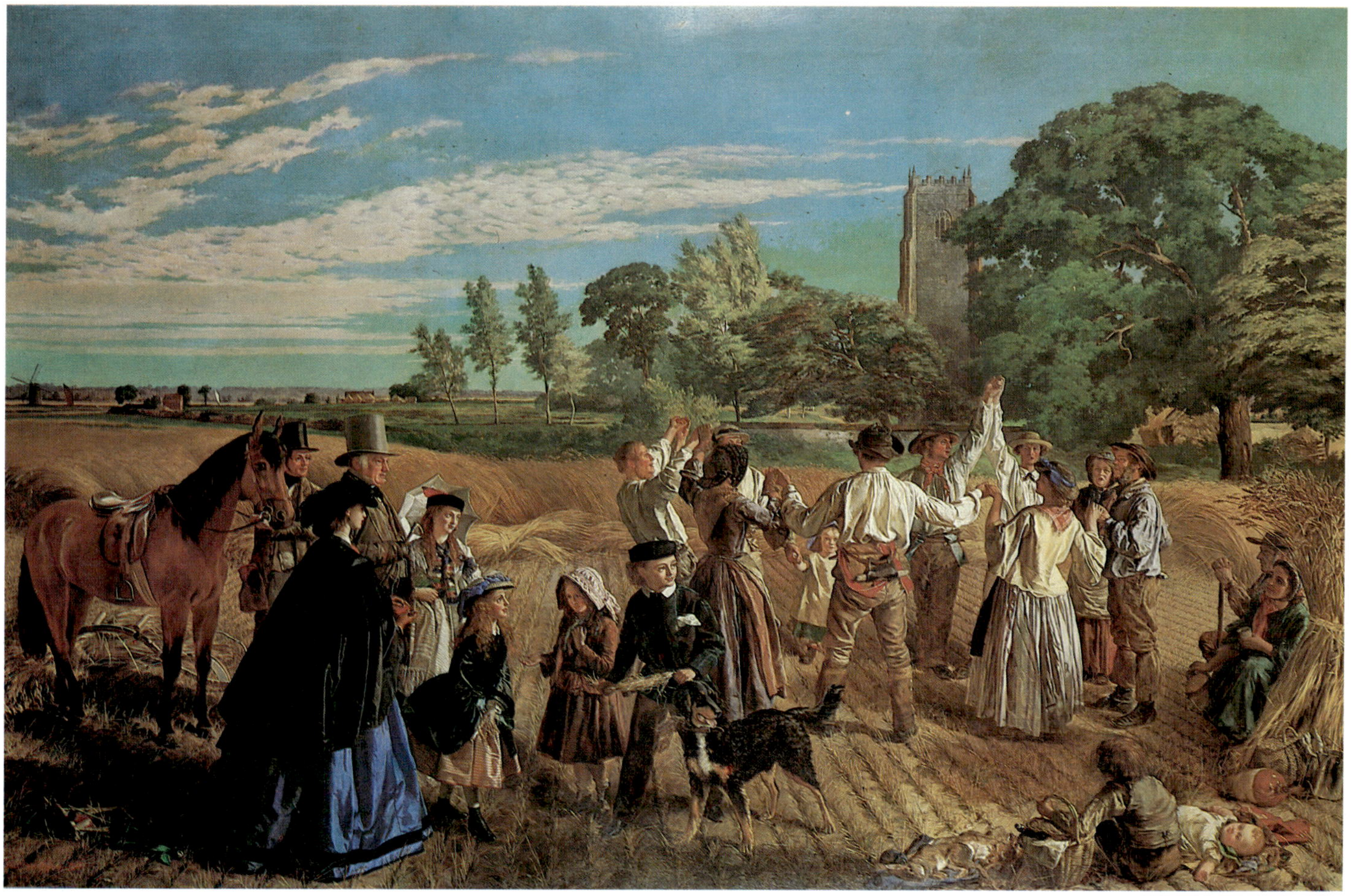

68
William Maw Egley
*Hullo, Largess! A Harvest Scene in Norfolk*

times, especially on seasonal jobs like harvesting. Flora Thompson recalled that several of the older women did farm work, not only to earn extra money, but also for the pleasure of working in the open air: '. . . Strong, healthy, weather-beaten, hard as nails, they worked through all but the very worst weathers and declared they would go "stark staring mad" if they had to be shut up in a house all day.' Specially hired gangs of women and children, with an overseer, were also common in the nineteenth century. Flora Thompson described them as 'lawless, slatternly creatures, some of whom had thought nothing of having four or five children out of wedlock'. But by the 1880s, they were rapidly dying out, as it was generally recognised that they were one of the greatest evils of the countryside. Joseph Arch also recalled that 'the gang system was in full force when I was a young man'. The overseer was generally a 'rough, bullying fellow' and the foul language and immoral habits of the women were notorious. Sometimes children were employed when barely able to walk. One great admirer of women workers was that curious Victorian figure, Arthur Joseph Munby. Secretly married to a maid-of-all-work, but thought by all his friends to be a bachelor, Munby was obsessed by strong, muscular, labouring women, and left a huge number of diaries and notes recording his conversations with them. His poem *Dorothy* constantly harps on the theme of romance between an upper-class man and a working girl. Dorothy herself is a heroic figure:

> Also, when harvest was come, she work'd in the field with
> her sickle;
> Wheat, and barley, and beans fell to the sweep of her blade;
> She could keep up with the men at reaping, and binding and
> stacking;
> She could keep up with the men; she could leave laggards
> behind.

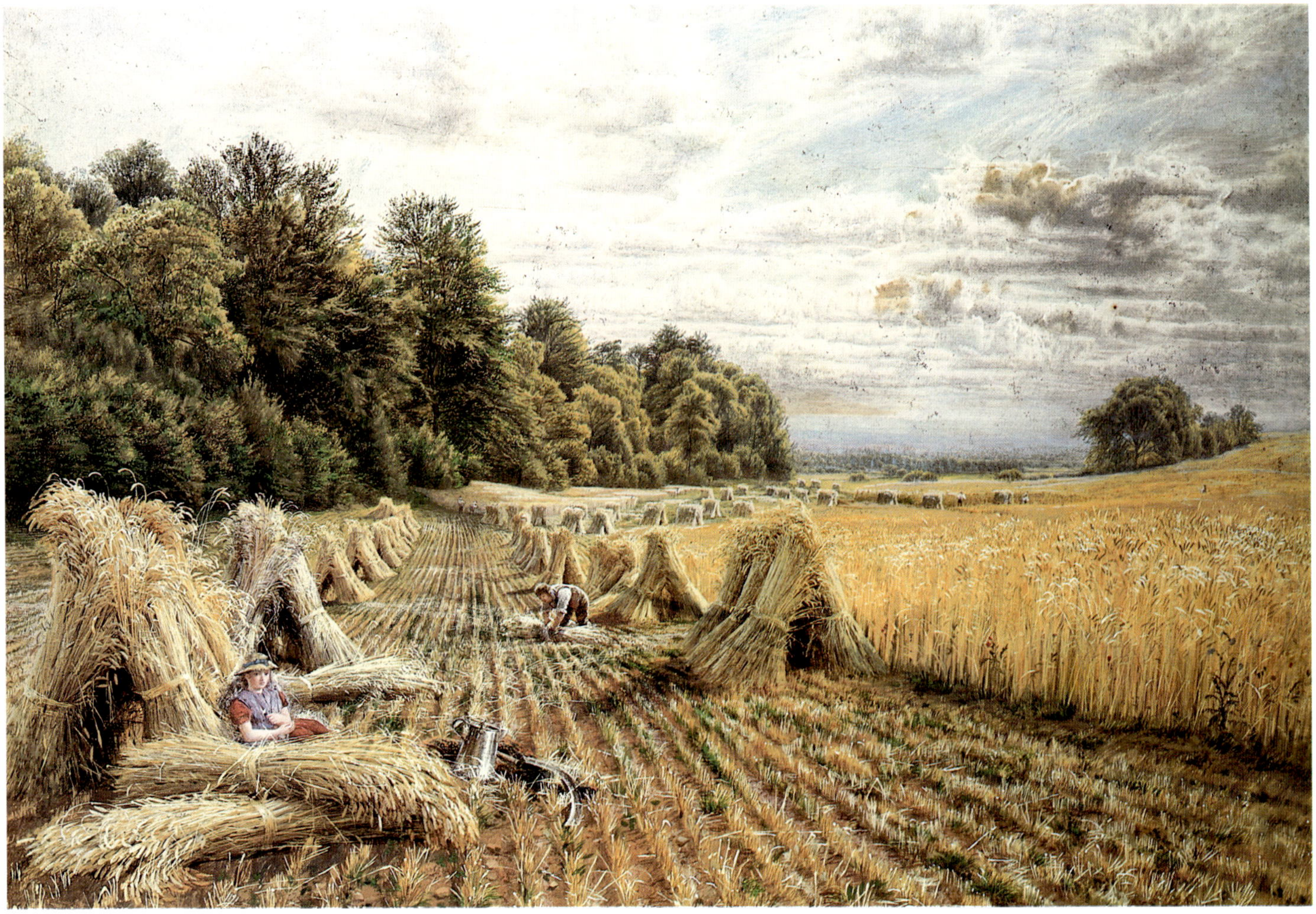

69
EDMUND GEORGE WARREN
*Amongst the Corn Stooks*

Most Victorian painters, however, preferred to show the men working, and the women and children resting among the sheaves, as in E.G. Warren's *Amongst the Corn Stooks* of 1865 (69), and George Vicat Cole's *Harvesting* (71). In both pictures, the corn is obviously being cut by the age-old method of the sickle and the crook. Mechanical reapers were commonplace by the 1880s, but binding machines did not come in until much later. The binding into sheaves was all done by hand, often by women and children. One can also clearly see in these pictures the quantity of wild flowers growing in among the corn. Alfred Williams wrote of the wonderful smell of the harvest-field: 'The thick white campion is sweetly fragrant too; then there are the scabious, corn-cockle, corn sow-thistle, pink and white convolvulus twining and clinging to the straws, and, sweetest of all, the deliciously scented corn-mint, growing everywhere through the field; the whole air is redolent with it. . . .

Great superstition surrounded the cutting of the last ears of corn in the field. They were usually cut with great reverence, and made into a corn dolly. After the corn was bound into sheaves, it was then stacked into stooks, usually consisting of four or five sheaves together. This required considerable skill, so that the stooks were strong enough to withstand the wind. When they were dry enough, the sheaves were piled onto the waggons, and taken to the farm. The harvest waggon was another favourite image, as in George Cole's picture *Harvest Time* (70). George Cole was the father of the better-known George Vicat Cole, and both father and son painted many fine harvest scenes, recording just how beautiful a field of golden corn could be. William Edward Millner also introduces a straw waggon into his picture *The End of the Day* (67). Millner was one of the very few artists to paint farm work realistically and honestly. Here as usual he avoids the picturesqueness and sentimentality found in so many Victorian paintings of this type.

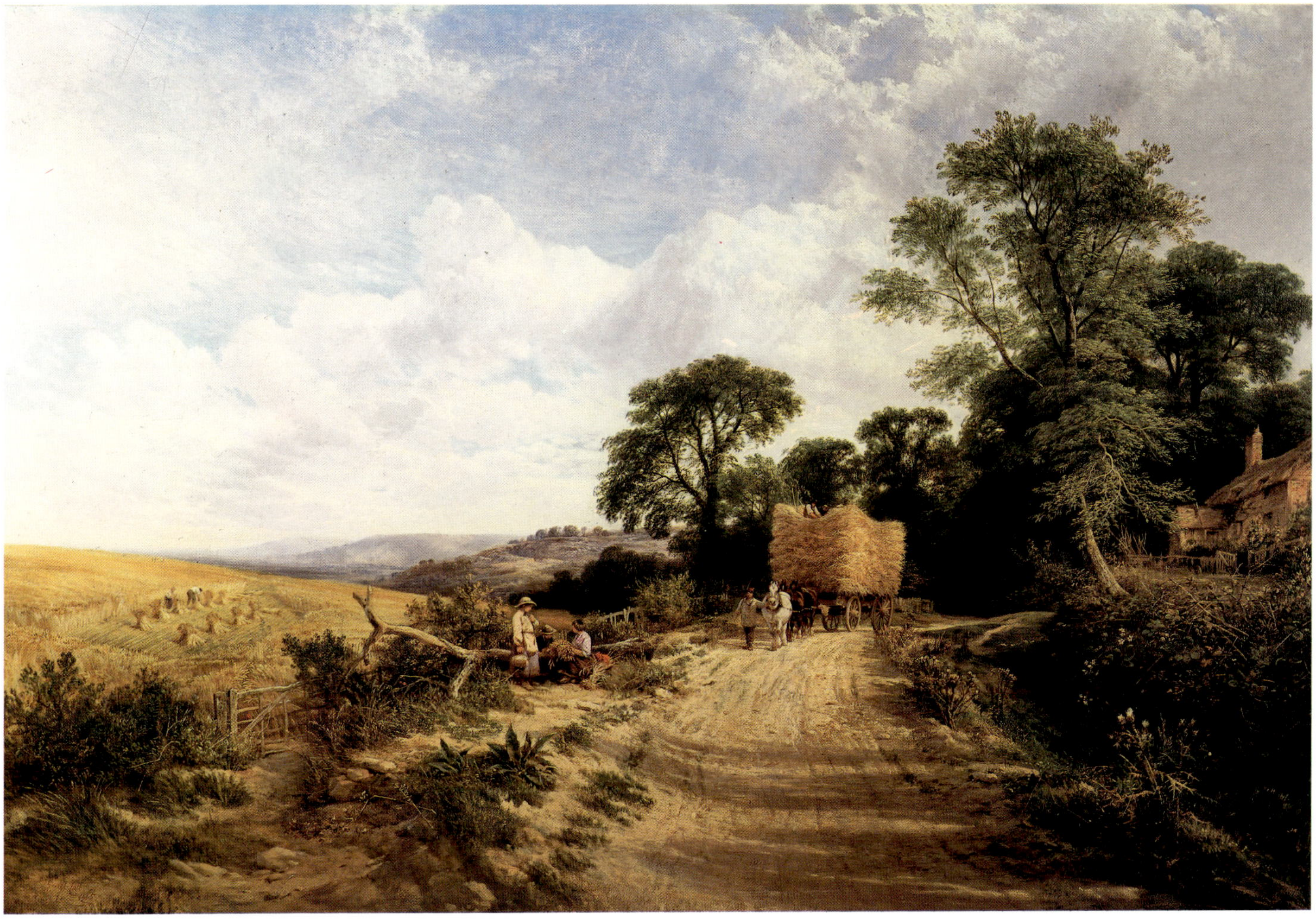

GEORGE COLE
*Harvest Time*

The most banal, and the most common, of all Victorian harvest scenes was a picture of a pretty girl holding a sheaf of corn; it was usually entitled *The Fair Reaper*. Some artists, like James John Hill and Charles Sillem Lidderdale, made a living painting nothing else.

One of the greatest painters of harvesting scenes was John Linnell. With its symbolic and biblical connotations, the harvest was for him an obvious subject. For Linnell, the harvest was not an agricultural event, it was a symbol of God's goodness, as manifested in the bounty of nature, and the fruits of the earth. As he wrote to Samuel Palmer in 1828, in that pseudo-religious language so typical of the Victorian chapelgoer: 'Pray inform me . . . if the harvest is begun in your part yet for I should like to see something of that glorious type of the ever-lasting harvest of spirits, the gathering of saints . . .' and he added sanctimoniously, 'hoping that none of us will be found among the tares'.

Linnell's harvest scenes are intensely idyllic. In *The Harvest Cradle* (72), another subject much beloved of the Victorians, he shows a baby asleep among the corn sheaves, while other children frolic about happily. The custom of taking babies out into the fields was an ancient one. Alfred Williams described how Granny Bowles had wrapped her children in a shawl, 'and set them down under the hedge while she worked away, as they did in olden times'. The same custom is recorded as early as the fourteenth century in Langland's *Piers Plowman*. For Linnell, the figures are unusually characterful, although the faces are rather expressionless, bathed in the ruddy glow of the golden harvest field. As Thomas Hardy wrote in *Tess*, 'a field-woman is a portion of the field; she has somehow lost her own margin, imbibed the essence of her surrounding, and assimilated herself with it'. Beyond them, the stooping figures of the harvesters recall the pictures of George Stubbs or even Brueghel.

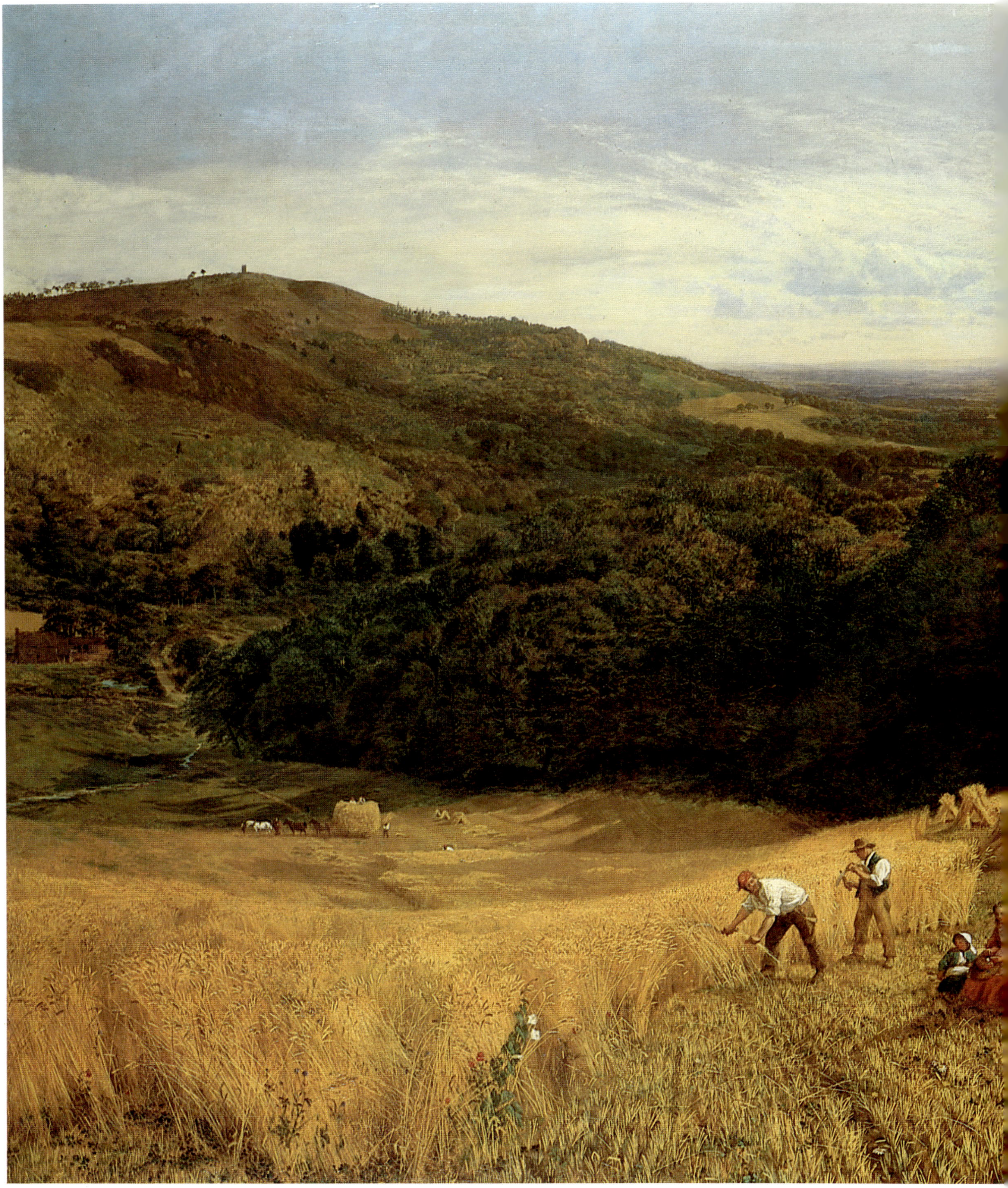

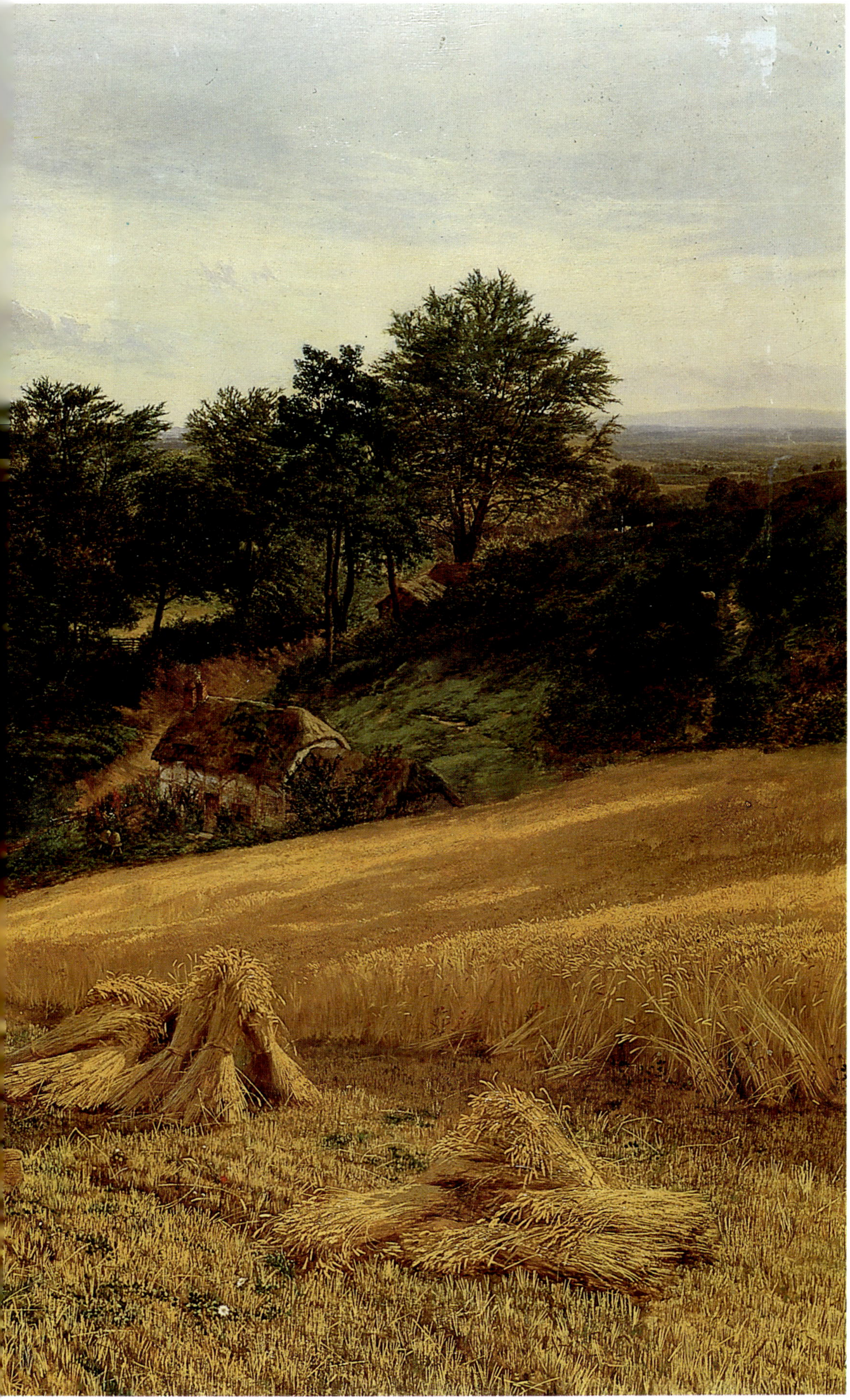

71
George Vicat Cole
*Harvesting*

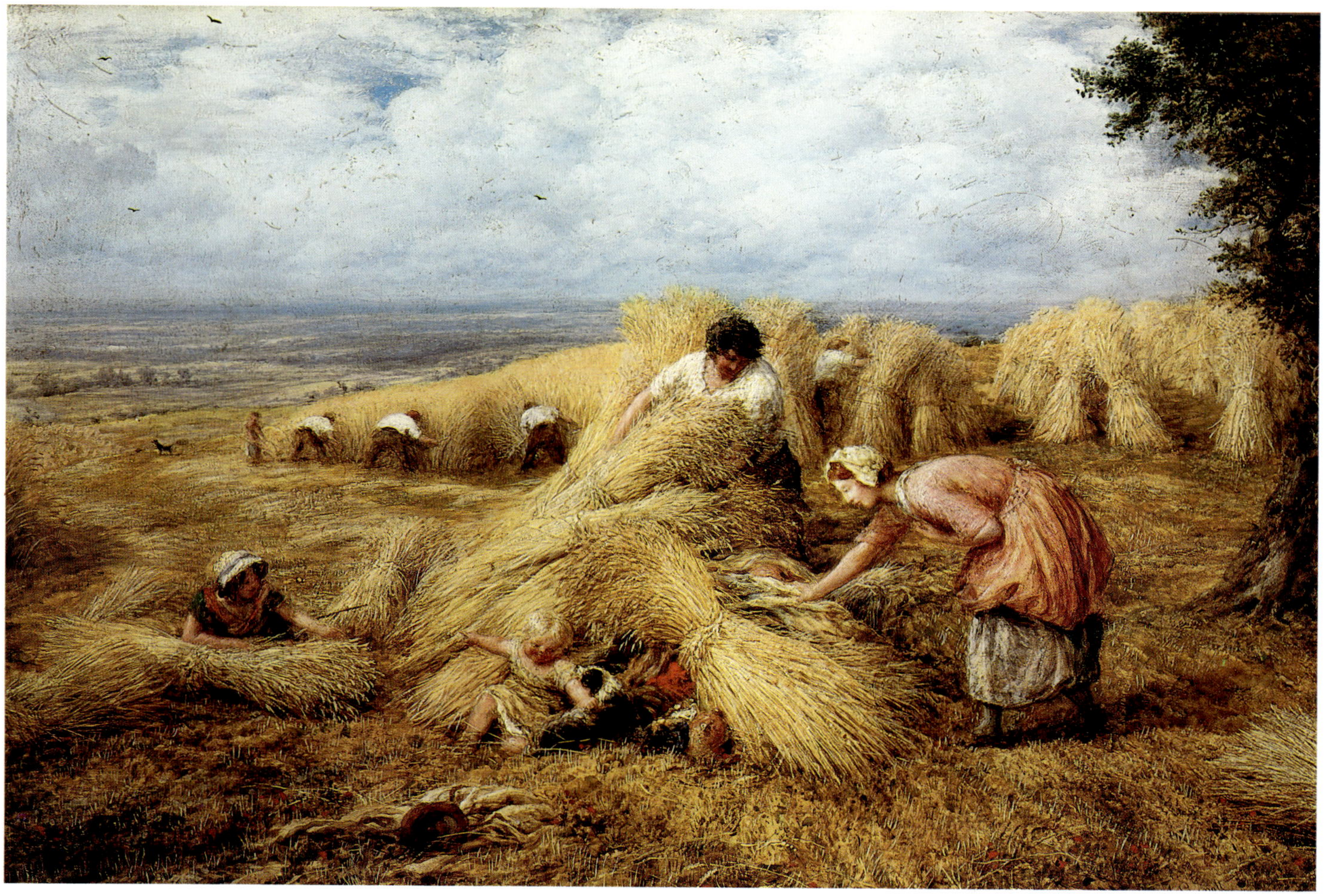

72
JOHN LINNELL
*The Harvest Cradle*

Even more idyllic is *The Noonday Rest* (73), in which the sleeping figures are absorbed completely into the overpowering atmosphere of heat and sunlight. It is a marvellously soporific and drowsy picture of an English summer's day. The harvesters would probably have started work at dawn, and so would have needed a rest. Very few Victorian pictures actually convey the sense of physical strain and grinding labour that harvesting involved. W.H. Barrett, in his *East Anglian Folklore and Other Tales* (1976), recalled that

> The hell of the life was the harvest. . . . It were the first three days which were hell. After that your muscles got used to it. I seen a strong man stand up and howl like a child, especially if there were a lot of green stuff in the corn that made it harder. . . . Clean corn was all right . . . but if there was a lot of bindweed or scratch weed, that was like pulling a truck off a railway line.

Barrett also added sarcastically that 'you'd see some lovely paintings of men at harvest'.

The harvest was at an end when the last waggon-load of corn was brought in. This was known as the 'Last Load', and was attended with much traditional rejoicing, usually known as the Harvest-Home. Linnell's picture of it is attended by a suitably apocalyptic sunset (74) bathing the whole scene in an intensely romantic and lyrical glow. Flora Thompson has left us one of the best descriptions:

> At last, in the cool dusk of an August evening, the last load was brought in, with a nest of merry boys' faces among the sheaves on top, and the men walking alongside with pitchforks on shoulders. As they passed along the roads they shouted:
>
> 'Harvest home! Harvest home!
> Merry, merry, merry harvest home!'

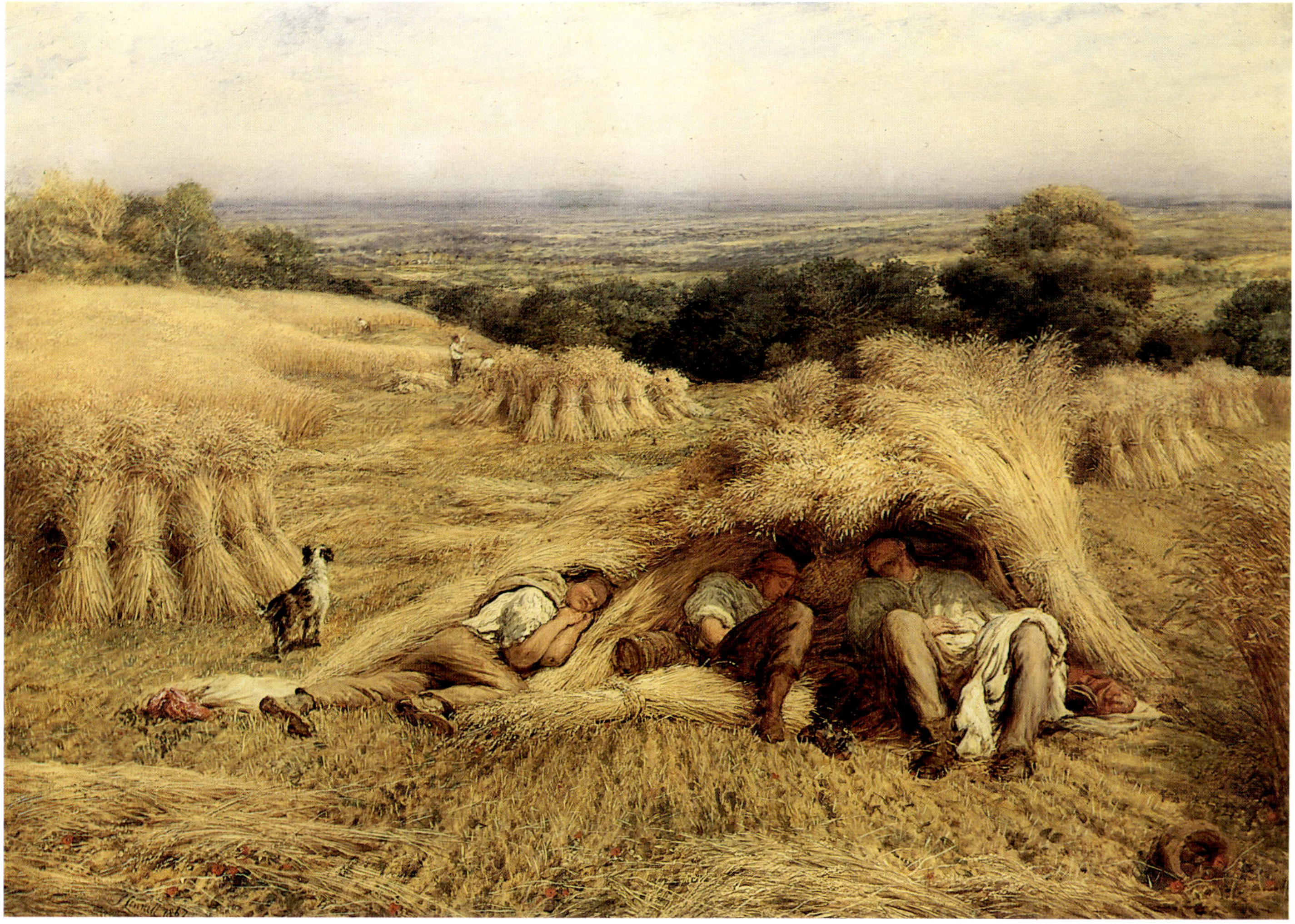

73
JOHN LINNELL
*The Noonday Rest*

and women came to their cottage gates and waved, and the few passers-by looked up and smiled their congratulations. The joy and pleasure of the labourers in their task well done was pathetic, considering their very small share in the gain. But it was genuine enough; for they still loved the soil and rejoiced in their own work and skill in bringing forth the fruits of the soil, and harvest-home put the crown on their year's work.

A few days later followed the harvest-home dinner, given by the farmer to all his harvest workers. 'And what a feast it was!' wrote Flora Thompson. 'Such a bustling in the farmhouse kitchen for days beforehand; such boiling of hams and roasting of sirloins; such a stacking of plum puddings . . . such a tapping of eighteen-gallon casks and baking of plum loaves could astonish those accustomed to the appetites of today.' After the dinner, there were sports, games, and finally dancing. As the century wore on, this good old custom declined, and a cash bonus was substituted in its place. No good Victorian picture seems to exist of a harvest-home supper, although La Thangue did paint *The Harvesters' Supper* (75), a more humble affair, taking place by the light of a fire out in the fields. The light of the fire illuminating the figures is handled with marvellous skill.

As one might expect, Clausen conveys more of a sense of actual labour in his *Harvest – Tying the Sheaves* of 1902 (77). This work is typical of Clausen's impressionist style at this period. But Clausen was not primarily a social commentator – his writings and lectures show little or no interest in social reform. His approach was that of a naturalist, or 'ruralist' as he was sometimes called. He wanted to depict man at work in his natural environment, with the minimum of sentiment or artifice. His work exudes not only a sense of physical exertion, but also great feeling for the English countryside, in all its moods. He has left us with some of the most memorable of all images of

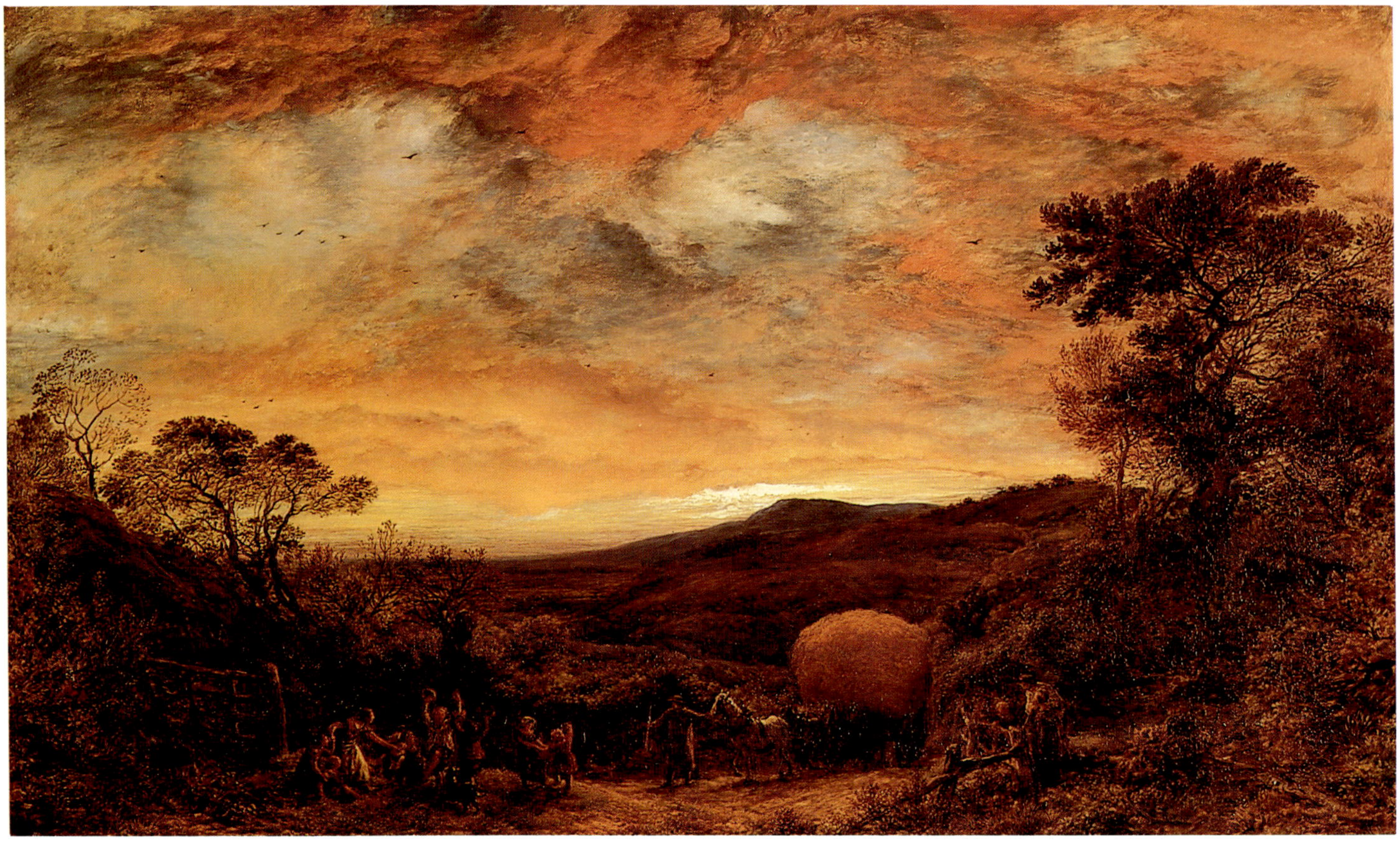

74
JOHN LINNELL
*The Last Load*

country life in English art. Later his work becomes almost Turneresque in its total preoccupation with the effects of light. But he never lost his interest in painting farm work, and the farm labourer, who in his pictures is always a noble and heroic figure.

Another subject painted by Clausen was threshing by hand with a flail. By this time, threshing by hand was almost extinct. Even Francis Kilvert, writing in rural Wales in 1874, 'heard in Greenway Lane the old familiar sound once so common, the sound of the flail on the barn floor. I had not heard it for years. I looked in at the barn door and found a man threshing out his barley.' Threshing was a stuffy and sweaty job, done in the autumn after the harvest was over, and in Victorian times it had been taken over by the threshing machine. This was usually the property of a contractor, who visited the farms in turn. The threshing machine greatly speeded the task of threshing, but feeding the corn into the revolving drum of the machine was extremely demanding work. Hardy describes Tess doing it, and disliking it intensely, at Flintcomb Ash: 'It was the ceaselessness of the work which tried her so severely.' Carrying the heavy sacks of grain into the barn was also an extremely arduous task, testing even the strongest worker.

After the corn was cut, and the field cleared, another important activity was gleaning, or 'leazing' as it was sometimes called. This was collecting up ears of corn dropped on the ground by the harvesters, and the farmers were usually happy to let the women and children of the village gather it up. It was an old tradition and often features in both painting and literature. John Clare had written in *The Shepherd's Calendar*:

> The reapers leave their beds before the sun
> And gleaners follow when home toils are done
> To pick the littered ear the reaper leaves
> And glean in open fields among the sheaves.

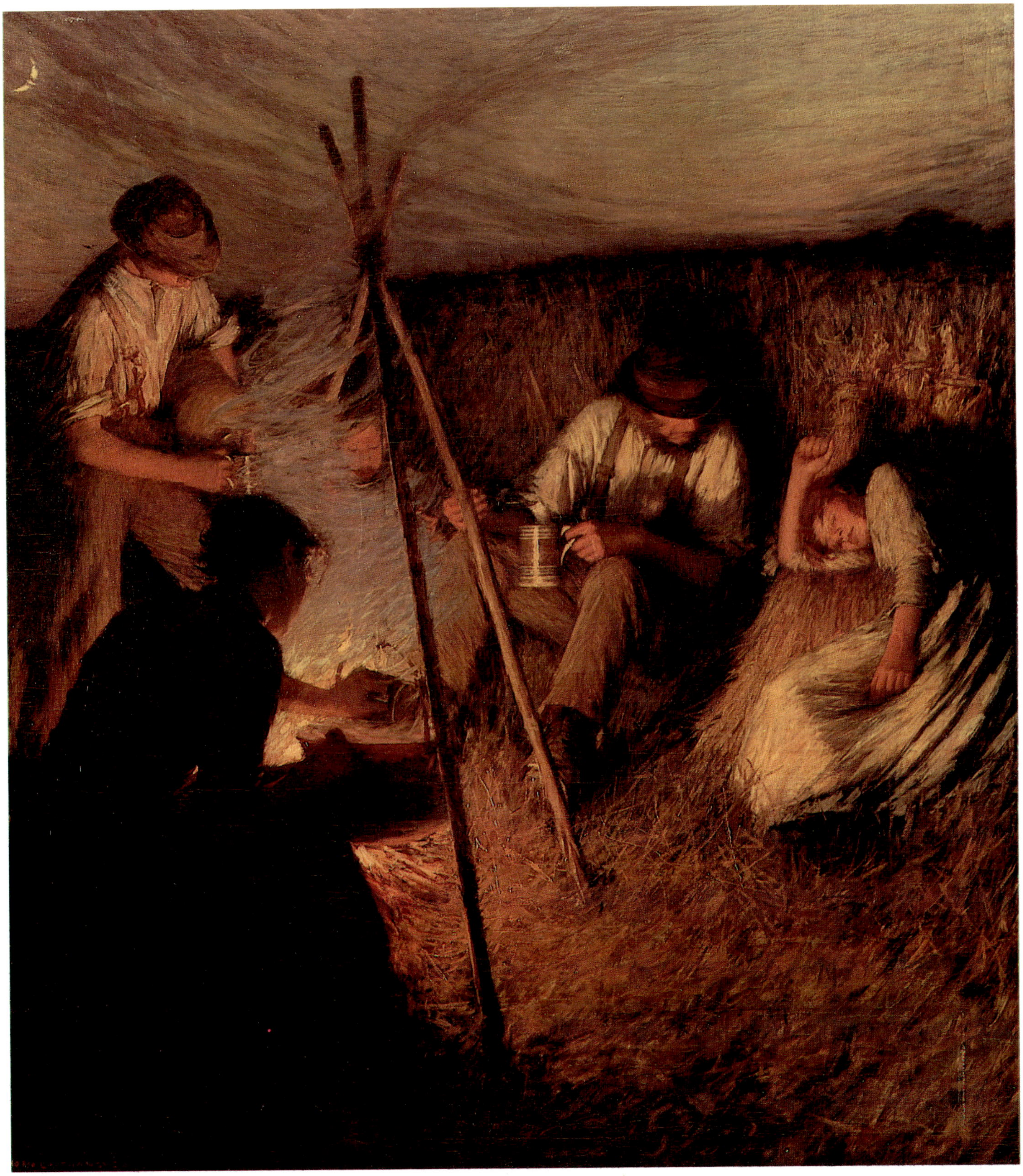

75
Henry Herbert La Thangue
*The Harvesters' Supper*

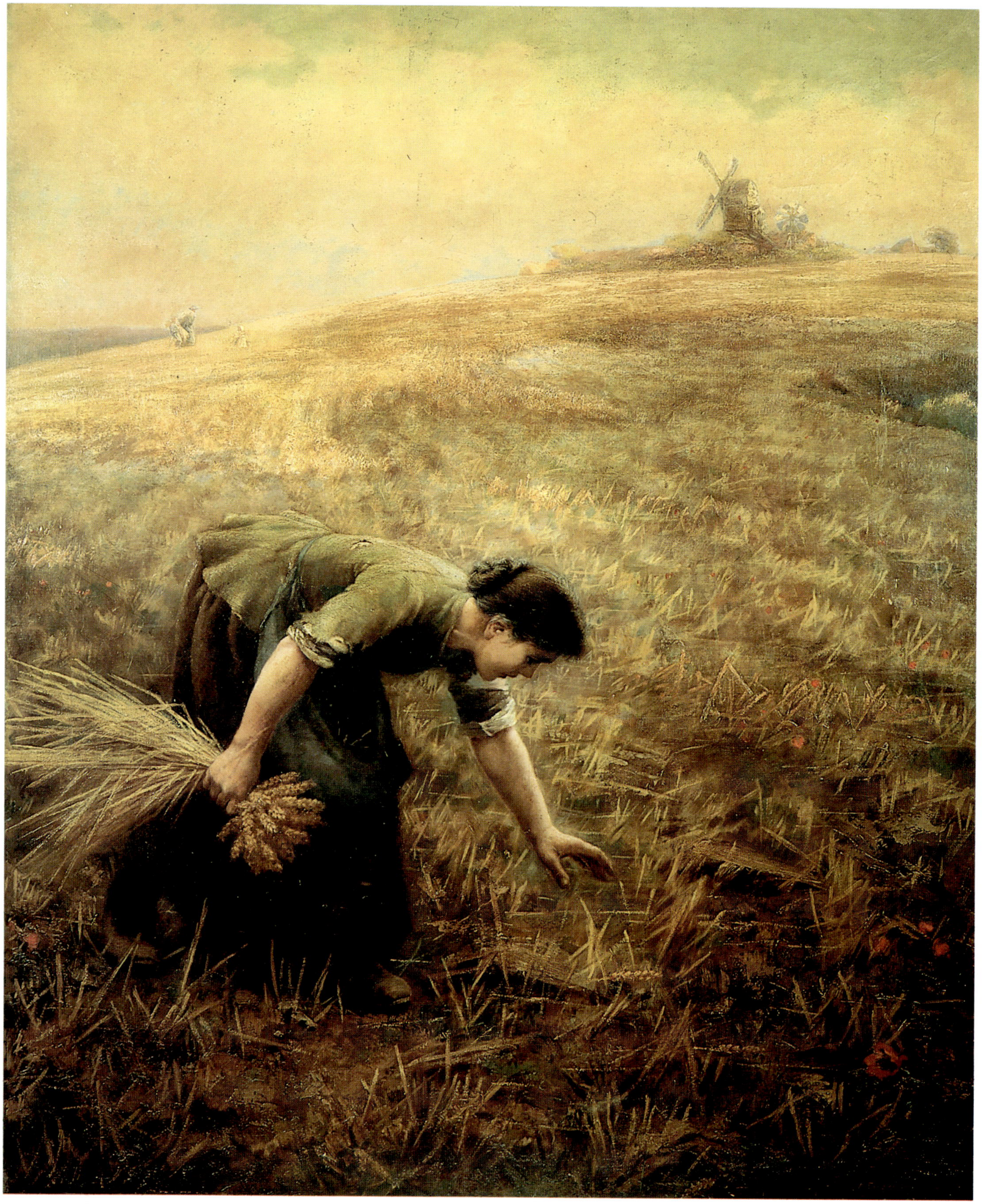

76
ARTHUR FOORD HUGHES
*Gleaning*

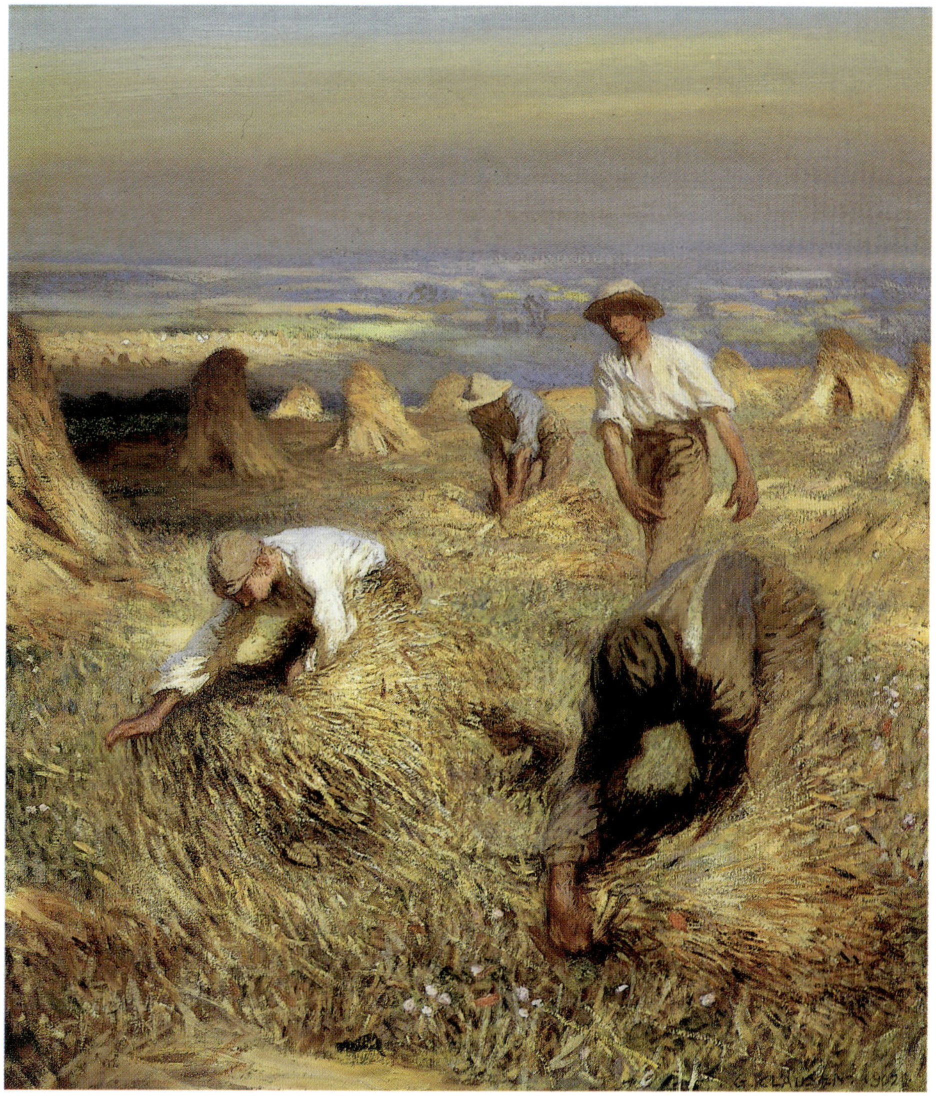

77
SIR GEORGE CLAUSEN
*Harvest – Tying the Sheaves*

A sack or two of corn would be taken to the local miller, to be ground into flour, and this might last a prudent housewife through the winter. Gleaning, because it was done by women and children, was a popular subject with Victorian painters. Arthur Foord Hughes makes an honest and sympathetic picture of it in his *Gleaning* (76). His pose corresponds very much with Flora Thompson's description: 'Up and down and over and over the stubble they hurried, backs bent, eyes on the ground, one hand outstretched to pick up the ears, the other resting on the small of the back with the "handful".' Alfred Williams recalled that 'The Village Schools were always closed for gleaning. This was the harvest holidays.' But by the beginning of this century, gleaning was beginning to die out. Some farmers prohibited it, and the villagers were less inclined to bother. Williams lamented the change: 'The young wife thinks there is no need to glean corn in the field; everything is different . . . it is nearly ten years since I saw gleaners in the field.'

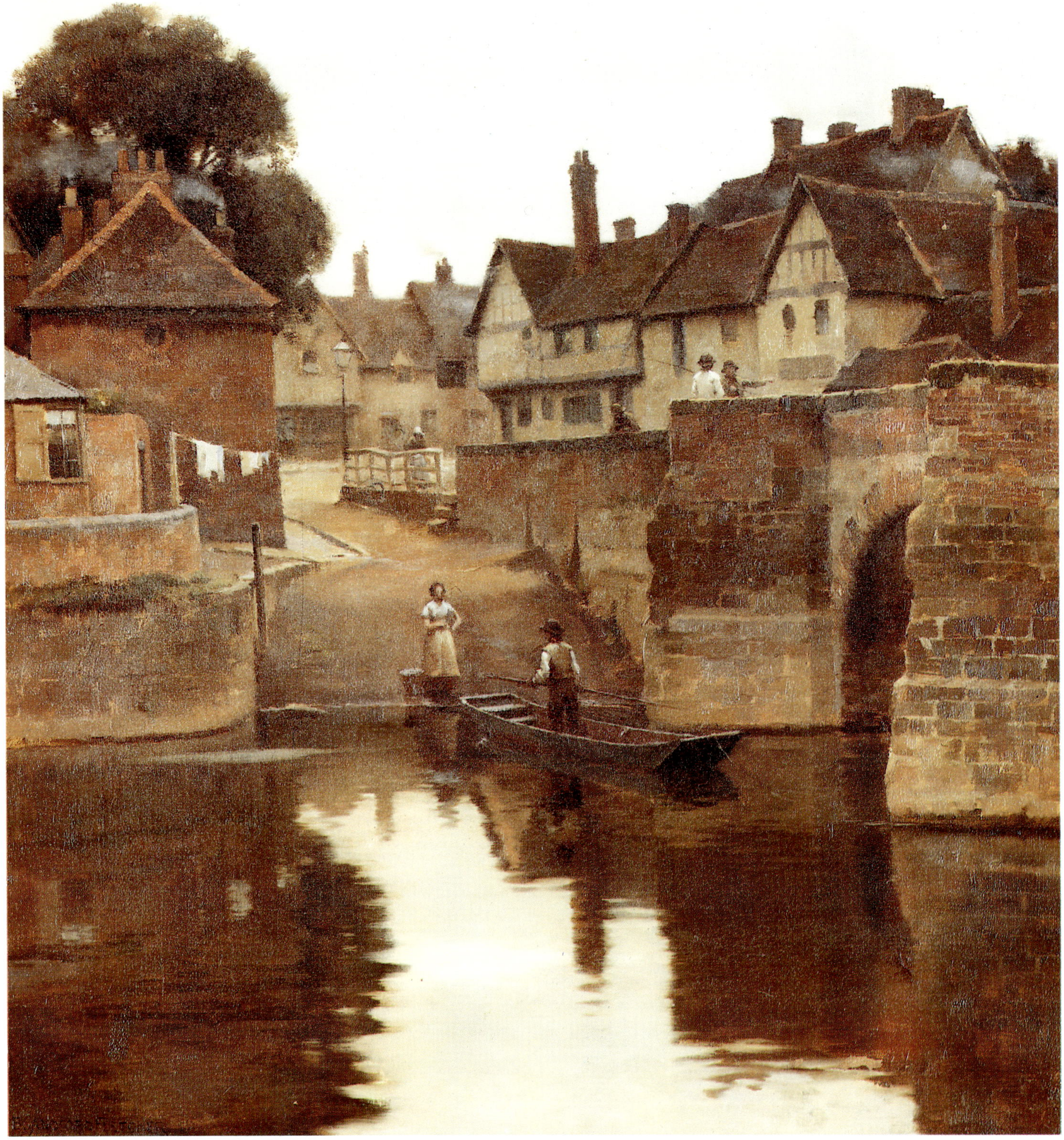

78
WILLIAM TEULON BLANDFORD FLETCHER
*King John's Bridge, Tewkesbury*

# Chapter Six

# THE VILLAGE

People were poorer, and had not the comforts, amusements or knowledge we have today, but they were happier

FLORA THOMPSON, *Lark Rise to Candleford*

THE VILLAGE WAS ANOTHER ESSENTIAL ELEMENT in the rural paradise, representing tradition, stability, innocence – all those things that were not to be found in the ugly, sprawling new cities. The contrast between the town and the country is a constant theme in Victorian literature. Even the Christian radical writers whose aim was to alleviate some of the horrors experienced by the poorest members of Victorian society, such as Elizabeth Gaskell, Charles Kingsley, or Thomas Carlyle, contrasted village life favourably with city life, concentrating their efforts mainly on the problems of the sprawling new industrial areas.

In Gaskell's novels *Mary Barton* and *North and South*, the country is depicted as a haven of lost innocence, by contrast with Manchester. Mary Burrows in her *Sketches of Our Village* (1852), a very popular early Victorian poem, captures perfectly the Victorian ideal of the village:

Scattered around the verdant village green
The peasants' humble cottages are seen;
Some almost hidden by the clust'ring flowers,
The produce of their evenings' leisure hours.
Within these small abodes the eye may see
The neat and careful hand of industry.

Painters on the whole were quite happy to perpetuate the popular view. Robert Gallon's *Village Scene* (79) looks typically English, with the rustic inn on the right, and charming old cottages with smoke coming out of the chimneys. In the road there are groups of children playing, the girls in long, white pinafores and straw hats, another inevitable element in the rural idyll. Gallon was a late Victorian landscape painter, who painted in a pretty, naturalist style similar to that of Leader and Vicat Cole. He was also fond of including cottages and villages in his pictures, and does not sentimentalise them. At its worst,

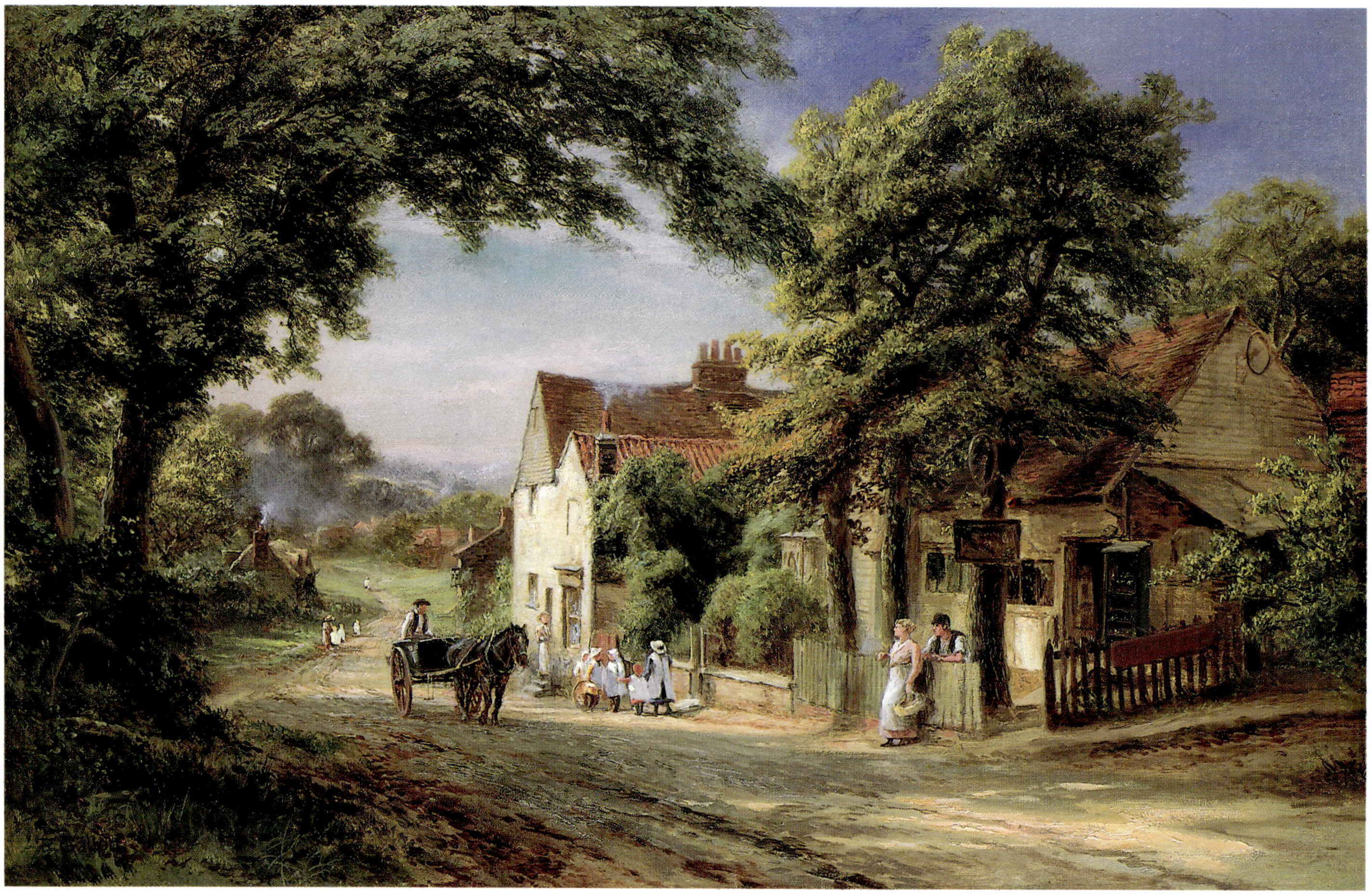

79
ROBERT GALLON
*A Village Scene*

the Victorian village picture is a picture-postcard affair, full of ancient thatched cottages, hollyhocks, and little girls in white bonnets. Henry John Sylvester Stannard was one of the better practitioners of this particular recipe, but unfortunately he spawned a host of inferior imitators.

It comes as a relief to find a picture like Blandford Fletcher's *Bridge* (78) where the figures are secondary to the splendidly mellow old buildings, which look as if they might belong to a larger market town, Dorchester rather than Lark Rise. Fletcher was one of the Newlyn School, and normally a painter of landscapes and rural scenes. Clausen's splendidly characterful *Old Woman* (80) is also a reminder that most of the people in the village would be old too. With many of the young men working elsewhere, and the girls out in service, the village population often consisted mainly of the old and the very young. Lark Rise had several old women, Old Queenie, with her lace-making and beehives, Old Sally with her brewing and bacon to cure, and Old Mrs Prout – 'crusty old dames', but a mine of information about old customs, cures and recipes. Witchcraft and magic were still potent forces in the nineteenth century, and a 'wise woman' or 'cunning man' might enjoy a tremendous local reputation for curing the ailments of both animals and humans. As late as 1871, it was explained to Francis Kilvert that the affliction of the celebrated 'frog-woman' of Presteigne who hopped from her house to the Primitive Methodist Chapel and back, was the result of a curse laid on her mother when pregnant. Witchcraft was still widely feared, and a whole range of protective devices were used to combat it: crossed knives, horse-shoes, rowan twigs.

But these remains of a primitive folk culture were of little interest to painters. Birket Foster, predictably, focuses on the happier side of village life in such pictures as *The Country Inn* (81). Here he has cleverly combined several old favourites – Herring-style piglets and ducks in the foreground, horses

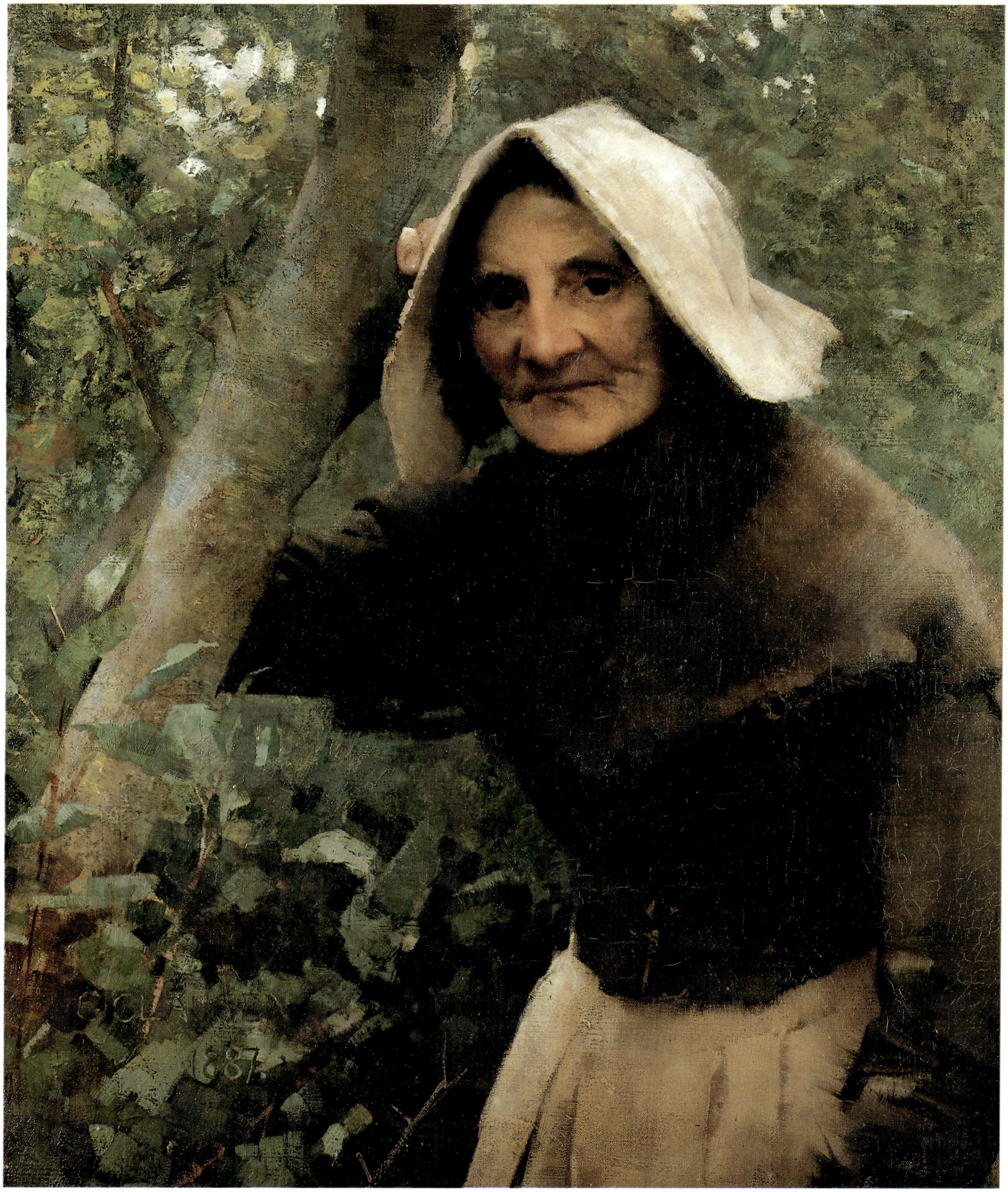

80
SIR GEORGE CLAUSEN
*An Old Woman*

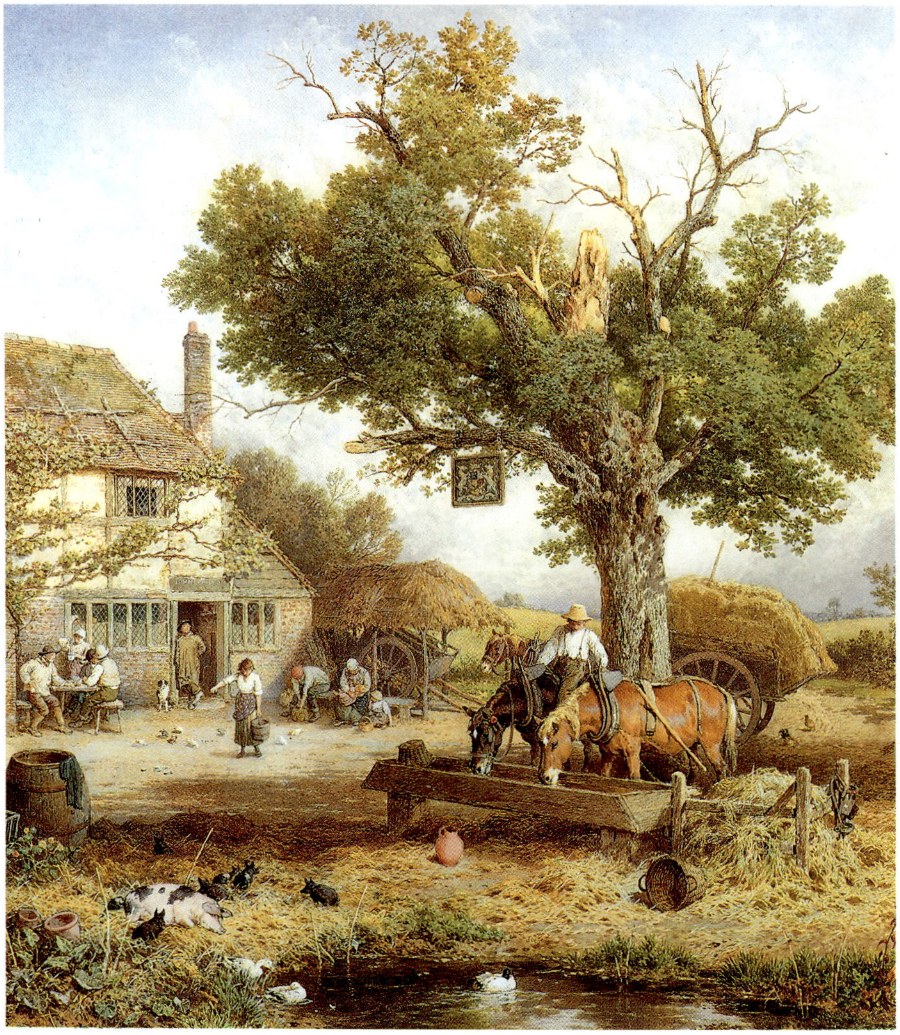

81
Myles Birket Foster
*The Country Inn*

drinking at a wooden trough, the farm cart laden with straw. In the background, the rustics sit at a table out-of-doors with their mugs of ale. In most villages, the real centre of the community was the local pub, though it may not have been as picturesque as a Birket Foster. For the agricultural labourer, wrote Richard Jefferies, the alehouse 'is at once his stock-exchange, his reading-room, his club, and his assembly rooms. It is here that his benefit society holds its annual dinner. . . . Here he learns the news of the day. . . . As a rule the beerhouse is the only place of amusement to which he can resort; it is his theatre, his music-hall, picture-gallery, and Crystal Palace.' At Lark Rise, the Waggon and Horses was very much the centre of village life, but only the men went there: 'The adult male population gathered every evening, to sip its half-pints, drop by drop, to make them last, and to discuss local events, wrangle over politics or farming methods. . . . It was an innocent gathering. None of them got drunk. . . .' Not all villagers were so abstemious. Kilvert often encountered drunkenness and fighting in and around the pubs in his parish. One thing all country writers agree on was the importance of singing in the pubs. Almost everyone was called upon to sing a song, and even in a small hamlet like Lark Rise the number of old and traditional songs the villagers knew was remarkable. The evening at the Waggon and Horses usually ended with the oldest inhabitant, Old David, singing his favourite song 'The Outlandish Knight'. David only knew this one song, and 'he had heard his own grandfather sing it. Probably a long chain of grandfathers had sung it; but David was fated to be the last of them.' When the women in the village heard the old man singing, they said to each other, 'They'll soon be out now. Poor old Dave's just singing his "Outlandish Knight".'

Almost every village in Victorian England had a number of craftsmen among the population. Most important were the blacksmith and the wheelwright, but there might also be car-

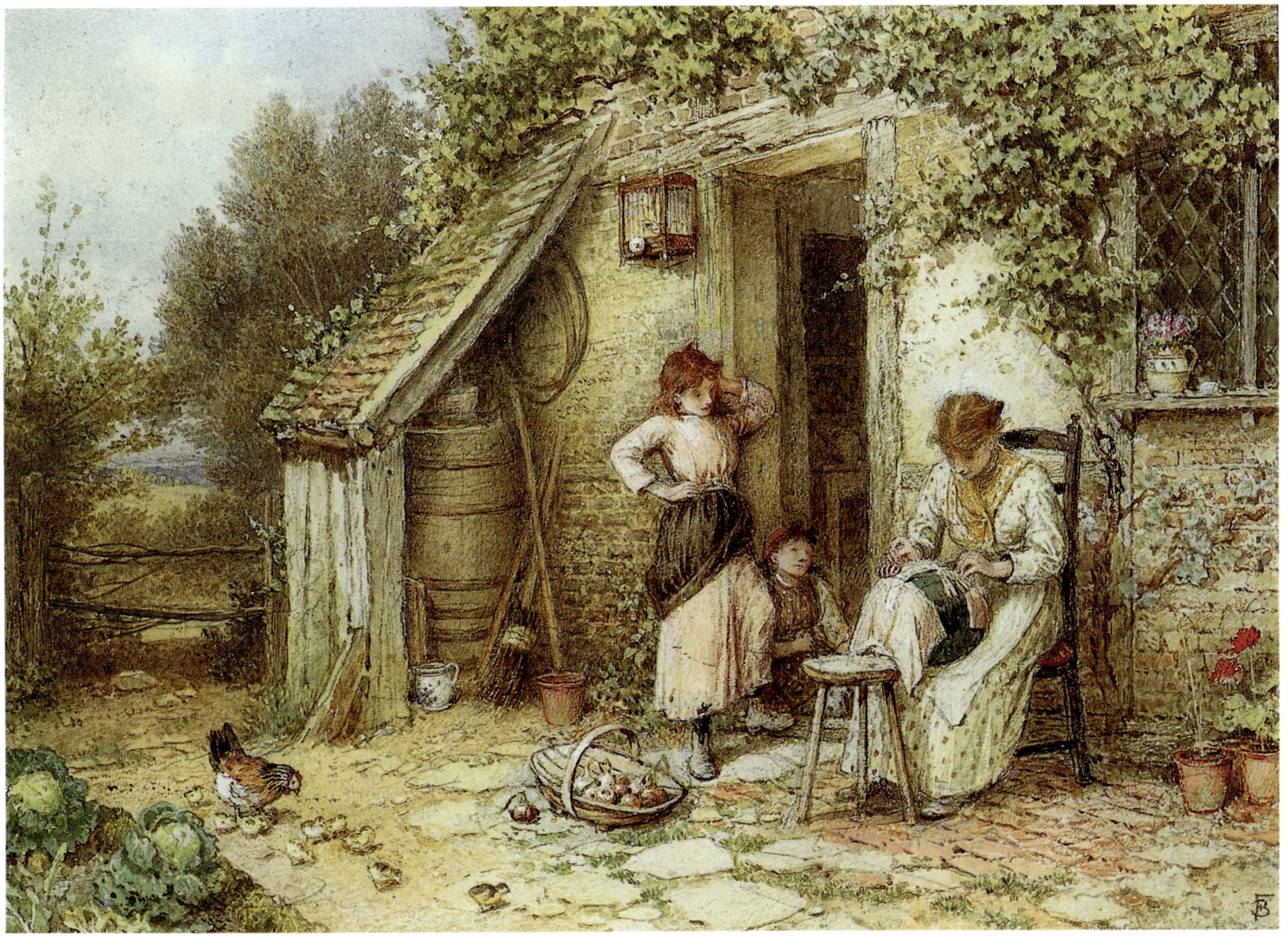

82
MYLES BIRKET FOSTER
*The Lacemaker*

penters, painters, plumbers, glaziers, thatchers, masons and shoemakers. Cottage industries also survived in some areas, particularly basket-work, glove and lace-making; but all of these were in decline in the country as a whole. Perhaps because they were under threat from mechanisation and competition from the towns, crafts were an attractive subject for painters. Birket Foster shows us a lace-maker outside a cottage (82) although it was a skill already probably confined to the older women. In Lark Rise: 'Queenie at her lace-making was a constant attraction to the children. They loved to see the bobbins tossed hither and thither, at random it seemed to them, every bobbin weighted with its bunch of bright beads and every bunch with its own story . . .' By the 1880s, lace-making was in decline, and Queenie lamented, 'things were different. . . . This nasty machine-made stuff had killed the lace-making.' Much the same thing happened to another cottage craft, glove-making, recorded by George William Mote (83).

Another profession that attracted the attention of painters was that of shoemaker. Every village of a reasonable size would be likely to have a local shoemaker or cobbler. The 1851 census revealed that there were 274,000 of them, more than coalminers or factory workers. Boots were expensive, but essential to life in the country. Often old and patched pairs were handed down to the children. Alexander Rossi shows the interior of what is obviously a modest village shoemaker's shop (84). Rossi was a frequent painter of children, but usually in rather smarter settings than this. Alfred Williams remembered his village shoemaker '. . . used to make many pairs of boots for the villagers; good, strong, substantial footwear, just the stuff for country places, and especially to wear about the farms in the wet and cold of winter; but this is at an end now. The village cobbler . . . is very nearly extinct.' Flora Thompson's Uncle Tom in Candleford was a shoemaker, but of a rather higher class, making ladies' shoes, and hunting boots for the gentry.

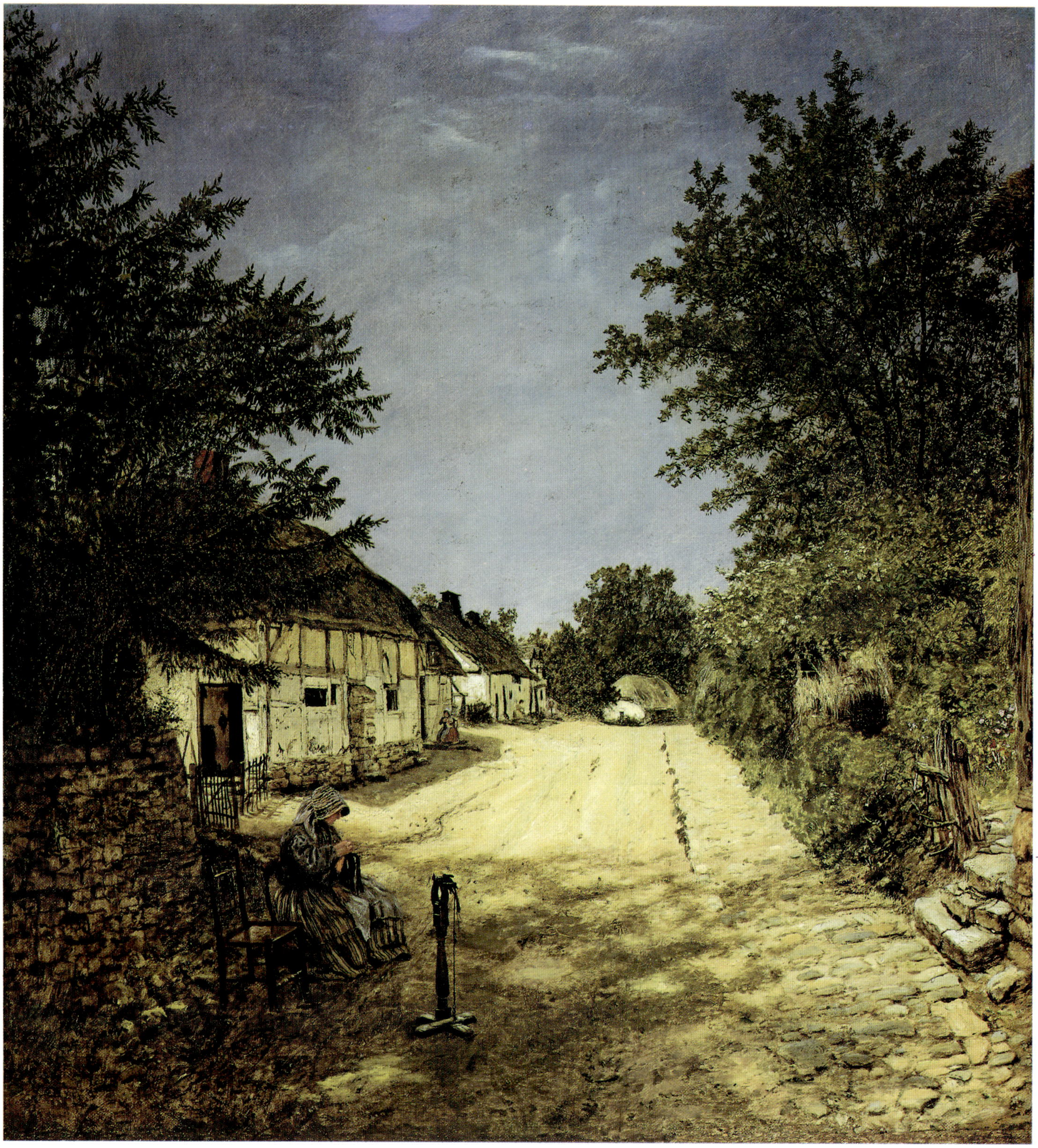

83
GEORGE WILLIAM MOTE
*Glovemaking*

85
*Overleaf* JOHN ROBERTSON REID
*A Country Cricket Match*

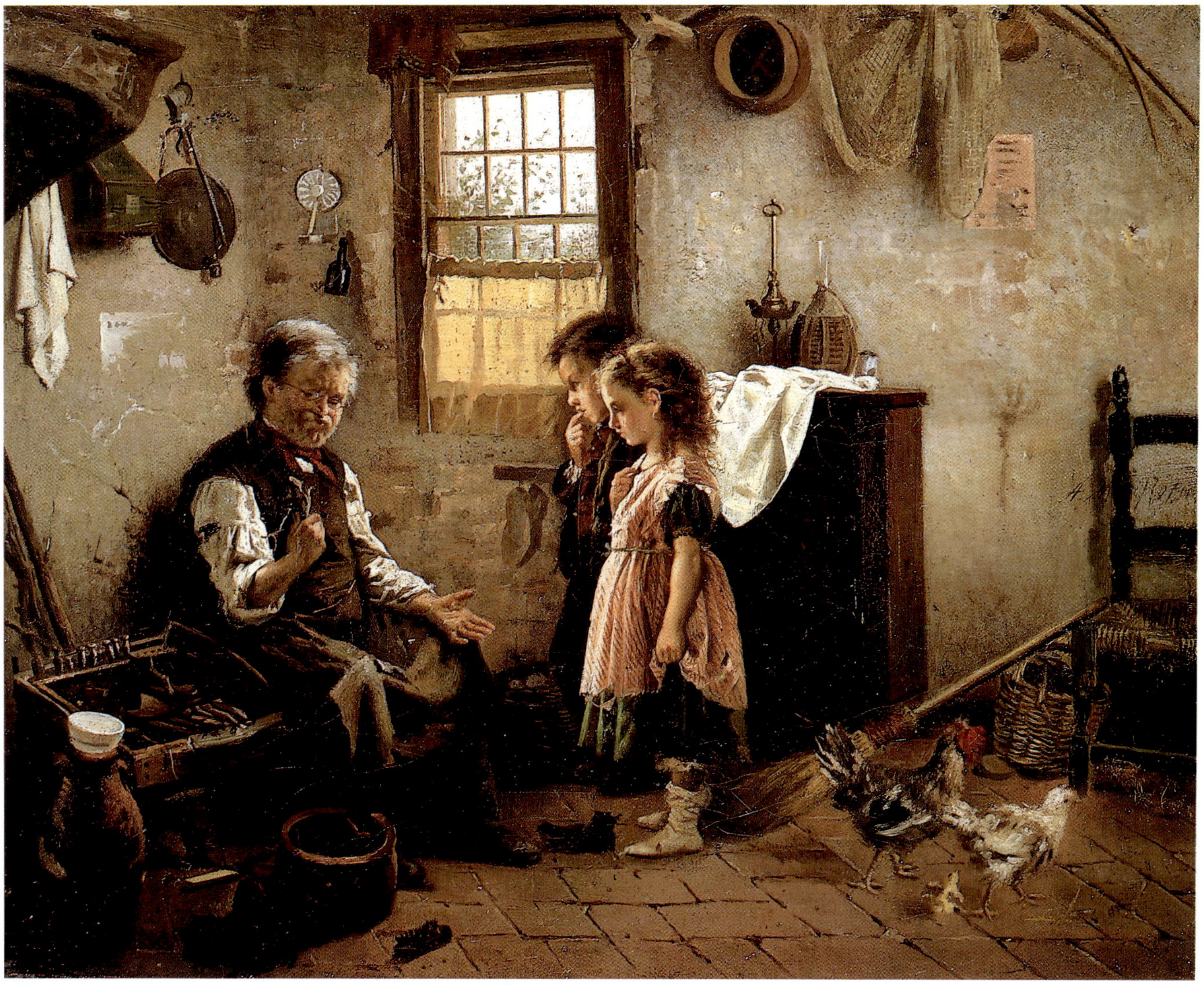

84
ALEXANDER M. ROSSI
*A Visit to the Cobbler*

These skilled craftsmen formed a proud, independent class of their own, a cut above the farm workers. They were often better educated, usually chapelgoers, sometimes trade unionists. And they often went bankrupt, because of competition or the fluctuations of trade. The interior of a blacksmith's or carpenter's shop was also a popular subject, with its picturesque clutter of tools, and the pleasing spectacle of the exercise of skill. In James Hayllar's picture of 1859, *A Controversy*, work has been suspended while an argument is in progress. The pub and the blacksmith's shop were the main exchanges for village news. Every village had its professional gossip. In Lark Rise it was Mrs Mullins, a bore dreaded by the whole village, 'the worst of all bores, a melancholy bore, and at the sight of her door-key and little black shawl the pleasantest of little gossiping groups would scatter'. James Hayllar, who lived in Wallingford-on-Thames, was a frequent painter of village life, using models from his own village.

Every village, however small, would have organised leisure activities of some kind. Depending on the population, these might include cricket, football, amateur dramatics, an orchestra or brass band, hockey, archery, swimming or the volunteers. Village cricket was the game most approved of by the Victorians, and it inspired one masterpiece in John Robertson Reid's *Country Cricket Match* (85). Cricket was, of course, a great public school game, and also inspired Sir Henry Newbolt's poem *Vitae Lampada* with the immortal words 'Play up, play up, and play the game!' But it was also democratic, and could unite the village and the manor house on the village green. Francis Kilvert played in 'a very good cricket match on the Common between Langley Burrell and the Chippenham 2nd XI. We were beaten by 2 runs, and up to the last moment it was anybody's match. I scored.' At Candleford, an imperious lady arrived in her carriage to ask the village bowler to get up a team to play 'the young gentlemen' but added 'don't bring *too* good a

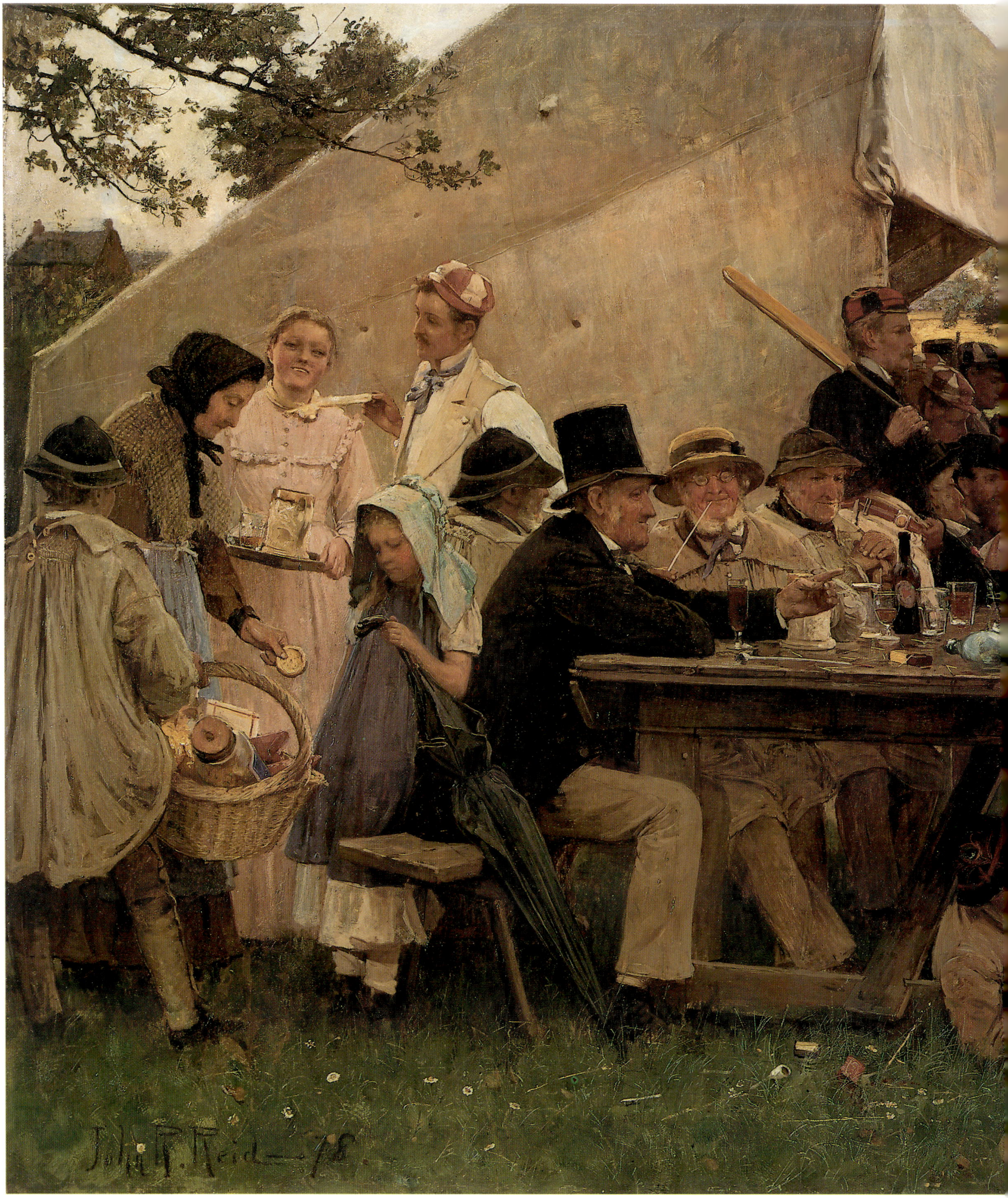

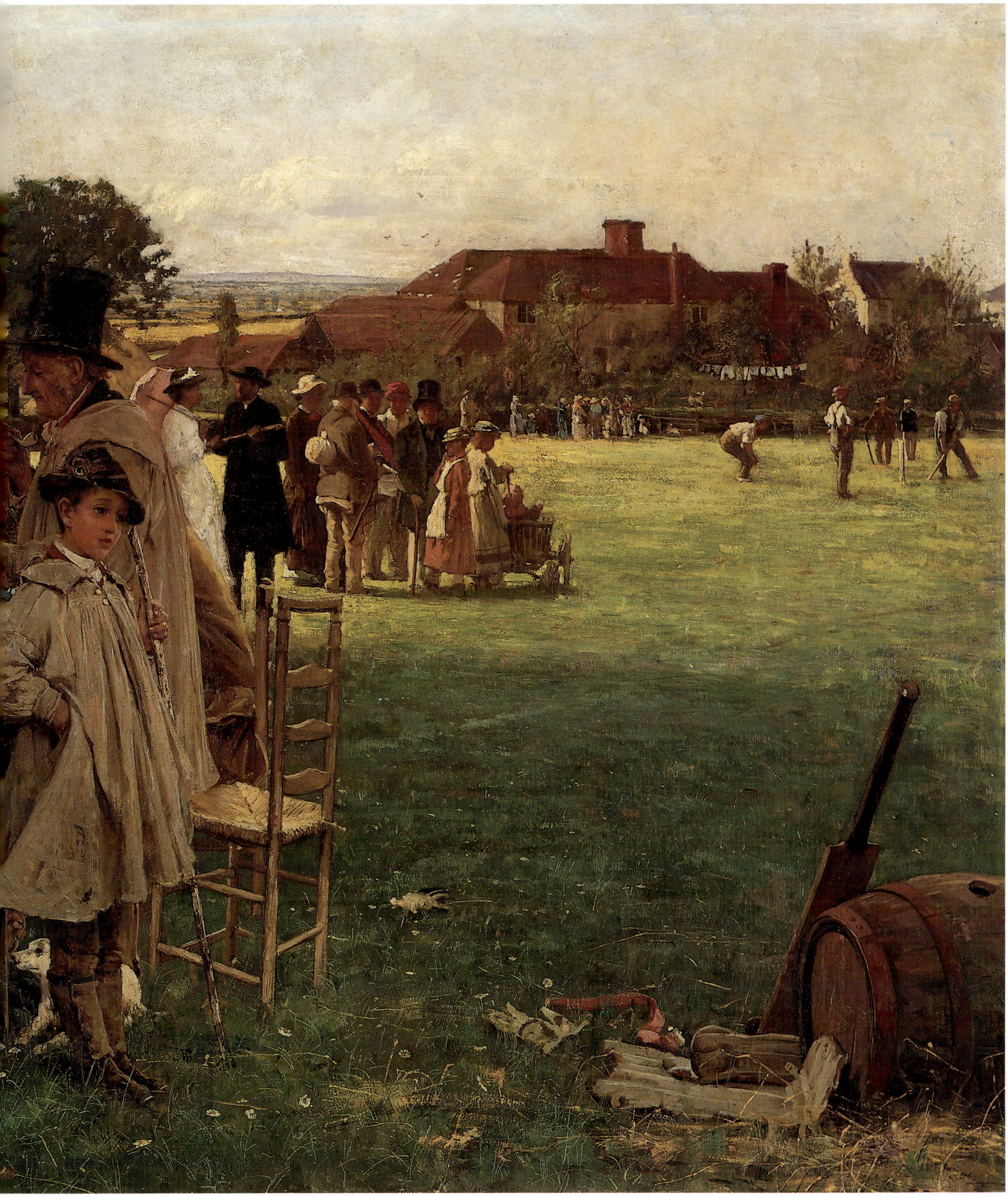

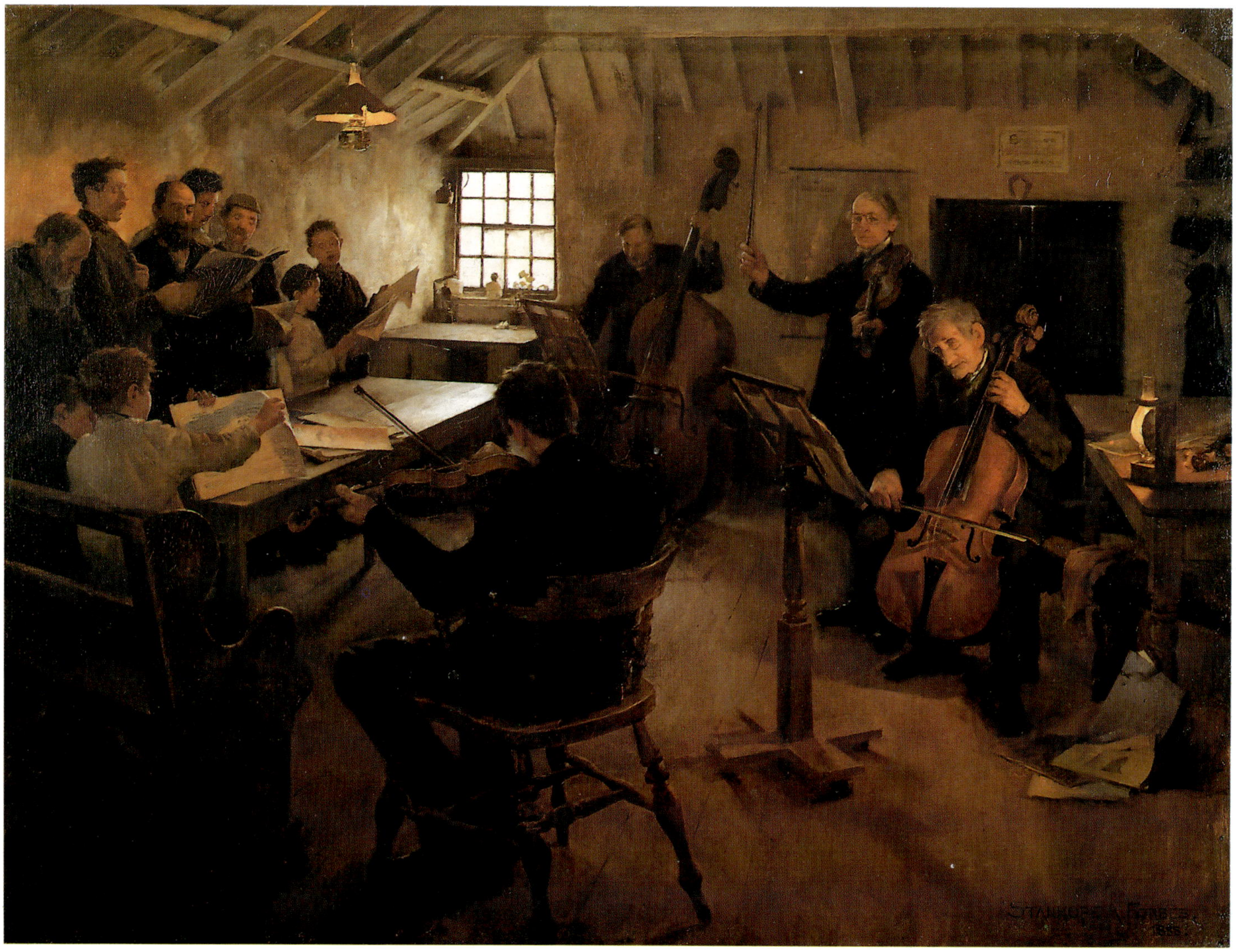

86
STANHOPE FORBES
*The Village Philharmonic*

team. They wouldn't want to be beaten.' J.R. Reid was a friend and neighbour of Clausen's for a time in Hampstead, and Reid's success at the Royal Academy with pictures of country life like the *Cricket Match* had some influence on Clausen around the late 1870s. Reid was one of the many good Scottish painters to settle in England in the nineteenth century, and he later turned mostly to coastal scenes.

Some villages might have their own orchestra, as shown in Stanhope Forbes's *Village Philharmonic* (86). This was painted in the Village Institute in Newlyn, where Forbes himself played the 'cello. Forbes posed several locals for the picture regardless of whether they could play an instrument or not. Every village would at least have an annual concert of some kind. At Lark Rise it was organised by the local squire, who played the banjo in the Negro Minstrel Troupe, consisting of village youths with their hands and faces blackened with burnt cork. Piano duets and songs followed, 'as the performers worked their conscientious way through the show piano pieces and popular drawing-room ballads of the moment'. Penny-readings and lectures, often given by the local vicar or curate, were also popular. Kilvert recorded in January 1873, 'A satisfactory lecture. I spoke about Noah's vineyard and drunkenness, the Tower of Babel, Babylon and the confusion of tongues, the death of the Emperor Napoleon III and the Great Coram Street Murder.'

The greatest of the village festivals was the feast. This was purely a village occasion, and the vicar and gentry would usually absent themselves. Probably a survival of pagan days, it was a real holiday for the village people alone. It was often combined with the club day of the local Friendly Society, such as the Ancient Order of Buffaloes in Wiltshire. These societies provided mutual help and benefit for their members and their families, particularly in the event of death, sickness or unemployment, in return for a small annual subscription. There would be a parade, sports, fairground stalls and amusements,

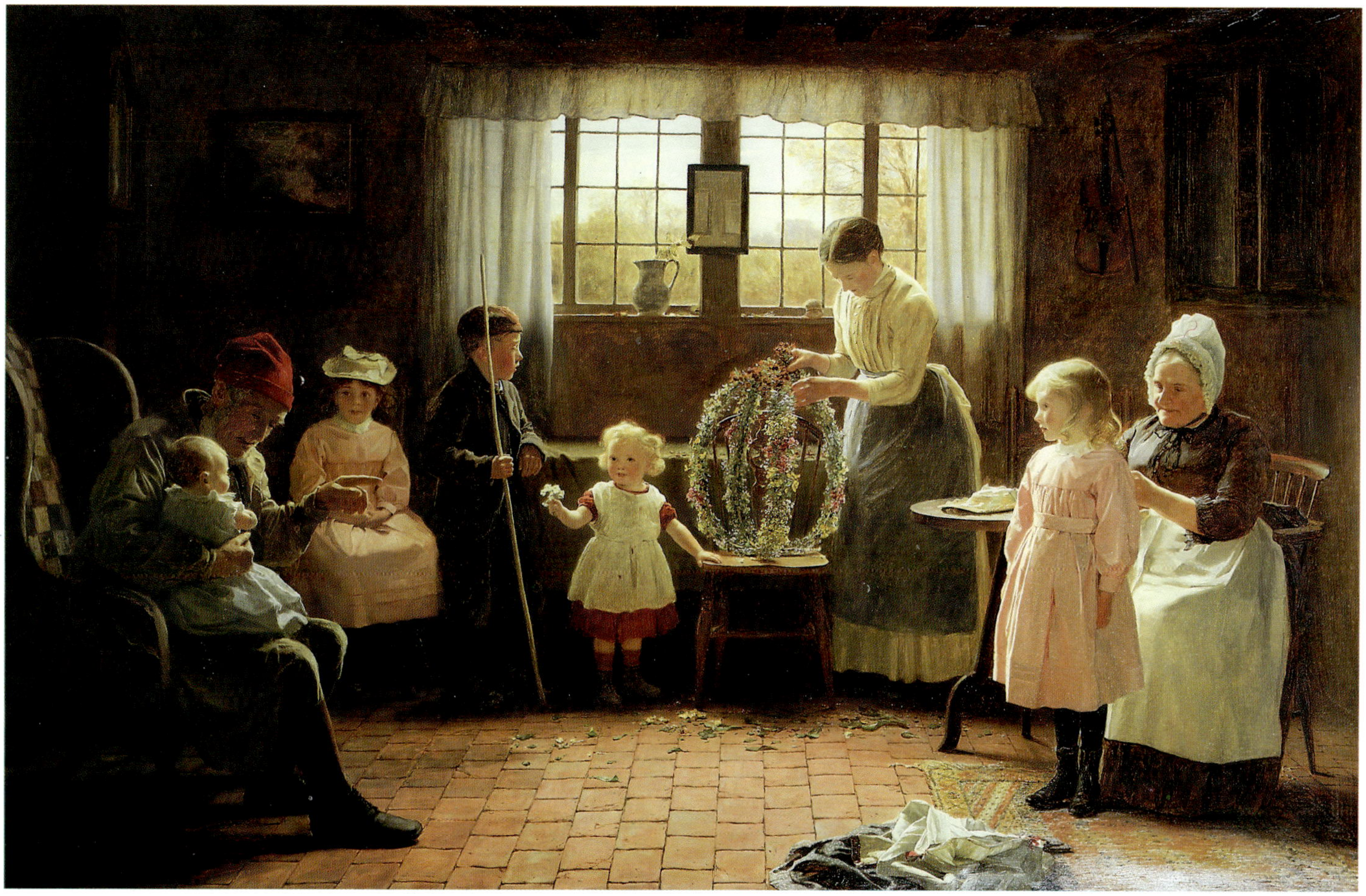

87
James Hayllar
*May Day*

and a huge amount of eating and drinking. Gradually the traditional village feast day began to die out by the end of the century, another victim of Victorian morality and respectability. The gentry and the middle-classes tended to disapprove of rowdy village festivals. As Alfred Williams wrote, 'they could see all manner of evil in it, it was nothing but a drunken, rowdy show, a public pest, and a nuisance.' Williams lamented this change: 'The old sports and festivals used to brighten up the year for farm people, and if they were rude and simple, noisy and boisterous, they served their purpose very well, and were always hailed with unfeigned joy and delight.'

Much more to Victorian taste was May Day, another traditional holiday, which became in the nineteenth century wholly associated with children. The maypole, may games and may dances had by then entirely died out, but the tradition of May Day garlands survived. These were garlands of flowers, usually arranged on a wooden framework, that were carried in procession by the children. In the centre of the leading garland a china doll, or 'lady', would be placed. The girls of the village would also elect a May Queen. James Hayllar's picture (87) shows a family preparing their garland, and getting the children ready. Then they would form in procession, to a strictly traditional pattern, and move off down the village. In Hardy's novel *Tess of the d'Urbervilles*, the heroine first appears as a girl in a May Day procession. The first stop would usually be the vicar's house, or the squire's. Here the girls would show off their garlands, sing a song, and ask for a contribution to the money box. There were many different May Day songs, but one very traditional one was:

Good morning, ladies and gentlemen, it is the first of May
And we are come to garlanding because it is new May Day;
A bunch of flowers we've brought you, and at your door we stay,
So please give us what you can, and then we'll go away.

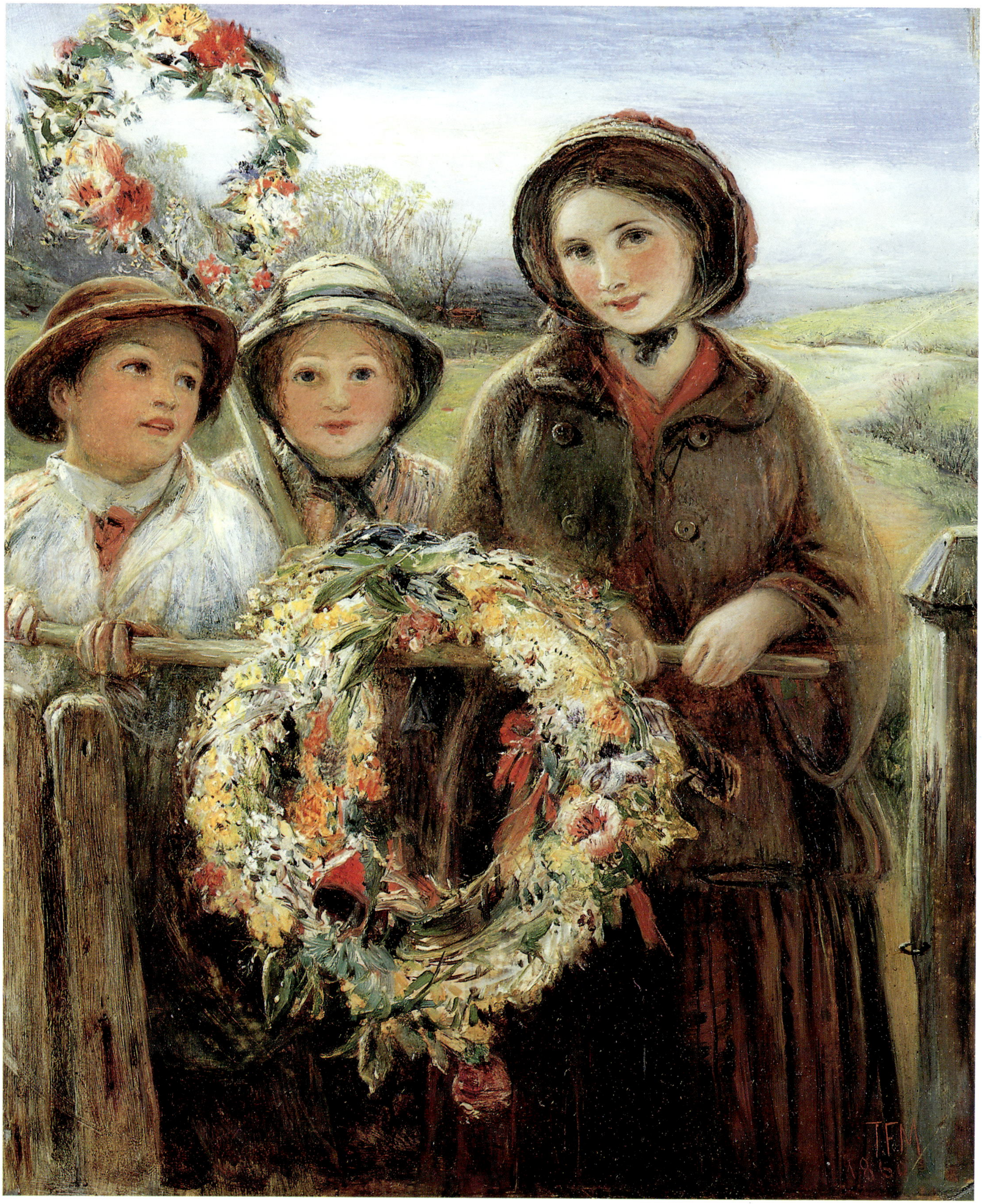

88
THOMAS FALCON MARSHALL
*May Day Garlands*

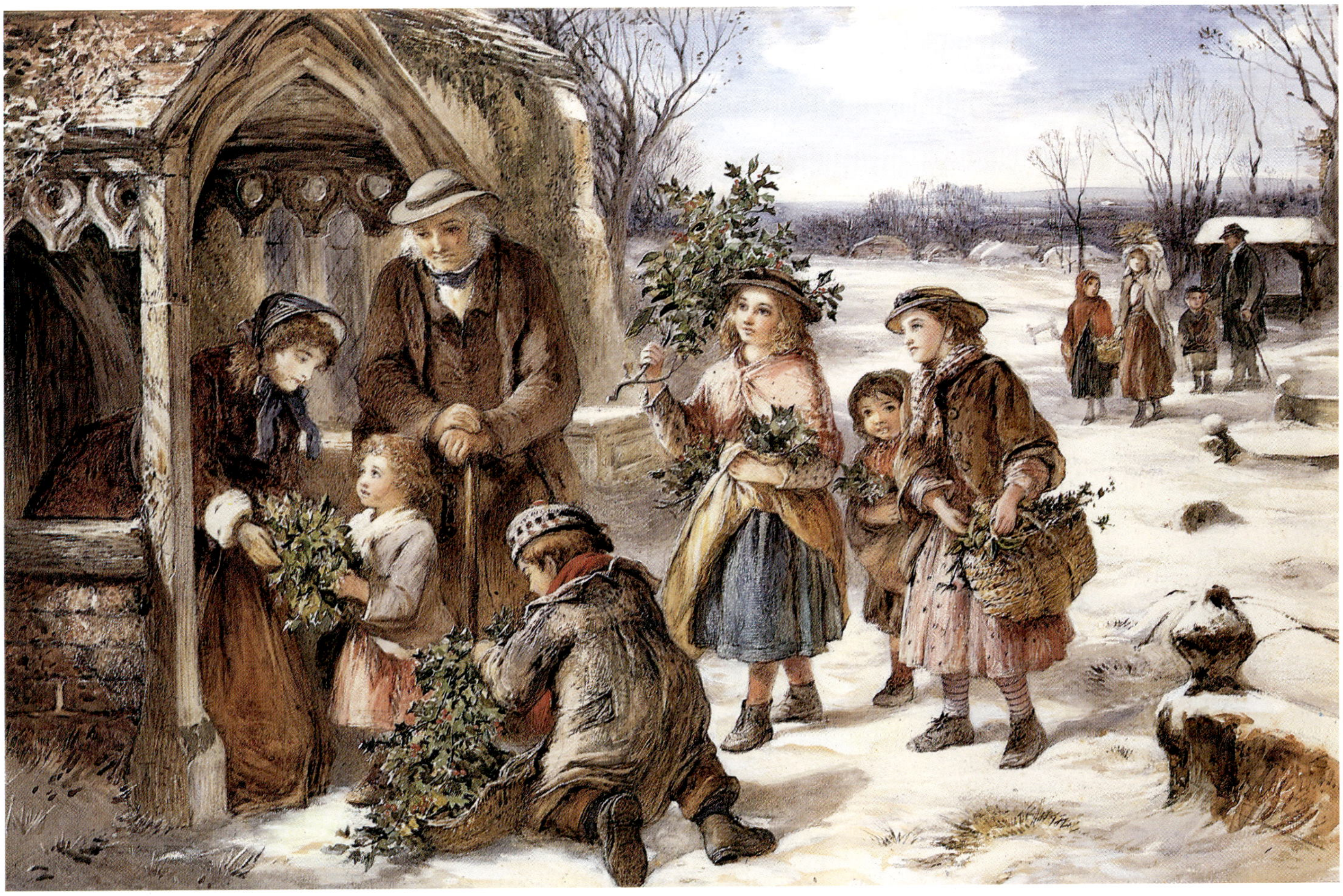

89
THOMAS FALCON MARSHALL
*Christmas Holly*

Thomas Falcon Marshall's picture (88) shows us a group of children with their garlands, at the gate of a house or cottage. After the vicar and the squire, they would then visit the steward's, the head-gardener's, and other houses on the estate, other local farms and cottages, before returning tired but usually happy in the evening. For Flora Thompson as a child, this was 'a day as near to perfection as anything can be in human life.'

Thomas Falcon Marshall, like so many Victorian artists, tended to see all village festivals in terms of the children. In his Christmas scene children are bringing baskets of holly to decorate the church (89). Christmas was an important church festival, but in small villages it was not celebrated in the same spirit as the Village Feast, or May Day. In Lark Rise 'Christmas Day passed very quietly'. In Wiltshire, Alfred Williams remembers bands of mummers and ballad-singers would go round the villages in the days leading up to Christmas. The mummers were groups of actors who performed traditional plays; they are described by Thomas Hardy in *The Return of the Native*. The ballad-singers would carry a large bowl of ale, and sing:

> Wassail, wassail, all over the town
> Our toast is white, and our ale is brown;
> Our bowl it is made of a sycamore tree
> And a wassailing bowl I will drink unto thee.'

In Kilvert's rural parish, Christmas was still full of ancient superstitions. There was a Holy Thorn, which always blossomed on Christmas Eve, and was greatly revered by the local people. One old farm worker told Kilvert another favourite story, about the oxen: 'I was watching them on old Christmas Eve and at 12 o' clock the oxen that were standing knelt down upon their knees and those that were lying down rose up on their knees and there they stayed kneeling and moaning, the tears running down their faces.'

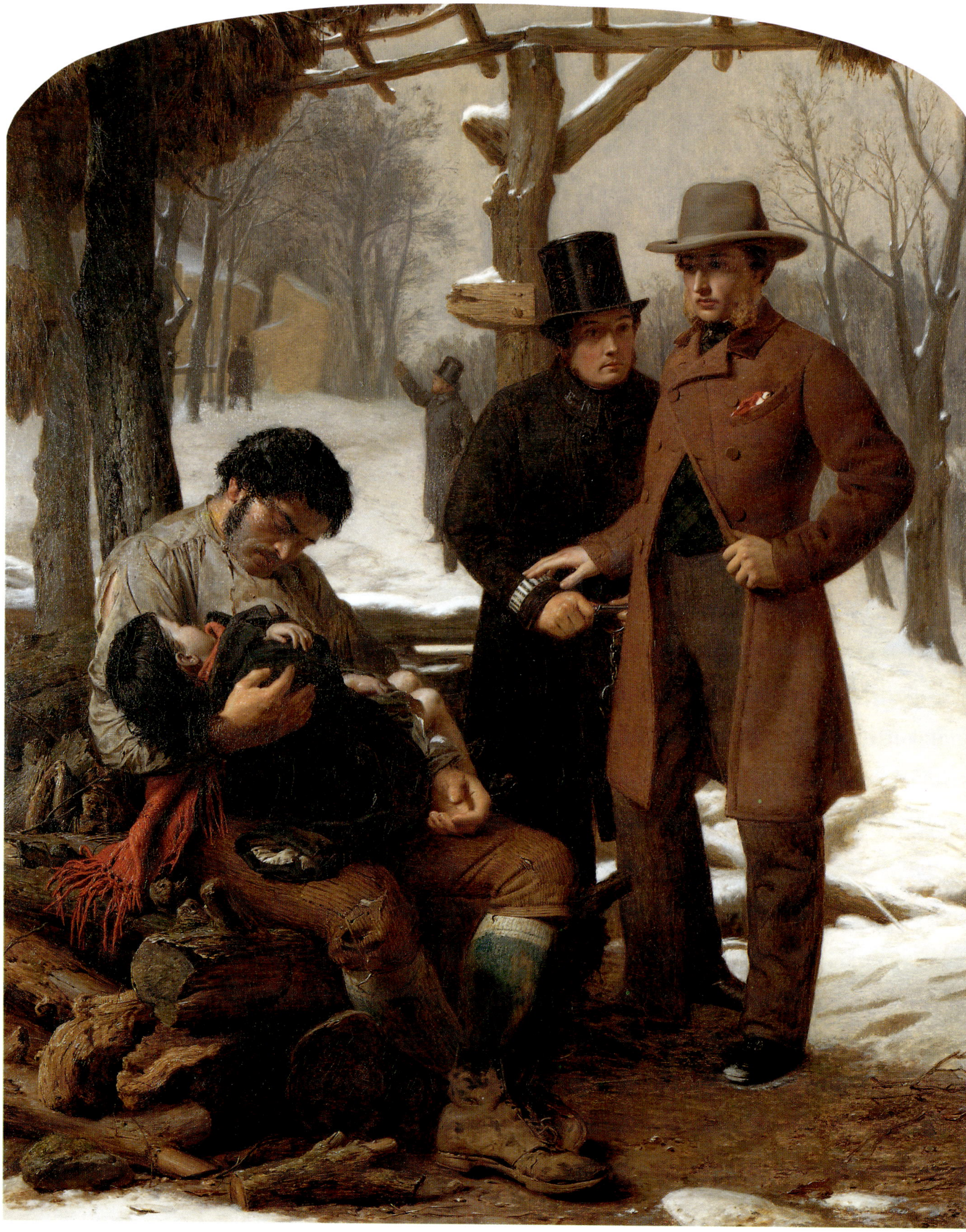

90
MARCUS STONE
*Silent Pleading*

## Chapter Seven

# LEAVING HOME

Farewell happy fields
Where joy forever dwells . . .

JOHN MILTON, *Paradise Lost*

MANY VILLAGE PEOPLE STRAYED NO FURTHER than five or ten miles from their birthplace throughout their entire lives. In an age when travel was so rare, leaving home could be a dramatic and sad occasion. Its poignant nature, in a country setting, made it a popular subject for painters. The two most common reasons for leaving were emigration or going into service in an upper-class household, often in the towns. Many good examples of both subjects survive.

The motives for emigration were usually poverty and lack of work. Poverty in rural areas was as common a problem as in the towns, as is shown in Marcus Stone's picture *Silent Pleading* (90). Here we see a labourer, clearly fallen on hard times, though a strong, able-bodied man, asleep on a bench with a child in his arms. A policeman is about to arrest him, but is deterred from doing so by a country gentleman. The picture was exhibited at the Royal Academy in 1859, with a quotation from Shakespeare's *The Tempest,* 'Him and his innocent child. The picture was much admired, appealing as it did to the socially concerned mid-Victorian audience, who had read their Thomas Carlyle, and were worried about the problems of poverty and vagrant children. Emigration was one of the solutions proposed for the problems of unemployment and vagrancy. Charles Kingsley, for instance, asked rhetorically in *Town Geology* (1873): 'Are none of you going to emigrate? If you have courage and wisdom, emigrate you will.' Between 1850 and 1900 about ten million people emigrated from the British Isles. The majority went to the United States, with Canada and Australia next in popularity. Many of the emigrants were farm workers and people from poor villages and small country towns. In *Jude the Obscure* Jude's first wife, Arabella, leaves him soon after their disastrous marriage, and emigrates with her family to Australia.

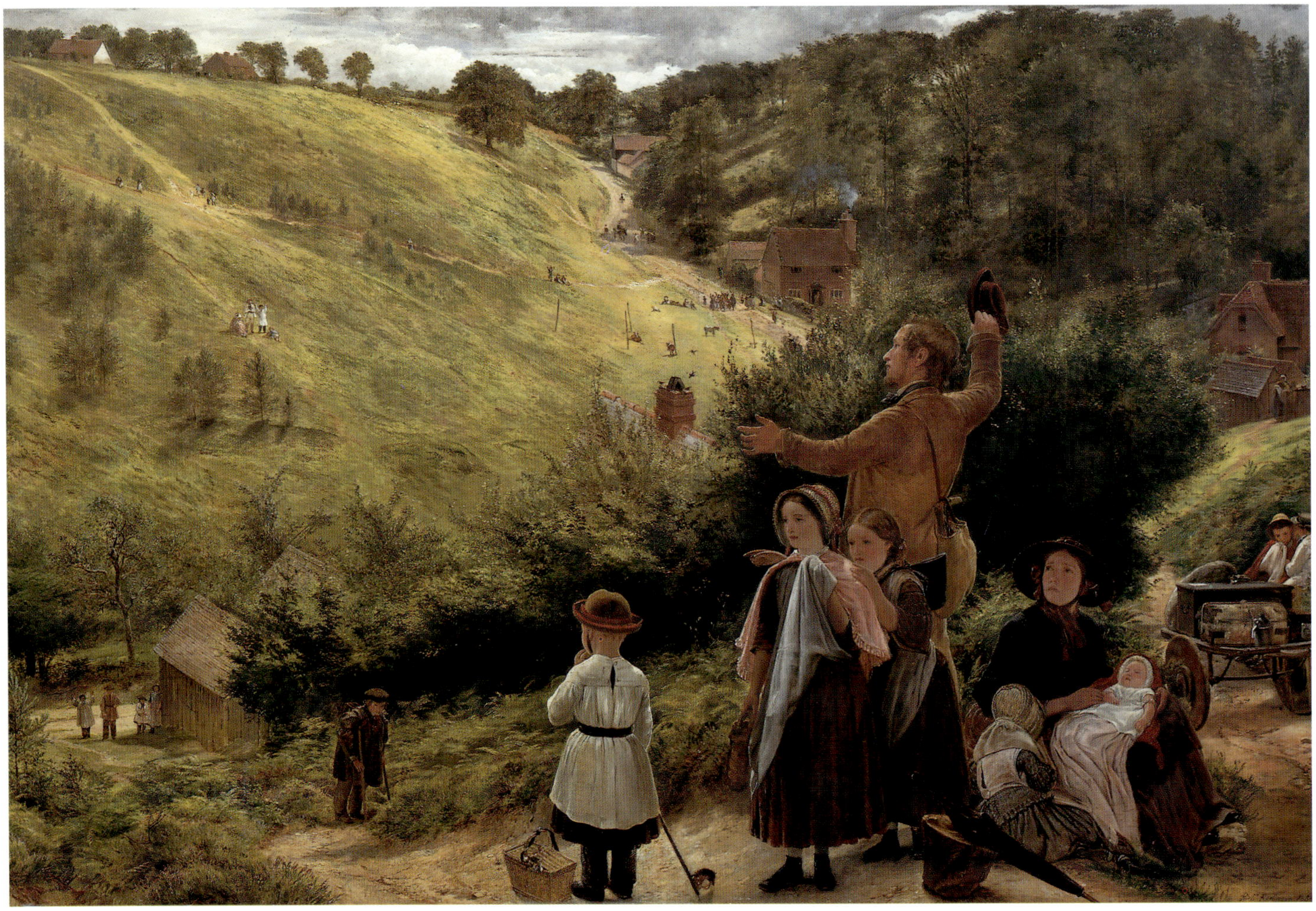

91
Richard Redgrave
*The Emigrant's Last Sight of Home*

The most famous of all emigration pictures is *The Last of England* by Ford Madox Brown, too well-known to need reproducing here. Emigration was at its height in the 1850s, and it was personal experience that inspired Brown to paint the subject. In 1852 he visited Gravesend to say farewell to his friend Thomas Woolner, the Pre-Raphaelite sculptor, who was emigrating to Australia. The models were the artist himself and his wife Emma, and with typical Pre-Raphaelite thoroughness Brown took three years to complete the picture. None of the other Pre-Raphaelites took up the emigration theme except for James Collinson, briefly a member of the Brotherhood mainly because of his engagement to Christina Rossetti, and noted for his tendency to fall asleep at their meetings. Although his paintings of *The Emigration Scheme* and *Answering the Emigrant's Letter* are both primarily cottage scenes rather than actual emigration pictures, they show how profoundly emigration affected the families concerned, especially the country poor, and how they tried to keep in touch with their absent relations through letters.

Less well-known than *The Last of England*, but just as moving and even more beautiful, is Richard Redgrave's *The Emigrant's Last Sight of Home* (91). It was painted at Leith Hill, near Abinger in Surrey, where Redgrave had a house, and was exhibited at the Royal Academy in 1859. Redgrave seems to have concentrated on the landscape, as if to emphasise the sadness of the emigrants at having to leave it. Ruskin praised its 'beautiful distance', and the *Art Journal* also commented on the landscape. It is the beauty of the landscape that dominates the picture, not the fact that it is about emigration. A much more direct approach is taken by Charles Joseph Staniland's *Emigrant Ship* (94), which shows a crowded quayside at the moment of the departure. At the centre of the crowd is a rustic figure in a smock waving goodbye with his stick. It recalls the famous emigration scene in *David Copperfield*, when the Micawbers, Mr

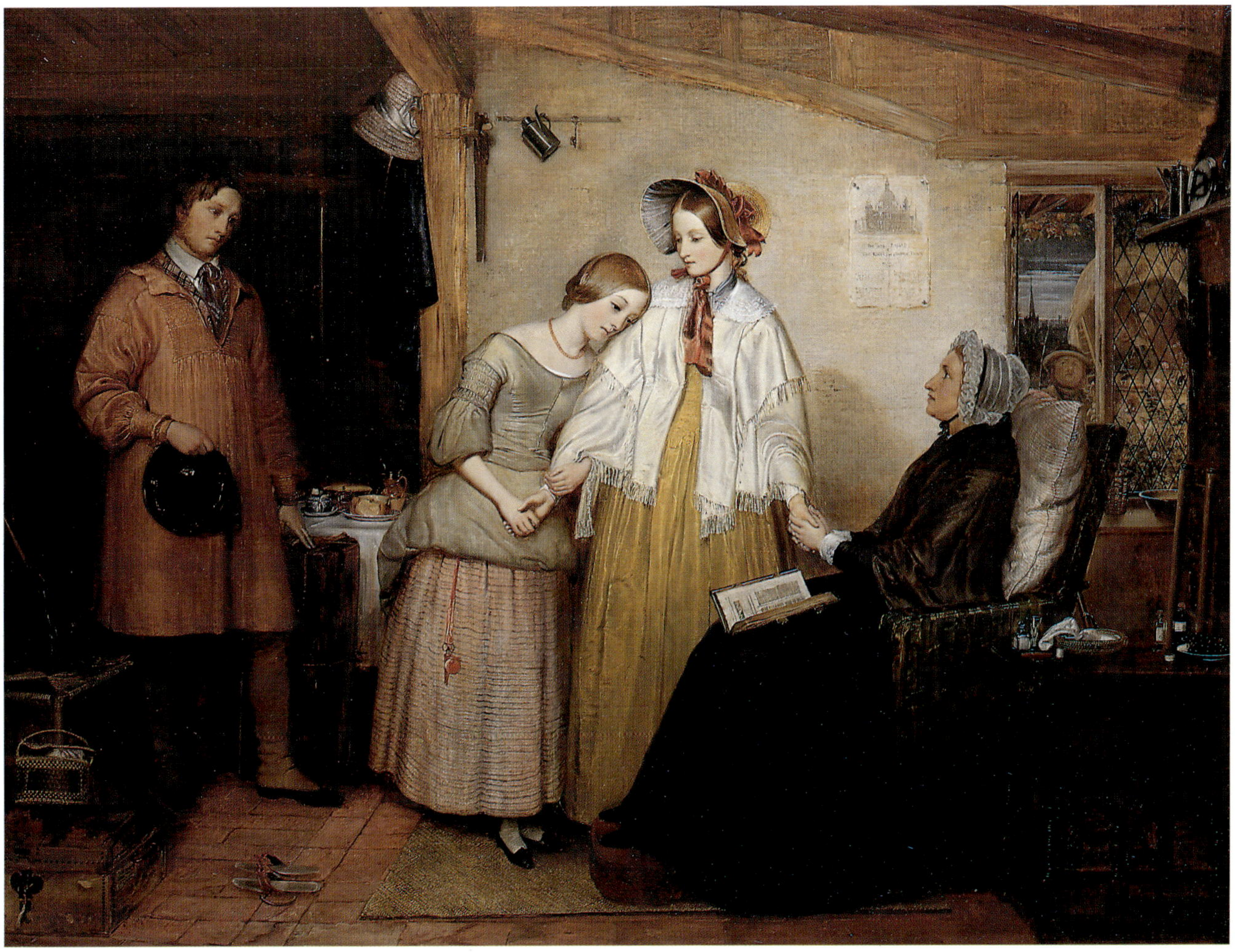

92
Richard Redgrave
*Going into Service*

Peggotty, Emily and Martha depart for Australia. Staniland was a painter and illustrator of historical scenes, and this was one of his very few forays into modern-life subjects. One can only wish that he had done more of them.

Girls leaving home to go into service also made a poignant subject, but at least the girls were not leaving for ever, and would come home for a two-week holiday once a year. At Lark Rise, 'There was no girl over twelve or thirteen living permanently at home. Some were sent out to their first place at eleven.' The first place was called a 'petty place', and was not expected to last more than a year. Then they moved up the scale, as housemaids, kitchenmaids or nurserymaids. Richard Redgrave's *Going into Service* (92) shows a girl about to leave home, bidding farewell to her old mother, seated with a bible on her knees, and her brother and sister. The girl is obviously already too old for a petty place. Her smart bonnet and shawl suggest that she might become a lady's maid, rather than a mere house or kitchenmaid. Redgrave was deeply concerned about the exploitation of female workers, and in the 1840s he painted several pictures about their plight, notably *The Poor Teacher* – also known as *The Governess* – *The Seamstress* and *The Outcast*. He was one of the pioneers among painters of social realist subjects.

La Thangue also painted a *Leaving Home* (93) with his usual sensitivity to the quiet pathos of country life. At Lark Rise, Laura had seen many girls going off into service: '. . . They would leave . . . perhaps before it was quite light on a winter morning, the girl in her best, would-be fashionable clothes and the mother carrying the baby of the family, rolled in its shawl.' Neighbours would gather to say goodbye and give advice and encouragement. For most girls, it was their first train journey ever. Eventually Laura herself went off to Candleford Green to work in the Post Office: . . . So, one morning in May, Polly and the spring-cart drew up at the gate, and Laura's little trunk, all

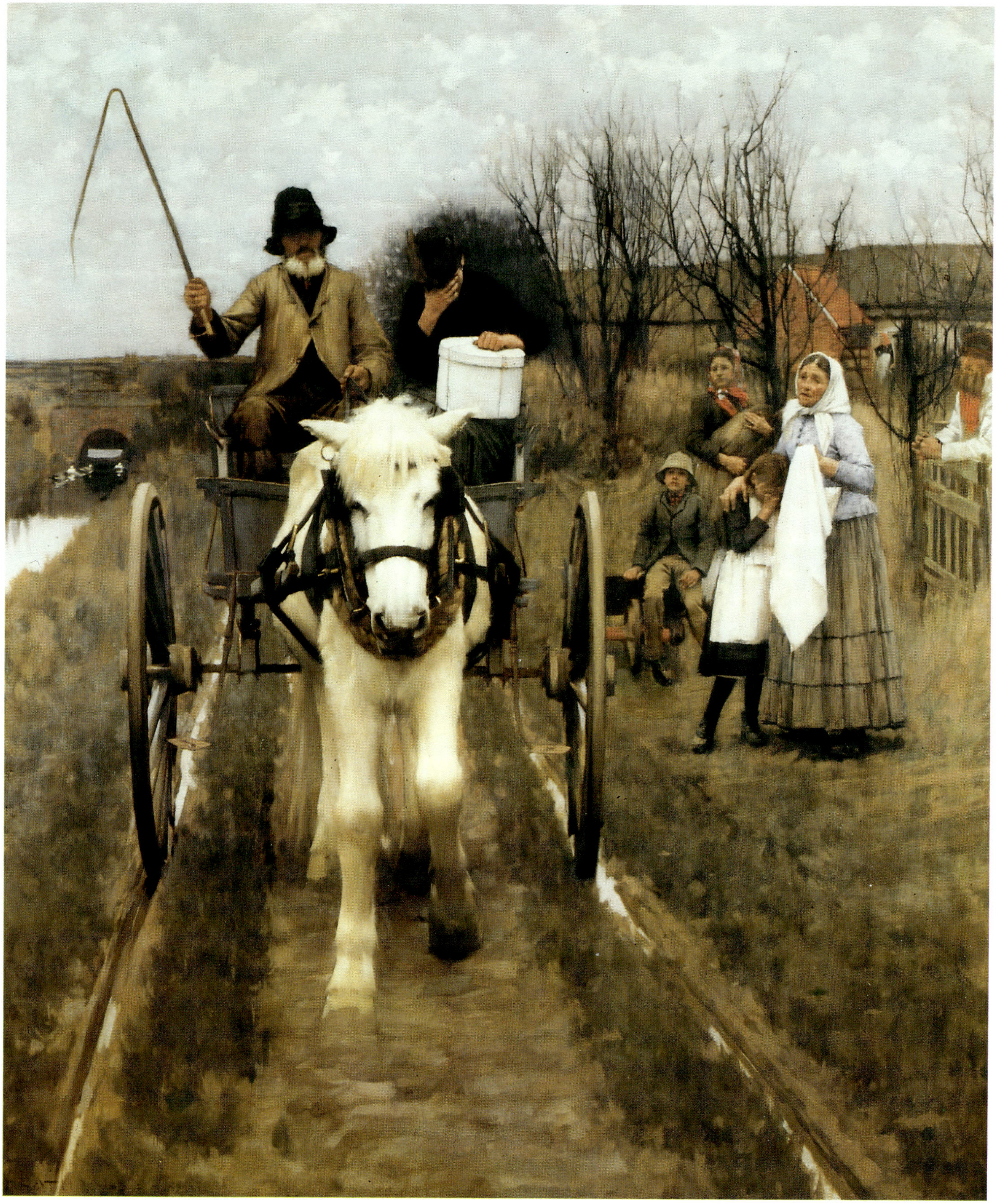

93
HENRY HERBERT LA THANGUE
*Leaving Home*

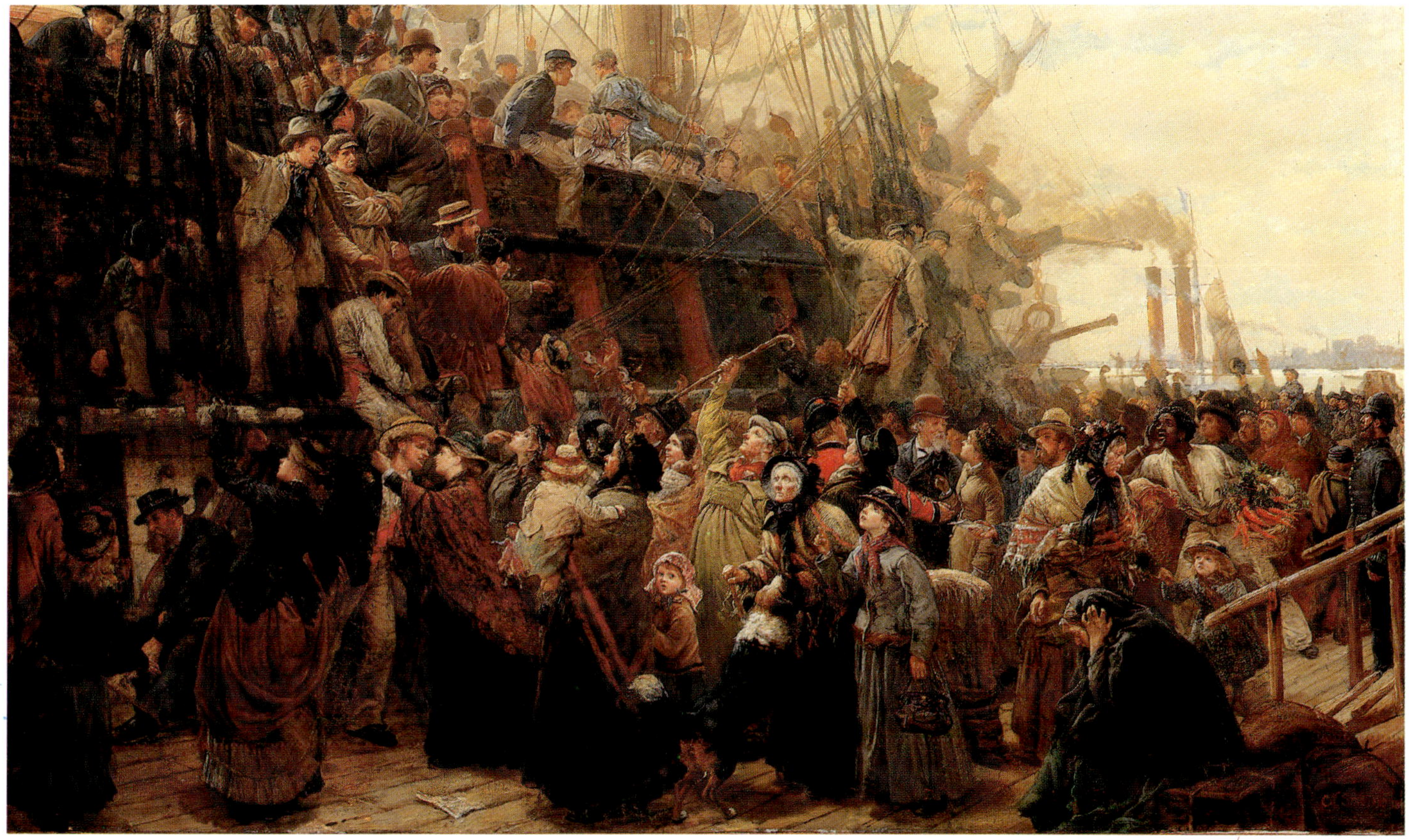

94
CHARLES JOSEPH STANILAND
*The Emigrant Ship*

new and shiny black with her initials in brass-headed nails, was hoisted into the back seat, and Laura in a new frock – grey cashmere with a white lace collar . . . climbed up beside her father, who was taking the day off to drive Polly.' Later, the girls would come back for their holidays, looking smart in their town clothes, including gloves and veil, and their mothers would insist on them wearing their best every time they went out, in order to impress the neighbours.

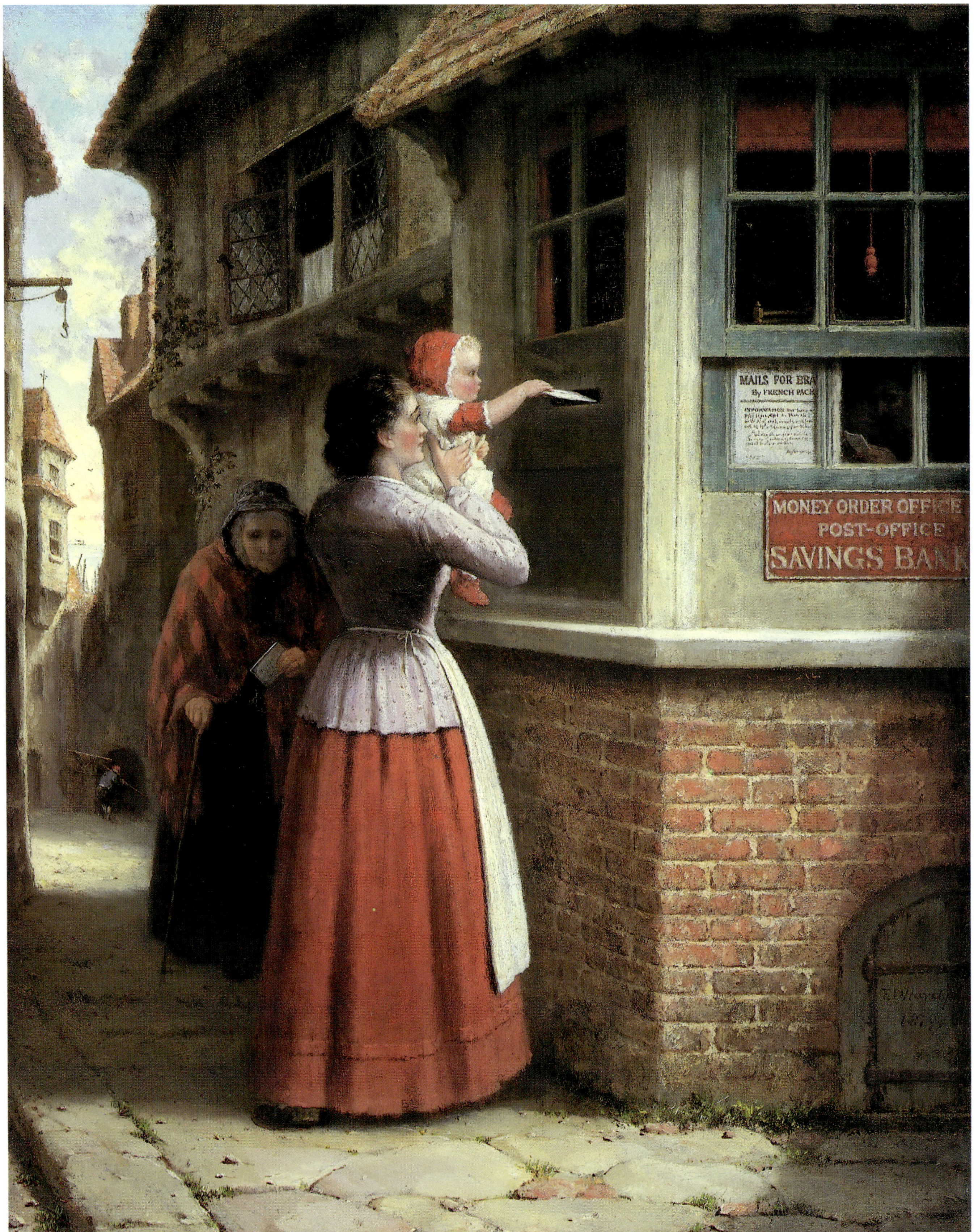
MAILS FOR BRA
By FRENCH PACK
MONEY ORDER OFFICE
POST-OFFICE
SAVINGS BAN

# Chapter Eight

# VILLAGE VISITORS

Today I sent my first post cards . . . They are capital things, simple, useful and handy. A happy invention.

*Kilvert's Diary*

THE PENNY POST, INTRODUCED IN 1840 BY THE reformer Rowland Hill, caused a revolution in most people's lives, both in the town and the country. It was a great help to business, but also enabled poor people to write to their relations and friends, anywhere in the world, for the first time in history. As a result the Victorians became prodigious, even obsessive, letter writers. Anthony Trollope, who himself worked for the postal service, wrote in *Phineas Redux*, 'what a blessing is the penny post'. The Post Office quickly became an important feature of life, especially in the country, as we can see in Frederick Daniel Hardy's picture *Posting a Letter* (95). The village postmistress, like Miss Dorcas Lane of Candleford Green, was an important personage in any village. Miss Lane took great pride in her work, and especially in the telegraph machine; occasions for using it were rare and caused excitement in the village.

Victorian painters brought the post into the service of art in many different ways. Letters play an important role in narrative pictures, as they do in Victorian novels, and the arrival of the post was a favourite subject for painters of village life. Letters from abroad were the most popular subject. One of the earliest of these was James Collinson's *Answering the Emigrant's Letter* (96), showing a family composing a reply to a letter from one of their relatives who has emigrated. The father, on the right, holds the letter, and a map of Australia.

Another letter from abroad has arrived in Thomas Webster's picture (97) of 1852. The postman is asking for payment on delivery of this letter, which does not please the old lady. Webster was one of a group of artists who settled in Cranbrook, in Kent, and devoted themselves to scenes of domestic and village life. F.D. Hardy was also a member of this Cranbrook Colony. Also a prolific painter of similar subjects was George Smith. His picture *As cold water is to a thirsty soul, etc.*

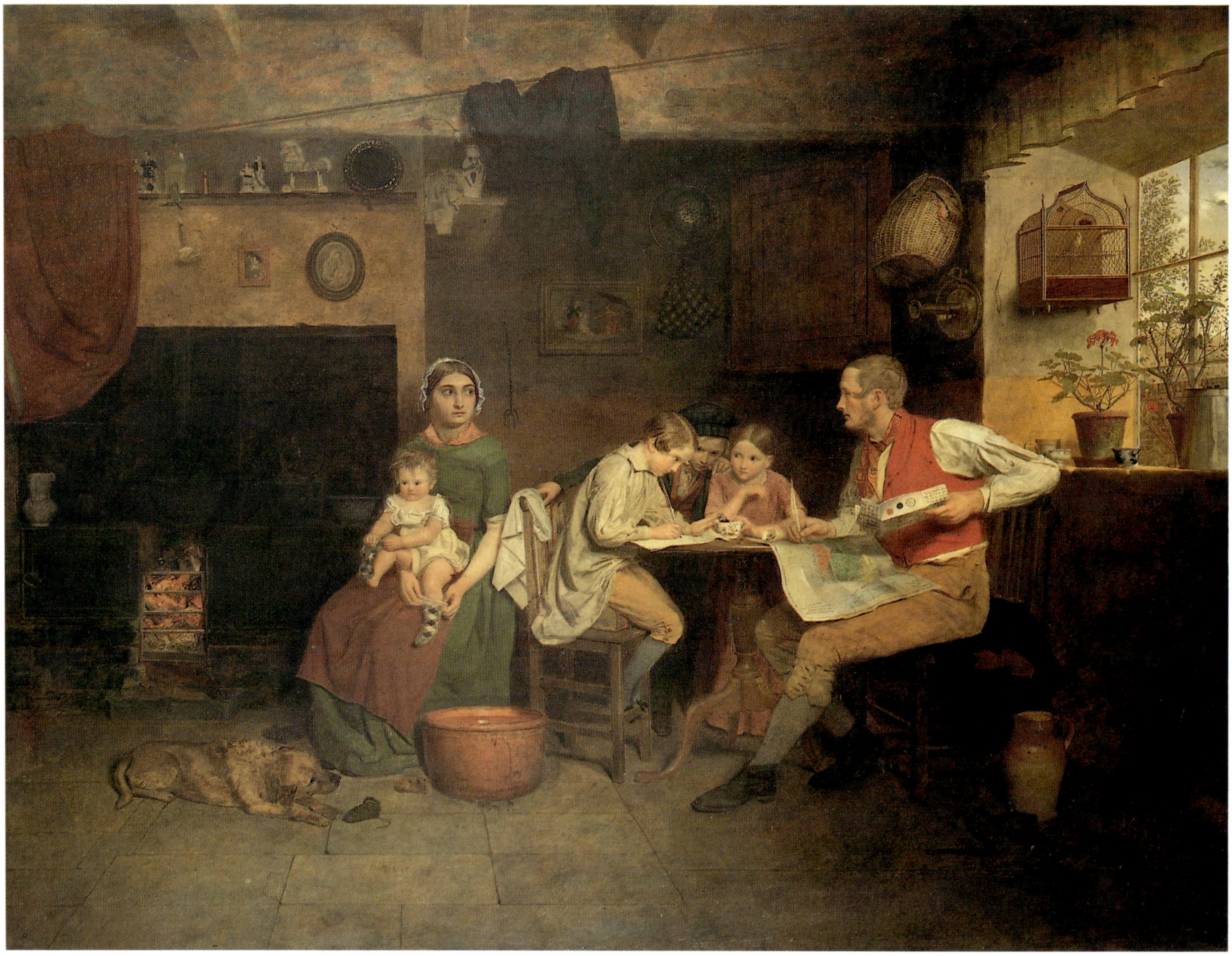

96
JAMES COLLINSON
*Answering the Emigrant's Letter*

(98) shows the whole family gathering around to hear a letter read out. Even the boys on the left look up from their model boat to listen in.

Liverpool also produced a thriving school of artists in the Victorian period, one of whom was James Campbell. His picture *News from my Lad* (99) shows an old locksmith receiving a letter from his son serving in India. The letter is dated from Lucknow, so the son must be fighting in the Indian Mutiny, and it begins, 'My dear old Daddy, I daresay you will read this in the old Shop. . . .' Campbell, like many of the Liverpool School, was influenced by the Pre-Raphaelite Brotherhood and his work is distinguished by its intense detail, pale tonality, and Dickensian characterisation.

Lark Rise had one postal delivery a day, made by a crotchety and bad-tempered postman known as 'Old Postie'. He usually had only two or three letters for the village, and took particular delight in telling some anxious ladies that he had nothing for them. He would also comment on the thinness of some letters, comparing it to the fatness of others he had just delivered. Everyone in the village longed for a letter, even if they did not expect one – this was known as 'yearning'. The young lady in William Hemsley's picture (100) is clearly yearning for a letter, doubtless from an admirer. The 'Old Postie' looks just as crotchety as the Lark Rise postman, and is doubtless going to enjoy telling her he has nothing for her. Eventually Old Postie, who had 'been a postman forty years and had walked an incredible number of miles in all weathers . . . was pensioned off and a smart, obliging young postman took his place . . . .' Even more interesting to the Lark Rise residents were occasional parcels of clothing, sent by their daughters out in service, probably a gift from their mistresses. 'As soon as a parcel was taken indoors, neighbours who had seen Old Postie arrive with it would drop in, as though by accident, and stay to admire, or sometimes to criticise, the contents.'

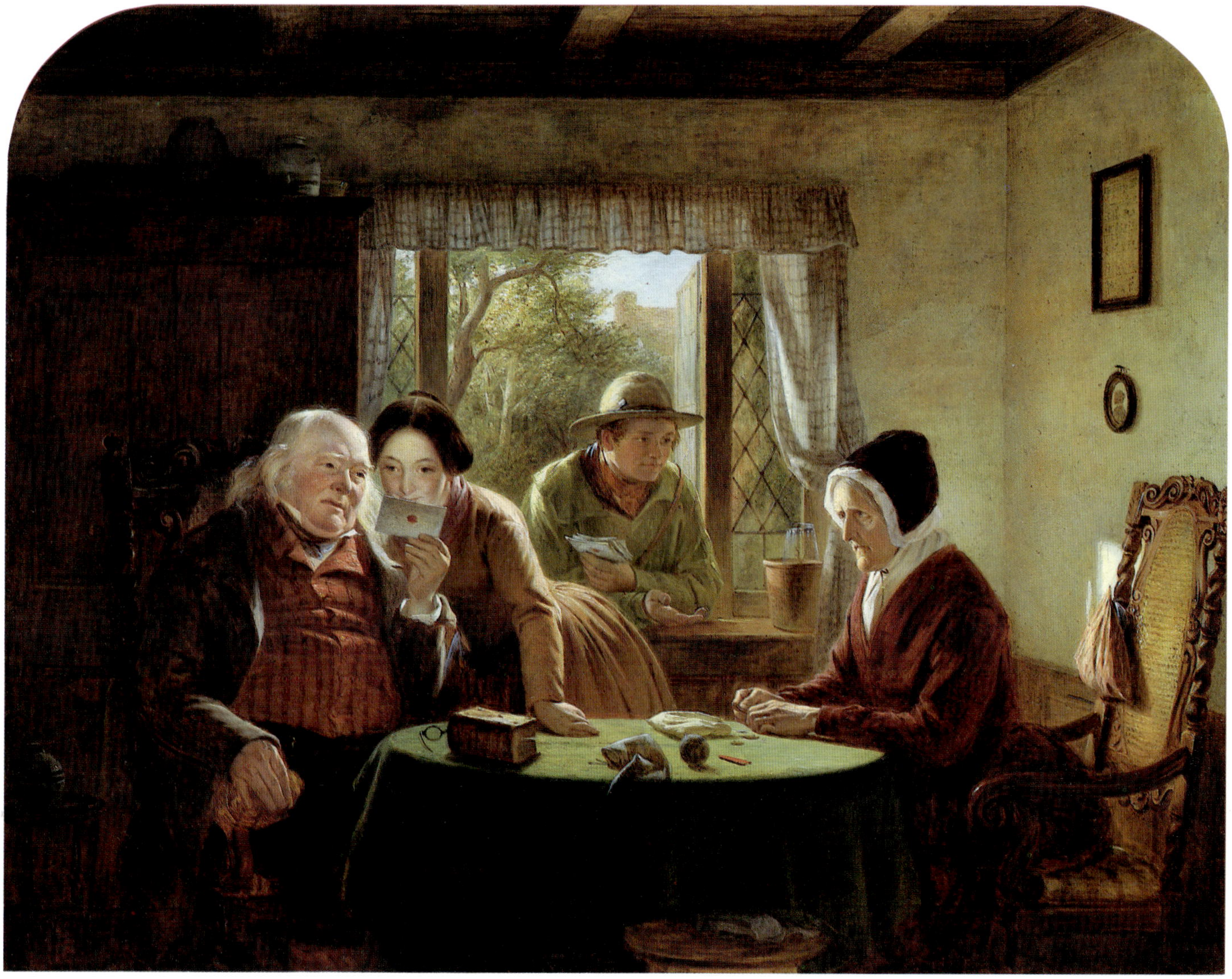

97
THOMAS WEBSTER
*A Letter from the Colonies*

As well as the postman, there were many other visitors to the village whose appearance would cause excitement. These included all kinds of travelling salesmen, tinkers and pedlars, cheap-jacks, and toy and sweet sellers. There were also travelling entertainers and showmen with their Punch and Judy shows, peep shows, and even dancing bears and pet monkeys. Lark Rise was visited every year by a German brass band. There were the Irish workers who came every summer to help with the harvest. There were vagrants, tramps and gipsies. The carter was also an important person in small villages, going round collecting things to take to market, and bringing back goods from the town. Flora Thompson's grandfather followed the traditional trade of eggler, going round farms and cottages collecting eggs, and taking them in his horse and cart to sell in the local market. Another important visitor was the local doctor. In small villages his appearance would be rare, as the villagers probably relied on traditional herbal remedies or the advice of a local 'wise woman'. The doctor, the parson and the squire or local landowner were probably the only educated people to visit a small village and were the only link between the villagers and the social world above their own. The doctor in Heywood Hardy's picture *Duty* (101) is certainly a distinguished and smartly-dressed figure, on a handsome horse. He is stopping to ask a young shepherd boy the way, perhaps to a small hamlet or an outlying farm. Alfred Williams's local doctor in Wiltshire used to accept payment in kind – corn from the farmers, bacon from the villagers; it was a common practice in the nineteenth century.

All these visitors made picturesque and popular subjects for painters. Birket Foster was particularly fond of painting cottages with a travelling salesman or craftsman calling at the door. Among others, he painted a china pedlar (103), a broom seller, and a chair mender (104). He was able to make a happy combination of several popular ingredients: a cottage,

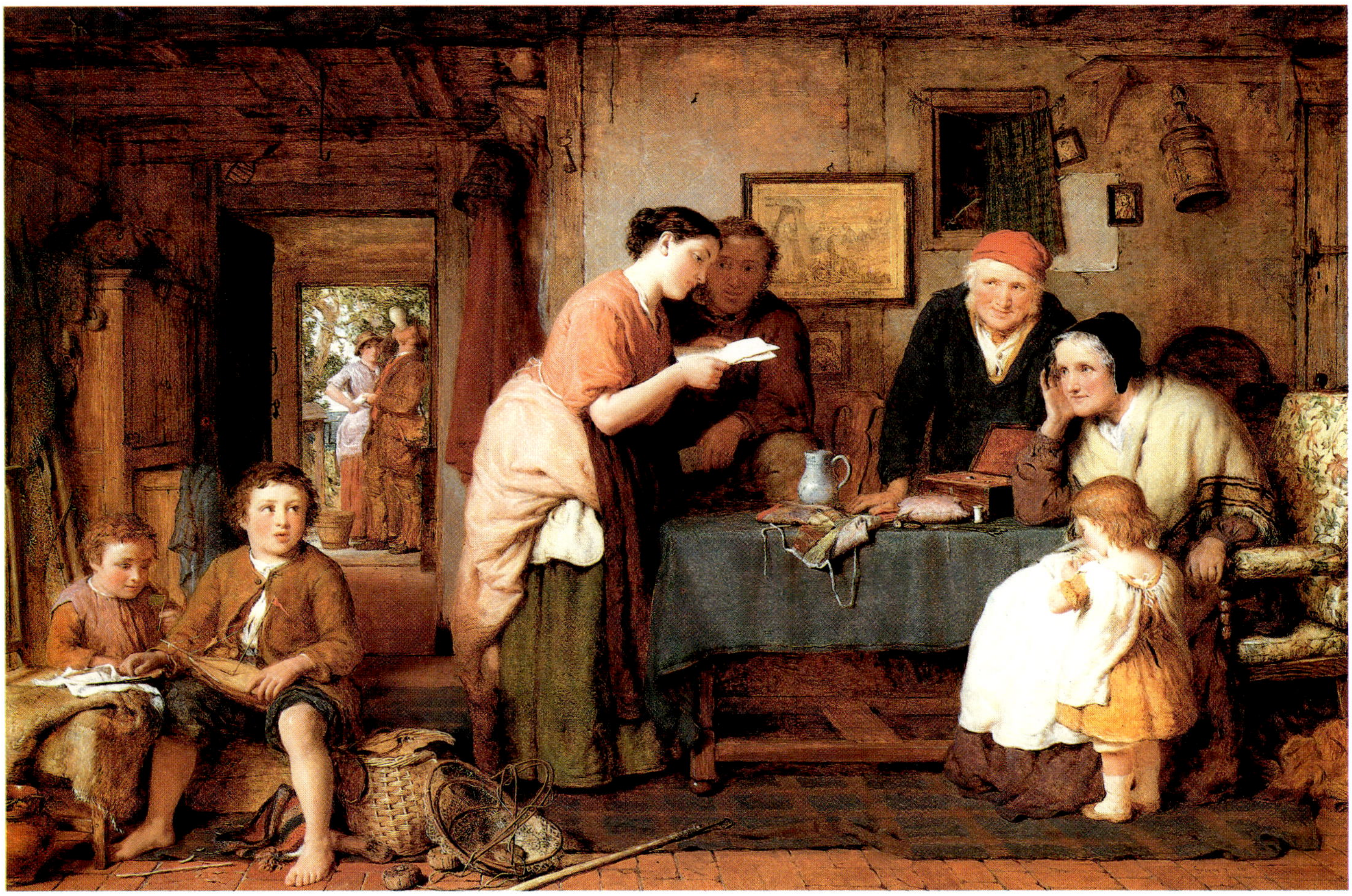

98
GEORGE SMITH
*'As cold water is to a thirsty soul, so is good news from a far country'*

pretty girls and children outside it, and the picturesque figure of the tradesman or craftsman. At Lark Rise, the packman or pedlar was a familiar figure, but already beginning to die out in the 1880s, as people began to shop in the nearby market towns. Sometimes a tallyman, or Johnny Fortnight, would call to try and sell furniture on the instalment plan. Occasionally, a cheap-jack would arrive, with a cartload of crockery and glassware, and shout 'Come buy! Come buy!' At Lark Rise he sold very little, as the villagers had little or no spare cash, and he never returned there. That year was remembered thereafter as 'that time the cheap-jack came'. Tinkers would also call, singing as they walked through the village:

> Any razors or scissors to grind?
> Or anything else in the tinker's line?
> Any old pots or kettles to mend?

Knifegrinding was often a separate profession of its own, and the visit of the knifegrinder, seated at his pedal-operated workbench on wheels, was recorded by James Charles in a delightful picture of 1887. Knifegrinders were a proverbially hard-up and impoverished class, as in George Canning's poem *The Friend of Humanity and the Knife Grinder*:

> Needy knife-grinder! Whither are you going?
> Rough is the road, your wheel is out of order –
> Bleak blows the blast; – your hat has got a hole in't,
> So have your breeches.

F.D. Hardy, one of the Cranbrook group, was also fond of painting visiting tradesmen, usually inside a cottage rather than outside. In *Try this Pair* (107) he shows us a visiting spectacle

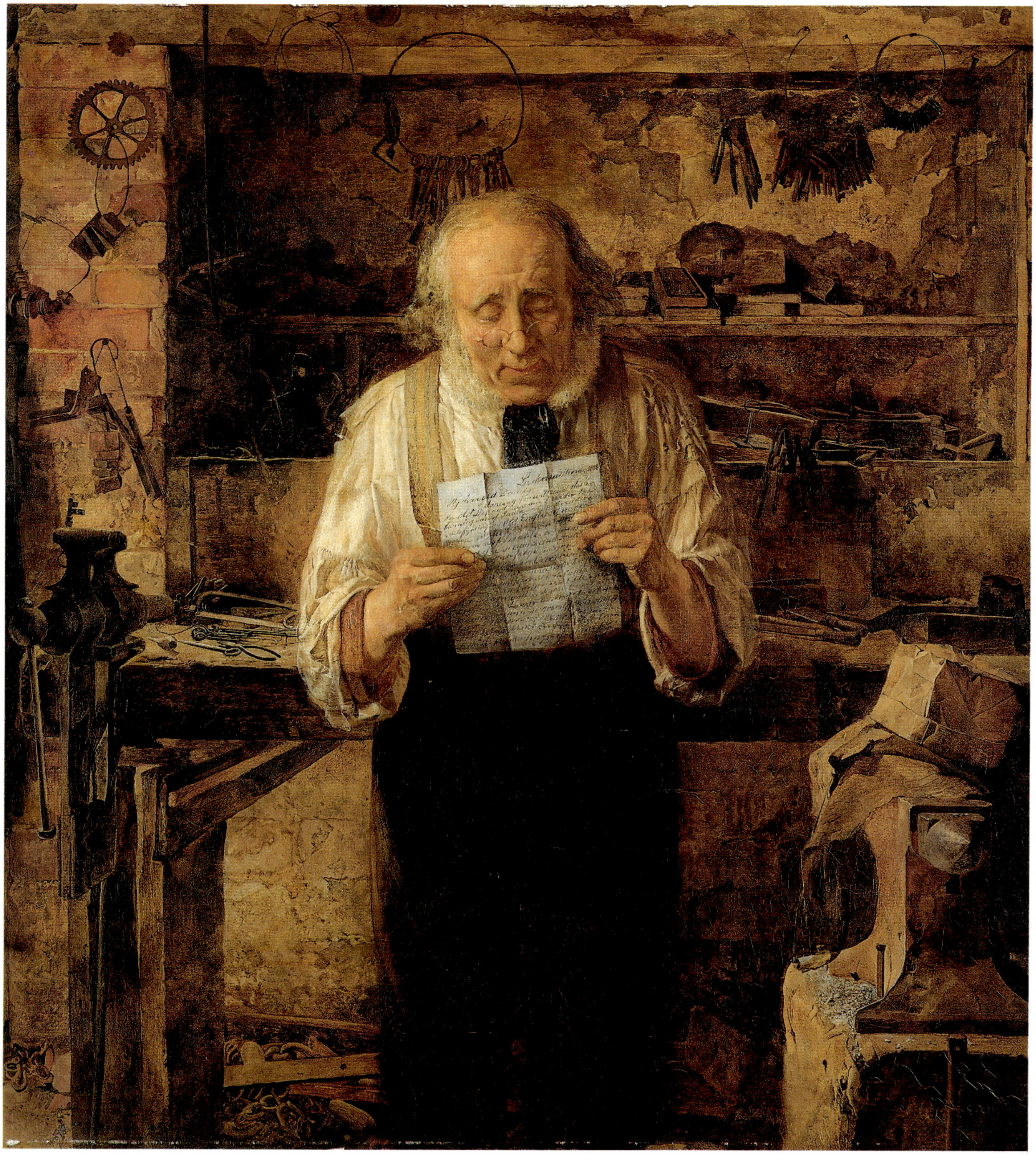

99
JAMES CAMPBELL
*News from my Lad*

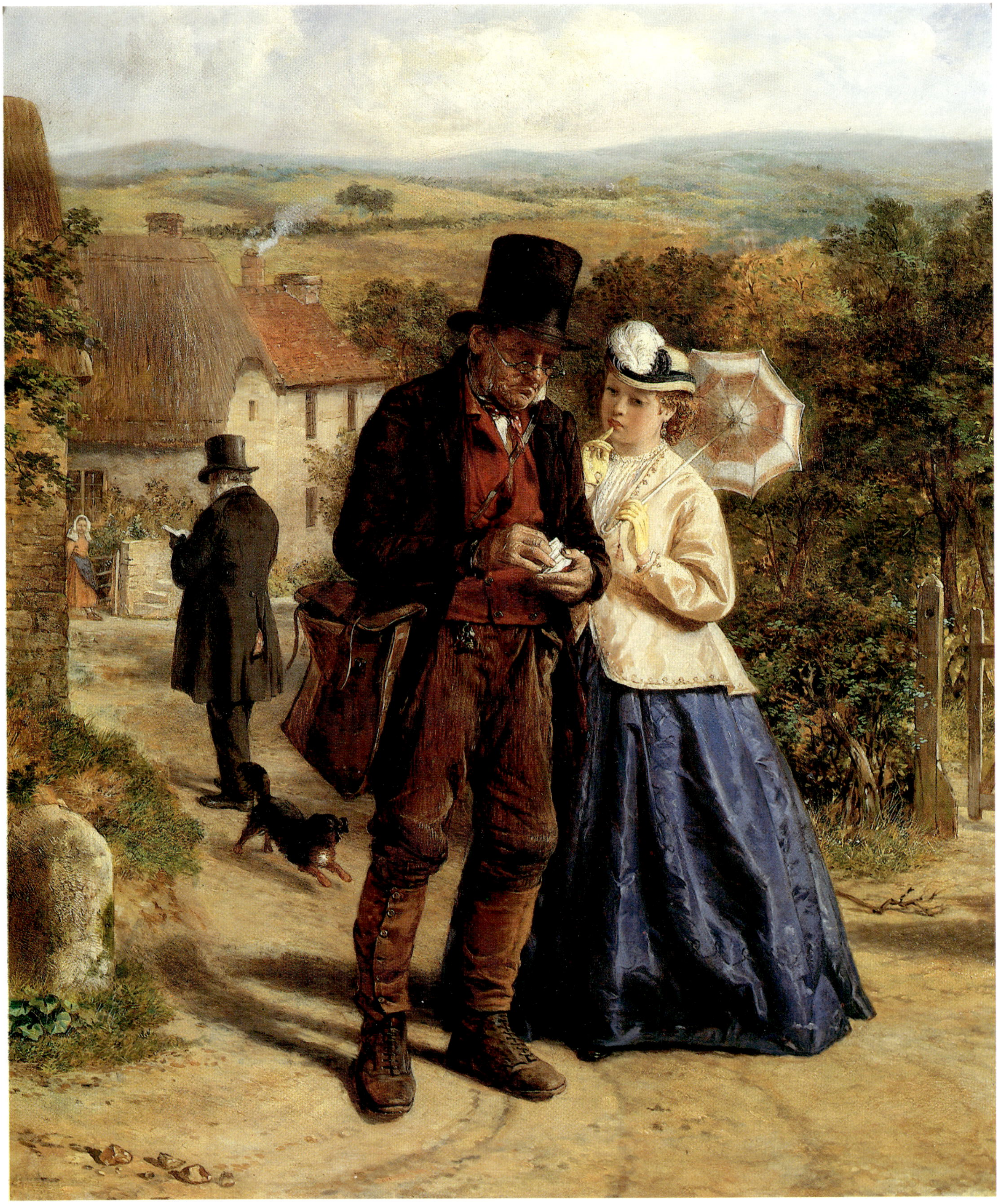

100
William Hemsley
*The Village Postman*

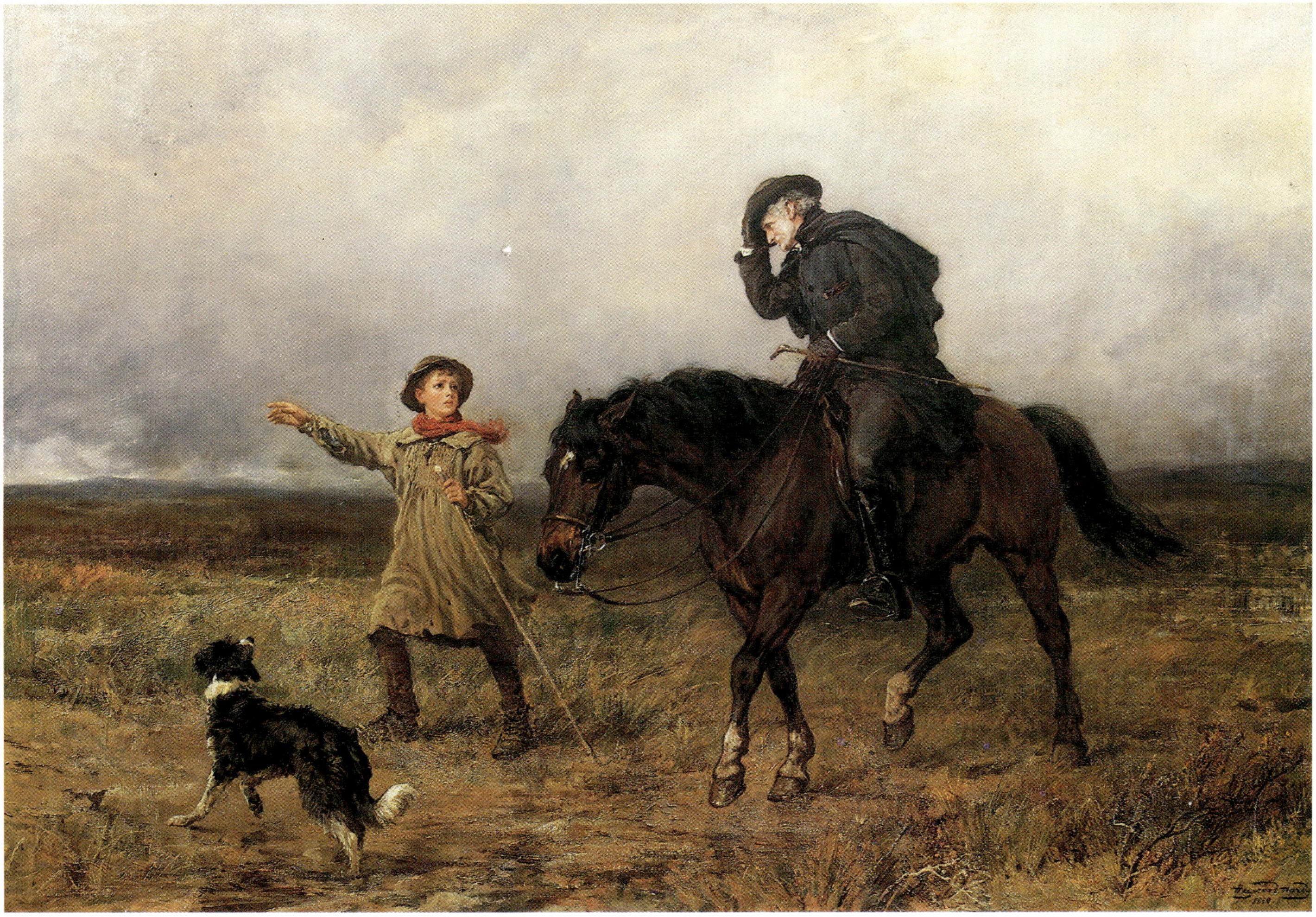

101
HEYWOOD HARDY
*Duty*

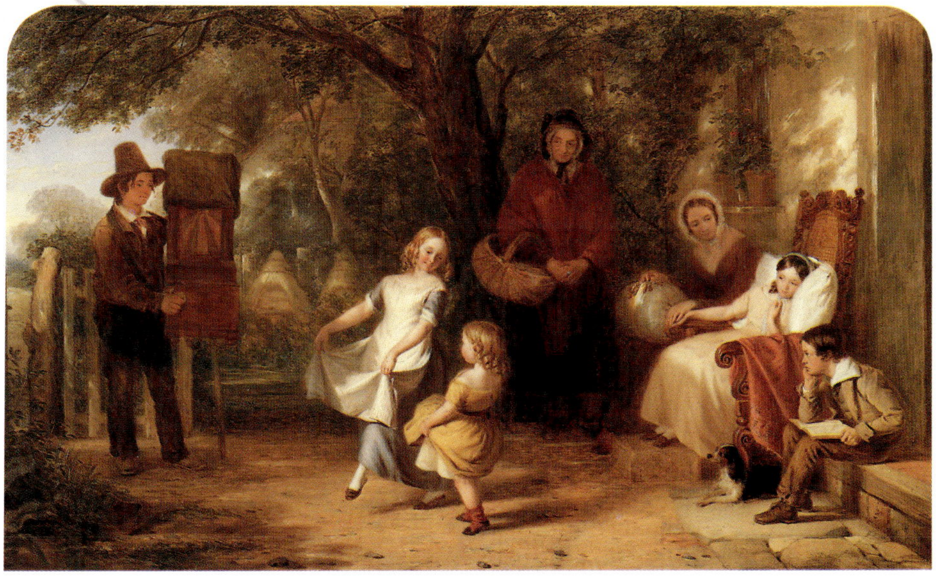

102
THOMAS WEBSTER
*Sickness and Health*

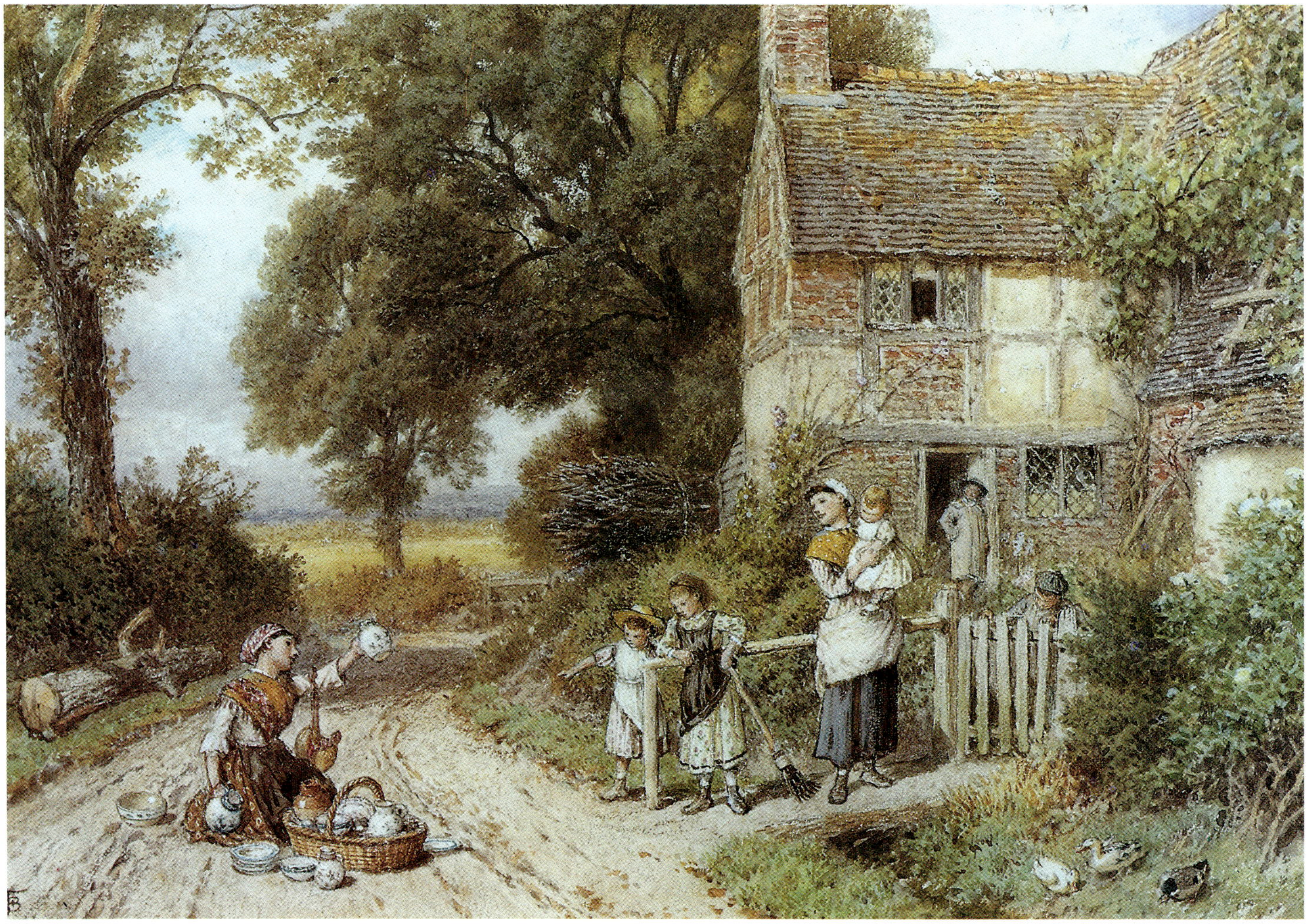

103
MYLES BIRKET FOSTER
*The China Pedlar*

salesman, a grey-haired, rabbinical old figure, producing his wares out of a wooden chest. On the floor beside him are his stick and travelling bag. Everyone is taking an interest, and the children are trying spectacles on as well. At the door appears a young man with a gun, a dog, and a rabbit, which suggests that this must be a farmer's or a gamekeeper's house. The shooting of rabbits, and all ground game, had for centuries been a jealously preserved right of the landowner, and it was not until quite late in the nineteenth century that a tenant was allowed to shoot rabbits on his farm. The growth of shops in country towns meant that travelling salesmen like this spectacle seller were gradually disappearing from the countryside. They could not compete with the lower price of mass-produced goods in the shops. At Lark Rise, the only pedlar who came was 'an old white-headed, white-bearded man, still hale and rosy,' but he was the 'last survivor of the once numerous clan' that used to visit the village.

Particularly enjoyed by the children were the toy seller and the sweet seller. James Stokeld, a north-eastern artist born in Sunderland, painted a particularly good picture of a travelling toy-maker with his donkey in 1864. In the background is what looks like a typical village in Stokeld's native County Durham. John Morgan and his son Frederick Morgan were both prolific Victorian painters of children, and John Morgan recorded the visit of a sweet seller (106), his basket full of oranges, biscuits, and stone bottles of lemonade or ginger beer.

Travelling showmen and entertainers were among the few forms of entertainment available to the poor, both in the country and the town, but they were already beginning to die out in Victorian times. One of the earliest Victorian painters to paint village scenes was William Frederick Witherington. His picture *The Dancing Bear* (105) records the excitement caused by the arrival of not only a bear, but a monkey and a performing dog. Other showmen exhibited performing fleas, birds and

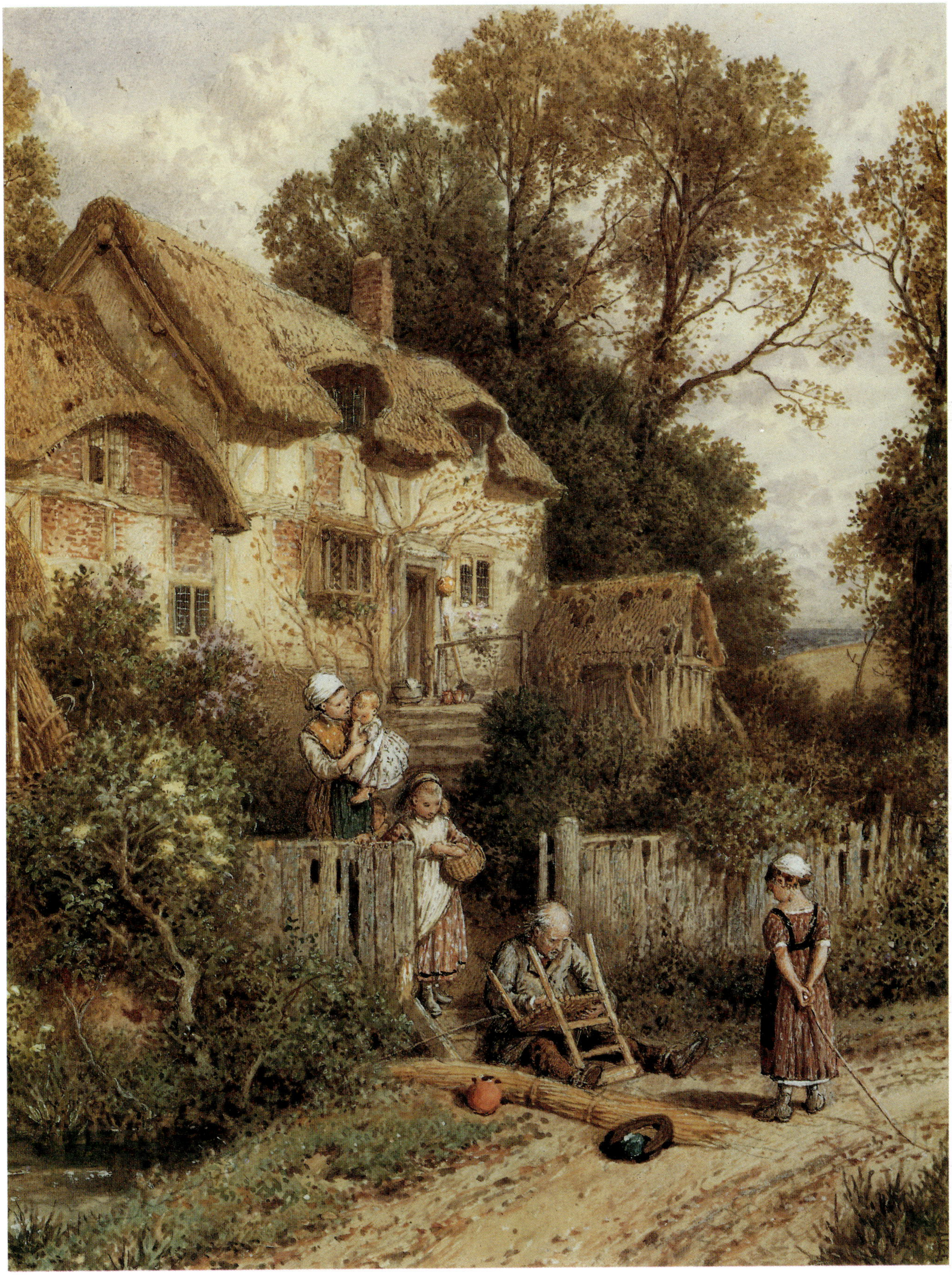

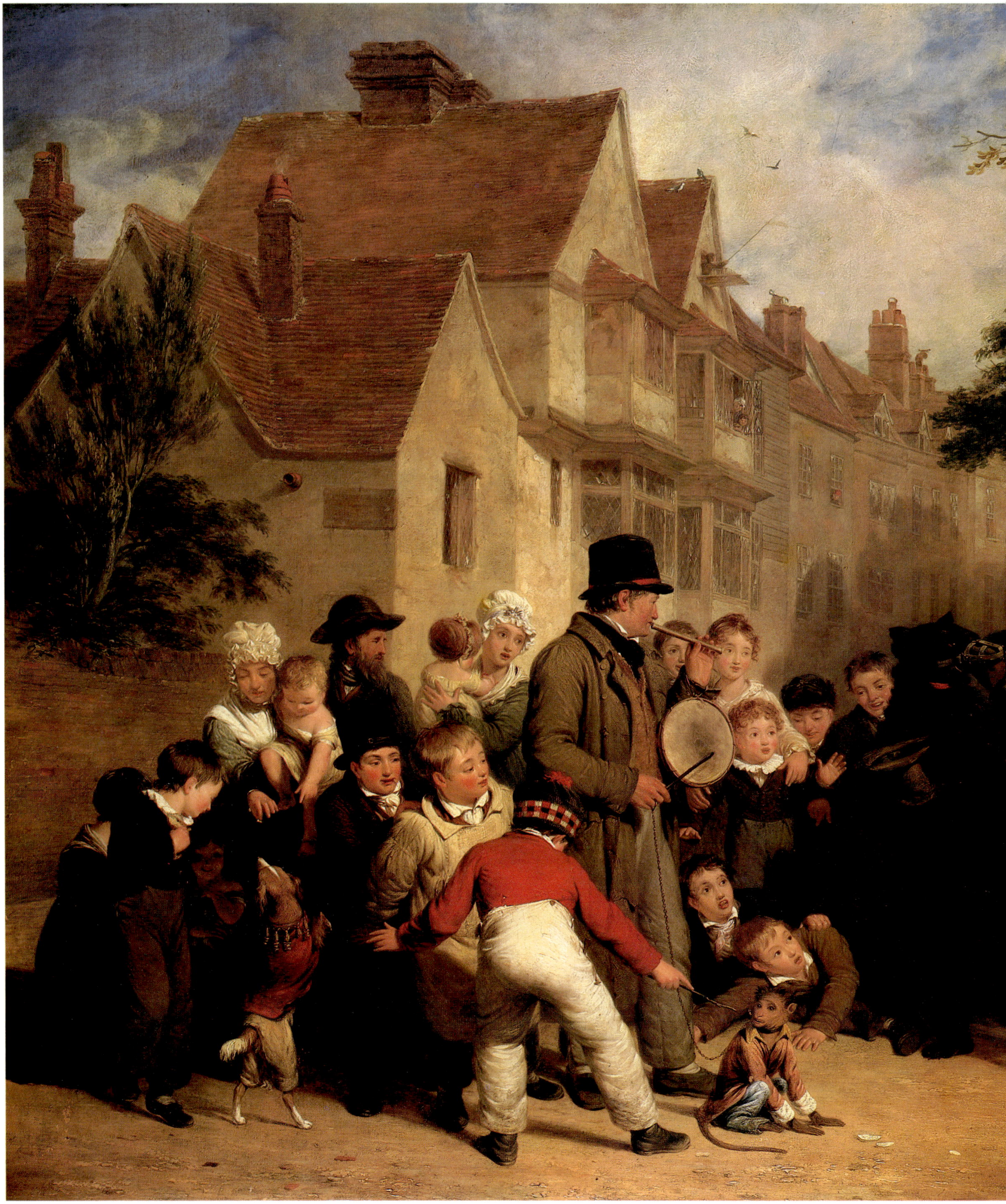

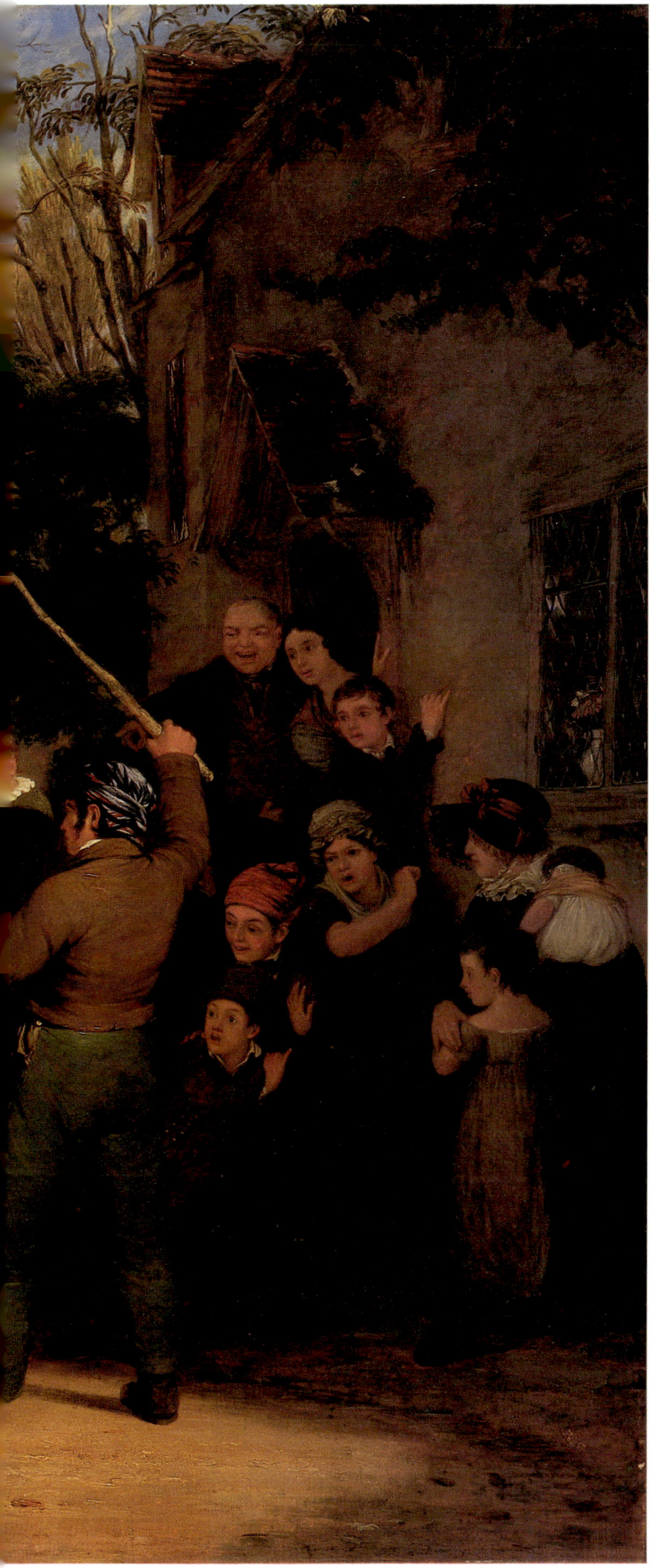

105
William Frederick Witherington
*The Dancing Bear*

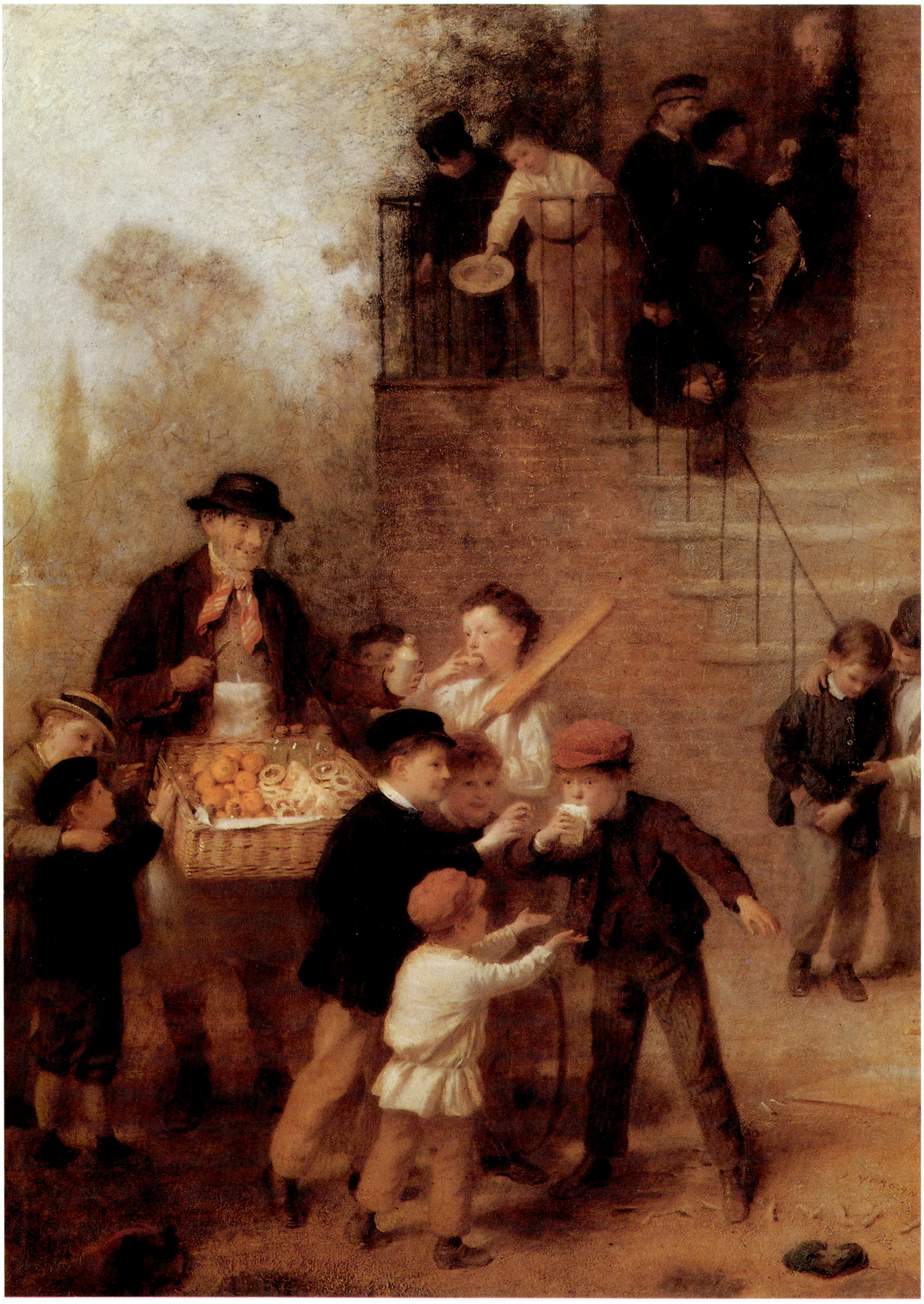

106
John Morgan
*The Sweet Seller*

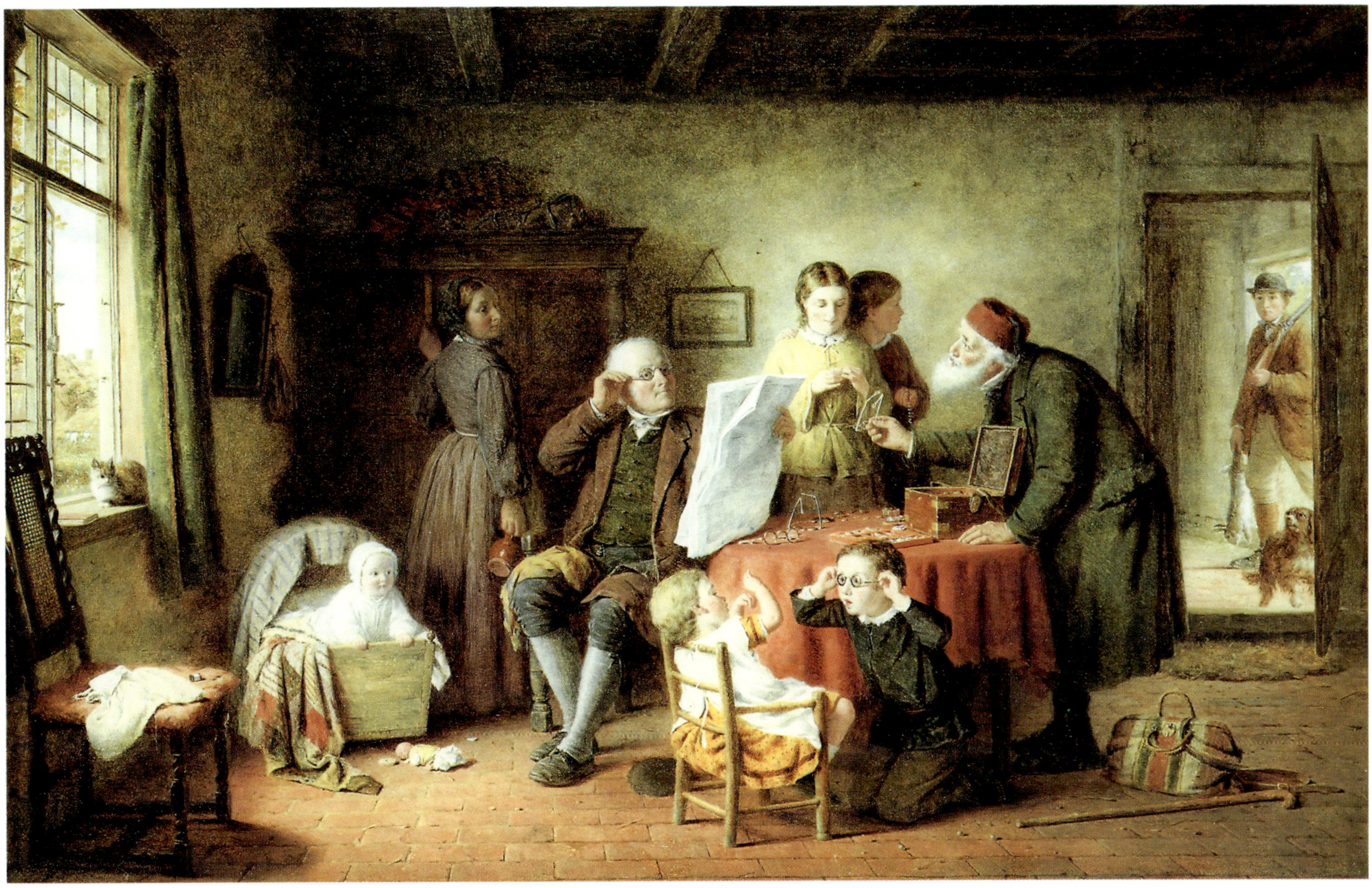

107
FREDERICK DANIEL HARDY
*Try this Pair*

mice, though we do not seem to have any paintings of these creatures. F.D. Hardy and the Cranbrook painters also liked to paint visiting entertainers, such as the hurdy-gurdy player with his pet monkey. Thomas Webster's *Sickness and Health* (102) shows two girls dancing to the music of an itinerant barrel-organ player. This picture, from 1843, is a sentimental genre picture typical of the period, contrasting the sick girl in her chair with her healthy sisters dancing. Although the sickness and death of young children were a harsh reality of the times, this little invalid does not look very ill, and the implication is that she will recover.

The travelling peep-show was popular with both children and adults, and is recorded in two delightful pictures, one by the Scottish artist John Burr (109), and the other by Edward John Cobbett (108). Henry Mayhew, in his encyclopaedic work *London Labour and London Poor*, interviewed a peep-show man, who said that 'Before the theatres lowered, a peep-show man could make 3s or 4s a day, at least, in fine weather, and on Saturday night about double that money'. He also observed that 'We takes more from children than grown people in London, and more from grown people than children in the country'. As far as the tastes of country people were concerned, he found that 'theatrical plays ain't no good for country towns, 'cause they don't understand such things there. People is werry fond of battles in the country, but a murder wot is well known is worth more than all the fights'. Other features of his show included The Dog of Montargis and the Forest of Bonday, The Forty Thieves, The Devil and Dr Faustus, The Death of Lord Nelson, Napoleon at Waterloo, and 'Queen Victoria embarking to start for Scotland, from the Dockyard at Voolich'.

Gipsies were a familiar sight in the Victorian countryside, with their painted caravans, and cavalcades of horses, goats and children. In Fred Walker's *Vagrants* (110) the models were a family of gipsies painted at Beddington, in Surrey. *The Vagrants*

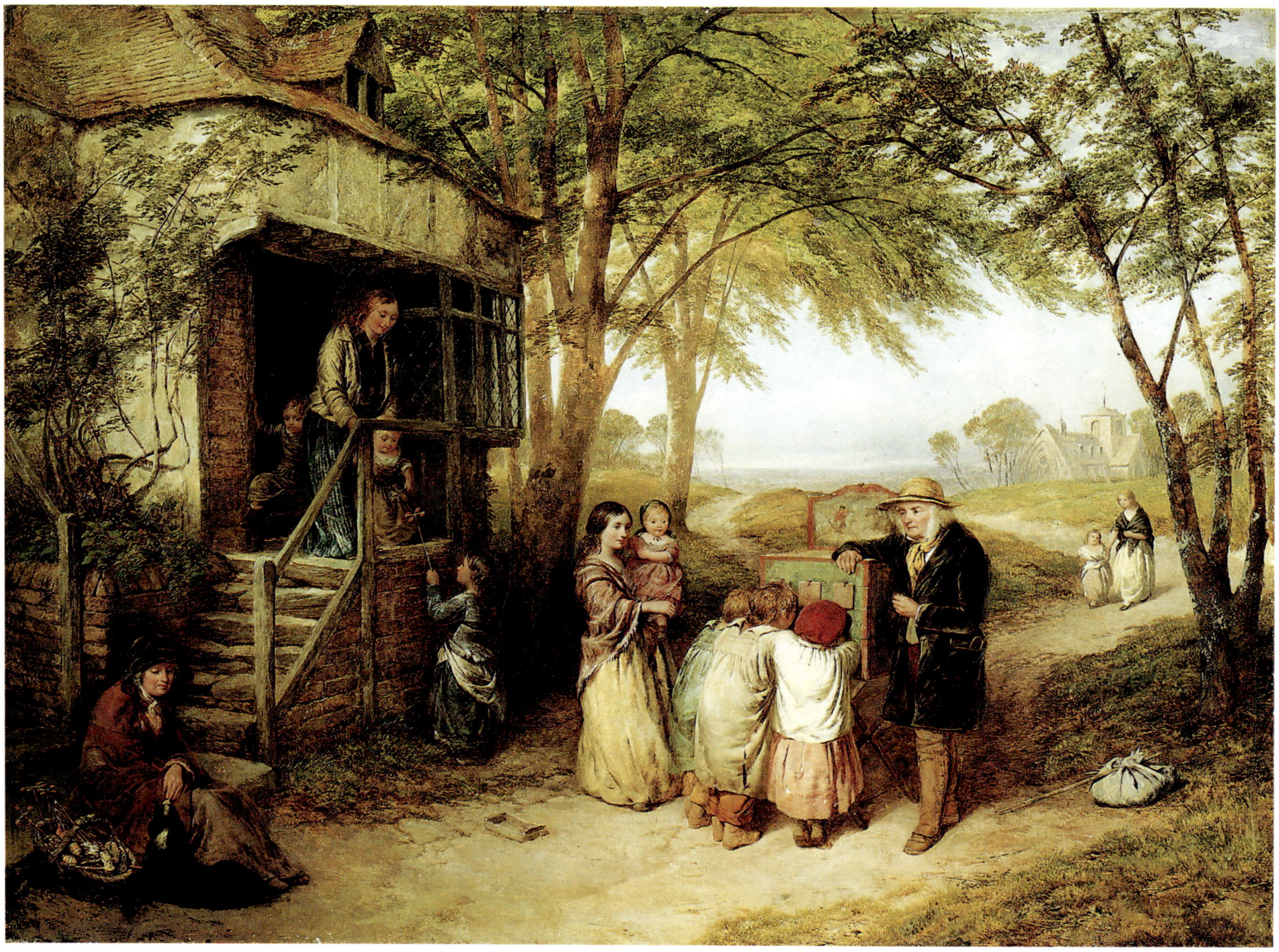

108
EDWARD JOHN COBBETT
*The Showman*

is typical of Walker's combination of poetic landscape and Millet-like peasants. The figures have wistful expressions, but deliberately-posed monumental attitudes, especially the girl on the right, who was posed in the studio. The Victorian fascination with gipsies is reflected in novels like George Borrow's *Lavengro*, and *Aylwin* by Theodore Watts-Dunton. The gipsy beauty was often a *femme fatale*: Jane Morris, wife of William Morris, or Keomi, mistress and model of the painter Frederick Sandys. Francis Kilvert was much taken with the beauty of 'Gipsy Lizzie', a young girl in his reading class, and wrote of her, 'How is the indescribable beauty of that most lovely face to be described . . .?'

Laura, in *Lark Rise*, was afraid of gipsies, having been warned by her mother that they stole children. But all the same she was fascinated by them: '. . . the gipsies were there, their painted caravan drawn up, their poor old skeleton horse turned loose to graze, and their fire with a cooking pot over it, as though the whole road belonged to them . . . full of dark, wild life, foreign to the hamlet children and fascinating, yet terrifying.' One artist who was equally fascinated by gipsies was Alfred Munnings, whose many pictures of them conjure up the air of exotic unfamiliarity they must have brought to the Victorian countryside. Munnings loved painting 'the gippoes' as he called them, and used them in his pictures of Hampshire hop-pickers, and also many other pictures of gipsy camps and horse fairs. 'The families that I got to know,' he wrote in his autobiography, 'had picturesque children, dogs and horses. The women had, somewhere in the back of each caravan, great black hats with ostrich feathers, laid away for gala days. . . . Nobody could beat their style of dress. . . .' Munnings, like many artists of his generation, loved the gipsies not only for their exotic looks, and their skill with horses, but also for their bohemian way of life, which many a Bloomsbury artist tried to imitate.

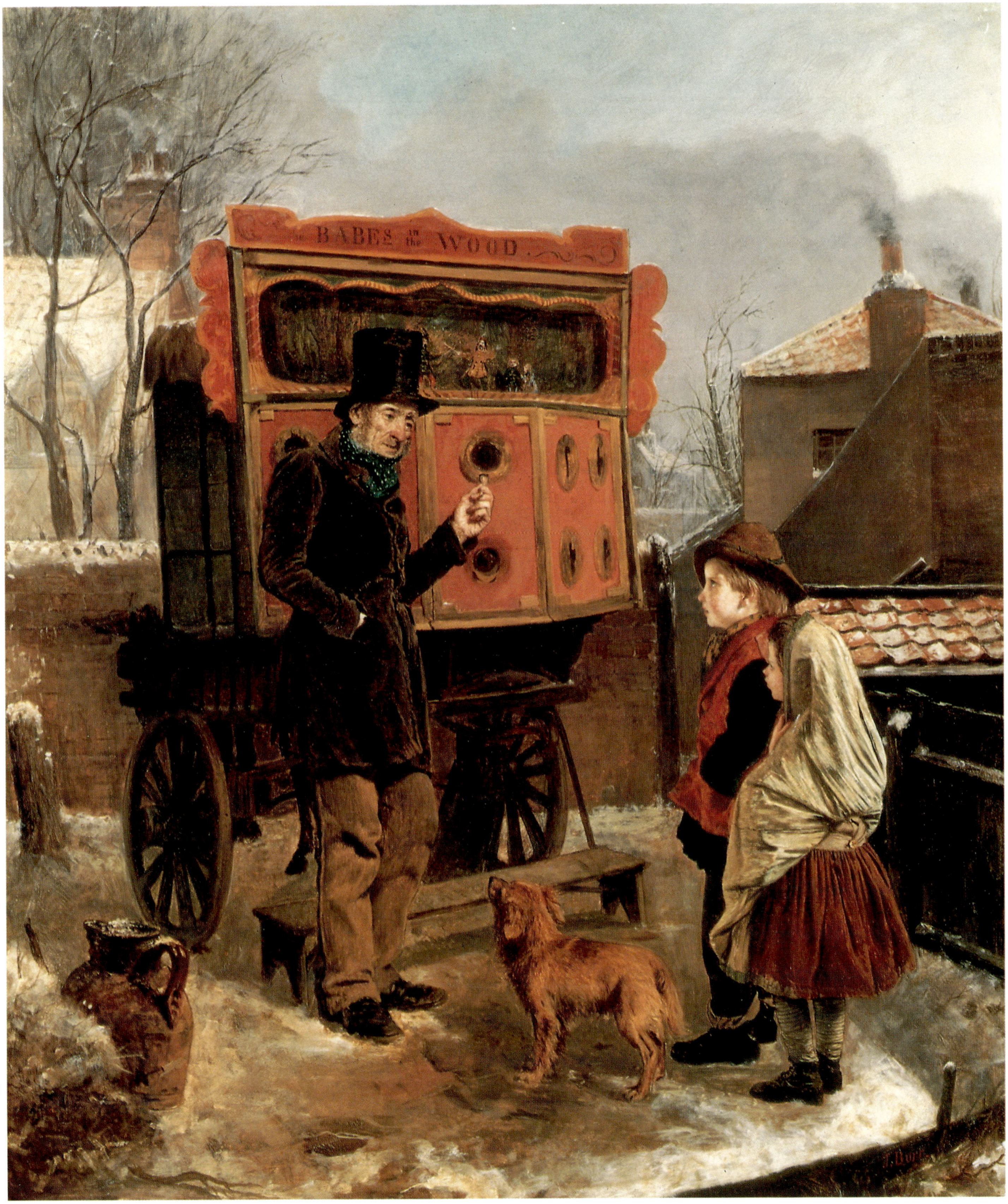


109
JOHN BURR
*The Peepshow*

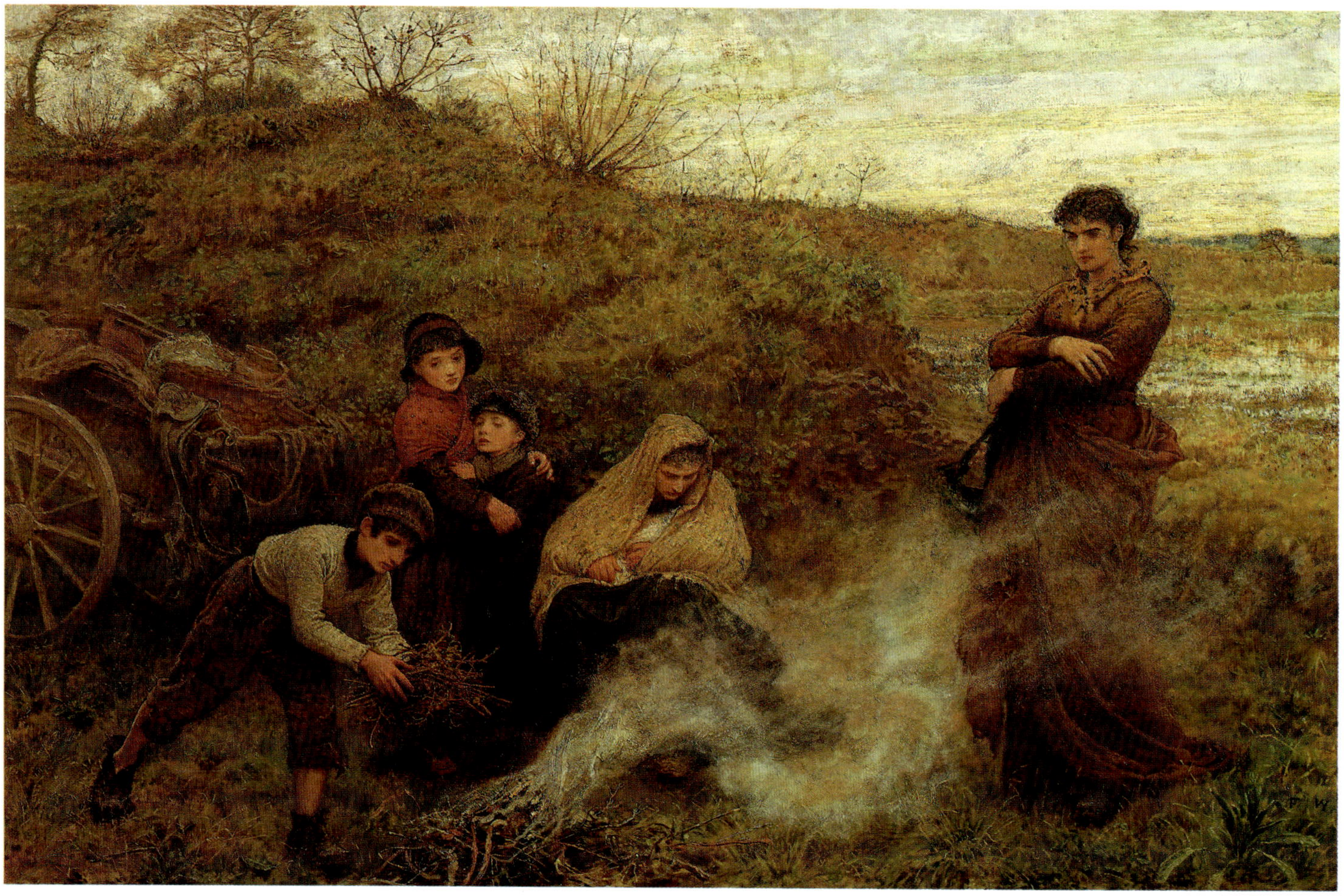

110
FRED WALKER
*The Vagrants*

Vagrants and tramps were also a common sight in the countryside, and children tended also to give them a wide berth, like the gipsies. When out for a walk, or on her way to school, Laura of *Lark Rise* would often see 'a dirty, unshaven man, his rags topped with a battered bowler, lighting a fire of sticks by the roadside to boil his tea-can'. Sometimes whole families could be seen on the march, and Laura's father once found a family of five peeping out at him from a ditch by the roadside. These vagrants were generally harmless, and the villagers were usually kind to them, giving them food and drink, or letting them sleep in a barn or under a rick. More alarming to children must have been the appearance of a 'reddleman', a traditional west-country figure who specialised in the red dye used for marking sheep. In Hardy's novel *The Return of the Native*, the reddleman Diggory Venn is one of the main characters of the story, and an inhabitant of the forbidding Egdon Heath.

The greatest excitement of the year was the local fair. This only took place once a year, in the nearest market-town, but people flocked to it from all the villages and farms for miles around. A travelling theatre might set up, and there would be all kinds of competitions, such as climbing a greasy pole for the prize of a leg of mutton at the top. Alfred Williams's local fair was Highworth Michaelmas Fair. Like many fairs, this was a market, a hiring fair and a fun-fair all rolled into one. 'This used to be a great muster,' wrote Williams:

> vast crowds flocked in from all the villages round; the town was quite full of sight-seers, especially in the evening – carters and carter-boys, cowmen and shepherds, with their wives and families; old and young, children and grey-beards together. . . . The fair was held in the market-place; but the whole of the principal streets were packed with booths and shows, swings, roundabouts, and other means of amusement; you could scarcely move for the crowds of people.

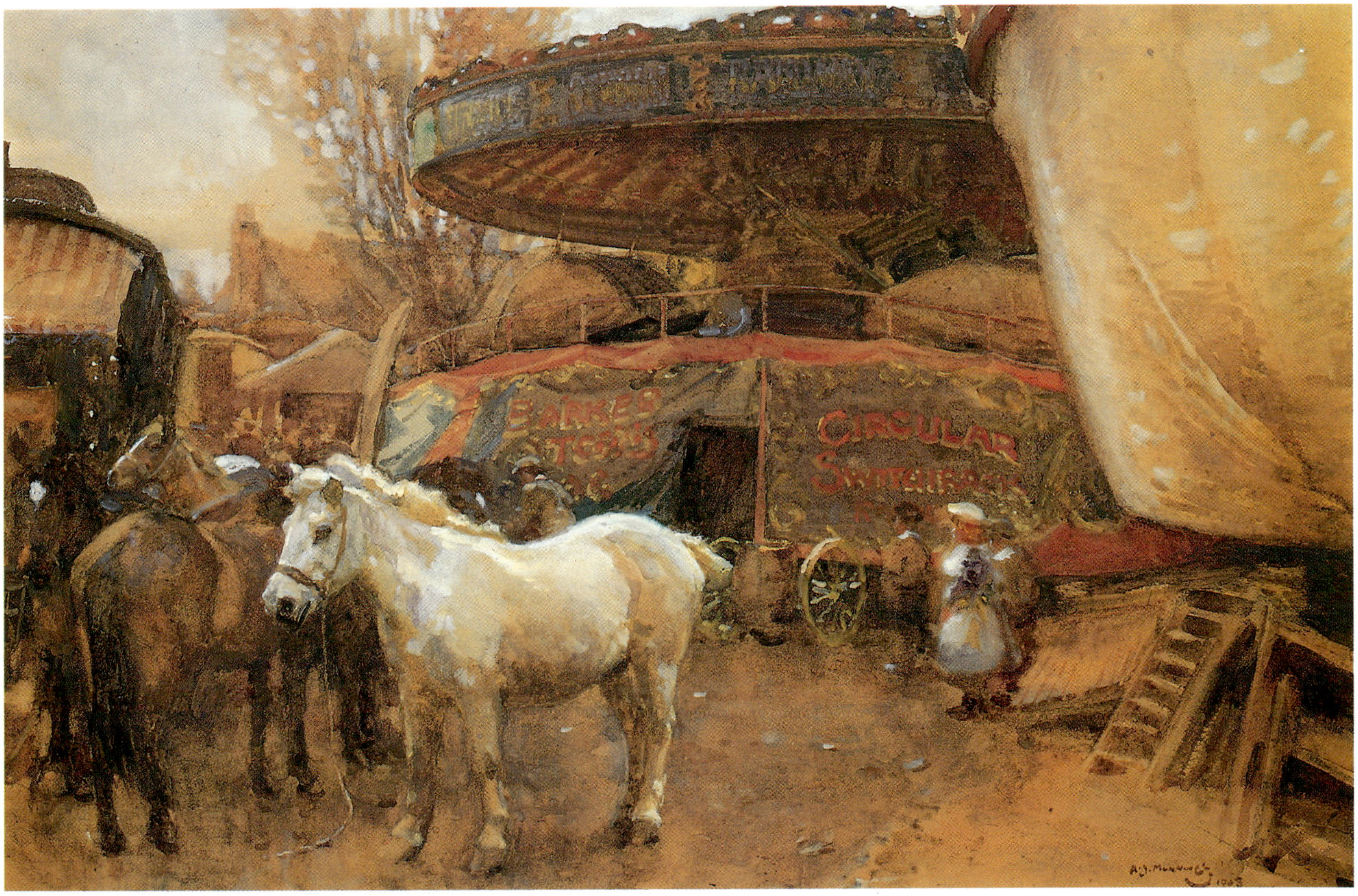


111
SIR ALFRED MUNNINGS
*The Fair has Come*

For many country people the local fair or feast day was one of their few days a year off work; something to be looked forward to with intense excitement and anticipation. Some of the great fairs, such as the Nottingham Goose Fair, or St. Giles's Fair in Oxford, became bigger and more popular than ever during the Victorian period. Another important function of these great country fairs was the hiring of workers by the local farmers. Williams recorded that at Highworth, the men who wanted a job put whipcord in their coats or hats, and stood on the pathway around the marketplace. The farmer then:

> walked down the street, eyeing them all up and down till he saw one that pleased him: then he went up to him and asked him a series of questions – where he had worked, and for how long, whether he was married, the number and age of his children, and what he expected to receive in wages. If the answers were satisfactory, he offered the man a shilling; if the other accepted it the bargain was considered as made: there was no setting the bond aside afterwards.

Something of the excitement of the fair is conveyed by Munnings's watercolour of 1908, *The Fair has Come* (111).

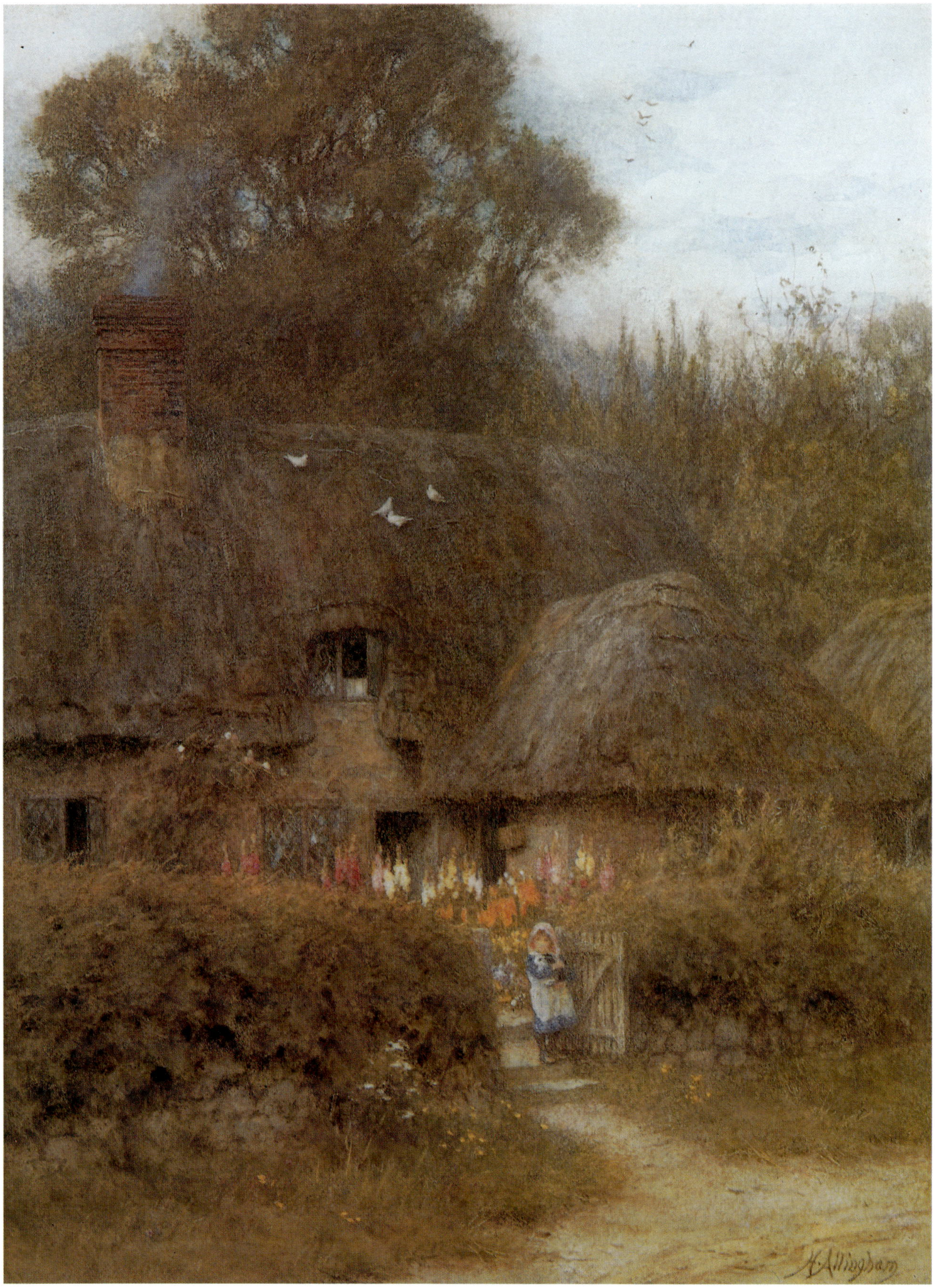

112
HELEN ALLINGHAM
*At the Cottage Gate*

## *Chapter Nine*

# THE COTTAGE

A tent pitched in a world not aright
It seemed, whose inmates, every one,
On tranquil faces bore the light
Of duties beautifully done.

COVENTRY PATMORE, *The Angel in the House*

THE COTTAGE WAS FOR THE VICTORIANS MORE than just a small house in the country – it was a cherished symbol of an innocence they felt they had lost, and the epitome of a way of life that they knew to be disappearing. Paintings of home and family life are the most common of all Victorian narrative pictures. The cosy room, the fireside, the children and pets would feature in countless pictures at the Royal Academy every year – small, sentimental, often exquisitely painted, and always extolling the joys of domestic happiness. Many pictures might be of middle-class or prosperous families, but the cottage was far and away the most popular symbol of homely domesticity.

The home and the family were, after all, the central institutions of Victorian life. In an age of sweeping social change, the family provided security and continuity. The very competitiveness and uncertainty of Victorian life seem to have encouraged a corresponding elevation of the spiritual values of domesticity. For Ruskin, home was 'a sacred place, a vestal temple, a temple of the hearth watched over by household gods'. Presiding over the temple was the wife, the 'Angel in the House' as Coventry Patmore described her: dutiful, submissive, obedient, faithful, pure and decorative. Lord Tennyson had confirmed that a woman's place was in the home in his poem *The Princess*:

Man for the field and woman for the hearth;
Man for the sword, and for the needle she;
Man with the head, and woman with the heart;
Man to command, and woman to obey.

The most prolific and the most passionate delineator of the English cottage was Helen Allingham. Her exquisitely delicate watercolours of old thatched cottages in Surrey and Wiltshire

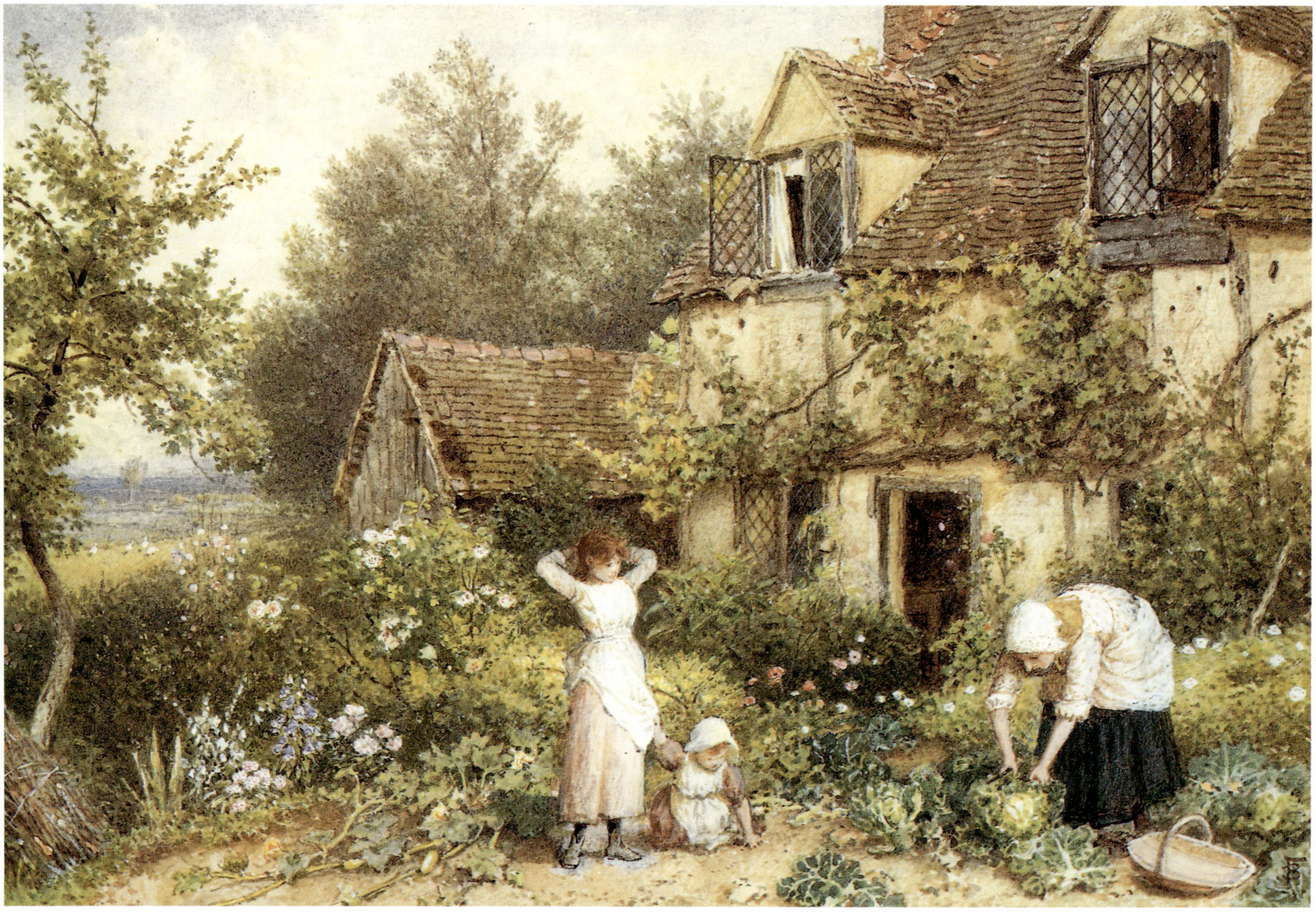

113
MYLES BIRKET FOSTER
*At the Cottage Door*

are now probably the most famous of all images of the English cottage (2, 112). Her two best-known books, *Happy England* (1903) and *The Cottage Homes of England* (1909), have also helped to establish her reputation as the leading exponent of the cottage idyll. She not only painted cottages, but village scenes as well, often with women and children, cottage interiors, again often with figures, and also wonderful landscapes with wild flowers, as we have already seen in Chapter 1. People often think that Helen Allingham's cottages are too sentimental, and yet her purpose in painting them was as much preservationist as artistic. She realised that they represented a rapidly disappearing way of life, and would soon be swept away or drastically altered. She wanted to record them before it was too late. Her watercolours are therefore not so much sentimental as nostalgic. They are no more sentimental than the writings of Flora Thompson, who was also describing a vanishing way of life.

Allingham came to painting cottages by a curious route. She was born Helen Paterson, the daughter of a Scottish doctor living in Burton-on-Trent, studied at the Royal Academy schools, and first earned her living as an illustrator for the *Graphic*. She also illustrated Thomas Hardy's *Far from the Madding Crowd*, although a more unlikely illustrator for Hardy could hardly be imagined. According to Marcus Huish, author of *Happy England*, Hardy was 'fairly complimentary' about the illustrations, which was probably a tactful way of saying he thought them quite unsuitable. In 1874, she married William Allingham, the Irish poet, joining a literary circle that included Carlyle, Tennyson, Browning and Ruskin. In 1881 she and her husband moved out of London to the Surrey village of Witley, near Haslemere. It was here that her interest in painting cottages and village life really blossomed.

Stylistically, Allingham's work might be described as by Fred Walker out of Birket Foster. At Witley she was a neigh-

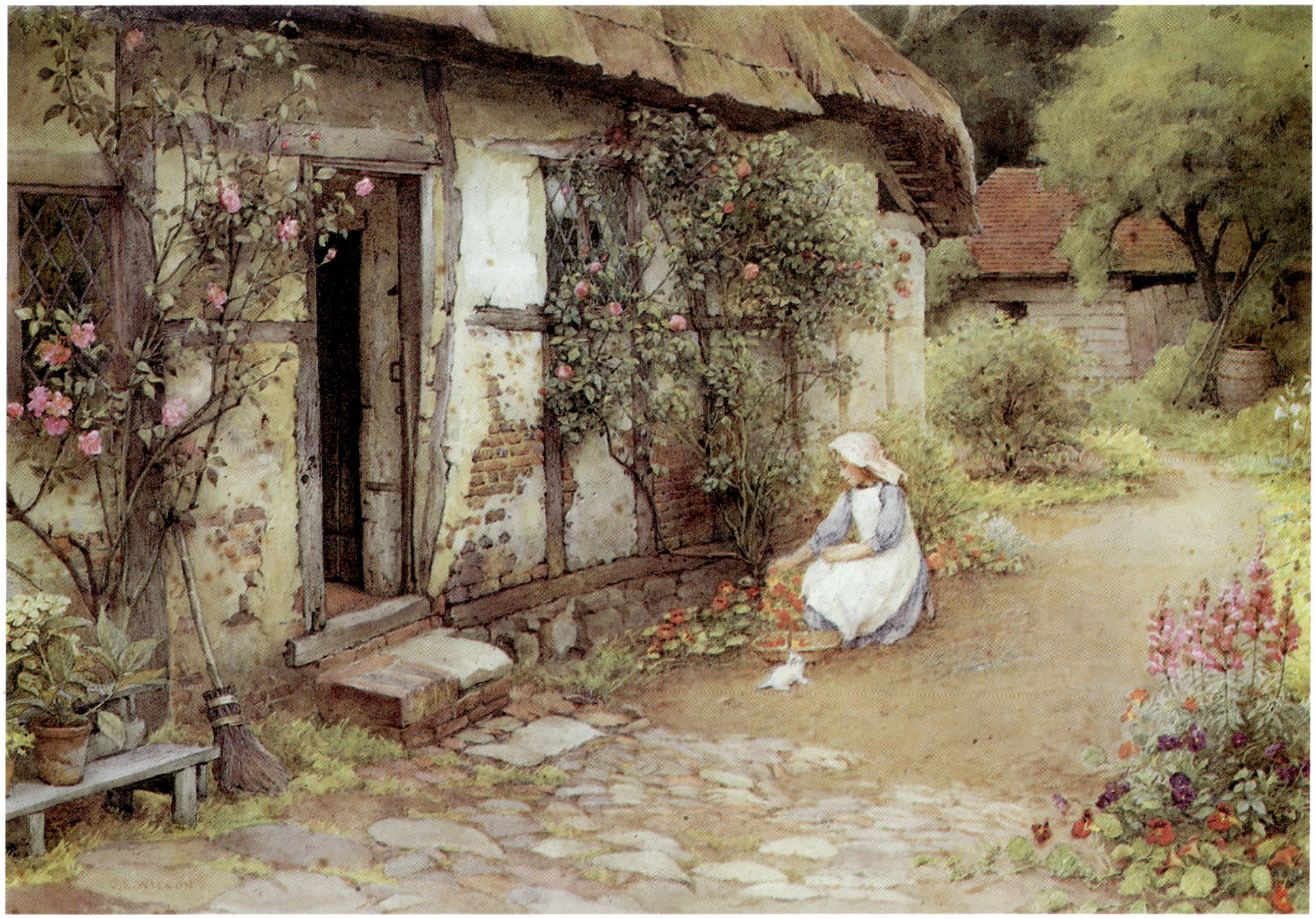

114
CHARLES EDWARD WILSON
*Outside a Cottage*

bour of Foster's, and there is no doubt that she greatly admired his work and to some extent imitated his subjects. But she also learned much from Fred Walker, her fellow-illustrator on the *Graphic*: in particular her simplicity and directness of approach. Her work is considerably more poetic and subtle than that of Foster, whose cottage scenes can seem quite garish when compared directly with hers (113). Allingham's colours are wonderfully soft and delicate; she was unquestionably one of the greatest of all Victorian watercolourists. Ruskin greatly admired her work, and in *The Art of England* (1884) compared her to Kate Greenaway, praising her skill at capturing 'the gesture, character and humour of charming children in country landscapes'. W. Graham Robertson compared Allingham favourably with Birket Foster in his memoirs, *Time Was* (1931). 'Her lovely little transcripts of the Surrey lanes and woodlands, of the school of Birket Foster – but, to me, fresher, more fragrant, and closer to nature than the work of the elder painter – are delights to the eye and lasting memorials of the fast-vanishing beauty of our countryside.'

Foster and Allingham had many imitators, but few equals. *At the Cottage Door* painters were extremely numerous in the last quarter of the nineteenth century, and the genre remained popular even up to 1914 and beyond. Among the best of this school were Arthur Claude Strachan, Henry J. Johnstone, Ethel Hughes, William Affleck, and Charles Edward Wilson (114), another Surrey artist who lived at Addiscombe, near Croydon.

The cottage hearth was an equally popular subject. One assiduous recorder of interiors was F.D. Hardy (115). Some of his early works of this kind are beautifully observed, and quite unsentimental, omitting the usual children, pets and other familiar props of the cottage idyll painters. The old kitchen, illustrated here, is delineated as dispassionately as a Dutch seventeenth-century kitchen by Ostade or Brekelenkamp. Another keen observer of cottage interiors, often with old

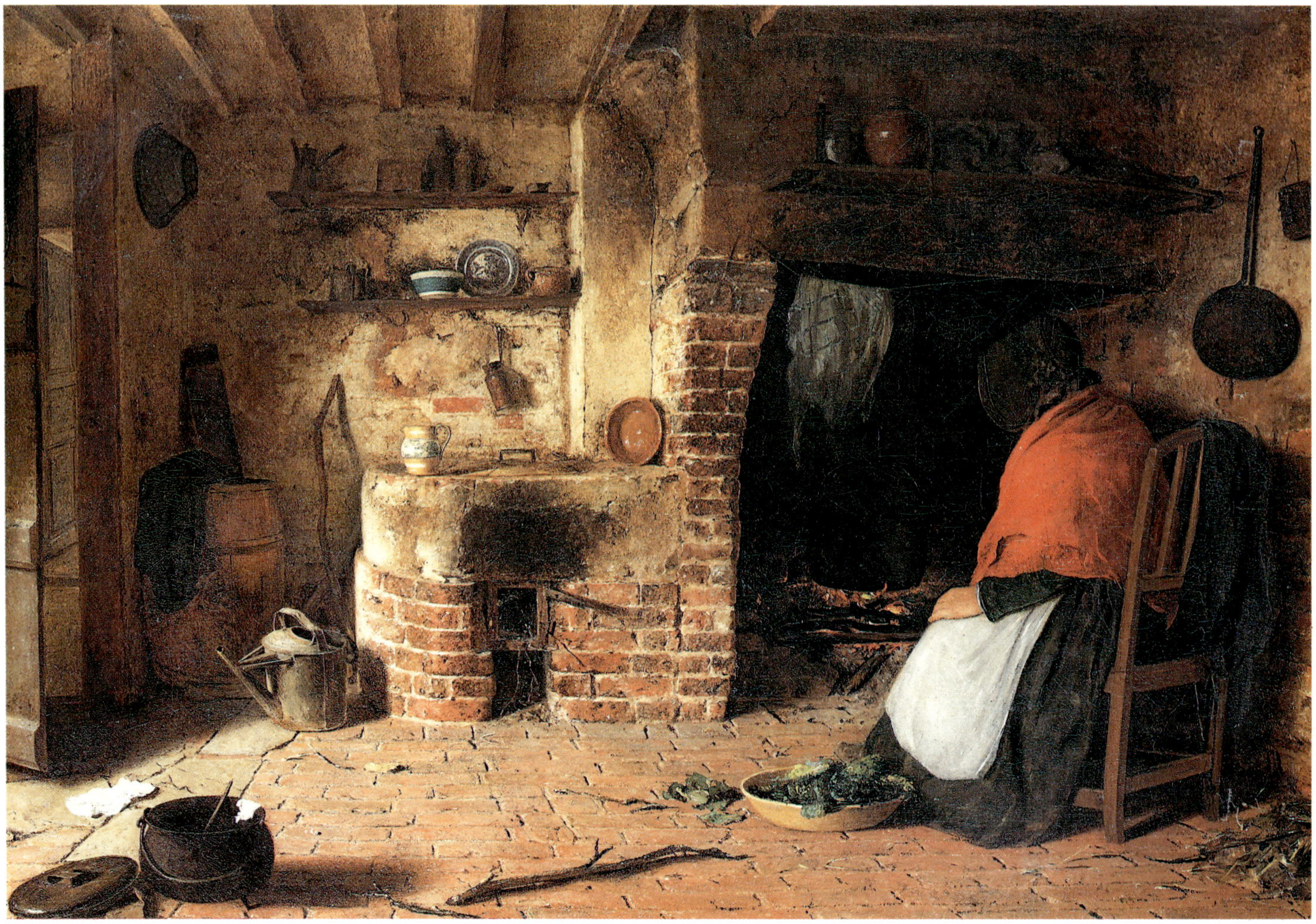

115
FREDERICK DANIEL HARDY
*A Cottage Fireside*

couples sitting by the fireplace, was the little-known Henry Spernon Tozer (118), who worked almost entirely in watercolour. His interiors always look as if they are based on real observation: the valance over the fireplace and the cluster of objects on the mantelpiece look quite authentic. Alfred Williams described his local Wiltshire cottages and farmhouses as 'full of curious odds and ends . . . and numerous quaint bits of furniture, beautiful old-fashioned chinaware, coloured prints, ancient guns and implements, cups, utensils, and every description of ornament.'

Tozer was unusual in painting old people in their cottages; the vast majority of cottage interiors, as we have seen, are concerned with children and family life. The cottage is almost invariably portrayed as a place of peace, security, and domestic happiness. Sentimentality is implicit in most of these pictures, to varying degrees, but one of the most restrained of the cottage artists was Joseph Clark. His *Chimney Corner* (116) has an authentic feel to it, and his *Labourer's Welcome* (117) is also a genuine if somewhat idealised picture of a relatively prosperous cottage. Here we see a farm labourer, reflected in the mirror, returning to his cosy home. His wife is both pretty and domesticated, and keeps their cottage in a pleasing state of organised clutter. The grandfather clock tells us that it is five past six – the hour when most farmworkers would return from work.

People in cottage pictures always look happy and cheerful, even on washing day, as we see in Pierre Edouard Frere's picture (120). Frere was a French artist, but a regular exhibitor of cottage scenes at the Royal Academy. Flora Thompson described Miss Dorcas Lane's wash-day in detail. She kept to the 'old middle-class country custom of one huge washing of linen every six weeks', and a local washerwoman came in for two days to help. Miss Lane had a separate wash-house, although the average cottager would have to do the washing in

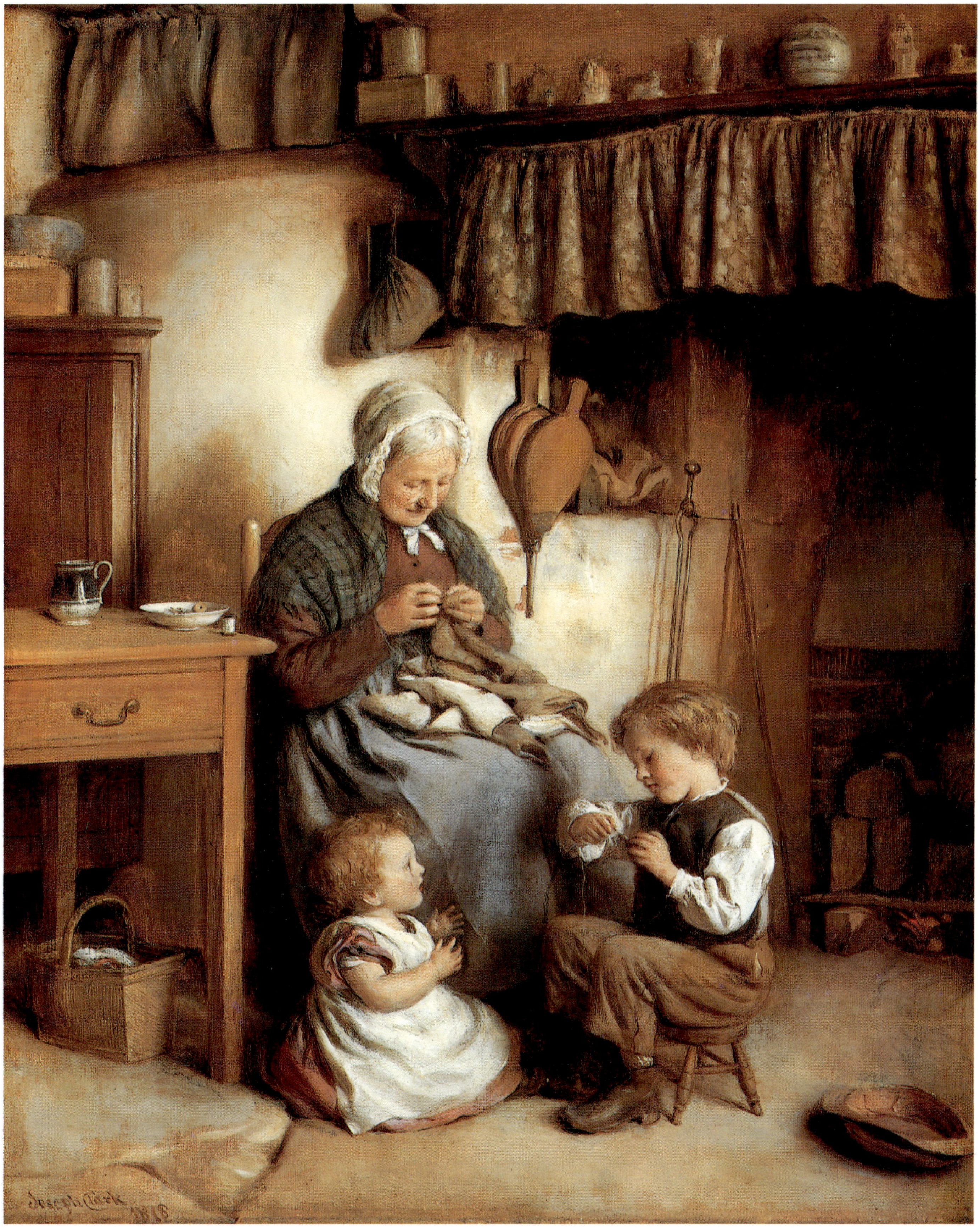

116
JOSEPH CLARK
*The Chimney Corner*

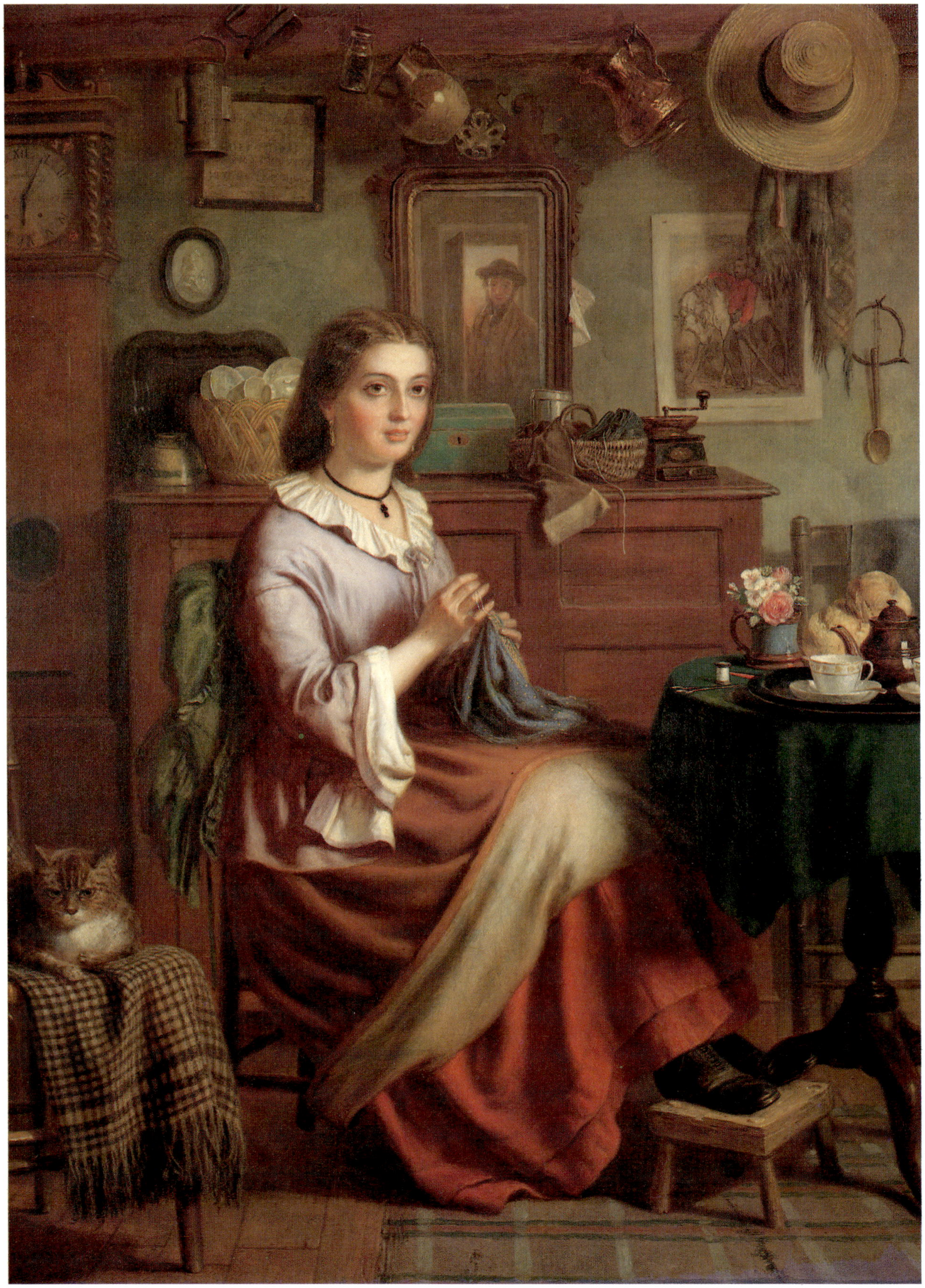

117
JOSEPH CLARK
*The Labourer's Welcome*

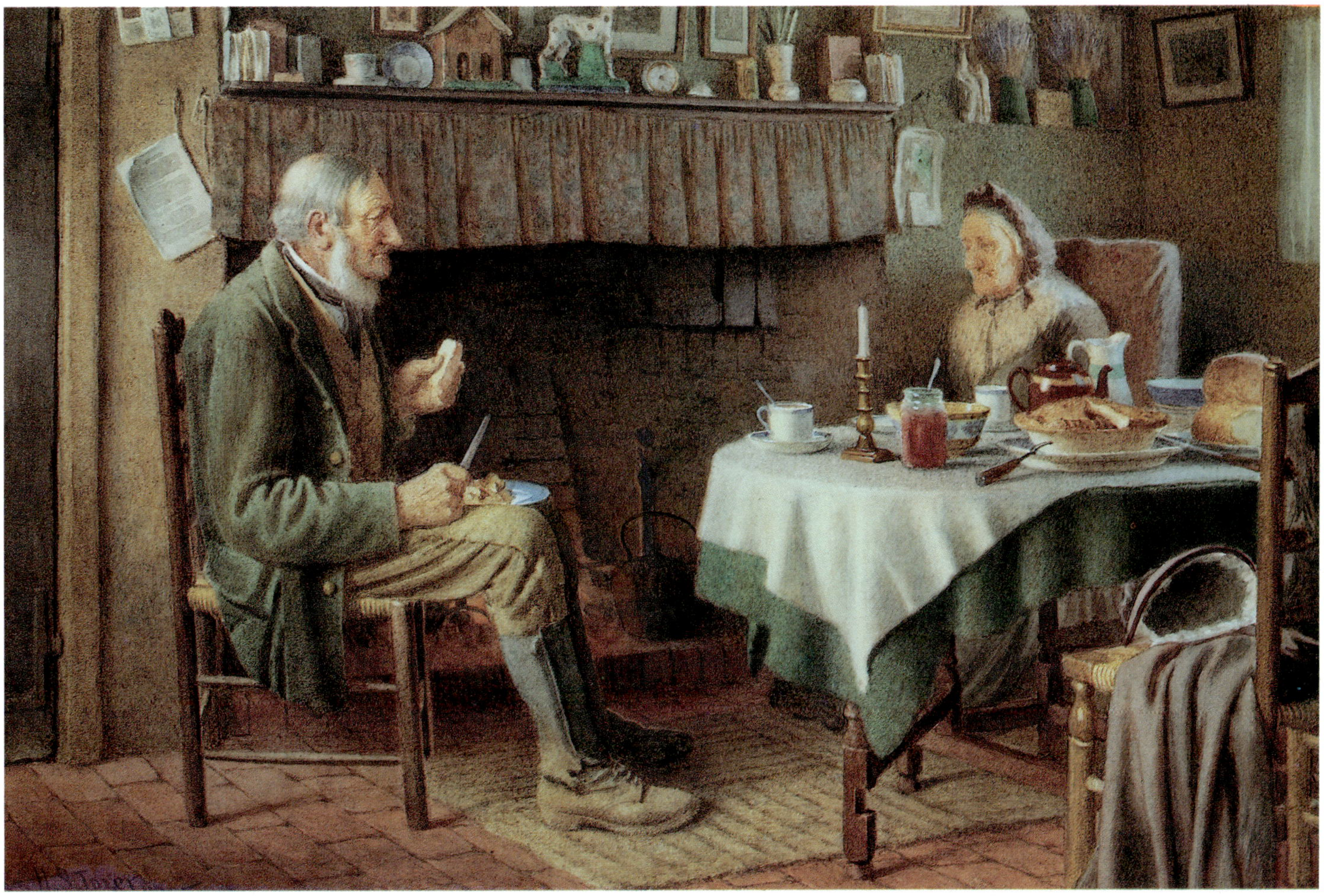

118
HENRY SPERNON TOZER
*The Evening Meal*

the main room, in front of the fire, as in Frere's picture. Afterwards 'sheets and pillow-cases and towels were billowing in the wind on a line the whole length of the garden, while Miss Lane's more intimate personal wear dried modestly on a line by the hen-house, "out of the men's sight".'

Painters also liked to show cottage industry still flourishing, as in Katherine L. Beard's *Spinning* (121). By the time this picture was painted, in the 1890s, the spinning of wool was no longer a cottage industry. It had long since been killed off by the factories and textile mills, and was only practised in a few places and for domestic use only. Most Victorian paintings of cottage life are, like this one, therefore harking back to an earlier, happier time, when the cottage housewife could supplement her income by practising one of the cottage crafts. The truth was that cottage industries had always been exploited, usually by the middleman, who came round to buy their products and take them to the local market. Much as writers like William Morris, or Ebenezer Elliott, author of the *Corn Law Rhymes*, deplored the decline of crafts in the countryside, it was an absolutely inevitable economic process.

Over all these cottage pictures hangs an atmosphere of rosy unreality. We know from contemporary reports that most cottages were cramped, insanitary and damp. The more picturesque the cottage the more likely it was to be unhealthy. Dickens pointed out what fast friends picturesqueness and typhoid usually were. Painters simply gloss over unpleasant facts by omitting them. We never see a privy, or the family pig. We see beds, but no suggestion of the fact that three or four people might have to share them. Cottages usually look reasonably tidy and well-furnished, although we know that the cottages of the very poor contained practically no furniture at all. But the Victorian spectator preferred to cling to the myth of the cottage idyll, and the painters willingly collaborated in perpetuating it.

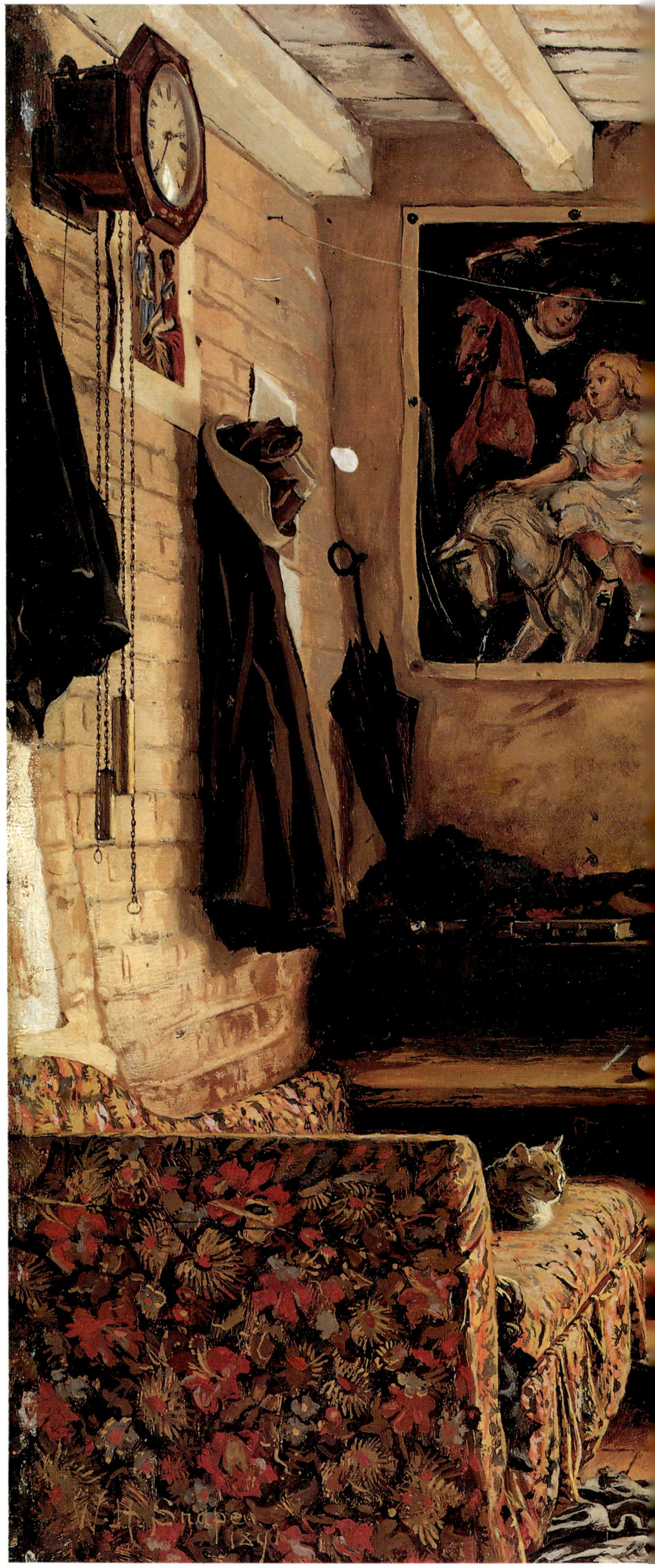

119
WILLIAM H. SNAPE
*A Cottage Scene*

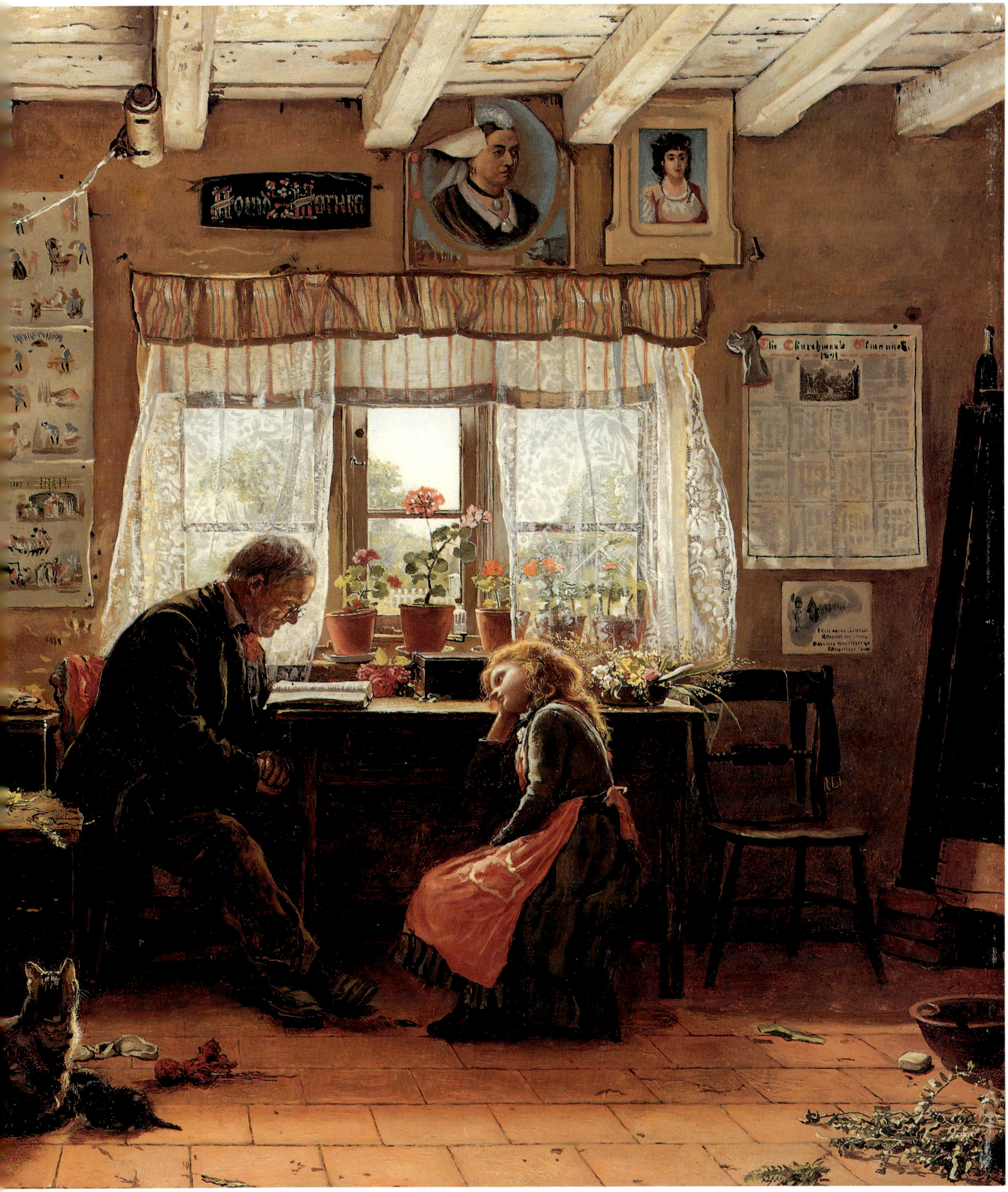

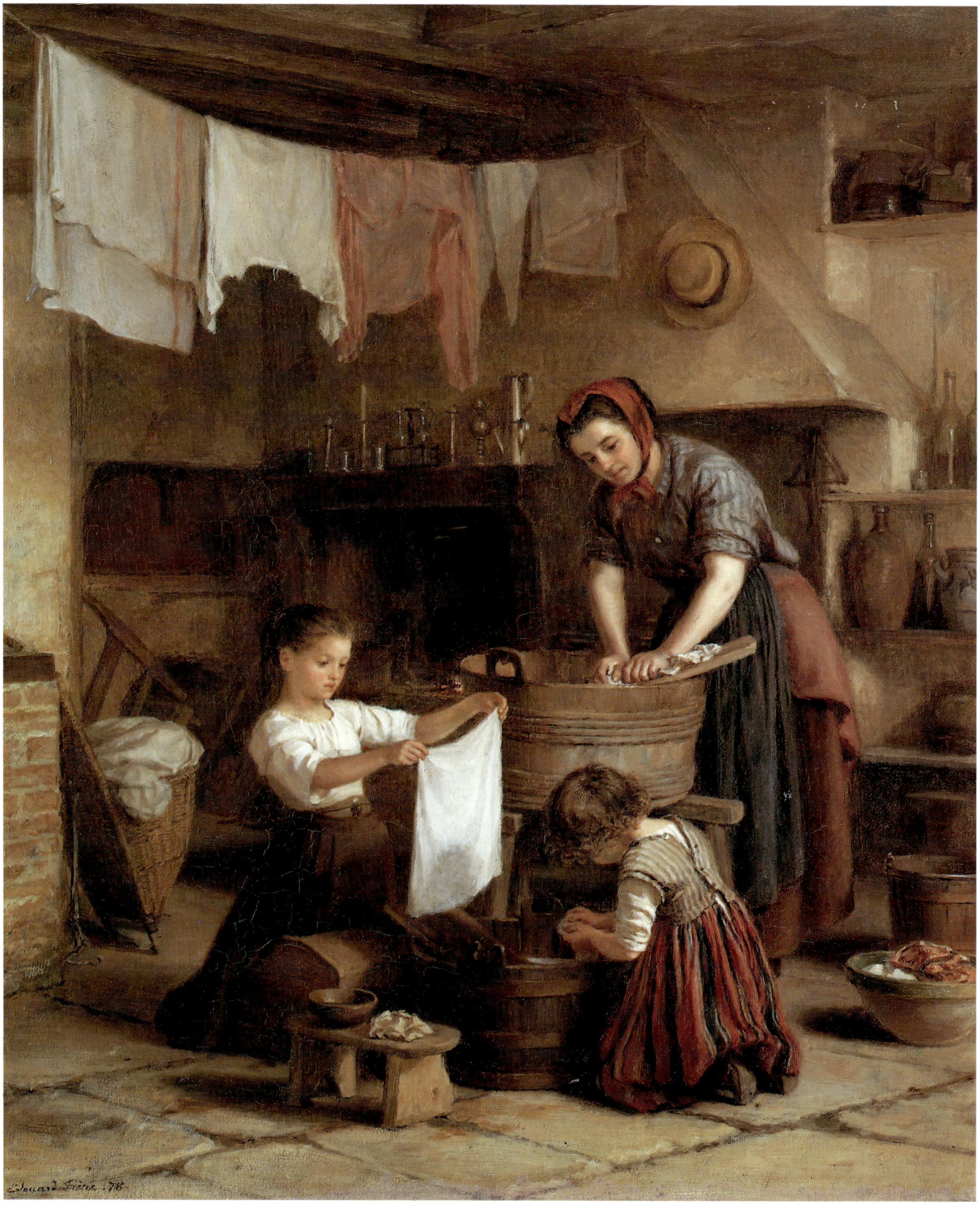

120
PIERRE EDOUARD FRERE
*Washing Day*

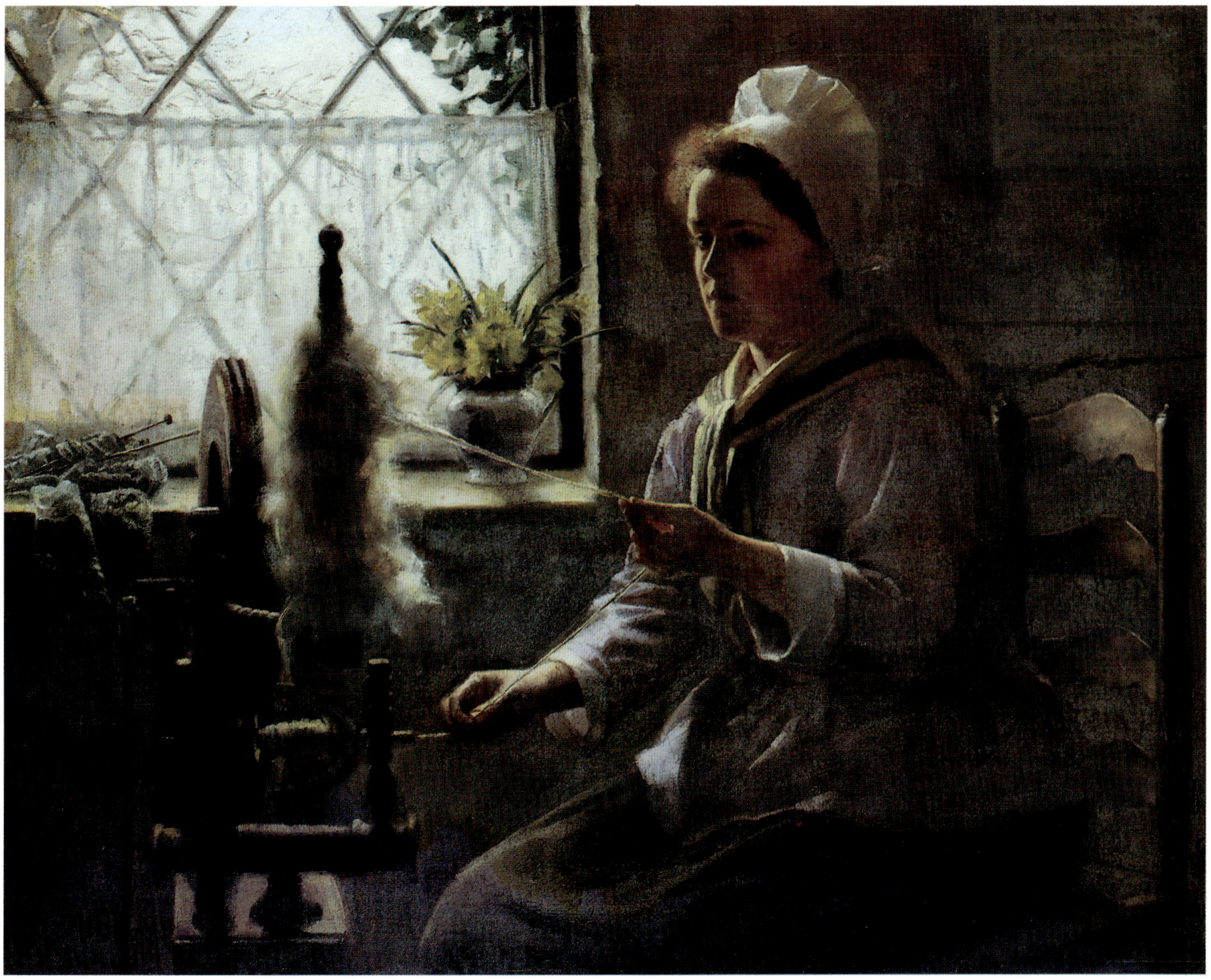

121
KATHERINE L. BEARD
*Spinning*

Another essential element of the cottage myth was rustic piety. The Victorians cherished the idea that the rustic was a simple, pious soul, who went to church every Sunday, and also read the family bible, possibly every day. Thomas Webster's *Sunday Evening* (123) is perhaps not too fanciful a picture of what cottage life might be like on a Sunday evening. Certainly the family bible, often the only book in a country cottage, was a treasured possession, handed down from generation to generation, and often inscribed with the names and birthdates of all the family. In William H. Snape's delightful cottage (119) an old grandfather is reading the bible to his grand-daughter. On the wall the posters include The Churchman's Almanac, the Queen, and the motto 'Home and Mother', thus reinforcing the Victorian belief that the cottage was both the repository and the breeding-ground of sound values. This pretty and seemingly innocent picture is, in fact, a catalogue of cottage virtues – piety, patriotism and family love. At Lark Rise, too, many of the cottages had 'pots of geraniums, fuchsias and old-fashioned sweet-smelling musk on the window-sills'.

The Victorians also liked to think of country children saying their prayers. Pictures of girls praying was a favourite subject for many painters, for example Henry Le Jeune, another delightful painter of country children. Le Jeune was one of many Victorian artists to make a living painting pictures of little girls as Bo-Peep or Little Red Riding Hood. James Hayllar's old rustic in his smock (122) is teaching his very pretty little grandchild to say her prayers. The rather ponderous title *As the Twig is bent, so the Tree is inclined* once more enshrines the myth of the cottage as the best place to bring up children.

The Victorian obsession with the cottage is inseparable from their idea of childhood. Life might have been harder and less comfortable in a cottage, but it was happier and more innocent, and as such the perfect atmosphere in which children could grow up healthy and pure. The Victorian middle-class

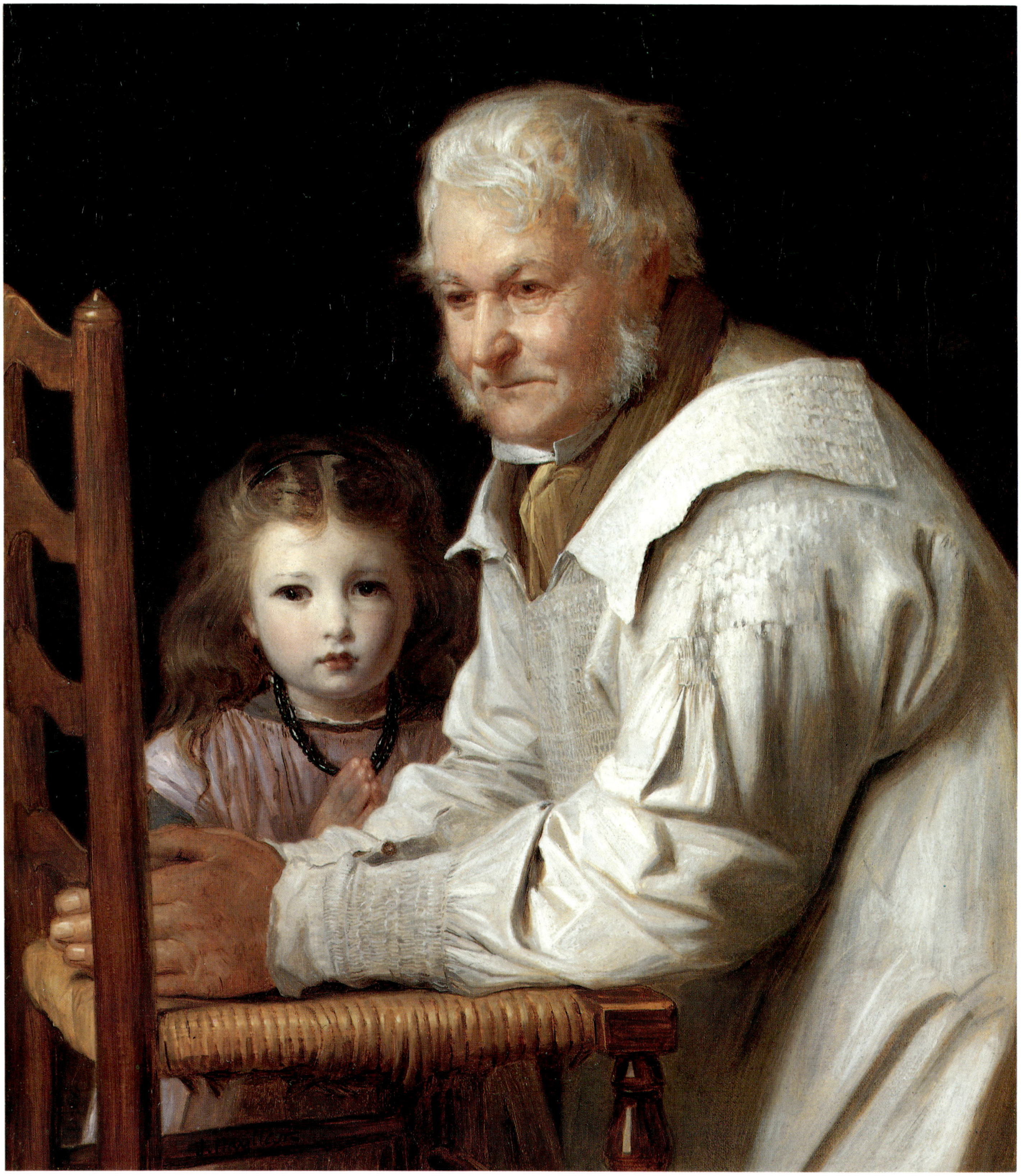

122
JAMES HAYLLAR
*'As the Twig is bent, so the Tree is inclined'*

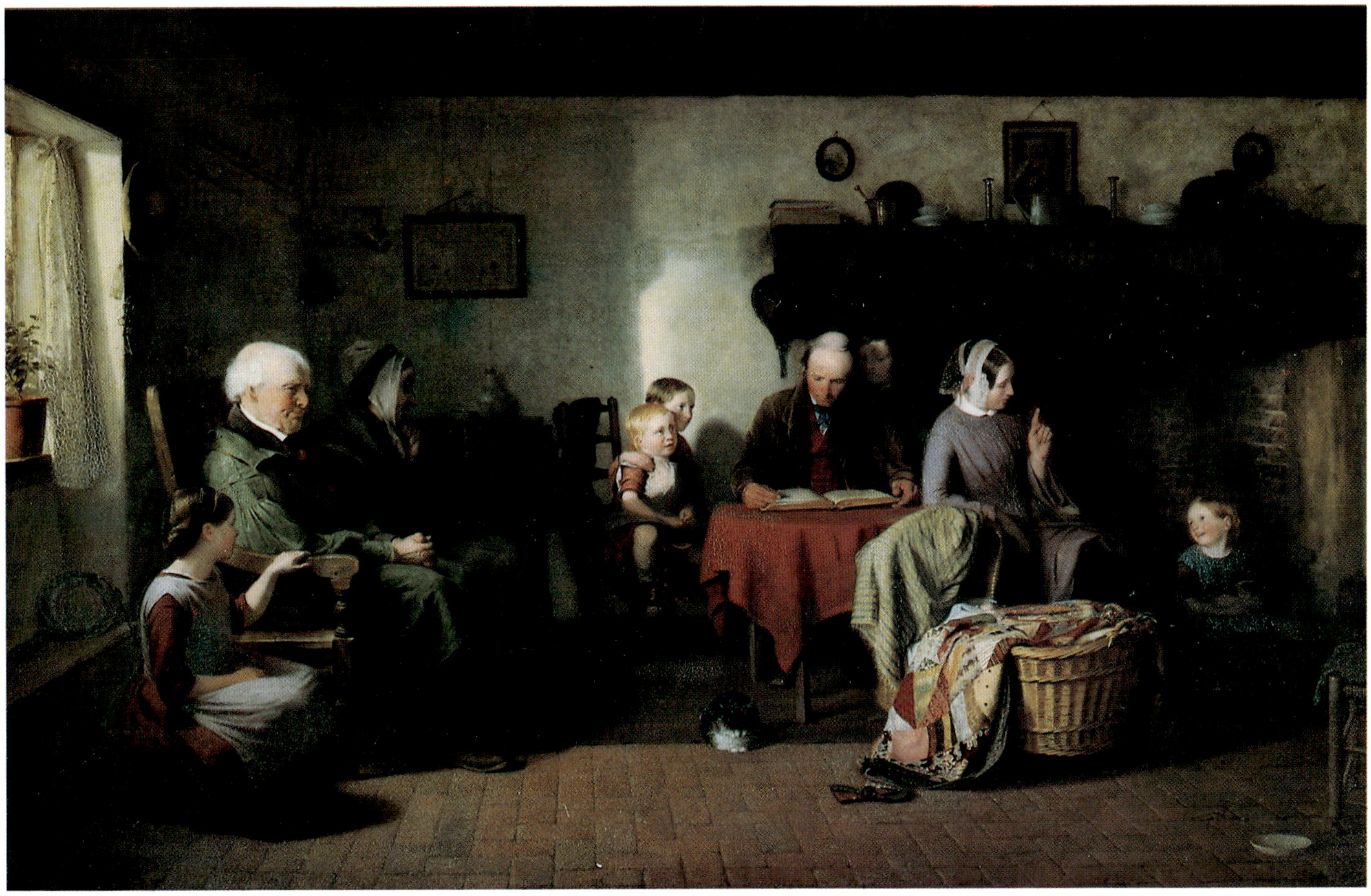

123
THOMAS WEBSTER
*Sunday Evening*

viewer might know nothing about farming or agriculture, but he did understand the importance of family life, and cottage life was something he could identify with. He or his immediate forebears might well have been born in a cottage. Although his cottage might not have looked like any of these pictures, this is how he wanted to remember it. The cottage is one of the most sacred of all Victorian myths, an icon at the centre of their concept of country life. This was the real paradise they had lost, or so they thought. Unfortunately, the gap between the image and reality was usually a wide one. No wonder Lord Shaftesbury, the greatest of all Victorian philanthropists, was so shocked when, on inheriting his father's estate, he found that the cottages were in an appalling state: 'I have passed my life in rating others for allowing rotten houses and immoral, unhealthy dwellings; and now I come into an estate rife with abominations! Why, there are things here to make one's flesh creep. . . .' The Rev. James Fraser, writing in 1867, reported that:

> The majority of the cottages that exist in rural parishes are deficient in almost every requisite that should constitute a home for a Christian family in a civilized community. They are deficient in bedroom accommodation . . . in drainage and sanitary arrangements . . . and in many instances are lamentably dilapidated and out of repair . . . 'I only wonder,' writes one clergyman to me, 'that our agricultural poor are as moral as they are.'

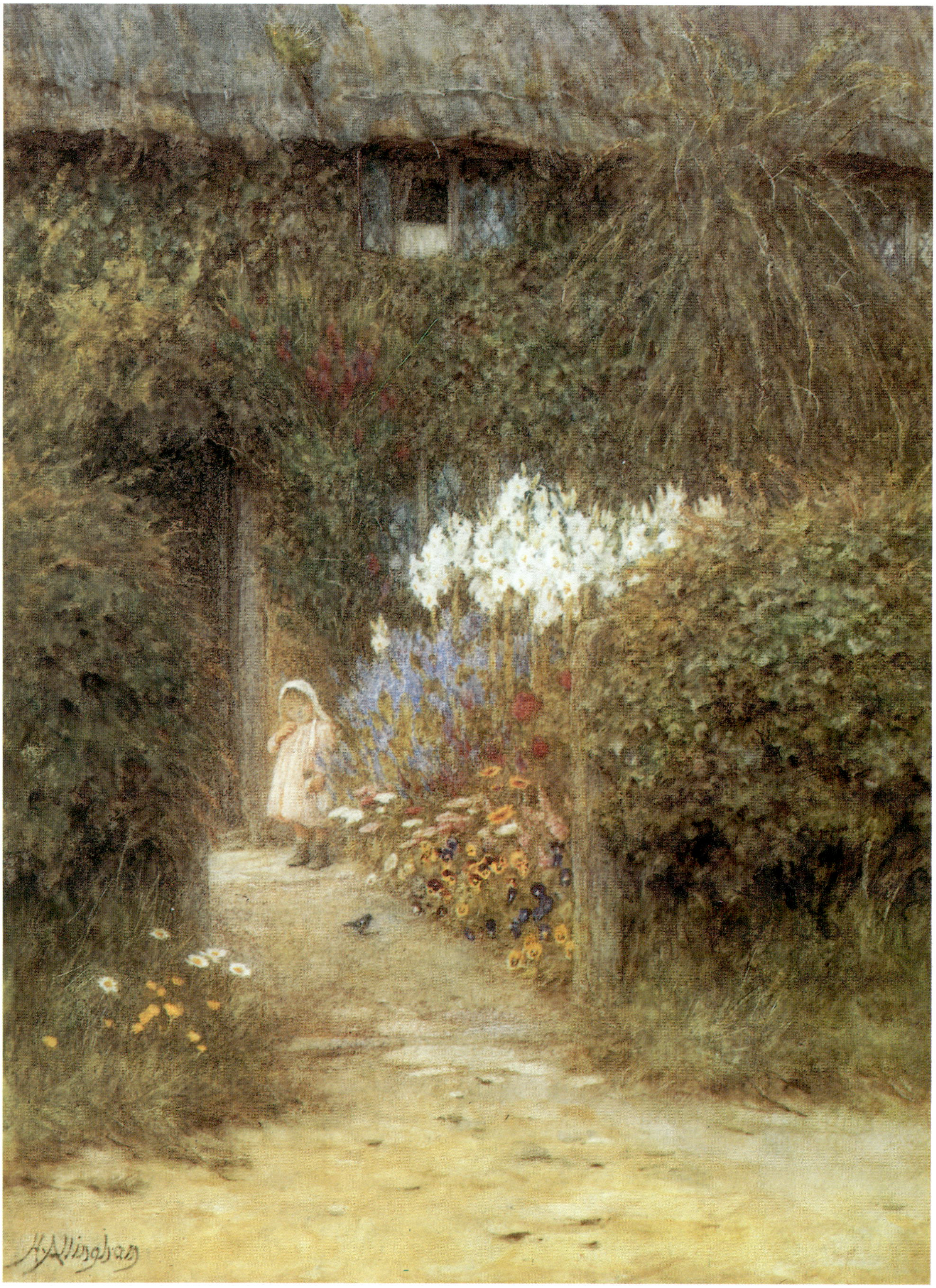

124
HELEN ALLINGHAM
*Redlynch, Wiltshire*

# Chapter Ten

# THE COTTAGE GARDEN

Take of English flowers these –
Spring's full-faced primroses,
Summer's wild wide-hearted rose,
Autumn's wall-flower of the close. . .

RUDYARD KIPLING, *A Charm*

THE COTTAGE GARDEN IS AN INSEPARABLE PART of the cottage idyll. Many of the same artists who painted cottages, in particular Helen Allingham and Birket Foster, also depicted their gardens. In many of Allingham's pictures we get a glimpse of the cottage garden, sometimes just a few sunflowers peeping over a hedge, sometimes a garden path leading to a cottage, as in the delightful watercolour of *Redlynch, Wiltshire* (124). This is a classic Allingham image: the thatched cottage, the garden path lined with a profusion of old-fashioned flowers, the little girl in a white bonnet. We do not know just how idealised Allingham's cottage gardens are, but there can be no doubt that many Victorian cottage-dwellers took great pride in their gardens, and spent a great deal of time working in them. In Birket Foster's watercolour (125) the children are helping to water and weed the flower beds around the cottage. Flowers line the paths, but the middle of the bed is planted with vegetables, and we can see cabbages on the left. Growing vegetables was much more important to the cottage gardener, because they provided the family with fresh and much-needed food to supplement their diet; flowers usually took second place. In W.S. Coleman's cottage garden (126) the same pattern is followed – vegetables and marrows in the centre, flowers along the path. In the background are the inevitable sunflowers and old-fashioned beehives. Both Coleman and his sister, Helen Cordelia Coleman, painted pretty cottage scenes and landscapes in the Birket Foster vein.

At Lark Rise, most of the men worked in their gardens for an hour or two after their tea-supper. 'They were first-class gardeners and it was their pride to have the earliest and best of the different kinds of vegetables. . . . The energy they brought to their gardening after a hard day's work in the fields was marvellous. They grudged no effort and never seemed to tire.' Some-

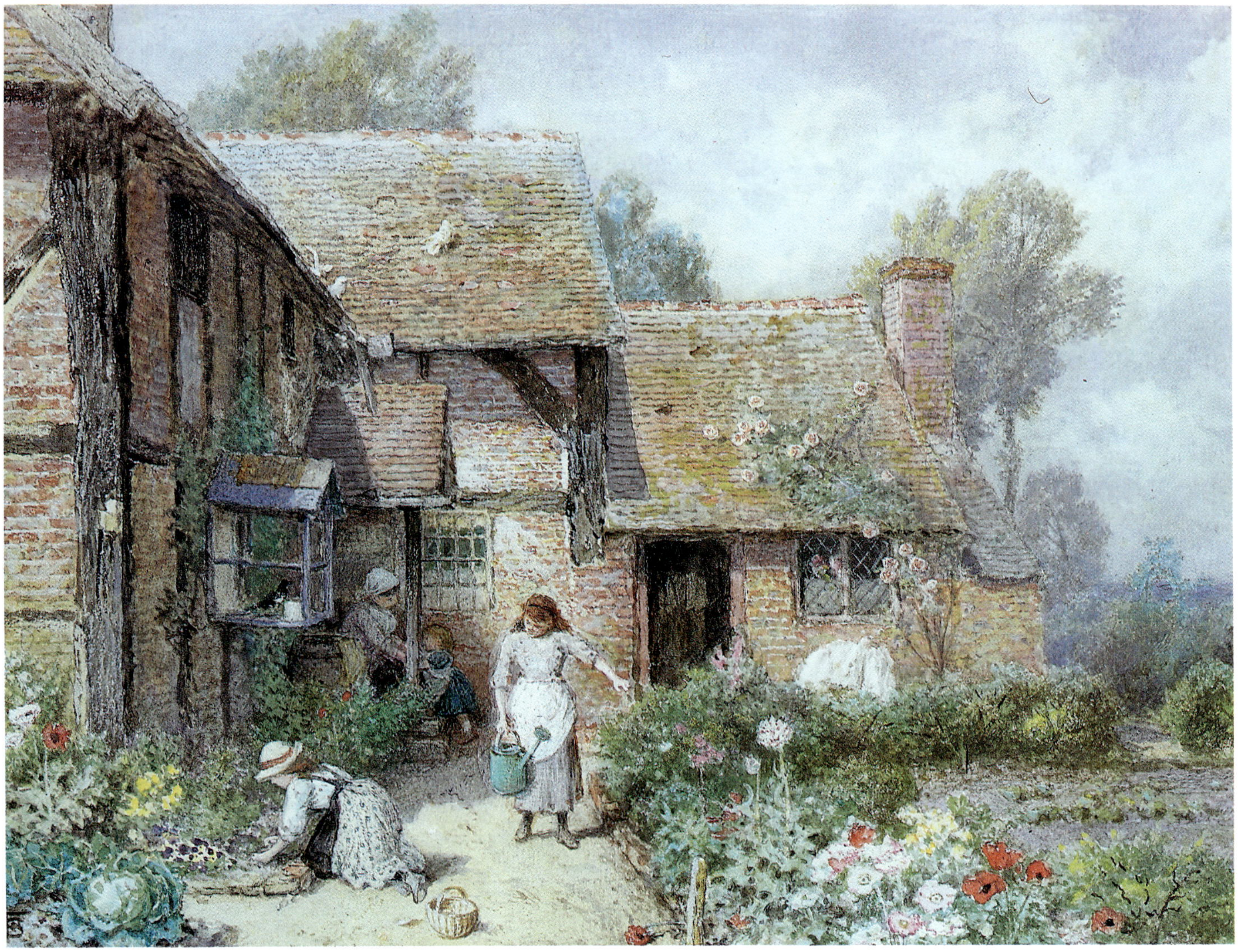

125
Myles Birket Foster
*An Afternoon in the Garden*

times, they even worked on in the dark. Some might have an allotment as well as a garden, but the garden 'was reserved for green vegetables, currant and gooseberry bushes, and a few old-fashioned flowers'. Their greatest pride and care was reserved for their potatoes, for these had to last them the whole year round. Especially large ones were taken to the inn to be shown off, and weighed on the only pair of scales in the village.

Many cottagers kept bees, and the old-fashioned, straw-covered hives can be seen in many cottage pictures, as in the W.S. Coleman, and another example by Frank Walton (129). At Lark Rise, the main keeper of bees was 'Old Queenie'. Every day, through the summer, she sat out watching them, and occasionally talking to them. It was traditional practice to inform the bees of any deaths in the village and in some parts of the country they were actually credited with foreknowledge of such deaths – the sign being when a swarm settled on a piece of dry wood. Alfred Williams recorded the superstition in Wiltshire. Another tradition was that of 'ringing' the bees to call them back to their hive after they had swarmed. An old village custom decreed that if the owner did not 'ring' the bees, usually done by banging a tin with a spoon, they could be claimed by the person on whose property they landed. Old Queenie used to run after them with a spoon and a shovel, for losing a swarm in summer was a serious loss. The old rhyme went:

> A swarm in May's worth a rick of hay;
> And a swarm in June's worth a silver spoon;
> A swarm in July isn't worth a fly.

Like Old Queenie, the girl in Frederick James Shields's *Young Beekeeper* (130) is sitting watching the hive, and maybe talking to the bees. The girl has a crutch beside her on the ground, and so may be crippled, something all too common

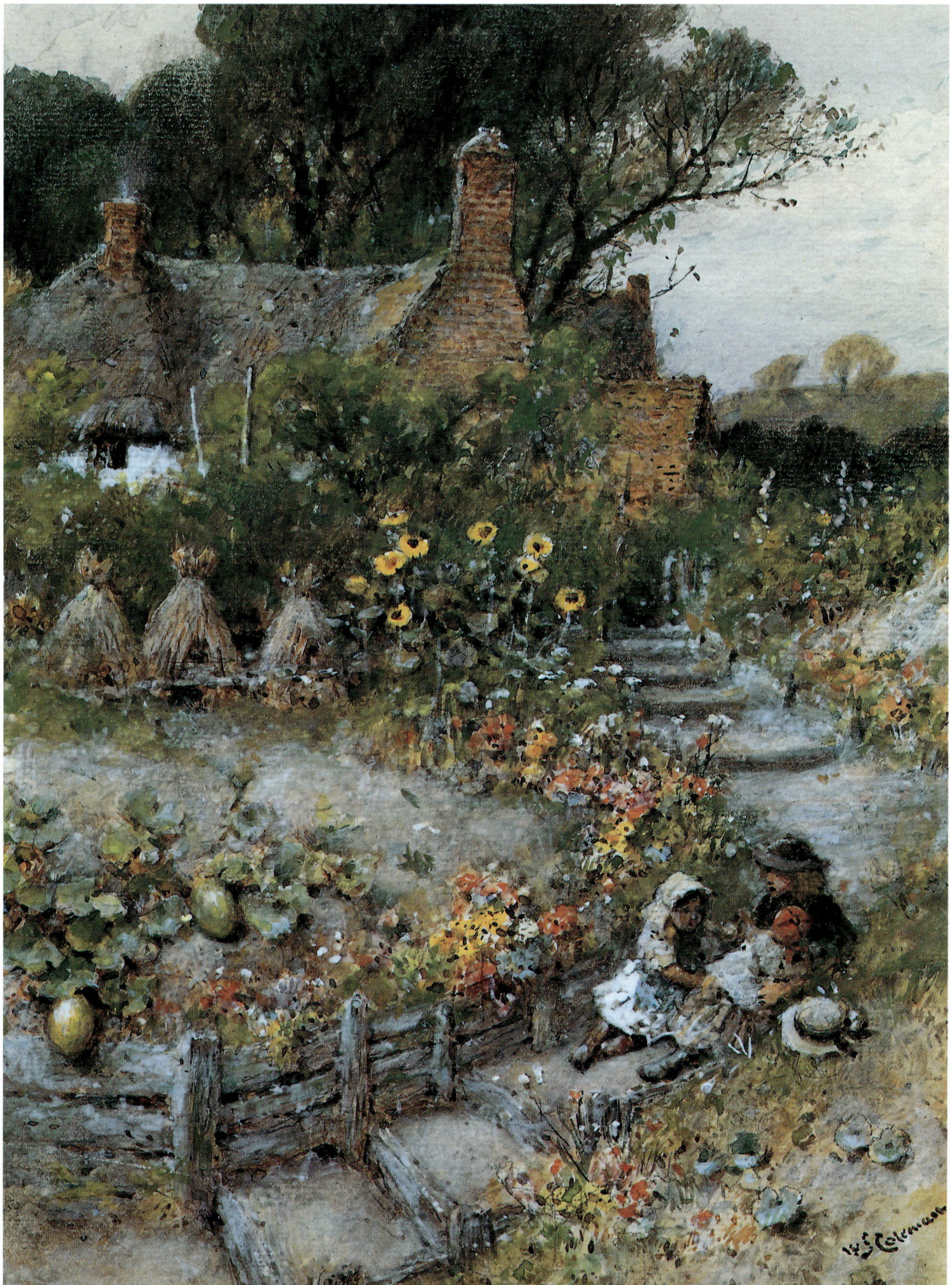

126
WILLIAM STEPHEN COLEMAN
*A Cottage Garden*

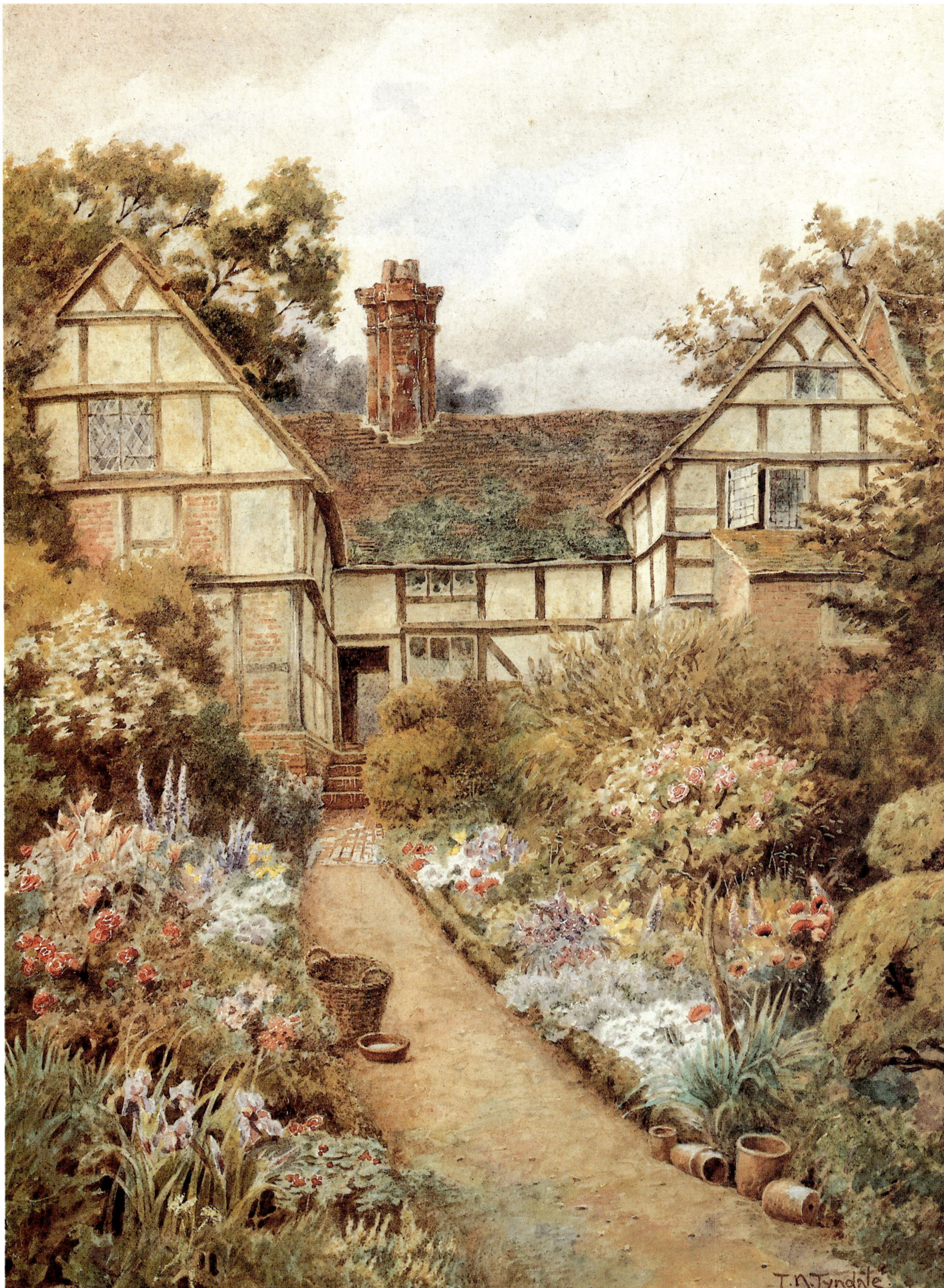


127
THOMAS TYNDALE
*A Cottage Garden*

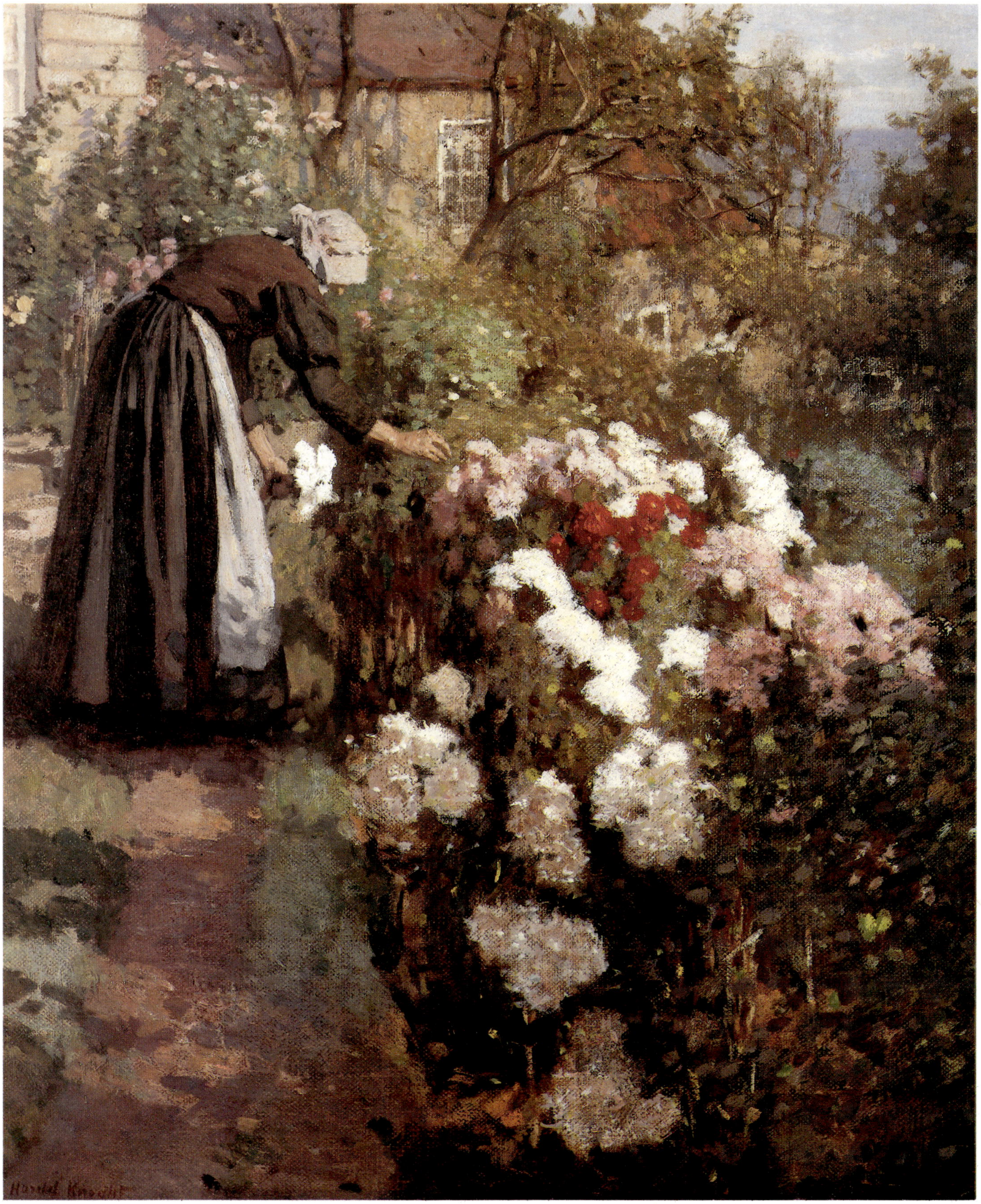

128
HAROLD KNIGHT
*The Cottage Garden*

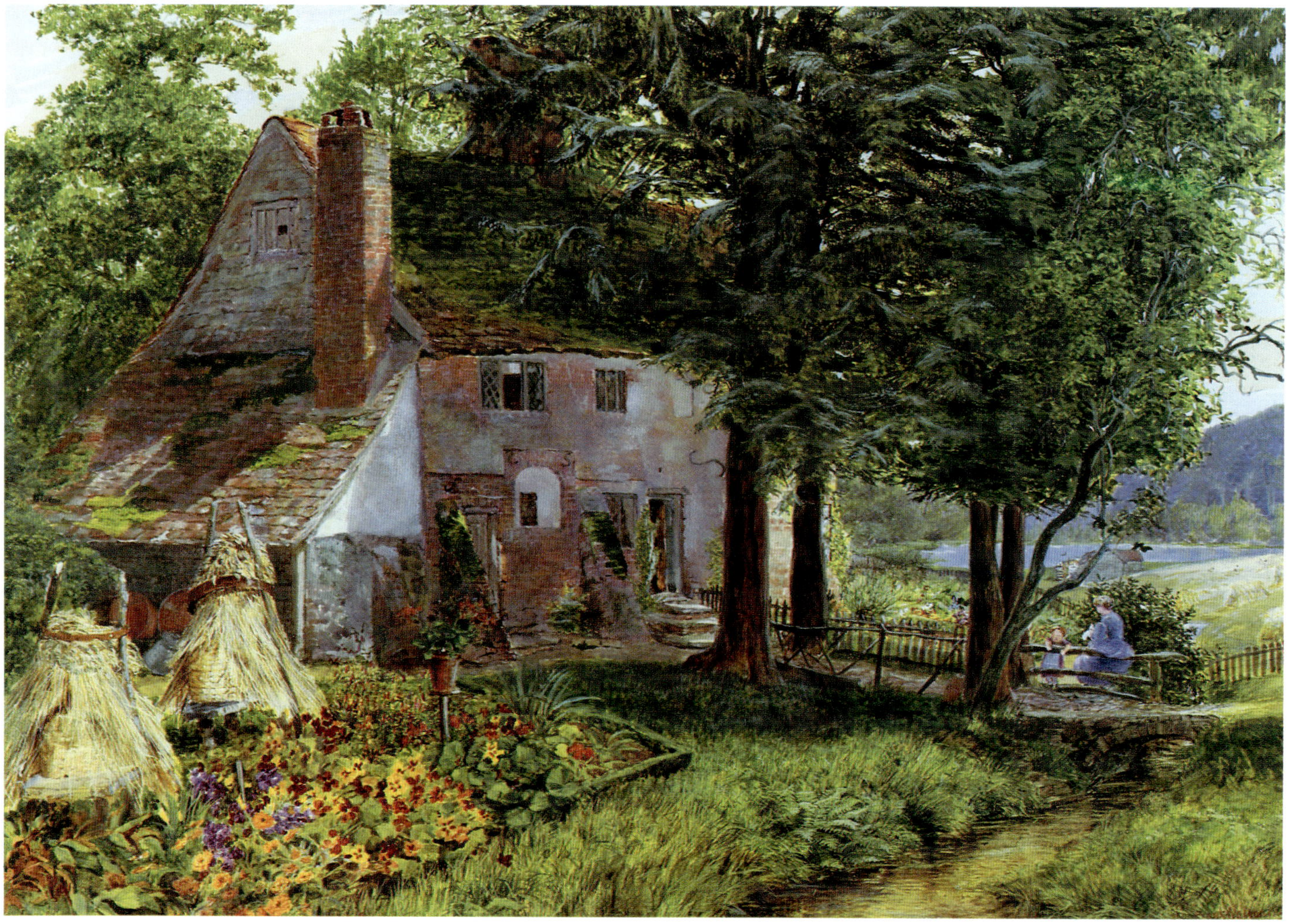

129
FRANK WALTON
*A Summer Afternoon*

among country children in the nineteenth century. Shields as we have seen was a Liverpool follower of the Pre-Raphaelites. He was both deeply religious and concerned about the widespread poverty of his countrymen. Many of his pictures are about social issues. It was typical of him to include a crippled girl in what is normally a very picturesque cottage subject. We would not find any cripples in the work of Birket Foster or Helen Allingham.

In the late Victorian period there was a steady revival of interest in old English gardens, and the cult of the cottage garden was part of this tendency. The Arts and Crafts movement also helped to foster an interest in old English gardens and traditional flowers. Both William Morris and Ruskin advocated the old English style, and the free planting of old-fashioned English flowers – roses, lilies, daisies, poppies. The children's books of Walter Crane and Kate Greenaway are part of the same movement, projecting an 'olde-worlde' image of old-fashioned gardens, with yew arbours, bowling greens and orchards. Garden writers like Gertrude Jekyll urged gardeners to study cottage gardens, and learn from them. Even George Samuel Elgood, a painter of grand and formal gardens, would occasionally paint a cottage garden if he found a particularly attractive one.

'Olde-worlde' is very much the image projected by the watercolours of Millicent Sowerby. Her work is very similar in spirit to that of Kate Greenaway, and her delicate watercolours abound in little girls in white dresses and mob caps taking tea in old English gardens. Thomas Tyndale was another painter of gardens, who loved to include old, half-timbered buildings in the background (127). Although Victorian landowners and farmers built many new cottages and model villages throughout the century, you would not think so from looking at these watercolours. The Victorian imagination demanded that every villager must live in an ancient cottage, preferably thatched and half-timbered.

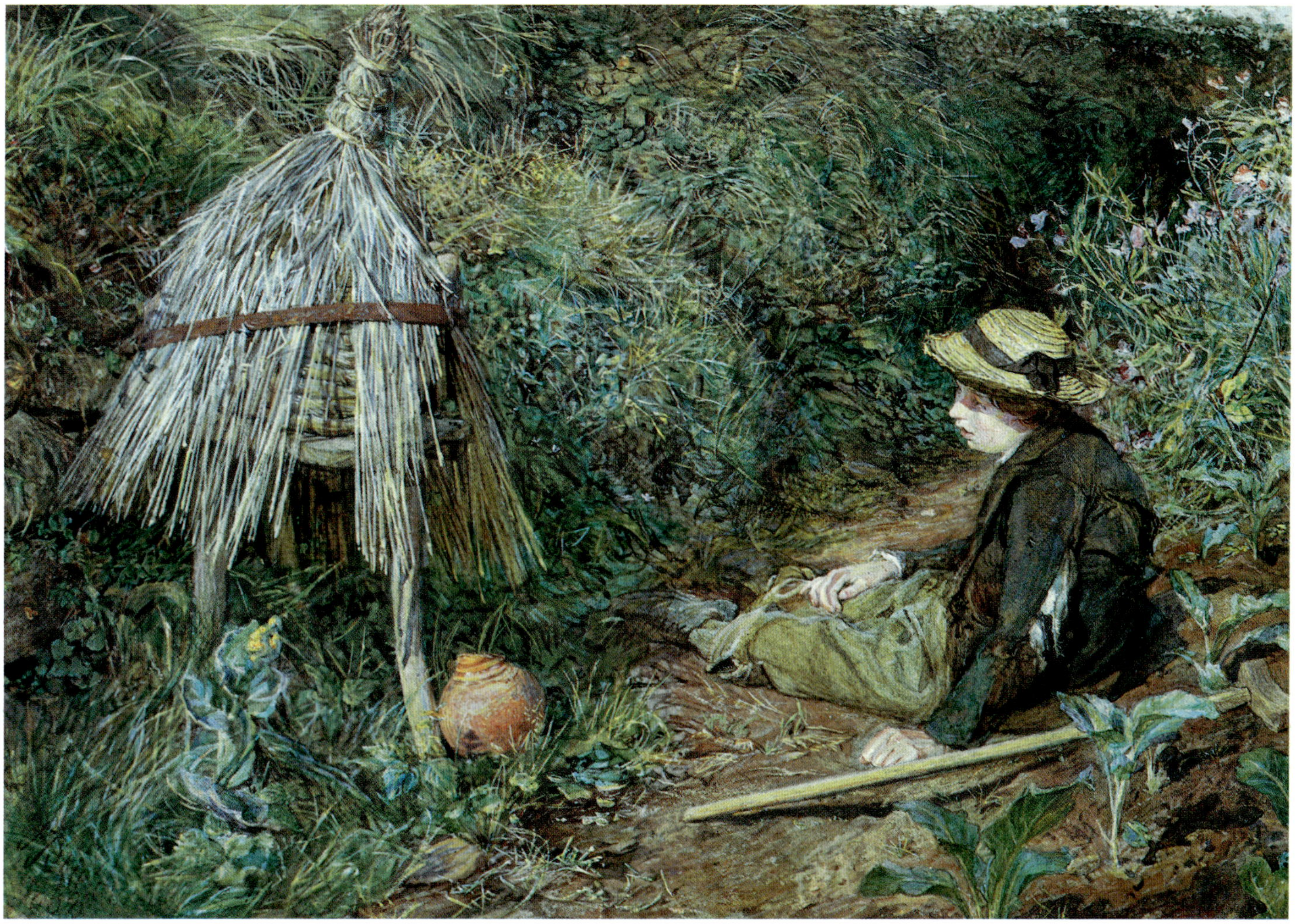

130
FREDERICK JAMES SHIELDS
*The Young Beekeeper*

The cottage garden kept its appeal even for late Victorian and impressionist painters. Walter Langley, one of the Newlyn School, again gives us the ancient thatched cottage, but with a rather pleasingly untidy garden in front (132). In it, a standard rose battles forlornly with a huge patch of rhubarb, weeds and onions gone to seed. Most cottage housewives grew their own herbs, used both for flavouring food and drink, and for remedies. Home-made wines, jam and jelly were also made by all but the very poorest. Harold Knight, another Newlyn artist, and the husband of Dame Laura Knight, painted a charming scene of a woman picking flowers in her cottage garden (128). Alfred Glendening, Junior, a painter of impressionist landscapes, preferred the humbler cabbage patch (131), a subject which seemed to appeal to painters in the impressionist style. Clausen, as one might expect, also painted men at work in gardens. *The Allotment Garden* (133) shows a man and woman working on their allotment rather than at home. According to Flora Thompson, 'The allotment plots were divided into two, and one half planted with potatoes and the other half with wheat or barley.' Allotments became increasingly popular in the nineteenth century, both in towns and villages, as a means whereby working-class people could improve their diet. Social reformers and the clergy pressed for the extension of allotments throughout the nineteenth century, and by 1833 forty two per cent of English parishes had an allotment scheme of some kind. The Liberal victory of 1885 gave added impetus to the movement; this was the election in which Joseph Arch was elected as a member for North-West Norfolk, using the slogan 'Three acres and a cow'. Further legislation in 1887 gave local councils compulsory powers to purchase land for the purpose of allotments or smallholdings.

Vegetable, fruit and flower shows also increased in size and importance, and the competition for prizes was fierce. These shows were encouraged and supported by the gentry,

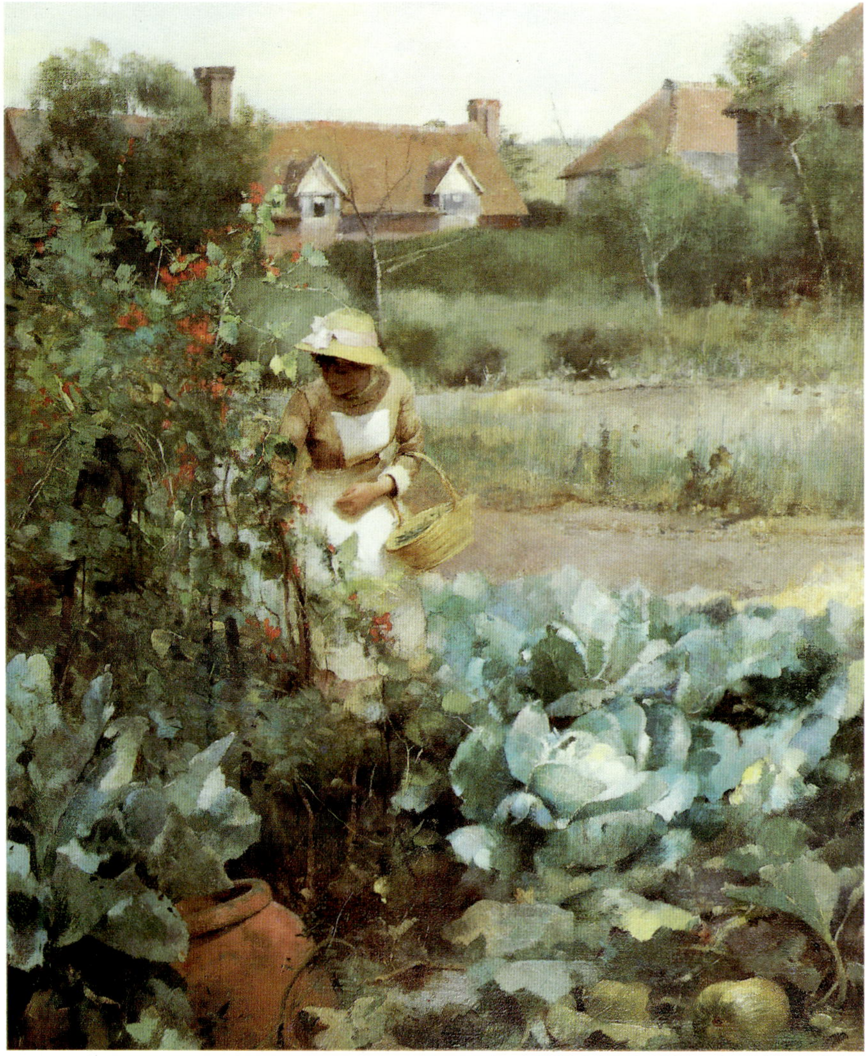

131
Alfred Glendening, Junior
*The Cabbage Patch*

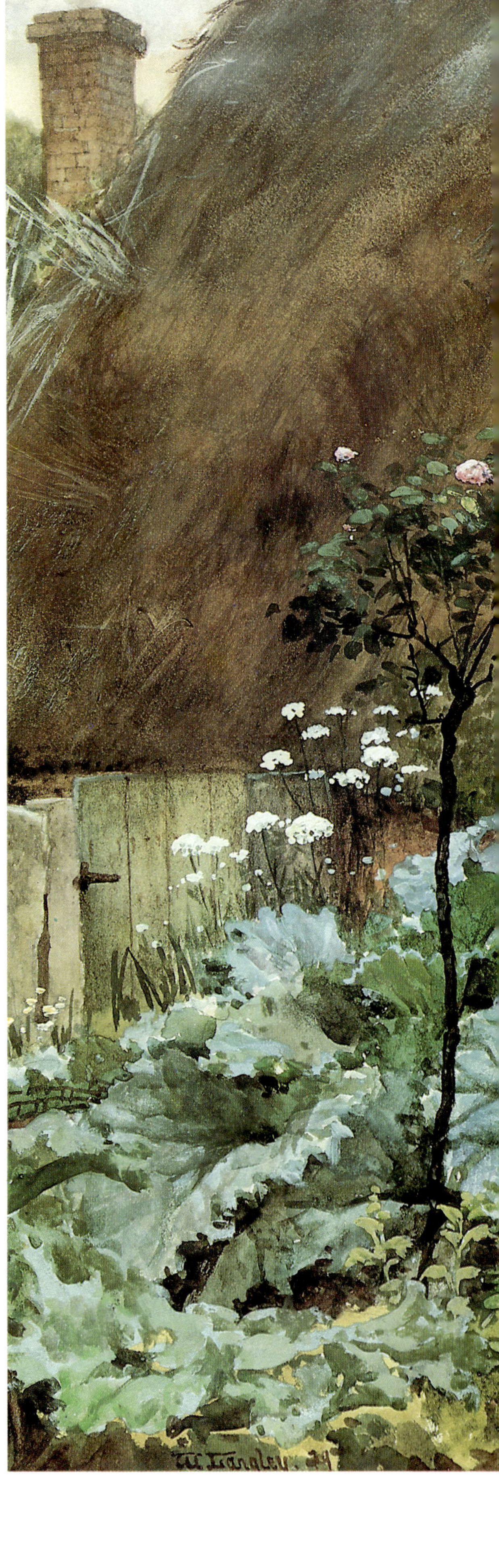

132
Walter Langley
*A Cottage Garden*

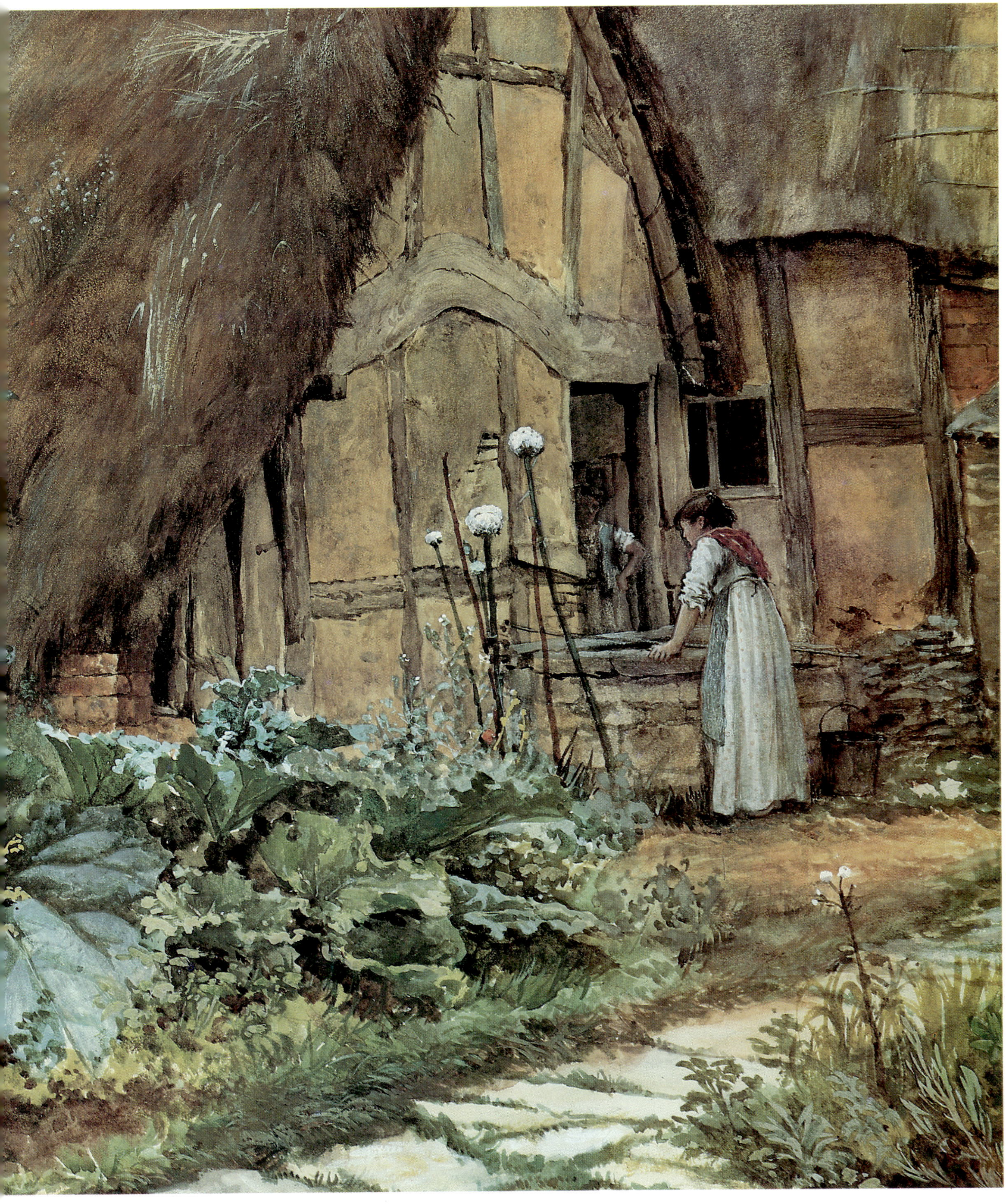

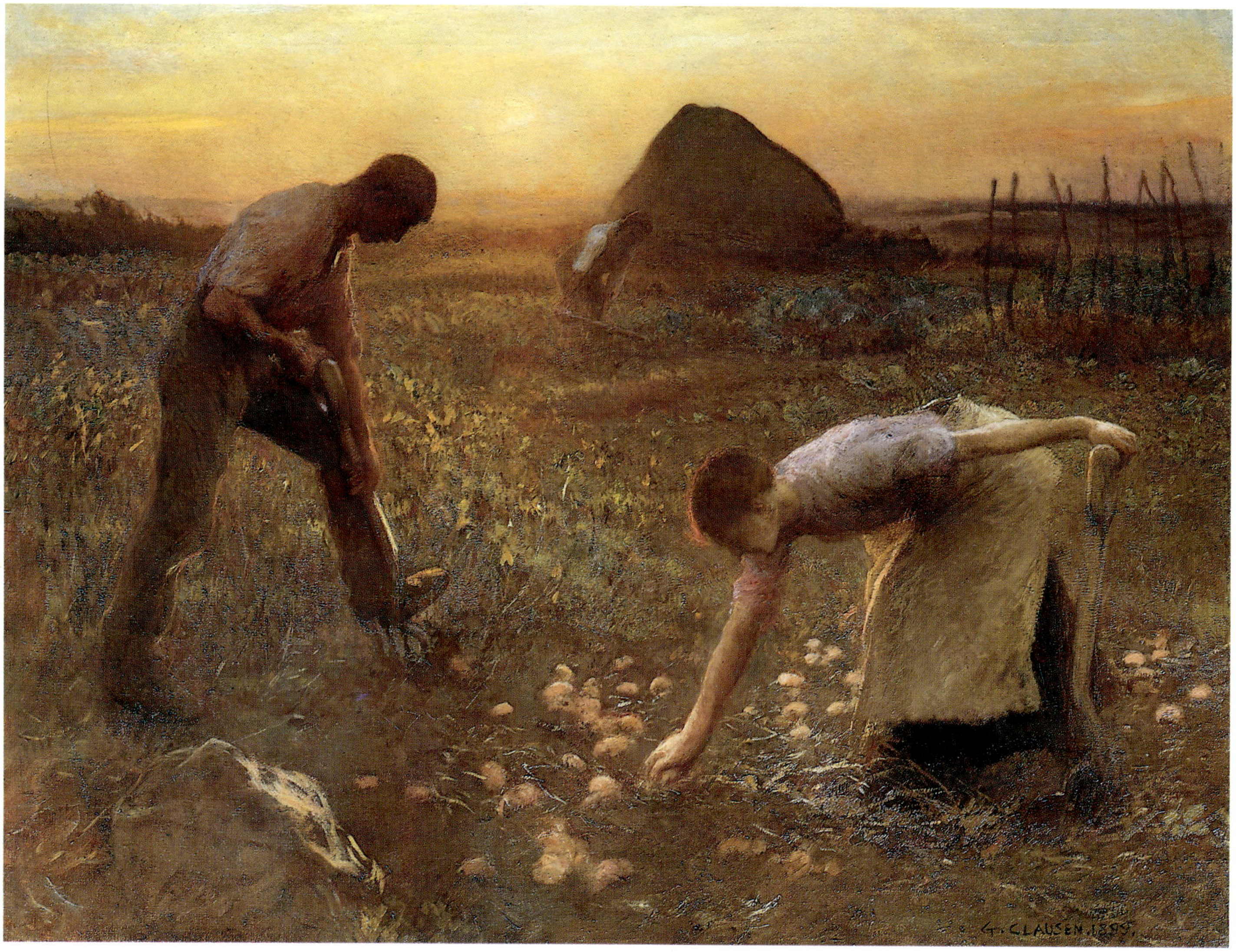

133
SIR GEORGE CLAUSEN
*The Allotment Garden*

and the lady of the manor was usually called upon to give the prizes away. Francis Kilvert went to Hay Flower Show in August 1870, 'the first they have had, a very successful one. A nice large tent, the poles prettily wreathed with hop vine, and the flowers, fruit and vegetables prettily arranged. The town was hung with flags. The whole country was there.' Kilvert, typically, was more diverted by a row of pretty girls sitting on a bench who fell over backwards, 'the whole row sprawling on their backs, with their heels in the air. . . . It was a case of being "on view" and "open to the public" and "no reserve".'

# Chapter Eleven

# CHILDHOOD

I remember, I remember,
The house where I was born.

THOMAS HOOD, *Past and Present*

IN ALMOST ALL PICTURES OF COTTAGE AND VILLAGE life, children play a major part. The Victorians raised large families, and were often strict parents, but they had nonetheless great affection for their children. The love of mothers for their babies is reflected in many delightful Victorian pictures. Carlton Alfred Smith's *New Baby* (134), Charles James Lewis's *Mother and Child* (135) or Fred Elwell's *First Born* (136) reveal a feeling of tenderness and affection that may surprise those who think of Victorian family life only in terms of repression and discipline. Lewis was one of the most delightful painters of cottage scenes and country children; C.A. Smith was a watercolourist who specialised in cottage interiors, usually with mothers and children. Their pictures manage to avoid the sickly sentimentality and cloying insincerity that is the fault with so many Victorian pictures of children. At their best Victorian painters brought a refreshingly secular atmosphere to the age-old tradition of the Madonna and Child. The nineteenth century produced many of the most delightful pictures of children in the whole of English art, and many of them are pictures of country children.

A child born in a cottage was not likely to start life attended by any of the ceremonial common to the birth of children in other sections of society. A doctor was not likely to be present; more likely a local midwife, or neighbour, would come in to help, returning to nurse the mother and baby for a few days after the birth. The child was likely to be one of a large family, anything from four to eight children being common in the Victorian period. Most cottages only had one or possibly two bedrooms, so the whole family would have to sleep together, often sharing beds. Rooms were often divided up by hanging old sheets or counterpanes across the room, as we can see in Charles Sillem Lidderdale's picture *Happy* (12). 'Poor but happy' is indeed the message to be gleaned from nearly all

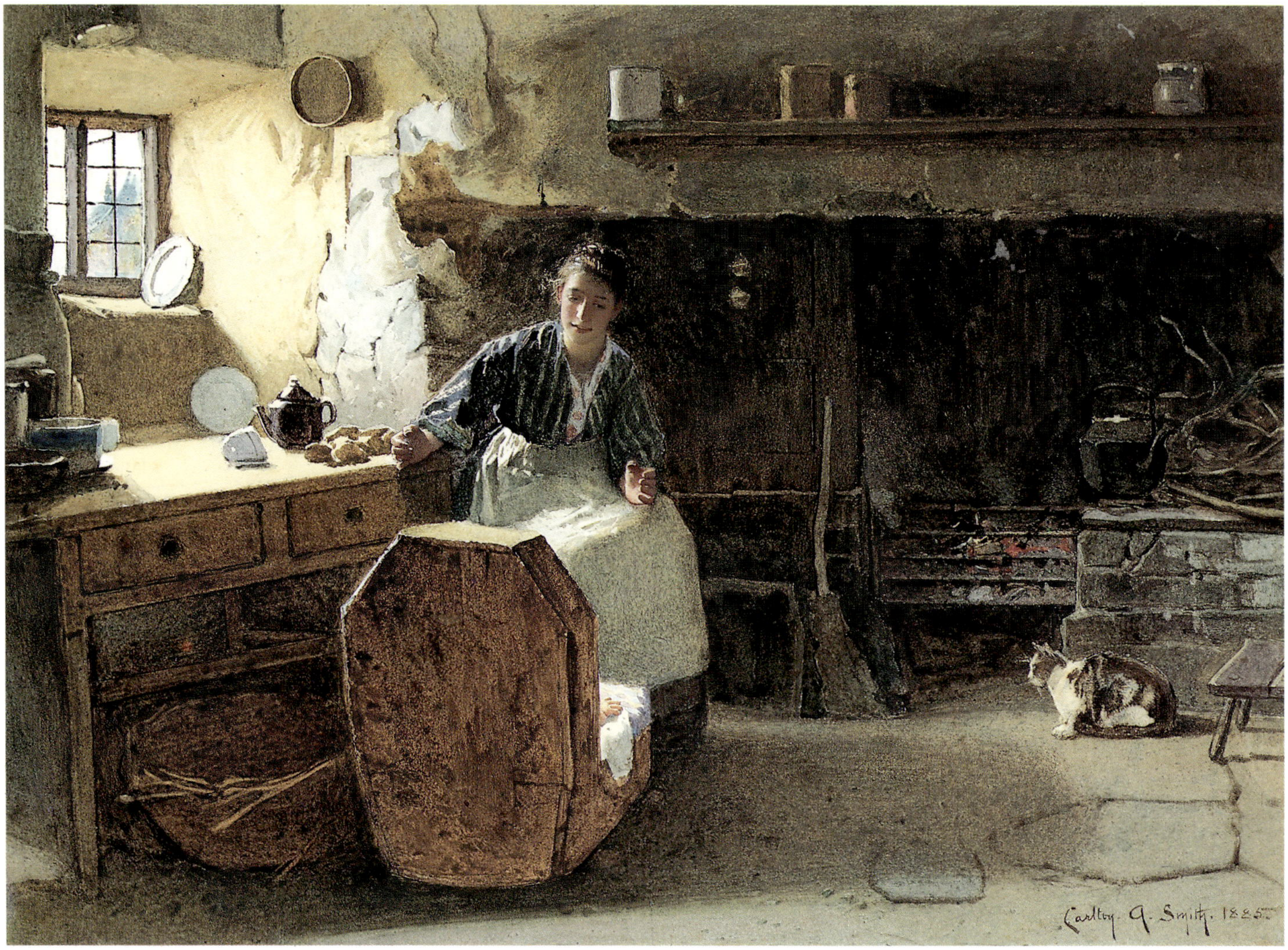


134
CARLTON ALFRED SMITH
*The New Baby*

these pictures. Lidderdale spent his whole career painting pictures of pretty farm-girls; this picture is a rare example of a cottage interior by him.

Paintings of domestic life in cottages were painted literally by the thousand in the Victorian period, and we have space for only a few examples by some of the better artists. We have encountered some of these before, such as George Smith. His picture *Here's Granny* (137) is typical of his output, and typical of many other Victorian cottage scenes. Granny is at the door, with a basket and a doll to give the children; the mother sits sewing by the fire with her other children; the baby is asleep in its cot. The cottage is simply furnished but extremely clean. It has a tiled floor, although most Victorian cottages probably had a floor of beaten earth, on which sand was usually scattered.

New babies were always made much of, as we see in William Henry Knight's *Youngest Child* (139) and F.D. Hardy's *First Birthday Party* (13). W.H. Knight was one of many painters in the mid-Victorian period to devote himself to pictures of children. Like those of George Smith, his pictures are usually on panel, small in size, beautifully observed and executed. They are the Victorian equivalent of the Dutch interiors of the seventeenth century. Hardy's picture is typical of his style, and clearly shows a fairly prosperous cottage. The room is quite well furnished, there is plenty of china on the table, food seems plentiful, and a plate of toast warms in front of the fire. On the left we can see that the wife is a seamstress, and is at work on a uniform. At the doorway stand the grandparents, poor but respectably dressed, bringing a doll for the baby, and a basket of provisions. This cottage, one feels, belongs to a small tradesman or farmer; an ordinary farm labourer could hardly have enjoyed such comforts.

Once the babies grew into children they would, however, begin to feel the weight of parental authority. Parents of all classes felt it was their moral duty to subject the wills of their

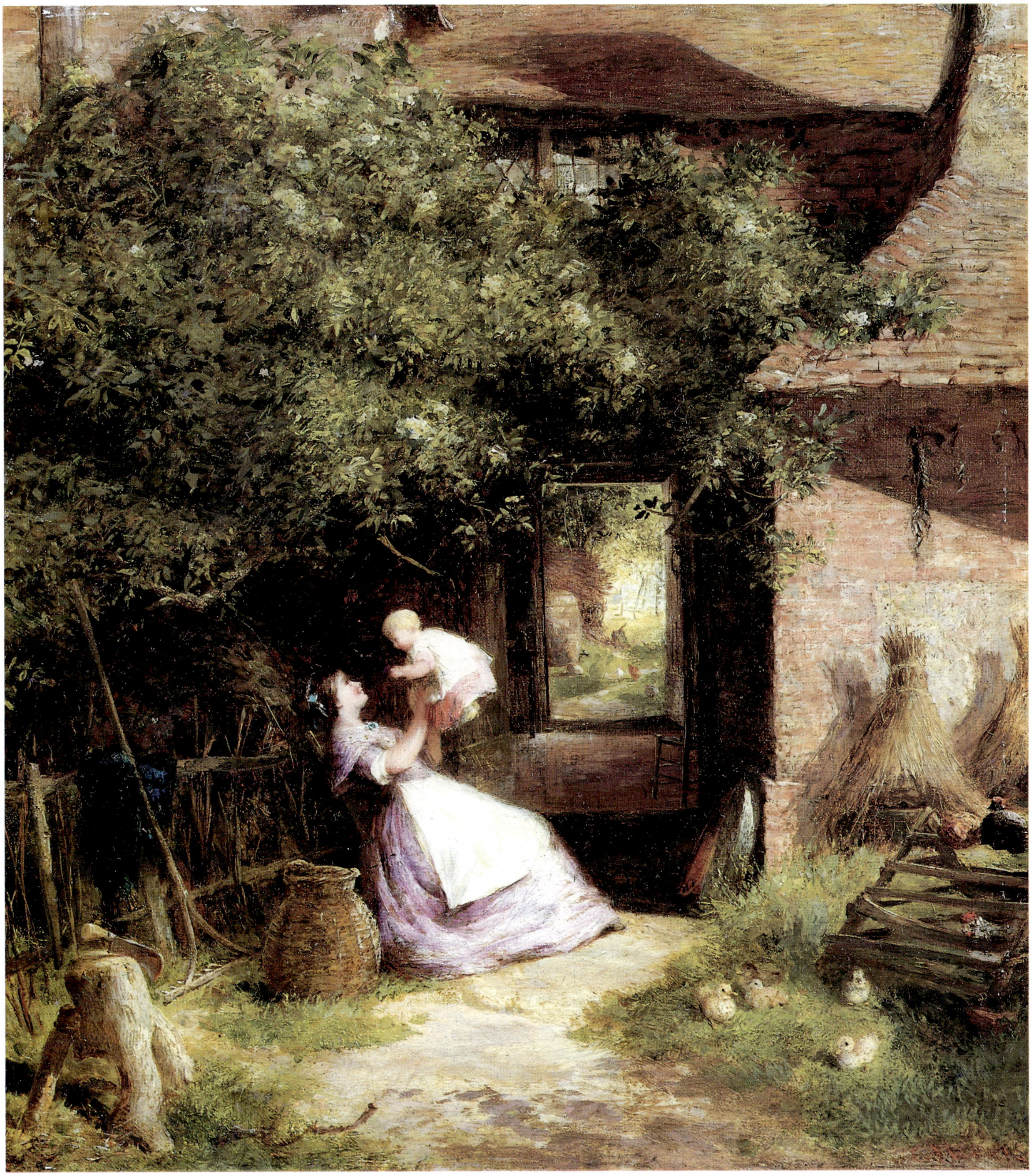

135
CHARLES JAMES LEWIS
*Mother and Child*

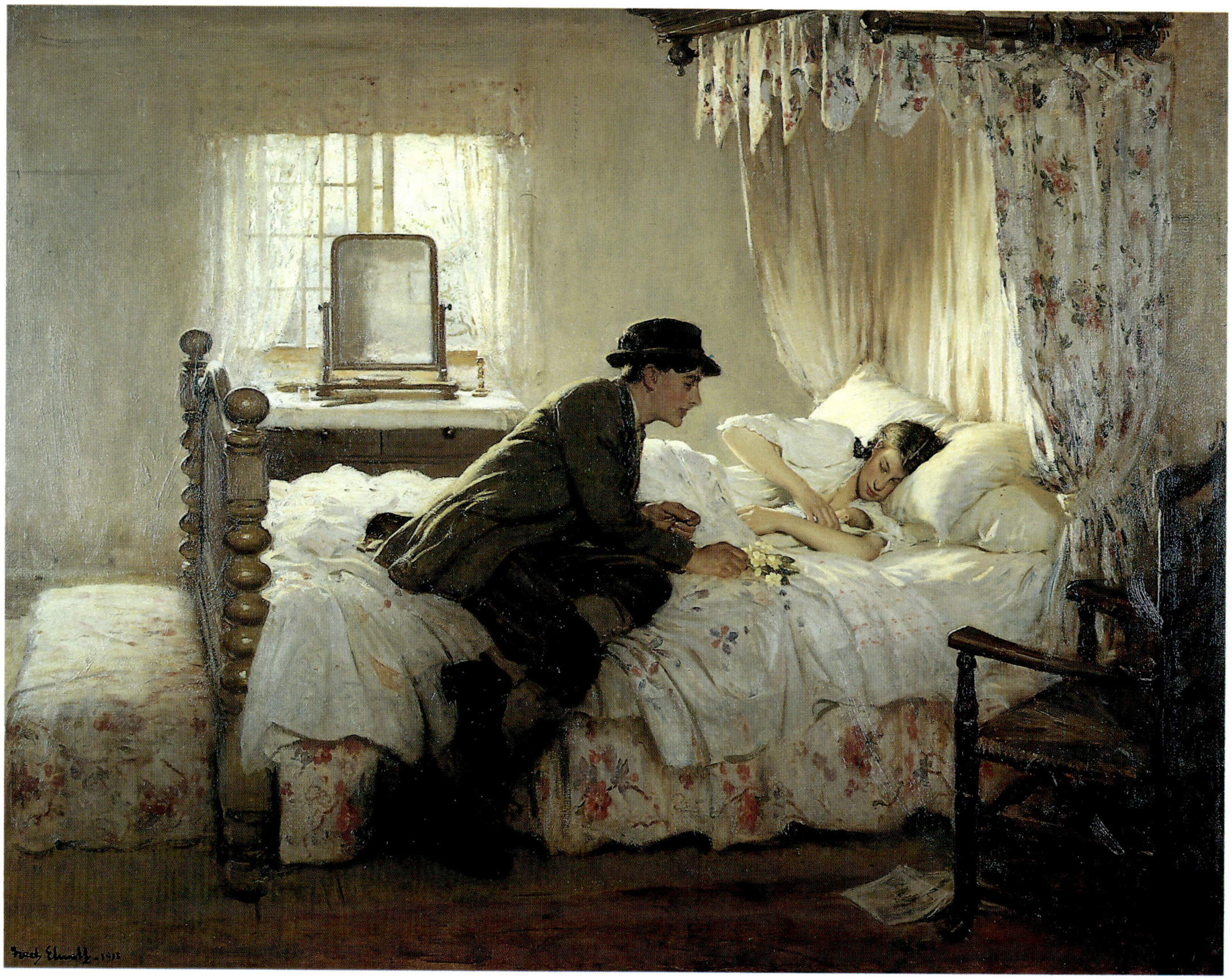

136
FREDERICK WILLIAM ELWELL
*The First Born*

children. In the words of Samuel Butler, 'At that time, it was universally admitted that to spare the rod was to spoil the child, and Saint Paul had placed disobedience to parents in very ugly company.' Even a gentle character like Francis Kilvert was in favour of physical punishment, and advised one parishioner to correct her naughty daughter, Fanny. 'I do flog her,' replied the mother, 'And the other morning . . . I held her hands while Joseph and Charlie whipped her on her naked bottom as hard as ever they were able to flog her.' This was not the type of scene likely to find its way into Victorian cottage pictures.

A more suitable subject was a family sitting down to a meal, as in Harry Brooker's *Breakfast Time* (138). This too looks like a reasonably prosperous household, with some old furniture, china on the table, and evidence of plenty of food. The children are quite tidy and well-dressed, although dressing a large family was always a great problem for a country mother. Clothes would be endlessly patched, repaired and handed on to the next child. Many of them might have been presents given to daughters in service by their employers; mothers relied upon their elder children to supply garments in this way. Boots were expensive, and they too had to be handed down. The diet of most country families was likely to be meagre, consisting mainly of bread and tea, supplemented by vegetables grown in the garden, and occasionally a little cheese or bacon. In 1867 a shepherd's wife from Blandford in Dorset, one of the poorest counties, described her family diet:

> We don't have a bit of butcher's meat for half a year, not from Christmas to Christmas; we sometimes get a bit of mutton at 3d the lb when a giddy sheep is killed on the farm. . . . We have a pig; sometimes we kill, perhaps, two in the year. We live on potatoes, bread and pig-meat, and are very thankful if we can get a bit of pig-meat; we often sit down to dry bread. . . . We never have a bit of milk.

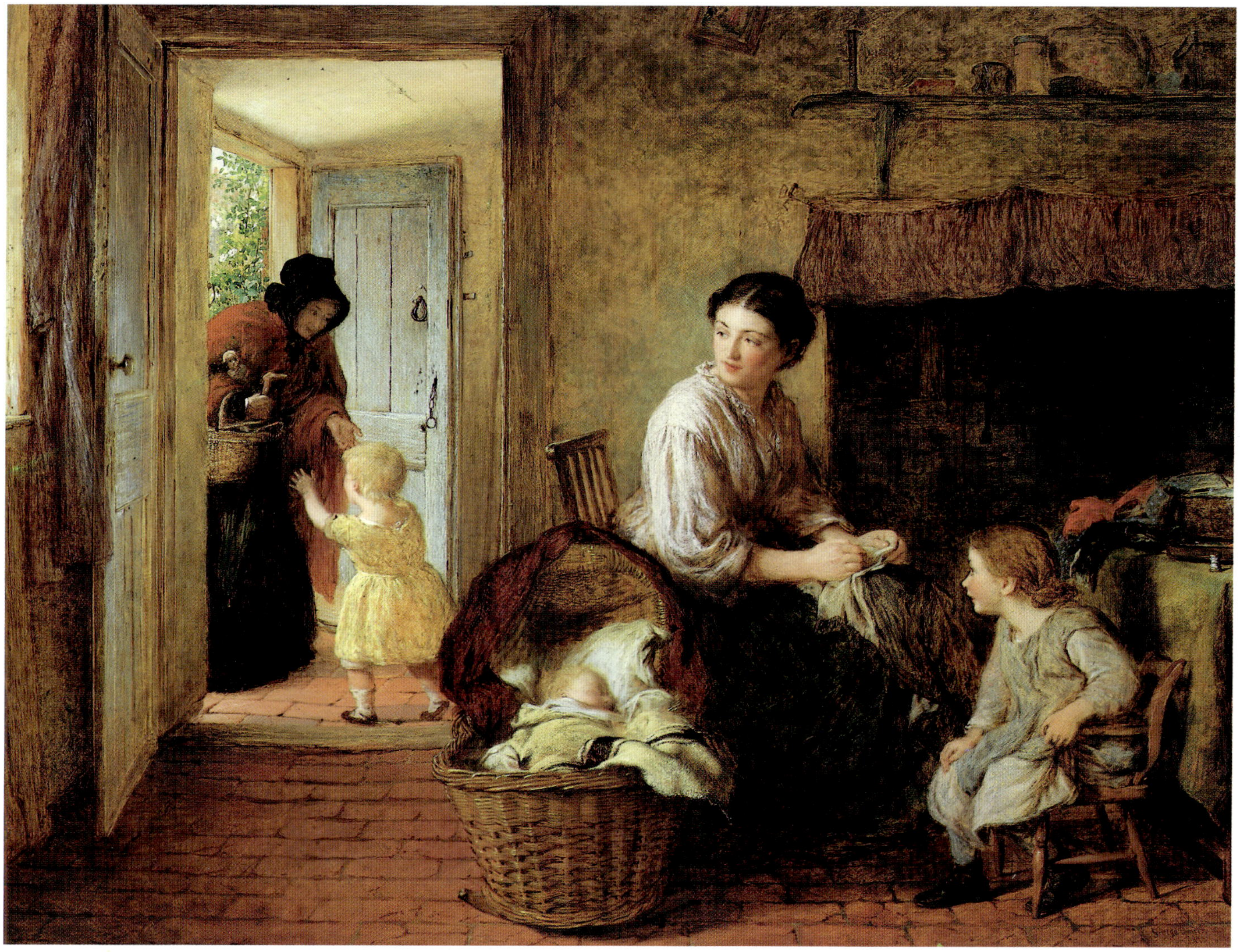

137
GEORGE SMITH
*Here's Granny*

The family pig was the great mainstay of the cottage diet in the nineteenth century, but this important member of the family is never to be found in a painting. By the time Brooker's picture was painted, in 1901, the diet of country people had greatly improved. Cheap foreign imports had brought fresh meat within the reach of all but the poorest pockets. Other foods like tinned meats, fish, jam, pickles, coffee, cocoa, currants and cake were available in the shops in market towns, or were brought round in vans and carts by travelling butchers and grocers.

The bringing up of large numbers of children in insanitary cottages meant that illness and child mortality were commonplace. Child deaths were not as common in the country as in towns, but nonetheless the figures were very high in the middle of the century. In Oxfordshire, for example, 33 per cent of all deaths in 1865 were of children under five. Illnesses like scarlet fever, diphtheria, measles and whooping cough were still highly dangerous to children; tuberculosis was common, and bad water led to regular outbreaks of typhoid. Almost every Victorian family, rich or poor, had to suffer the death of children. Although medicine made enormous progress during the period, treatment could still be rudimentary and painful. Country people relied heavily on traditional remedies and herbal cures, which were not always effective.

Painters responded to the theme of sickness in different ways. William Hemsley, generally a painter of children's games, turned it into a fairly light-hearted affair in his picture *The Doctor*, where the doctor is shown taking the pulse of an apprehensive, but extremely healthy-looking child. Generally, a doctor would not be called to a cottage unless it was something much more serious. Mrs Alexander Farmer's *An Anxious Hour* (140) strikes a much more serious note. This is a simple but moving picture of a mother watching over her sick child, and is typical of the more honest approach to modern-life sub-

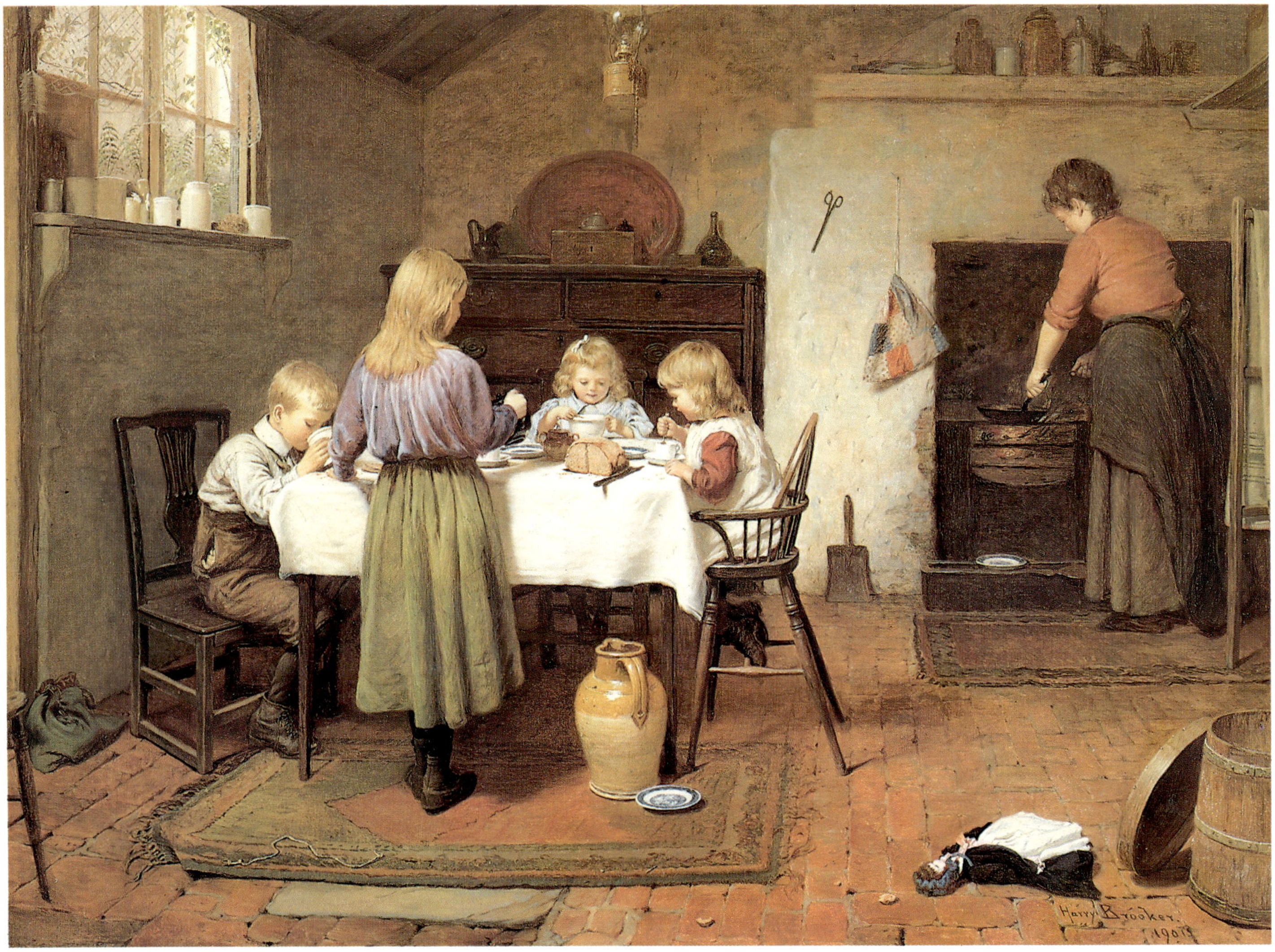


138
HARRY BROOKER
*Breakfast Time*

jects of the 1850s and 60s. The sickness and death of children was one of the most poignant themes in Victorian literature – Paul Dombey, or Little Nell, for example, in the works of Dickens. In 1891 Luke Fildes took up the theme, and created one of the most popular pictures of the century, *The Doctor* (141). It was the death of his own first child, on Christmas Day 1877, watched over by the family doctor Dr Murray, that gave him the idea for the subject. Fildes's elaborate preparations for the picture are typical of the Victorian artist's search for authenticity. After sketching fishermen's cottages in Devon for a week, Fildes built a full-size replica of a cottage interior in his studio in Melbury Road, complete with rafters, walls, and the window on the right through which the dawn light was to glimmer. Fildes was well-rewarded for his trouble; the picture was an instant success at the Royal Academy of 1891, and over a million engravings of it were sold around the world. Sir Henry Tate, its purchaser, gave it to the nation along with his collection, and for years it has been one of the most popular pictures in the Tate Gallery – apart, that is, from its relegation to the basement during the philistine years of the 1920s and 30s.

Children playing, rather than dying, was a much more popular subject. 'Old art waited reverently in the forum' complained Ruskin; 'ours plays happily in the nursery'. Many of the artists we have already encountered painted pictures of children's games. Thomas Webster, that specialist in the doings of the Victorian schoolboy, shows us a rustic *See-Saw* (144); F.D. Hardy, also of the Cranbrook group, a game of *Hide and Seek* (142). Hardy enjoyed the views upstairs and through doorways to other rooms that these interiors offered, just as Pieter de Hoogh had done in Holland two centuries earlier. William Hemsley, in one of his typically cheerful scenes, shows children blowing bubbles (143), and William Bromley a game of marbles (145). John Morgan gives us two

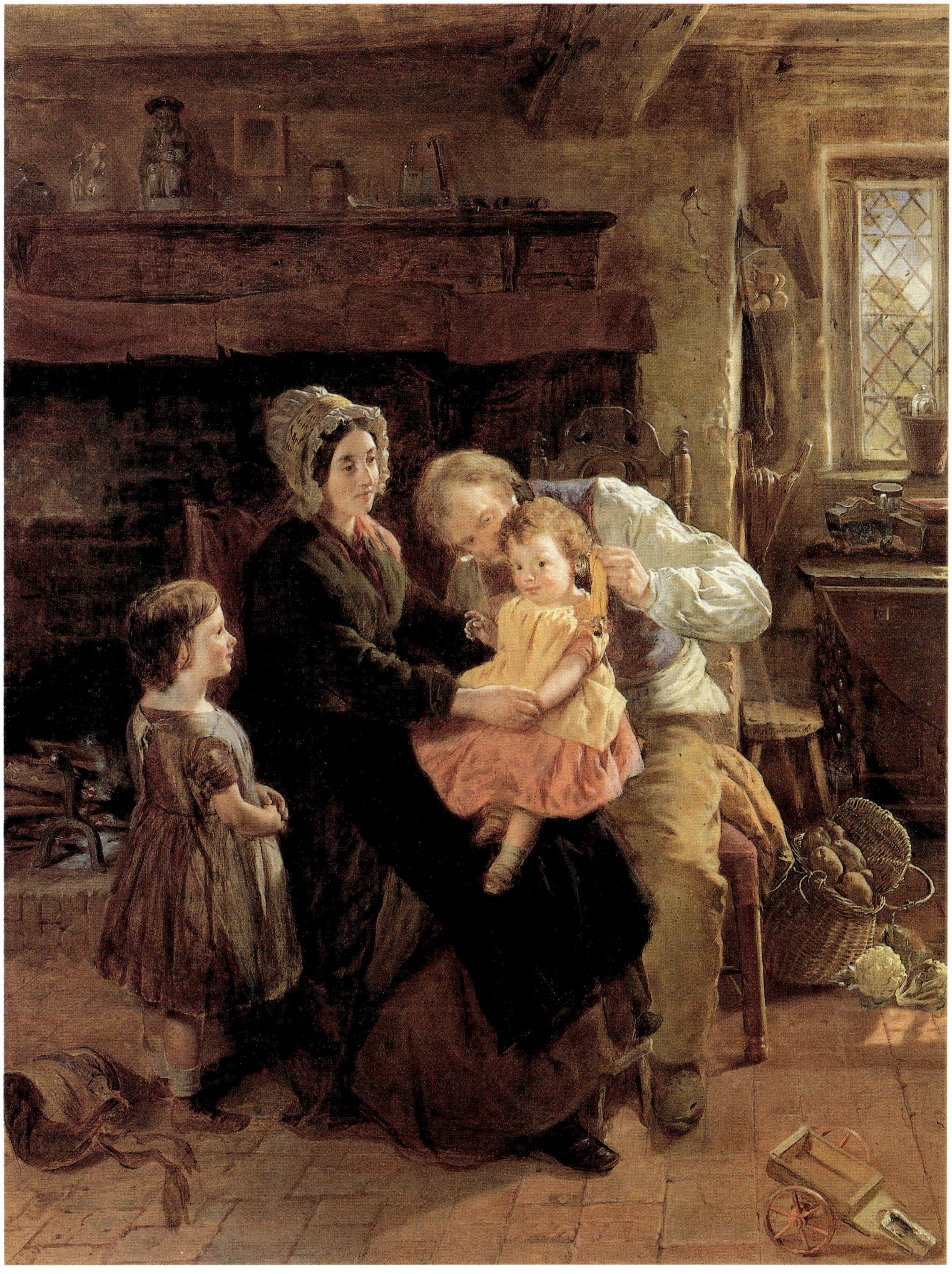

139
William Henry Knight
*The Youngest Child*

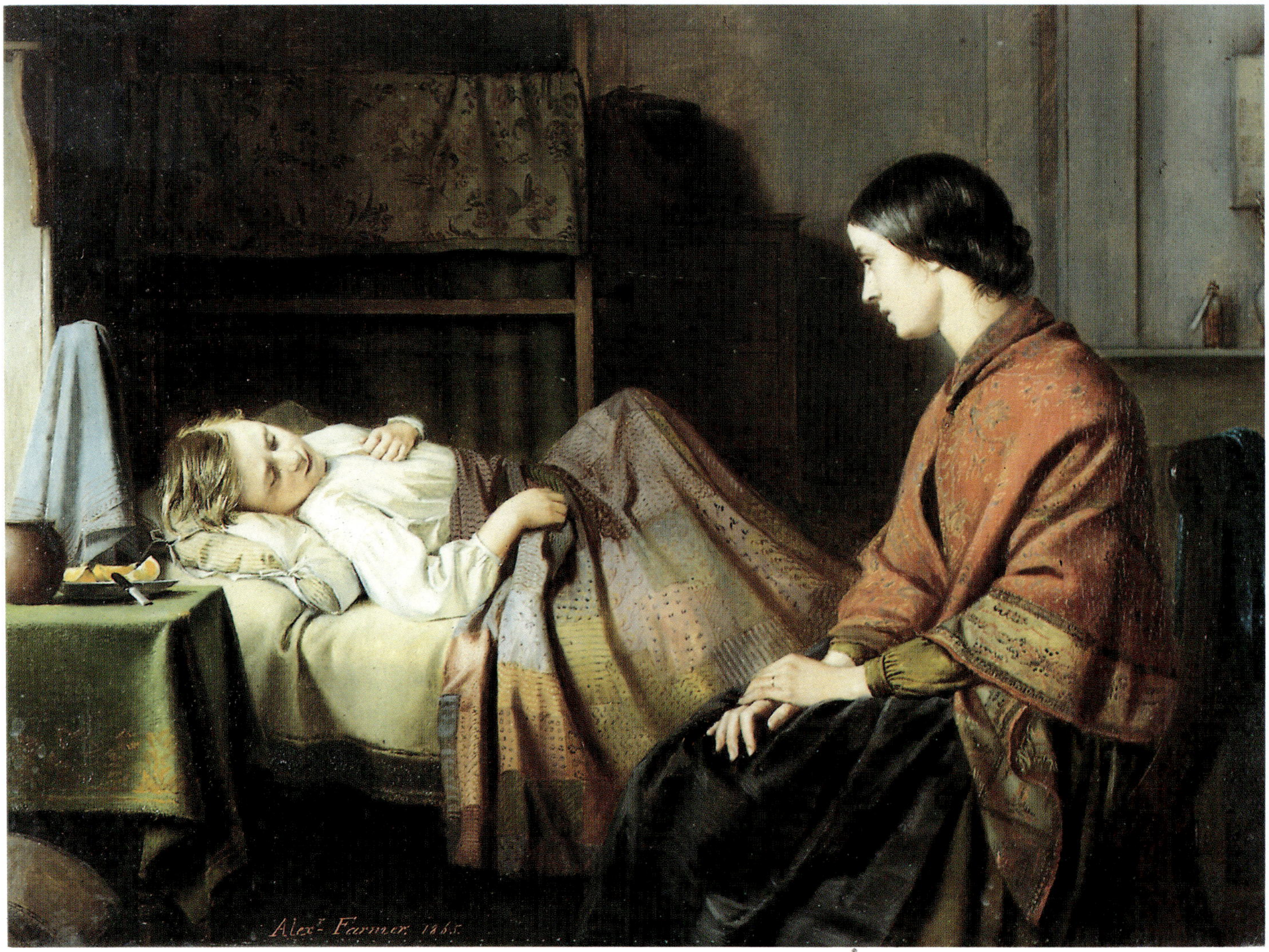

140
Mrs Alexander Farmer
*An Anxious Hour*

boys squaring up for a fight, encouraged by the other boys and a group of rustics (149). An older man is trying to intervene, without success, and in the background is a cricket match, which may be the source of the quarrel. These pictures only show us a few of the games played by children – unfortunately many games seem never to have been made the subject of paintings. At Lark Rise, the girls would take part in an extraordinary number of traditional games and dances. Some are still remembered, such as Oranges and Lemons, or London Bridge, but others have been completely forgotten, such as Here Come Three Tinkers, Thread the Tailor's Needle, Honeypots, Waly Waly Wallflower, Green Gravel, Queen Anne, and many more.

Another favourite occupation of children was blackberrying, and this was painted by many artists. Victorian children found much that was edible in the hedgerows and fields. Alfred Williams remembered that Wiltshire children ate many things:

> In the spring they eat the large buds and young leaves of the hawthorn, commonly known as 'bread and cheese' . . . later they devour primrose and cowslip petals and stems, the juicy leaves of the sorrel; afterward they dig up the underground nuts. . . . Then, in the summer, there is the fruit of the maple tree, 'hatchet and bill-hooks', crabs and wilderns; and in the autumn blackberries, acorns, beech and hazel nuts. When these are gone there remain slans (or sloes), peggles (hawthorn fruit), hipsons (the wild-briar berries) and the rich berries of the year. All these things are gathered and devoured by the youngsters of the countryside, to say nothing of raw wheat and barley, peas and beans, with turnips, swedes, and mangolds from the field.

Obviously there were many ways Victorian country children could supplement their diet. Sophie Anderson's little girl in *Windfalls* (147) is gathering apples, though by the look of her rosy cheeks she is not thinking of stealing any. Sophie Ander-

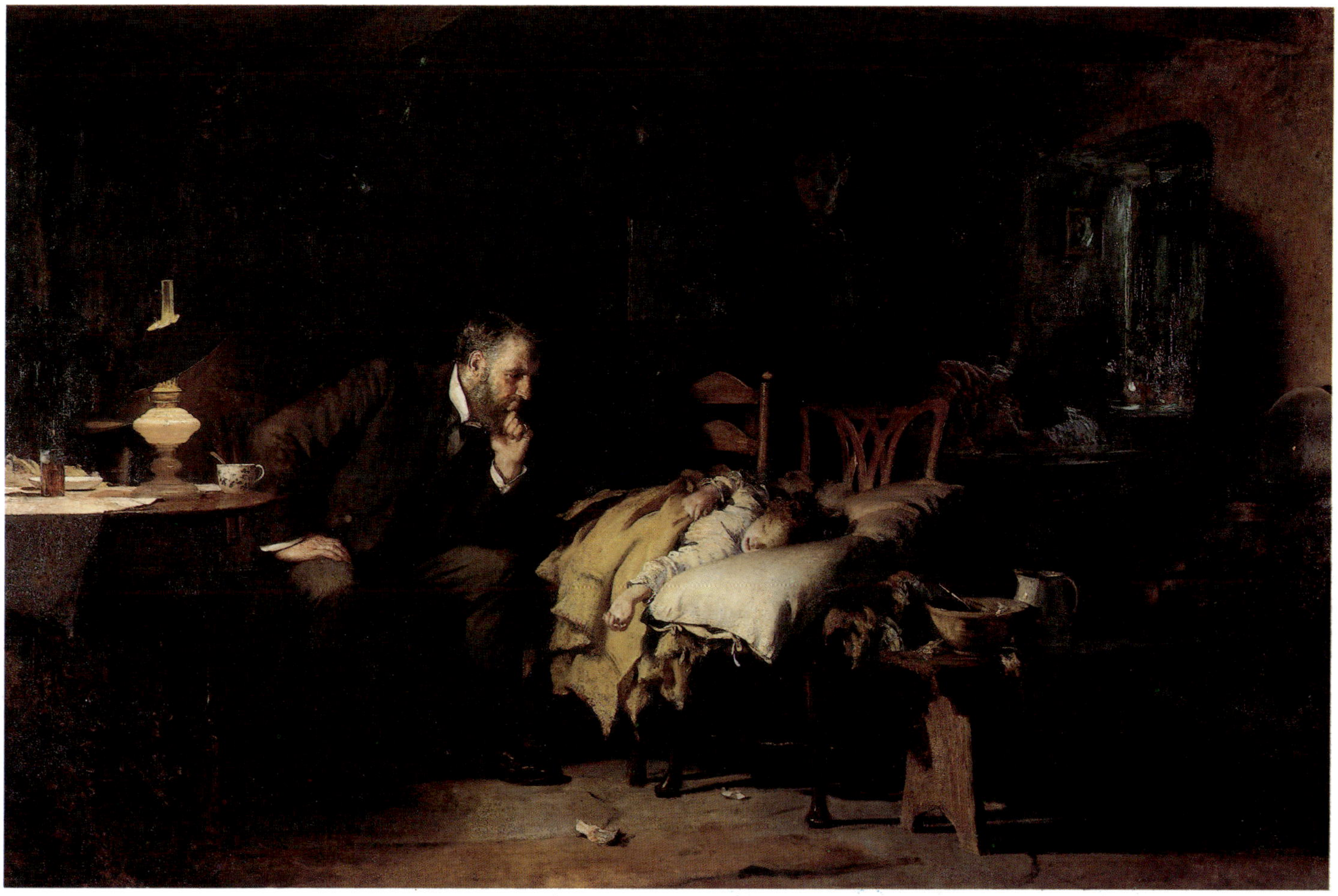

141
SIR LUKE FILDES
*The Doctor*

son was another of the many Victorian painters of pretty little girls in landscapes. So too was William Gunning King, though his works are later and more impressionistic in style. His delightful *Saturday Afternoon* (148) shows two children by a river fishing for minnows to put in their glass jar.

What very few of these pictures even hint at is the fact that most of these children would be sent out to work in the fields by the age of eight or nine. Frederick J. Shields's moving *One of our Breadwatchers* (146) acts as a stern and necessary reminder. At Porlock, in Somerset, Shields observed the practice of leaving children out in the snow all day to scare the birds off the newly-sown corn, using rattles. The children sat in rudely constructed shelters made of gorse and hurdles, heated by tiny fires, as shown in the picture. Shields himself 'worked for three days in a snow-covered, ploughed field sharing the privations which his little model and many other boys and girls endured for the poorest wage'. A *Times* reviewer in 1866 thought the title 'of questionable taste' but went on to praise the picture for its pathos: 'It will be a good time for the art when our painters have learnt what a wealth of subjects there is about us to be realised without falsehood, exaggeration or sickliness.' Children were widely used for all kinds of farm work, not only light jobs such as bird-scaring, weeding, watching animals, stone-picking and gleaning, but also in nearly all the harvests, hay, corn, hop-picking, potato-picking, and apple-gathering. The revelation that very young children were employed in gangs, often with a brutal and cruel overseer, shocked public opinion and Parliament into the passing of the Gangs Act of 1867. This prohibited the employment of children under eight in gangs, and prohibited mixed gangs of boys and girls. It stopped some of the worst abuses, but did not prevent children going to work after the age of eight. Numerous Education Acts followed in the 1870s and 80s, and gradually parents were forced to send their children to school until they were older.

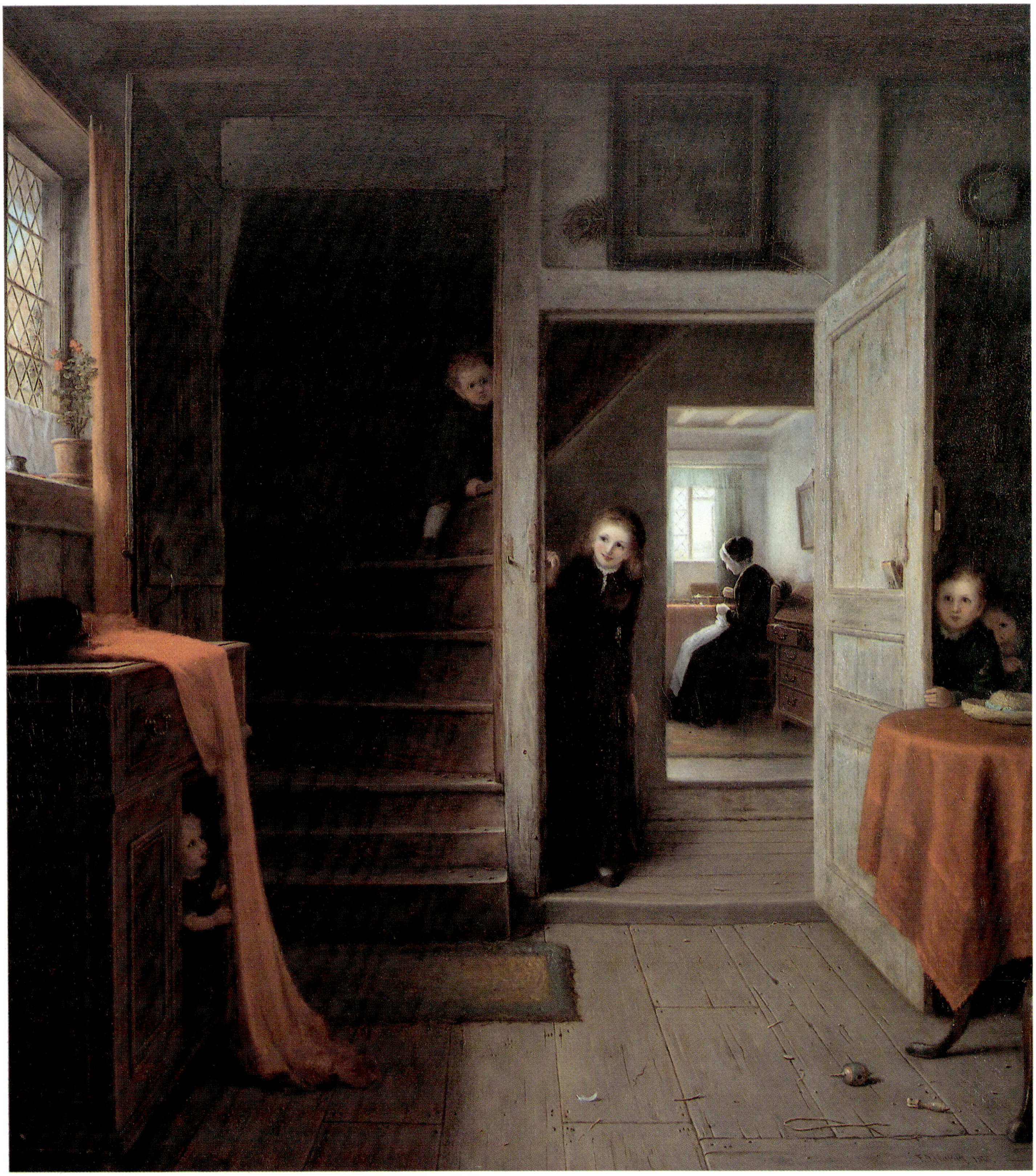

142
FREDERICK DANIEL HARDY
*Hide and Seek*

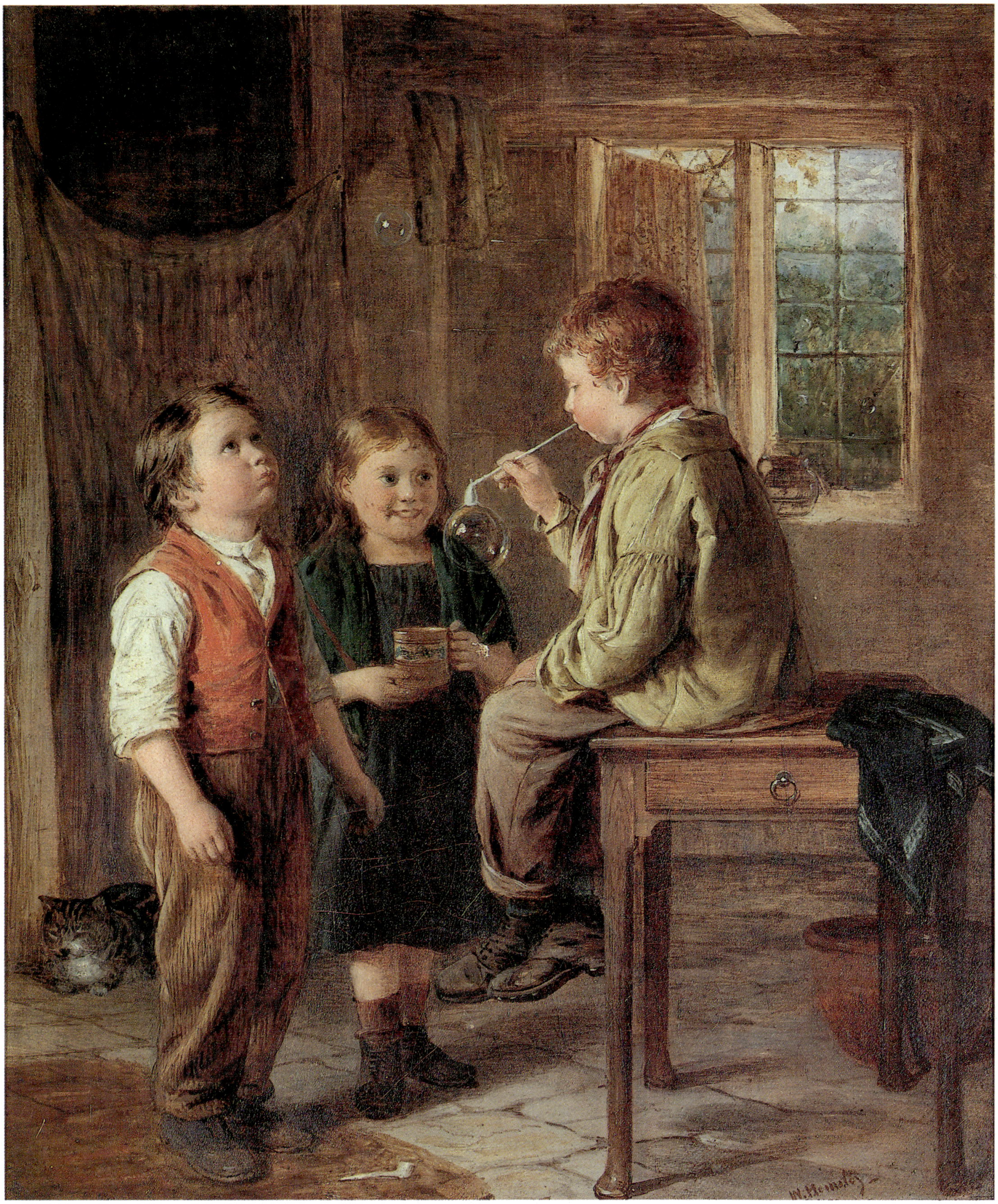

143
William Hemsley
*Bubbles*

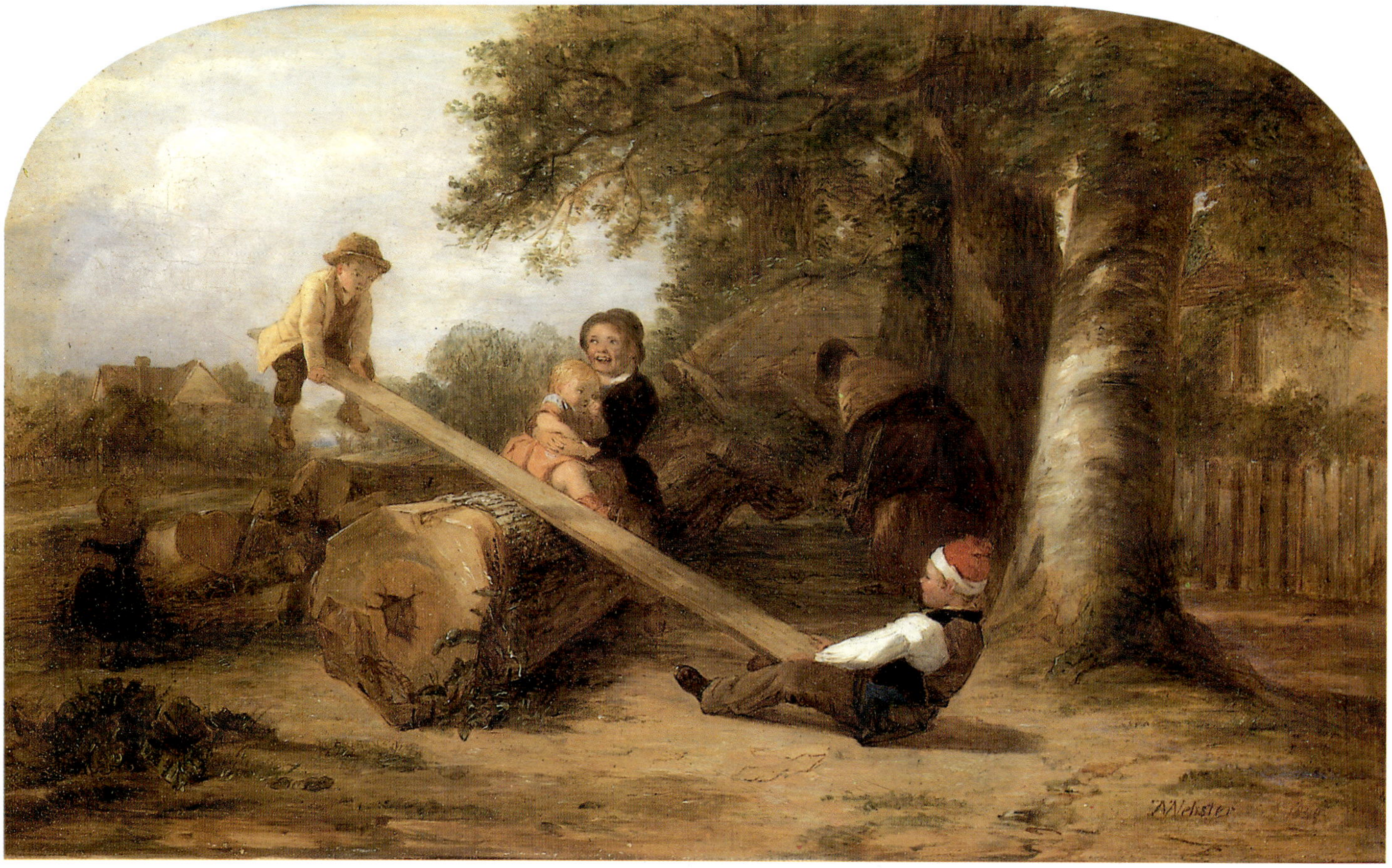

144
THOMAS WEBSTER
*The See-Saw*

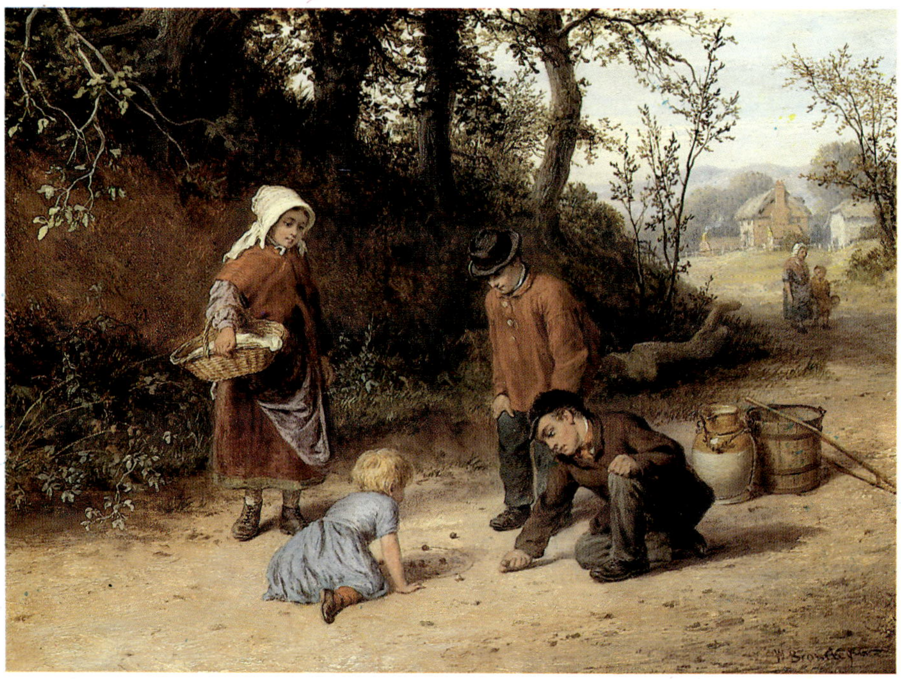

145
WILLIAM BROMLEY
*A Game of Marbles*

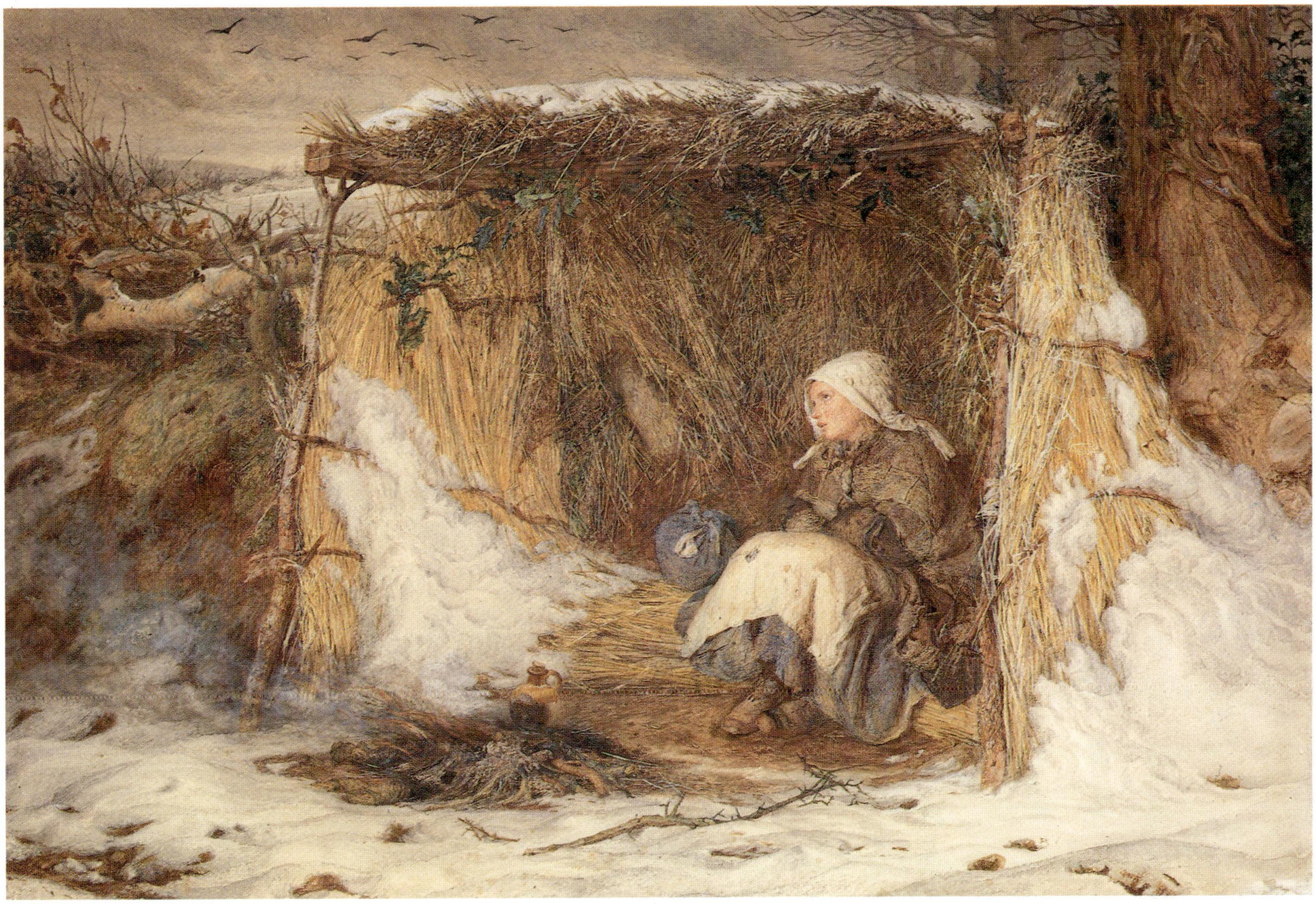

146
FREDERICK JAMES SHIELDS
*One of our Breadwatchers*

'In the very short schooling that I obtained, I learnt neither grammar nor writing. On the day that I was eight years of age, I left school, and began to work fourteen hours a day in the fields, with from forty to fifty other children of whom, even at that early age, I was the eldest. We were followed all day long by an old man carrying a long whip in his hand, which he did not forget to use.' Thus wrote Mrs Burrows in her recollections of 'A Childhood in the Fens about 1850-60'. Her experience was probably fairly typical. The quality of education received by country children in the nineteenth century was poor, but varied considerably according to local conditions. Some villages had a small endowment sufficient to pay a local 'dame', who taught the village children to read and write. Others had parochial schools supported by rates or endowments; an increasing number had national schools, which were partly funded locally and partly by government grant. On large estates there was often a school built and maintained by the landowner, especially if one of his sons was rector of the local parish, which was often the case with landed families. There were also church schools, both Church of England and nonconformist, and many of these had Sunday schools which taught reading as well as giving religious instruction.

The most common type of village school was the so-called 'dame' school, and this was the one which particularly appealed to painters. Both Alfred Rankley (150) and William Bromley (151) painted pictures of ancient dames, in their widow's caps, teaching small numbers of children in their own cottages. Both the cottages are extremely snug and cheerful. Very few small villages actually had a school building of their own, so the vestry, the church hall, a cottage, or even someone's kitchen was used instead. The standard in these small village schools was likely to be low; a child might learn to read only, not to write properly or do sums. A Hampshire Schools inspector wrote in the 1880s of children at a poor

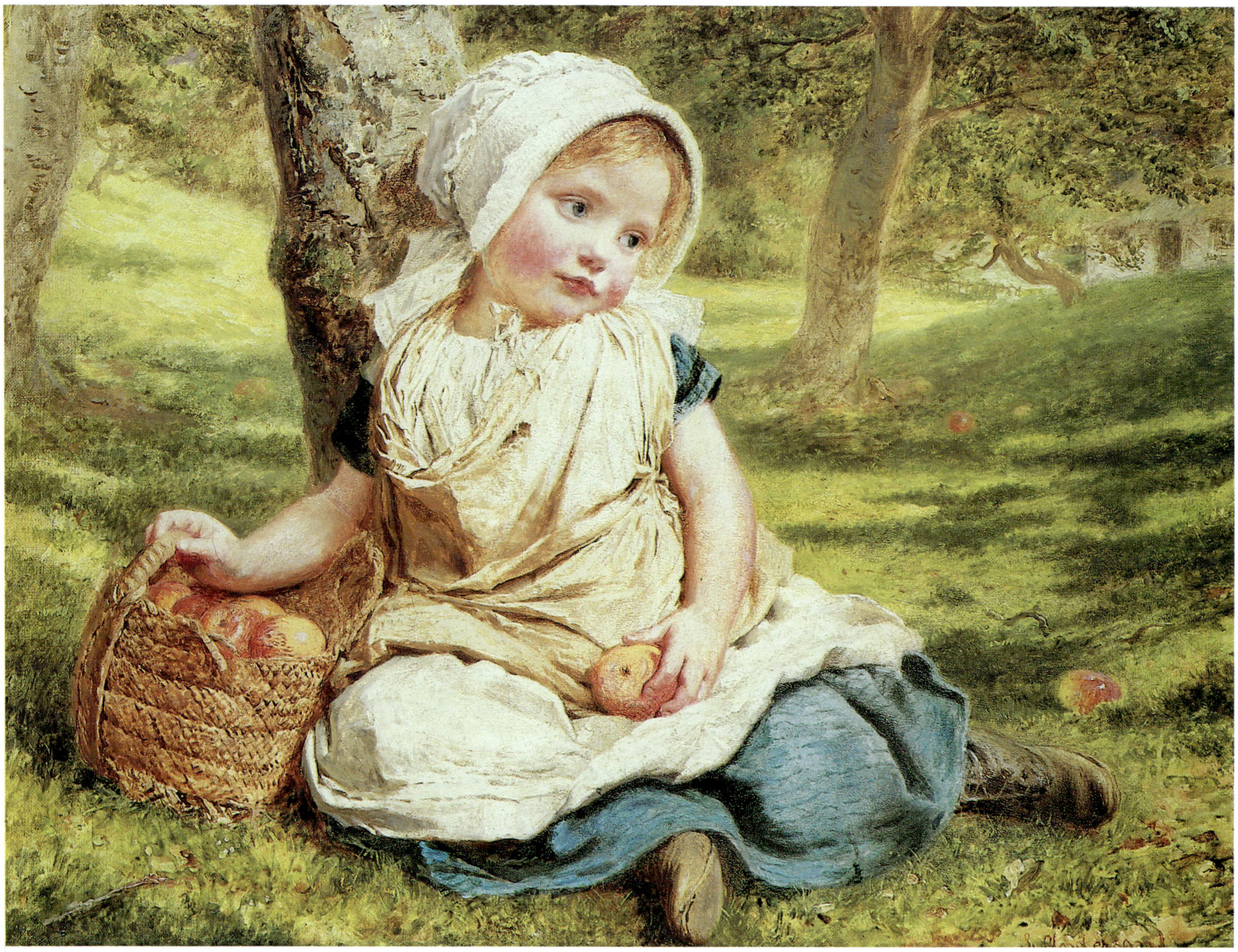

147
SOPHIE ANDERSON
*Windfalls*

school: 'in the hands of a dull monitor, frequently packed away in a dark corner of the main room or in a dingy classroom, where the luckless little creatures have only the opportunity of learning how, without crying, to sit still for hours together, with dangling legs and aching backs.' The little girl in C.J. Lewis's picture *Dreaming* (152) is certainly dozing over her lessons.

Lark Rise was fortunate in having a national school in the nearby village of Fordlow, presided over by a schoolmistress, or 'governess' as she was called. Leaving home at seven in the morning, the children walked there and back every day, a journey of a mile and a half each way, carrying their dinner-baskets with them. In cold weather some of them carried two hot potatoes which had been in the oven all night, to warm their hands on the way and to eat on arrival. The school had about forty-five children and consisted of just one large classroom. Flora Thompson described the childrens' appearance:

Even then, to an outsider, it would have appeared a quaint, old-fashioned little gathering; the girls in their ankle-length frocks and long, straight pinafores, with their hair strained back from their brows and secured on their crowns by a ribbon or black tape or a bootlace; the bigger boys in corduroys and hobnailed boots, and the smaller ones in home-made sailor suits or, until they were six or seven, in petticoats.

The entry of the governess was greeted with 'good morning ma'am', and much curtseying and pulling of forelocks. The day then began with hymns on the harmonium, and prayers. Every morning the local rector arrived to take the older children for scripture. He was one of the old school, 'as far as possible removed by birth, education and worldly circumstances from the lambs of his flock', and saw to it that the phrase 'to order myself lowly and reverently before my betters' was underlined in the catechism. If he found the boys ragging or misbehaving,

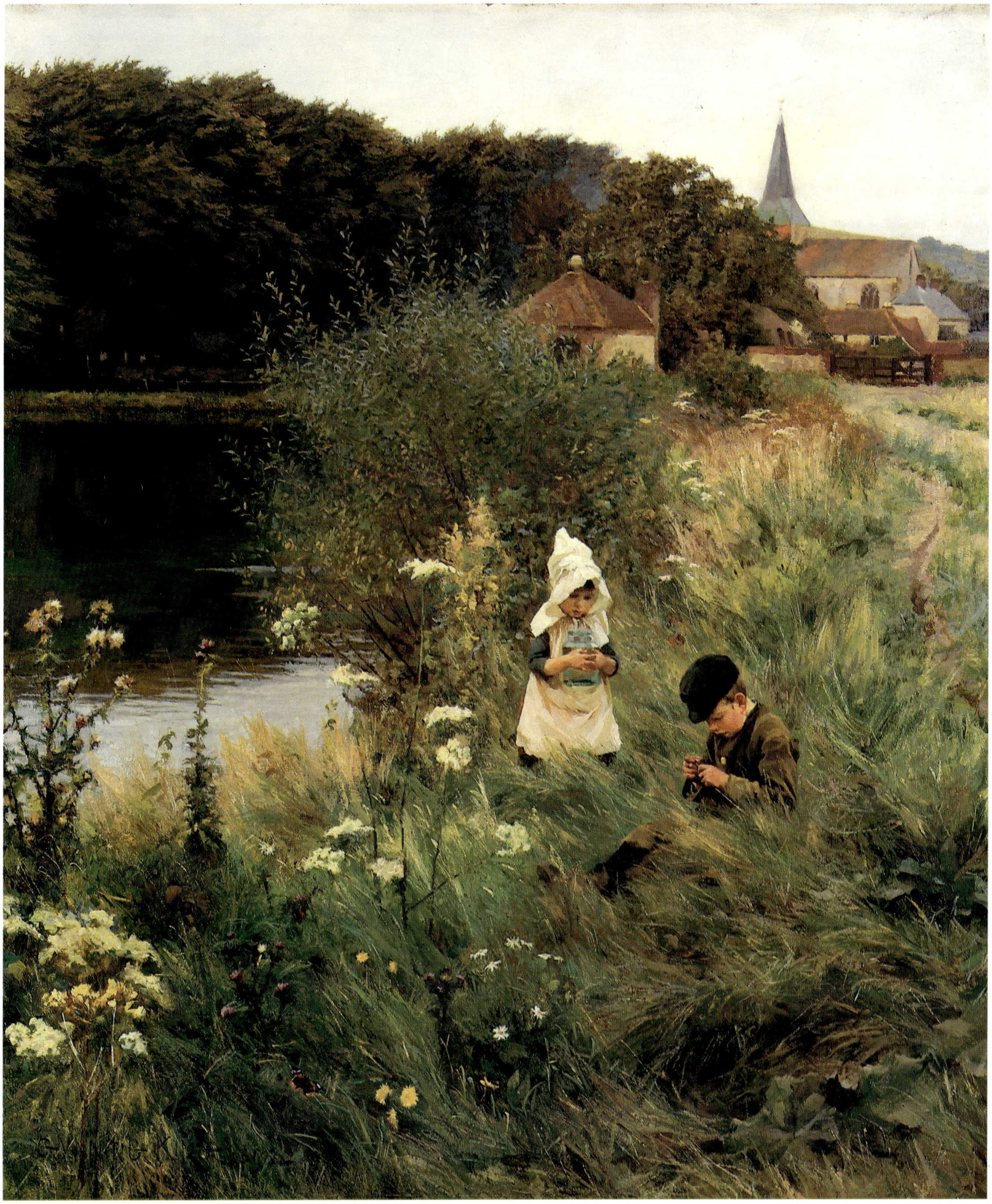

148
WILLIAM GUNNING KING
*Saturday Afternoon*

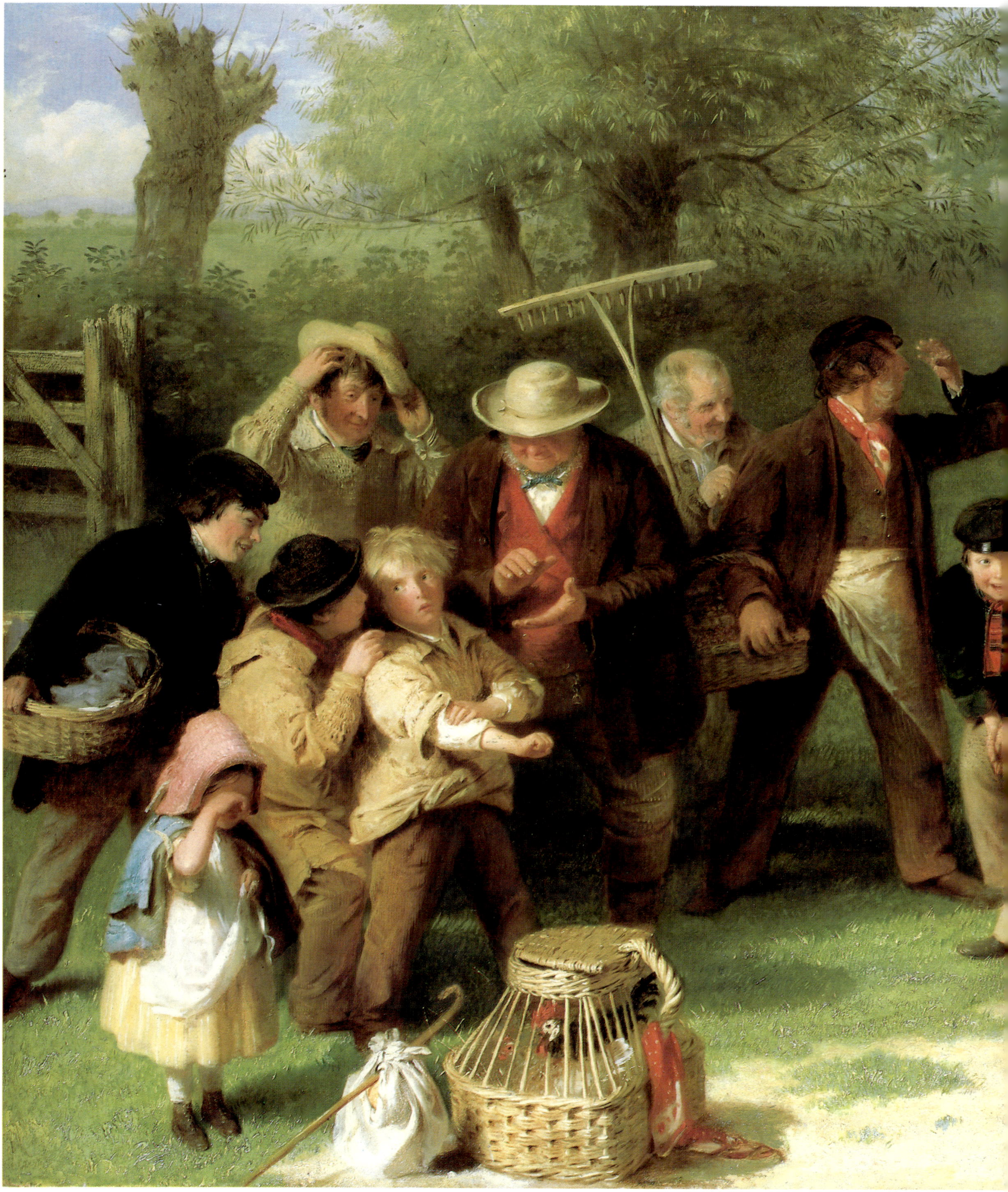

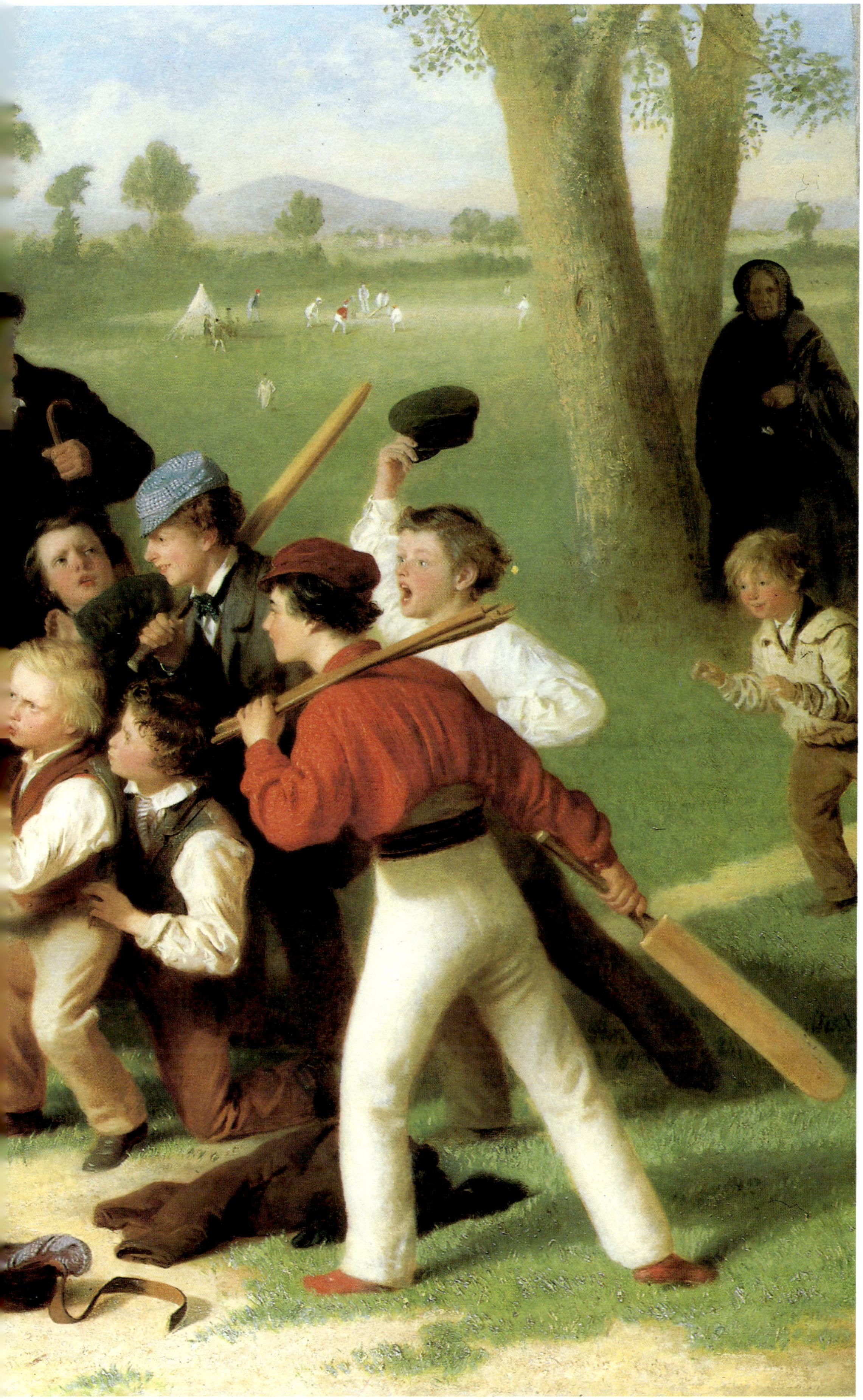

149
JOHN MORGAN
*The Cricket Match*

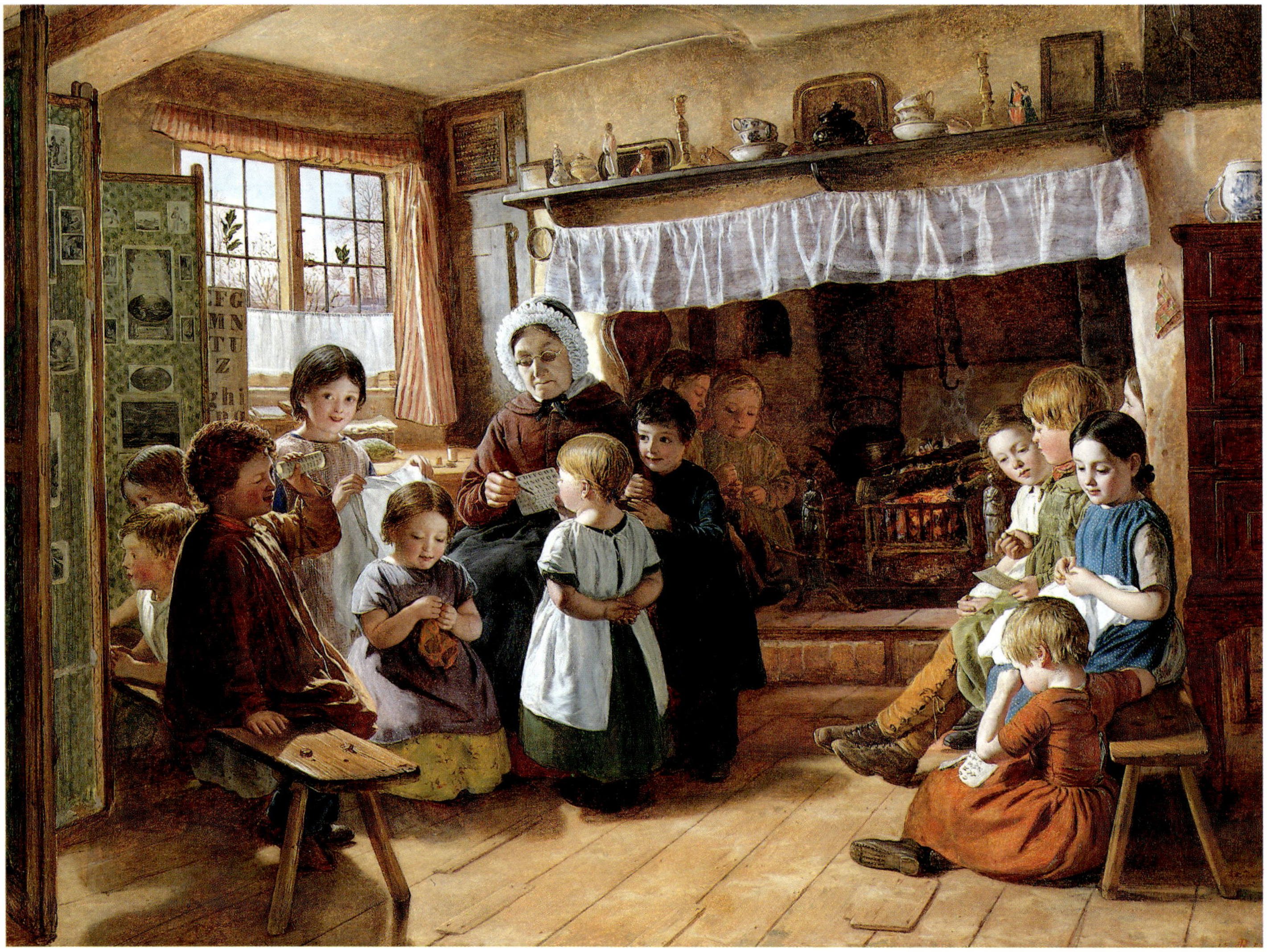

150
ALFRED RANKLEY
*The Village School*

he would not hesitate to use the cane. The lady of the manor would also appear occasionally to inspect the children, and in particular the girls' needlework. Alfred Williams's description of his village school in Wiltshire matches that of Lark Rise almost exactly. They too were 'subject to visits from the vicar and the lady of the manor', who expected deference and good behaviour. 'Little boy, where are your manners?' the lady would say to some recalcitrant boy. 'Ain't got none miss' would be his cheeky reply, before running off.

George Washington Brownlow has left us a very interesting picture of *A Straw-Plaiting School in Essex* (153). Straw-plaiting and basket-making were important industries in the south of England, especially in Buckinghamshire, Bedfordshire, Hertfordshire and Essex. Children started to learn the technique of straw-plaiting very young; even as young as two or three they could clip off the loose ends; at four they would start to plait. Then they would be sent to a nearby 'craft' or plaiting school, where they not only learnt, but produced finished work for sale. The children in Brownlow's picture all look very cheerful and rosy, but this was not the case in the inspectors' reports. One inspector in 1871 reported that young children were crowded into small rooms, generally presided over by a master or mistress 'with cane in hand to remind the idler of his duty. . . . I have been told that one of the reasons why parents send their children to the plaiting school instead of allowing them to plait at home is because the master or mistress "gets more work out of them" than they could venture to attempt themselves.' Also, a child who went to a craft school would not be able to pursue an ordinary education, so many of them remained deficient in the three Rs. Eventually, the Workshops Regulation Act of 1867 prohibited the employment of children under eight in any handicraft. But parents and employers contrived to get round the Act for many years, and no-one could prevent children working at home. Straw-plaiting remained a profitable

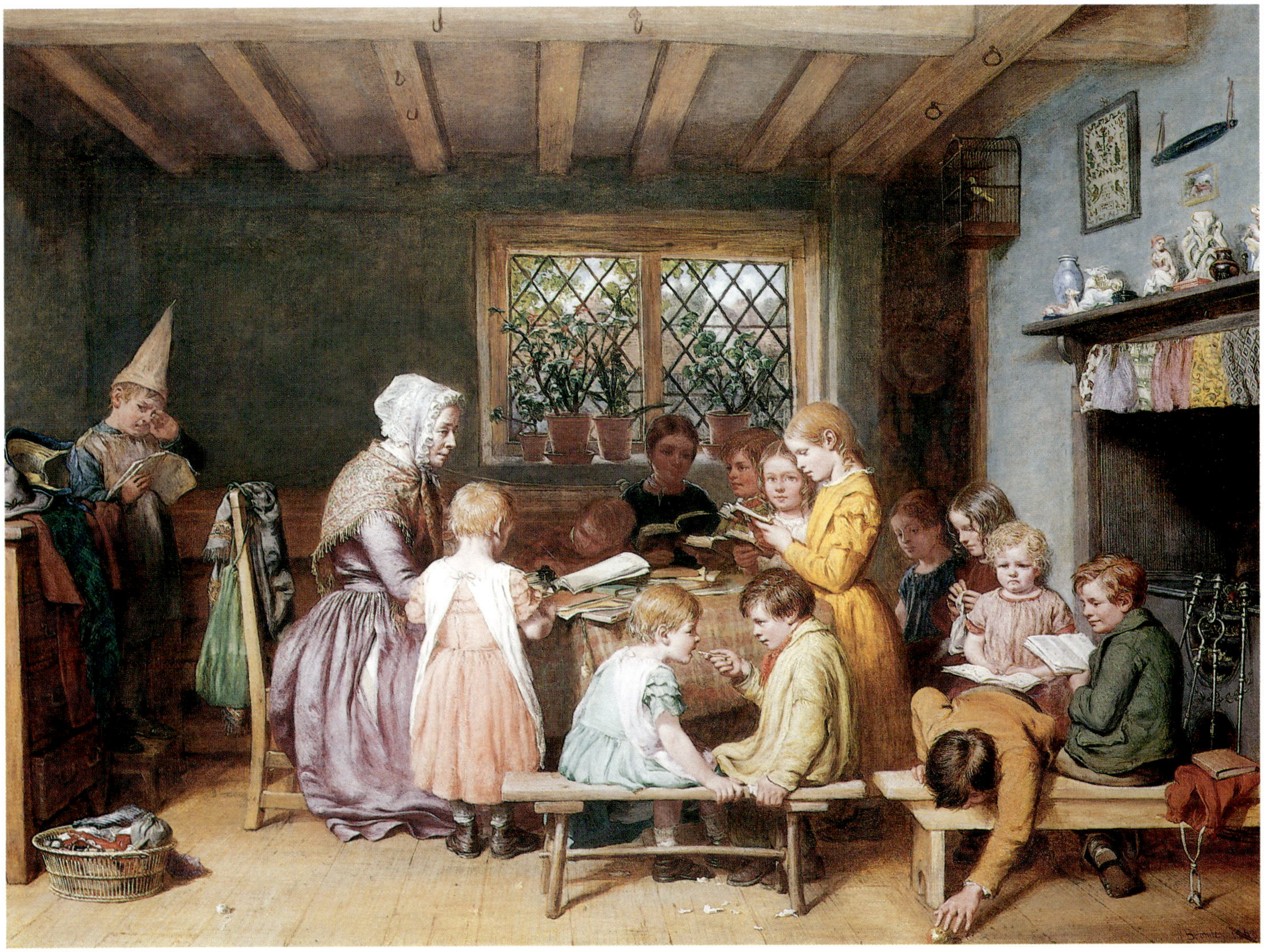

151
William Bromley
*The Schoolroom*

industry right up to the end of the century, before it was finally killed off by machinery, but it was always a lowly-paid occupation. As always, the plaiters were powerless to resist exploitation by the middle-man who bought their goods and took them to sell in the local towns.

After the first Education Act of 1870, things began to improve. New schools were built, teachers trained, inspectors appointed. Children were forbidden to work under the age of ten, and schooling was made compulsory up to the age of thirteen. In the country, however, the new laws were simply disregarded. Many children continued to work in the fields, and take time off for harvesting and gleaning. Absenteeism was rife, and was encouraged by many parents who resented the fact that their children could no longer go out and earn a living. 'What do our Alf want wi' a lot o' book larnin?' said one parent in Lark Rise. 'He can read and write and add up as much money as he's ever likely to get. What more do he want?' School inspectors found it difficult to bring about any improvements in country schools, and their reports are full of frustrations and complaints during the 1880s and 90s. The arrival of the Inspector was an event dreaded at Fordlow School. He was an elderly clergyman, reputed to be strict: '. . . His voice was an exasperated roar and his criticism was a blend of outraged learning and sarcasm . . . he did not care for or understand children. . . .' It took twenty years and several more Education Acts before schooling finally became compulsory for all children in the country. The paradox is that all the Victorian concern for education only served in the end to drive people off the land. No-one wanted to be a farmer's drudge when he could go off and become a clerk or a porter on the railway. The Victorians were driven by their social conscience to educate the people, but they shrank from the social consequences. They feared social mobility, hence the endless insistence on schools inculcating in their pupils the injunction to 'be happy in that

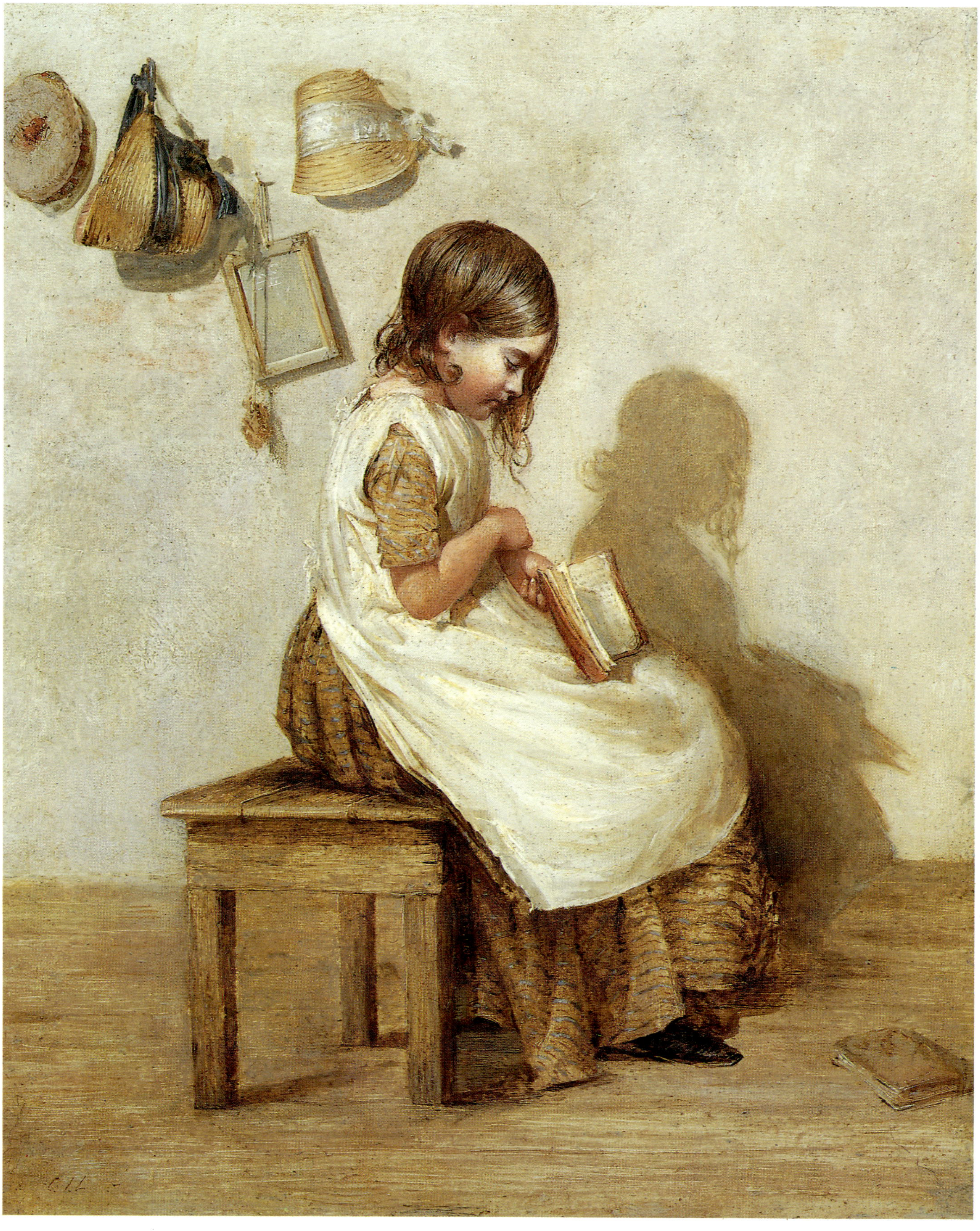

152
Charles James Lewis
*Dreaming*

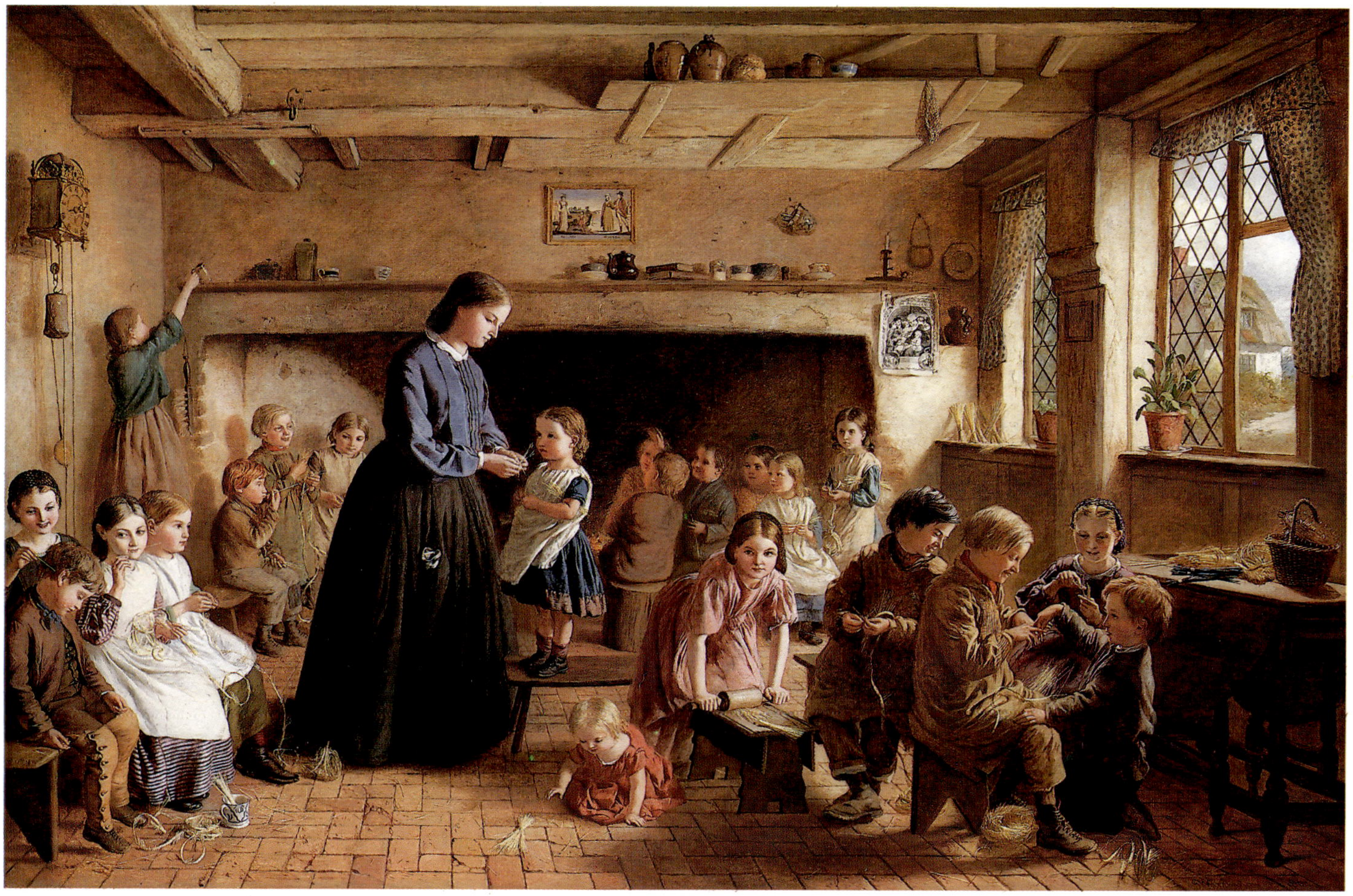

153
GEORGE WASHINGTON BROWNLOW
*A Straw-Plaiting School in Essex*

station in which God had seen fit to place them' – in other words, the bottom. This sentiment was even enshrined in a verse of that quintessentially Victorian hymn 'All things bright and beautiful':

> The rich man in his castle,
> The poor man at his gate,
> He made them high or lowly,
> And ordered their estate.

Rider Haggard, in his book *Rural England*, confirmed that by 1902: 'Education has certainly done much to depopulate the rural districts, for if a lad cannot read and write and do a sum he is no use in the town, and what he otherwise learns at school has no reference and no value to country life and farm labour.' Agriculture was at its lowest ebb when Haggard was writing, and he commented 'It is now common for only the dullards, the vicious, or the wastrels to stay upon the land, because they are unfitted for any other life.'

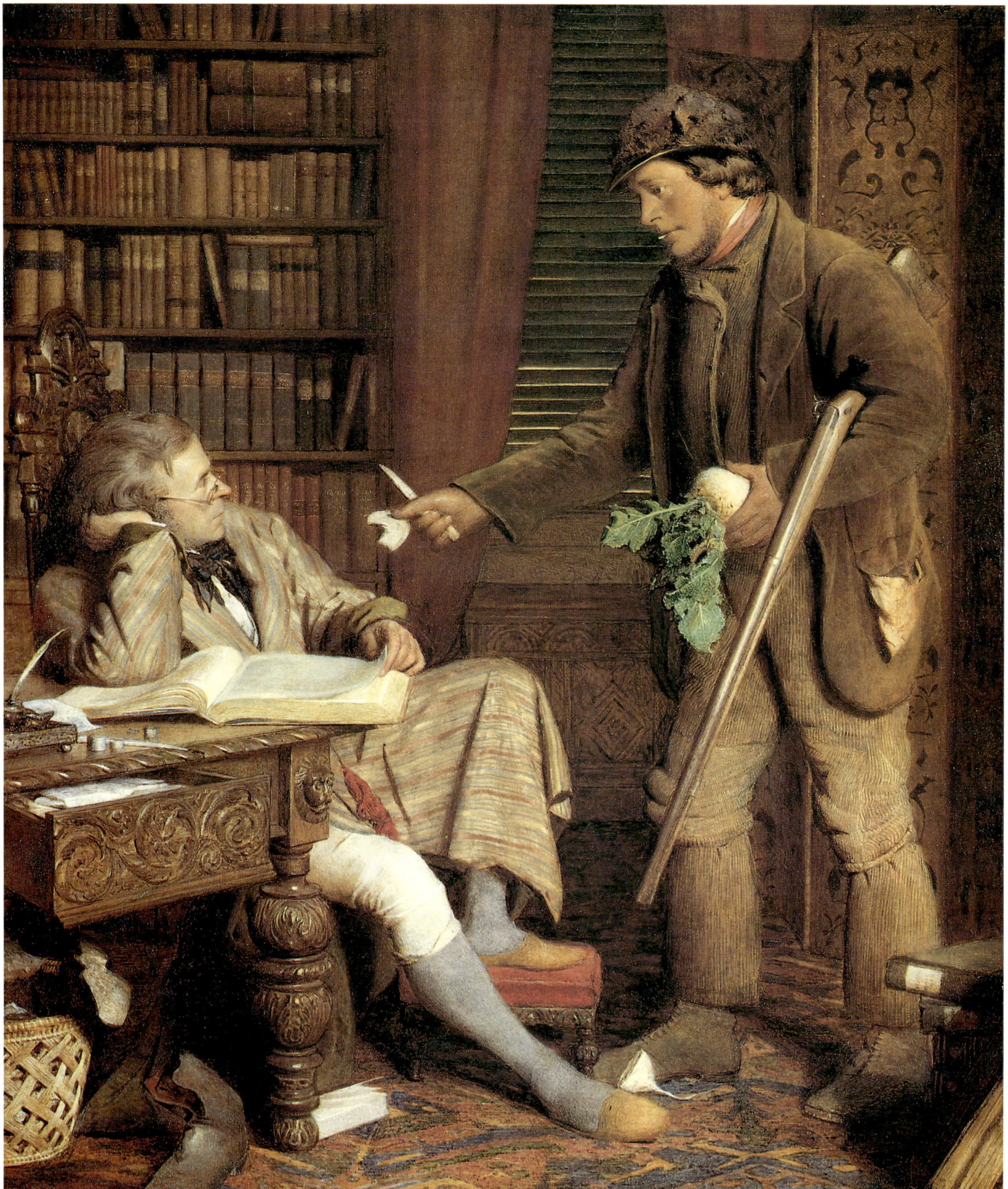

154
James Lobley
*The Squire and the Gamekeeper*

# Chapter Twelve

# THE SQUIRE

O let us love our occupations,
Bless the squire and his relations,
Live upon our daily rations,
And always know our proper stations.

CHARLES DICKENS, *The Chimes*

ALEXANDER II OF RUSSIA THOUGHT THAT THE next best thing to being Tsar of Russia was to be an English country gentleman. Certainly, it was a pleasant thing to be a member of the English aristocracy or landed gentry in the nineteenth century. They were at the zenith of their power, prestige and wealth. Most of the land belonged to them. Income from city property, mining and commerce had made many of them richer than ever before. Whether Whigs or Tories, their political influence was immense, and most of the Prime Ministers of the nineteenth century, except Disraeli and Gladstone, were hereditary peers. On their own estates, they were absolute rulers. As magistrates, justices of the peace, or members of local councils, they kept local affairs under their control. The local vicar, whose appointment they often controlled, was often a relation. If the landowner was a sportsman, hunting, shooting and fishing were his to command, and the Game Laws gave him draconian powers to protect these sports from poachers. He could decree who lived on his estate and who could not.

Social prestige was still associated principally with land ownership; as Walter Bagshot phrased it, 'All opulence gravitates towards the land.' The new rich, with fortunes made in commerce or industry, hastened to seek respectability by buying themselves country estates. It was an almost unprecedented era of country-house building, largely funded with new money derived from biscuits, banking, guano, ostrich feathers, and a host of other trades. Industrialists in their dozens strove to realise the Victorian dream of 'an estate in the country, a glistening new country house with thick carpets and plate-glass windows, the grateful villagers, at the door of their picturesque cottages, touching their caps to their new landlord, J.P., High Sheriff perhaps, with his sons at Eton and Christchurch and his clean, blooming daughters teaching in the Sunday School' (Mark

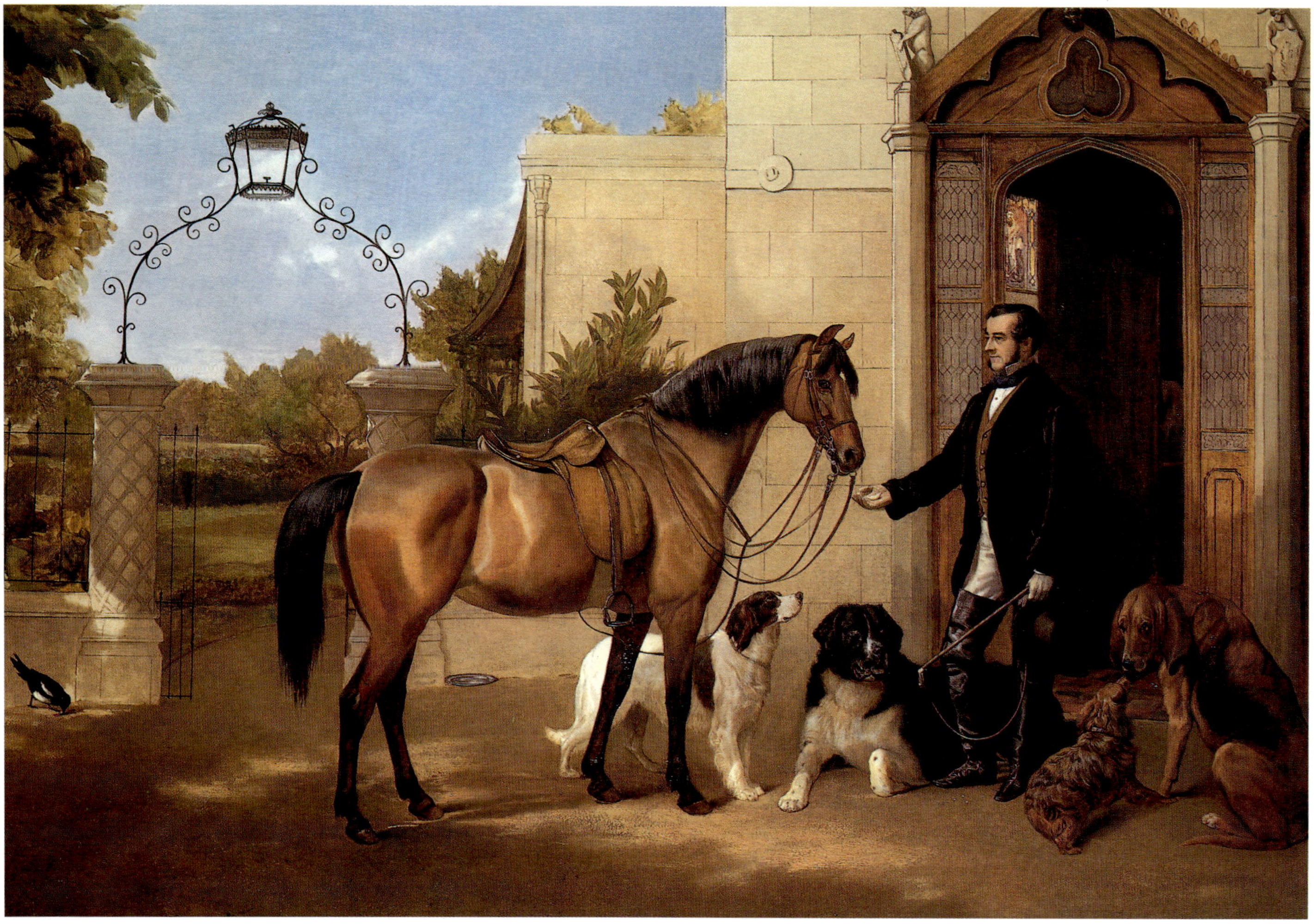

155
FREDERICK WILLIAM KEYL
*Portrait of a Gentleman with his Horse and Dogs*

Girouard, *The Victorian Country House*, 1981). In time they could hope for the ultimate accolade, an entry in *Burke's Landed Gentry*.

Victorian landowners generally were benevolent autocrats. They took their responsibilities seriously, and many of them took a keen interest in agricultural improvements. But in return they expected both obedience and deference. They expected the villagers to doff their caps and their womenfolk to curtsey. Lark Rise only had a minor and impoverished squire, yet as Flora Thompson wrote: 'It would be impossible for anyone born in this century to imagine the pride and importance of such small country gentlepeople in the 1880s.' In spite of being poor, '. . . they expected to reign over their poorer neighbours and to be treated by them with the deference due to royalty. Like royalty, too, they could be charming to those who pleased them. Those who did not had to beware.' Joseph Arch wrote bitterly that

> We labourers had no lack of lords and masters. There were the parson and his wife at the rectory. There was the squire, with his hand of iron overshadowing us all. There was no velvet glove on that hard hand. . . . At the sight of the squire, the people trembled. He lorded it right feudally over his tenants, the farmers; the farmers in their turn tyrannised over the labourers; the labourers were no better than toads under a harrow.

Arch, who founded the National Union of Agricultural Labourers in 1872, started life as a hedge-cutter in Warwickshire. He combined lay-preaching for the Primitive Methodists with campaigning for better pay and conditions for farm workers. In 1889 he became a member of Parliament and although the landed classes regarded him as a dangerous radical, for many ordinary labourers he was a hero, the only real farm worker's friend. In the Waggon and Horses in Lark Rise, for example, 'Sam, the man with advanced opinions,

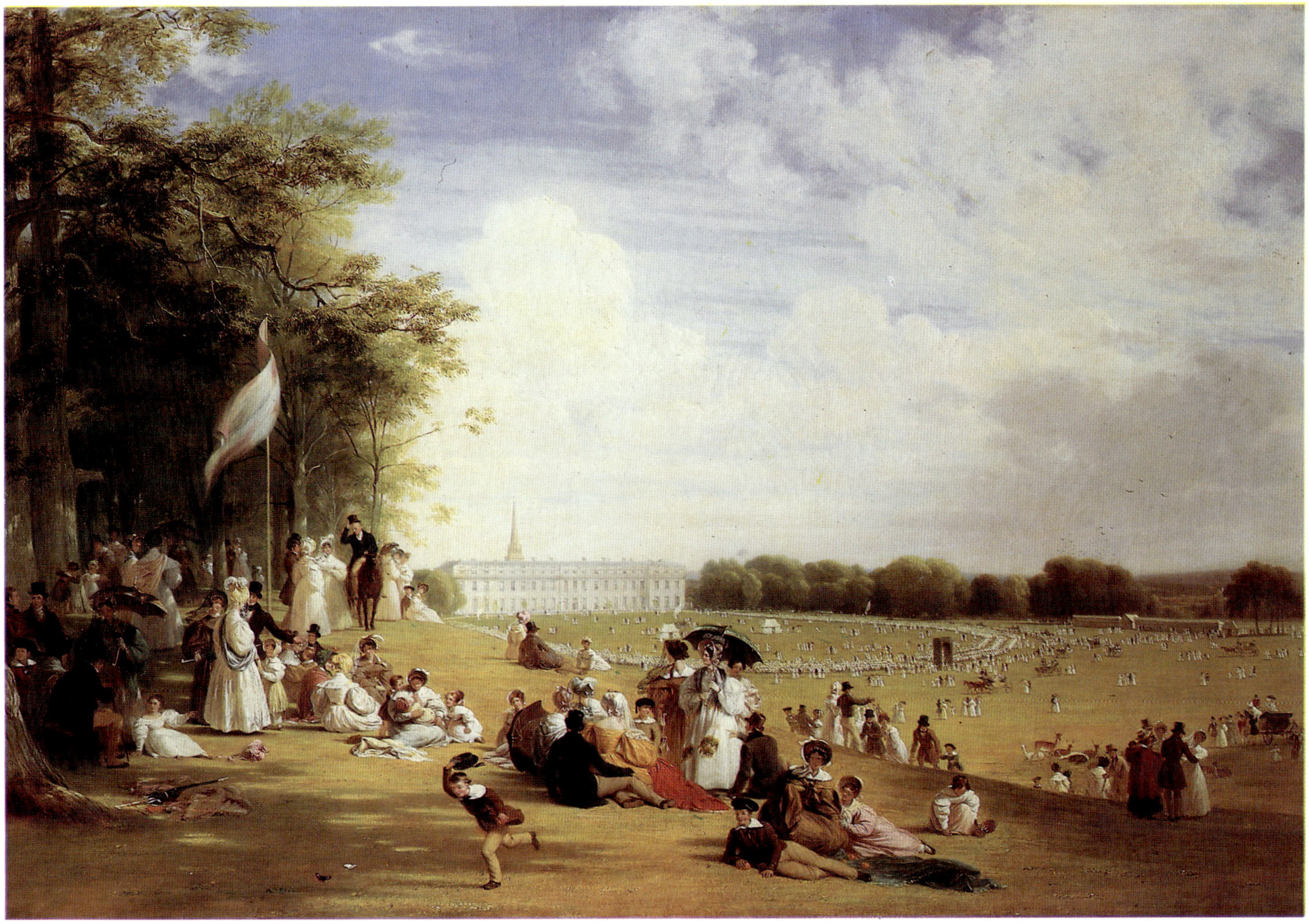

156
William Frederick Witherington
*A Fete in Petworth Park*

would relate with reverent pride the story of his meeting and shaking hands with Joseph Arch, the farm worker's champion', thumping the table, and waving his pewter mug.

The squire mainly features in Victorian art in pictures of sport, as we shall see in the next chapter. Sport was his most public, and his most ornamental role in the countryside, and the one that brought him most into contact with the farmers, tenants, and people of the neighbourhood. Most portraits of Victorian squires, like the one by Frederick William Keyl (155), show him with his favourite horse and dogs. No sign of the wife and children here. This squire is standing outside what looks like a Victorian country house of recent construction. Keyl was a German painter who became a pupil of Sir Edwin Landseer. Through Landseer he met Queen Victoria and Prince Albert, who commissioned him to paint a great many of their favourite dogs, horses, and other animals.

One very interesting and rare picture shows us a rather different kind of squire, sitting in his library poring over books – *The Squire and the Gamekeeper* by James Lobley (154). This squire is clearly not interested in farming, or even in the rent, which sits on the table beside him. So absorbed is he in his books that he has the blinds pulled down to keep out the light. The gamekeeper seems to be complaining that he and his wife have to live on turnips, and cuts off a piece of turnip to give to his master. This is the kind of squire of whom William and Mary Howitt complained in their *Rural Life of England* (1838): 'The aristocracy shut themselves up in their houses and parks, and are rarely seen beyond them. . . . They know nothing and therefore can feel nothing for the toiling class.' This squire is clearly well-meaning, but content just to leave things as they are. If he was not a sportsman or keen on farming, then it was probable that his tenants and employees would rarely see him. Not all Victorian landlords were builders and improvers.

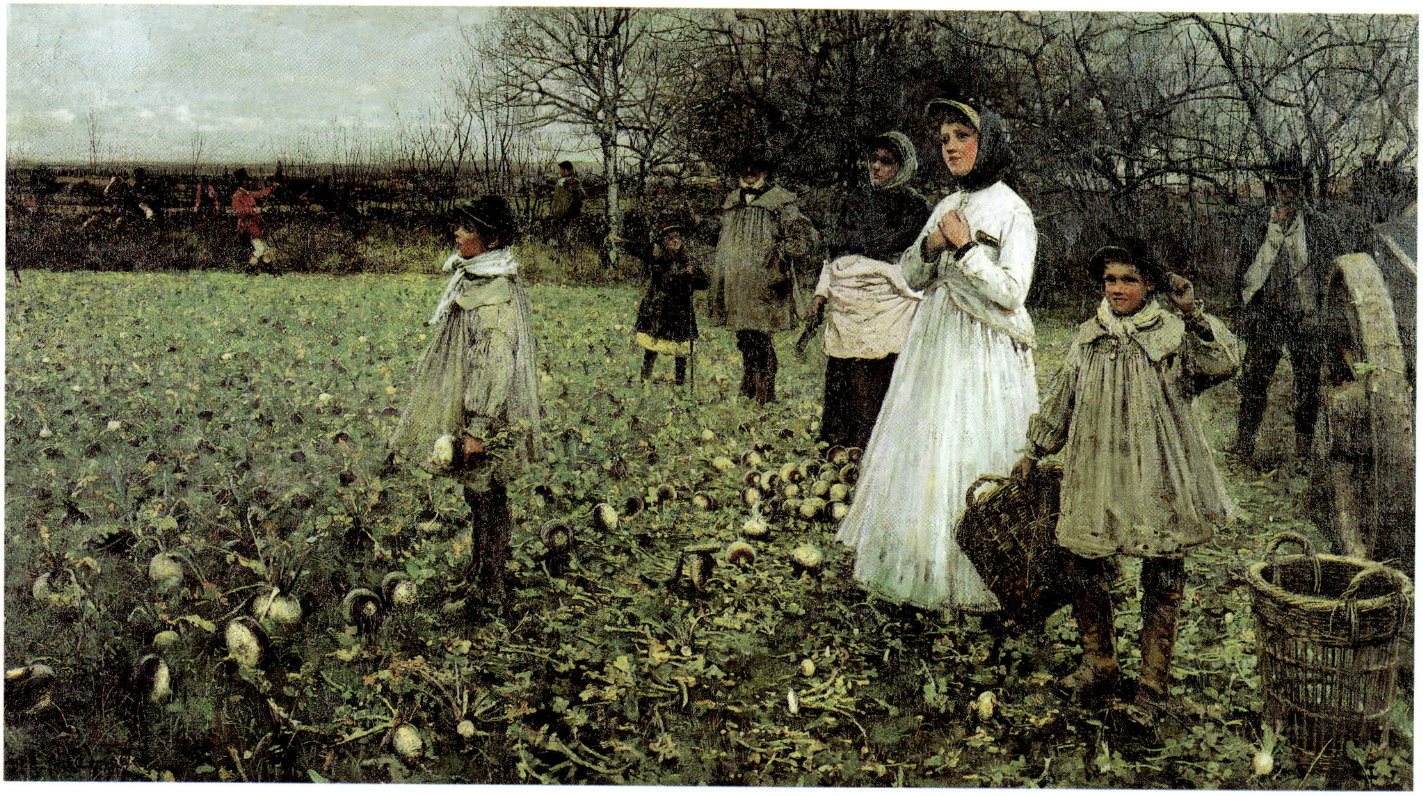

157
JOHN ROBERTSON REID
*Toil and Pleasure*

Very few pictures attempt to contrast the life of the gentry with the life of ordinary people. One which does is *Toil and Pleasure* by the Scottish painter John Robertson Reid (157). The picture shows the hunt passing a group of workers in a turnip field. As a young man, Reid was a friend of Clausen, and had a studio near him in Hampstead. Both Clausen and Reid were, at this period, becoming interested in French naturalism, but Clausen was never so concerned with social issues as Reid. Clausen preferred to show people at work in their environment rather than make the kind of social comment implicit in *Toil and Pleasure*. Flora Thompson, as usual, neatly describes how country people saw the gentry, as they 'flitted across the scene like kingfishers crossing a flock of hedgerow sparrows. They saw them sweeping through the hamlet in their carriages, the ladies billowing in silks and satins, with tiny chenille-fringed parasols held at an angle to protect their complexions.' Nonetheless, the wife of a squire felt it part of her duty to look after the local villagers, and most of them did a certain amount of charitable work, visiting the sick and the old, dispensing food, medicines, clothes, and money. The 'lady bountiful' was an ideal to which all Victorian country ladies aspired, and before the advent of the welfare state, it was probably the only source of help available to poor country people.

Occasionally a great landowner would dispense largess, as we see in W.F. Witherington's *A Fete in Petworth Park* (156), painted in 1835. Lord Egremont, owner of Petworth, was a great Sussex landowner, a collector, and a patron of J.M.W. Turner. He could well afford to entertain his tenants and employees, and is doing so here on an immense scale. Races, sports and entertainments of all kinds are taking place, and doubtless plenty of food and drink is on offer too. This is the aristocracy playing its grand, feudal role, an ideal much encouraged by the young Disraeli and others of the young England group in the 1840s. Inspired by the romantic novels of

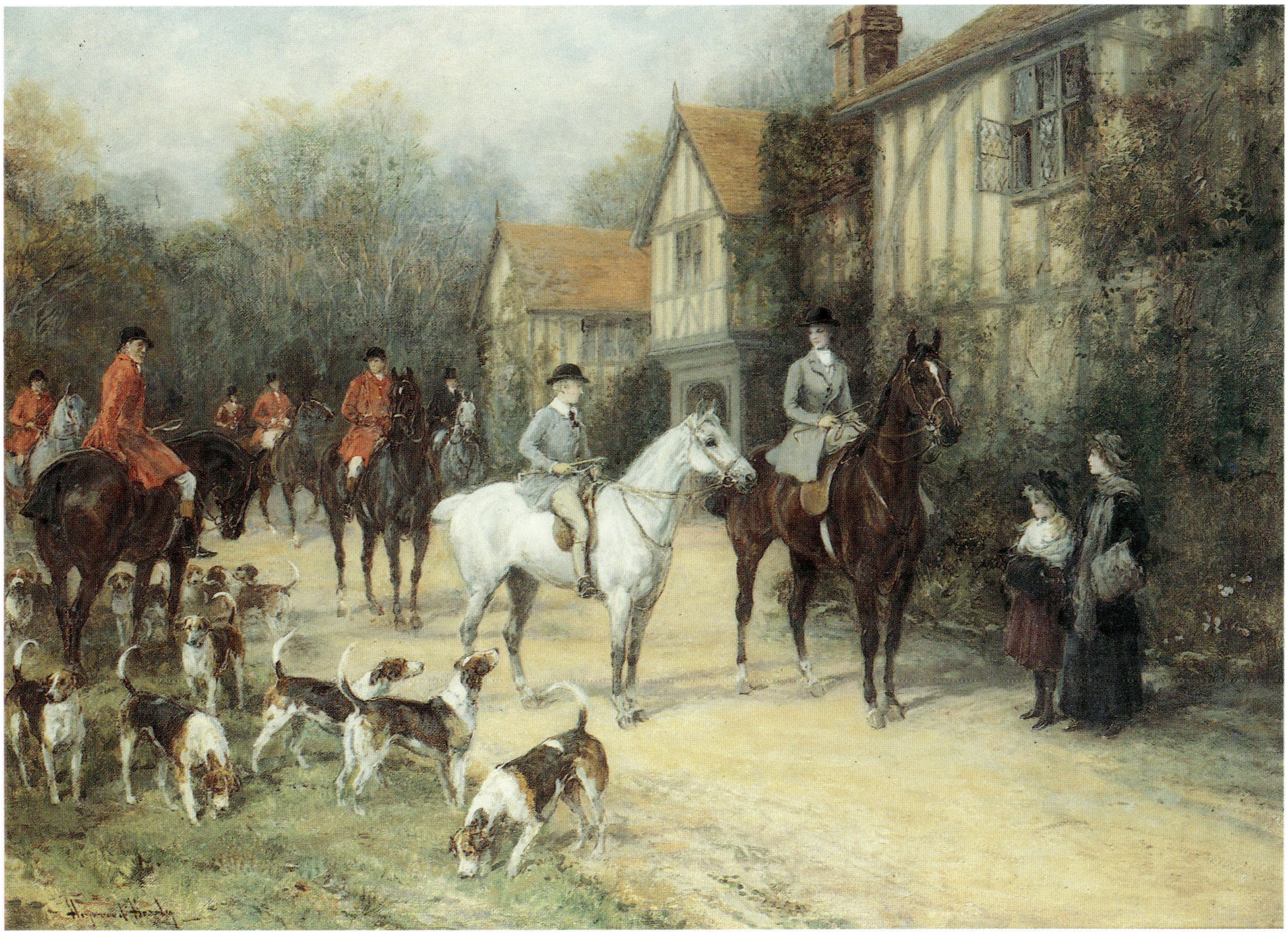

158
HEYWOOD HARDY
*The Young Squire*

Walter Scott, they believed that the solution to social problems was for the aristocracy and gentry to rally the populace around their ancestral estates and to dispense charity and benevolent guidance to a humble and suitably grateful peasantry. It was a romantic, chivalric ideal, and some Victorian landowners tried very hard to live up to it. But such attempts to turn the social clock backwards were doomed to failure. Young England mainly manifested itself in aristocratic extravaganzas like the Eglinton Tournament, when the young Lord Eglinton invited all his friends to his castle in Scotland to take part in a medieval tournament, complete with jousting knights, and a Queen of the Tournament. Sadly, it was dogged by almost continuous rain, and the expense of it all left poor Lord Eglinton virtually bankrupt.

Someone also entitled to a good deal of deference was the 'young squire', or the heir to the estate. This is reflected in a good many paintings, even historical ones such as Frith's *Coming of Age in the Olden Tyme*. This shows a young son and heir standing on the steps of his ancestral mansion, while his tenantry and retainers feast and make merry in the courtyard below. Heywood Hardy's *Young Squire* (158) partakes of this rosy, romantic vision of the gentry and their role. Here the young squire on his grey pony is the centre of attention at the hunt, while his handsome mother looks on proudly from her horse, and two pretty sisters stand by admiringly. Hardy usually painted hunting and other country scenes, with the figures in vaguely Regency or eighteenth-century dress. They are the visual equivalent of Georgette Heyer novels, and much the same atmosphere hangs about his *Young Squire*. Much more down-to-earth is George Goodwin Kilburne's *The Heir* (159). Here a cocky, bumptious-looking little boy is paying a visit to the stables. The groom looks on indulgently as this incredibly smart little figure, in his tweed suit, gaiters and bowler hat struts about the yard.

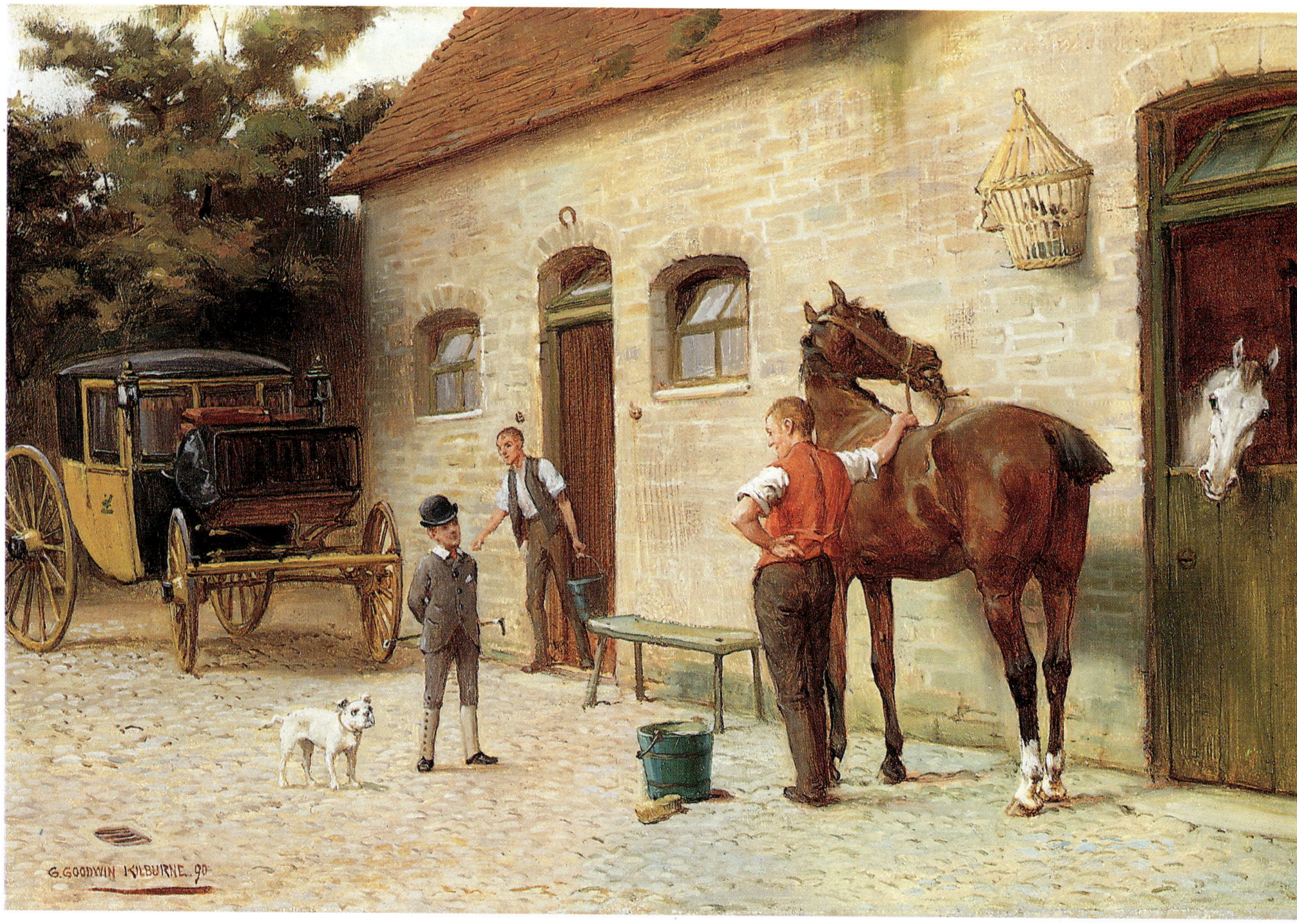


159
George Goodwin Kilburne
*The Heir*

Occasionally, the villagers might be invited to the big house and be shown round, which is the scene depicted in James Hayllar's *Visiting the Hall* (160). Here a smartly-dressed little girl is showing a group of rustics round the pictures. The woman is wearing a traditional shawl and bonnet; the man a long smock or overall, with a straw hat in his hand. The old man behind them is wearing the traditional smock-frock, becoming old-fashioned by this time, but still worn by many older village people. Hayllar lived at Castle Priory, a house on the river Thames at Wallingford, and painted most of his pictures in and around the house. The scene shown here is a room in Castle Priory, and the rustics would have been modelled from local people. Hayllar is also remarkable for having produced four artistic daughters, Edith, Jessica, Kate and Mary, all of whom painted extremely well, and all of whom exhibited at the Royal Academy, yet another unbeaten Victorian record.

By the end of Queen Victoria's reign, the power and influence of the landed classes was already on the wane. A combination of social and economic changes, particularly the agricultural depressions of the 1880s and 1890s, had undermined the foundations of their wealth, power and influence. In the 1830s and 40s, three-quarters of the members of the House of Commons were landowners; by the 1850s and 60s their numbers had fallen to two-thirds; from 1885 to 1905 they shrunk to only one-third. The real centres of political power, prestige and wealth had begun to shift elsewhere. Gradually, the large estates which had formed the foundation of the landowners' power began to be broken up. Taxes and the First World War dealt further blows, and only the richest and most adaptable were able to survive. Lloyd George, architect of the Liberal Party's taxation reforms, denounced dukes as an expensive anachronism, claiming that one duke cost as much to maintain as a dreadnought. In Oscar Wilde's play *The Importance of Being Earnest*, one of Lady Bracknell's quips always

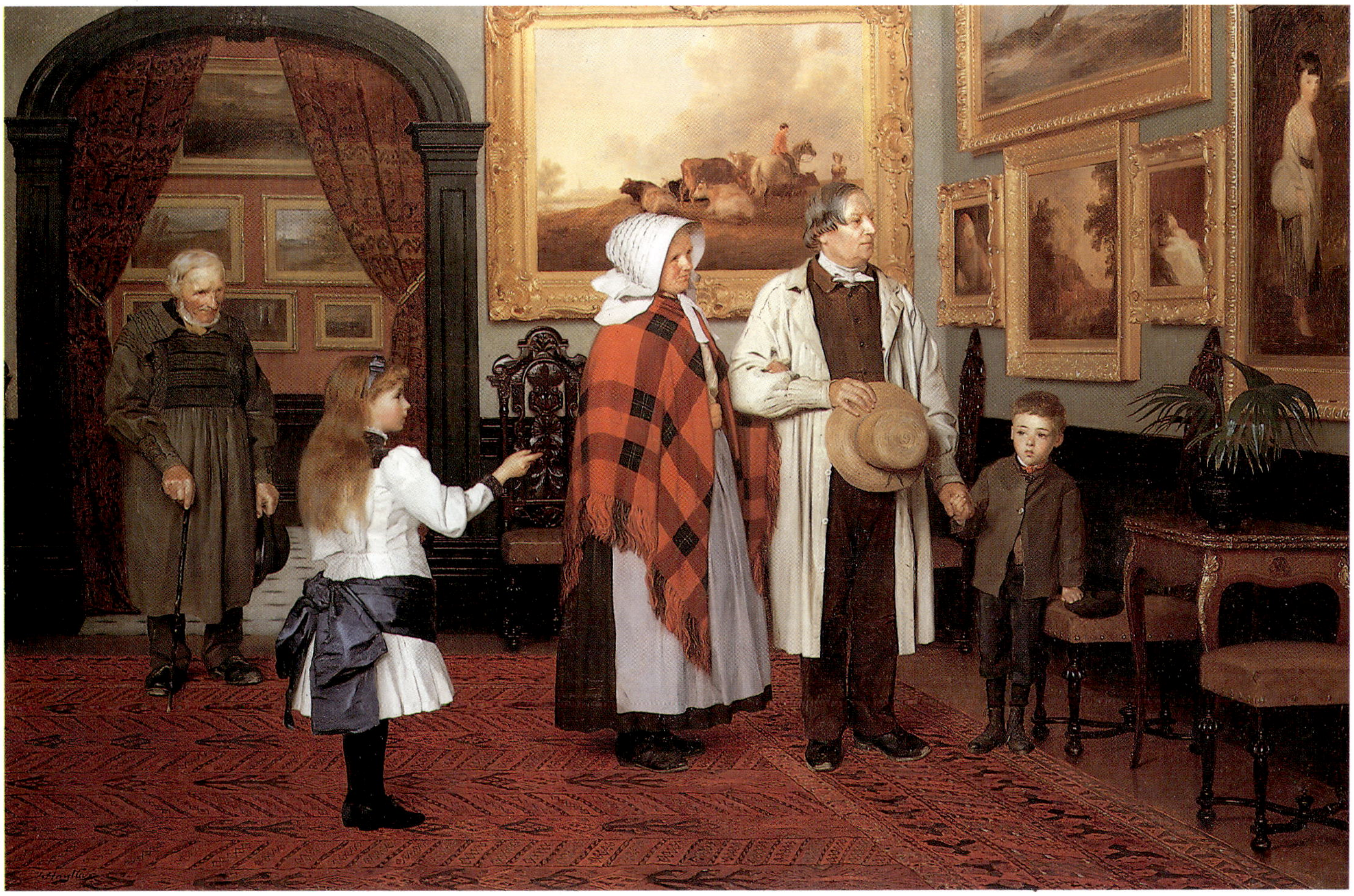

160
JAMES HAYLLAR
*Visiting the Hall*

raised sympathetic applause from a Victorian audience: 'What between the duties expected of one during one's lifetime, and the duties extracted from one after one's death, land has ceased to be either a profit or a pleasure. It gives one position, and prevents one from keeping it up.'

By the 1890s, there was a glut of country houses and large country estates on the market. Most successful businessmen by then preferred to buy or build a more modest country house, in its own grounds, thus avoiding the bother of owning land.

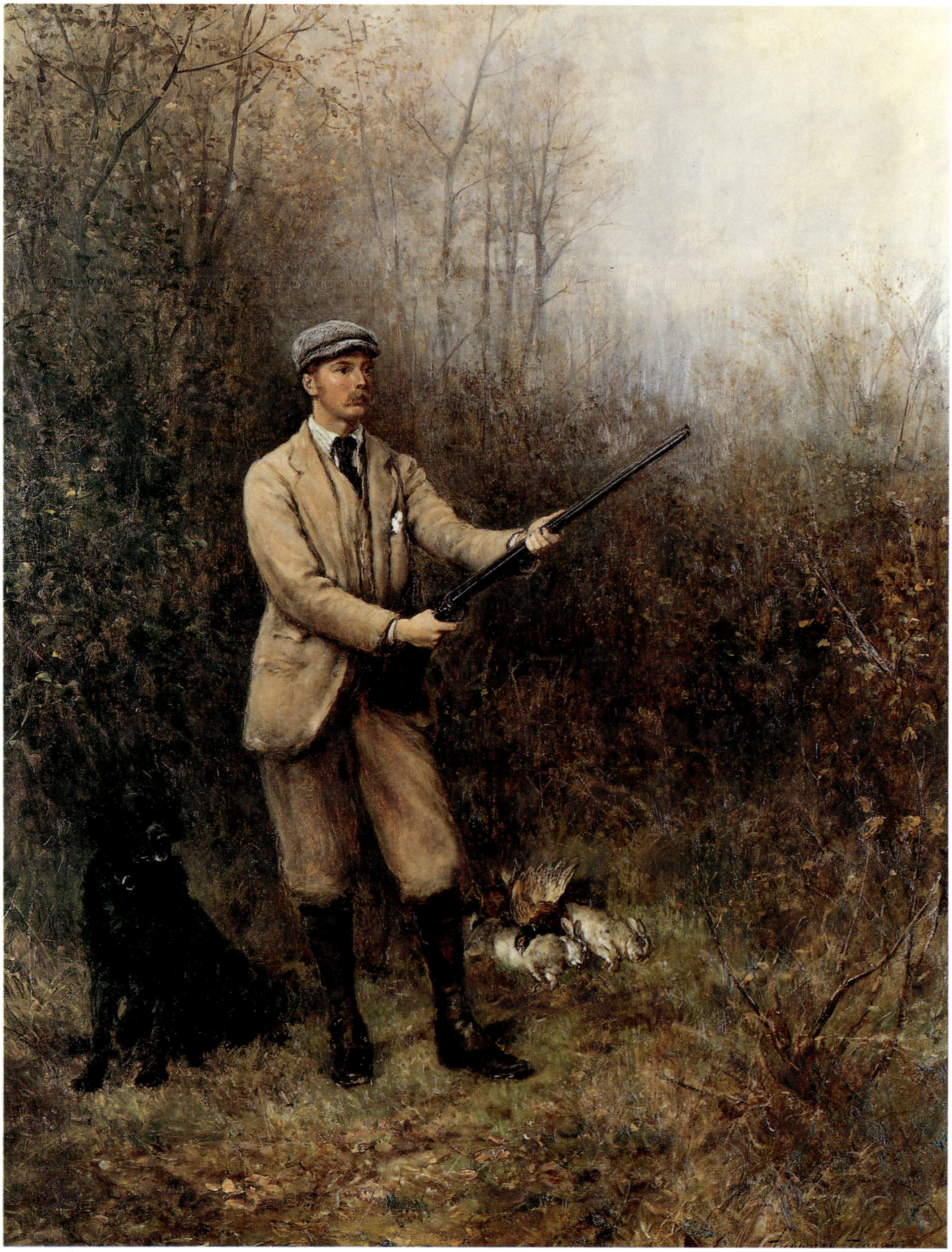

161
Heywood Hardy
*A Waiting Gun*

# Chapter Thirteen

# ~ SPORT ~

Play up, play up, and play the game!

Sir Henry Newbolt, *Vitae Lampada*

It was in pursuit of sport, particularly hunting and shooting, that the landed classes manifested the full extent of their power in the countryside. For many of the aristocracy and gentry, especially if they were not involved in politics, sport was the chief benefit to be had from owning a country estate. For the sake of sport, they were prepared to use to the full their land, their influence, and occasionally their coercive powers. Like a feudal lord marshalling his retainers, the landowner would summon up the maximum amount of help and co-operation from his tenants, his staff, and the workforce on the estate – driving the pheasants out of the woods, stopping foxes' earths, and so on – to enable him and his friends to enjoy the sport of their choice.

Hunting and shooting were the main sports enjoyed by the gentry, as they still are today. Some might do both, but landowners tended to prefer one or the other. Conflict of interest between the hunting and shooting fraternities was one of the chief causes of friction between the landowning classes, and it can still stir violent passions today. Hunting was in general more popular in the Victorian period; shooting in the Edwardian. As with so many things, the Victorians tidied up hunting. The masters of the Regency and early Victorian periods had been wild characters; hard riders, drinkers, womanisers, and gamblers. The Victorian master, as described in the novels of Trollope (himself a keen hunting man), is a very different figure – autocratic, professional, disciplined, a kind of rural general, admired, respected and obeyed. Instead of the aristocratic private packs of the eighteenth century, the nineteenth century saw the rise of the subscription pack, open to anyone with the necessary money and enthusiasm. The railway too made it possible to work in London and hunt in the country. Sir Robert Foster, MP for the City of London, went from Paddington Station to Gloucestershire to hunt with the

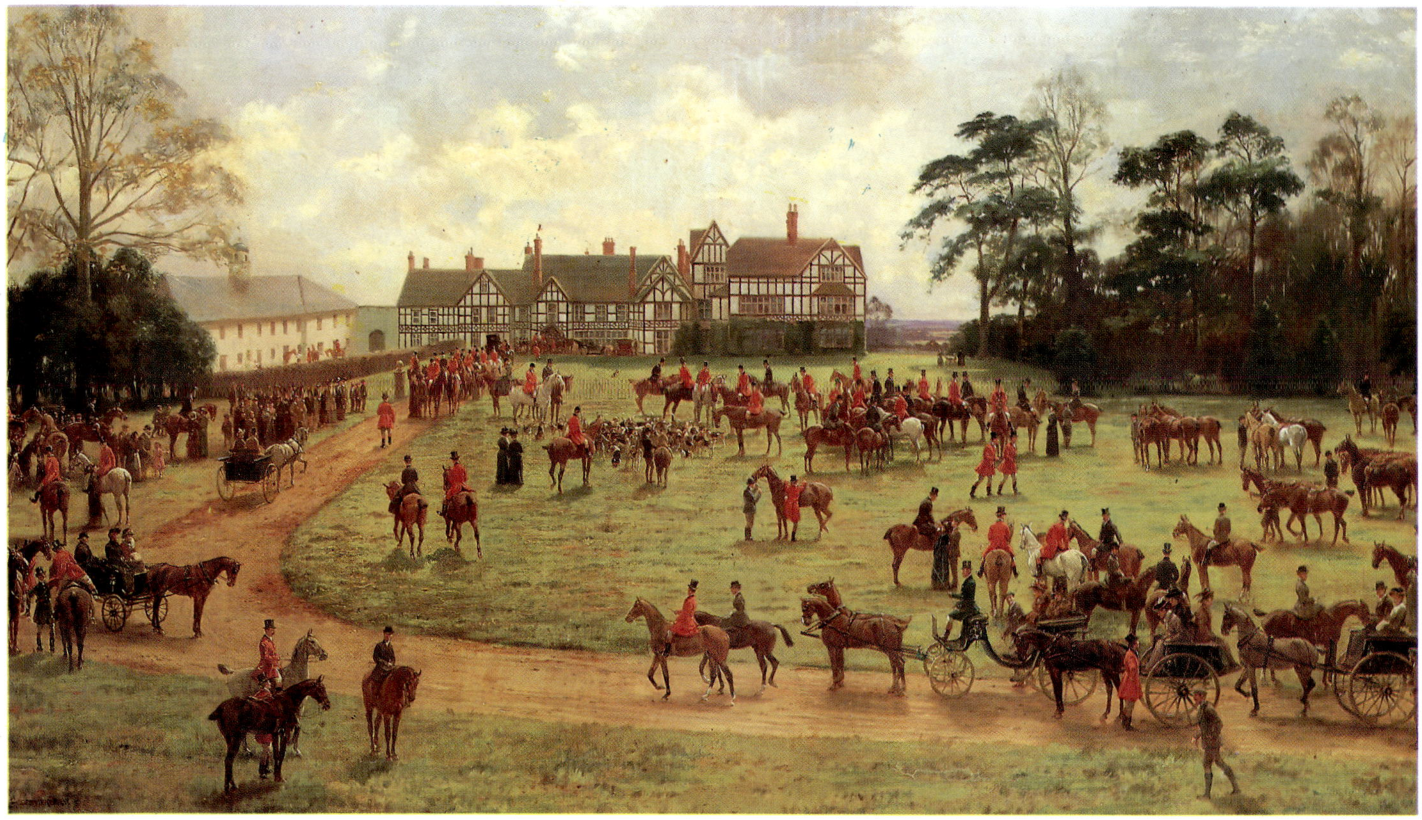

162
GEORGE GOODWIN KILBURNE
*The Meet*

Beaufort; hacking back to the station, he passed the time by reciting a chapter of Hallam's *Middle Ages*. Another Victorian development was the arrival of women on the hunting field. Their presence was undoubtedly a civilising influence, and figures like the Empress Elizabeth of Austria, or 'Skittles' the famous Victorian courtesan, gave added social *piquance* to the sport. When the hunt passed Lark Rise, the villagers marvelled at 'the women sitting in their side-saddle with hour-glass figures encased in skin-tight black habits', and commented, 'Looks for all the world as if she'd been melted and poured into it, now don't she?'

'The true charm of cricket and hunting,' wrote Tom Hughes, author of *Tom Brown's Schooldays*, 'is that they are still more or less sociable and universal; there's a place for every man who will come and take his part.' Every man, that is, who could ride, and could afford to pay for horses and equipment. In reality, that meant the gentry, the professional classes, the farmers, and such tradesmen or businessmen who enjoyed the sport. Mr Jorrocks, the hero of Surtees' sporting novels, was a city grocer, who describes the charm of hunting as 'The dash of the 'ound, the feathering for the scent, the picking it out, the challenge when it's found, the rush of the pack to the cry – the werry sight of the beauteous mottled intelligent h'animals is enough to set my werry blood boiling.' The fashionable hunting world was centred on Melton Mowbray in Leicestershire, from whence one could hunt with the famous Quorn, Pytchley, Cottesmore or Belvoir packs. The size and splendour of these great hunts were recorded by such sporting artists as Henry Alken, John Ferneley, J.F. Herring, R.B. Davis, and the Barraud brothers. These artists carried on the Regency tradition of sporting painting, quite outside the mainstream of Victorian art. Very few of them bothered to exhibit. They worked entirely for private patrons, moving from house to house, or racecourse to racecourse. Pictures of shooting and fishing were often

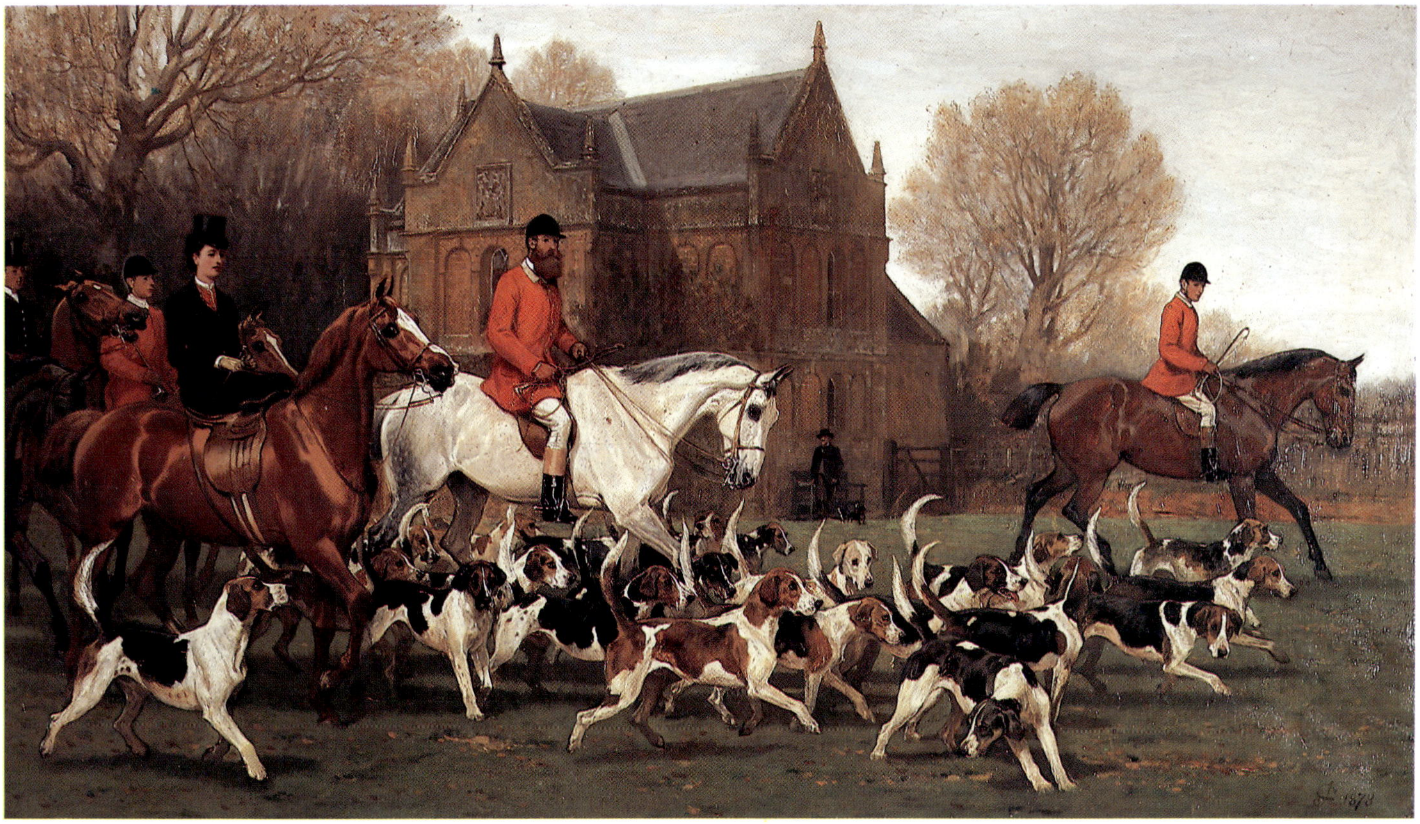

163
JOHN CHARLTON
*Earl and Countess Spencer with Hounds in Althorp Park*

privately commissioned also. A good example of this type of picture is John Charlton's painting of Earl and Countess Spencer with the hounds in Althorp Park (163). Here is the famous 'Red' Earl Spencer, so-called because of his red beard and forceful character, going out with the Pytchley, passing the falconry building in the park at Althorp.

The hunt meet was always a major social event for country people, especially if it took place in a local town, or in the park of a great country house. G.G. Kilburne's *Meet* (162) shows us a typical Victorian gathering, in front of a large, half-timbered, old manor-house, with the stable-block on the left. Drinks, the so-called stirrup-cup, were handed round on trays, and when the Master decided that everything was ready, the horn would sound, and the hunt moved off. Some of the spectators, especially the children, would follow the hunt as far as they could. Some would follow all day, in the hope of earning sixpence for opening a gate, giving directions, or helping a faller.

Thomas Blinks, one of the best late Victorian painters of hunting scenes, and of foxhounds, shows us a hunt in *Full Cry* (164) scattering a flock of geese. In front is the Master, or possibly the Huntsman, and behind him the rest of the field. To the left, the less adventurous riders are using the road, and one rider is falling off as he attempts to jump a hedge. One of the main problems of hunting was the maintaining of good relations with the farmers. Permission had to be sought to hunt over their land, and compensation paid for damage to crops, fences or livestock. Many farmers themselves hunted, which of course enraged poor Cobbett. If they were tenant farmers, a sporting landlord might well insist on the right of the hunt to cross their land being written into the lease.

To meet the hounds passing though the countryside was always a moment of excitement. When this happened near Lark Rise, 'the men at work there would drop their tools and climb on the five-barred gates for a better view, or stop their

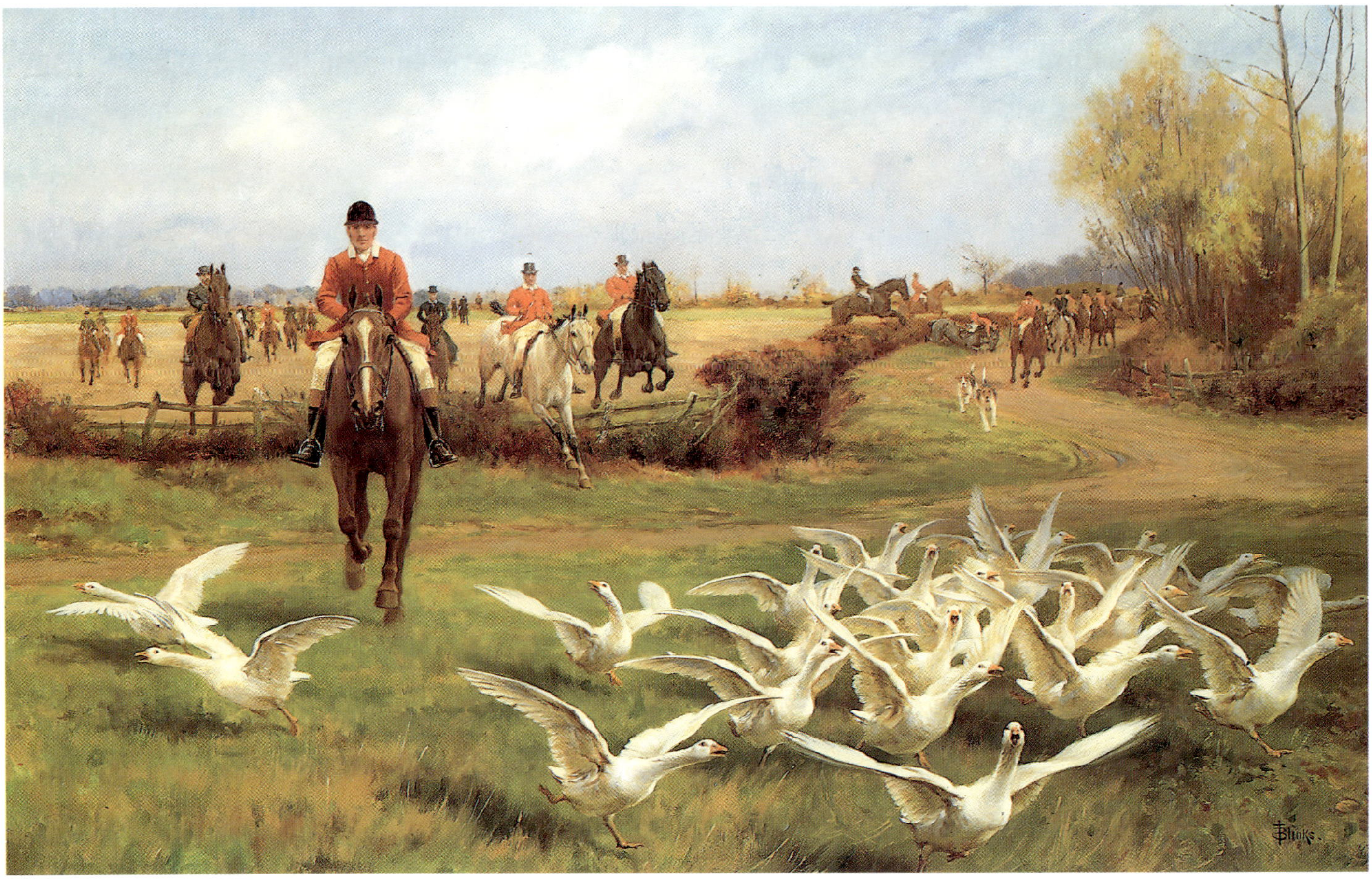

164
THOMAS BLINKS
*Full Cry*

teams and straighten their backs at the plough-tail to cup their hands to their mouths and shout "Tally-ho: A-gallop, a-gallop, a-lye, a-lye, Tally ho!"' In Birket Foster's watercolour, *A Peep at the Hounds* (165), the girl by the hedge looks as if she is shouting 'Tally-ho!' too. Birket Foster, typically, concentrates on the spectators rather than the hunt, which is seen at a distance, converting it into an idyllic part of the landscape rather than a blood sport. Hunting is, of course, just as popular a sport in the twentieth century as it was in the nineteenth, and therefore this is a part of the paradise that we have not lost. But hunting, like everything else, has changed, mainly because the patterns of farming and land-ownership have changed. The power of the Victorian landowners ensured that their estates were designed to facilitate hunting, and therefore it was a golden age for the sport.

Shooting, on the other hand, was and remains a sport exclusively for the rich. The fact that the Prince of Wales, later King Edward VII, was a keen shot gave an immense boost to the fashion for shooting. The late Victorian period was the age of the *grande battue*: armies of beaters and keepers, thousands of driven birds, huge bags. A shoot was often the focal point of a grand country-house weekend. If it was a famous shoot, then one of the famous 'big shots' might be invited, Lord Walsingham or Lord de Grey, whose astonishing exploits with the gun are recorded in the elaborately kept game books of the period. Heywood Hardy's sportsman waiting for the birds (161) shows what a typical Victorian gun might look like, with his retriever beside him, and some rabbits and a pheasant on the ground. This is obviously quite a modest shoot; at a big shoot the guns would usually have a loader, and use two or three shotguns in succession. The birds would be picked up by dogs and pickers behind him. In Edith Hayllar's *The First of October* (166), three Victorian sportsmen relax over the lunch table after a morning's pheasant shooting. The bag is a modest one; no *grande*

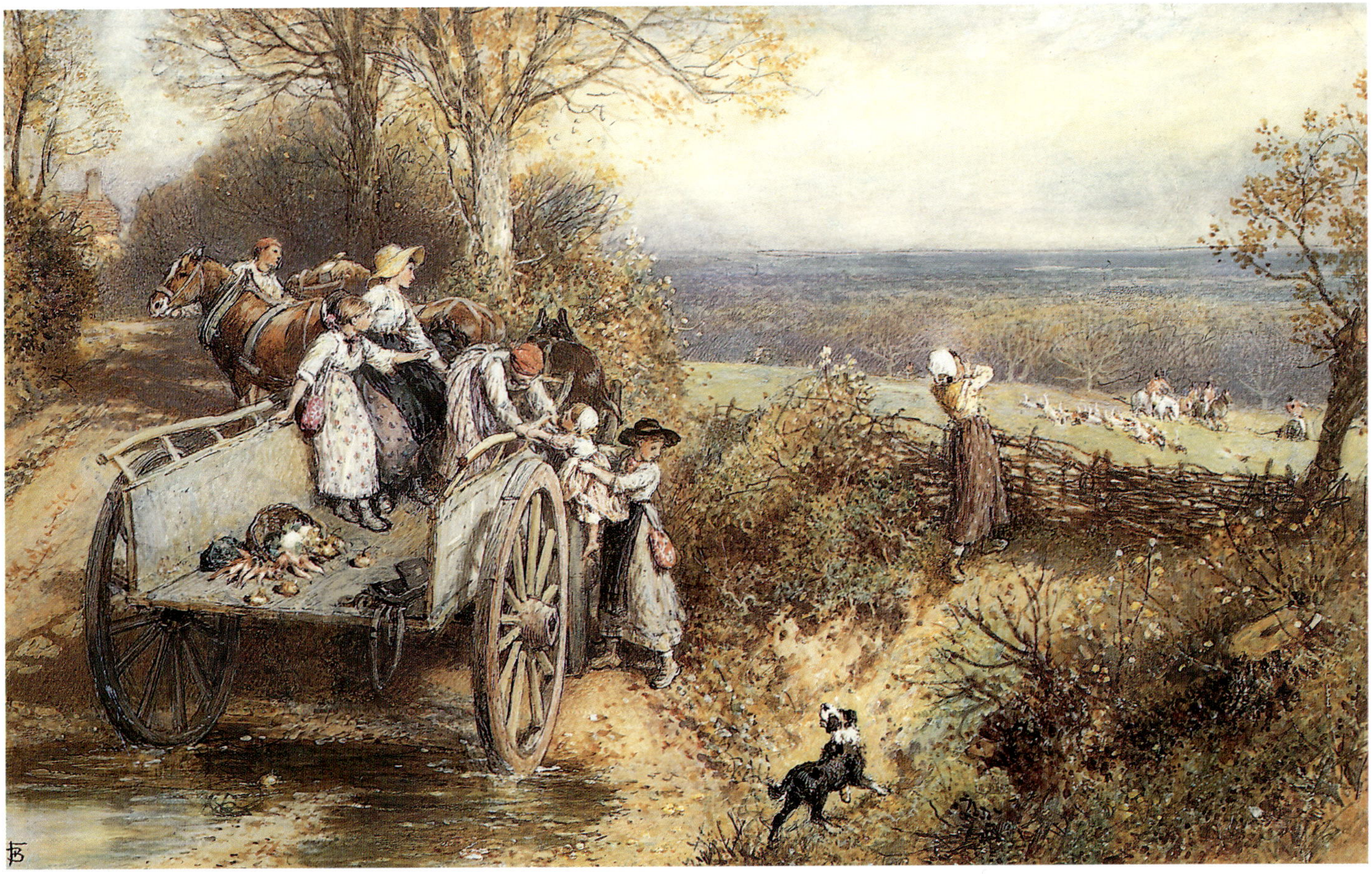

165
Myles Birket Foster
*A Peep at the Hounds, here they come!*

*battue* here. Many old-fashioned sportsmen despised the grand and fashionable shoots with quantities of hand-reared pheasants, preferring to walk up a few wild birds with their dogs in the traditional way.

In order to preserve and protect his game, the landowner would employ one or more gamekeepers. By 1911, there were twice as many gamekeepers as there were country policemen. The Game Laws had always prohibited anyone except the landowner from shooting game birds, hares or rabbits on his land. This was a law which the sporting landlord was prepared to enforce, and as he was probably a Magistrate or Justice of the Peace himself, he was in a position to do so. The increasing abundance of game, and the fact that the labouring population often did not have enough to eat, led to even more widespread poaching. Countrymen in general hated the Game Laws, did not believe in them, and secretly supported and encouraged poaching. 'We labourers,' wrote Joseph Arch, 'do not believe hares and rabbits belong to any individual, not any more than thrushes and blackbirds do.' The poacher might be a lone individual, or a highly-organised gang. Not infrequently there were bloody fights between gamekeepers and poachers. 'There was a murderous affray with poachers at the Moor last night,' wrote Kilvert. 'Two keepers beaten fearfully about the head with bludgeons and one poacher, Cartwright, a Hay sawyer, stabbed and his life despaired of.'

The Night Poaching Act of 1862 gave the police powers to stop and search anyone in the countryside suspected of poaching. This meant that any rustic with bulging pockets could be stopped and searched; gamekeepers would often take these powers upon themselves. In John Templeton Lucas's curious picture *The Poacher Caught* (167), a gamekeeper has found a rabbit in the pocket of a poor travelling entertainer, on the road with his wife and children. Gipsies, vagrants and other travellers were always prime poaching suspects, although the gipsies

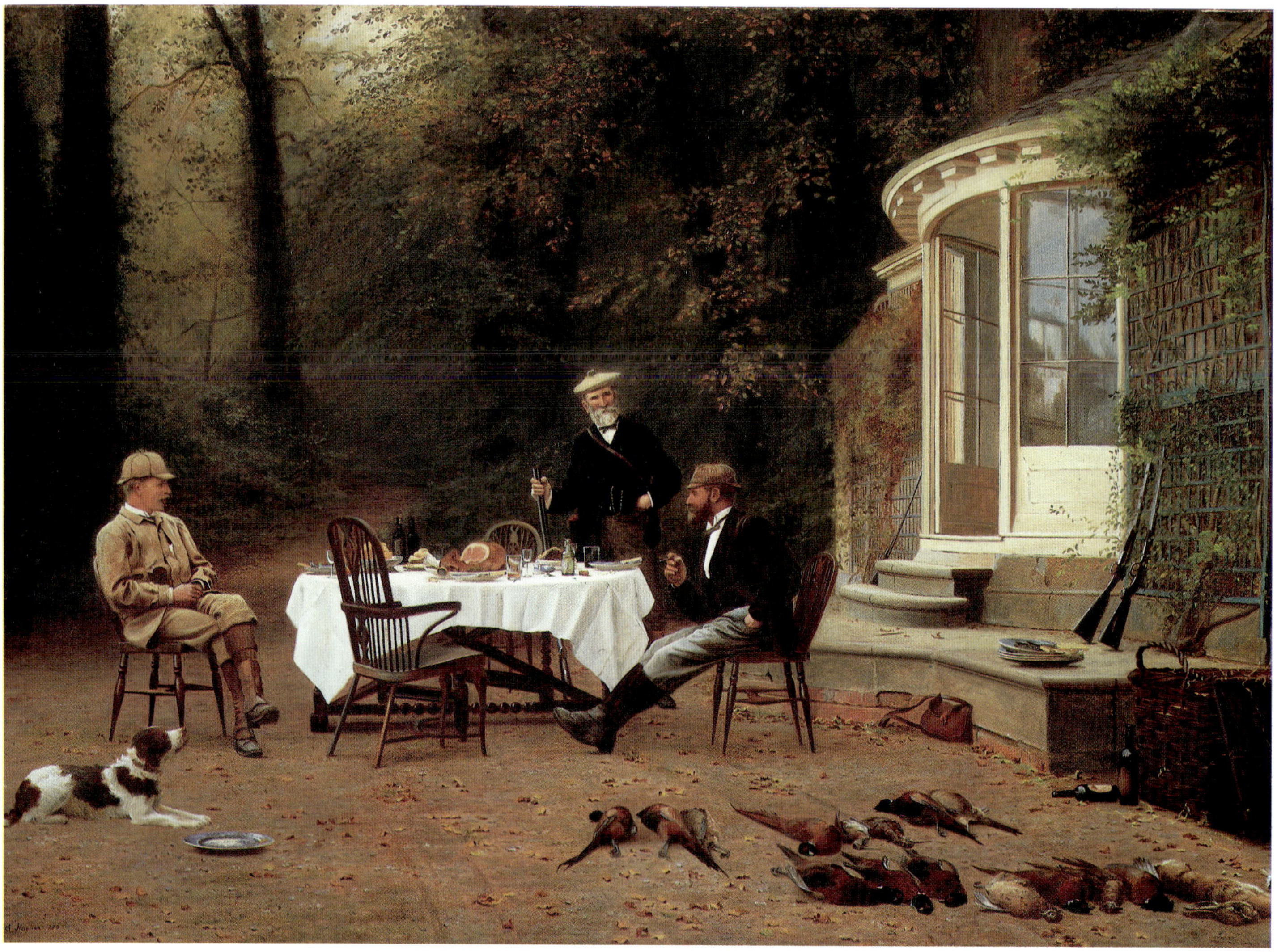

166
EDITH HAYLLAR
*The First of October*

were usually too clever to get caught. Gamekeepers were usually unpopular figures in the countryside, disliked equally by farmers and labourers, for it was they who had to do the landowners' dirty work for them. But nonetheless the gamekeeper was a dedicated and knowledgeable countryman, and a great deal of legend grew up around him. Probably the most famous gamekeeper in Victorian literature is in Richard Jefferies's *The Gamekeeper at Home* (1878). The original of this character was a Wiltshire keeper called Benny Haylock, an eccentric and irascible fellow, who fiercely protected his woods and had no respect for anyone, the squire included. If any of the guns brought a dog into the woods, he would immediately order it and its owner out; if they failed to hit a bird, he would make the most scathing comments on their marksmanship. But a wise landowner would take all this in good part. A good gamekeeper, however rude, was a loyal and relentless defender of his woods and game.

Shooting, much more than hunting, was productive of friction, resentment and bad feeling in the countryside. Between the landowner wishing to preserve his pheasants and village people with not enough to eat, there was bound to be a difference of opinion. If legend and myth grew up around the gamekeeper, much more surrounded the poacher, who was regarded in the village as a folk-hero, his exploits related endlessly in the pub. There are numerous traditional poems that celebrate the skill and bravery of the poachers, such as *The Sledmere Poachers*, a Yorkshire folk tale. Charles Kingsley, in his poem *The Bad Squire*, mounted a much more bitter and scathing attack on shooting and the preserving of game:

> You have sold the labouring-man, squire,
> Body and soul to shame,
> To pay for your seat in the House, squire,
> And to pay for the feed of your game.

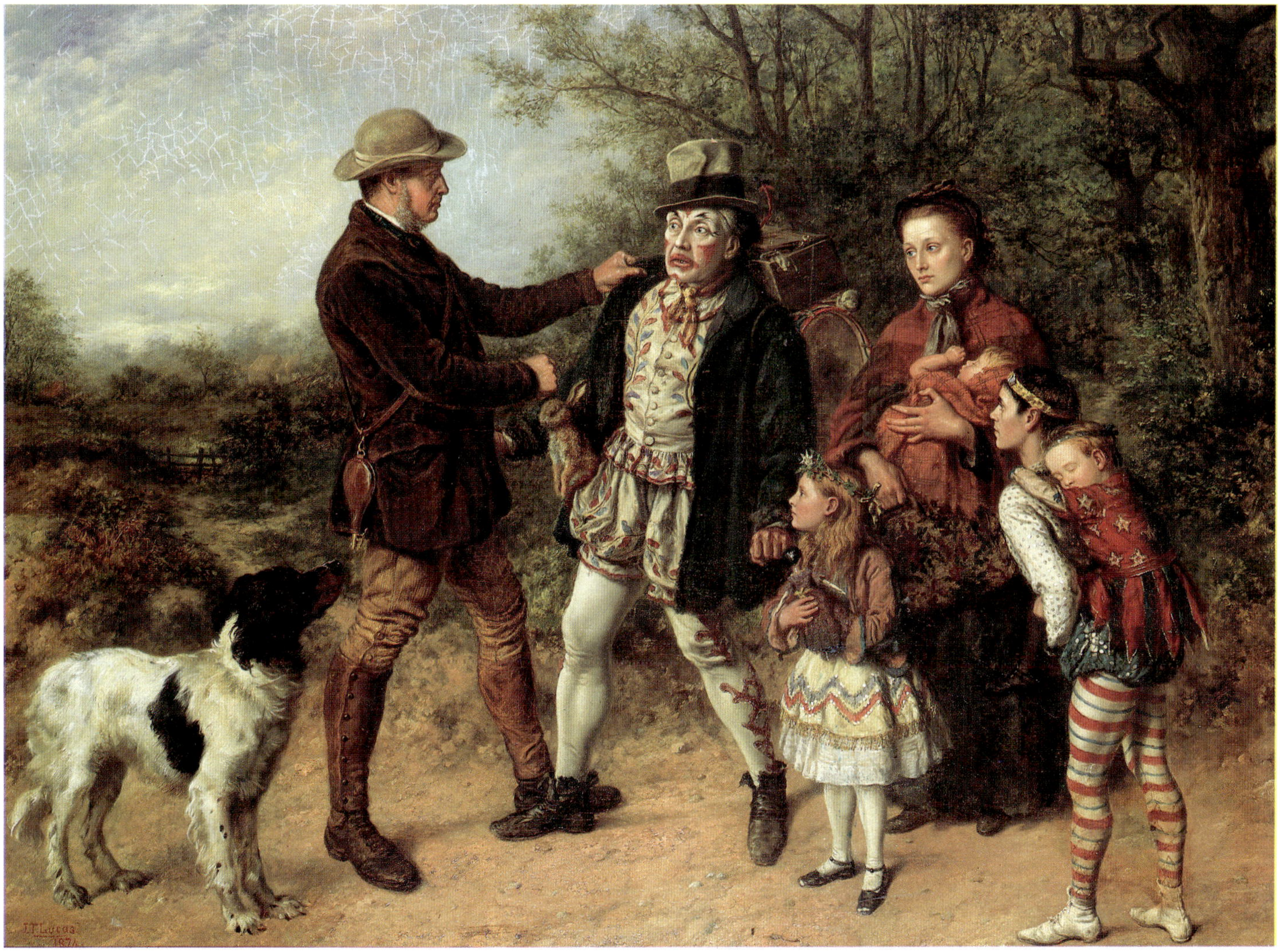

167
John Templeton Lucas
*The Poacher Caught*

You made him a poacher yourself, squire,
When you'd give neither work nor meat,
And your barley-fed hares robbed the garden,
At our starving children's feet.

Kingsley was a passionate reformer, preacher and writer on social issues, which he explored in his novels *Alton Locke* and *Yeast*. Yet he was not a revolutionary; he believed that the existing system was best, if it could be reformed and administered by a benevolent and enlightened ruling class. Kingsley was the scourge of the ruling classes, but at the same time one of Queen Victoria's favourite preachers. This is a typically Victorian paradox. That sage monarch also reprimanded her son, the Prince of Wales, for his excessive enthusiasm for shooting at Sandringham, urging him 'to do away a little with the *exclusive* character of shooting'. The Queen had put her finger on the problem: shooting was a great divider of rich and poor. The threat of poaching has receded, but shooting is still, as it always was, a rich man's sport, mainly enjoyed by syndicates of paying guns. But for sheer size, glamour and organisation there can have been nothing like a great Edwardian shoot.

Hunting and shooting both thrived in the Victorian period, but the bloodthirsty pleasures of the Regency – prize-fighting, bear-baiting, ratting, cock-fighting – were driven underground by a heavy blanket of moral disapproval. They were replaced by more civilised Victorian games, such as cricket, football, tennis, archery, croquet and cycling. These sports form the subject of many Victorian pictures. The most popular country-house game in the mid-Victorian period was croquet. It could be played by ladies wearing hats and voluminous skirts, as we see in George Elgar Hicks's charming sketch (168). Frederick Locker-Lampson, in his poem *Mr. Placid's Flirtation*, had some advice for the Victorian player:

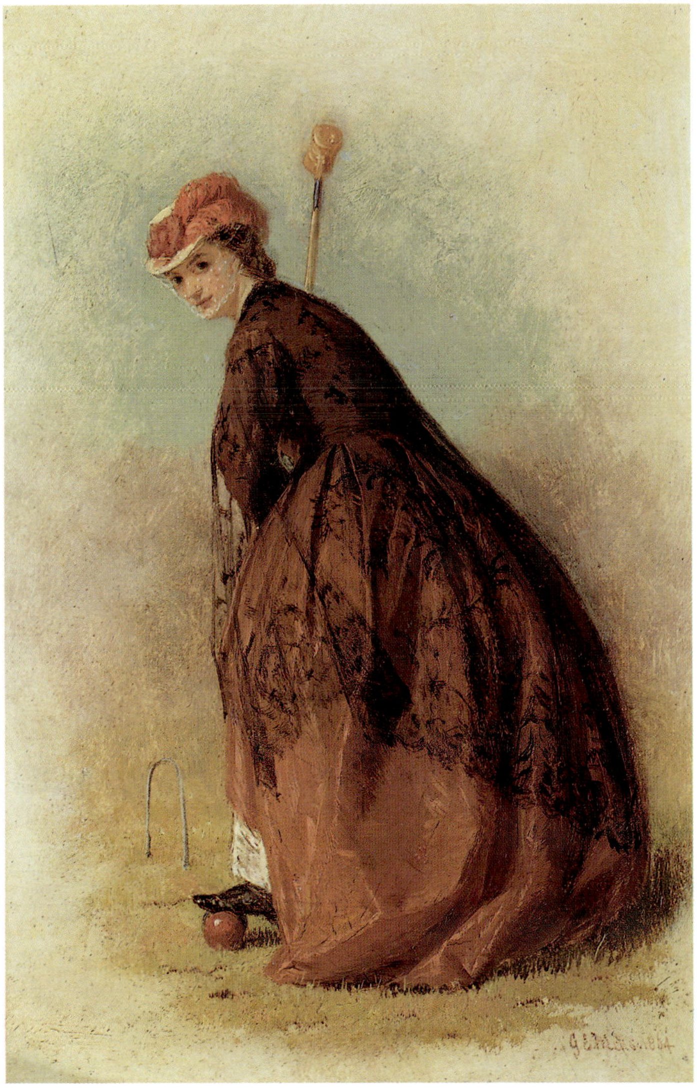

168
George Elgar Hicks
*Croquet*

> A luncheon despatch'd, we adjourn'd to croquet,
> A dainty, but difficult sport in its way.
> Thus I counsel the sage, who to play at it stoops,
> Belabour thy neighbour, and spoon through thy hoops.

The croquet lawn was the traditional place for flirtation. Douglas Jerrold even asserted that 'It may be said that a man is nearer the church-door when he has a mallet in his hand, than when to the strains of Godfrey, he has his arm round a lady's waist.' Francis Kilvert, like all Victorian curates, was much in demand on the croquet lawn, and it was here that he met his beloved Daisy Thomas, the vicar's daughter, whom he hoped to marry. Alas, her father forbade the marriage because Kilvert had no money and inadequate prospects, so poor Kilvert pined. He later married an older woman, but the marriage was not happy.

Another popular mid-Victorian sport was archery, which also offered exciting opportunities for flirtation and romance. The pretty Gwendolen first caught the attention of Grandcourt at an archery contest in George Eliot's novel *Daniel Deronda*. 'Who can deny,' wrote Eliot, 'that bows and arrows are among the prettiest weapons in the world for feminine forms to play with?' William Powell Frith used his three daughters, Alice, Fanny and Louisa, as models for his *English Archers, 19th Century* (169), and wrote in his *Autobiography* that 'the girls are true to nature, and the dresses will be a record of female habiliments of the time'. All the accessories are correct – from the waist of the girl on the right hangs a large tassel for cleaning arrows, a grease-box for beeswax and lard into which the gloved fingers were dipped, two ornamental acorns, and an ivory pencil for scoring. Kilvert often wrote about archery in his diary, and in September 1875 proudly recorded his meeting with 'Major Fisher, the Champion Archer of England. After

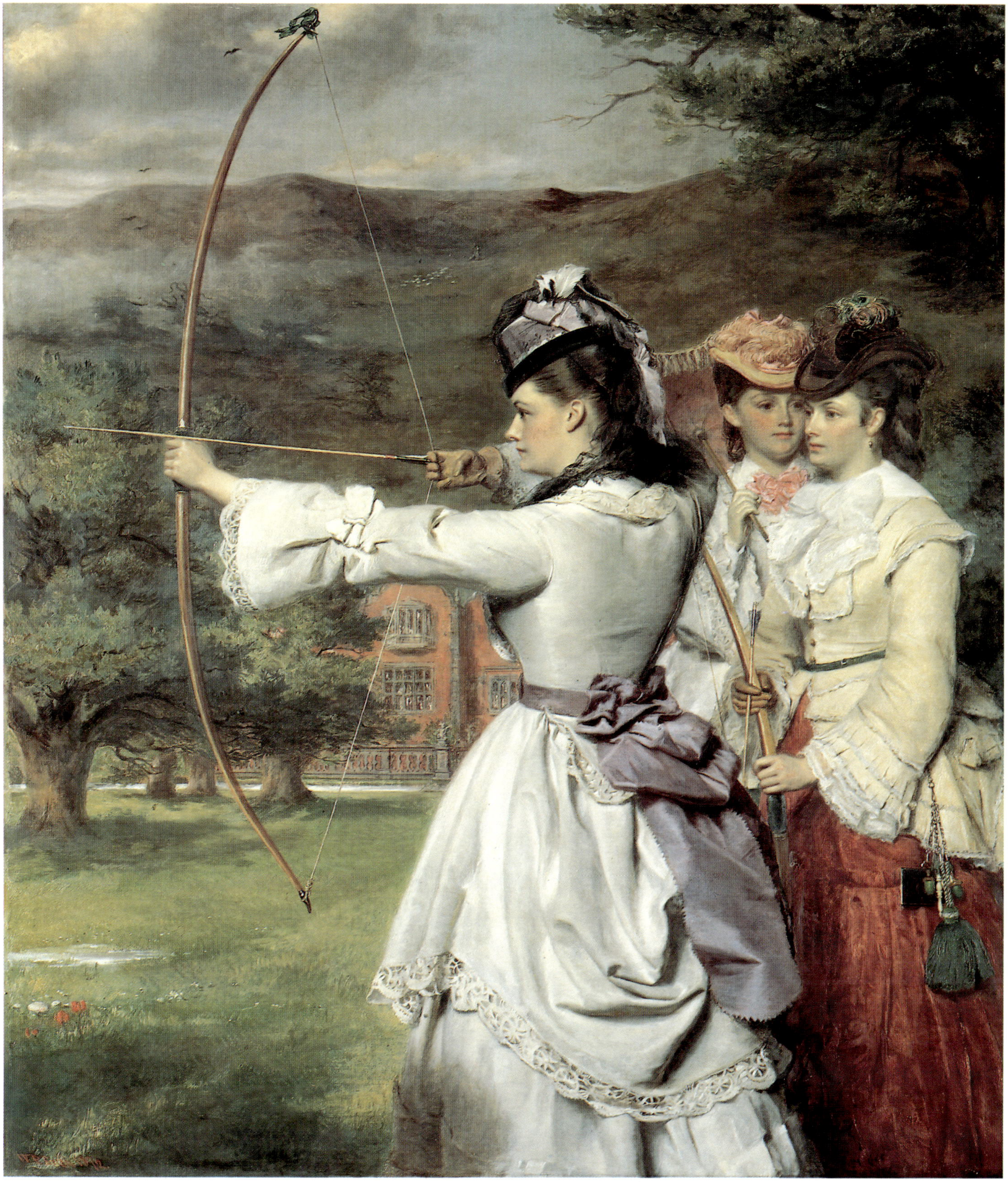

169
William Powell Frith
*English Archers, 19th Century*

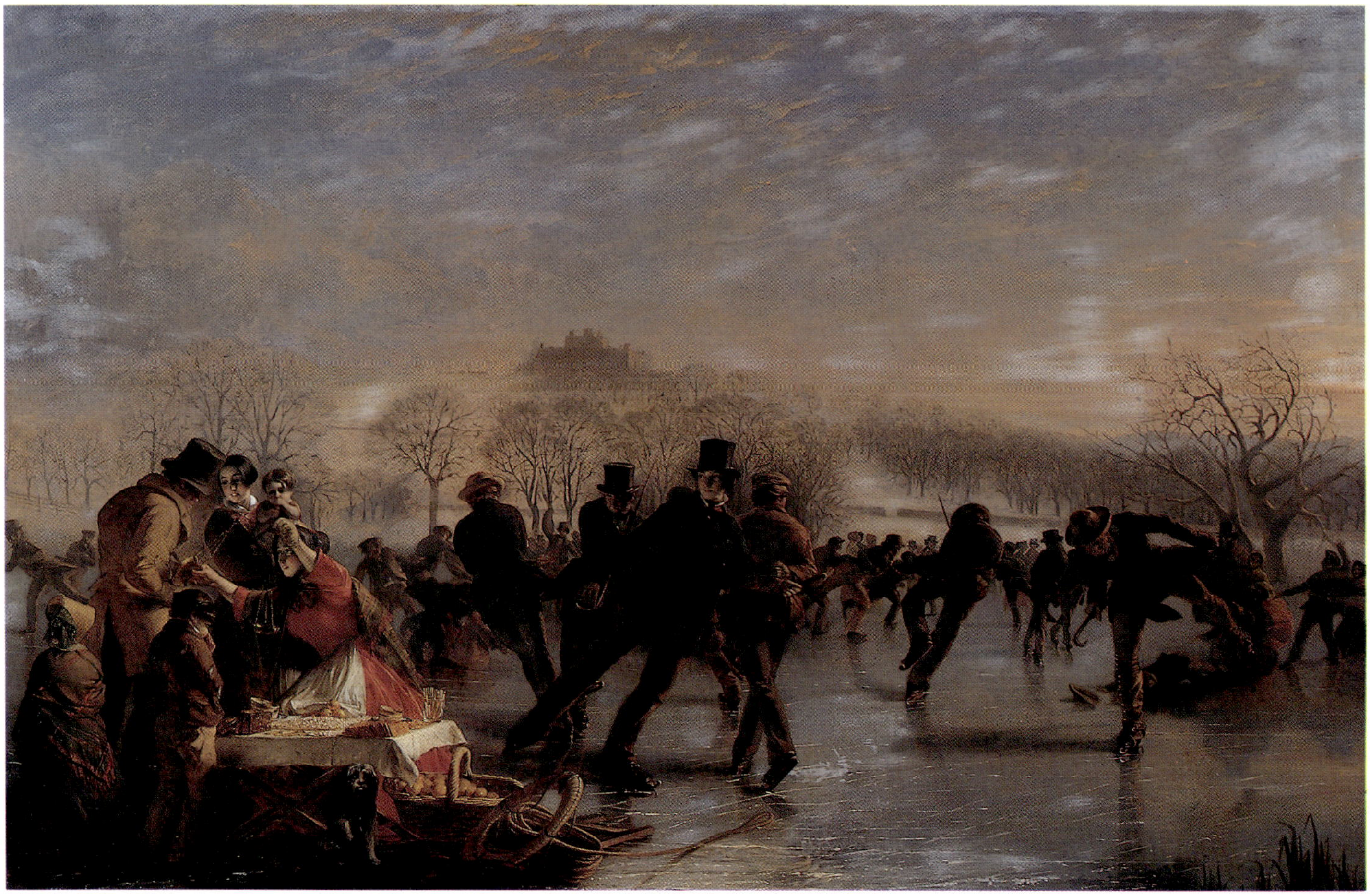

170
CHARLES LEES
*Skaters, a Scene on Duddingston Loch*

luncheon the archers went out to shoot at a beautiful archery ground by the riverside. The ladies sat watching under the trees while the arrows flashed past with a whistling rush. . . .' Jerrold wrote that 'Archery and croquet are two out-of-door amusements of fashionable London which no foreigner understands. They are conducted with demureness and serious, business-like precision, that look more like performances of strict duty, than the *abandon* of pleasure. . . .' Skating, and roller-skating, also enjoyed a vogue. Here again Kilvert was to the fore, writing in December 1870: 'There was distinguished company on the ice . . . I had the honour of being knocked down by Lord Royston. . . . Hatty Audry skated beautifully and jumped over a half-sunken punt.' Skating could be enjoyed by lesser mortals too, as we can see in Charles Lees's *Skaters, A Scene on Duddingston Loch* (170). Lees was a Scottish painter who made a speciality of sporting subjects, including golf. Duddingston Loch is near Edinburgh, and Craigmillar Castle is in the distance.

Both croquet and archery were put in the shade by lawn tennis, invented in 1874. It quickly became the most popular of all social games in the country, especially with the young. It was more exciting than croquet or archery, and better exercise. Kilvert, inevitably, was in the thick of it. Already by 28 July 1874 he was writing: 'This morning Teddy set up the net and poles in the field just opposite the dining-room windows and we began to play "sphairistike" or lawn tennis, a capital game, but rather too hot for a summer's day.' The game, as played by Kilvert, must have looked very like that in Horace H. Cauty's picture (172), and it must have indeed been hot work playing in full Victorian dress. Many artists and illustrators painted tennis matches and parties – Lavery, Mote, and du Maurier to name only a few – but perhaps most delightful of all is Edith Hayllar's *Summer Shower* (171). Painted at the Hayllars' house at Wallingford, it shows a tennis party taking refuge indoors from a shower of rain. The men wear knickerbockers and stockings,

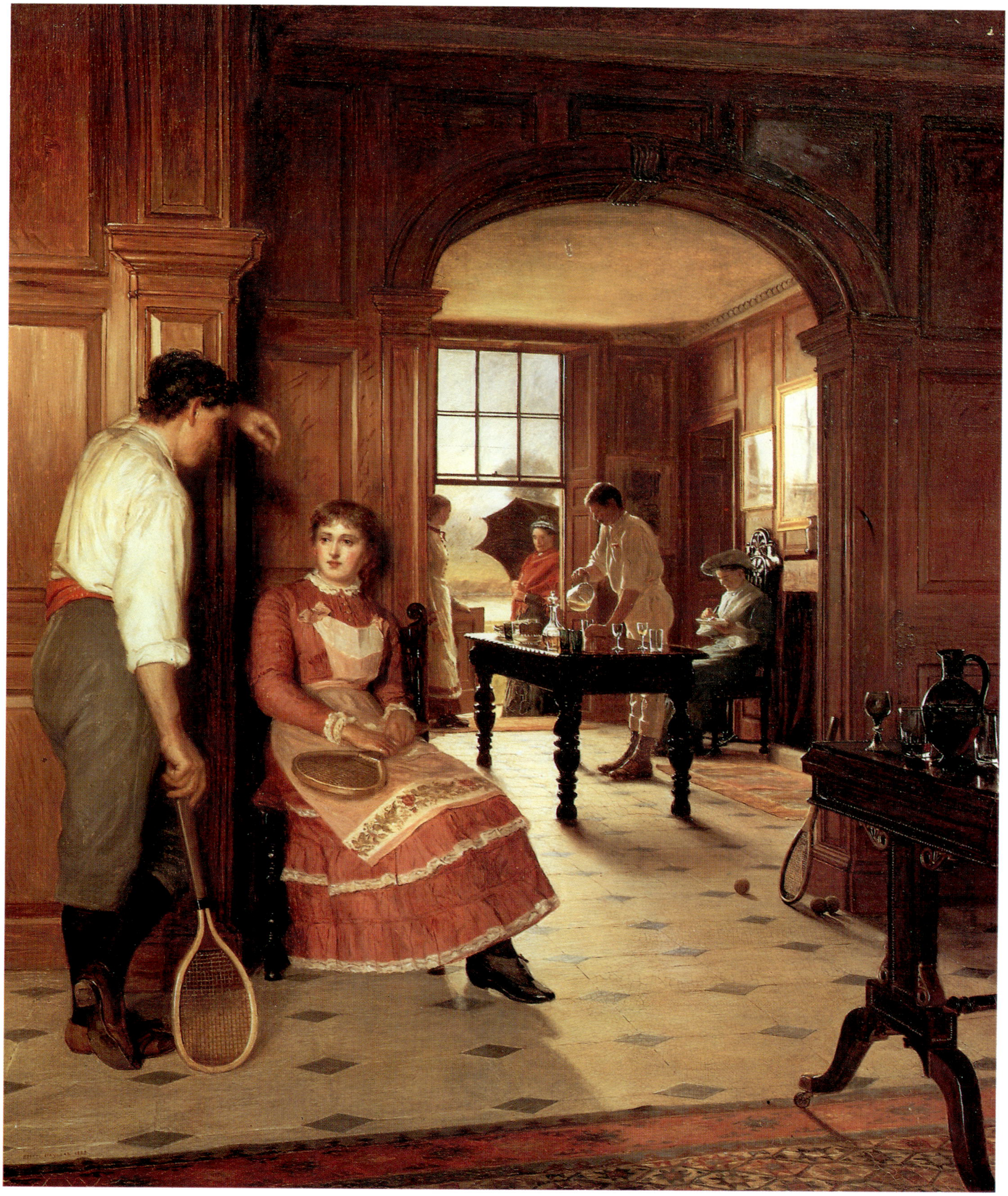

171
EDITH HAYLLAR
*A Summer Shower*

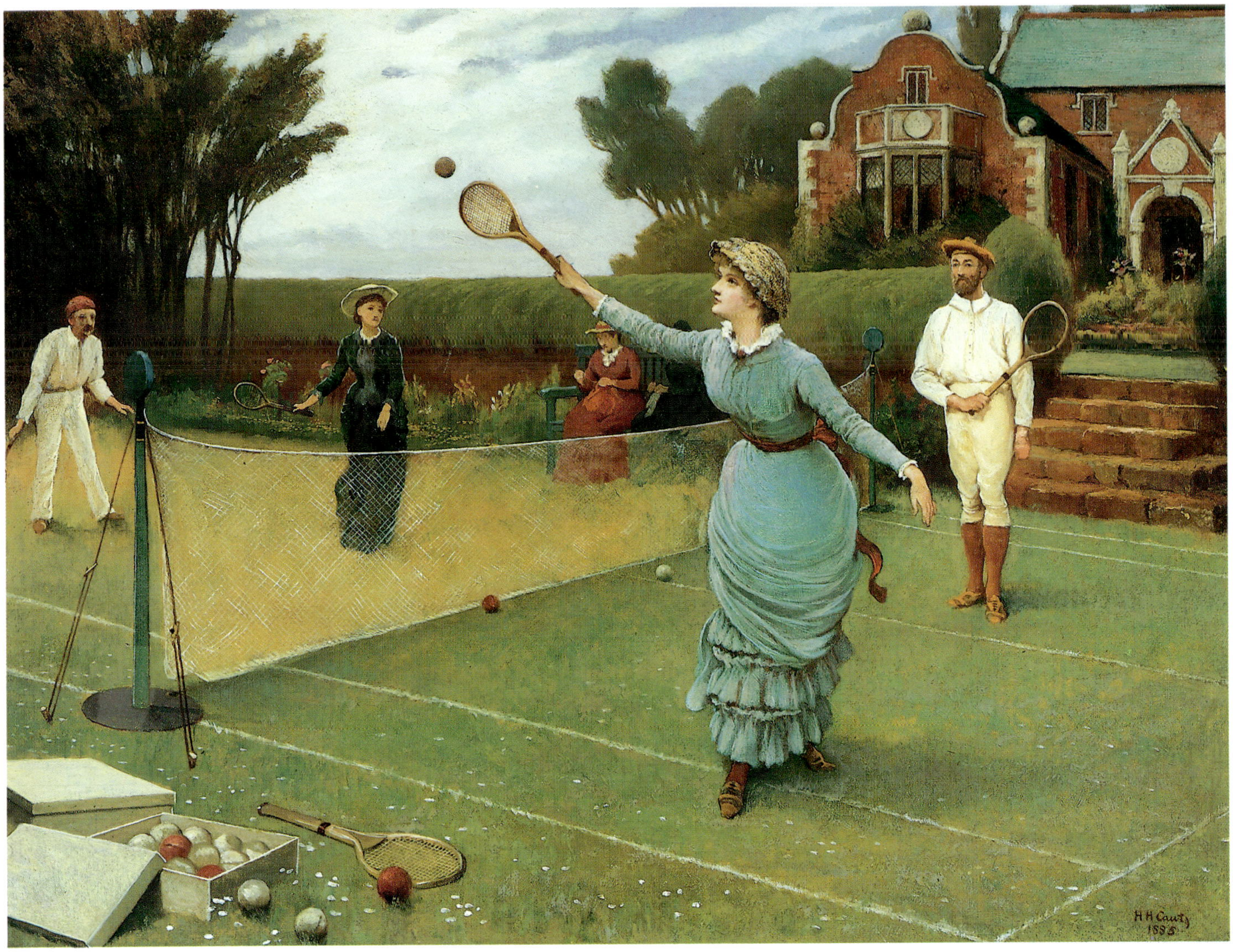

172
HORACE HENRY CAUTY
*The Tennis Match*

and coloured scarves as belts; the ladies have tied their long dresses back with aprons, with pockets for spare tennis balls. When playing, they usually wore small straw hats. There is no picture quite so redolent of a Victorian summer afternoon, with gentle sets of tennis, showers, lemonade, tea and cucumber sandwiches.

The more democratic the sport, the less painters seemed to like it. Croquet, archery and tennis were of course country-house games, and this made them an attractive subject for Victorian painters. Fishing was a more genuinely democratic sport, but fishermen usually only appear in Victorian landscapes as incidental figures. Football, arguably the most popular of all village sports, did not seem to appeal to painters at all.

# Chapter Fourteen

# ~ LOVE ~ AND MARRIAGE

Find even ash or four-leaved clover
An' you'll see your true lover before the day's over.

TRADITIONAL

PICTURES OF FLIRTATION AND ROMANCE IN THE countryside were a uniquely Victorian speciality. They provided nature with romantic interest, and an excuse for painting pretty girls in nice dresses. Many Victorians were passionate walkers, and in a society in which conventions were so repressive an innocent country walk might afford a rare opportunity for a young man and a young woman to meet and talk, without the inhibition of parental supervision. Lovers could meet secretly in some out-of-the-way spot, and the seduction of village girls and servants usually began in this way. Arthur Donnithorne had secret trysts with Hetty Sorrel in *Adam Bede*; the seduced girl in H.G. Jebb's novel *Out of the Depths* (1859) was a lady's maid who met her lover by an old well not far from the big house. Tess of the d'Urbervilles met her fate in the same way. Both in literature and in life, the countryside was the place for love.

The most famous Victorian picture of flirtation in the countryside is probably Holman Hunt's *Hireling Shepherd* (173). Hunt intended this to be an elaborate moral and biblical fable, and wrote in his memoirs that the shepherd symbolised the church neglecting its flock, in the shape of the sheep straying into the corn, and the lamb eating green apples. We can enjoy it, however, as a simple scene of rustic flirtation, set in a breathtakingly beautiful summer landscape. It was painted in 1851 near Ewell, in Surrey, where an uncle of Hunt's owned a farm. The model for the girl was Emma Watkins, a farm girl who lived nearby. Millais also came to stay at Ewell, and worked on his *Ophelia* at the same time. Two of the most beautiful of all Pre-Raphaelite landscapes were being painted at Ewell that summer.

The Pre-Raphaelite movement produced surprisingly few other pictures of romance in the countryside, except for *April Love* by Arthur Hughes. Most painters preferred to follow John

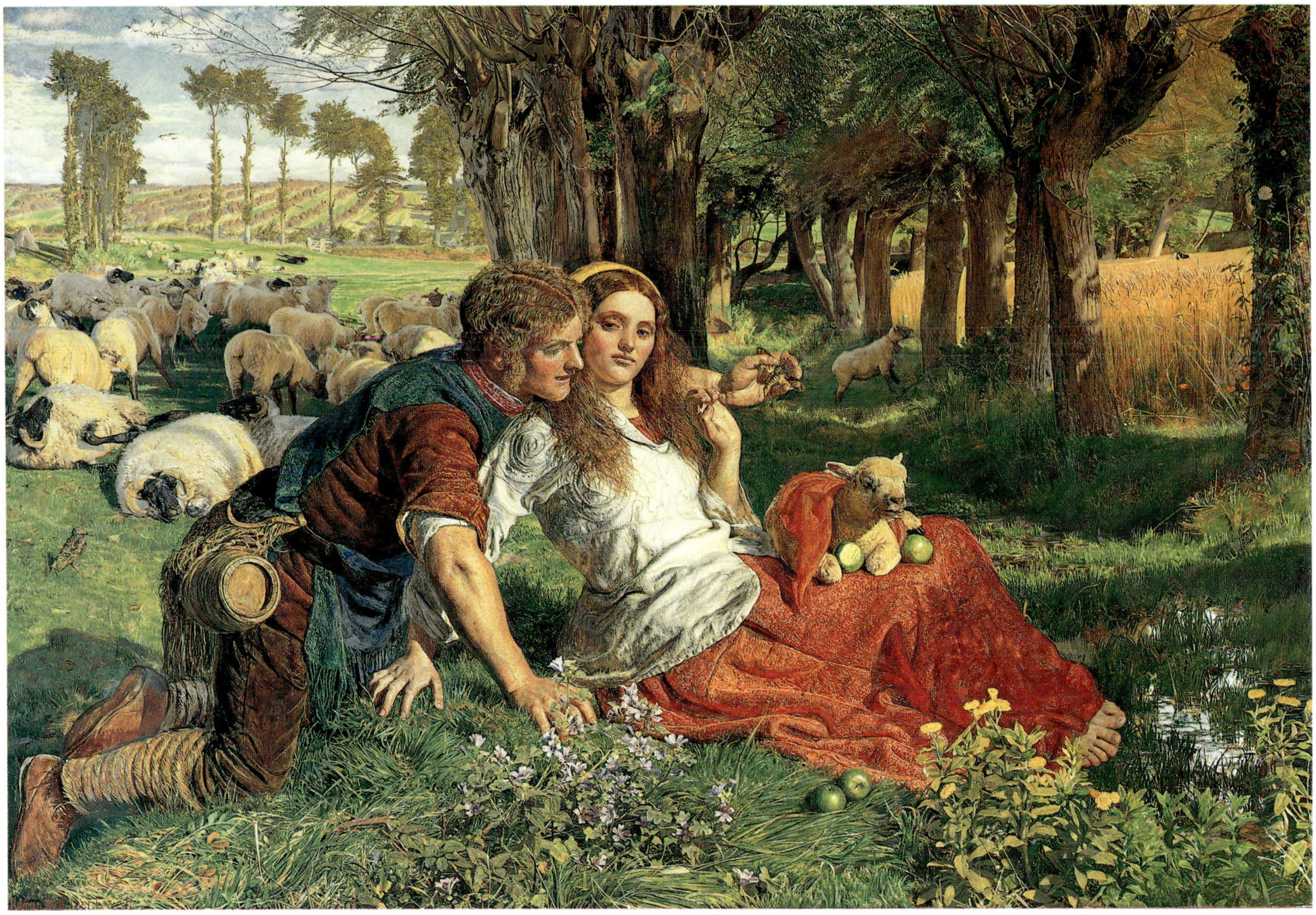

173
William Holman Hunt
*The Hireling Shepherd*

Callcott Horsley's simpler recipe of 'sunshine and pretty women'. His *Showing a Preference* (174) is a Victorian classic of the genre. A young sailor, in this case a junior officer, is escorting two pretty girls beside a cornfield, and is paying more attention to the one on the left. *Punch* thought the officer was 'showing a preference in a very indiscreet and decided manner. The very poppies hang their heads in shame. Let us hope, however, that he has made a fitting choice and that his charmer will become a mate before he is a commander.' Sailors often appear in these pictures, and 'A. Sailor and his Lass' was a favourite title. The Victorians seemed to look more indulgently on their flirtations than those of mere landlubbers; it was assumed that sailors were always incorrigibly amorous. Horsley himself was a noted prude: as rector of the Royal Academy schools, he forbade the use of nude models, particularly because there were lady students present, and was therefore dubbed 'Clothes-Horsley' by his pupils.

All Victorian love affairs – if we are to judge by the novels of the period, at least – were beset by tiffs and misunderstandings. The couple in Jacob Thompson's *The Course of True Love* (175) seem to have run into one of these little difficulties. Lengthy periods of courting, lengthy engagements, and a high level of parental interference must have ensured that the path of true Victorian lovers rarely ran smooth. Thompson exhibited a longer version at the Royal Academy in 1854, in which he introduced an angry lady, obviously the girl's mother, approaching over a stile, and providing an even more tangible obstacle to their courtship. Thompson was a Cumbrian artist who lived near Penrith, and most of his narrative pictures are set amid the dramatic scenery of Cumberland and Westmorland. More touching, and more genuinely rustic, are the couple in Frederick Smallfield's *Early Lovers* (176) holding hands over a stile. Smallfield was mainly a watercolourist, and produced a number of works showing Pre-Raphaelite influence in the

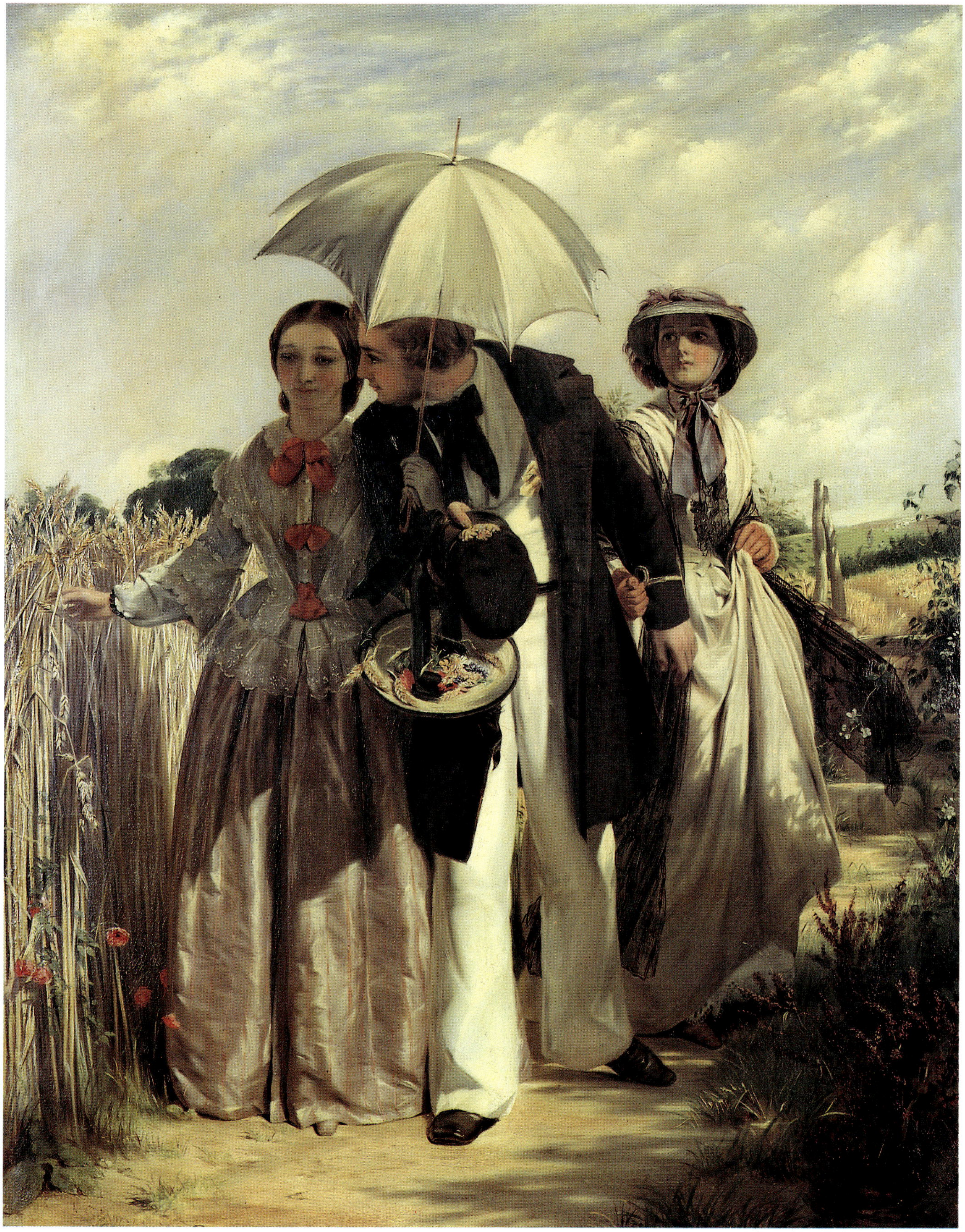

174
JOHN CALLCOTT HORSLEY
*Showing a Preference*

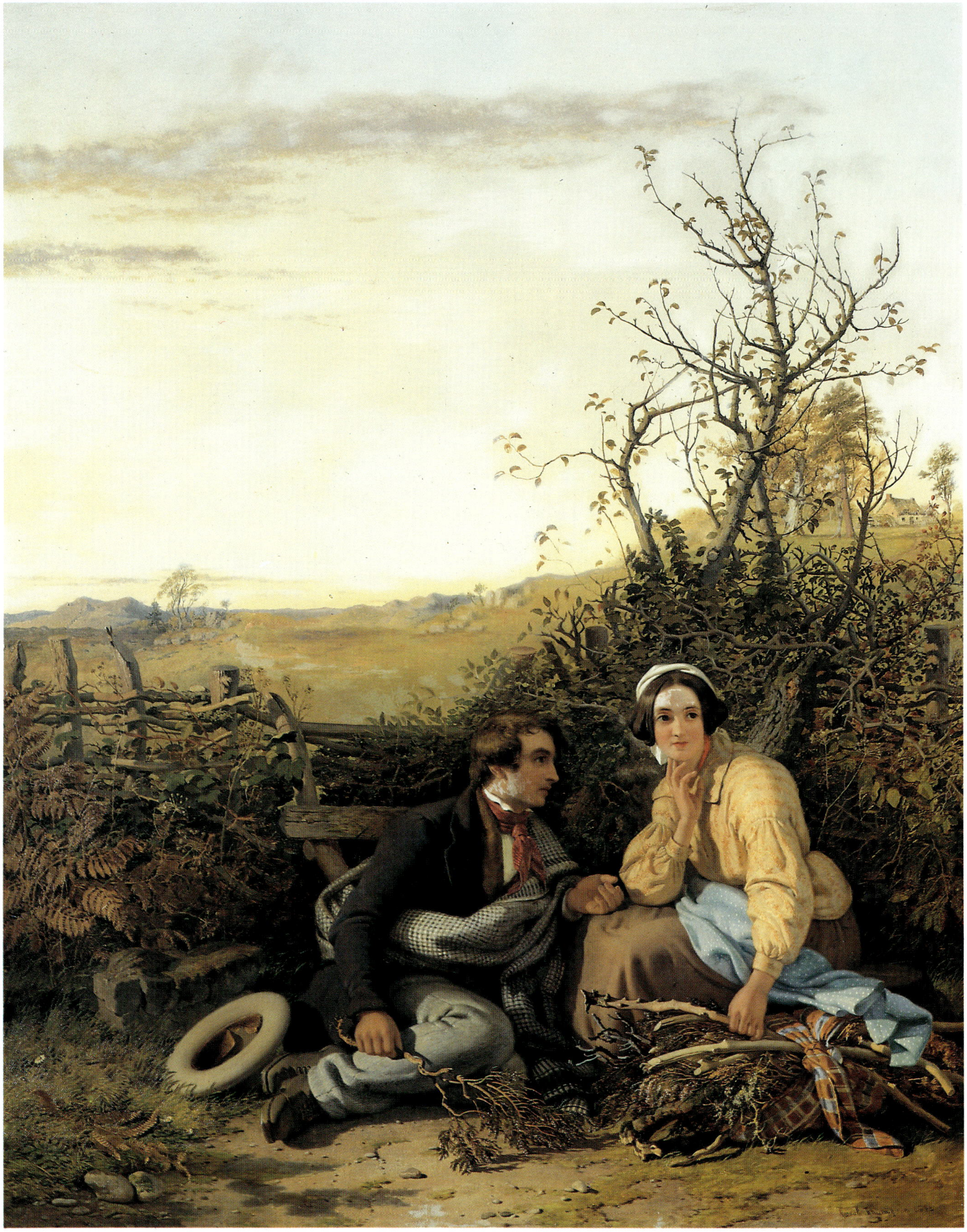

175
Jacob Thompson
*The Course of True Love Never did Run Smooth*

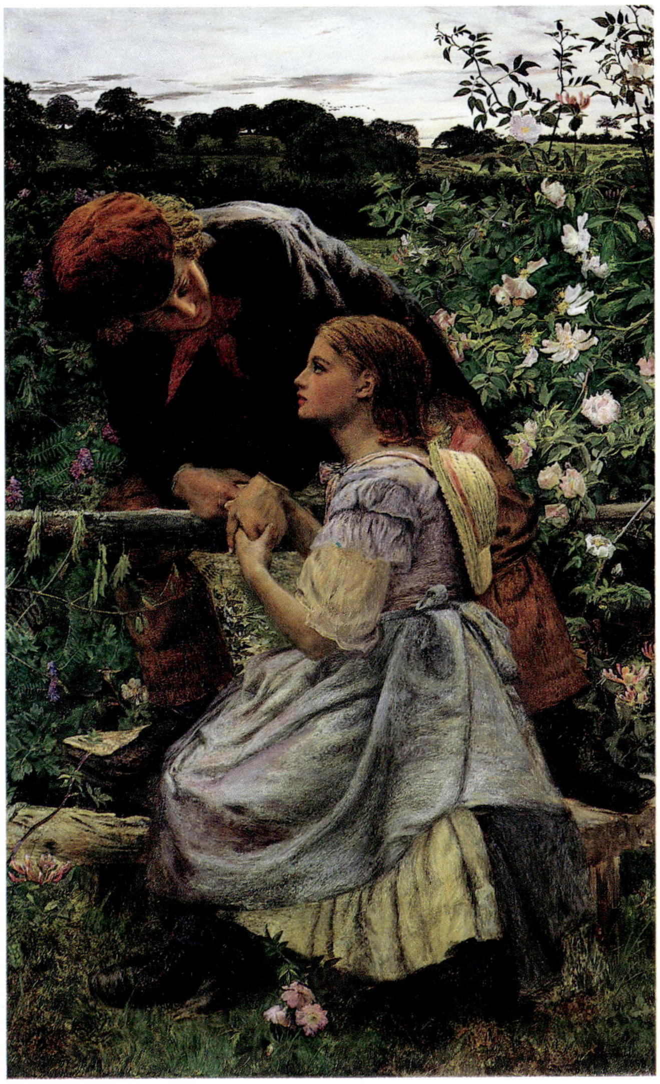

176
FREDERICK SMALLFIELD
*Early Lovers*

1850s and 1860s. *Early Lovers* is an example, combining tender emotion with a beautiful background of landscape and flowers. The rustic tryst kept its appeal right through the century, and reappears even in a much later work, such as *The Edge of the Wood* (3) by Elizabeth Stanhope Forbes, who was the wife of the Newlyn artist, Stanhope Forbes.

The cottage also formed a perfect setting for courtship and flirtation. 'Love in a cottage' was the theme or the title of many a mid-Victorian picture. George Smith, that tireless exponent of the cottage idyll, explored it in his *Gamekeeper's Courtship* (179). Here, a girl is hiding behind a door while the Jefferies-like figure of the gamekeeper is talking to her mother, but his dog has spotted her. Another frequent painter of rustic courtship was William Henry Midwood (180). Here the girl has been interrupted at her spinning-wheel, and does not seem pleased. The tam-o-shanter on the back of the chair suggests that the rustic swain is a Scotsman.

Among the Victorian middle and upper classes, a man was not thought to be able to marry until he had established himself in a trade or profession, or already had sufficient means to support a wife and children. Among country people, who did not have much money anyway, marriage was taken more lightly, and couples often married very young. But even in the country, long engagements were commonplace: usually a year or two, and sometimes five or even ten years. Arthur Hughes's famous *Long Engagement* (181) has captured with touching pathos the plight of these dutiful children, forbidden by their parents to marry year after year. The lover is a poor young curate, just like Francis Kilvert, whose meagre stipend was obviously considered inadequate. He must wait, therefore, for promotion and a higher salary. Hughes's couple have already been engaged so long that the ivy is climbing over her name 'Amy' carved on the tree. In *Lark Rise*, Flora Thompson described one such couple, known as Chokey and Bess.

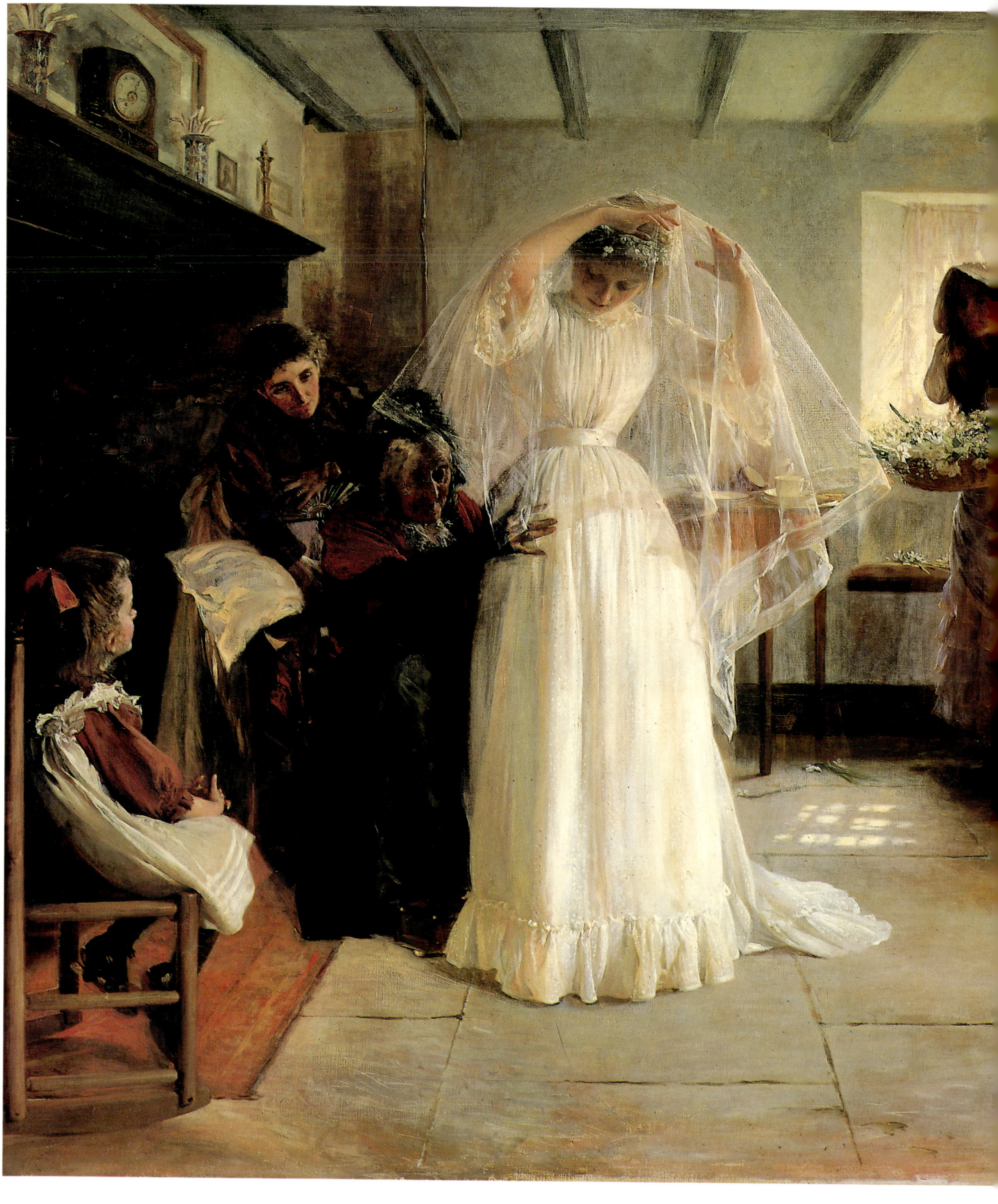

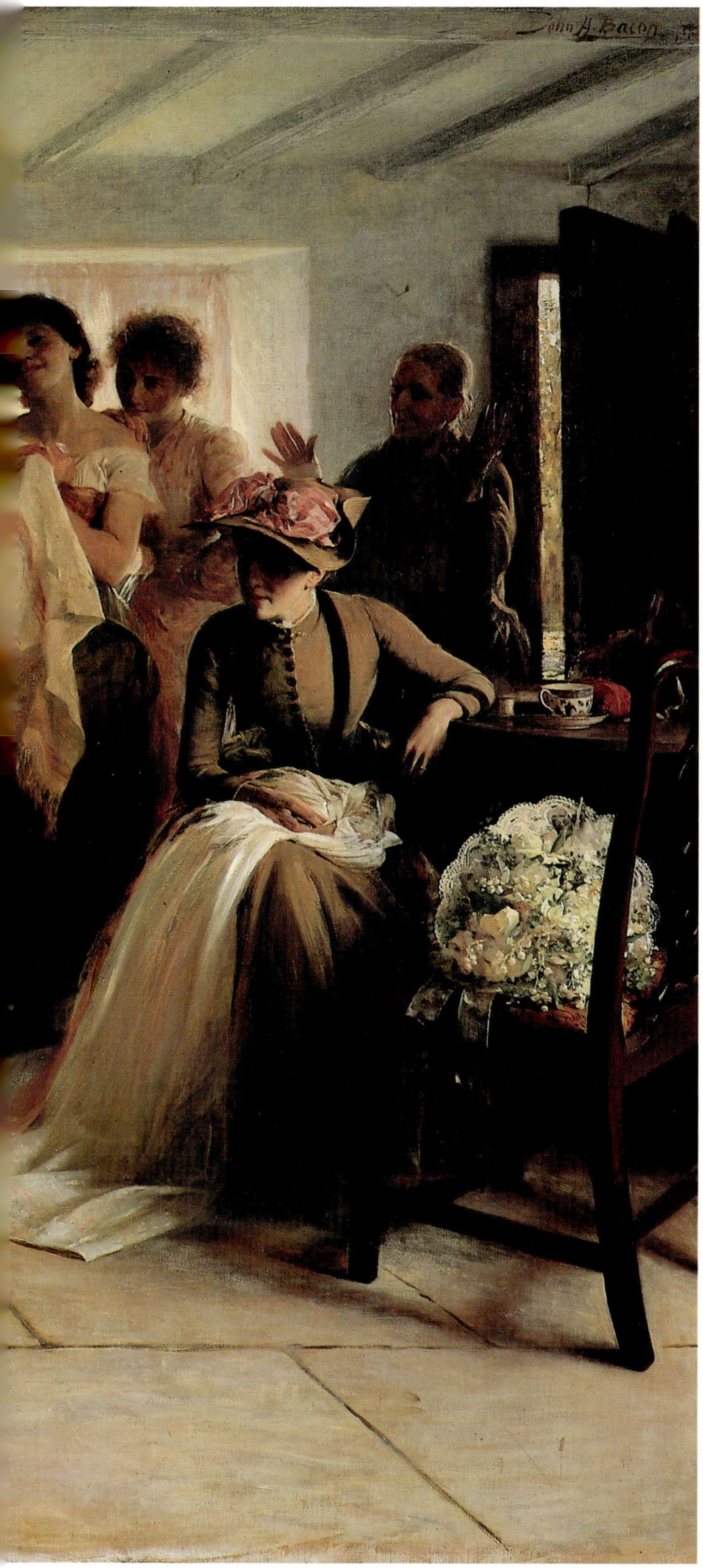


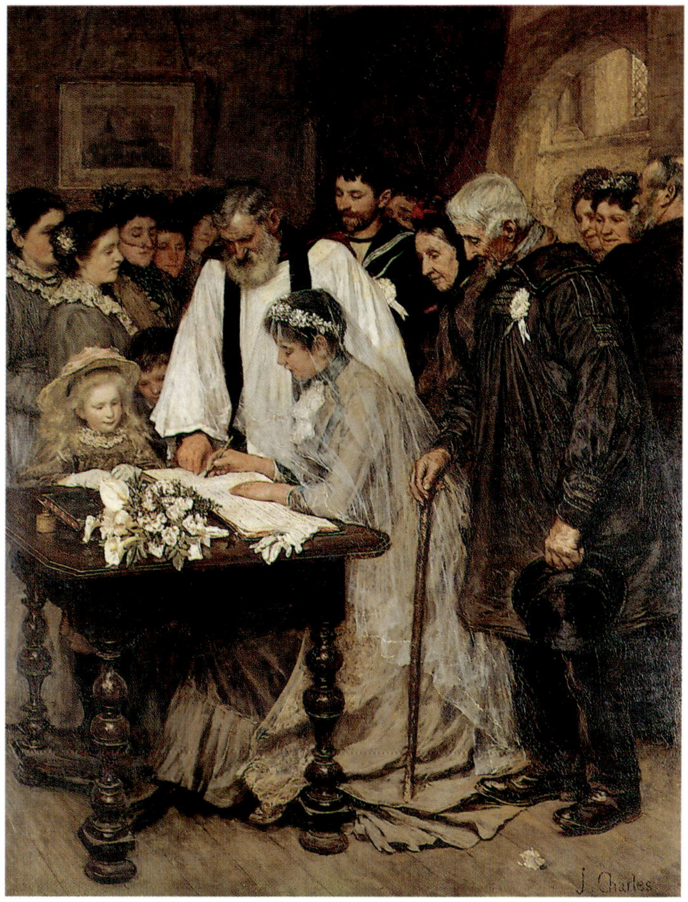


178
JAMES CHARLES
*Signing the Marriage Register*

177
JOHN HENRY F. BACON
*A Wedding Morning*

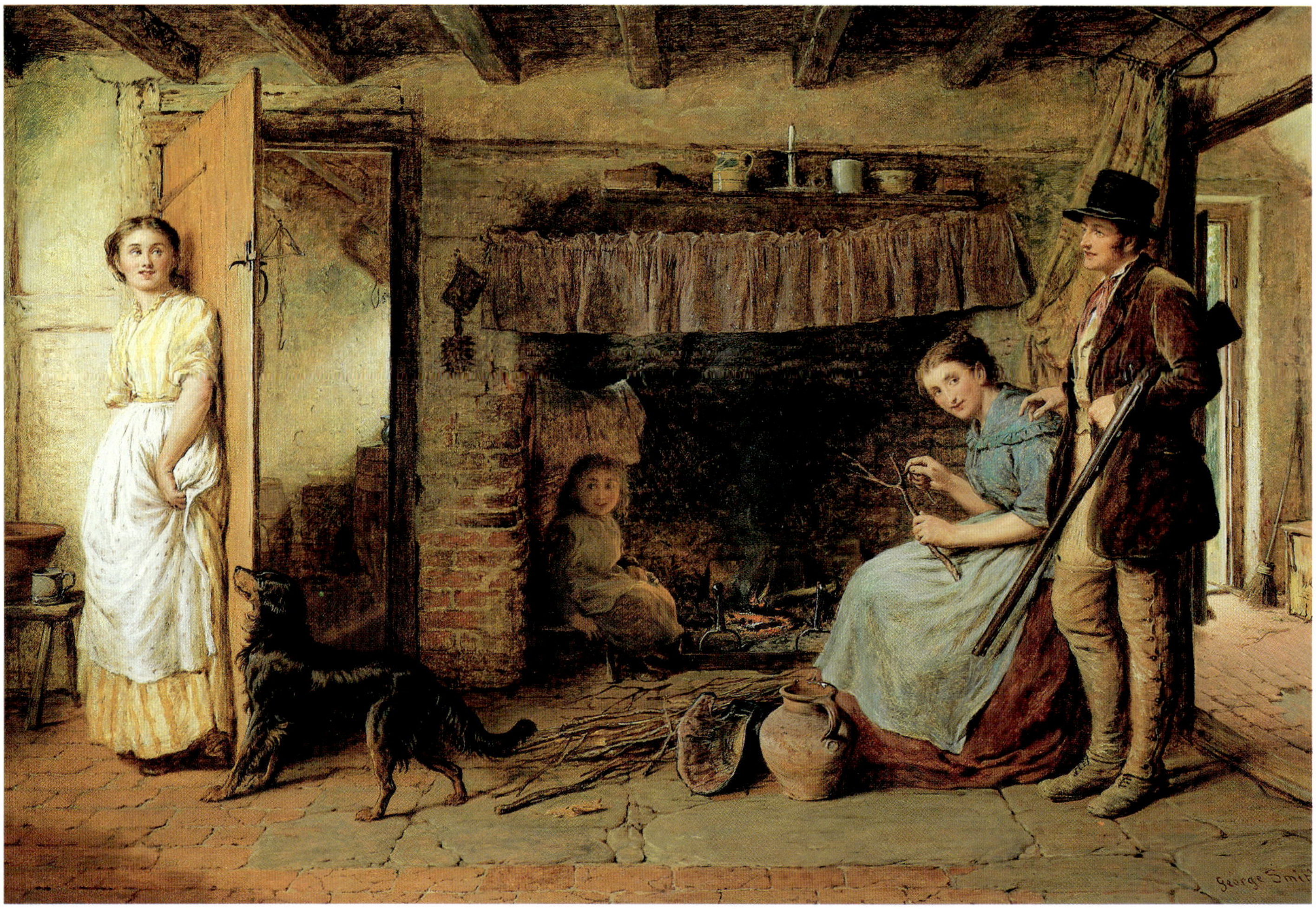


179
George Smith
*The Gamekeeper's Courtship*

Refused permission to get married, they walked out together every evening for about ten or twelve years, and did not finally marry until some fifteen years had passed.

Even in a small village, feelings would be outraged if such rules were not observed. At Lark Rise, an adulterous couple were treated by the villagers to 'rough music. . . . Effigies of the pair had been made and carried aloft on poles by torchlight to the house of the woman, to the accompaniment of the banging of pots, pans and coal shovels, the screeching of tin whistles and mouth-organs, and cat-calls, hoots, and jeers.' The guilty pair very soon left the village. In Hardy's *Jude the Obscure*, Jude Fawley and Sue Bridehead suffer continual prejudice and persecution because they are not legally married. Hardy also railed against the selfishness of parents in not allowing their daughters to marry without their permission, in his poem *The Orphaned Old Maid*, which begins: 'I wanted to marry, but father said No . . .'

But once the engagement was over, and the date fixed, then came the momentous event, the wedding day. The whole paraphernalia of the white wedding was largely a Victorian invention, although Jane Welsh Carlyle thought it 'something betwixt a religious ceremony and a pantomime'. Most of the characteristics of an English wedding – the church packed with friends and relations, the bride in white dress and veil attended by bridesmaids, the nervous groom with his best man, Mendelssohn's *Wedding March*, the wedding breakfast with champagne, toasts and a cake, the presents on display, the honeymoon – were established in the Victorian period. The bride in her white floating veil symbolised the Victorian attitude to women – an angel on a pedestal, pure, innocent, faithful, and above all, ignorant. Victorian brides almost always wore orange-blossom. This was a curious survival of a pagan fertility symbol, but the Victorians seem to have overlooked the fact. 'Custom and romance have raised the chaplet of orange-

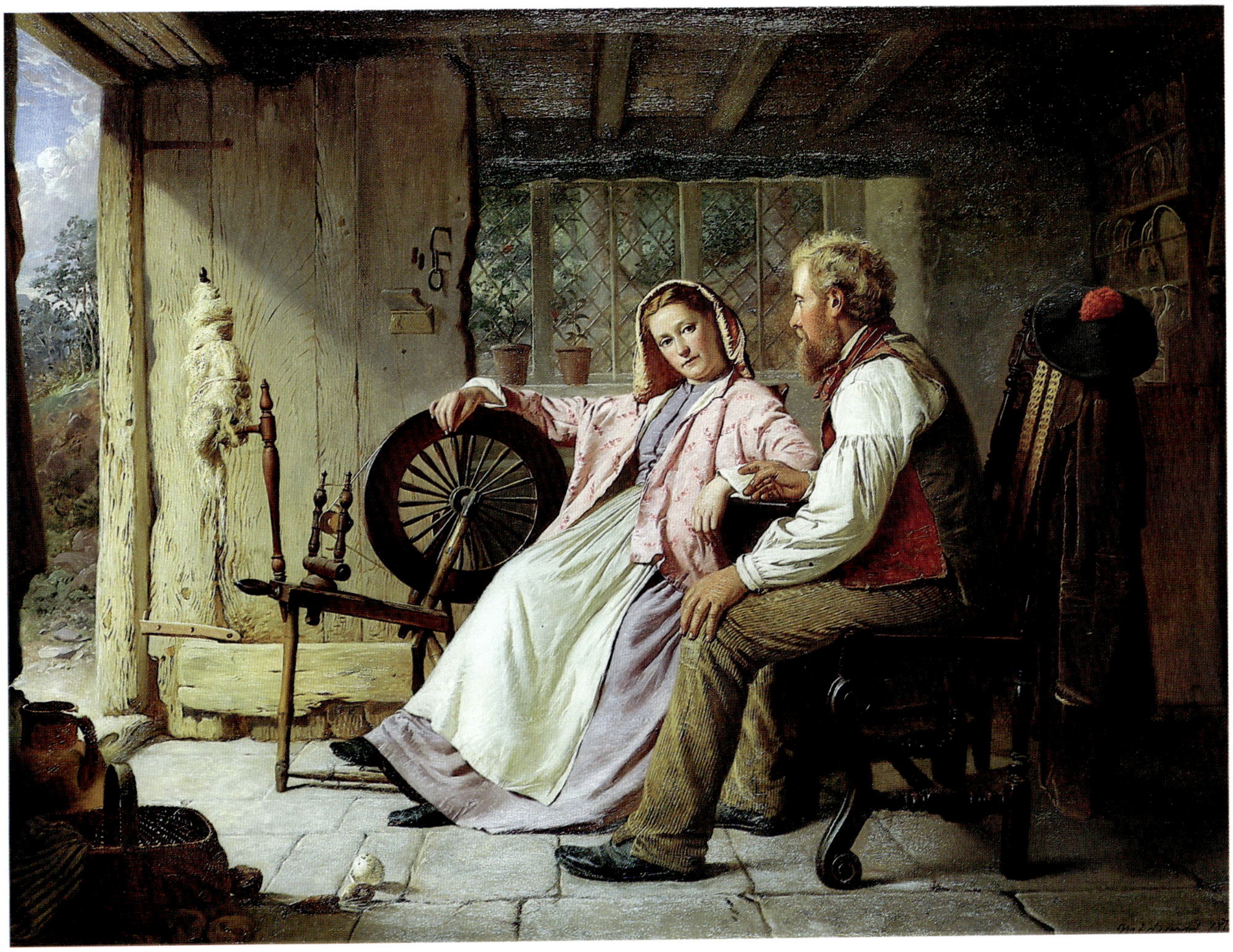

180
WILLIAM HENRY MIDWOOD
*Rustic Courtship*

blossom to unmerited respect,' wrote John Cordy Jeaffreson, author of *Brides and Bridals* in 1870, suggesting that some other flower should take its place. None did, and most of the brides depicted here are wearing it.

Frith painted a London wedding, in his picture *For Better, For Worse* of 1881, but most painters preferred the simple charm of a country wedding. John H.F. Bacon shows us *A Wedding Morning* (177) with the bride putting the finishing touches to her preparations, accompanied by relatives and friends. Her dress is very simple and white, with a long veil, and on her head is the inevitable orange-blossom. Grandmother is helping her, as is another girl at the table – perhaps her chief bridesmaid. Other bridesmaids and friends are arriving with more flowers, and their expressions of delight at the bride's appearance are unaffected and natural. It is a beautiful picture, and reminiscent of the wedding scene in Hardy's *Under the Greenwood Tree*.

Then the bride and her bridesmaids would be off to the church. John White's *Village Wedding* (182) shows the carriage waiting outside the church for the bride and groom, and the villagers assembling to get a good view. A wedding was always an exciting day for everyone in the village, and pennies would be scattered for the children. Inside the church, the service over, the bride and groom with their close relations would go to the vestry to sign the register (178). In James Charles's wonderful picture, the old father and mother look on as their daughter signs. She is dressed very like the bride in Bacon's picture, complete with orange-blossom. The father wears the traditional smock-frock with a white favour, but does not seem aware that both his stick and his boot are on the hem of her wedding-dress. The bridesmaids wear simple dresses of the same colour trimmed with flowers, reflecting not only economy but a change of fashion. The bridegroom, once again, is a sailor.

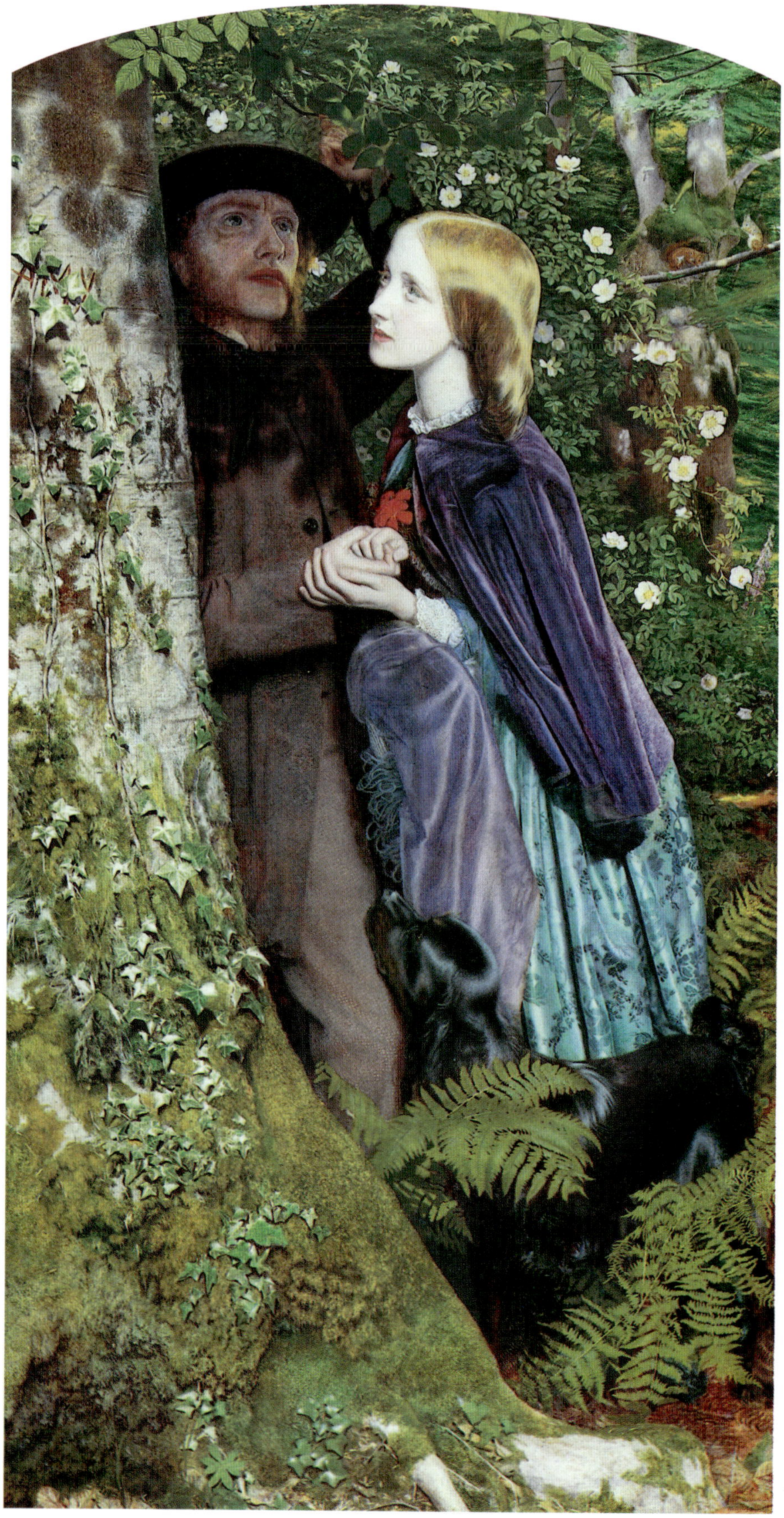

181
Arthur Hughes
*The Long Engagement*

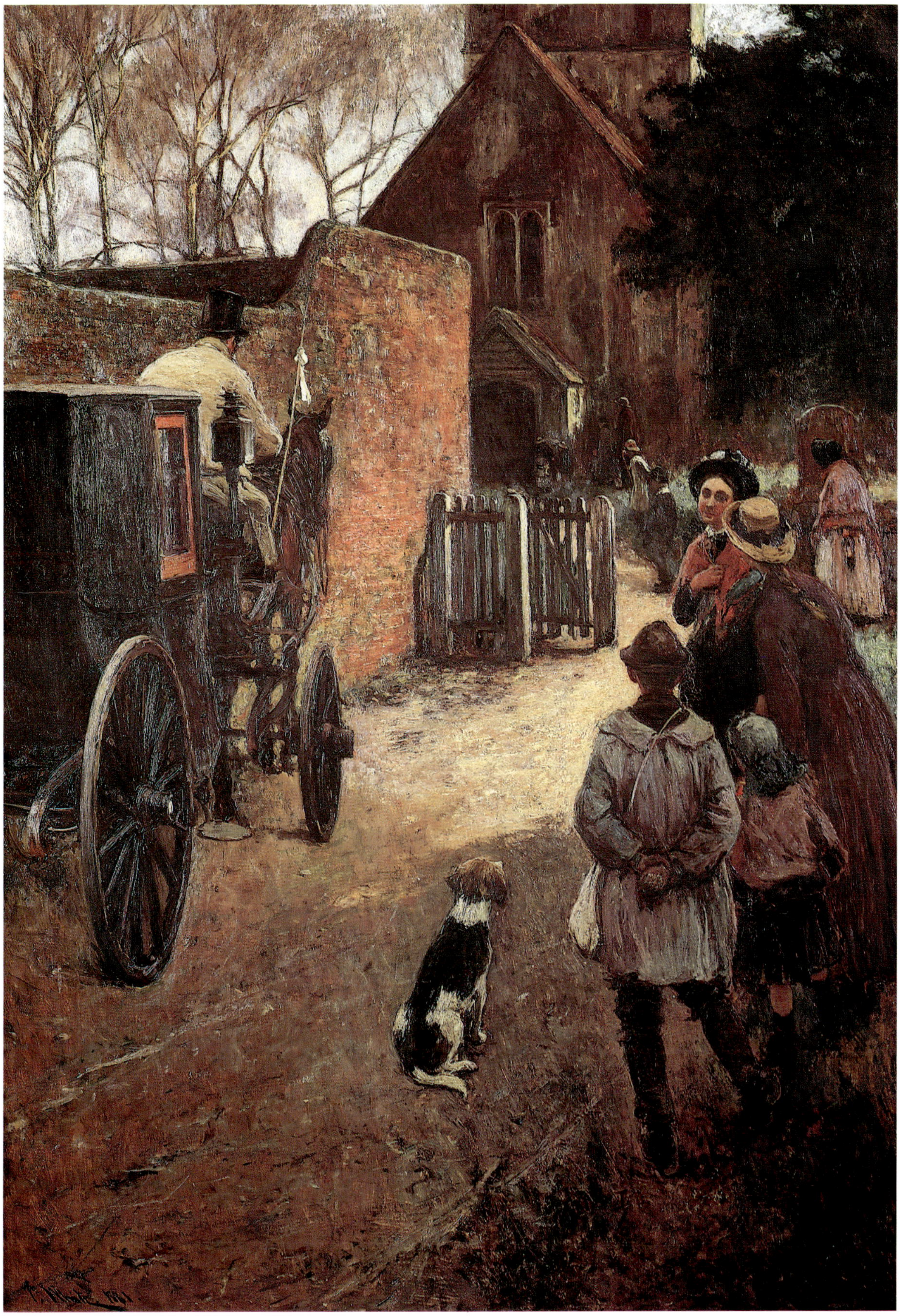

182
JOHN WHITE
*A Village Wedding*

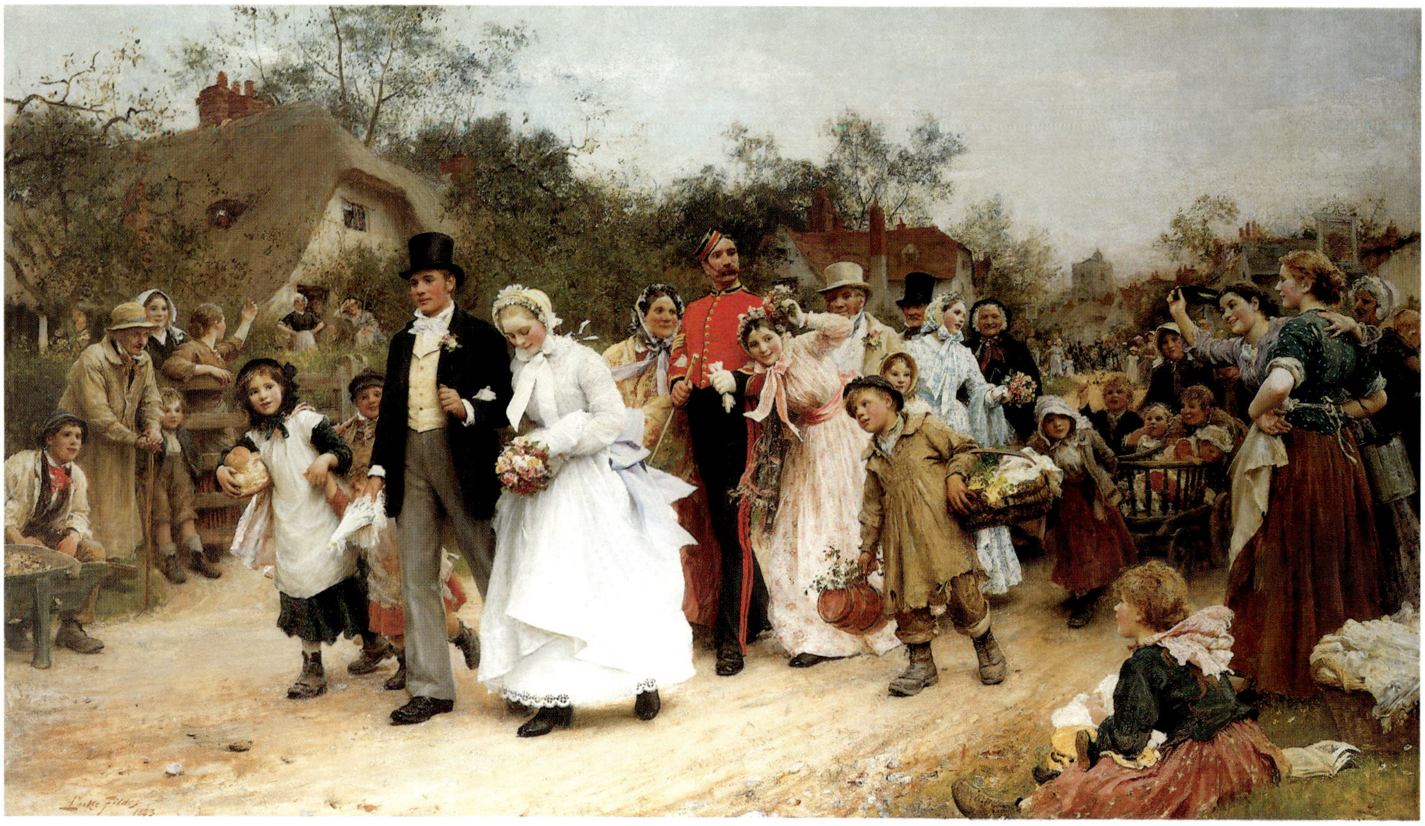

183
SIR LUKE FILDES
*The Village Wedding*

The country wedding inspired two of the greatest Victorian narrative pictures, Luke Fildes's *Village Wedding* (183), and *The Health of the Bride* by Stanhope Forbes (184). Fildes's picture is the most spectacular evocation of a country wedding of the period. Although he painted it in 1883, Fildes tried to recapture the spirit of the village as he remembered it in his boyhood – in other words in the early Victorian period. 'I left London', he wrote, 'with the idea of painting this "Village Wedding" quite in modern costume, but . . . it is so ugly and nasty I cannot bring myself to do it. I don't mean the people in their everyday clothes – they are just passable – but I mean those in their wedding attire, all Reading and Wallingford shop goods degrading in every aspect. . . .' The painting is set in the Oxfordshire village of Aston Tirrold, and the models were mostly local people. The Trooper in the Life Guards was modelled in the studio in London, and Fildes's son recalled, in his life of his father, that

> He used to come down to Melbury Road from the New Cavalry Barracks in Knightsbridge and was glad to have a shilling for the morning's work and his bus fare. The two girls in the forefront, one of whom throws an old shoe at the bridal pair, were my mother's parlourmaid and head-housemaid and great would be . . . the flutterings 'below stairs' on the mornings when the gallant Life Guardsman was due to come for a sitting.

Fildes had made his name before this with gloomy social realist subjects, such as the famous *Applicants for Admission to a Casual Ward*. He painted *The Village Wedding* in order to prove that he could also paint happy subjects, and succeeded brilliantly. The picture was an instant success when it was shown at the Royal Academy in 1883. This is one of the most joyous, celebratory pictures of country life of the whole Victorian period – and a triumphant portrait of the paradise that the Victorians felt they had lost.

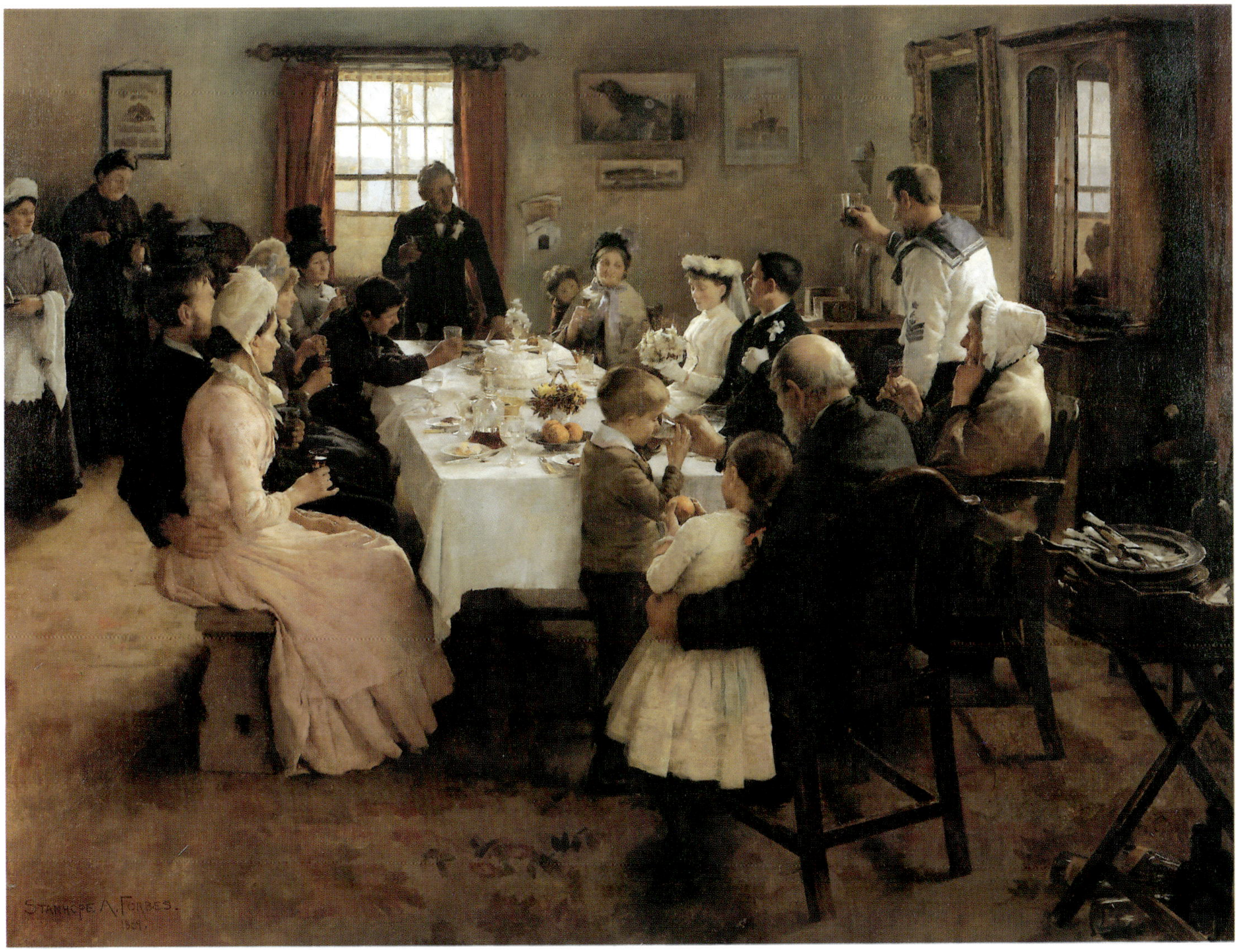

184
STANHOPE FORBES
*The Health of the Bride*

Stanhope Forbes's *Health of the Bride* was painted in his studio in Newlyn, Cornwall, and was modelled on the interior of the village inn. All the models were local characters. The man at the head of the table is rising to propose a toast to the bride. Everyone is raising their glass, and the sailor on the right stands up. The bride and groom sit quietly at the table, perhaps rather overawed by the occasion. This is one of the outstanding social realist pictures of the nineteenth century, and has for many years been one of the best-loved paintings in the Tate Gallery. Shortly after its completion it was sold to Sir Henry Tate, the founder of the gallery, whereupon Forbes felt able to marry the painter Elizabeth Armstrong, to whom he had been engaged for several years. Forbes wrote to Sir Henry Tate about his marriage, saying that 'It was inevitable after painting this picture', although it is probable that the handsome price paid by Sir Henry was an equally important factor.

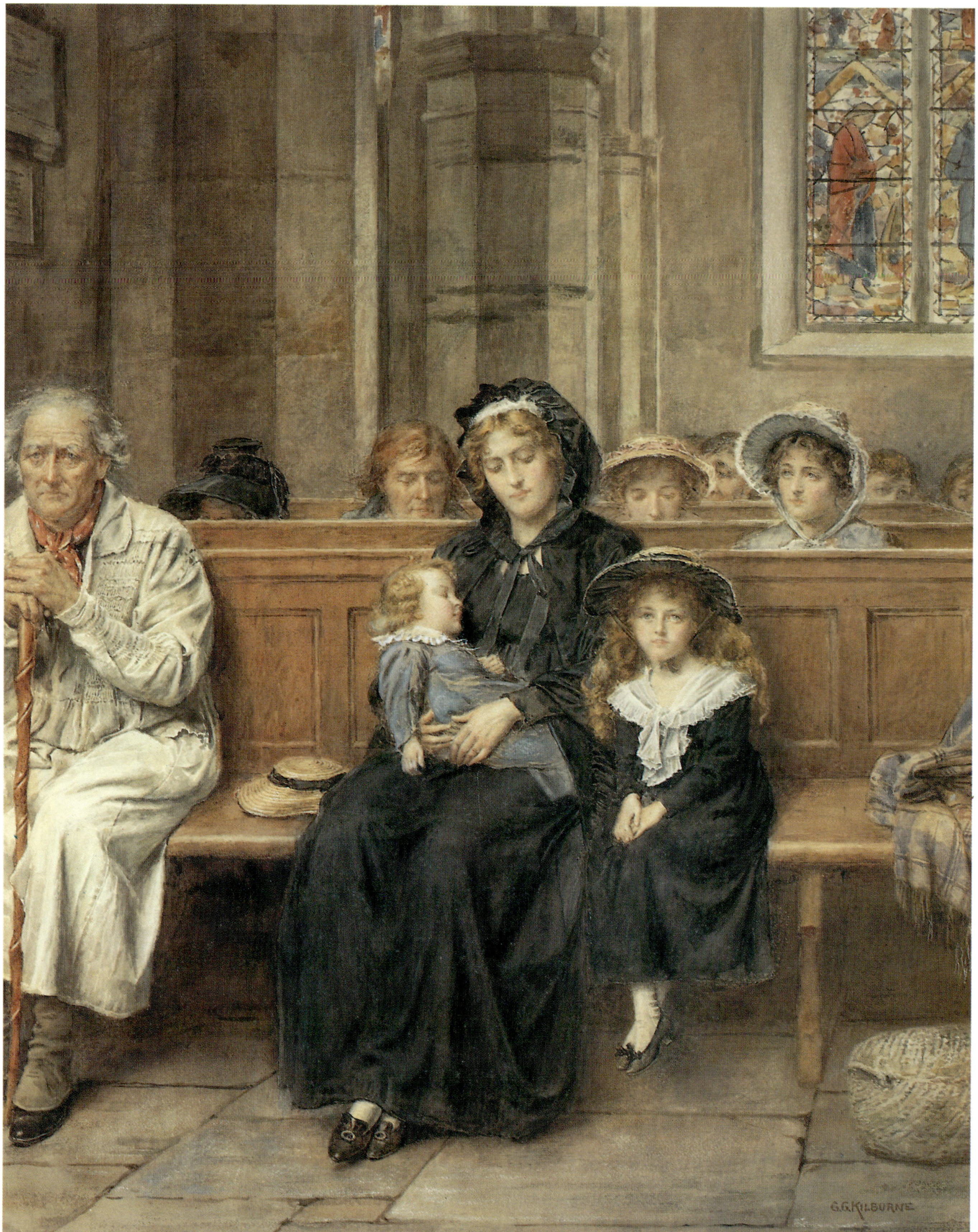


185
George Goodwin Kilburne
*In Church*

# Chapter Fifteen

# THE VILLAGE CHURCH

On afternoons of drowsy calm
We stood in the panelled pew,
Singing one-voiced a Tate-and-Brady psalm,
To the tune of 'Cambridge New'.

THOMAS HARDY, *Afternoon Service at Mellstock*

THE VILLAGE CHURCH WAS AN IMPORTANT focal point in any village. It was probably an extremely ancient building, medieval or even older, although the Victorians were notorious over-restorers of old churches and builders of new ones. It was bad restoration of old churches that led William Morris to found the Society for the Protection of Ancient Buildings in 1877. The vicar was also likely to be an important person in the village, possibly the only educated man there, and often the only link with the social world beyond the village. In the early Victorian period, most parsons were relations of the gentry, or younger sons of landowning families. This was the age of the 'squarson', when the parson was 'a country gentleman in orders, who rode to hounds, and shot and danced and farmed, and often did worse things', according to Dean Church, in his *Life and Letters* (1894). This close relationship between the squire and the parson was often resented in the countryside, particularly as the parson was often also a magistrate. Many independent-minded country people, if they went to church at all, preferred the Methodist or Baptist chapels, where there was no need for deference to squire or parson, and the preacher and congregation were people of their own class.

By the last quarter of the century, the squarson was already an anachronism. The hunting parson, according to Trollope, 'is making himself to stink in the nostrils of his bishop, and is becoming a stumbling block and rock of offence to his brethren.' After 1870, fewer public schoolboys took holy orders, and the country vicar became a more professional, middle-class figure. Most country clergymen were liked and respected, provided they did not interfere or dominate too much. Most of them were charitable, and did good works, visiting the sick and the poor of the village. At Lark Rise, the parson's wife had a box

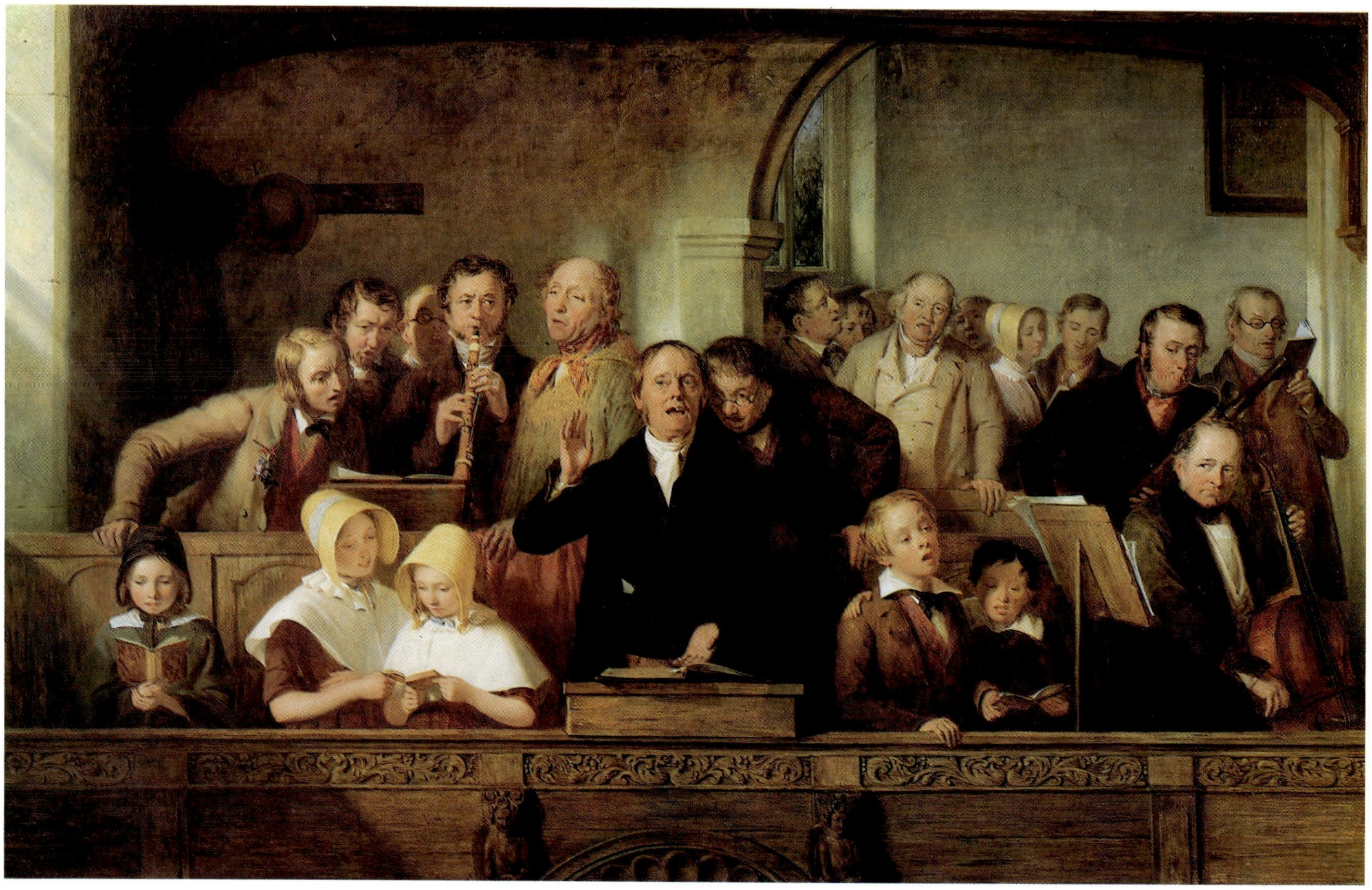

186
THOMAS WEBSTER
*The Village Choir*

of baby clothes and equipment which she lent out to any new mothers in need.

A vicar in a large parish might well have a curate to help him. Like Francis Kilvert, curates were generally poor bachelors, hard-working and dedicated, and much loved by their parishioners, who might find the vicar a little too grand and lofty. Anyone who thinks that a Victorian curate had an easy life should read Kilvert's description of having a bath on a frosty December morning: 'I sat down in my bath upon a sheet of thick ice which broke in the middle into large pieces, whilst sharp points and jagged edges stuck all around the sides of the tub like chevaux de frise. . . . The ice-water stung and scorched like fire. . . .' But there were compensations. The countryside in Kilvert's parish was extremely beautiful, and he greatly enjoyed walking around it, visiting his parishioners. In Robert Gallon's picture *On the Way to Church* (1), we see people walking through a beautiful summery landscape to a church among the trees. Kilvert's diary was often equally ecstatic: 'I have rarely seen Langley Church and Churchyard look more beautiful than they did this morning. The weather was lovely and round the quiet church the trees were gorgeous, the elms dazzling golden and the beeches burning crimson.'

Those that did go to church on Sunday might go to both morning and evening service. During the rest of the day, practically no activity of any kind was allowed except eating, walking, and reading the bible or some approved literature such as the *Sunday Book*. Most villagers worked in their gardens, but in some places even this was disapproved of. One rector of Kilvert's acquaintance found boys playing football on a Sunday, and stabbed the ball with his knife to stop them playing. For children it was a day of sometimes paralysing boredom. They had to accompany their parents to church, and the nonconformists often organised Sunday schools as well. In G.G. Kilburne's watercolour *In Church* (185), a mother sits with her two

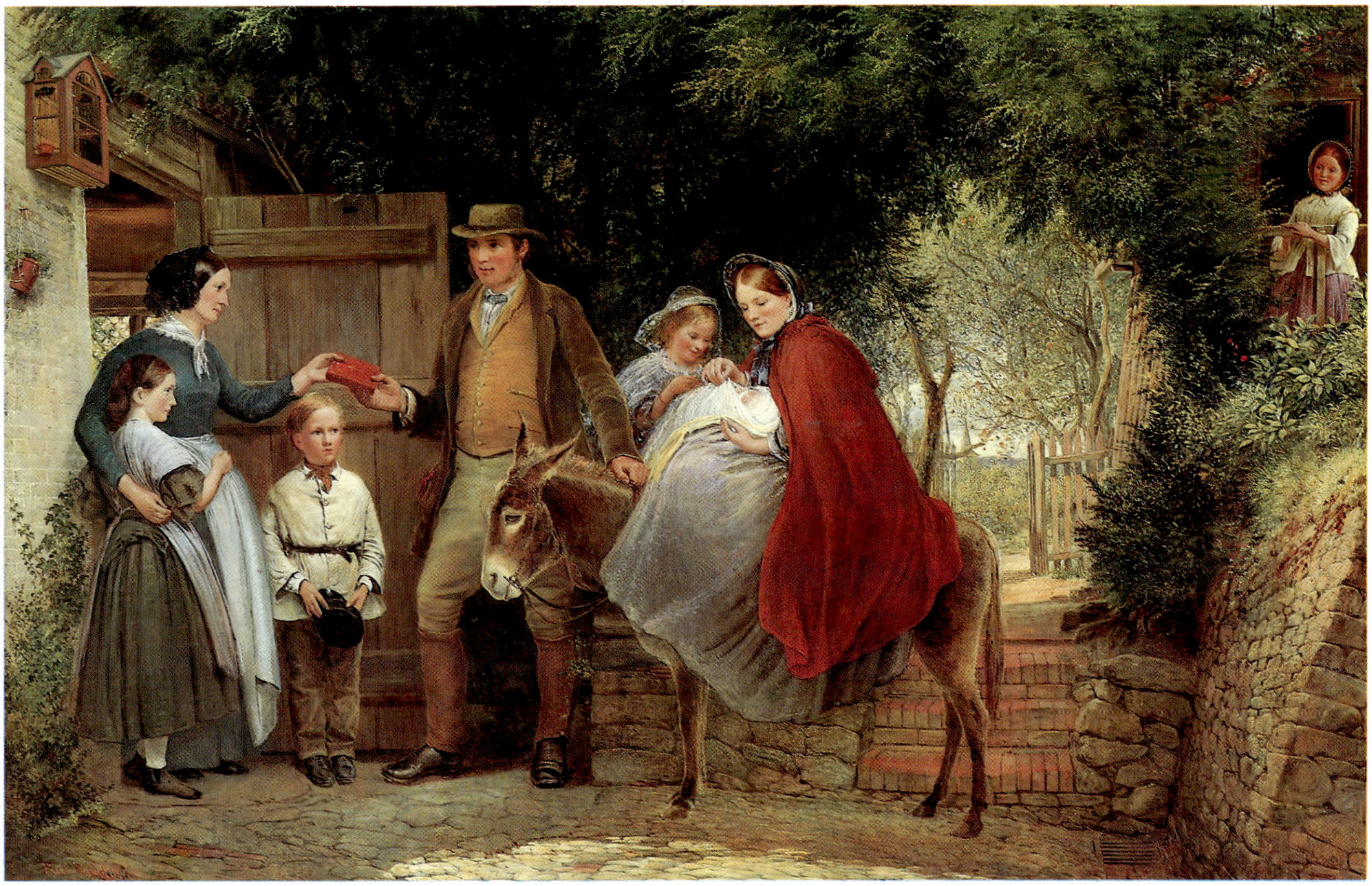

187
RICHARD REDGRAVE
*Starting for the Christening*

children, an old rustic in his smock alongside. At Lark Rise, Flora Thompson recalled the tedium of afternoon service; 'the school-children, under the stern eye of the manor-house, dared not so much as wriggle; they sat in their stiff, stuffy, best clothes, their stomachs lined with heavy Sunday dinner, in a kind of waking doze, through which Tom's Amens rang like a bell, and the Rector's voice buzzed beelike.' Every child had to learn its catechism, and Kilvert was sometimes extremely surprised by the answers. He asked one young girl, 'Who died for us on the Cross?', to which she answered promptly 'Lord Chesterfield'.

Kilvert also had great difficulty persuading his local squire, Mr Ashe, to install a harmonium in the church. Mr Ashe 'disapproved of any music in a church besides the human voice. . . .' Eventually, the villagers and local farmers subscribed enough money to buy a harmonium, and it was installed in spite of the squire's disapproval. Mr Ashe was obviously somewhat old-fashioned in his views. His family probably had their own pew in the church, often with high enough partitions to enable the occupants to doze off. Arthur J. Ashton in *As I Went on My Way* (1924) recalled a country squire who had his own fire in his family pew, and just before the sermon 'poked the fire, opened a cupboard, took out a glass, and then a bottle of golden wine, poured out a glassful of the elixir, drank it, sat down again and went to sleep'. Thomas Webster's *Village Choir* of 1847 (186), although set in an earlier period, still records the atmosphere that must have existed in many village churches well into the nineteenth century. Before organs and harmoniums were installed most village churches had an orchestra, who sat and played among the choir or in the gallery above the nave. Webster was painting from experience, as he had been a Chapel Royal choirboy in his youth.

Another important reason for attending church was the christening of a new baby. Redgrave's picture *Starting for the*

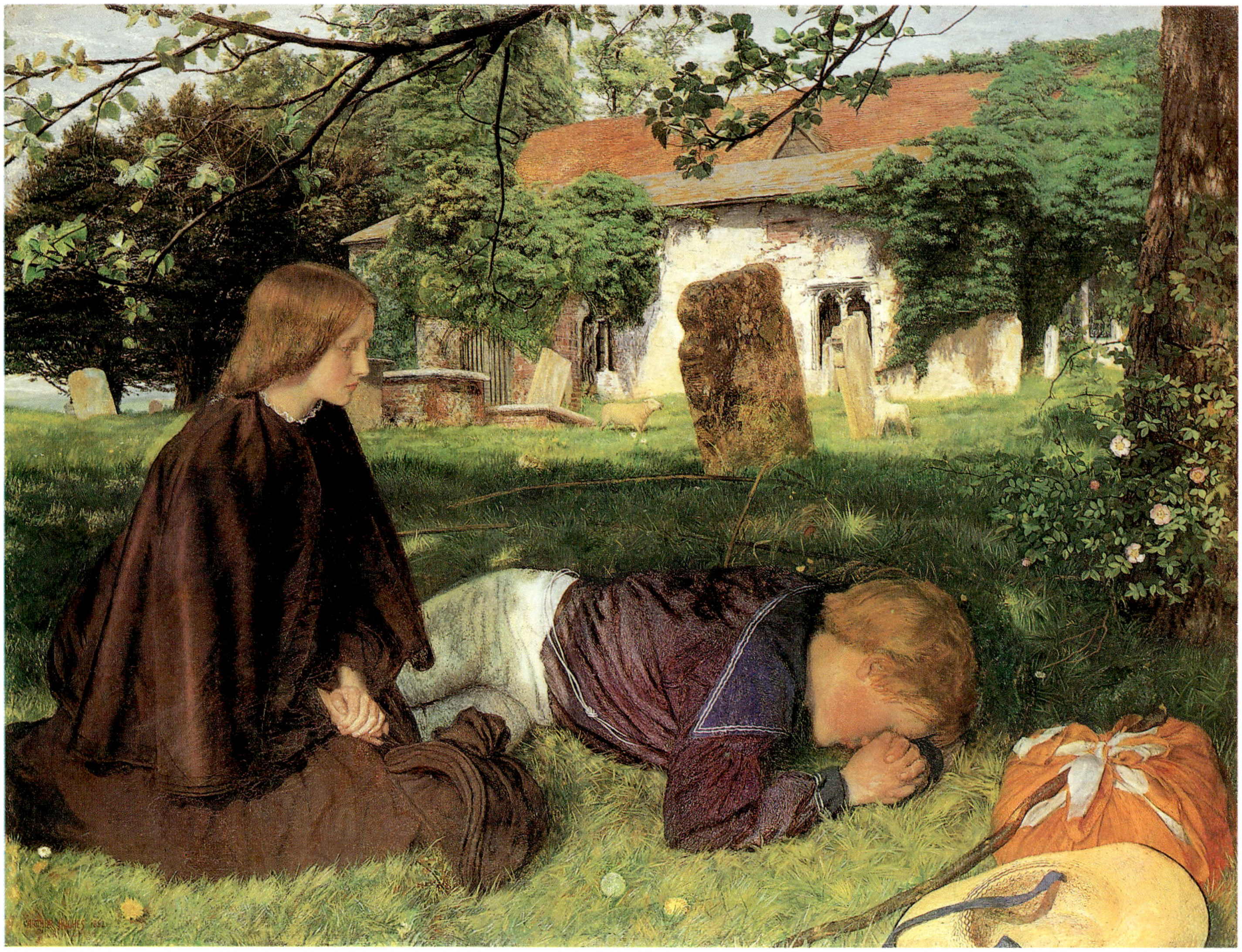

188
Arthur Hughes
*Home from the Sea*

*Christening* (187) shows a family about to go off to church, the mother and the new baby mounted on a donkey. Francis Kilvert found one remote church in Dorset where the clerk told him there was never any water in the font: 'The last parson never used no water. He spit into his hand.' At James Charles's more fashionable church in his picture *Christening Sunday* (1887), things would have been conducted with more decorum. The artist shows a smarter-looking gathering, with a coachman waiting to pick up his master or mistress. There is also a woman in a veil carrying another baby, which suggests that there may have been more than one baptism taking place.

The Victorian cult of death meant that lovers of art were not squeamish about pictures of churchyards. A pretty girl in a graveyard was a favourite subject, and Henry Bowler's *The Doubt – Can these Dry Bones live?* is probably the most famous example. Children in churchyards were quite acceptable too, and Arthur Hughes's *Home from the Sea* (188) is a classic of this genre. A sailor boy has come home to find that his mother has died. With his sister, he is sorrowing at her grave. The picture was begun in 1856, in the old churchyard at Chingford in Essex. A more conventional type of churchyard picture is Mann's *The Child's Grave* (189). One or two of the children are a little tearful, but the rest seem to be quite happy, romping among the tombstones. Death here has become a matter for sentimental reverie, not real emotion.

By complete contrast, Frank Holl's *Her Firstborn* (190) is a genuine and moving cry of anguish. The background was painted in the churchyard at Shere, in Surrey. It shows a procession led by four young girls carrying the tiny coffin. The parents and grandparents following look quite weighed down with grief. 'Mr Holl, we are sure, never painted better or made the onlooker sadder,' wrote the *Art Journal*. Holl, with his penchant for the heart-rending, had already painted another moving picture of a country funeral, *'I am the Resurrection and the*

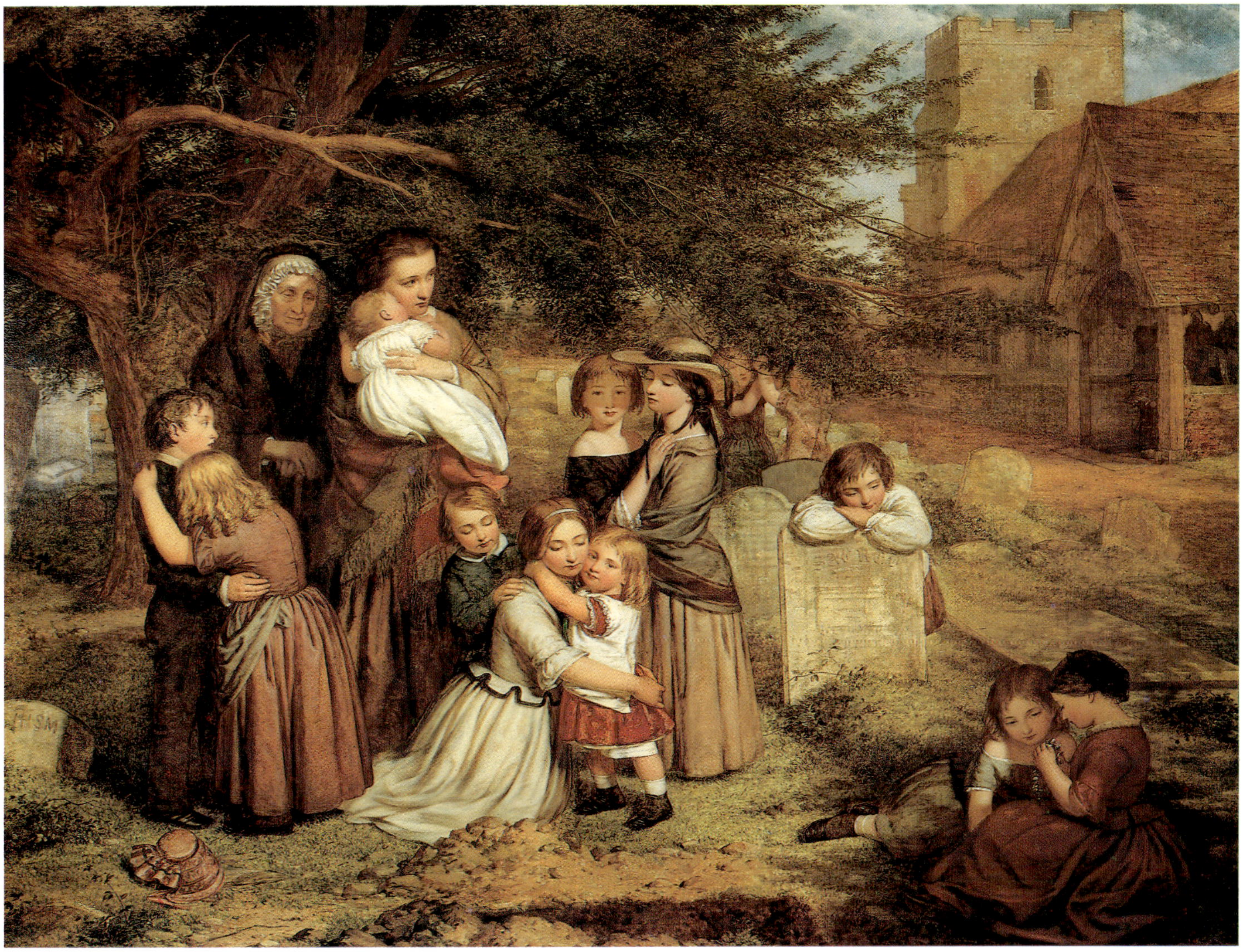

189
JOSHUA HARGRAVE SAMS MANN
*The Child's Grave*

*Life'* of 1872. Many Victorians were struck by the contrast between the elaborate, formal funerals of the rich, which left no room for genuine sorrow, and the simple but moving funerals of the poor. Flora Thompson noticed it even as a child: 'Against the earth's spring loveliness, the heavy black procession looked dreamlike, like a great black shadow . . . in spite of the lavish display of mourning, it did not touch her as the country funerals did with their farm-waggon hearse and few poor, walking mourners crying into their handkerchiefs.' William Morris deliberately rejected the hypocrisy of the age when he chose in 1896 a simple country burial at Kelmscott in Oxfordshire. His plain coffin, covered with flowers, was drawn to the churchyard by a farm horse and cart.

In Alfred Williams's Wiltshire village, he recalled that 'When a death occurs the bell is tolled from the tower, the little one for an infant, the heavy one for one of riper years; all the cottage blinds in the vicinity are drawn. . . .' It was traditional to go and view the corpse, and to touch it, as that ensured you would not dream about the dead. After the funeral, there was always a tea or a feast, and at Candleford Green one widow told Laura proudly, 'We buried 'im with 'am'. Williams wrote that 'The villagers are calm and philosophic, though very reverent, in the presence of death. . . . That is the stoicism of the countryside.' Also stoical is the old lady in the churchyard in Perugini's *Faithful* (191). Perugini has bravely painted a picture of an old lady grieving for her loved one, and the result is more moving than the endless Victorian pictures of pretty young widows. Victorian mourning customs decreed that a widow wear black crepe for at least a year after her husband's death. She then had to go into half-mourning, which meant dresses of grey or black only, for another six months. Queen Victoria herself set an example of irreproachable widowhood for her subjects to follow. She preferred wearing black to the end of her life and made widowhood into a way of life. She enjoyed talk-

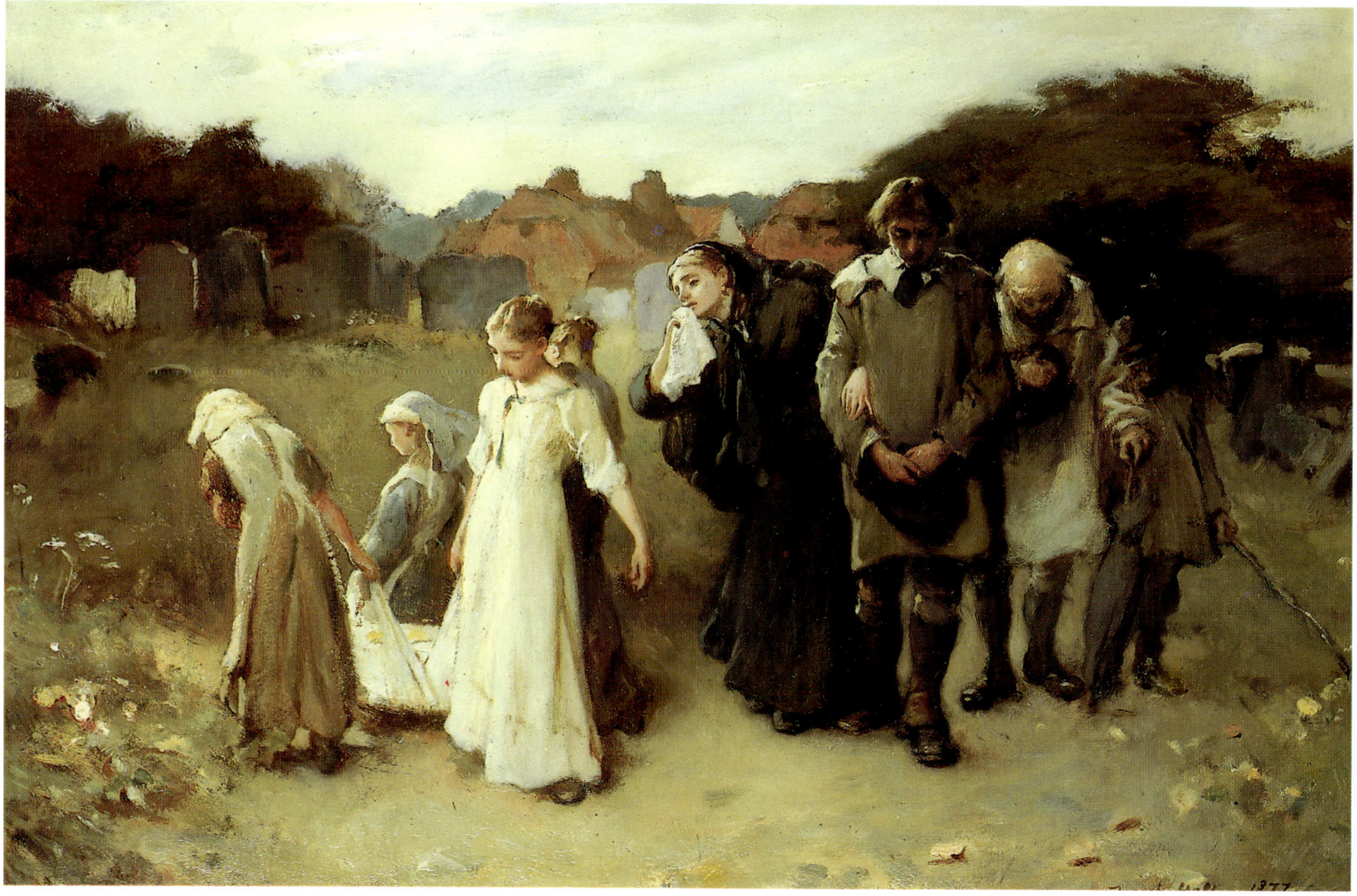

190
FRANK HOLL
*Her Firstborn*

ing to other widows, of any class, and commiserating with them. She also collected Frank Holl's pictures, because their gloomy themes appealed to her. All this meant that the widow was a powerful emotional symbol, irresistible to painters.

The death of children, being an experience suffered by every Victorian family, rich or poor, was a particularly emotional theme. The empty cradle and the child's grave were a reality, not just a painter's fancy. H.H. La Thangue handled the theme with restrained pathos in his *Man with the Scythe*. A mother has come out of her cottage to find that her sick daughter has just died, propped up on a pillow in a chair. At the gate stands the symbolic figure of death, the reaper, an old man carrying a scythe. The simple setting, outside a cottage with a row of cabbages by the path, makes the scene infinitely more moving. Much more powerful, and monumental, is La Thangue's *Last Furrow* (192). Here an old ploughman has died at his work, and has slumped over the handle of the plough just as it was turning. The horses have stopped, and one is looking round as if sympathetically. It is a large, striking and intensely moving picture, and implies not only death but the hardship of a life of unremitting toil. But better this than a slow death in the workhouse, that most dreaded of all Victorian institutions. Alfred Williams described a heartrending scene in his village when an old man, Mark Titcomb, unable to look after himself any longer, was taken forcibly to the workhouse, protesting bitterly.

He died, heartbroken, not long after arriving there. The Victorian poor preferred starvation to the workhouse, which was regarded as a disgrace, and an admission of defeat. It was not the hardship they feared, as conditions were probably much the same in poor cottages. Not surprisingly, the workhouse was not a popular subject with artists, although Herkomer painted a scene in the Westminster Workhouse for old women.

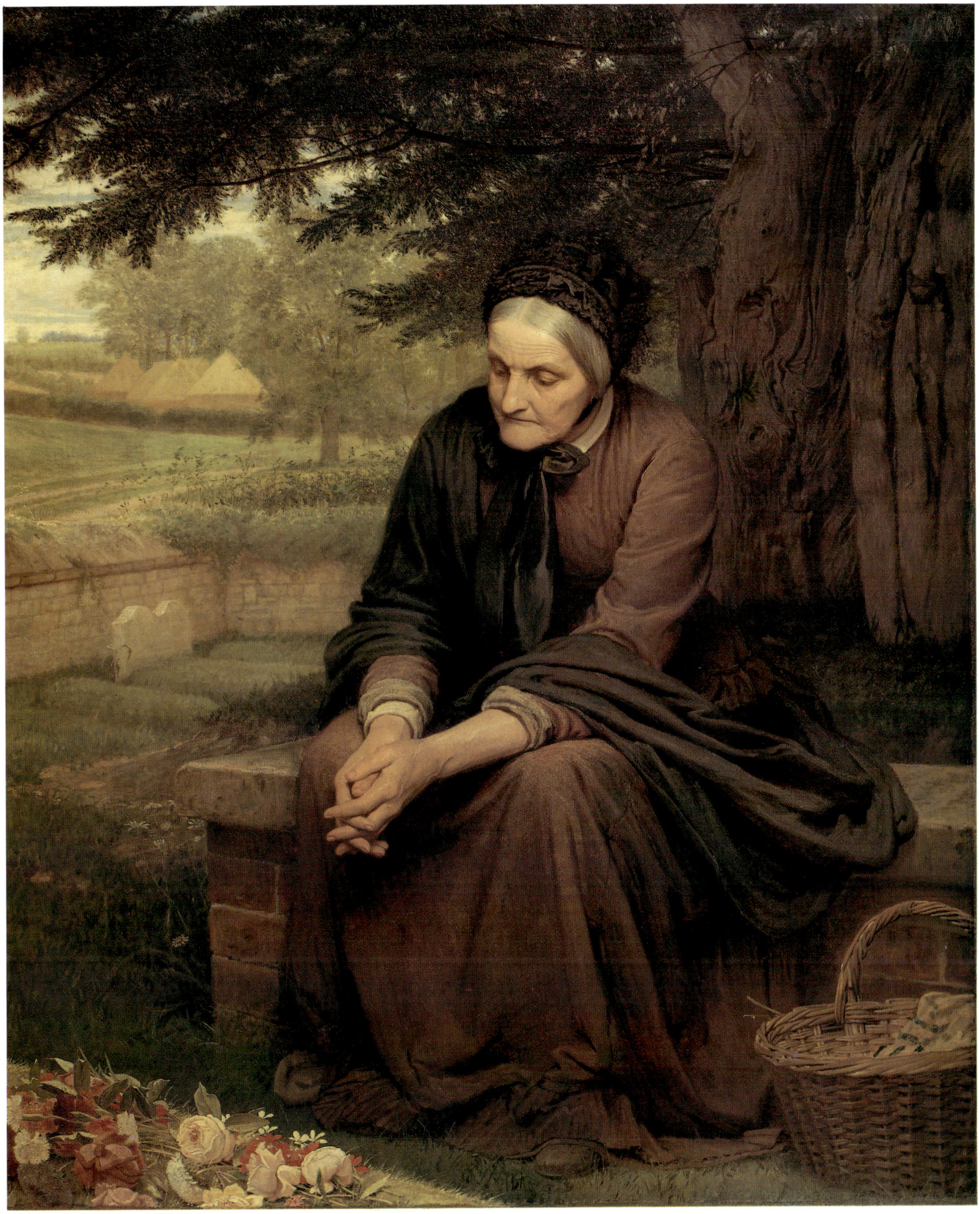

191
CHARLES EDWARD PERUGINI
*Faithful*

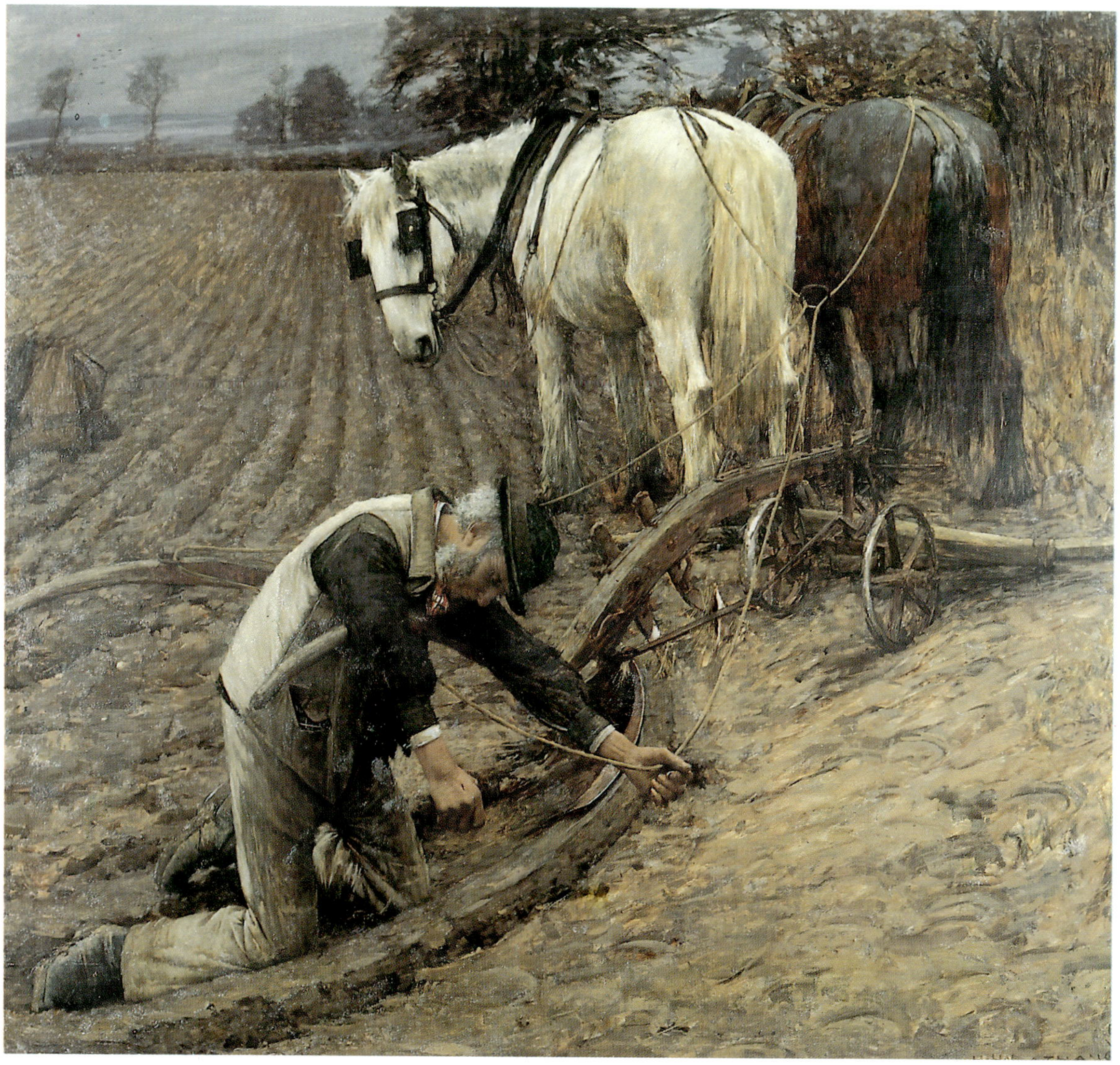

192
HENRY HERBERT LA THANGUE
*The Last Furrow*

Both Alfred Williams and Flora Thompson wrote their books in the twentieth century, looking back to Victorian childhoods. Their conclusions were the same – that in spite of all the hardship, and all the poverty, country people were happier in the nineteenth century. Their horizons were narrow, but they expected less from life, and therefore made the best of what little they had. 'Poverty's no disgrace,' Flora Thompson's mother would say, 'but 'tis a great inconvenience.' Country people were proud of their ability to survive hard times, and to make do. At Lark Rise, 'their favourite virtue was endurance. Not to flinch from pain or hardship was their ideal.' Williams said much the same thing: 'It is work and hardship that brings out all that is finest in us.' It can stand as a fitting epitaph for our Paradise Lost.

# *List of Illustrations*

Abbreviations for sources: BAL Bridgeman Art Library; CWG Christopher Wood Gallery; FAPL Fine Art Photographic Library; PC private collection; RGG Richard Green Gallery; SB Sotheby's Bond Street; TG Tate Gallery; V&A Victoria & Albert Museum.

52 Sir George Clausen (1852-1944) *Winter Work*, 1883-4; oil; SB.
53 Sir George Clausen (1852-1944) *Bird-Scaring*, 1896; oil; BAL/ Harris Museum and Art Gallery, Preston.
54 Sir George Clausen (1852-1944) *The Return from the Fields (Boy and Man)*, 1882; oil; SB.
55 Sir George Clausen (1852-1944) *Ploughing*, 1889; oil; BAL/ Aberdeen Art Gallery and Museums.
56 William Caldwell Crawford (working 1898-1936) *Ploughing*, 1905; oil; SB.
57 Stanhope Forbes (1857-1947) *The Drinking Place*, 1900; oil; Oldham Art Gallery.
58 Harold Harvey (1874-1941) *Watering the Horse*, 1909; oil; SB.
59 Rowland Wheelwright (1870-1955) *On the Towpath*; oil; SB.
60 Thomas Blinks (1860-1912) *Bread Winners*, 1905; oil; SB.
61 John Sargent Noble (1848-1896) *At the Blacksmith's*, 1883; oil; Kurt Schon Gallery.
62 Sir Alfred Munnings (1878-1959) *A Michaelmas Sale on a Suffolk Farm*, 1900; oil; RGG.
63 Sir Alfred Munnings (1878-1959) *Bungay Races*; watercolour; SB.
64 Sir George Clausen (1852-1944) *The Mowers*, 1891; oil; Usher Art Gallery, Lincoln.
65 Arthur Hopkins (1848-1930) *Loading Hay*, 1913; watercolour; SB.
66 George Vicat Cole (1833-1893) *The Hayrick*, 1866; oil; SB.
67 William Edward Millner (1849-1895) *The End of the Day*; oil; SB.
68 William Maw Egley (1826-1916) *Hullo, Largess! A Harvest Scene in Norfolk*, 1862; oil; Mrs C. Hussey.
69 Edmund George Warren (1834-1909) *Amongst the Corn Stooks*, 1865; watercolour; FAPL.
70 George Cole (1810-1883) *Harvest Time*, 1865; oil; Bristol Art Gallery.
71 George Vicat Cole (1833-1893) *Harvesting*; oil; SB.
72 John Linnell (1792-1882) *The Harvest Cradle*, 1859; oil; City of York Art Gallery.
73 John Linnell (1792-1882) *The Noonday Rest*, 1862; oil; Christie's.
74 John Linnell (1792-1882) *The Last Load*, 1853; oil; TG.
75 Henry Herbert La Thangue (1859-1929) *The Harvesters' Supper*; oil; Bradford Art Gallery.
76 Arthur Foord Hughes (1856-*c*.1927) *Gleaning*; oil; FAPL.
77 Sir George Clausen (1852-1944) *Harvest – Tying the Sheaves*, 1902; oil; RGG.
78 William Teulon Blandford Fletcher (1858-1936) *The Bridge*; oil; SB.
79 Robert Gallon (1845-1925) *A Village Scene*; oil; RGG.
80 Sir George Clausen (1852-1944) *An Old Woman*, 1887; oil; SB.
81 Myles Birket Foster (1825-1899) *The Country Inn*; watercolour; RGG.
82 Myles Birket Foster (1825-1899) *The Lacemaker*; watercolour; FAPL.
83 George William Mote (1832-1909) *Glovemaking*; oil; FAPL.
84 Alexander M. Rossi (working 1870-1903) *A Visit to the Cobbler*; oil; FAPL.
85 John Robertson Reid (1851-1926) *A Country Cricket Match*, 1878; oil; TG.
86 Stanhope Forbes (1857-1947) *The Village Philharmonic*, 1888; oil; Birmingham Museum and Art Gallery.
87 James Hayllar (1829-1920) *May Day*; oil; SB.
88 Thomas Falcon Marshall (1818-1878) *May Day Garlands*; oil; CWG.
89 Thomas Falcon Marshall (1818-1878) *Christmas Holly*, 1865; watercolour; CWG.
90 Marcus Stone (1840-1921) *Silent Pleading*, 1859; oil; Calderdale Museums, Halifax.
91 Richard Redgrave (1804-1888) *The Emigrant's Last Sight of Home*, 1858; oil; TG.
92 Richard Redgrave (1804-1888) *Going into Service*; oil; SB.
93 Henry Herbert La Thangue (1859-1929) *Leaving Home*; oil; SB.
94 Charles Joseph Staniland (1838-1916) *The Emigrant Ship*; oil; Bradford Art Gallery.
95 Frederick Daniel Hardy (1826-1911) *Posting a Letter*, 1879; oil; PC.
96 James Collinson (1825-1881) *Answering the Emigrant's Letter*, 1850; oil; Manchester City Art Gallery
97 Thomas Webster (1800-1886) *A Letter from the Colonies*, 1852; oil; TG.
98 George Smith (1829-1901) *'As cold water is to a thirsty soul, so is good news from a far country'*, 1864; oil; RGG.
99 James Campbell (*c*.1925-1893) *News from my Lad*, 1859; oil; Walker Art Gallery, Liverpool.
100 William Hemsley (1819-*c*.1893) *The Village Postman*; oil; SB.
101 Heywood Hardy (1843-1933) *Duty*, 1888; oil; BAL/Guildhall Art Gallery, London.
102 Thomas Webster (1800-1886) *Sickness and Health*, 1843; oil; BAL/V&A.
103 Myles Birket Foster (1825-1899) *The China Pedlar*; watercolour; FAPL.
104 Myles Birket Foster (1825-1899) *The Chair Mender*; watercolour; BAL/V&A.
105 William Frederick Witherington (1785-1865) *The Dancing Bear*; oil; Walker Art Gallery, Liverpool.
106 John Morgan (1823-1886) *The Sweet Seller*; oil; SB.
107 Frederick Daniel Hardy (1826-1911) *Try this Pair*, 1864; oil; SB.
108 Edward John Cobbett (1815-1899) *The Showman*, 1878; oil; Walker Art Gallery, Liverpool.
109 John Burr (1834-1893) *The Peepshow*; oil; BAL/Forbes Collection, New York.
110 Fred Walker (1840-1875) *The Vagrants*; oil; TG.
111 Sir Alfred Munnings (1878-1959) *The Fair has Come*, 1908; watercolour; RGG.
112 Helen Allingham (1848-1926) *At the Cottage Gate*; watercolour; SB.
113 Myles Birket Foster (1825-1899) *At the Cottage Door*; watercolour; RGG.
114 Charles Edward Wilson (working 1891-1936) *Outside a Cottage*; watercolour; FAPL.
115 Frederick Daniel Hardy (1826-1911) *A Cottage Fireside*, 1850; oil; PC.
116 Joseph Clark (1834-1912) *The Chimney Corner*, 1878; oil; CWG.
117 Joseph Clark (1834-1912) *The Labourer's Welcome*; oil; Sheffield Art Galleries.
118 Henry Spernon Tozer (working *c*.1900-1910) *The Evening Meal*; watercolour; SB.
119 William H. Snape (working 1885-1892) *A Cottage Scene*, 1891; oil; CWG.
120 Pierre Edouard Frere (1819-1886) *Washing Day*, 1878; oil; FAPL.
121 Katherine L. Beard (working 1885-1890) *Spinning*; oil; FAPL.
122 James Hayllar (1829-1920) *'As the Twig is bent, so the Tree is inclined'*; oil; CWG.
123 Thomas Webster (1800-1886) *Sunday Evening*; oil; Proby Collection, Elton Hall.

124 Helen Allingham (1848-1926) *Redlynch, Wiltshire*; watercolour; CWG.
125 Myles Birket Foster (1825-1899) *An Afternoon in the Garden*; watercolour; RGG.
126 William Stephen Coleman (1829-1904) *A Cottage Garden*; watercolour; CWG.
127 Thomas Tyndale (working *c.*1900-1910) *A Cottage Garden*; watercolour, CWG.
128 Harold Knight (1874-1961) *The Cottage Garden*; oil; MacConnal Mason Gallery.
129 Frank Walton (1840-1928) *A Summer Afternoon*; watercolour; FAPL.
130 Frederick James Shields (1833-1911) *The Young Beekeeper*; watercolour; FAPL.
131 Alfred Glendening, Junior (1861-1907) *The Cabbage Patch*, 1884; oil; CWG.
132 Walter Langley (1852-1922) *A Cottage Garden*, 1879; watercolour; PC.
133 Sir George Clausen (1852-1944) *The Allotment Garden*, 1899; oil; Fine Art Society.
134 Carlton Alfred Smith (1853-1946) *The New Baby*, 1885; watercolour; SB.
135 Charles James Lewis (1830-1892) *Mother and Child*; oil; BAL/ CWG.
136 Frederick William Elwell (1870-1958) *The First Born*, 1913; oil; Ferens Art Gallery, Hull.
137 George Smith (1829-1901) *Here's Granny*; oil; CWG.
138 Harry Brooker (1848-1940) *Breakfast Time*, 1901; oil; RGG.
139 William Henry Knight (1823-1863) *The Youngest Child*; oil; SB.
140 Mrs Alexander Farmer (working 1855-1867) *An Anxious Hour*, 1865; oil; V&A.
141 Sir Luke Fildes (1843-1927) *The Doctor*, 1891; oil; TG.
142 Frederick Daniel Hardy (1826-1911) *Hide and Seek*; oil; SB.
143 William Hemsley (1819-*c.*1893) *Bubbles*; oil; SB.
144 Thomas Webster (1800-1886) *The See-Saw*; oil; BAL/Guildhall Art Gallery, London.
145 William Bromley (working 1835-1888) *A Game of Marbles*; oil; SB.
146 Frederick James Shields (1833-1911) *One of our Breadwatchers*; watercolour; Manchester City Art Gallery.
147 Sophie Anderson (1823-1903) *Windfalls*; oil; Edmund and Suzanne McCormick Collection.
148 William Gunning King (1859-1940) *Saturday Afternoon*; oil; Bradford Art Gallery.
149 John Morgan (1823-1886) *The Cricket Match*; oil; RGG.
150 Alfred Rankley (1819-1872) *The Village School*, 1855; oil; CWG.
151 William Bromley (working 1835-1888) *The Schoolroom*; oil; RGG.
152 Charles James Lewis (1830-1892) *Dreaming*; oil; CWG.
153 George Washington Brownlow (1835-1876) *A Straw-Plaiting School in Essex*, 1864; oil; RGG.
154 James Lobley (1829-1888) *The Squire and the Gamekeeper*; oil; Private Collection.
155 Frederick William Keyl (1823-1871) *Portrait of a Gentleman with his Horse and Dogs*, 1854; oil; CWG.
156 William Frederick Witherington (1785-1865) *A Fete in Petworth Park*, 1835; National Trust, Petworth, Sussex.
157 John Robertson Reid (1851-1926) *Toil and Pleasure*, 1879; oil; TG.
158 Heywood Hardy (1843-1933) *The Young Squire*; oil; SB.
159 George Goodwin Kilburne (1839-1924) *The Heir*, 1890; oil; RGG.
160 James Hayllar (1829-1920) *Visiting the Hall*; oil; SB.
161 Heywood Hardy (1843-1933) *A Waiting Gun*, 1890; oil; SB.
162 George Goodwin Kilburne (1839-1924) *The Meet*; oil; SB.
163 John Charlton (1849-1917) *Earl and Countess Spencer with Hounds in Althorp Park*, 1878; oil; BAL/Earl Spencer Collection.
164 Thomas Blinks (1860-1912) *Full Cry*; oil; RGG.
165 Myles Birket Foster (1825-1899) *A Peep at the Hounds, here they come!*; watercolour; RGG.
166 Edith Hayllar (1860-1948) *The First of October*, 1888; oil; SB.
167 John Templeton Lucas (1836-1880) *The Poacher Caught*, 1874; oil; SB.
168 George Elgar Hicks (1824-1914) *Croquet*, 1864; oil; PC.
169 William Powell Frith (1819-1909) *English Archers, 19th Century*, 1872; BAL/Royal Albert Memorial Museum, Exeter.
170 Charles Lees (1800-1880) *Skaters, a Scene on Duddingston Loch*, 1853; oil; Trafalgar Galleries, London.
171 Edith Hayllar (1860-1948) *A Summer Shower*, 1883; oil; BAL/ Forbes Collection, New York.
172 Horace Henry Cauty (1846-1909) *The Tennis Match*, 1885; oil; CWG.
173 William Holman Hunt (1827-1910) *The Hireling Shepherd*, 1851; oil; Manchester City Art Gallery.
174 John Callcott Horsley (1817-1903) *Showing a Preference*, 1850; oil; Private Collection.
175 Jacob Thompson (1806-1879) *The Course of True Love Never did Run Smooth*, 1854; oil; Private Collection.
176 Frederick Smallfield (1829-1915) *Early Lovers*, 1858; oil; Manchester City Art Gallery.
177 John Henry F. Bacon (1868-1914) *A Wedding Morning*, 1892; oil; Lady Lever Art Gallery, Port Sunlight.
178 James Charles (1851-1906) *Signing the Marriage Register*; oil; Bradford City Art Gallery.
179 George Smith (1829-1901) *The Gamekeeper's Courtship*; oil; RGG.
180 William Henry Midwood (working 1867-1871) *Rustic Courtship*, 1876; oil; SB.
181 Arthur Hughes (1832-1915) *The Long Engagement*, 1859, oil; Birmingham City Art Gallery.
182 John White (1851-1933) *A Village Wedding*, 1881; oil; Royal Albert Memorial Museum, Exeter.
183 Sir Luke Fildes (1843-1927) *The Village Wedding*, 1883; oil; the Manney Collection.
184 Stanhope Forbes (1857-1947) *The Health of the Bride*, 1889; oil; TG.
185 George Goodwin Kilburne (1839-1924) *In Church*; watercolour; SB.
186 Thomas Webster (1800-1886) *The Village Choir*, 1847; oil; BAL/V&A.
187 Richard Redgrave (1804-1888) *Starting for the Christening*; oil; RGG.
188 Arthur Hughes (1832-1915) *Home from the Sea*, 1862; oil; Ashmolean Museum, Oxford.
189 Joshua Hargrave Sams Mann (working 1849-1884) *The Child's Grave*; oil; PC.
190 Frank Holl (1845-1888) *Her Firstborn*, 1877; oil; SB.
191 Charles Edward Perugini (1839-1918) *Faithful*; oil; Walker Art Gallery, Liverpool.
192 Henry Herbert La Thangue (1859-1929) *The Last Furrow*, 1895; oil; Oldham Art Gallery.

# *Select Bibliography*


General Reading

*The Diaries of the Rev. Francis Kilvert* 1870-1879, Jonathan Cape, 1938-1940.

Flora Thompson, *Lark Rise to Candleford*, Penguin Books, 1945.

Derek Hudson, *Munby, Man of Two Worlds*, John Murray, 1972.

Merryn Williams, *Thomas Hardy and Rural England*, Macmillan, 1972.

Richard Jefferies, *The Gamekeeper at Home*, Oxford University Press, 1978.

Alan Hurst, *Hardy – an Illustrated Dictionary*, Macmillan, 1980.

G. E. Mingay (editor), *The Victorian Countryside*, 2 vols., Routledge Kegan Paul, 1981.

Alfred Williams, *In a Wiltshire Village*, Alan Sutton, 1981.

*Between Earth and Sky* – poetry and prose edited by Neil Philip, Penguin Books, 1984.

*Country Voices, Life and Lore in Farm and Village,* compiled by Charles Kightly, Thames & Hudson, 1984.

Books and Catalogues on Victorian Painting

John Ruskin, *Academy Notes* 1855-9, 1875.

Graham Reynolds, *Paintings of the Victorian Scene*, Batsford, 1953.

Jeremy Maas, *Victorian Painters*, Barrie & Jenkins, 1969.

Christopher Wood, *Dictionary of Victorian Painters,* 2nd ed., Antique Collectors' Club, 1978.

Alan Staley, *Pre-Raphaelite Landscape*, Oxford University Press, 1973.

Christopher Wood, *Victorian Panorama – Paintings of Victorian Life*, Faber, 1976.

Christopher Wood, *The Pre-Raphaelites*, Weidenfeld & Nicolson, 1983.

*Painting in Newlyn,* Catalogue of Exhibition at the Barbican Art Gallery, London, 1985.

*Hard Times,* Catalogue of Exhibition at Manchester City Art Gallery, 1987.

Books on Individual Artists

| | |
|---|---|
| Clausen | *Sir George Clausen RA*, Catalogue of Exhibition at Bradford Art Gallery, 1980. |
| Cole | T.J. Barringer, *The Cole Family*, Catalogue of Exhibition at Portsmouth Art Gallery, 1988. |
| Cooper | T.S. Cooper, RA, *My Life*, 2 vols., 1890. |
| Fildes | L.V. Fildes, *Luke Fildes RA, A Victorian Painter*, Michael Joseph, 1968. |
| Foster | Jan Reynolds, *Birket Foster*, Batsford, 1984. |
| Frith | W.P. Frith, *My Autobiography and Reminiscences*, 3 vols., 1887-8. |
| Hayllar | Christopher Wood, *The Artistic Family Hayllar, Connoisseur*, April-May 1974. |
| Herkomer | J. Saxon Mills, *The Life and Letters of Sir H. von Herkomer RA*, 1923. |
| Holl | A.M. Reynolds, *The Life and Work of Frank Holl*, 1912. |
| Leader | Frank Lewis, *B.W. Leader RA*, F. Lewis, 1971. |
| Linnell | Catalogue of John Linnell Exhibition, Fitzwilliam Museum, Cambridge, 1982. |
| Munnings | Sir Alfred Munnings, *An Artist's Life*, 1955. |
| Redgrave | *Richard Redgrave,* Catalogue of Exhibition at the Victoria and Albert Museum, 1988. |
| Waite | *E.W. Waite*, Catalogue of Exhibition at Gainsborough's House, Suffolk, 1983. |
| Walker | J.G. Marks, *Life and Letters of Frederick Walker ARA*, 1896. |

# Index

*Illustration page numbers in italics*